INTERNATIONAL AND TRANSNATIONAL CRIME AND JUSTICE

International crime and justice is an emerging field that covers crime and justice from a global perspective. This book introduces the nature of international and transnational crimes; theoretical foundations to understanding the relationship between social change and the waxing and waning of the crime opportunity structure; globalization; migration; culture conflicts and the emerging legal frameworks for their prevention and control. It presents the challenges involved in delivering justice and international cooperative efforts to deter, detect, and respond to international and transnational crimes, and the need for international research and data resources to go beyond anecdote and impressionistic accounts to testing and developing theories to build the discipline that bring tangible improvements to the peace, security, and well-being of the globalizing world. This books is a timely analysis of the complex subject of international crime and justice for students, scholars, policy makers, and advocates who strive for the pursuit of justice for millions of victims.

Mangai Natarajan is a professor in the Department of Criminal Justice at John Jay College of Criminal Justice, The City University of New York. She is an award-winning policy-oriented researcher who has published widely in international criminal justice. To date she has edited ten books, including a special issue on Crime in Developing Countries for *Crime Science Journal*, and authored a monograph, *Women Policing in a Changing Society: Back Door to Equality* (2008). She is the founding director of the International Criminal Justice major at John Jay College.

INTERNATIONAL AND TRANSNATIONAL CRIME AND JUSTICE

Second Edition

Edited by

Mangai Natarajan
The John Jay College of Criminal Justice,
City University of New York

CAMBRIDGE
UNIVERSITY PRESS

CAMBRIDGE
UNIVERSITY PRESS

University Printing House, Cambridge CB2 8BS, United Kingdom

One Liberty Plaza, 20th Floor, New York, NY 10006, USA

477 Williamstown Road, Port Melbourne, VIC 3207, Australia

314-321, 3rd Floor, Plot 3, Splendor Forum, Jasola District Centre, New Delhi - 110025, India

79 Anson Road, #06-04/06, Singapore 079906

Cambridge University Press is part of the University of Cambridge.

It furthers the University's mission by disseminating knowledge in the pursuit of education, learning and research at the highest international levels of excellence.

www.cambridge.org
Information on this title: www.cambridge.org/9781108497879
DOI: 10.1017/9781108597296

© Cambridge University Press 2011, 2019

First published 2011
Second edition 2019

A catalogue record for this publication is available from the British Library

Library of Congress Cataloging in Publication data
Names: Natarajan, Mangai, editor.
Title: International and transnational crime and justice / edited by Mangai Natarajan.
Description: Second edition. | New York: Cambridge University Press, 2019. |
Includes bibliographical references and index.
Identifiers: LCCN 2019000704 | ISBN 9781108497879 (hardback) |
ISBN 9781108708838 (paperback)
Subjects: LCSH: Transnational crime. | Criminology – Cross cultural studies. |
Victims of crimes – Legal status, laws, etc. | Criminal justice, Administration
of – International cooperation. | Criminal justice, Administration
of – Cross-cultural studies. | BISAC: SOCIAL SCIENCE / Criminology.
Classification: LCC HV6252 .I56 2019 | DDC 364.1/35–dc23
LC record available at https://lccn.loc.gov/2019000704

ISBN 978-1-108-49787-9 Hardback
ISBN 978-1-108-70883-8 Paperback

Contents

Figures and Tables

FIGURES

TABLES

Preface

*"The structure of world peace cannot be the work of one man, or one party, or one nation...
It cannot be a peace of large nations – or of small nations. It must be a peace which rests
on the cooperative effort of the whole world."* Franklin Roosevelt, quoted by Barack Obama,
44th President of the United States, in his Address to the UN General Assembly, September
23, 2009

In furtherance of world peace, many educational institutions are now broadening their
curricula to improve understanding of the global realities of the present-day world. Crime
undeniably poses a serious threat to social order and tranquillity and it is certain that the
rule of law, coupled with an efficient criminal justice system, is fundamental to social and
economic progress. This is true of every sovereign state. The disciplines of criminology
and criminal justice have a vital role to play in improving the understanding of crimes that
threaten the peace and security of nations and in finding the best way to deal with them.

The rapid increase in globalization at the end of the twentieth century led criminologists
to study "transnational crimes," i.e., criminal acts that span national borders and that violate
the laws of more than one country. This resulted in the creation of a new field of study, "comparative criminology and criminal justice," though it is also known by many other names,
including international criminology and criminal justice, global criminology and criminal
justice, supranational criminology, and cross-cultural criminology. Meanwhile, growing
international awareness of the millions of victims of genocide, crimes against humanity,
and war crimes in the late twentieth century, compelled the international community to
pay attention to these "gravest crimes" that threaten the peace, security, and well-being of
the world. These crimes were given formal recognition in the Rome Statute of 1998 (now
signed by more than half the member states of the United Nations), which established the
International Criminal Court to deal with them.

The disaster of September 11, 2001, accelerated the need to study international crime
and criminal justice, not just in the USA but all around the world. A new undergraduate
major – International Criminal Justice (ICJ) – was established at John Jay College of
Criminal Justice in 2001 and subsequently, in 2010, a companion master's ICJ program was
also started. Other universities and colleges are now beginning to offer similar programs
at the undergraduate and graduate levels. The programs will help to expand the boundaries of criminology and criminal justice and will open many new career opportunities for
students of these fields.

As the founding director of John Jay's undergraduate ICJ program, I soon realized that there was urgent need for a student text that would provide concise, up-to-date information on the broad array of topics covered by international crime and justice. I was fortunate in being able to persuade McGraw-Hill to custom publish in 2005 and subsequently, in 2011, I was proud that Cambridge University Press agreed to publish a new edition, with an updated and expanded content, as a textbook for the national and international market. That version of the book was produced with hard cover, paperback, and as an ebook. Apart from John Jay College of Criminal Justice, the book has been adopted by many other universities in the USA as a source book and textbook for courses on international crime and justice.

The unique feature of the Cambridge University Press 2011 edited volume is that it was designed to be flexible in terms of future editions, which will add more topics, research ideas, references, etc. It has become the primary source for anyone interested in learning about international criminal justice. The book serves as a source of knowledge on this evolving field in criminology and criminal justice and is popular among students and others for its short, clear, and concise chapters, written by 77 authors, many of whom are world-renowned experts.

International crime and justice is an evolving field and there is a constant need to update the materials and the focus. Many universities around the world are introducing transnational crime and justice, and international criminal justice in their BA and MA programs. This book is an enhanced edition, with the existing chapters of the Cambridge University Press 2011 edition and new chapters that are relevant to studying international and transnational crime and justice issues. It contains 84 chapters by 89 authors.

My role in developing international criminal justice programs, teaching the courses, and undertaking research – presenting at international conferences and supervising dissertations and theses on ICJ topics at John Jay since 2000 – has provided me with the extensive contacts needed in putting together this book. I hope it is more than a textbook. The short chapters, specially written by many of the world experts in this new field, are intended to give students an understanding of the main concepts covered by each topic and to sensitize students to the complex nature of the problems. Given the enormous interest in this field, I confidently expect new editions of the book in the future years.

My sincere thanks go to each and every one of the 89 authors for accepting my invitations to write the chapters. Because of their broad expertise, I had to twist the arms of some of them to write more than one chapter. Many of them not only wrote chapters but helped by reviewing the chapters of other authors. I also thank some other reviewers who are not authors, including Patricia Brantingham, John Braithwaite, Carlos Carcach, Richard Culp, James Finckenauer, Dinni Gorden, Dennis Kenney, Edward Kleemans, Dana Miller, Mahesh Nalla, Carlos Ponce, Sheetal Ranjan, Phil Reichel, Aiden Sidebottom, Janet Smith, Nick Tilley, and Cathy Widom, who reviewed the 2011 and the present edition. Without the help of all these friends and colleagues, this project would not have been possible. I am fortunate to have such a wonderful group of international experts as friends. It was a pleasure to work with them as well as a great learning experience. I also thank the anonymous reviewers of the book proposal, selected by Cambridge University Press, whose comments helped me to improve the book and gave me confidence that I was on the right track.

I have been blessed by having many hard-working, talented, eager-to-learn students in the ICJ program. Some of them read the chapters, gave feedback, and helped to check and proofread the references.

There is nothing like having the help of mentors in facing the challenges of an academic career. I thank Professor Ronald V. Clarke, my mentor, or rather my guru(!), for teaching me to be rigorous and self-critical ever since my time at Rutgers. I am also grateful for many brainstorming sessions with him that helped shape this book.

I must acknowledge my special thanks to Professor Roger S. Clark, an optimistic human being and inspirational teacher, who has directed me over the years or so on the right path toward understanding international criminal law.

Encouragement can work wonders for one's confidence and I thank Professor Graeme Newman, a founding scholar of global crime and justice, for his encouraging comments when I started thinking about a book on international crime and justice. I am grandly indebted to him for his unequivocal support in my international crime and justice career.

Two other people of great importance in my career in international criminal justice are Professors Gerhard Mueller and Freda Adler. In 2005, before his death, Professor Mueller paid me the honor of writing the foreword for the earlier, custom edition of this book, published by McGraw-Hill.

There are many other people who contributed to the development of the book. First, I would like to thank ex-Provost Basil Wilson, who conceived the idea of an ICJ major at John Jay and who asked me to run the program. Thanks also to John Jay administrators for their constant and continued support and thanks to the colleagues in my department for their patience with this preoccupied colleague. My sincere thanks to the young scholars who teach and use the textbook at John Jay for constantly providing feedback in improving this edition.

My special thanks to Lauren Wilson, Rutgers University PhD candidate, for her assistance in compiling the manuscript; Lidia Vasquez, a JJ PhD candidate in assisting with reference checks; and the JJ's Office of Advanced Research (OAR) for providing me a research assistant support to this book project.

One of my ICJ students, Ray Hilker, wrote to me (Tuesday, July 25, 2017), "I decided to purchase your book, *International Crime and Justice*. When I last rented it, I had not read the preface, only the chapters for assignments. But today, I decided to read it from cover to cover. I'm not sure if you did, but for the future you should assign the preface as a part of the class reading requirement. Your words give purpose to what we study, and once again have reminded me of why I am here, and why I will continue to work to reach the same goals that you write of in your text." I am indeed touched by students and their remarks about the book.

I would also like to thank Robert Dreesen, Senior Editor of Cambridge University Press, for his confidence in me and enthusiasm about the book; Claire Sissen, Gail Welsh, and Dan Shutt for production assistance; and Jackie Grant for facilitating the production.

Finally, thanks to all my friends – they knew who they are – for constantly cheering me up whenever I have begun to droop under the burden of producing the book. Above all, thanks to Jithendranath Vaidyanathan, my best friend, for his unwavering commitment to my professional success.

Ever since I entered the world of criminology, my passion and ambition has been to understand victimization and to help prevent it. I therefore dedicate this book to the victims of international and transnational crimes, in the hope it might help in the future to reduce the terrible harms that they suffer.

About the Editor

Mangai Natarajan PhD is a full professor in the Department of Criminal Justice and director of the International Criminal Justice major at John Jay College of Criminal Justice, City University of New York. She moved to the USA from India in 1985 to pursue her doctoral studies and obtained a Rutgers University PhD (Criminal Justice) in 1991. She is an active policy-oriented researcher who has published widely in three areas: drug trafficking, women police, and domestic violence. Her books include Natarajan, M. (2008). *Women Police in a Changing Society: Back Door to Equality*, Aldershot; Natarajan, M. (Ed.) (2007). *Domestic Violence: The Five Big Questions*. International Library of Criminology, Criminal Justice and Penology, Aldershot; Natarajan, M. (Ed.) (2005). *Women Police*. International Library of Criminology, Criminal Justice and Penology, Aldershot; Natarajan, M. and Hough, M. (Ed.) (2000). *Illegal Drug Markets: From Research to Policy, Crime Prevention Studies Volume 11*, Monsey, NY; Natarajan, M. (Ed.) (2010). *Drugs of Abuse: The International Scene (Volume 1); Drugs and Crime (Volume 2); Prevention and Treatment of Drug Abuse (Volume 3)*, Taylor & Francis, London; Natarajan, M. (Ed.) (2011). *Crime Opportunity Theories: Routine Activity, Rational Choice and Their Variants*, Aldershot; Natarajan, M. (Ed.) (2005). *Introduction to International Criminal Justice*, New York; Natarajan, M. (Ed.) (2011). *International Crime and Justice*, New York: Cambridge University Press. Recently (2015–2016), she edited a special issue on *Crime in Developing Countries* for *Crime Science*.

Her wider academic interests revolve around crime theories that promote crime reduction policy thinking and her related areas of expertise include social network analysis, crime mapping and crime analysis, problem-oriented policing, and situational crime prevention. As well as being an active researcher, Dr. Natarajan is a curriculum developer and a dedicated teacher, teaching in the undergraduate, graduate, and PhD programs. She is the founding director of the International Criminal Justice major, one of the fastest-growing and most popular majors at John Jay. She has been recognized for Excellence Research on Improving Policing for Women by the Australasian Council of Women and Policing and the Law Council of Australia in August 2013 and, in June 2017, she obtained the annual "ECCA" Award for Fundamental Contributions to Environmental Criminology and Crime Analysis.

Notes on Contributors

Marcelo F. Aebi is Full Professor of Criminology and Vice Director of the School of Criminal Sciences at the University of Lausanne, Switzerland. He is the Executive Secretary of the European Society of Criminology, a member of the group of experts that produces the *European Sourcebook of Crime and Criminal Justice Statistics* and, as a consultant expert of the Council of Europe, he is responsible for the *Council of Europe Annual Penal Statistics* (*SPACE*). He has published extensively, and in several languages, in the fields of comparative criminology, crime measurement, crime trends, drugs, corrections, and alternatives to imprisonment. He is also a part-time Visiting Professor at the Autonomous University of Barcelona, Spain.

Jay S. Albanese is Professor in the Wilder School of Government & Public Affairs at Virginia Commonwealth University. He served as chief of the International Center at the National Institute of Justice, the research arm of the US Department of Justice. He is the author or editor of 20 books, including *Organized Crime: From the Mob to Transnational Organized Crime* (2015), *Professional Ethics in Criminal Justice: Being Ethical When No One is Looking* (4th ed., 2016) and *Transnational Crime in the 21st Century* (2011). Dr Albanese has served as executive director of the International Association for the Study of Organized Crime and is past president and fellow of the Academy of Criminal Justice Sciences. He is United Nations Liaison for the American Society of Criminology.

Alex Alexandrou is Assistant Professor in the Department of Security, Fire, and Emergency Management at John Jay College of Criminal Justice. Dr Alexandrou has worked extensively in both business and academic environments. He has over 18 years of professional experience in healthcare IT, including software integration, biometric and access control systems, deploying virtualization by transitioned use of physical servers into virtualization technology, realigning IT architecture with cloud-based networks and security platforms/technologies. His current research interests include mobile forensics investigation, mobile devices vulnerabilities and threats, wireless networking and wireless vulnerabilities and exploits, security, and privacy.

George Andreopoulos is Professor of Political Science and Criminal Justice at the City University of New York. He has written extensively on international organizations, international human rights, and humanitarian law issues. He is currently completing a book on the authority and legitimacy of the United Nations Security Council.

Xabier Agirre Aranburu has been Senior Analyst at the Office of the Prosecutor (OTP) of the ICC (International Criminal Court) since 2004, when he joined the first team that established the office. For the last 20 years he has worked in the investigation of international crimes (war crimes, crimes against humanity, genocide) as well as the training of prosecutors and judges around the world with the UN ICTY (United Nations International Criminal Tribunal for the former Yugoslavia), ICRC (International Committee of the Red Cross), UN OHCHR (UN Office of the High Commissioner for Human Rights), ICTJ (International Center for Transitional Justice), and several universities and NGOs. He is the author of a number of academic publications on related subjects.

Enrique Desmond Arias is the Marxe Chair in Western Hemisphere Affairs at Baruch College, City University of New York. He is the author of *Criminal Enterprises and Governance in Latin America and the Caribbean* (Cambridge University Press, 2017), *Drugs and Democracy in Rio de Janeiro: Trafficking, Social Networks, and Public Security* (2006), and co-editor of *Violent Democracies in Latin America* (2010). His writing has appeared in *Comparative Politics*, *Perspectives on Politics*, the *Latin American Research Review*, *Current Sociology*, the *Journal of Latin American Studies*, *Policing and Society*, *Qualitative Sociology*, *Latin American Politics and Society*, *America's Quarterly*, and *Studies in Comparative International Development*.

Alexis A. Aronowitz is Senior Assistant Professor in the Social Science Department at University College Utrecht, the Netherlands. She has served as a staff member and consultant on projects in the field of human trafficking for the United Nations Interregional Crime and Justice Research Institute, the United Nations Office on Drugs and Crime, the Organization for Security and Cooperation in Europe, the International Organization for Migration, and other international organizations. She continues to work as an independent consultant on human trafficking and has published extensively on the topic.

Jana Arsovska is Associate Professor at the Sociology Department at John Jay College of Criminal Justice. She holds a PhD degree in Criminology from the University of Leuven, where she studied organized crime. She has published widely on Balkan criminality and organized crime.

G. S. Bajpai serves as Chairperson at the Centre for Criminology & Victimology, National Law University Delhi, India. His areas of interests include criminology, criminal justice, victimology, and research methods. He has held several international assignments, including the Commonwealth Academic Staff Fellowship in the UK, and visits under cultural exchange programs for undertaking advanced research in France, Japan, and the Netherlands, among other countries.

Rosemary Barberet is Professor in the Sociology Department of John Jay College of Criminal Justice, where she teaches International Criminal Justice courses. Her publications have dealt with victimology, women and crime, crime indicators, and comparative methodology. Dr Barberet has received the Herbert Bloch Award of the American Society of Criminology and the Rafael Salillas Award of the Sociedad Española de Investigación Criminológica. She currently represents the International Sociological Association at the United Nations and is an active member of Criminologists without Borders.

Stefan Barriga is Liechtenstein's Deputy Head of Mission to the European Union in Brussels. He acted as legal adviser to the Chairman of the Special Working Group on the Crime of Aggression between 2003 and 2009 and continued to advise the chief negotiators on the crime of aggression up to the successful conclusion of this process at the Review Conference 2010. Since 2002, he has represented Liechtenstein in numerous negotiations on legal issues, in particular in the context of the Sixth Committee (legal) of the UN General Assembly and the ICC Assembly of States Parties. Mr Barriga holds a doctoral degree in Law from the University of Vienna (Austria) and an LLM from Columbia University.

Popy Begum is a doctoral student at the School of Criminal Justice, Rutgers University (NJ). She received her Bachelor's in International Criminal Justice in 2013 from John Jay College of Criminal Justice, and her Master's in Criminology and Criminal Justice Research Methods in 2014 from Oxford University. Her research interests include honor-based violence, and she has published on the topic.

Roberta Belli is Senior Security Information Analyst for the United Nations Department of Safety and Security (UNDSS), currently based in Jerusalem. Prior to joining the United Nations, she was a researcher and project manager for the United States Extremist Crime Database (ECDB). Her research interests include social network analysis as applied to the crime-terror nexus, the financial criminality of far-right and Islamic extremists, and counter-terrorism strategies focusing on intelligence-led operations, threat and risk assessments, and situational crime prevention.

Gisela Bichler is a professor at California State University, San Bernardino. She is also the director of the Center for Criminal Justice Research. Her interest in maritime crime stems from her doctoral research on commercial passenger ship casualties. Recently, Dr Bichler has become heavily involved in various research initiatives using social network analysis to understand criminal networks and their operations, both on land and on the water.

Steven Block is Associate Professor in the Department of Criminology and Criminal Justice at Central Connecticut State University. He has recently published articles in *Deviant Behavior*, *Journal of School Violence,* and *Newspaper Research Journal.*

Alfred Blumstein is J. Erik Jonsson Professor Emeritus of Urban Systems and Operations Research at Carnegie Mellon University. His research over the past 20 years has covered many aspects of crime and criminal justice, including crime measurement, criminal careers, sentencing, deterrence and incapacitation, prison populations, juvenile violence, redemption, and drug policy. Among other accolades, he has received the American Society of Criminology's Sutherland Award, the Wolfgang Award for Distinguished Achievement in Criminology, and the 2007 Stockholm Prize in Criminology.

Rick Brown is Deputy Director of the Australian Institute of Criminology and a Visiting Fellow of Policing and Criminal Justice at the University of Derby. He has previously run a crime and justice research consultancy and worked for the Home Office Police Research Group in London. He has published over 50 government reports, book chapters, and journal articles.

Gloria J. Browne-Marshall is Professor of Constitutional Law at John Jay College of Criminal Justice. Professor Browne-Marshall's publications include *Race, Law, and American Society: 1607 to Present, The Voting Rights War: The NAACP and the Ongoing Struggle for Justice* (2016) and *The Constitution: Major Cases and Conflicts* (2011) as well as several articles and book chapters. She is an award-winning legal correspondent reporting on the United Nations and the US Supreme Court.

Francesco Calderoni is Associate Professor of Criminology at the Faculty of Social and Political Sciences at Università Cattolica del Sacro Cuore of Milan. He has been a researcher at Transcrime since September 2005. At Università Cattolica, he coordinates the major in Policies for Security in the master's in Public Policy, and the international PhD in Criminology. His areas of interest are the mafias, organized crime, illegal markets, criminal justice and policies against organized crime, and criminal networks.

Paolo Campana is Lecturer in Criminology and Complex Networks at the Institute of Criminology, University of Cambridge. His work specializes in organized crime and forms of extra-legal governance; migrant smuggling and human trafficking; and trust, reputation, and mechanisms of cooperation in illegal settings. He has a strong interest in the application of network analysis techniques to the study of organized forms of criminality.

David Donat Cattin is Secretary-General at Parliamentarians for Global Action (www.pgaction.org), New York. He is also Adjunct Professor of International Law at the Center for Global Affairs at New York University (NYU), a lecturer of the Salzburg Law School on International Criminal Law at University of Salzburg (Austria) and a founding member of the Victims' Rights Working Group (1997), an informal group of NGOs and activists who played a significant role in ICC-related negotiations.

Kerry Clamp is Assistant Professor in the School of Sociology and Social Policy at the University of Nottingham. She has degrees from the University of South Africa, Sheffield, and Leeds. Kerry has written widely on the conceptualization and application of restorative justice within transitional settings as well as police use of restorative justice and practice. She is Chair of the Editorial Board and Editor of the Newsletter for the European Forum for Restorative Justice.

Roger S. Clark is Board of Governors Professor of International Law at Rutgers University School of Law in Camden, New Jersey. He holds advanced doctorates in Law from Victoria University of Wellington in New Zealand and from Columbia Law School in New York. Between 1986 and 1990, he was a member of the United Nations Committee on Crime Prevention and Control, a group of independent experts elected by the Economic and Social Council ("ECOSOC"). The Committee supervised the criminal justice work of the United Nations. (It has since been replaced by the Commission on Crime Prevention and Criminal Justice, which is composed of representatives of states.) Since 1995, he has represented the government of Samoa in negotiations to create the International Criminal Court and to get it up and running. He was actively involved in the process to extend the Court's jurisdictional reach to the crime of aggression, which was completed in December 2017.

Ronald V. Clarke is University Professor at the Rutgers School of Criminal Justice. He was employed for 15 years in the British Government's criminology research department, where he had a significant role in the development of situational crime prevention. Dr Clarke is author or joint author of more than 300 publications. He was awarded the Stockholm Prize in Criminology in 2015.

Harry R. Dammer is Professor of Criminal Justice and Criminology and Associate Dean of the College of Arts and Sciences at the University of Scranton, PA. Dr Dammer received his Bachelor's and Master's from the University of Dayton (OH) and his PhD from the Rutgers University School of Criminal Justice (NJ). He has received two Fulbright Scholar Awards and is the former Chair of the International Section of the Academy of Criminal Justice Sciences. He has authored or co-authored seven books and published numerous articles, manuals, and professional reports on a variety of criminal justice topics, mainly in the areas of comparative criminal justice, corrections, and the practice of religion in the correctional environment. He has visited prisons in more than a dozen countries, including China, South Africa, Israel, and South Korea, and throughout Europe.

Meredith Dank is Research Professor at John Jay College of Criminal Justice, focusing on human trafficking, gender-based violence, and qualitative methods. She has been the Principal Investigator on over a dozen government-funded and privately funded research grants, and has conducted research in over a dozen countries.

Sarah Durrant is Investigative Analyst at the Department of Health and Human Services – Office of Inspector General. During her undergraduate degree at Marist College, Sarah held a US Secret Service internship where she was exposed to investigating financial crimes involving bitcoin. In 2018, she received her Master's degree in International Crime and Justice at John Jay College. Her thesis research focused on cryptocurrencies and their use in fueling transnational crimes.

Marcia Esparza is Associate Professor in the Department of Criminal Justice at John Jay College. Her research areas include state violence, genocide, collective memory-silence in the aftermath of mass killings and military sociology in Latin America and more recently in Spain, and in the Balearic Island of Mallorca. Her research experience includes her work for the United Nations-sponsored Truth Commission in Guatemala (1997–1999). Dr. Esparza is the Founder and Director of the Historical Memory Project, a forum for documenting and promoting the historical memory of state violence. She is an author of a monograph *Silenced Communities: Legacies of Militarization and Militarism in a Rural Guatemalan Town* (2017) and coauthor of the following edited books: *Remembering the Rescuers of Victims of Human Rights Crimes in Latin America* (2016) and *State Violence and Genocide in Latin America: The Cold War Years* (2009).

Marcus Felson is the originator of the routine activity approach and author of *Crime and Everyday Life* (2010) and *Crime and Nature* (2006), and Professor at Texas State University in San Marcos, Texas. He has a BA from the University of Chicago, an MA and PhD from the University of Michigan, and received the 2014 Honoris Causa from the Universidad Miguel Hernandez in Spain. Professor Felson has been given the Ronald Clarke Award by the Environmental Criminology and Crime Analysis group, and the Paul Tappan Award of the Western Society of Criminology. He has been a guest lecturer in Abu Dhabi, Argentina, Australia, Belgium, Brazil, Canada, Chile, China, Denmark, Ecuador, El Salvador, England, Finland, France, Germany, Hong Kong, Hungary, Italy, Japan, Mexico, the Netherlands, New Zealand, Norway, Poland, Scotland, Spain, South Africa, Sweden, and Switzerland. He has applied routine activity thinking to many topics, including theft, violence, child molesting, white-collar crime, and corruption.

Joshua D. Freilich is a member of the Criminal Justice Department at John Jay College and is Chair (2017–2019) of the American Society of Criminology's Division on Terrorism and

Bias Crimes. He is the creator and co-director of the United States Extremist Crime Database (ECDB). Freilich's research has been funded by DHS and NIJ and focuses on the causes of and responses to terrorism, measurement issues, and criminological theory, especially crime prevention.

Martin Gottschalk is Chair of the Departments of Criminal Justice and Sociology at the University of North Dakota. In addition to his primary research interest in evolution and the sociology and social psychology of punishment, he has worked with the US Probation and Pretrial Services System to examine the effects of manualized cognitive behavioral therapy. He has authored or co-authored works appearing in journals such as *International Journal of Comparative and Applied Criminal Justice*, *Criminal Justice Policy Review*, and *Critical Criminology*.

Adam Graycar has worked at senior levels of government and has also been the director of the Australian Institute of Criminology, Dean of the School of Criminal Justice at Rutgers University, New Jersey, and Professor at the Australian National University. He is now a professor at Flinders University.

Rob Guerette is Associate Professor of Criminology and Criminal Justice at Florida International University. His research focuses largely on the prevention of crime, particularly transnational crimes, through both the analysis of crime patterns and opportunities to inform strategic preventive action and through evaluation of programs and policies designed to address crime problems.

Pieter Hartel is Professor of Cyber Security at Delft University of Technology. He also holds part-time professorial positions at the University of Twente and at Singapore University of Technology and Design. He has 25 years of research and teaching experience in Cyber Security in the Netherlands, the UK, the USA, Malaysia, and Singapore. His research interests include the human factor in cyber security, cybercrime, crypto markets, and blockchain technology.

David C. Hicks has worked with enforcement, intelligence, nongovernment, and government institutions in Canada. He is currently Senior Lecturer in Criminology at the University of Derby and has previously taught at Cardiff University and the University of Ottawa.

Gregory J. Howard is Associate Professor of Sociology at Western Michigan University where he teaches undergraduate courses on courts, media and crime, and environmental justice and graduate courses on sociological theory, criminological theory, as well as surveillance and mobilities. His research investigates mobilities involving horses and drones to understand the relationship between power, surveillance, and the movement of people, goods, and ideas. He has contributed research on comparative criminology to the *International Journal of Comparative and Applied Criminal Justice* and edited books by Carolina Academic Press, Routledge, McGraw Hill, HEUNI, NIJ, and Oxford University Press. He earned a B.A. in Social Ecology from the University of California at Irvine and an M.A. and Ph.D. in criminal justice from the State University of New York at Albany.

Andrea Hughes is Research Associate at John Jay College of Criminal Justice, focusing on human trafficking and gender-based violence. She is also a licensed social worker with extensive experience providing therapy and supervising programs that serve survivors of human trafficking, domestic violence, sexual assault, and homicide.

Emily Hurren is Lecturer in the School of Criminology and Criminal Justice at Griffith University, and an adjunct member of the Griffith Criminology Institute. She conducts research on child maltreatment and is particularly interested in the links between child maltreatment and developmental outcomes. She uses linked, longitudinal administrative data from various government departments, particularly including the child protection and youth justice systems in Queensland (Australia). Her work is guided by the developmental and life-course criminology perspective and developmental systems theories.

Douglas Irvin-Erickson is Assistant Professor, Director of the Genocide Prevention Program, and Fellow of Peacemaking Practice at the School for Conflict Analysis and Resolution, George Mason University. He is the author of a recent book, *Raphael Lemkin and the Concept of Genocide* (2016), and is currently writing a book based on his genocide prevention work in the African Great Lakes region and in Southeast Asia.

Matti Joutsen received the degree of Doctor of Laws (J.S.D.[hab.]) at the University of Helsinki. Currently, he is Special Advisor at the Thailand Institute of Justice. Previously, he served as Director of the European Institute for Crime Prevention and Control, affiliated with the United Nations (HEUNI). In Finland, he has also served as a court judge and as the Director of International Affairs at the Ministry of Justice. Dr Joutsen has been an active participant in the work of the United Nations crime prevention and criminal justice program for over 40 years. He served as interregional adviser for the UN on crime prevention and criminal justice and was a key negotiator on the UN Convention against Transnational Organized Crime, and in the review process for the UN Convention against Corruption.

Helen Kapstein is Associate Professor in the English Department at John Jay College, City University of New York. She earned her PhD in English and Comparative Literature from Columbia University. A postcolonial scholar, her areas of interest include South African literature and culture, cultural and media studies, and tourism and museum studies. Her book *Postcolonial Nations, Islands, and Tourism: Reading Real and Imagined Spaces* was published in 2017. Her work has appeared in *Postcolonial Text*, *English Studies in Canada*, and *Safundi: The Journal of South African and American Studies*, among other venues.

Maria Kiriakova is Assistant Professor and Associate Librarian for Technical Services at John Jay College of Criminal Justice. She has contributed articles to various reference books in the area of criminal justice, such as the *Encyclopedia of Crime and Punishment* (2002) and the *Encyclopedia of Law Enforcement* (2004).

Antigona Kukaj, an ICJ graduate of John Jay College, holds a Master's in Human Rights Studies (with a focus on genocide studies and transitional justice) from the Columbia University Graduate School of Arts & Sciences. She has participated in many United Nations activities relating to the International Criminal Court and the work of international courts and tribunals. She is currently pursuing her legal studies at the Mississippi College School of Law.

Justin Kurland is Senior Lecturer in Security and Crime Science at the University of Waikato and received his Bachelor's from Rutgers University, his Master's from Boston University, and his PhD from University College London (UCL). He is interested in the spatiotemporal analysis of crime in and around large-scale sport and event venues, crowd control, wildlife and conservation crimes, and how methods from other disciplines can inform our understanding of crime and security issues, as well as prevention.

Leona Lee is a faculty member in the Sociology Department of John Jay College of Criminal Justice. She received her PhD in criminal justice from Rutgers University and her MPhil from Cambridge University. Her research interests are in juvenile delinquency, juvenile justice, sentencing, and comparative studies. She has published in the *Journal of Criminal Justice*, *Journal of Crime and Justice*, *Juvenile and Family Court Journal*, and *Youth and Society*.

Theodore Leggett has been researching crime for the United Nations Office on Drugs and Crime in Vienna since 2004 and is best known for a series of regional organized crime threat assessments. Before joining UNODC, Ted spent nine years doing field research on crime in Africa, first at the School of Development Studies at the University of Natal in Durban, and then at the Institute for Security Studies in Pretoria. Most recently, he was responsible for UNODC's first *World Wildlife Crime Report*. His contribution is written in his private capacity and does not reflect the views of the United Nations.

A. M. Lemieux studied Biochemistry and Molecular Biophysics at the University of Arizona (BS 2005, MS 2006). He subsequently earned a Master's (2008) and PhD (2010) in Criminal Justice from Rutgers University. His doctoral research examined the risk of violent victimization Americans are exposed to in different activities and places. Since 2010, he has worked at the Netherlands Institute for the Study of Crime and Law Enforcement (NSCR) as a post-doc and then as a researcher. His current research focuses on the spatial and temporal elements of wildlife crime within protected areas with a specialization in understanding and planning ranger patrols.

Eric G. Lesneskie is Associate Professor in the Department of Sociology, Social Work, and Criminal Justice at Bloomsburg University. His current research interests include offender risk assessment, school crime, and organized crime.

Michael Levi holds degrees from Oxford, Cambridge, Southampton, and Cardiff and has been Professor of Criminology at Cardiff University, Wales since 1991. He has researched and published widely on international fraud, money laundering, and organized crime, as well as on violent crime and policing. Recent and pending books include *Drugs and Money: White-Collar Crime and its Victims*. Professor Levi's contribution was funded via EPSRC's grant EP/N028112/1.

Simon Mackenzie is Professor of Criminology at Victoria University of Wellington and Professor of Criminology, Law and Society at the Scottish Centre for Crime and Justice Research, University of Glasgow. Dr Mackenzie's main research interests are in international criminal markets, white-collar crime, organized crime, and policing. He is a director of Trafficking Culture, which maintains a website on evidence and policy in antiquities trafficking, and has worked with the UN on crime prevention in this field.

Shannon Magnuson is a doctoral student at George Mason University. Her research interests include organizational change, implementation science, and translational criminology. Her work across many justice settings takes a hands-on approach to improving how agencies use evidence and science to prevent crime and improve justice outcomes for clients.

Marissa Mandala is a research analyst at the New York City Police Department's Office of Management, Analysis & Planning. She graduated in 2018 with her PhD in Criminal

Justice from John Jay College at the CUNY Graduate Center. She received her Master's in Criminology from the University of Pennsylvania in 2013, and her Bachelor's in International Relations and Political Science from the University of Southern California in 2009. Her research interests include situational crime prevention, environmental criminology, and the terrorist tactic of assassination.

Marie-Helen Maras is a tenured Associate Professor at John Jay College of Criminal Justice, with a DPhil in Law and an MPhil and MSc in Criminology and Criminal Justice from the University of Oxford. She has numerous peer-reviewed journal articles covering cybercrime, digital forensics, and related issues, and is the author of several peer-reviewed books, the most recent of which is *Cybercriminology* (2016). Prior to her academic post, she served in the US Navy for approximately seven years, gaining significant experience in security and law enforcement from her posts as a Navy Law Enforcement Specialist and Command Investigator.

Estee Marchi is a PhD student of Criminal Justice and Assistant Editor of the *Criminal Law and Criminal Justice Books Review Journal* at Rutgers University, Newark. Her research specialties include lone-wolf terrorism and media and crime relationships.

Ineke Haen Marshall has a joint appointment in Sociology and Criminal Justice at Northeastern University. She received her Master's in Sociology from Tilburg University (the Netherlands) and her PhD from Bowling Green State University. She specializes in the study of comparative and global criminology, ethnicity and crime, self-report methodology, juvenile delinquency, and criminal careers. She is the chair of the Steering Committee of the International Self-Report Study of Delinquency (ISRD3) and co-author of *Delinquency in an International Perspective: The International Self-Report Delinquency Study* (2003), *Juvenile Delinquency in Europe and Beyond: Results of the Second International Self-report Delinquency Study* (2010), *The Many Faces of Youth Crime: Contrasting Theoretical Perspectives on Juvenile Delinquency across Countries and Cultures* (2012), and *A Global Perspective on Young People as Offenders and Victims* (2018).

Rob Mawby is Visiting Professor of Rural Criminology at Harper Adams University, Shropshire, England. His research interests cover comparative policing, victimology, crime reduction, and tourism and crime. He is the editor of *Crime Prevention and Community Safety: An International Journal* and is the author of eight books and more than 100 articles. Outside academia he has worked with police and other criminal justice agencies in a variety of capacities and was a member of police science subcommittee (2004–2007) of the European Police College (CEPOL) and expert advisor to EFUS on the Security and Tourism initiative.

Michael G. Maxfield is Professor of Criminal Justice at John Jay College of Criminal Justice. He is the author of numerous articles and books on a variety of topics, including victimization, policing, homicide, community corrections, and long-term consequences of child abuse and neglect. He is the co-author (with Earl Babbie) of the textbook, *Research Methods for Criminal Justice and Criminology*, now in its eighth edition (2018). Professor Maxfield served as editor of the *Journal of Research in Crime and Delinquency* from 2008 through 2016.

José Luis Morín is Professor in and Chairperson of the Latin American and Latina/o Studies Department at John Jay College of Criminal Justice. He teaches in the areas of international and domestic criminal justice, civil rights, international human rights, and Latin American and Latina/o studies. He has taught courses on international law and indigenous rights at the University of Hawai'i at Mānoa and worked many years as a civil rights and international human rights attorney.

Katharina Neissl is a doctoral candidate at Northeastern University. Her research interests include juvenile justice and delinquency, issues of gender, race and ethnicity, and comparative criminology. She was the project leader of the ISRD3 study in the USA.

Graeme Newman is Distinguished Professor Emeritus at the School of Criminal Justice, University at Albany and has published works in the fields of the history and philosophy of punishment, comparative criminal justice, private security, situational crime prevention, and information technology. Among his authored and co-authored books are: *Super Highway Robbery* (2003); *Migration, Culture Conflict and Crime* (2002); *The Global Report on Crime and Justice* (1998); *Rational Choice and Situational Crime Prevention* (1997); *The Punishment Response, Second Edition* (1985); and *Comparative Deviance: Law and Perception in Six Cultures* (1976).

Elenice Oliveira is Assistant Professor at Montclair State University, New Jersey. She has taught a course on Gender Issues in International Criminal Justice at John Jay College. Her research focuses on analyzing crime, policing, and prevention strategies in the USA and developing countries.

Stephan Parmentier studied Law, Political Science, and Sociology at the Catholic University of Leuven, Belgium and the University of Minnesota-Twin Cities. Since 1997 he has been Professor of Sociology of Crime, Law, and Human Rights at the Faculty of Law of the University of Leuven. He was elected Secretary-General of the International Society of Criminology in 2010 and is an Advisory Board member of the Oxford Centre for Criminology and the International Centre of Transitional Justice, New York.

Gohar Petrossian is Assistant Professor at John Jay College of Criminal Justice, Department of Criminal Justice. Her research focuses on applying environmental criminology theories to study crimes against wildlife, with a particular focus on illegal fishing.

Stephen Pires is Associate Professor of Criminology and Criminal Justice at Florida International University. His expertise is on the illegal wildlife trade and kidnappings for ransom with a particular focus on the opportunity structures of offending and the implications for prevention.

Carla L. Reyes is Assistant Professor of Law and Director of Legal RnD at the Center for Legal Services Innovation at Michigan State University College of Law, and serves as Faculty Associate at the Berkman Klein Center for Internet & Society at Harvard University.

Diana Rodriguez-Spahia is a PhD candidate at John Jay College of Criminal Justice Graduate Center, New York City. She also teaches courses in the International Criminal Justice and Sociology programs. Her research interests include terrorism, the crime-gender nexus, and policy development.

Vincenzo Ruggiero is Professor of Sociology at Middlesex University and at the University of Pisa, Italy. He has worked for the United Nations on a number of projects on transnational crime, human trafficking, and political corruption. Among his books are: *La Roba* (1992), *Eurodrugs* (1995), *European Penal Systems* (1995), *Organized and Corporate Crime in Europe* (1996), *Economie sporche* (1996), *The New European Criminology* (1998), *Crime and Markets* (2000), *Movements in the City* (2001), *Crime in Literature* (2003), *Understanding Political Violence* (2005), *Social Movements: A Reader* (2008), *Penal Abolitionism* (2010), *Corruption and Organized Crime in Europe* (2012), *Punishment in Europe* (2013), *The Crimes of the Economy* (2013), *Power and Crime* (2015), and *Dirty Money* (2017).

Ernesto U. Savona is Professor of Criminology at the Catholic University of Milan and director of Transcrime, Joint Research Centre on Transnational Crime – Università Cattolica del Sacro Cuore (Italy).

Phyllis A. Schultze is Librarian at the Don M. Gottfredson Library of Criminal Justice, Rutgers University, Newark. She also serves as Managing Editor of the online book review journal *Criminal Law and Criminal Justice Books*, and is the compiler of the Rutgers Criminal Justice Gray Literature Database.

Jon M. Shane is Associate Professor of Criminal Justice at John Jay College of Criminal Justice. His research is focused on police policy and practice issues, situational crime prevention, and problem-oriented policing; his theoretical interests include rational choice, routine activities, environmental criminology, and social disorganization. He has published extensively in leading policing and criminal justice journals on these topics, with a focus on police management.

Louise Shelley is University Professor and Omer and Nancy Hirst Endowed Chair at the Schar School of Policy and Government at George Mason University and the founder and director of the Terrorism, Transnational Crime and Corruption Center. She has published *Human Trafficking: A Global Perspective* (2010), *Dirty Entanglements: Corruption, Crime and Terrorism* (Cambridge University Press, 2014), and *Dark Commerce: How A New Illicit Economy is Threatening our Future* (2018). She is the author of many articles and book chapters on different aspects of transnational crime and testifies before Congress on these issues. She is a member of Global Initiative on Transnational Organized Crime.

Bir Pal Singh is presently working as Assistant Professor at the National Law Institute University, Bhopal (MP), India. His teaching and research interests include sociology, sociology of law, social-cultural anthropology, tribal and customary laws, legal anthropology, and empowerment of weaker sections.

Edward Snajdr is Associate Professor of Anthropology at John Jay College of Criminal Justice, CUNY. His research focuses on domestic violence, gender, crime, social justice, and how anthropology can be applied in the fields of criminology and development. He has conducted ethnographic field research in Eastern Europe, Central Asia, and the USA. His book, *Nature Protests: The End of Ecology in Slovakia*, was published in 2008. His forthcoming book, *What the Signs Say: Language, Gentrification and Place-making in Brooklyn* (with Shonna Trinch), will be published in 2020. At John Jay, he teaches Cultural Anthropology, Culture and Crime, and Systems of Law.

Itai Sneh is tenured at the Department of History in John Jay College of Criminal Justice and completed his doctorate at Columbia University. He holds a degree in Law and a Master's in Eastern European Jewish History from McGill University in Montreal, Canada, and a BA in Jewish History (with minors in International Relations, Biblical Studies, and Yiddish Language and Culture) from Hebrew University in Jerusalem, Israel. His research interests, presentations, and publications include books, articles, and lectures on the history of human rights; American presidential, diplomatic, legal, and political history; international law; terrorism; genocide; and the Middle East. He serves as a peer reviewer in the *Interdisciplinary Journal of Human Rights Law,* the *Journal of American History,* and *Peace & Change.*

Anna Stewart is Professor in the School of Criminology and Criminal Justice at Griffith University. Her research interests are built around opportunities provided by government administrative data. She has examined the lifetime contacts individuals have with child protection, criminal justice and mental health systems, system responses to youth offending and domestic violence, management of risk, diversionary responses, and system modeling. Her recent interests focus on translational research, moving research findings into policy and practice.

Alexander Sukharenko is Director of the Research Center of New Challenges and Threats to the National Security of the Russian Federation (Vladivostok, Russia) and an independent anti-corruption expert. Also he is a columnist in *Nezavisimaya gazeta* (Moscow) and business weekly *Konkurent* (Vladivostok). He is the author of more than 200 articles, policy memos and book chapters on organized and economic crime, illicit fishing, corruption, and terrorism. His latest releases are: *Russian Organized Crime: Transnational Aspects* (Moscow, 2014), *Anti-Corruption in the Countries of the Asia-Pacific Region: Organizational and Legal Aspects* (Moscow, 2017) and *Anti-Corruption in China: Legislation and Enforcement* (Moscow, 2018). He has numerous departmental and academic awards.

Anamika Twyman-Ghoshal is Associate Professor of Criminology at Stonehill College in Massachusetts. Her main research interests include global crime, crimes of the powerful, maritime piracy, and terrorism. She holds a Bachelor's in Law from the University of Wolverhampton, a Master's in International Business Law from Queen Mary, University of London, and a PhD from Northeastern University in Massachusetts. Her publications have focused on piracy, terrorism, corruption, and crimes of the powerful. Prior to joining academia, Dr Twyman-Ghoshal worked for the International Maritime Bureau in London investigating international fraud. She is fluent in English, German, Polish, and French and conversational Bengali.

Cécile Van de Voorde is a cultural criminologist and social documentary photographer whose ethnographic fieldwork focuses on violations of international human rights and humanitarian law, notably sexual and gender-based violence in armed conflict.

Jan J. M. van Dijk is Emeritus Professor of Victimology at the International Victimology Institute Tilburg (INTERVICT), and was born in Amsterdam, the Netherlands. He received his PhD in Criminology from Nijmegen University in 1977, initiated the International Crime

Victim Surveys in 1988, and acted as president of the World Society of Victimology between 1997 and 2000. Among his professional achievements are the Sellin-Glueck Award (2008), the Stockholm Prize in Criminology (2012), and the European Criminology Award (2017).

Rolf van Wegberg is a cybercrime researcher at Delft University of Technology and the Cyber Security & Resilience division at TNO. He conducts research and teaches at the intersection of crime and IT.

Klaus von Lampe is Professor in the Department of Law, Police Science and Criminal Justice Administration at John Jay College of Criminal Justice. He has been studying the illegal cigarette trade in Europe, China, and the USA over some 20 years. His other research interests include drug trafficking, underworld power structures, strategic crime analysis, and international law enforcement cooperation. Dr von Lampe is the author, co-author, or co-editor of numerous publications on organized and international crime, including the award-winning and critically acclaimed book *Organized Crime: Analyzing Illegal Activities, Criminal Structures, and Extra-legal Governance* (2016).

Noah Weisbord is Associate Professor of Law at Queen's University in Canada. He was a law clerk and visiting professional in the Immediate Office of the Prosecutor of the International Criminal Court and served as an expert on the working group charged by the ICC's Assembly of States Parties with drafting the crime of aggression.

Elmar Weitekamp holds a Master's in Social Work in Mönchengladbach, a Master's in Criminology, and a PhD in Criminology from the University of Pennsylvania. He served as Professor of Victimology and Restorative Justice at the University of Leuven and as Research Professor at the University of Tübingen. He is a long-time board member of the World Society of Victimology, and has been Visiting Professor at the University of Melbourne (Australia). His research interests and publications relate to victimology, restorative justice, and juvenile gangs.

Rob White is Professor of Criminology at the University of Tasmania, Australia. Recent books include *Environmental Harm: An Eco-Justice Perspective* (2013); *Green Criminology* (with Diane Heckenberg, 2014); and *Climate Change Criminology* (2018).

Lauren Wilson is a PhD candidate at the Rutgers School of Criminal Justice and a research associate at the Center for Conservation Criminology and Ecology. Her previous work includes sustainable management for zoo and aquarium animal populations, molecular genetics research, and ecological monitoring.

Richard Wortley is Director of the Jill Dando Institute of Security and Crime Science at University College London. He is a former prison psychologist and a past national chair of the Australian College of Forensic Psychologists. His main research interest is crime prevention and, in particular, the prevention of sexual offences against children, both contact and online. He has published internationally in this area, including the following books (with Stephen Smallbone): *Situational Prevention of Sexual Offenses Against Children* (2006), *Child Pornography on the Internet* (2006), *Preventing Child Sexual Abuse* (2008), and *Internet Child Pornography: Causes, Investigation & Prevention* (2012).

Yuliya Zabyelina is Assistant Professor in the Political Science department at John Jay College of Criminal Justice. She holds a doctoral degree in International Studies from the University of Trento in Italy, where she studied the role of state failure in furthering opportunities for transnational organized crime. Before moving to the USA, she held a postdoctoral position at the University of Edinburgh School of Law and lectured at Masaryk University in the Czech Republic. At John Jay College, she primarily teaches in the BA and MA programs in International Criminal Justice. She has been recognized with several professional awards, including the Newton International Fellowship (2013), SAGE Junior Faculty Teaching Award (2015), Aleksanteri Institute Visiting Scholar Fellowship (2015), Donald EJ MacNamara Junior Faculty Award (2016), and Faculty Scholarly Excellence Award (2018). She has also worked as a consultant for the United Nations Office on Drugs and Crime.

Marco Zanella is an Italian lawyer with a PhD in Criminology from the Catholic University of Milan. He has been a research assistant at the John Jay College of Criminal Justice and a visiting student at the Faculty of Law of the Erasmus University Rotterdam. He served as an intern at the United Nations Office on Drugs and Crime (UNODC) within the Terrorism Prevention Branch (TPB), Division for Treaty Affairs (DTA), and between 2006 and 2009 he cooperated at TRANSCRIME, the Joint Research Centre on Transnational Crime, at the University of Trento and the Catholic University of Milan.

Introduction

Mangai Natarajan

Criminology seeks to explain the nature, extent, causes, and consequences of crime, while the discipline of criminal justice deals with society's response to crime – how this is conceived, organized, administered, delivered, and evaluated. For most of their histories, these disciplines have focused on lower-class offenders committing "street" crimes that impact local neighborhoods and cities. They have paid relatively little attention to corporate or white-collar crimes and they have paid even less attention to studying the cross-cultural context of crime and the different national responses to crime.

In the past two decades, scholars have broken out of this mold and have begun to extend the boundaries of criminology and criminal justice. Specifically, they began to study crime patterns and evolving criminal justice practices in other parts of the world, using their own countries as a benchmark comparison. Their pioneering work resulted in "comparative criminology" and "comparative criminal justice" becoming established sub-fields of the broader disciplines (Mannheim, 1965; Mueller & Wise, 1965, 1975; Clinard & Abbott, 1973; Chang, 1976; Newman, 1976; Shelley, 1981a, 1981b; Terrill, 1982; Adler, 1983; Johnson, 1983; Bayley, 1990). One of the facts exposed by this body of work, increasingly recognized by the United Nations and the World Bank, is that the rule of law is not simply the result of economic and social progress; rather, it is a necessary condition for this progress to be achieved.

The acceleration in globalization that began in the 1990s has made clear that criminologists must take one step further than that made in comparative criminology (Fairchild, 1993; Adler, 1996; Yacoubain, 1998, Reichel, 1999). They must study not just the crimes and criminal justice systems of other countries, but also "transnational" crimes that span two or more countries. These crimes include cybercrimes, international money laundering, and various forms of trafficking (in drugs, humans, stolen antiquities, and endangered wildlife), which result from the huge expansion of world trade, the vast increase in migration, the internationalization of currency markets, and the explosions of international travel and electronic communications. While these consequences of globalization have been lauded by economists and others, criminologists, lawyers, and crime policy officials must now grapple with one of globalization's downsides – the opportunities it has created, together with the explosion of new technologies, for "transnational" crimes to emerge or be transformed into more serious forms (Newman, 1999).

No sooner had criminologists and criminal justice scholars wakened to this reality than developments in international relations and international law drew their attention to yet another large and important class of crimes that they had neglected, so-called international crimes (Yacoubain, 2000). These are crimes such as genocide and mass killings that occur within the boundaries of a sovereign state, but which are so horrific in their scale and consequences that they demand an international response. Some criminologists and criminal justice scholars (notably Hagan & Rymond-Richmond, 2009) have recently begun to conduct research on these crimes and it is becoming evident that a whole new field of study – international crime and justice – is being created. This field includes comparative criminology and criminal justice, and its subject matter is transnational crimes, international crimes, and the international responses to these crimes.

As will become apparent from this book, this new field departs in many important respects from traditional criminology and criminal justice. As discussed below, the international dimension of the field requires input from an even wider range of disciplines than those involved in criminology and criminal justice. Another important change is that moving the focus, first, from local crimes to transnational crimes, and then to international crimes, results in victims becoming increasingly more important. At the local level, the focus is mostly on offenders – explaining their crimes, apprehending them, and treating them. Relatively little attention is paid to the needs of victims for restitution, compensation, and protection. At the international level this relationship is reversed. There is considerably more concern with the harm to victims, and with restitution and compensation. This is because transnational and international crimes often involve multiple victims who suffer egregious harms and who have little recourse to justice. The victims are very visible, whereas the offenders are often difficult to identify, and even more difficult to apprehend. Thus, the implication for scholars is that victimology, the Cinderella of traditional criminology (Fattah, 1991), becomes much more important in international crime and justice.

Recognition of the increasing importance of transnational and international crimes led to the establishment of a undergraduate and graduate programs major in International Criminal Justice (Natarajan, 2002, 2008). This book is intended to serve the needs of the students in these programs for concise, up-to-date information on the broad array of topics covered by international crime and justice. Later sections of this introductory chapter detail the reasons for studying international criminal justice, lay out the elements of the interdisciplinary approach to the subject, and provide a brief description of the three parts of the book. The next two sections, however, provide more information about transnational and international crime.

DISTINGUISHING BETWEEN TRANSNATIONAL AND INTERNATIONAL CRIMES

Bassiouni (1986) provides a distinction between international criminal law enforceable by international criminal tribunals and crimes of international concern that are enforceable by national systems though they are also codified in international conventions. In line with Boister's (2003) four-fold distinction between international criminal law and transnational criminal law, Table I.1 highlights the main differences between transnational and international crimes.

Table I.1. Distinctive features of transnational and international crimes

Transnational Crimes	International Crimes
1. Have direct impact on the countries that are affected.	1. Have direct and indirect impact on the world peace and security.
2. Have jurisdictional and legal impact.	2. Have universal applicability.
3. Have no limitations to certain jurisdictions; can spread across countries.	3. Have domestic feature limiting the jurisdiction.
4. Have local crime groups organizing the activities through local and international networks or vice versa.	4. Have local governments and their agencies, social institutions including race, ethnicity, religion, caste, executing mass atrocities in their sovereign nations.
5. Not all international crimes are transnational in nature.	5. All transnational crimes are of international concern.

Distinguishing between transnational and international crime serves two important purposes: 1) it encourages the international community to focus its resources on the gravest crimes that threaten the peace and well-being of the world; 2) it encourages criminal justice resources and priorities including law enforcement to narrow their focus on the cross-national border crimes that affect specific countries' or regions' safety and security. For example, if cocaine trafficking happens between and within countries in the American region, these countries can collaborate and cooperate in developing extradition treaties and providing mutual legal assistance in controlling and preventing the trafficking in the region. This approach does not require Asian countries to become involved in the problems of the Americas; they can reserve their resources for the international or global causes. On the other hand, for example, in the case of genocide, a core international crime, the international communities or global response would help render and restore justice to the victims and assist in reconstructing the affected countries.

While transnational crimes can be dealt with by the cooperation of international agencies that focus on cross-national issues and border activities, including the United Nations Office of Drug Control (UNODC), the International Police Organization (INTERPOL), the European Union's Police Organization (EUROPOL), the Association of South-East Asian Nations Chiefs of Police (ASEANOPOL), and the World Customs Organization (WCO), to deal with international crimes *ad hoc*, or permanent institutions such as the International Criminal Court, international criminal tribunals that are beyond the sovereignty agreed upon by majority of countries of the world are essential.

Twenty-first-century crimes that span national borders, violating the laws of more than one country, are on the increase in volume and in numbers. The number of countries that are affected is also on the increase. Globalization has not only accelerated the commission of the crimes but also is involving countries that had not previously participated in the transnational crime business or activities.

Crimes such as honor-based violence and its variants are also increasing and spreading across countries affecting specific immigrant communities. Such crimes, which were once very much local and cultural, were not previously of interest worldwide. Crimes such as gender-based violence and child abuse are universal and ubiquitous, which is of concern to the international community, requiring domestic laws to take care of the crimes under their sovereignty context.

TRANSNATIONAL CRIMES

The Fourth United Nations Survey of Crime Trends and Operations of Criminal Justice Systems (1994) defined transnational crime as offenses whose inception, prevention, and/ or direct or indirect effects involves more than one country (Williams & Vlassis 2001). This was a follow-up of the Fifth United Nations Congress on the Prevention of Crime and the Treatment of Offenders, which coined the term "transnational crime." Gerhard Mueller (Mueller & Wise, 2001) argues that "the term 'transnational crime' did not have a juridical meaning then, and it does not have one now. It is a criminological term, under which may be lumped what is variously and differently defined in the penal codes of states, but with the common attribute of transcending the jurisdiction of any given state. We also observed then that, almost invariably, transnational criminality is organized criminality, although it is entirely imaginable that a single person can engage in transnational crime" (p. 13).

According to McDonald (1997), an offense is of transnational nature if:

1. it is committed in more than one state
2. it is committed in one state but a substantial part of its preparation, planning, direction, or control takes place in another state
3. it is committed in one state but involves an organized criminal group that engages in criminal activities in more than one state
4. it is committed in one state but has substantial effects in another state

This indeed reflects General Assembly Resolution 55/25 of November 15, 2000, United Nations Convention against Transnational Organized Crime, Article 3, section 2. Examples of transnational crimes include illegal immigration, sea piracy, airliner bombings, and various forms of international trafficking, which include trafficking in drugs, in stolen cars, in firearms, in antiquities and cultural objects, in endangered species, in human body parts, and in women for the sex trade.

Because transnational crimes span the borders of two or more countries, they require action by the specific countries where the laws have been violated. It is the need for cooperation between states, equally interested in protecting their legal values, which makes them willing to assist each other to prevent or prosecute such crimes. Reciprocity is therefore a guiding principle (Triffterer, 2006), but some cases where such reciprocity is absent require the attention of an international body, in particular the United Nations. An important example is the bombing of Pan Am Flight 103 over Lockerbie, Scotland in 1988, which killed all 259 people on board and eleven people in the village of Lockerbie. Though the aircraft was American-owned and many of the victims were US citizens, the airliner was brought down over Scotland. This meant that the case fell squarely under the jurisdiction of Scottish law. Because of the lack of extradition treaties, the Libyan leader Moammar El-Gadhafi refused to hand over the Libyan citizens suspected of the crime. This conflict was resolved by the United Nations' request to the government of Libya to comply by ensuring the appearance in the Netherlands of the two accused for the trial, as well as making available in the Netherlands any witnesses or evidence that might be requested by the court (for details, see Security

Council Resolution 1192 (1998) on the Lockerbie case). The Libyan leader eventually agreed to the trial being held in a neutral country, i.e., the Netherlands, though under Scottish law.

INTERNATIONAL CRIMES

The Rome Statute defines international crimes as the gravest crimes that threaten the peace, security, and well-being of the world and are of concern to the international community. This covers the "core crimes" of genocide, war crimes, crimes against humanity, and the crime of aggression (for details, see UN document PCNICC/2000/INF/3/Add.2, on Elements of Crime). The Preamble to the Rome Statute states in paragraph 6 that "it is the duty of every State to exercise its criminal jurisdiction over those responsible for international crimes." While there may be general agreement that the "core crimes" specified in the Statute are indeed "international crimes," there are many other crimes that in some circumstances might also qualify for this designation. Murphy (1999) has argued that international crimes are defined in a two-stage process. They are initially defined as crimes in a particular convention or agreement between two or more states. The primary focus of such agreements is the prosecution and punishment of individuals who perpetrate the crimes in question. Subsequently, after the agreement has been ratified by a large number of states and generally accepted even by states who do not become parties to the agreements, the crimes they cover may be regarded as crimes under customary international law. These crimes can be tried by countries that recognize them, or they can be tried by international criminal courts.

There is no authoritative listing of the acts that qualify, or might qualify, as international crimes, but a survey of conventions that criminalize certain acts produced the list of 24 such acts in Table I.2. These acts are categorized under the interests the conventions are designed to protect. The particular circumstances and conditions that might qualify them as international crimes, thus putting them under international jurisdiction, remain unclear. At first sight, many of the crimes would not be punishable under international law because they seem not to pose a threat to values inherent to the international community as a whole, in particular "the peace, security and wellbeing of the world," which includes the sovereignty and independence of each individual state. However, clearer specification and description of the crimes might reveal that in certain circumstances they do indeed constitute a threat to the integrity of the international community. The fact that such vital issues remain unclear reflects the immaturity of the field and the delayed recognition of its importance.

WHY STUDY INTERNATIONAL CRIME AND JUSTICE?

Students sometimes ask me why, as Americans, they should concern themselves with issues such as female genital mutilation and female infanticide that occur in distant lands. They ask, do we not have enough problems of our own to deal with and why should we interfere in the cultural practices of other countries? I try to explain that criminal justice scholars should be concerned with victimization and violations of human rights, not just in their own countries, but wherever they occur in the world. In many countries women are sorely oppressed and are subjected to inhumane treatment. Though the authorities in these countries might recognize the problems and develop measures to combat them, the problems tend to be accepted by local people and the measures have little or no impact. Again, one might question how the

Table I.2. Twenty-four "international crimes"

A. Protection of Peace
    1. Aggression
B. Humanitarian Protection During Armed Conflicts
    2. War crimes
    3. Unlawful use of weapons
    4. Mercenarism
C. Fundamental Human Rights
    5. Genocide
    6. Crimes against humanity
    7. Apartheid
    8. Slavery and related crimes
    9. Torture
    10. Unlawful human experimentation
D. Protection against Terror-Violence
    11. Piracy
    12. Aircraft hijacking and sabotage of aircrafts
    13. Force against internationally protected persons
	D. Protection against Terror-Violence (cont.)
	    14. Taking of civilian hostages
	    15. Attacks upon commercial vessels
	E. Protection of Social Interests
	    16. Drug offenses
	    17. International traffic in obscene publications
	F. Protection of cultural interests
	    18. Destruction and/or theft of national treasures
	G. Protection of the environment
	    19. Environmental protection
	    20. Theft of nuclear materials
	H. Protection of Communications
	    22. Interference with submarine cables
	I. Protection of Economic Interests
	    23. Falsification and counterfeiting
	    24. Bribery of foreign public officials

Source: Paust et al. (2000); Murphy (1999)

involvement of foreigners could help with these local problems, but there are some success stories of such intervention. For example, local reformers were only successful in putting an end to "sati," a cultural practice in India that required wives to immolate themselves on their husbands' funeral pyres, when they obtained the backing of the British colonial administration. More might be achieved, however, by raising international awareness about such problems through the United Nations and other international bodies, in the hope that coordinated international pressure can work to minimize the harms inflicted.

In the wake of the World Trade Center disaster, the general point is now easier to make that individual countries cannot on their own, without international help, successfully tackle some crimes. Perhaps the clearest example of this relates to the various bi-lateral and international agreements now in place to deal with terrorism. In fact, there are many good reasons to study international crime and justice. Twenty such reasons are identified below.

1. International crimes cause harm to hundreds and thousands of innocent people in all parts of the world. It is important to understand the magnitude and extent of this suffering.
2. International crimes are major human rights violations. We must study these violations in order to develop international law and appropriate institutions of justice to prevent and respond to these violations.
3. Victims of state crimes (government crimes against citizens) are not fully protected by international law. It is important to find ways of extending this protection through international treaties and agreements.
4. Differing views are held around the world as to what are appropriate or desirable ways to process offenders in the criminal justice system. We must examine these differences

from a comparative perspective to form some consensus in developing regulatory mechanisms.

5. It is important to understand the role of international relations in providing lawful resolution to atrocities committed around the world.

6. The perpetrators of international crimes are political figures who frequently escape the justice systems of their own countries and obtain sanctuary in other countries. We must try to uncover the political motivations of countries providing asylum to these criminals as a basis for developing more effective extradition treaties.

7. It is important to understand the historical and cultural backgrounds of crimes against humanity, such as slavery and apartheid, so as to find ways to eliminate the roots of these forms of discrimination.

8. Some international crimes are difficult to prosecute due to both political constraints involving state sovereignty issues and to the lack of resources of international institutions such as the United Nations. We must find ways around these problems so that an effective international justice system can be developed. It is also important to find ways to improve the effectiveness of regional forces such as "Eurojust."

9. The establishment of the International Criminal Court (ICC) is a major step in international criminal justice. We must find ways to improve the functioning of the court and to make it a force for world peace and justice.

10. Truth Commissions are a most encouraging development in the field of international criminal justice. It is important to understand how these commissions came to be established in order to improve their effectiveness in investigating the victimization of indigenous peoples and in rebuilding states.

11. In many parts of the world, women and children are subjected to many forms of violence. They are doubly victimized during times of armed conflict. It is important to find ways to improve the social status of women and children, as well as ways to develop international guarantees to preserve and protect their rights.

12. Globalization has resulted in the massive migration of people from one part of the world to another in search of better prospects. Local criminal groups often victimize innocent individuals in the process of migration. It is important to find ways of reducing the risks of victimization of migrants.

13. Many local crimes such as car theft span national borders. It is important to understand the factors that contribute to local crimes (including cultural, social, political, economic, and environmental conditions), so that effective situational controls can be implemented.

14. The proliferation of organized crime networks, with their extensive resources and sophisticated operations, is a serious threat to world security. We must study the operations of these organized crime networks and learn how they exploit a broad range of criminal opportunities.

15. Law enforcement strategies vary between and among nations. In order to reach some common ground for effective interdiction of international traffickers, it is important to develop international cooperative policing efforts. It is also important to learn how existing resources such as INTERPOL and EUROPOL can be made more effective.

16. International financial centers have opened doors for many organized criminal and terrorist groups to conceal their illegal proceeds. We must learn how to tighten

international banking safeguards so as to reduce opportunities for money laundering by these groups.

17. Transnational criminal activities affect all parts of the world, but the literature suggests that they most often originate in developing countries. It is important to understand the impact on crime of global economic development if developing countries are to be helped to combat transnational crimes.

18. Terrorism offers a serious threat to world peace and security. It is important to understand the political, social, economic, and cultural contexts in which terrorists operate if we are to develop effective measures to combat terrorism.

19. Technology has been a powerful force in bringing the world together. By the same token, it has opened new opportunities to commit crimes through the Internet. Traditional criminological explanations do not adequately explain such crimes, which seem little related to deprivation. We need a program of interdisciplinary research to learn how to design out these crimes from the Internet/cyberspace.

20. The mission of criminology and criminal justice has been to train people to assist in dealing with local crime problems. Expanding their mission to train people who are interested in making a career in international criminal justice will enrich both disciplines.

INTERNATIONAL CRIME AND JUSTICE: A COMPREHENSIVE INTERDISCIPLINARY APPROACH

Criminology and criminal justice are both interdisciplinary in nature. They draw upon many other disciplines in developing theories about crime, criminality, and the criminal justice process (including the apprehension, punishment, and treatment of offenders). These disciplines include economics, law, human geography, sociology, psychology, corrections, public administration, police science, and social work (see Figure I.1). An even wider range of disciplines must be invoked, however, in the service of understanding and dealing with transnational and international crimes. Victimology has already been mentioned in this context, but there are also important contributions to be made by international criminal law and human rights, international relations, political science, information technology, conservation and marine science, and global studies (see Figure I.1). Transnational and international crimes are local in origin, but their international reach ratchets up their level of complexity and changes their character in fundamental ways. Thus, once-simple frauds have now been transformed by globalization and advances in technology into massive Ponzi and pyramid schemes affecting many thousands of individuals across the world. And the difficulties of identifying offenders, arresting them, and bringing them to justice are multiplied many times when those offenders are engaged in international and transnational crimes. This increased complexity, requiring the contributions of scholars from many disciplines, poses daunting but exciting challenges to those studying international crime and justice.

ABOUT THE BOOK

As discussed above, there are many important reasons for studying international crime and justice, but until now there has been no single book offering a broad coverage of the many topics in this new field. This book is an attempt to meet this need. It provides an introduction

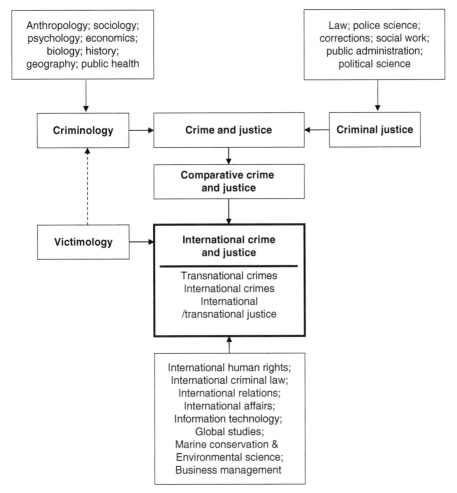

Figure I.1. International crime and justice: subject matter and contributory disciplines.
Source: Author

to the nature of international and transnational crimes and to the emerging legal frameworks for their prevention and control. Emphasis is placed on global aspects of the work of different criminal justice agencies and on international structures that have been created for crime prevention, punishment, and control.

The compact and informative chapters make the book suitable for both graduate and undergraduate courses. In many cases, because of the depth and breadth of the book's coverage, it could serve as the main text. In other cases, it might be more suitably used as a supplementary text. Courses that would most likely make use of the book as a course text include: Introduction to International Criminal Justice, Comparative Criminology/Criminal Justice, International Criminology/Global Criminology, International Perspectives on Crime and Justice, and Global Crime and Justice.

This book is arranged in three parts covering the subject matter of international crime and justice, including the topics on transnational and international core crimes and research.

Part I: Transnational Crime contains four subsections including an overview of transnational crimes; transnational organized crime groups; factors that facilitate transnational crimes: and the development of transnational justice.

Part Ia: Varieties of Transnational Crimes includes 26 chapters on transnational trafficking crimes: drug trafficking (Chapter 1); trafficking of human beings (Chapter 2); trafficking of children (Chapter 3); migrant smuggling (Chapter 4); international trafficking of stolen vehicles (Chapter 5); transnational firearms trafficking (Chapter 6); trafficking in art, antiquities, and cultural heritage (Chapter 7); the illegal cigarette trade (Chapter 8); and wildlife trafficking (Chapter 9). Further in this section transnational crimes with more general global implications are discussed. These include: cybercrime (Chapter 10); crime and online anonymous markets (Chapter 11); cryptocurrencies and money laundering (Chapter 12); money laundering (Chapter 13); international fraud (Chapter 14); ransom kidnapping (Chapter 15); child pornography (Chapter 16). Other crimes of international concern are also covered, including: transnational environmental crime (Chapter 17); one of the world's worst industrial disasters due to multinational corporate criminal negligence at Bhopal, India (Chapter 18); maritime crimes (Chapter 19); maritime piracy (Chapter 20); poaching of terrestrial animals and plants (Chapter 21); illegal commercial fishing (Chapter 22); corruption (Chapter 23); tourist and visitor crimes (Chapter 24) – which are very much local in character but have international repercussions. The section also covers crimes that have global impact with features of transnational crimes, including terrorism, with a review of practical ways to prevent terrorism (Chapter 25), and political assassinations (Chapter 26).

Part Ib: Transnational Organized Crime opens with a discussion of the important reasons for studying transnational organized crime (Chapter 27) and its patterns and trends (Chapter 28); transnational organized crime networks (Chapter 29); Italian organized crime (Chapter 30); extortion (Chapter 31); Russian organized crime (Chapter 32); and the rise of Balkan organized crime (Chapter 33). While the previous chapters deal with organized crime groups, specific chapters follow on some of the world's major organized crime groups, including those in Asia (Chapter 34) and drug cartels (Chapter 35). While there are various notions about the relationship between terrorists and organized crime groups, the chapter on the "nexus" between organized crime and terrorism (Chapter 36) provides an interesting perspective for further research.

Part Ic: Factors that Facilitate Transnational Crimes covers basic explanations of international and transnational crime, including the globalization of crime (Chapter 37); routine activities and transnational crime (Chapter 38); political aspects of violence (Chapter 39); migration, crime, and victimization (Chapter 40); and culture and crime (Chapter 41).

Part Id: Transnational Justice provides the legal framework for understanding variations in legal systems of the world (Chapter 42); punishment philosophies and practices around the world (Chapter 43); prisons around the world (Chapter 44); and world policing models (Chapter 45). It also provides an account of law enforcement activities and the development of regional police cooperation and cooperation among the judiciary directed against international and transnational crime, including cross-border policing

(Chapter 46); cybercrime laws and investigations (Chapter 47); the European Union and judicial cooperation in criminal matters (Chapter 48); extradition and mutual legal assistance (Chapter 49); international cooperation to combat money laundering (Chapter 50); and the role of major intergovernmental organizations and international agencies in combating transnational crime (Chapter 51). The section ends by discussing the major approaches to crime prevention that have been adopted around the world (Chapter 52).

Part II: International Crimes consists of three sections and provides detailed research accounts of the core international crimes of genocide, war crimes, crimes against humanity, and the crime of aggression, as well as some other international crimes.

Part IIa: Core International Crimes introduces the three core international crimes as defined by the Rome Statute, 1998 (Chapter 53). It also provides an account of historical dimensions of genocide (Chapter 54) and includes further chapters on understanding culture and conflict in preventing genocide (Chapter 55); war crimes (Chapter 56); and Apartheid (Chapter 57). Finally, in the context of the ICC, the section presents the latest discussion on crimes of aggression (Chapter 58) when committed by a state's leaders, as well as discussing crimes of the powerful (Chapter 59).

Part IIb: International Crime and Justice for Women and Children provides an account of women and international criminal justice (Chapter 60); domestic violence (Chapter 61); honor-based violence (Chapter 62); child maltreatment (Chapter 63); and children and international criminal justice (Chapter 64).

Part IIc: International Justice focuses on major developments in international criminal justice, including the role of the United Nations in preserving security and peace worldwide (Chapter 65) and a discussion of treaties and international criminal law (Chapter 66). Chapter 67 focuses on the newly introduced International Criminal Court (ICC) and describes its functioning; The ICC and the Darfur Investigation: Progress and Challenges (Chapter 68) explains how serious international crimes are investigated and how the ICC processes the cases; Chapter 69 discusses the attention paid by the ICC to victims' rights and the workings of major international criminal tribunals and international hybrid courts established in response to specific international crimes, including Nuremberg, Tokyo, Rwanda, Yugoslavia, and Sierra Leone (Chapter 70). Further, Chapters 71, 72, 73, and 74 describe the development of Human Rights Commissions and the Truth Commissions in South Africa and Guatemala and discuss the role of NGOs in international criminal justice. Finally, Chapter 75 discusses the need for restorative justice for transitional settings that are heading toward transformation.

Part III: International and Transnational Crime Research. Measuring the nature and extent of transnational and international crime is a prerequisite for the scientific discipline of international criminology. Chapters 76–81 review the main sources of crime and delinquency, victimization data that exist at national and international levels, and the role of qualitative methodology in studying the evolving nature of international and transnational crimes.

Further, this section describes information resources for international crime and justice. Chapter 82 describes the world criminal justice library network and Chapters 83 and 84 provide specific instructions for finding ICJ-related information from journals, databases, the Internet, and the mass media, and the role of Grey Literature in criminal justice research.

CONCLUSION

This short introduction has described the scope and coverage of the book. It has explained what is meant by transnational and international crimes and it has drawn attention to the rapid emergence of international crime and justice as an important new sub-field of criminology and criminal justice. In particular, it has explained how some pioneering criminologists and criminal justice scholars have responded to the growing realization of the threats to world order posed by international terrorism and transnational organized crime, scourges that have been enabled and facilitated by the acceleration of globalization. It has explained how this new field of study encompasses and enhances previous comparative research and why it demands the contribution of scholars from a wide range of disciplines.

It would be remiss, however, if this introduction closed without exhorting more scholars to follow the example of the pioneers who have expanded their horizons and broadened their focus beyond crimes occurring at the neighborhood and city levels. While these crimes continue to demand attention, the personal and financial harms they cause to their victims pale into insignificance compared with the gross violations of human rights, the suffering of millions, and the vast numbers of violent deaths resulting from international crimes brought daily to our attention in our comfortable homes by newspapers, television, and the Internet. As scholars, we can no longer ignore these crimes, but must find ways to use our disciplinary knowledge and skills in helping to prevent and control them. The chapters in this book point the way and provide a sure foundation for our future efforts.

REFERENCES

Adler, F. (1983). *Nations not obsessed with crime*. Littleton, CO: F.B. Rothman.
  (1996). A note on teaching "International". *Journal of Criminal Justice Education*, 7(2), 323–344.
Bassiouni, M (1986), *International criminal law*. Dobbs Ferry, NY: Transnational Publishers.
Boister, N. (2003) Transnational criminal law? *European Journal of International Law*, 14(5), 953–976.
Clinard, M. & Abbott, D. (1973). *Crime in developing countries: A comparative perspective*. New York: John Wiley.
Chang, H.D. (Ed.). (1976). *Criminology: a cross-cultural perspective*. Durham, NC: Carolina Academic Press.
Fairchild, E. S. (1993). *Comparative criminal justice systems*. Belmont, CA: Wadsworth.
Fattah, E. A. (1991). *Understanding criminal victimization*. Scarborough, Toronto: Prentice Hall.
Hagan, J. & Rymond-Richmond, W. (2009). *Darfur and the crime of genocide*. New York: Cambridge University Press.
Johnson, H. E. (1983). *International handbook of contemporary developments in criminology*. Westport, CT: Greenwood Press.
Mannheim, H. (1965). *Comparative criminology*. London: Routledge & Kegan Paul.
McDonald, W. (1997). *Crime and law enforcement in the global village*. Cincinnati, OH: Anderson Publishing.
Mueller, G. O. W. & Wise, M. E. (Eds). (1965). *International criminal law*. Publications of the Comparative Criminal Law Project, vol. 2. South Hackensack, NJ: Rothman.
  (1975). *Studies in comparative criminal law*. Springfield, IL: Thomas.

(2001). Transnational crime: Definitions and concepts. In P. Williams & D. Vlassis (Eds), *Combating transnational crime: Concepts, activities, and responses* (p. 13). New York: Frank Cass Publishers.

Murphy, J. F. (1999). Civil liability for the commission of international crimes as an alternative to criminal prosecution. *Harvard Human Rights Journal*, 12. Retrieved February 25, 2010, from www.law.harvard.edu/students/orgs/hrj/iss12/murphy.shtml#fn22.

Natarajan, M. (2002). International criminal justice education: A note on curricular resources. *Journal of Criminal Justice Education*, 13(2), 479–500.

(2008). John Jay's bachelor's degree in international criminal justice. In K. Aromaa & Redo, S. (Eds), *The rule of law: Criminal justice teaching and training across the world*. Helsinki, Finland: The European Institute for Crime Prevention and Control.

Newman, G. (1976). *Comparative deviance: Perceptions and law in six cultures*. New York: Elsevier.

(Ed.). (1980). *Crime and deviance: A comparative perspective*. Beverly Hills, CA: Sage.

(Ed.). (1999). *Global report on crime*. New York: Oxford University Press.

Paust, J., Bassiouni, M., Scharf, M., Gurule, J., Sadat, L., Zagaris, B., & Williams, S. (2000). *International criminal law*. Durham, NC: Carolina Academic Press.

Reichel, P. L. (1999). *Comparative criminal justice systems – A topical approach*. Upper Saddle River, NJ: Prentice Hall.

Shelley, L. (1981a). *Crime and modernization. The impact of industrialization and modernization on crime*. Carbondale, IL: Southern Illinois University Press.

(Ed.). (1981b). *Readings in comparative criminology*, Carbondale, IL: Southern Illinois University Press.

Terrill, J. R. (1982). Approaches for teaching comparative criminal justice to undergraduates. *Criminal Justice Review*, 7(1), 23–27.

Triffterer, O. (2006). Concluding remarks. In The Austrian Federal Ministry for Foreign Affairs / Salzburg Law School on International Criminal Law, Humanitarian Law and Human Rights Law (Eds.), *The future of the international criminal court – Salzburg retreat*, 25–27 May 2006. www.sbg .ac.at/salzburglawschool/Retreat.pdf.

Williams, P. & Vlassis, D. (2001). *Combating transnational crime: Concepts, activities, and responses*. New York: Frank Cass Publishers.

Yacoubain, G. S. (1998). Underestimating the magnitude of international crime: Implications of genocidal behavior for the discipline of criminology. *The World Bulletin*, 14, 23–36.

(2000). The (in)significance of genocide behavior to the discipline of criminology, *Crime, Law & Social Change*, 34(1), 7–19.

PART I

OVERVIEW: TRANSNATIONAL CRIME

Varieties of Transnational Crimes

Transnational crimes are criminal acts and transactions that span national borders. Globalization and advances in technology have led to a vast increase in these often-complex crimes that include cybercrimes, international money laundering, and various forms of trafficking. Drug trafficking is perhaps the pre-eminent transnational crime. Ever since the Shanghai Convention in 1909, the serious threat to human well-being caused by drug abuse has led nations around the world to take action to deal with their drug problems. Indeed, for many decades drug trafficking absorbed most of the United Nations' efforts devoted to the control of transnational crimes. More recently, recognition of the wide-scale violations of human rights resulting from trafficking of humans, especially of women and children for sexual exploitation and servitude, have galvanized international cooperation. But countries whose laws have been violated do not always have an equal interest in stopping transnational crimes. For example, some poorer countries may turn a blind eye to illegal migration of their nationals seeking employment in wealthier countries. This is because the migrants often remit a large portion of their earnings back home, thus benefiting the local economy.

A 2017 report of Global Financial Integrity by Channing Mavrellis, CAMS (March 2), titled "*Transnational crime and the developing world*," illustrates that the business of transnational crime is valued at an average of $1.6 trillion to $2.2 trillion annually. Of the 11 transnational crimes (the trafficking of drugs, arms, humans, human organs, and cultural property; counterfeiting, illegal wildlife crime, illegal fishing, illegal logging, illegal mining, and crude oil theft), counterfeiting ($923 billion to $1.13 trillion) and drug trafficking ($426 billion to $652 billion) have the highest and second-highest values, respectively; illegal logging is the most valuable natural resource crime ($52 billion to $157 billion). Transnational crime is a lucrative money-making business.

Many examples of the generalizations made above can be found in the chapters (1–26) collected together in this section, which cover a wide range of transnational crimes, as follows: international drug trafficking (Chapter 1: Mangai Natarajan); trafficking in human beings (Chapter 2: Alexis A. Aronowitz) and children (Chapter 3: Meredith Dank and Andrea Hughes); migrant smuggling (Chapter 4: Paolo Campana); the international trafficking of stolen vehicles (Chapter 5: Rick Brown and Ronald V. Clarke); small arms trafficking (Chapter 6: Theodore Leggett); trafficking in art, antiquities, and cultural heritage (Chapter 7: Simon Mackenzie); cigarette smuggling (Chapter 8: Klaus von Lampe); wildlife trafficking (Chapter 9: Justin Kurland); cyber crime (Chapter 10: Alex Alexandrou); crime and online anonymous markets (Chapter 11: Pieter Hartel and Rolf van Wegberg); cryptocurrencies and money laundering opportunities (Chapter 12: Sarah Durrant and Mangai Natarajan); money laundering (Chapter 13: David C. Hicks and Adam Graycar); international fraud (Chapter 14: Michael Levi); ransom kidnapping (Chapter 15: Stephen Pires and Rob Guerette); and child pornography (Chapter 16: Richard Wortley).

While there is no single definition for transnational crimes, in the early 1990s scholars defined transnational crimes to include offences whose inception, prevention, and/or direct or indirect effects involve more than one country. The above-mentioned crimes fit the definition, and there are other crimes that are local but have transnational impact. Some of these crimes are discussed at length in this section. They are: transnational environmental crime (Chapter 17: Rob White); industrial disasters due to corporate criminal negligence (Chapter 18: G. S. Bajpai and Bir Pal Singh); maritime crimes (Chapter 19: Gisela Bichler); maritime piracy (Chapter 20: Jon M. Shane and Shannon Magnuson); poaching of terrestrial wild animals and plants (Chapter 21: Lauren Wilson and Ronald V. Clarke); illegal commercial fishing (Chapter 22: Gohar Petrossian and Ronald V. Clarke); corruption (Chapter 23: Adam Graycar); tourist and visitor crimes (Chapter 24: A. M. Lemieux and Marcus Felson); terrorism (Chapter 25: Graeme Newman and Ronald V. Clarke); and political assassinations (Chapter 26: Marissa Mandala). These crimes have distinctive features, explanations, nature, and extent, and require transnational cooperation, legal instruments, and strategic responses to prevent them from happening.

1 Drug Trafficking

Mangai Natarajan

INTRODUCTION

Ever since the Shanghai Opium Commission in 1909, many countries around the world have found themselves grappling with problems of drug abuse and many conventions have formulated proposals to reduce the international trade in illicit substances. International collaborative efforts and policies have mostly been geared to obstructing the supply of drugs, while efforts to control demand have been left to national governments. Judged by world seizures, various forms of illicit drugs continue to be sold and used at unacceptably high levels in many parts of the world. Moreover, with the advent of globalization, drugs are traveling across borders much more commonly than they once did. Many countries without histories of drug use, particularly developing countries, are now reporting problems of abuse because they have become transit points for international drug trafficking. This has not only become a threat to public health but also to public safety and security.

Because of lucrative profits, drug traffickers will always find a way to meet the demand for drugs. Traffickers are opportunistic and can be expected to: market new drugs; seek out new routes to smuggle drugs; seek new partners among organized crime groups in different countries; exploit new manufacturing and communication technologies; recruit vulnerable individuals into the work of trafficking; and find ways to launder the proceeds. This chapter provides a descriptive account of international drug trafficking intended to assist understanding of its complex nature and of the challenges involved in its control.

DEFINITION

Drug trafficking is a crucial link in the chain between illicit drug production and consumption (World Drug Report, 1997, p. 131) and involves the following sequential stages of distribution:

- growing or producing
- manufacturing
- importing or smuggling
- wholesale distribution
- regional distribution
- street-level distribution

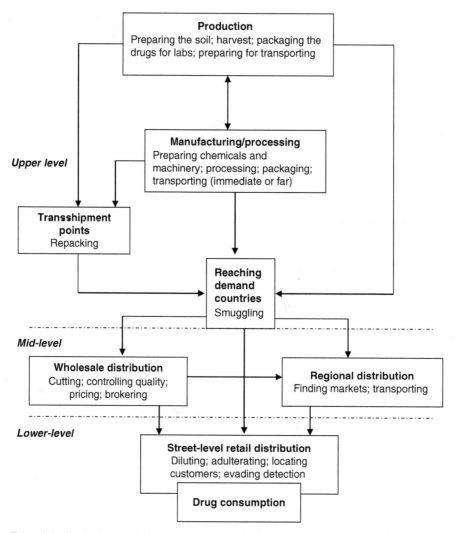

Figure 1.1. Sequential steps in international drug trafficking.

As usually defined, it does not encompass retail operations and street-level drug dealing but involves all the earlier stages in the drug distribution chain, including the tasks of production, manufacturing, smuggling, and wholesale and regional distribution that involve multi-kilo operation. Figure 1.1 distinguishes three levels of distribution as follows: upper-level drug trafficking denotes the movement of drugs in bulk from the producing countries to the demand countries; mid-level operations involve the wholesale distribution of the smuggled drugs to different regions; and lower-level distribution involves retail level sales to the consumer markets within the demand countries.

These distinctions provide the framework for understanding the mechanics of drug trafficking operations and for undertaking international, national, and local-level supply reduction strategies.

DRUG SUPPLY

According to the 2018 World Drug Report, the production of opium and the manufacture of cocaine has increased. In 2017, a total of 10,500 metric tons of opium was produced around the world. The major producers are Afghanistan, Myanmar, and the Lao People's Democratic Republic – countries that are part of the Golden Triangle and Golden Crescent. The Andes region (Colombia, Peru, and Bolivia) is the major source of supply of cocaine to world markets.

There is an emerging trend of the misuse of non-medical opioids (hydrocodone, oxycodone, codeine, and tramadol) and medical/pharmaceutical opioids (methadone, buprenorphine, and fentanyl). Hundreds of new psychoactive substances (NPSs) are also now available on the market worldwide. Amphetamine has dominated synthetic drug markets in the Near and Middle East and Western and Central Europe, but recently its manufacture has increased in North Africa and North America. The methamphetamine market is growing in East and Southeast Asia and North America and in Oceania, and now accounts for the largest share of global quantities of amphetamine-type stimulants (ATSs) seized.

According to the European Monitoring Centre for Drugs and Drug Addiction (EMCDDA, 2018) and the European Union Agency for Law Enforcement Cooperation (EUROPOL), Belgium and the Netherlands are key countries for the manufacture of ecstasy (MDMA) in Europe. These substances are also produced in many other European countries, including Belgium, Germany, the United Kingdom, Greece, Portugal, the Nordic states, Poland, Estonia, Lithuania, and the Czech Republic. They are also produced in Australia, North America, South Africa, China, and Southeast Asian countries (where they are much cheaper to produce than in Europe), and more recently in South and Central America.

Finally, cannabis is the most widely used drug around the world. Colombia and Jamaica are now the main source of cannabis for the United Kingdom and the USA, while Morocco and Albania are the main sources for continental Europe.

Complexities of International Drug Trafficking

As can be seen from Figure 1.1, drug trafficking involves many stages of operation from production to consumption. Unlike legal international businesses, the illegal drug trade requires clandestine strategies and techniques to move the drugs from producing countries to the consumers. Understanding the ways in which drugs are trafficked (e.g., methods, techniques, and routes) and how the drug trade is organized (e.g., distribution strategies, structure of organizations, and organized crime networks) is important in finding ways to control the flow of drugs.

Variety of Methods, Techniques, and Routes Used to Transport Drugs

Globalization has greatly increased the volume of containerized trade, the frequency of international flights, the availability of international delivery services, and global access to the Internet. Depending upon the quantity and proximity of locations, illegal drugs are now finding their ways to consumer nations by air, sea, land, and postal services in the same way as legal commodities. E-trafficking of drugs has also been reported. High-powered motorboats, bulk cargo freighters, and containerized cargo ships remain the most common methods of moving multikilo-level quantities of cocaine and heroin. However, any available method may be used. For example, small submersibles are sometimes used in Central America for transporting cocaine, and cannabis resin is transported from Morocco to Spain using goods vehicles, in cars (by ferry), or using small boats. The drugs are then transported over land to France, the United Kingdom, the Netherlands, and other European countries.

Drugs have been swallowed or hidden in body cavities; hidden on the person; packed into luggage or belongings; stashed in cars, boats, or aircraft; and hidden in seemingly legitimate freight. The US Customs and Border Control has listed some of the more unusual methods of concealment.

- Drugs surgically implanted in a man's thigh.
- Contraband hidden in a woman's wig.
- Cocaine surgically implanted in a living dog.
- Marijuana concealed in the hollowed-out boards of wooden pallets.
- Cocaine masked in the soles of shoes.
- Marijuana bundles in manmade landscaping stones.
- Drugs stashed in the manifold of an engine.
- A variety of drugs in body cavities and ingested.
- A marijuana load in the floorboard of a trailer hauling two live bears.
- Drugs concealed in new furniture.
- Marijuana hidden in metal cans disguised as food products.

The World Customs Organization (2017) reports a seizure of 142 bricks of cocaine (156 kg) in two electric generators from Chile to the seaport of Limassol, Cyprus. In March 2016, 468 kg of heroin was found in 114 out of 1800 boxes containing raisins from Iran.

VARIED ROUTES

Drug traffickers are constantly looking for new routes that are convenient and safe from interdiction. In order to increase their profits, traffickers have also developed markets for drugs in the transshipping points or countries. Consequently, there has been a surge in drug use among the general population in Nigeria and other African countries as well as in the Indian subcontinent.

Drug traffickers are undoubtedly rational actors who weigh the pros and cons of different routes to move drugs from supply to demand countries. Reuter (2014) describes three criteria they use: 1. They generally prefer countries where corruption is rife and where there are fewer law enforcement resources. 2. They prefer routes that are near to the supply or demand countries, saving them time and money. 3. They prefer countries with ready supplies of local manpower to help with the transport and distribution of drugs.

A possible fourth attractive criterion, made possible by the advent of the darknet or cryptonet, is the availability of the virtual delivery of drugs, which helps to conceal the identity of all involved parties. A recent study by Rhumorbarbe et al. (2016) found that 2700 vendors from 70 countries claimed to sell illicit drug products by this method. The drugs sold included cannabis-related products, ecstasy (MDMA), and stimulants (cocaine, speed). According to Dolliver (2015), of the 19 countries that were identified as distinct source countries for drugs, the USA is both the number-one country of origin for drug sales on Silk Road 2 (a small darknet site that was merged after the shutdown of the larger Silk Road) and the number-one destination country.

Varieties of Trafficking Organizations and Distribution Strategies

Traffickers must develop routine ways of transacting business and the distribution systems that have been developed in some cases are highly complex. Large drug networks are organized with extensive human "trust" contacts between supply and destination points (Decker & Townsend, 2008) and with a distinct hierarchical structure similar to some business corporations. They may be controlled by so-called "kingpins" who negotiate transactions with other drug organizations. Within the networks, middle managers oversee operations on behalf of the kingpins; couriers transport drugs within and between the demand countries; and wholesalers distribute the drugs to retailers (or street dealers) who in turn supply the users. They use all available technology, including personal computers, public telephones, cell phones, pagers, and facsimile machines, in their daily operations.

The enormous profits available from drug trafficking attract a wide spectrum of participants. These range from individuals working alone to major organized crime syndicates involving a variety of ethnic groups that undertake a variety of tasks. The organized crime groups include: the Italian and Sicilian Mafia; the Neapolitan Camorra and Calabrian 'Ndrangheta; Asian Triads and Tongs; the Japanese Yakuza; Mexican cartels; the Cuban and Russian Mafias; and many other criminal groups from the Middle East, the Caribbean, and Europe. They take part in all stages of distribution (from setting up connections with the producers, to transshipping and distributing to the retailers) by networking with one another. Colombian and Italian groups supply cocaine in cooperation with other groups (e.g., Dutch, British, and Spanish) and West African, especially Nigerian, groups are also active in transporting cocaine from Africa to Europe; Balkan organized crime groups (OCGs) are emerging actors. The activities of these groups have become a major challenge for law enforcement. Analyses of 78 drug trafficking organizations prosecuted in New York City from 1985 to 2007 found four main kinds of organization – "freelance," "family-based businesses," "communal businesses," and "corporations" (Natarajan & Belnager, 1998; Natarajan, Zanella, & Yu, 2015). A high degree of specialization exists in the tasks performed by some of the trafficking enterprises in order to minimize the risks of detection and arrest (Desroches, 2005).

Not only have the changes discussed above expanded the opportunities for drug trafficking, but they have diversified these opportunities through divergence of supplies, proliferation of substances, and expansion of trafficking routes and methods. These forces have created niche markets that large established drug trafficking organizations might not be sufficiently nimble to exploit. Instead, the markets become the preserve of *ad hoc* networks of sometimes hastily formed groups of criminal entrepreneurs, who might forge business deals with first one entity and then another as opportunity dictates (Natarajan, 2006). Consistent with this view, recent research has argued that drug trafficking organizations are now more likely to consist of networks of a relatively small number of criminal entrepreneurs, with informal links between their members and a flattened hierarchy, than in the past, when they primarily comprised large, hierarchical criminal syndicates characterized by the use of violence, threat, or intimidation.

Global Strategies to Combat the Supply and Demand of Illegal Drugs

Various international organizations have important roles in controlling drug supplies and the demand for drugs around the world. These include the United Nations International Drug Control Programme, the United Nations Educational Scientific and Cultural Organization (UNESCO), the International Narcotics Control Board (INCB), the World Health Organization, INTERPOL, EUROPOL, and the World Customs Organization (WCO). The United Nations Office on Drugs and Crime (UNODC), which functions as a global leader in this field, has extensive liaison arrangements with these agencies and with regional enforcement authorities in order to develop and strengthen cross-border and regional cooperation in apprehending traffickers and seizing drugs. Despite these global efforts and despite stringent enforcement at the street level, illegal drugs still reach the hands of millions of users.

It is difficult to set in place a unified mechanism to combat the illicit supply of drugs due to variations in legal systems, law enforcement tactics, cultures (languages and cultural practices), financial institutions and banking systems, political and economic conditions, and tolerance levels of drugs and ideologies. However, it is imperative to develop increased international cooperation in apprehending the traffickers and disrupting supplies. There is also an urgent need to develop international regulatory controls with high standards for entry in banking and financial institutions to control the money laundering of the proceeds from drug trafficking.

SUMMARY

The 2018 World Drug Report shows no evidence that the global drug problem has been reduced; instead, there has been an increase in drug production, in the range of drugs produced, and in the diversity of drug markets. Without interdiction efforts, drug supplies might have skyrocketed and so might have the numbers of users. The fundamental economic point is that so long as there is the demand, and the rewards of meeting this demand are sufficiently great, there will be criminal groups willing to supply the drugs. Globalization has increased the crime opportunities through divergence of supplies, proliferation of substances, and expansion of trafficking routes, including virtual routes. Recent research has argued that drug trafficking organizations are now more likely to consist of networks of a relatively small number of criminal entrepreneurs, with informal links between their members (Natarajan, 2006). A handful of evaluations show some positive impact of crackdowns on street-level local markets, but hardly any empirical evaluations exist of supply reduction efforts aimed at higher-level markets. This lack of scientific research is due largely to the difficulty of collecting data on the complex, constantly changing nature of drug trafficking. Finding a solution to this difficulty presents an urgent challenge to the community of researchers concerned with combating drug trafficking.

REFERENCES

Decker, S. H. & Townsend, M. (2008). *Drug smugglers on drug smuggling: Lessons from the inside.* Philadelphia, PA: Temple University Press.

Desroches, F. (2005). *The crime that pays: Drug trafficking and organized crime in Canada.* Toronto: Canadian Scholar's Press.

Dolliver, D. S. (2015). Evaluating drug trafficking on the Tor Network: Silk Road 2, the sequel. *International Journal of Drug Policy*, 26(11), 1113–1123.

European Monitoring Centre for Drugs and Drug Addiction (EMCDDA). (2018). European Drug Report 2018: Trends and Developments. Retrieved from www.emcdda.europa.eu/system/files/publications/8585/20181816_TDAT18001ENN_PDF.pdf.

Natarajan, M. (2006). Understanding the structure of a large heroin distribution network: A quantitative analysis of qualitative data. *Quantitative Journal of Criminology*, 22(2), 171–192.

Natarajan, M. & Belanger, M. (1998). Varieties of upper-level drug dealing organizations: A typology of cases prosecuted in New York City. *Journal of Drug Issues*, 28(4), 1005–1026.

Natarajan, M., Zanella, M., & Yu, C. (2015). Classifying the variety of drug trafficking organizations. *Journal of Drug Issues*, 45(4), 409–430.

Reuter, P. H. (2014). The mobility of drug trafficking. In J. Collins (Ed.), *Ending the drug wars* (pp. 33–40). London: The London School of Economics and Political Science.

Rhumorbarbe, D., Staehli, L., Broséus, J., Rossy, Q., & Esseiva, P. (2016). Buying drugs on a Darknet market: A better deal? Studying the online illicit drug market through the analysis of digital, physical and chemical data. *Forensic Science International*, 267, 173–182.

United Nations International Drug Control Programme. (1997). *World drug report.* New York: Oxford University Press.

United Nations Office on Drugs and Crime (UNODC). (2018) *World drug report 2018.* New York: United Nations.

World Customs Organization. (2017). *Illicit trade.* Brussels: World Customs Organization.

2 Understanding the Complexity of Trafficking in Human Beings

Alexis A. Aronowitz

INTRODUCTION

The US Department of State (2017) has documented trafficking in human beings and their exploitation in 187 countries around the world. Trafficking affects the most vulnerable in many of the poorest societies, often women and children. With promises of good jobs and salaries, educational opportunities, or marriage, unsuspecting victims are lured into virtual slavery that is often coupled with psychological, physical, and sexual abuse. The International Labour Organization (2017) estimated, in 2016, that 25 million people worldwide were exploited in forced labor. The trafficking industry is estimated to be worth billions of US dollars annually.

While much attention has been focused on the trafficking of women and children for sexual exploitation, trafficking can occur in any industry in which there is a demand for cheap labor. Trafficking and exploitation have been documented in the construction, brick making, domestic, and food service industries, on farms, in mines, and on fishing boats. Trafficking also occurs for the purpose of child soldiering, forced begging, and other criminal activities, and organ harvesting. New forms of human trafficking, such as selling children for adoption, forced marriage, and for forced surrogacy, have been identified. The markets and industries differ across regions and countries and within countries and cities (United Nations Office on Drugs and Crime [UNODC], 2016; US Department of State, 2017).

Human trafficking may occur:

(1) internally, within a country's borders, either within a city or from a rural area or village to a metropolitan area in a country;
(2) intra-regionally, with children and adults being trafficked, for example, throughout the West and Central Africa and Southeast Asia regions;
(3) internationally, for example, from Africa to Europe, or from Russia and Southeast Asia to the USA.

DEFINITION

The Protocol to Prevent, Suppress and Punish Trafficking in Persons, Especially Women and Children, supplementing the United Nations Convention against Transnational Organized Crime (hereafter referred to as the Trafficking Protocol) defines trafficking in persons as (*acts*) the recruitment, transportation, transfer, harboring or receipt of persons, by (*means*) means of the threat or use of force or other forms of coercion, of abduction, of fraud, of deception, of the abuse of power or of a position of vulnerability or of the giving or receiving of payments or benefits to achieve the consent of a person having control over another person, for the purpose of exploitation. Exploitation (*goals*) shall include, at a minimum, the exploitation of the prostitution of others or other forms of sexual exploitation, forced labor or services, slavery or practices similar to slavery, servitude or the removal of organs.

This trafficking definition contains three separate elements: *criminal acts*, the *means* used to commit these acts, and *goals*. At least one element from each of these three groups is required before the definition applies. The consent of a victim of trafficking in persons to the intended exploitation is deemed irrelevant if consent was obtained through threat or use of force, coercion, abduction, fraud, or deception. In the case of children, trafficking can exist in the absence of abduction, coercion, fraud, or deception, and the Trafficking Protocol literally excludes the possibility of consent to trafficking by a person under the age of 18.

Human trafficking can be viewed as a process involving distinct phases: recruitment, transportation (movement within or into a country), exploitation, and victim disposal. During each of these phases, numerous crimes ranging from kidnapping, threats of violence, and theft of documents to assault, rape, or death can be perpetrated against the individual victims. Violence, both psychological and physical, occurs most often in the exploitation phase (Aronowitz, 2017).

TRENDS AND STATISTICS

Due to its clandestine nature, accurate statistics on the magnitude of the problem are elusive and unreliable. This is due to a number of reasons. Foremost is the fact that – out of fear of the police or their traffickers, shame, unwillingness to recognize their victimization, or the fact that they may be in love with or dependent upon their traffickers – victims rarely report their victimization. Further, definitions of trafficking may vary, government officials still view trafficked persons as illegal migrants and freelance sex workers, failing to recognize and register victims, and there may be no centralized agency systematically collecting such data. Between 2012 and 2014, 63,251 victims were detected in 106 countries and territories worldwide (UNODC, 2016).

There is a large discrepancy between the number of known cases of identified victims (in the tens of thousands) and estimates (in the tens of millions). In the past, estimates have been criticized as unreliable, in part, because the methodology was rarely given. The United Nations Office on Drugs and Crime has developed a methodology, the Multiple Systems Estimate, to produce more reliable estimates of undetected victims. The methodology involves a capture-recapture method used with lists of victims maintained by different local authorities (UNODC, 2016).

The United Nations Office on Drugs and Crimes (2016) reports that for the 85 countries on which data on victims were disaggregated into gender and age, 51 percent of the victims were women, 20 percent girls, 8 percent boys, and 21 percent men. This represents a changing pattern over the years, in which more men are identified as victims of trafficking.

Aggregate statistics hide regional differences and in Eastern Europe and Central Asia, for example, 53 percent of victims were men, and in Sub-Saharan Africa, 64 percent of identified victims were children (UNODC, 2016). Arrests and prosecutions are limited. In 2016, The US Department of State (2017) reported 14,897 prosecutions and only 9,071 convictions for human trafficking worldwide. These low numbers may indicate that trafficking is prosecuted under other legislation or may reflect problems in reporting or recording offenses.

FACTORS THAT CONTRIBUTE TO TRAFFICKING

The root causes of trafficking can be explained in terms of "push" and "pull" factors. Push factors include economic, political, and social conditions in the countries of origin that encourage individuals to migrate in search of a better life elsewhere. Specifically, rapid growth of population, persistent poverty, high unemployment, internal conflicts resulting in widespread violence and civil disorder, oppressive political regimes, corruption, gender discrimination, and grave violations of human rights push people from developing and poorer nations to migrate (Aronowitz, 2017, Bales, 2007).

Pull factors, or reasons why migration occurs to a particular country, can be attributed to the high demand for cheap manual labor and paid sex in destination countries. Children and women are targeted for the trade due to their powerlessness, innocence, and inability to protect themselves. They are easier to exploit and are less able to claim their rights.

Other factors that facilitate trafficking are the involvement of organized crime groups and corruption in countries of origin, transit, and destination.

TRAFFICKERS AND THEIR ORGANIZATIONS

Trafficking operations range from single individuals exploiting a single victim within a city or country, to highly sophisticated organizations that are able to move large numbers of people across numerous countries with the use of fraudulent documentation and the assistance of corrupt border guards. These organizations are then able to place their victims in various brothels, factories, construction sites, farms, or households. Somewhere in between these two extremes are loose networks of criminals (Aronowitz, 2009, 2017). Women play a major role in the crime of human trafficking and of the 6,800 persons who were convicted of trafficking during the years 2012–2014, about 40 percent were female (UNODC, 2016). Depending upon the complexity of the operation, the distance between the source and destination country, the number of people being moved, and the possible use of fraudulent documentation, trafficking units can be divided into several sub-units that specialize in a particular part or sequence of the operation. These sub-units provide various services from recruitment and escort to logistical support (Schloenhardt, 1999).

METHODS OF RECRUITMENT AND MARKETS OF EXPLOITATION

Methods of recruitment and the deceit used to lure the victim vary depending upon the source country, age, and gender of victims. False promises of marriage are used to traffic young girls from rural areas in Albania who are later forced into prostitution in Italy and other Western European countries. This *modus operandi* has been documented as the "loverboy" practice in the Netherlands. In Western Africa, children are promised a good education, an internship, a job, or some small token such as a bicycle or radio. The children often leave willingly and are later forced into often life-threatening situations involving harsh manual labor. In Edo State, Nigeria, young female victims reportedly sign contracts promising to repay debts of up to $50,000 prior to their departure for Western European countries where they are forced into prostitution. To ensure repayment, priests use a personal item from the victims to perform a voodoo ritual and thus bind the young women to their traffickers. In the Philippines, women have been known to travel to destinations such as Japan on formal contracts and "entertainer visas," subsequently being forced into prostitution in clubs, while men from India and Nepal are lured to the Gulf States through employment agencies and exploited in the construction industry. The USA has documented domestic sex trafficking of minors as well as a number of cases in which male migrant workers were lured to the country on false promises of good wages in agriculture and held in virtual bondage.

HARM TO VICTIMS: HUMAN RIGHTS AND PUBLIC HEALTH CONCERNS

Victims of trafficking are almost always subjected to various forms of physical, sexual, and psychological abuse. Their documents may be seized and their freedom restricted. Adult women forced into prostitution are also frequently coerced into taking drugs and alcohol. Many trafficked victims are subjected to abhorrent working, living, and sanitary conditions (Bales, 1999), during which time their movements are restricted and they are denied food, medical care, and proper shelter. If they come to the attention of immigration and enforcement officials in many destination countries, they are viewed not as victims of trafficking, but as illegal immigrants and willing accomplices in smuggling schemes. They are subsequently incarcerated and frequently deported without medical or psychological support or protection. Upon return to their countries of origin they are often vulnerable to "retrafficking" or retaliation if they cooperate with criminal justice authorities.

In addition to these human rights violations, a strong link has been established between trafficking in persons for prostitution and HIV/AIDS infection. Girls and young women are often forced to have unprotected sexual contacts with multiple partners, greatly increasing their risk of contracting sexually transmitted diseases (STDs) including HIV/AIDS. There is also a risk of unwanted pregnancy, early motherhood, and illnesses that might affect future reproductive ability (Oram et al., 2012). A study of trafficked victims in Nepal (Tsutsumi et al., 2008) found symptoms of depression, anxiety, and PTSD among victims of trafficking for both sexual and labor exploitation.

ENDING HUMAN TRAFFICKING AND VICTIMIZATION

Ending trafficking will require focusing upon the four Ps: prevention, prosecution, victim protection, and partnerships – between governmental and nongovernmental organizations, private industry, and faith-based organizations – at the grassroots, local, national, and international levels. The United Nations Office on Drugs and Crime, together with other international and local partners, has implemented various antitrafficking projects with services around the globe: providing advice on drafting and revising relevant legislation, advice and assistance on establishing and strengthening antitrafficking offices and units, training for law enforcement officers, prosecutors, and judges, strengthening victim and witness support, and promoting awareness-raising. The International Organization for Migration, the International Labour Organization, the Organization for Security and Cooperation in Europe, and the United Nations Children's Fund have also been active in providing training to law enforcement, immigration, and judicial officers, in running awareness-raising campaigns targeting the general public and populations at risk, and in providing shelter, rehabilitation, skills training, and microcredit programs to repatriated victims.

A more permanent solution requires changes in social and economic policies, historical, gender, and cultural practices, and national-level initiatives to prevent vulnerable persons from falling prey to traffickers. Only long-term sustainable strategies, such as the eradication of poverty and corruption and the provision of education, job, and career opportunities for the most vulnerable populations in the society will truly eradicate trafficking (Aronowitz, 2017).

SUMMARY AND CONCLUSION

Human trafficking is a horrific crime covering a broad range of activities resulting in the exploitation of persons in prostitution, other forms of sexual exploitation, forced labor, slavery-like practices, or the removal of organs. It is an offense that may involve the exploitation and enslavement of a victim for a period of days to years. Trafficking is a sophisticated crime, almost always involving a degree of organization. It should be dealt with through investigation and prosecution of offenders for trafficking and any other criminal activities in which they engage.

Trafficking must be recognized as a human rights, public health, and criminal justice issue. Trafficked persons must be seen as victims of crime, and victim support and protection are important humanitarian objectives. Only by protecting victims can governments respect their human rights, restore their dignity, and hope to secure their cooperation in the prosecution of offenders. Failure to secure conviction of offenders and compensation for victims will allow traffickers to thrive on the countless number of those seeking a better future for themselves and their families.

REFERENCES

Aronowitz, A. A. (2009). *Human trafficking, human misery: The global trade in human beings.* Westport, CT: Praeger Publishers.
    (2017). *Human trafficking: A reference handbook.* Santa Barbara, CA: ABC-CLIO.
Bales, K. (1999). *Disposable people.* Berkeley, CA: University of California Press.
    (2007). What predicts human trafficking. *International Journal of Comparative and Applied Criminal Justice,* 31(2), 269–279.
International Labour Organization. (2017). *Global estimates of modern slavery: Forced labour and forced marriage.* Geneva. Retrieved from www.ilo.org/wcmsp5/groups/public/---dgreports/---dcomm/documents/publication/wcms_575479.pdf.
Oram, S., Stöckl, H., Busza, J. Howard, L, & Zimmerman, C. (2012). Prevalence and risk of violence and the physical, mental, and sexual health problems associated with human trafficking: Systematic review. *Plos Medicine.* Retrieved from https://doi.org/10.1371/journal.pmed.1001224.
Schloenhardt, A. (1999). Organized crime and the business of migrant trafficking. *Crime, Law and Social Change,* 32, 203–233.

Tsutsumi, A., Izutsu. T., Poudyal, A., Kato, S., & Marui, E. (2008). Mental health of female survivors of human trafficking in Nepal. *Social Science & Medicine,* 66, 1841–1847.

United Nations Office on Drugs and Crime (UNODC). (2016). *Global report on trafficking in persons.* Vienna. Retrieved from www.unodc.org/documents/data-and-analysis/glotip/2016_Global_Report_on_Trafficking_in_Persons.pdf.

US Department of State. (2017). *Trafficking in persons report 2017.* Washington, DC. Retrieved from www.state.gov/documents/organization/271339.pdf.

WEBSITES

Anti-Slavery International. www.antislaveryinternational.org.

International Labour Organization. www.ilo.org.

International Organization for Migration (IOM). www.iom.int.

US Department of State Office to Monitor and Combat Trafficking in Persons. www.state.gov/g/tip.

United Nations Office on Drugs and Crime. www.unodc.org/unodc/en/human-trafficking/what-is-human-trafficking.html.

3   The Trafficking of Children in the USA

Meredith Dank and Andrea Hughes

INTRODUCTION

Around the world, children and adolescents are being exploited for sex and labor. They may be forced to work in a variety of situations, such as begging for money in the street, working in brothels, or packaging and selling drugs. Human trafficking has garnered much attention over the past 20 years; however, little is understood about the varied and complex experiences of children and adolescents who are victims of human trafficking.

Children and adolescents may experience specific life circumstances that would make them more vulnerable to trafficking. Research has shown children who are subjected to physical and sexual abuse in their homes run away as a means to protect themselves (Dank et al., 2015; Bigelsen & Vuotto, 2013). Runaway and homeless youth are especially vulnerable as there are not enough shelters and services to take care of them so they are forced to survive on the street (Dank, 2011; Freeman & Hamilton, 2008). Traffickers are adept at recognizing people who are struggling and targeting them by initially providing the financial and emotional support the young people crave. Children and youth who are in the child welfare system are also highly vulnerable to exploitation (Dank et al., 2017). Poverty and lack of resources and services make it difficult for children and adolescents to fully leave exploitative situations.

There have been a number of studies focused on domestic minor sex trafficking in the USA, but almost no research has been conducted looking at the labor trafficking of children. Children are not granted specific oversight in labor policies, particularly within agriculture, making them vulnerable to exploitation and labor trafficking (Walts, 2017). The little research that has been conducted in the USA on child labor trafficking has found that youth are most likely to be forced to pack and sell drugs by familial networks and gangs (Murphy, 2016).

Research has helped us to better understand many of the push/pull factors involved in how and why young people are trafficked; however, few promising practices have been identified to help with the prevention and intervention of child trafficking. The USA has traditionally taken a criminal justice approach, focused on creating laws, arresting perpetrators, and prosecution. Creating avenues to capture and punish traffickers may be necessary to address human trafficking to a certain extent, but a more holistic approach is needed to help victims access badly needed services and have the opportunities necessary to create a life that would make them less vulnerable to further exploitation (Dank et al., 2015).

DEFINITIONS, TRENDS, AND STATISTICS

While no good prevalence estimates exist on child trafficking in the USA, the National Human Trafficking Hotline, operated by the Polaris Project, received 8,524 reported cases of human trafficking in 2017, of which 2,495 of those cases were minors.

In the USA, the Trafficking Victims Protection Act (TVPA) of 2000 was the first federal law to address human trafficking and has been reauthorized multiple times. The law includes both sex and labor trafficking.

> **Sex trafficking** is the recruitment, harboring, transportation, provision, obtaining, patronizing, or soliciting of a person for the purposes of a commercial sex act, in which the commercial sex act is induced by force, fraud, or coercion, or in which the person induced to perform such an act has not attained 18 years of age (*22 USC § 7102*).

> **Labor trafficking** is the recruitment, harboring, transportation, provision, or obtaining of a person for labor or services, through the use of force, fraud, or coercion for the purposes of subjection to involuntary servitude, peonage, debt bondage, or slavery (*22 USC § 7102*).

The legal definition of sex trafficking does not require the use of force, fraud, or coercion for individuals under the age of 18. This definition complicates the experiences of youth who engage in survival sex. In addition, there is no such stipulation in the legal definition for labor trafficking, meaning children who experience labor trafficking are required to demonstrate force, fraud, or coercion at the same standard as adults. These issues in the definition open the door to debates as to what exactly constitutes child trafficking.

While all states have a human trafficking law, they differ by state. Most of the state laws focus on sex trafficking and prosecution of offenders. Few laws mandate funding for victim assistance, which is necessary to help victims recover from trafficking and decrease the chances for revictimization.

WHO IS MOST AT RISK OF BEING TRAFFICKED?

Although any young person is at risk of being trafficked for sex and/or labor in the USA, research has shown that youth with specific types of backgrounds and vulnerabilities are more likely to be trafficked than others. Young people involved in the child welfare (CW) and/or runaway and homeless youth (RHY) systems – youth populations that often overlap – are particularly vulnerable to sex and labor exploitation (Dank et al., 2017). RHY and CW youth often have limited economic resources, unstable living environments, previous experiences with parental or caretaker abuse and neglect, and struggles with health and substance abuse issues (Tucker et al., 2011). Each of these realities puts RHY and CW youth at heightened risk for trafficking exploitation and related traumatic victimization, including exchanging commercial sex on their own to meet basic needs or for something of value (Dank et al., 2015).

Child Welfare-Involved Youth

Young people placed in foster care, kinship care, state and private residential settings, and other out-of-home care, including emergency shelters, are at especially high risk of trafficking. Several studies of young people exchanging sex on their own for something of value and those who experienced physical or sexual victimization have found high rates of prior CW system involvement. One study found that 75 percent of identified sex-trafficking victims had experienced a foster care placement (Gragg et al., 2007). The same study found that 69 percent of trafficked victims had prior CW involvement in the form of an abuse or neglect investigation (Gragg et al., 2007).

Runaway and Homeless Youth

As with studies of CW-involved victims of human trafficking, studies of youth involved in trafficking have found high rates of running away, or of homelessness after running away or after an adult caretaker kicked them out of their homes without providing alternative residential arrangements. Gragg and coauthors (2007) found that all commercial sexual exploited (CSE) youth they surveyed had run away from home at least once, and most of the sexual exploitation youth experienced occurred when they were away from home. Another New York City-based study found that nearly all sampled CSE victims were homeless or had experienced frequent residential instability (Dank, 2011). Housing instability and a lack of basic resources elevate the risk that RHY youth will be targeted by exploiters (Williams & Frederick, 2009).

Lesbian, Gay, Bisexual, Transgender, and Questioning Youth

Approximately 40 percent of runaway and homeless youth identify as lesbian, gay, bisexual, transgender, or questioning/queer (LGBTQ); these youth are at highest risk for human trafficking. Several studies have found that LGBTQ youth make up a disproportionate fraction of RHY (Durso & Gates, 2012). Further, homeless LGBTQ youth frequently engage in illegal activities to support themselves, including exchanging sex for monetary and nonmonetary resources to survive – even more so than heterosexual RHY (Freeman & Hamilton 2008). According to a survey of nearly 1,000 homeless youth in New York City, young men were three times more likely than young women to have traded sex for a place to stay, and LGBTQ youth were seven times more likely than heterosexual youth to have done so (Freeman & Hamilton, 2008). Transgender youth in New York City have been found eight times more likely than non-transgender youth to trade sex for a safe place to stay (Freeman & Hamilton, 2008).

CHILD LABOR TRAFFICKING

While there have been numerous studies examining the sex trafficking of minors in the USA, there has been very little research conducted on the labor trafficking of domestic children and adolescents. Covenant House conducted a 2012 survey of RHY and found that 5 out of 174 individuals met the US federal definition of labor trafficking; there were also several more cases where the authors found indications of trafficking but were unable to clearly designate it as such. The authors noted that, much like sex traffickers, labor traffickers often prey on vulnerable and isolated youth (Bigelsen & Vuotto, 2013). The Polaris Project also found that victims of child labor trafficking often suffer from isolation and may not be permitted to attend school or communicate with their family. Some children are also vulnerable to familial labor trafficking, meaning that a family member forces the child to work in domestic servitude or in a family-owned business.

IMPACTS OF BEING TRAFFICKED

The physical and emotional consequences of sex trafficking of both adults and youth can include, but are not limited to: arrest and incarceration, sexually transmitted infection (STI), post-traumatic stress disorder and other related psychiatric disability development, physical assault and injuries, sexual assault, family dissolution, and premature death. The effects of sex trafficking on youth can include reduced educational attainment; public health and emergency medical expenses associated with teen pregnancy; STI transmission; sexual and physical assault and injuries; and increased involvement in delinquent activities (Thukral & Ditmore, 2003).

Although youth victims of sex trafficking often come into contact with various service systems and institutions, such as the police, judges, therapists, and teachers, they face significant barriers to being identified as victims and to accessing services that could help them find safe and autonomous means of survival. The services that youth victims receive are often not tailored to address the specific needs that a youth has after they have been the victim of trafficking and the service providers often lack specific training in addressing the needs of youth (Gragg et al., 2007; Williams & Frederick, 2009). In particular, despite the severity of their victimization, most states treat commercially exploited children and adolescents as criminals (Institute of Medicine & National Research Council, 2013), adding arrest, detention, adjudication, conviction, commitment, incarceration, and a criminal record to the possible ramifications of their exploitation. States also frequently assume that detention is the only viable means to remove juveniles from unsafe environments that expose them to CSE (Fernandez, 2013). Because victims of sex trafficking face significant social stigma and difficulty accessing appropriate social services, it is particularly important that service providers are simultaneously trained to assess whether youth are victims of trafficking and how to best link them to services that will address their victimization needs.

SUMMARY AND CONCLUSION

Research has shown that the experiences of children and youth who have been trafficked are multifaceted and frequently stem from life situations that make them initially vulnerable to exploitation and then difficult to escape. US law and policies have traditionally focused on the criminal justice approach to addressing human trafficking, but research demonstrates a need for a more holistic response that includes allocating resources to shelters and other services and addressing social justice issues.

Children and youth need support if they are to be able to fully escape and recover from human trafficking. Stable housing, education, employment opportunities with a livable wage, and physical and mental health services are all necessary for prevention and recovery. Services should be provided in a manner that is sensitive to the experiences of this population and the trauma, stigma, and shame that often accompanies this victimization. In addition, services must address the specific needs of LGBTQ youth.

Youth who are engaged in survival sex or human trafficking are vulnerable to being arrested for prostitution, selling drugs, or any other activity related to their exploitation. Having a criminal record makes it more difficult for youth to exit exploitative situations because it is especially difficult to obtain employment. While there have been laws developed and implemented in a number of states to protect children and youth from arrest related to human trafficking, research is needed to fully understand how they are being utilized and applied.

More attention must be brought to the issue of labor trafficking of children. Limited research exists on children's experiences of labor trafficking, and on labor trafficking in general. Labor and antitrafficking laws and policies need to address children who are forced to work to ensure they have the same protections and recourses as adults. Social services, law enforcement, and the legal community should be trained to recognize the labor trafficking of children and make assessment a regular practice to ensure victims are being identified and subsequently receive the help they require.

Lastly, the USA is not unique in its struggles in dealing with child trafficking. This issue is pervasive in both developing and developed societies. The more we learn through research, such as what has already been conducted in the USA, the more countries all over the world can determine the most effective ways in which to combat child trafficking.

In conclusion, the lives and experiences of children and youth who have experienced labor or sex trafficking are complex, and require more research, attention, and response. Prevention and recovery efforts should include a tailored, informed, victim-centered criminal justice response and more importantly must provide for the short- and long-term economic and health needs of the victims, as well as the social injustices that cause the proliferation of human trafficking in the first place.

REFERENCES

Bigelsen, J. & Vuotto, S. (2013). *Homelessness, survival sex and human trafficking: As experienced by the youth of Covenant House*. New York: Covenant House.

Dank, M. (2011). *The commercial sexual exploitation of children in New York City*. El Paso, TX: LFB Scholarly Publishing.

Dank, M., Yahner, J., Madden, K., Banuelos, I., Yu, L., Ritchie, A., Mora, M., & Conner, B. (2015) *Surviving the streets of New York: Experiences of LGBTQ youth, YMSM, and YWSW engaged in survival sex*. Washington, DC: Urban Institute. Retrieved from www.urban.org/sites/default/files/publication/42186/2000119-Surviving-the-Streets-of-New-York.pdf.

Dank, M., Yahner, J., Yu, L., Vasquez-Noriega, C., Gelatt, J., & Pergamit, M. (2017). *Pre-testing a human trafficking screening tool in child welfare and runaway and homeless youth systems*. Washington, DC: Urban Institute. Retrieved from www.urban.org/sites/default/files/publication/93596/pretesting_tool_1.pdf.

Durso, L. E. & Gates, G. J. (2012). *Serving our youth: Findings from a national survey of service providers working with lesbian, gay, bisexual, and transgender youth who are homeless or at risk of becoming homeless*. Los Angeles, CA: The Williams Institute with True Colors Fund and the Palette Fund.

Fernandez, K. (2013). Victims or criminals? The intricacies of dealing with juvenile victims of sex trafficking and why the distinction matters. *Arizona State Law Journal*, 45, 859–890.

Freeman, L. & Hamilton D. (2008). *A count of homeless youth in New York City*. New York: Empire State Coalition of Youth and Family Services.

Gragg, F., Petta, I., Bernstein, H., Eisen, K., & Quinn, L. (2007). *New York prevalence study of commercially sexually exploited children.* Rockville, MD: Westat.

Institute of Medicine & National Research Council of the National Academies. (2013). *Confronting commercial sexual exploitation and sex trafficking of minors in the United States.* Washington, DC: The National Academy of Sciences.

Murphy, L. T. (2016). *Labor and sex trafficking among homeless youth. A ten city study (executive summary).* Retrieved from https://static1.squarespace.com/static/5887a2a61b631bfbbc1ad83a/t/59498e69197aea24a33a640b/1497992809780/CovenantHouseReport.pdf.

Thukral, J. & Ditmore, M. (2003). *Revolving door: An analysis of street-based prostitution in the intersection of domestic human trafficking with cw and rhy programs.* New York: Urban Justice Center Report.

Tucker, J. S., Edelen, M. O., Ellickson, P. L., & Klein, D. J. (2011). Running away from home: A longitudinal study of adolescent risk factors and young adult outcomes. *Journal of Adolescence*, 40(5), 507–518.

Walts, K. (2017). Child labor trafficking in the United States: A hidden crime. *Social Inclusion*, 5(2), 59–68.

Williams, L. M. & Frederick, M. E. (2009). *Pathways into and out of commercial sexual victimization of children: Understanding and responding to sexually exploited teens.* Lowell, MA: University of Massachusetts Lowell.

IMPORTANT READING

https://polarisproject.org/sites/default/files/Polaris-Typology-of-Modern-Slavery.pdf.

www.urban.org/research/publication/surviving-streets-new-york-experiences-lgbtq-youth-ymsm-and-ywsw-engaged-survival-sex.

www.ncjrs.gov/pdffiles1/nij/grants/225083.pdf.

4 Migrant Smuggling

Paolo Campana

INTRODUCTION

Human smuggling, also referred to as "migrant smuggling" or "people smuggling," is internationally defined by the UN Protocol against the Smuggling of Migrants by Land, Sea and Air (the Protocol). Adopted by the General Assembly in November 2000, the Protocol defines human smuggling as "the procurement, in order to obtain, directly or indirectly, a financial or other material benefit, of the illegal entry of a person into a State Party of which the person is not a national or a permanent resident" (Article 3). As of April 2018, 112 countries have signed the Protocol and made human smuggling a criminal offense.

Based on the UN definition, the commodity at stake is the illegal entry into a country. In the jargon of law enforcement agencies this same commodity is often defined as "illegal border crossing." This commodity is typically exchanged between a smuggler, or group of smugglers, and a prospective migrant. Human smuggling is primarily an offense against a state. When everything goes well in the smuggling process – i.e., the smuggler keeps his promise and the migrant safely reaches the chosen destination – the only victim is the state that has seen its borders and its right to exercise control over a given territory violated. This is a crucial point, as it separates human smuggling from human trafficking (see also Chapter 2). In the latter, the commodity at stake is control over a person for the purpose of exploitation. Human trafficking is, therefore, primarily an offense against an individual; the illegal entry into a country may be present, but it is an ancillary element and not a constitutive one (see Campana & Varese, 2016 for a discussion about the differences between trafficking and smuggling and the potential transitions from smuggling to trafficking). The two terms are often erroneously used interchangeably in the media coverage and public discourse, leading to confusion and thus hindering our ability to develop effective policies.

The UN definition also stipulates that, for the offense of human smuggling to be present, there has to be a financial or other material benefit for the smuggler. This places genuine humanitarian actions taken to help migrants in situations where such aid is needed to pro-tect their physical integrity with no financial gain for the helper outside of the definition of human smuggling. This humanitarian provision is sometimes disregarded by states.

ASSESSING THE SCALE OF THE PHENOMENON

Reliable statistics on human smuggling are difficult to compile. As noted by McAuliffe and Laczko (2016, p. 10), "only a minority of countries in the world produce comparable national data on the scale of migrant smuggling each year, and [...] there is no global estimate of the magnitude of migrant smuggling." There are a number of reasons why reliable evidence is difficult to obtain. First, human smuggling takes place under a condition of illegality, in which both smugglers and migrants may have an incentive not to leave traces during the smuggling process. Second, some states may lack the capacity and resources to collect data on smuggling. Furthermore, states too may have an incentive not to make such data publicly accessible, for both political and security reasons. For instance, in the case of Australia, the launch of the "military-led Operation Sovereign Borders in 2013 was accompanied by new and substantial restrictions on the release of information about smuggled migrants and SIEVs [Suspected Illegal Entry Vessels]" (Gallagher & McAuliffe, 2016, p. 223).

Some countries might report aggregate data on irregular migration rather than human smuggling. Assessing human smuggling based on such data, however, can be challenging as not all the cases of irregular migration involve the assistance of a smuggler. The number of asylum applications is sometimes used as a proxy for human smuggling. However, not all asylum seekers have necessarily used the service of a smuggler, nor have all of the smuggled individuals lodged an asylum application. Furthermore, in certain circumstances, individuals might lodge more than one asylum application.

The official data available on human smuggling tend to be produced by law enforcement agencies, for instance in the form of detected illegal border crossings. Law enforcement statistics are characterized by a number of limitations. First, numbers may be influenced by changes in the level of policing rather than changes in the actual phenomenon. Second, statistics normally refer to crossings rather than individuals; when the smuggling process extends across countries, there is a concrete risk of double-counting the same individuals. In addition, law enforcement statistics do not include migrants and crossings that are not detected. This makes it difficult to take into account instances in which the journey has resulted in deaths. According to McAuliffe and Lackzo (2016, p. 12), "very few countries around the world collect official data on the number of deaths that occur when migrants try to cross borders with the help of smugglers." Yet, notwithstanding their limitations, law enforcement statistics often constitute the best – and sometimes the only – source of data available. The European Union, through its border and coast guard agency Frontex, produces quarterly risk analyses and annual reports that are made publicly available in a rather timely fashion. These publications include a wealth of statistics on illegal border crossings, returns, overstaying, and the use of fraudulent documents (see Figure 4.1). The International Organization for Migration (IOM) also collects and disseminates data on migration flows and missing migrants through a number of open databases (see the list of websites below). Other sources of data are the UN Refugee Agency (UNHCR) and the UN Office on Drugs and Crime (UNODC). UNODC's Global Study on the Smuggling of Migrants (2018) offers a very good overview of the phenomenon worldwide and an insightful starting point to explore current trends in human smuggling.

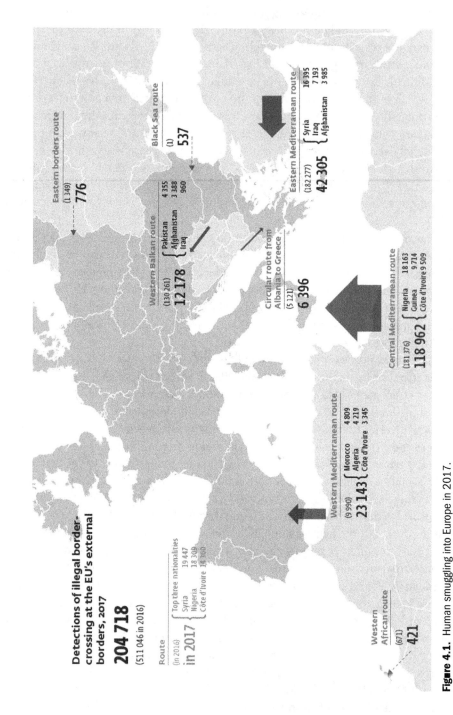

Detections of illegal border-crossing at the EU's external borders, 2017

204 718

(511 046 in 2016)

Route

(in 2016)	Top three nationalities
in 2017	Syria 19 447
	Nigeria 18 309
	Côte d'Ivoire 14 300

Eastern borders route
(1 349)
776

Western Balkan route
(130 261)
12 178
Pakistan 4 355
Afghanistan 3 388
Iraq 960

Black Sea route
(1)
537

Eastern Mediterranean route
(182 277)
42 305
Syria 16 395
Iraq 7 193
Afghanistan 3 985

Circular route from Albania to Greece
(5 121)
6 396

Central Mediterranean route
(181 376)
118 962
Nigeria 18 163
Guinea 9 714
Côte d'Ivoire 9 509

Western Mediterranean route
(9 990)
23 143
Morocco 4 809
Algeria 4 219
Côte d'Ivoire 3 345

Western African route
(671)
421

Figure 4.1. Human smuggling into Europe in 2017.

Source: Frontex Risk Analysis for 2018

26

THE MARKET FOR SMUGGLING SERVICES

Analytically, we can think of human smuggling as a market in which the commodity traded is the illegal entry into a country for a profit (Campana, 2017). Markets, by definition, are characterized by supply and demand. In this specific instance, migrants constitute the demand side of the market. They are willing to buy a service, i.e., illegal entry into a country, for a variety of reasons that include leaving war zones, extreme poverty, economic hardship, or persecution (although a discussion of the motivations to migrate is beyond the scope of this contribution). The demand for smuggling services is satisfied by a number of sellers. In this specific market, sellers are collectively defined as smugglers.

The market approach helps us understand how smuggling works in practice. By virtue of being a general framework, it also helps us draw comparisons across countries and smuggling routes. Bilger et al. (2006, p. 59) interpret human smuggling as a "transnational service industry linking service providers (human smugglers) with their clients." This specific industry is characterized by asymmetric information between smugglers and migrants, e.g., on the quality of the service provided by the former, as well as high risk and uncertainty.

Interpreting smuggling as a business is not the only approach. Some scholars have applied a socio-legal approach to investigate the tension between the rights of states and the rights of individuals. Other scholars have placed human smuggling within the broader migration literature or within a global political economy framework (see Baird & van Liempt, 2016, for a discussion). Each approach sheds light on a different aspect of human smuggling, and in so doing furthers our ability to gain a comprehensive understanding of the phenomenon. It is perhaps of little surprise that such a complex and multifaceted practice as human smuggling can be fruitfully tackled from different angles.

THE STRUCTURE OF HUMAN SMUGGLING

How are smuggling activities organized? Zhang and Chin (2002) have investigated the structure of smuggling operations between China and the USA and concluded that such operations "are made up of decentralized associations of criminals of diverse backgrounds, and the relationships among core members are mostly horizontal" (Zhang & Chin, 2002, p. 759). The smugglers were found to be a rather heterogeneous set including small business owners, handymen, taxi drivers, fruit stand owners, fast food restaurant owners, housewives, massage parlor owners, police officers, and government officials (Zhang & Chin, 2002, p. 745). Zhang and Chin describe the network of smugglers as a "task force, committed to one task or one operation at a time—that is, to deliver their clients to their destiny and get paid" (Zhang & Chin, 2002, p. 750). These task forces, they add, tend to be rather small in number with a core group of generally three or four individuals brought together purely by business arrangements.

İçduygu and Toktas (2002) have explored the organizational arrangements underpinning the movement of Iraqi and Iranian irregular migrants. They described the smuggling operations as "a loosely cast network, consisting of hundreds of independent smaller units which cooperate along the way" (İçduygu & Toktas, 2002, p. 46). Smugglers would adopt a "hand-to-hand" approach, that is, handing over migrants directly to another smuggler after a border crossing (İçduygu & Toktas, 2002, p. 46). Similarly, Sanchez (2015, p. 44) investigated smuggling operations between the USA and Mexico and found no evidence of "the existence of a single, centralized, power providing operational or logical support in any of the smuggling groups identified." The exact opposite seems to be the case, as she notes that "there was never any kind of leadership" (Sanchez, 2015, p. 44).

Campana (2018) offers the first formal modeling of human smuggling operations. Quantitative data on interactions among smugglers operating between the Horn of Africa and Northern Europe via Libya and Italy were extracted from court files and then analyzed using a set of statistical techniques for social network analysis. This work has shown that smuggling activities on this particular route are segmented and carried out by localized and very rudimentary hierarchies. The reach of these hierarchies tends to remain local in scope. Additionally, this work has found no evidence of a single hierarchical organization, but rather a collection of independent actors. Even in networks involved in the supply of a truly transnational commodity, namely the movement of people from the Horn of Africa to Northern Europe, the local dimension still appears to play an important role. For instance, smugglers who are involved in the same stage of the journey are more than six times more likely to coordinate. Furthermore, this work has found strong indications of competition among smugglers – a "far cry from the idea that smuggling markets are characterized by the presence of kingpins who can exert monopolistic control over a certain route" (Campana, 2018, p. 16).

The same work also found no evidence of any involvement of the Sicilian Mafia in smuggling activities taking place in Sicily or elsewhere, despite the Italian island being a key stage in the smuggling route. No payment of protection money was identified in Sicily, which indicates that the roles of smugglers and of racketeers are clearly distinct. This is a crucial point. A clear distinction between smugglers and militia members ("protectors") was also found on the African side of the operations. A statistical analysis of the interactions that took place in Libya has shown that smugglers are more likely to coordinate with fellow smugglers and militia members with other militia members. Again, the role of smuggler and that of protector appears to be clearly distinct. This does not, however, imply complete separation as cross-role interactions did take place in Libya, mostly in the form of smugglers paying bribes to militia members to be able to operate. A similar picture emerges in relation to the West African route explored by Brachet (2018, p. 29) using an ethnographic approach: "These so-called transnational networks are in fact rather fragmented and uncoordinated chains of actors […] There are no transnational criminal networks in Agadez but rather small-scale low-investment activities."

CONCLUSIONS

Human smuggling appears to be characterized by the presence of small-scale independent operators that show a high degree of segmentation and fragmentation in their operations. Smugglers do not tend to monopolize the market in which they operate. This is a far cry from how mafia-like organizations are structured and operate (see also Chapter 27). The polycentric nature of human smuggling and the presence of multiple independent, competing smugglers poses a formidable challenge to the authorities: following the removal of an individual smuggler, the remaining smugglers will try to seize this opportunity and expand their "market" share. Such challenges are exacerbated by the fact that, as an industry, human smuggling is characterized by low barriers to entry and a rather low level of required resources – i.e., low skill and low capital requirements (Campana, 2017; see also Zhang & Chin, 2002, p. 747; Brachet 2018, p. 29). Crucially, given the separation between protectors and smugglers, a more effective set of policies might target the former to reduce opportunities for the latter. In addition, a different set of policies can be devised to reduce the demand for smuggling services, e.g., the adoption of schemes that resettle refugees directly from conflict zones or the provision of a higher number of work and study visas.

Tackling human smuggling poses a number of moral dilemmas. For instance, an effective naval operation to rescue migrants at sea, such as the ones launched by Italy and the European Union, may increase the number of arrivals, as smugglers incorporate the rescue efforts into their modus operandi; however, in the absence of such operations, migrants would face death under the watch of developed countries. Rescue operations are just one example of the tension between humanitarian and securitarian approaches to human smuggling.

REFERENCES

Baird, T. & van Liempt, I. (2016). Scrutinising the double disadvantage: Knowledge production in the messy field of migrant smuggling. *Journal of Ethnic and Migration Studies*, 42(3), 400–417.

Bilger, V., Hofmann, M., & Jandl, M. (2006). Human smuggling as a transnational service industry: Evidence from Austria. *International Migration,* 44(4), 59–93.

Brachet, J. (2018). Manufacturing smugglers: From irregular to clandestine mobility in Sahara. *The Annals of The American Academy of Political and Social Science*, 676, 16–35.

Campana, P. (2018). Out of Africa: The organization of migrant smuggling across the Mediterranean. *European Journal of Criminology*, 15(4), 481–502, doi.org/10.1177/1477370817749179.

(2017). The market for human smuggling into Europe: A macro perspective. *In Policing*, 11(4), 448–456.

& Varese, F. (2016). Exploitation in human trafficking and smuggling. *European Journal on Criminal Policy and Research*, 22(1), 89–105.

Gallagher, A. & McAuliffe, M. L. (2016). South-East Asia and Australia. In M. L. McAuliffe and F. Laczko (Eds.), *Migrant smuggling data and research* (pp. 211–241). Geneva: International Organization for Migration.

Içduygu, A. & Toktas, S. (2002). How do smuggling and trafficking operate via irregular border crossings in the Middle East? Evidence from fieldwork in Turkey. *International Migration*, 40(6), 25–54

McAuliffe, M. L. & Laczko, F. (2016). Report overview. In M. L. McAuliffe and F. Laczko (Eds.), *Migrant smuggling data and research* (pp. 1–24). Geneva: International Organization for Migration.

Sanchez, G. E. (2015). *Human smuggling and border crossing*. Abingdon and New York: Routledge.

United Nations Office on Drugs and Crime (UNODC). (2018). *Global study on smuggling of migrants*. Vienna: United Nations Office on Drugs and Crime.

Zhang, S. & Chin, K. L. (2002). Enter the dragon: Inside Chinese human smuggling organisations. *Criminology*, 40(4), 737–768.

WEBSITES

UNODC Smuggling of Migrants Knowledge Portal. www.unodc.org/cld/en/v3/som/.

North Africa Mixed Migration Hub. www.mixedmigrationhub.org/.

Mixed Migration Monitoring Mechanism Initiative (4Mi). www.regionalmms.org/index.php/4mi-
    page/about-4mi.
Irregular Migration Research Database. https://gmdac.iom.int/research-database/.
IOM Migration Flows – Europe. http://migration.iom.int/europe/.
Missing Migrants Project. https://missingmigrants.iom.int/.
University of Queensland Migrant Smuggling Case Database. https://ssl.law.uq.edu.au/som-database/
    home.php.
European Border and Coast Guard Agency. https://frontex.europa.eu/.

International Trafficking of Stolen Vehicles

Rick Brown and Ronald V. Clarke

INTRODUCTION

For many years, cars stolen in the USA have been exported to countries in South America or the Caribbean using containers and ferries. Others have simply been driven across the border into Mexico. Thefts are sometimes organized on a massive scale, with criminal groups responsible for the trafficking of dozens of vehicles (Tremblay, Talon, & Hurley, 2001). Other thefts are more opportunistic, often committed by juvenile offenders, who might steal a car in the afternoon and sell it that same evening in Mexico (Resindez, 1998). There is now compelling evidence that vehicle theft hot spots in the USA are in counties bordering Mexico and those with busy ports (Highway Loss Data Institute, 2008; Block et al., 2011; Lantsman, 2013). There have also been reports of vehicles stolen in one country being traded for drugs in another (e.g., between the USA and Mexico and between Brazil and Bolivia).

Beyond the USA, the demise of the Soviet system in the early 1990s resulted in large numbers of cars being stolen in Western Europe and exported to Russia and other countries of Eastern Europe. The emerging market economies in those countries created a demand for cars (especially luxury models) that could not be met by domestic producers, and criminal entrepreneurs moved in to fill the gap. Increasing globalization has created similar conditions in other parts of the world with the result that many other countries have become markets for cars stolen abroad. Thus, the Middle East is now a destination for cars stolen in Europe and Australia, West Africa for cars stolen in the USA and the UK, and China and Southeast Asia for cars stolen in the USA and Japan. Regional theft markets have also developed. For example, Bolivia is the destination for cars stolen in Brazil and Argentina, Nepal for cars stolen in Northern India, Indonesia for cars stolen in Malaysia, Cambodia for cars stolen in Thailand, and other parts of Africa for cars stolen in South Africa. Japan has been a major source of exported stolen vehicles to Indonesia, the Russian Far East, the United Arab Emirates, Nigeria, and even the UK (Clarke & Brown, 2003). War zones have also created demand for stolen vehicles, with cars stolen in the USA being recovered during conflicts in Iraq and Syria.

No reliable figures exist for the scale of the problem. INTERPOL's stolen vehicle database recorded 118,000 vehicles that were stolen in one country and detected in another in 2017. Most of the trafficked vehicles are cars, exported whole with false identities. There is also a small export trade in stolen commercial vehicles and motorcycles and a large, though poorly measured, trade in stolen vehicle parts. The increased complexity and cost with exporting stolen vehicles compared with supplying domestic demand means that luxury models and newer vehicles are often preferred, although local variations exist. For example, in Mexico there is a preference for SUVs and pick-ups stolen from the USA (Block, 2012).

Whichever vehicles or countries are involved, the pattern is the same: the principal flow of stolen vehicles is from rich to poorer countries. This mirrors the wider global economy in which manufactured goods move from the developed to the less-developed world, but is contrary to most other forms of transnational crime, where the flow is in the other direction.

HOW IS TRAFFICKING IN STOLEN CARS ACCOMPLISHED?

In order to devise countermeasures, more needs to be known about the traffickers' methods. Unfortunately, our understanding is limited by the complexity of the crime, which is due to the following.

1. Each of the three main forms of vehicle trafficking has to be understood in detail. These are: 1) driving stolen cars across national borders or transporting them in ferries; 2) shipping them overseas in sealed containers; and 3) disassembling them and shipping them overseas for sale as spare parts.
2. Trafficking in stolen cars involves a complex sequence of actions, including the following:
   * preferred vehicles are identified and stolen, either to order or "on spec";
   * they may be moved to a safe place and monitored for police response to tracking devices;
   * their identities may be changed;
   * they may be stored, awaiting pick-up for transfer across the border;
   * depending on the method of transfer, they may be placed in sealed containers and loaded onto ships, or they may be driven across the border;
   * at the destinations they may be handed over to a local contact or collected by such a person from the docks;
   * they may be legally registered; and finally
   * they may be sold on the open market or to a private buyer.
3. Due to local conditions, many differences exist in methods employed. Thus, in South Africa, where stolen cars are mostly driven to neighboring countries, criminals often acquire the vehicles through carjacking – in other words, at gunpoint from their owners. This method is rarely used in other countries. At the export stage, traffickers use many different routes; Liukkonen (1997) identified six distinct routes in Europe alone. Some routes require only a single border crossing, while others require many border crossings, which increases the risks for the criminals involved. Lantsman (2013) noted a preference for direct shipping routes, rather than those with multiple ports of call.
4. The traffickers' methods, the routes they use, and the countries principally involved all undergo constant change in response to law enforcement initiatives or the changing opportunity structure for their crime. For instance, in the early 1990s, there were many reports of cars being exported from Hong Kong and Japan to China, but by the

mid-1990s the trade in illegal imports to China decreased, partly as a result of actions taken by the Chinese authorities, including banning the import of right-hand-drive vehicles.

WHAT FACILITATES TRAFFICKING IN STOLEN CARS?

At the most general level, trafficking in stolen cars relies upon a ready supply of attractive vehicles in one country or region, the demand for such vehicles in another, and a ready means of transporting them from origin to destination. Other conditions that facilitate trafficking in stolen cars should be noted because of their potential relevance to policy. These include the following.

- Vast numbers of cars cross national borders every day. As a result of trade agreements and worldwide increases in tourism, many border controls have been eased or lifted, in order to cope with the huge number of cars traversing national boundaries. Looking for stolen cars among this vast amount of legal traffic is like searching for the proverbial needle in the haystack.
- Huge volumes of containers are shipped from many ports in developed countries. Stolen cars and auto parts are frequently shipped in sealed containers to other countries. Many of the cars have been given new identities, but in some cases they are shipped in containers labeled as "kitchen equipment" or "household goods." Customs officials examine only about 1 percent of containers shipped from US ports, partly because cargo ships work in tight turnarounds.
- A substantial legal trade exists between countries in used cars. Large volumes of used cars are legally traded between developed countries and developing countries. Criminals involved in trafficking in stolen cars can shelter behind this trade, masking their activities as legitimate business.
- Customs controls focus on arrivals, not departures. This pattern holds worldwide because customs officers are responsible for levying duties on certain goods entering the country and keeping prohibited goods out. In the USA, this pattern has become more pronounced as fears of terrorism have increased.
- Law enforcement activity is inhibited by the commitment of developing countries to fostering international trade. Many countries encourage the swift export of goods in order to increase economic efficiency. This can result in law enforcement organizations needing to justify their actions in searching suspicious containers and may result in fewer checks being undertaken.
- Many countries have difficulties in even controlling the illegal import of cars that have not been stolen. Until countries can control illegal imports, they have little prospect of preventing the import of stolen cars.
- International standards for vehicle registration and ownership documents are non-existent. This makes it difficult for officials to detect forged or altered papers. Language barriers make the task even more difficult.
- There is great variation and lax enforcement of vehicle registration procedures among countries. Even in some developed countries, such as the UK, it is not necessary for the registering officer to see the vehicle. In many less-developed countries, vehicle registration requirements are very poorly enforced.

- Officials may be corrupt. This includes police officers who provide protection to car thieves, ports officials who ignore suspect shipments, and vehicle registration officials who allow stolen vehicles to be registered.
- Law enforcement give low priority to vehicle theft. Developing countries are faced with many more serious crime problems than the import of stolen cars and cannot be expected to give vehicle theft high priority. In developed countries, law enforcement action to reduce the export of stolen vehicles is eclipsed by the need to tackle other forms of organized crime (e.g., drugs importation, human trafficking, etc.).
- The number of offenders with the necessary contacts to undertake vehicle trafficking has increased, expanded by substantial migration into developed countries. Available evidence suggests that many of those involved in vehicle trafficking are immigrants, who discover and exploit the opportunities existing for this crime. They may already have the necessary contacts in their home countries and they may avoid prosecution by working in their own language, which may be unfamiliar to the police.

HOW ORGANIZED IS VEHICLE TRAFFICKING?

Recent research has suggested that organized crime is no longer dominated by the traditional "Mafia" of the textbooks. Instead, there are now many more small, loosely structured networks of criminal entrepreneurs, often with specialized knowledge, who come together to exploit specific opportunities for crime, such as credit card fraud or counterfeiting banknotes. It would, therefore, not be surprising if many people engaged in the trafficking of stolen cars were not members of organized crime groups, but were employed in vehicle repair garages, in selling used cars, or in legitimate export businesses. These individuals then discover that they can exploit their knowledge and contacts to make large profits in exporting stolen vehicles. (See Brown & Clarke, 2004, for a summary of the differences between traditional organized crime syndicates and more contemporary descriptions of "criminal entrepreneur" networks.)

WHAT IS BEING DONE TO REDUCE THE PROBLEM?

Despite the low priority accorded to vehicle theft by law enforcement authorities, much has been done over the years by the USA, INTERPOL, and the United Nations to tackle the problem, including the following.

- The USA has developed a model bi-lateral agreement for the repatriation of stolen vehicles (see United Nations, 1997) and has signed agreements with numerous countries in Latin America, although the recovery process is often long and cumbersome. US agents have provided training to customs officials in these countries in ways to identify stolen cars.
- The National Insurance Crime Bureau (which is supported by the American insurance industry) provides a repatriation service, which helps to recover detected stolen vehicles from other countries. X-ray machines are now being routinely used to inspect sealed containers in US ports. Documentation relating to any car for export must now be presented 72 hours prior to loading (US Customs and Border Protection, 2017).

- The US Motor Vehicle Theft and Law Enforcement Act of 1984 requires car manufacturers to mark the major body parts of high-risk models to deter their theft for chopping and for export.
- The stolen vehicle database maintained by the FBI's National Crime Information Center can be accessed by the Royal Canadian Mounted Police. INTERPOL has developed a similar database of stolen vehicles for access by member states, while EUCARIS, the European Car and Driving License Information System (www.eucaris.net), provides a similar service in Europe.
- Many countries have established committees or task forces to study auto theft and to make policy recommendations, including ways to curb the export of stolen vehicles (United Nations, 1997).

Much of this activity has been undertaken to assist the repatriation of stolen cars. Important as this is, it may play only a minor role in deterrence since very small numbers of trafficked cars are detected. Much greater attention should be devoted to the earlier stages of trafficking in an effort to prevent cars leaving the countries of origin.

CONCLUSIONS

Because of improved security on new cars and generally falling crime rates, auto theft in developed countries is declining. Trafficking in stolen cars will probably be immune to this trend because improvements in vehicle security provide little deterrent to professional thieves, who find ways of stealing vehicles with keys – for example, through carjackings or fraudulent rental and lease agreements. Furthermore, the demand for stolen cars in developing countries, fueled by increasing globalization, is unlikely to abate. While the problem may have been exaggerated in the past, there is some evidence that it is now increasing. Research could assist law enforcement efforts by uncovering the methods used by traffickers to circumvent licensing requirements and to avoid detection at customs and border checkpoints.

REFERENCES

Block, S. (2012). Characteristics of internationally trafficked stolen vehicles along the U.S.-Mexico border. *Western Criminology Review*, 13(3), 1–14.

Block, S., Clarke, R. V., Maxfield, M. G., & Petrossian, G. (2011). Estimating the number of U.S. vehicles stolen for export using crime location quotients. In M. A. Andresen & J. B. Kinney (Eds.), *Patterns, prevention and geometry of crime*. New York: Routledge.

Brown, R. & Clarke, R. V. (2004). Police intelligence and theft of vehicles for export: Recent UK experience. In M. G. Maxwell & R. V. Clarke (Eds.), *Crime prevention studies*, Vol. 17. Monsey, NY: Criminal Justice Press.

Clarke, R. V. & Brown, R. (2003). International trafficking in stolen vehicles. In M. Tonry (Ed.), *Crime and justice. A review of research*, Vol. 30. Chicago: University of Chicago Press.

Highway Loss Data Institute. (2008). *Insurance special report: Theft losses by county: 1999–2007 models*. Arlington, VA: The Institute.

Lantsman, L. (2013). "Moveable currency": The role of seaports in export oriented vehicle theft. *Crime, Law and Social Change*, 59, 157–184.

Liukkonen, M. (1997). Motor vehicle theft in Europe. Paper No. 9. Helsinki: HEUNI.

Resindez, R. (1998). International auto theft: An exploratory research of organization and organized crime on the U.S./Mexico border. *Criminal Organizations*, 12, 25–30.

Tremblay, P., Talon, B., & Hurley, D. (2001). Body switching and related adaptations in the resale of stolen vehicles: Script elaborations and aggregate crime learning curves. *British Journal of Criminology*, 41, 561–579.

US Customs and Border Protection. (2017) Exporting a motor vehicle: Interpretation and application of 19 CFR Part 192. Retrieved from www.cbp.gov/trade/basic-import-export/export-docs/motor-vehicle.

United Nations. (1997). International cooperation in combating transnational crime: Illicit trafficking in motor vehicles. *Commission on Crime Prevention and Criminal Justice*. Vienna: United Nations.

6   Transnational Firearms Trafficking

Guns for Crime and Conflict

Theodore Leggett

INTRODUCTION

The trafficking of firearms is unlike many of the other forms of trafficking discussed in this book because firearms are durable goods. Unlike drugs, pirated fish, or counterfeit pharmaceuticals, a well-maintained AK-47 will last indefinitely. As a result, there is little need for a continuous contraband flow. Trafficking tends to be episodic, often from an established stockpile to a region descending into crisis.

In addition, the modern pistol or assault rifle represents a "mature technology," so current weapons holders do not need to update their stock regularly to remain competitive. There has been very little innovation in small arms design in the last 50 years – it appears there are few ways to make small arms more accurate or deadlier than they are today. Consequently, the number of new small arms purchased each year is only about 1 percent of those already in circulation. Even the world's most innovative militaries only update their small arms every second decade or so.

As the global turnover in the licit arms industry is limited, the same is likely true for the illicit arms industry. Many still-functional weapons were distributed in developing countries during the Cold War and thereafter, and since the destruction of weapons has been limited in many parts of the world, there is little need to import new weapons into these regions today. Small Arms Survey, a Geneva-based arms monitoring group, estimated the global authorized trade in firearms at approximately US$1.58 billion in 2006, with unrecorded but licit transactions making up another US$100 million or so. The most commonly cited estimate for the size of the illicit market is 10 percent to 20 percent of the licit market, which would be about US$170 million to US$320 million per annum. This may sound like a lot of money, but it appears to be diffused among a large number of small players. It is also small compared to, for example, the value of drug markets, typically estimated to be in the tens of billions of dollars.

There are two primary markets for illicit arms: those who need weapons for criminal purposes, and those who need them for political ones.

GUNS FOR CRIME

For criminals, there are often more immediate sources of firearms than those trafficked internationally. In most cities in the developed world, there is limited use for military-type weapons (see Box 6.1), and so the demand is for concealable handguns. For example, despite the availability of a wide range of firearms in the USA, including semiautomatic assault rifles, about 90 percent of firearm murders in 2015 were committed with handguns. Firearms used in crime are often diverted from the legal handgun market that exists in many countries. If handgun controls are tight in one country, they may be looser in a neighboring one, and while the transborder movement of these weapons could be considered trafficking, the volumes are rarely big or concentrated enough to be deemed an organized trafficking flow.

For example, it is likely that the largest cross-border movement of firearms for criminal purposes today is the flow from the USA to Mexico. The USA has the greatest number of firearms per capita in the world, and the majority of gun shop owners polled say that it is too easy for criminals to acquire firearms. A survey of licensed firearm dealers in the USA in 2011 found that over two-thirds had experienced attempted "straw purchases" (i.e., people who are paid to buy guns on behalf of others) in the previous year. In contrast, in Mexico, firearms can only be purchased from the state, and handguns are restricted to lower-caliber models. Largely due to violence associated with the drug trade, there is a large illicit demand for firearms in Mexico, and the USA provides an abundant source. One study suggested that 2.2 percent of US domestic firearms sales between 2010 and 2012 involved weapons trafficked to Mexico, amounting to over 200,000 firearms per year.

All the available evidence suggests most of the firearms trafficking is done by small groups moving small amounts of weapons very frequently. The Mexican Attorney General's Office asserts, "At the present time, we have not detected in Mexico a criminal organization, domestic or foreign, dedicated to arms trafficking." Docket research by the Violence Policy Center suggests that most of these weapons were purchased legally in the USA, using "straw" purchasers. Similar to the smuggling of migrants, there are low barriers to entry for low-level criminals to participate in this market.

Box 6.1. Are Military Weapons Used in Street Crime?

Handguns have obvious advantages over long arms for use in street crime. They can be concealed and carried constantly; they are easier to use at close quarters; and they are every bit as deadly. But they can be difficult to find in many developing countries, since few can afford them. Criminals wishing to use firearms in poorer countries would have to make use of military arms left over from past conflicts, or somehow access (buy, rent, steal) handguns from the police or other licensed holders. Given that most people are unarmed and bullets are expensive, bladed weapons, which may also have agricultural uses, are often more commonly used in crime. For example, despite bordering several countries that have seen recent conflict, 76 percent of homicides in Tanzania in 2015 were committed with a bladed weapon, compared to only 2 percent that were committed with firearms.

In states where handguns are accessible, most criminals prefer to use them. Military weapons may be used, however, when criminal conflict becomes tantamount to a low-intensity military conflict. Some of the best-known examples include conflicts in the favelas of Brazil and some states in Mexico.

In Brazil, an analysis by a consortium including the local NGO Viva Rio of over 200,000 firearms seized over 30 years in the state of Rio de Janeiro found that just under 92 percent were civilian-type arms (68 percent were revolvers, 16 percent pistols, and 8 percent shotguns). Less than 2 percent were assault rifles or submachine guns, and 82 percent were manufactured in Brazil. Some 70 percent of the weapons seized chambered either 38 short or 32 short rounds. In other words, in one of the areas best known for the use of military arms, smaller weapons still comprised the vast majority of the seizures.

GUNS FOR WAR

The second source of demand for illicit weapons – demand from groups whose objectives are political rather than criminal – emerges when a set of militants finds the resources to equip an unauthorized force, or when a state subject to international embargoes attempts to circumvent these controls. Similar to criminals, insurgents may be able to access the weaponry desired from local sources or by stealing, renting, or purchasing weapons from the police and military. The looting of the Libyan armories after the fall of Kaddafi in 2011 was a major source of illicit military weapons to the region. State actors and some insurgent groups may have state allies willing to shuttle weaponry around the international agreements in what is often referred to as the "grey market." A recent study of weaponry used by ISIS found that most of the firearms had been diverted from other insurgent groups, who, in turn, had been illegally sourced by governments.

WHAT IS FIREARMS TRAFFICKING?

The Protocol against the Illicit Manufacturing of and Trafficking in Firearms, Their Parts and Components and Ammunition, supplementing the United Nations Convention against Transnational Organized Crime (the Protocol), defines a firearm as: "any portable barrelled weapon that expels, is designed to expel or may be readily converted to expel a shot, bullet or projectile by the action of an explosive…" Firearms are generally deemed a subset of the larger category of "small arms and light weapons," which also includes armaments such as heavy machine guns and grenades. "Firearms" include both handguns (such as pistols and revolvers), as well as long arms (such as rifles, shotguns, and assault rifles). "Craft weapons," produced by amateurs or artisans, are especially important in the developing world and may also be included.

   Under the Protocol, "illicit trafficking" is defined as "the import, export, acquisition, sale, delivery, movement or transfer of firearms … from or across the territory of one State Party to that of another State Party if any one of the States Parties concerned does not authorize it…" In practice, firearms trafficking is similar in nature to the trafficking of any other ostensibly licit good. Although clandestine cross-border movement does occur, it is often easier to ship the weapons through regular commercial channels, relying on false or fraudulently acquired paperwork and corrupt officials to ensure passage. To get to their final users, a combination of licit shipping and clandestine movement may be required. But, in theory, the "organized crime group" responsible for the trafficking could be as small as one well-placed broker and his conspirators on the receiving end. The rest of the people in the trafficking chain may be comporting themselves entirely within the ambit of the law.

   During the Cold War, much of the politically oriented firearms trafficking was conducted by agents of national governments, as antagonists armed their proxies in conflicts around the world. Following the collapse of the Soviet Union, a large number of surplus weapons became available for purchase. While nations continue to use firearms supply for geostrategic purposes, since the 1990s many of the actors have been profit-motivated criminals. However, as many commentators have noted, with the global proliferation of democracy, the number of international conflicts and civil wars has dropped dramatically since the mid-1990s. In short, there appears to have been an overall drop in demand for illicit military-grade firearms, although conflicts related to the Arab Spring have caused a lesser resurgence.

Global trends in the criminal acquisition and use of firearms are more difficult to discern. Most European and Asian countries have seen reductions in the amount of firearm homicides in recent years, as have some of the most violent countries, such as Colombia and South Africa. Others have apparently seen firearms violence levels rise, including the northern triangle of Central America, parts of the Caribbean, and Venezuela. But firearms were already widely available in most of the areas affected by criminal violence today, so there has been little apparent increase in demand.

WHY SOME AREAS ARE VULNERABLE TO GUN TRAFFICKING

While overall firearms trafficking may be in decline, the existence of large stockpiles of both military and civilian weapons pose a major source of vulnerability to future trafficking. Destruction of surplus arms is, therefore, both a form of crime prevention and conflict amelioration. Defining "surplus" is controversial, however, and even getting accurate information on firearms holdings can be difficult.

To get a sense of where the stockpiles are most acute in terms of military weapons, estimates of the size of the largest firearms arsenals in the world can be compared to the size of the active military in each country. Where there are many more weapons than there are soldiers to use them, there could be a vulnerability to firearms trafficking. The existence of reserve forces complicates this picture somewhat, as the combat readiness of these reserves varies substantially from country to country, but because these weapons are generally stored until needed, a risk of leakage exists.

After the dissolution of the former Soviet Union, Ukraine was left with large amounts of surplus weaponry. As a result, Ukraine represents a country that has been plagued by weapons surpluses, including decaying munitions stocks that have accidentally detonated on more than one occasion (see Figure 6.1). The country was allegedly a source of weapons for a number of notorious international firearms traffickers in the past, such as Victor Bout and Leonid Minin. In a transitional economy, there is considerable pressure to realize value for these assets, and licit sales to countries like Kenya and Chad appear to have been fed into conflict zones. It remains unclear how the recent conflict in Ukraine will affect these stocks, but large areas of the country are presently controlled by forces without international political accountability, compounding the risk.

On the crime side, civilian handgun holdings are more relevant. Small Arms Survey has also made estimates of the number of registered and unregistered civilian firearms in countries around the world. In these estimates, the USA appears to be the clear leader in terms of the number of weapons per capita. One-quarter of US citizens own a firearm, and many gun owners own several firearms (see Figure 6.2).

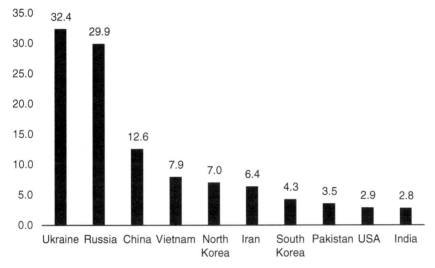

Figure 6.1. Firearms per active-duty soldier, top ten national firearms arsenals.
Source: Elaborated from data from Small Arms Survey 2018 and International Institute for Strategic Studies 2017 yearbooks

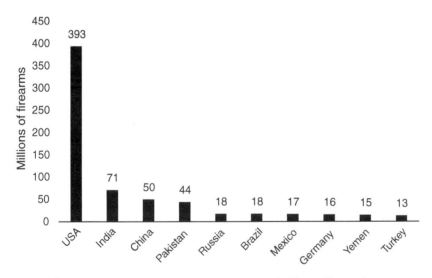

Figure 6.2. Total civilian firearms holdings, top ten countries (millions of firearms).
Source: Small Arms Survey 2018

For obvious reasons, criminals in the USA avoid using weapons registered in their names. Research among convicts in the USA shows that some purchased their weapon directly from a licensed dealer, but most acquired it through social networks or from criminal sources. The 2015 National Firearms Survey found that 2.5 percent of Americans had guns stolen within the past five years, producing an estimated 500,000 stolen firearms per year. This represents a large pool of firearms that can be used by criminals without fear of ownership traces. But transnational firearms traffickers may be less concerned about ownership traces, which is why straw purchases seem prevalent in the sourcing of weapons for Mexico's drug wars.

FURTHER READING

Azrael, D., Hepburn, L., Hemenway, D., & Miller, M. (2017). The stock and flow of U.S. firearms: Results from the 2015 National Firearms Survey. *The Russell Sage Foundation Journal of the Social Sciences*, 3(5), 38–57.

Conflict Armament Research. (2017). *Weapons of the Islamic State. A three-year investigation in Iraq and Syria*. London: Conflict Armament Research.

Martyniuk, A. (2017). *Measuring illicit arms flows: Ukraine*. Geneva: Small Arms Survey.

McDougal, T., Shirk, D., Muggah, R., & Patterson, J. (2015). The way of the gun: Estimating firearms trafficking across the US-Mexico border. *Journal of Economic Geography*, 15, 297–327.

Wintemute, G. (2013). Frequency of and responses to illegal activity related to commerce in firearms: Findings from the Firearms Licensee Survey. *Injury Prevention*, 19, 412–420.

7 Trafficking Antiquities

Simon Mackenzie

INTRODUCTION

Antiquities are old objects of cultural heritage. They can be very valuable and are often kept in museums or private collections. There is still much cultural heritage buried under the ground around the world, or otherwise *in situ* as part of a temple or other heritage structure like a church. Items can be illegally removed from temples or gravesites in one country (the source country) and trafficked internationally for sale in another (the market country). Source countries for antiquities tend to be developing countries, whereas market countries are richer, developed nations. In other words, looted antiquities tend to move from the poor countries where they are found to the rich countries where the buyers are (Mackenzie, 2005; Polk, 2000). Many countries suffer this kind of looting. High-profile cases of looting have for many years been occurring in countries such as Egypt, Turkey, Greece, and China, in South American countries such as Peru, and some Southeast Asian countries such as Cambodia and Thailand. Recently, high levels of antiquities looting have been observed in regions engaged in conflict, especially Iraq, Afghanistan, and Syria. Antiquities looting can destroy the archaeological context in which objects are found, diminishing our capacity to record knowledge about past civilizations. Looting and trafficking can also harm the objects themselves, and this is sometimes deliberate, such as when objects are cut or broken into pieces for ease of transport.

MEASUREMENT PROBLEMS

Trafficking antiquities typically involves clandestine excavation or theft, smuggling in transit, and either private sale or mixing with objects in the legitimate market. It is therefore difficult to arrive at reliable estimates of the size of the illicit market. We do, however, have continuing evidence of sometimes widespread looting in source countries (Brodie et al., 2001; Coggins, 1969), and case studies of specific types of objects have suggested that very high proportions of them have been looted (Gill & Chippindale, 1993). Researchers have developed innovative methods to achieve greater accuracy in estimating the size of the problem, such as by using auction catalogs or import and export records. Some research teams are using satellite imagery to track the development of looting issues on the ground (Parcak et al., 2016; Contreras & Brodie, 2010). Conventional crime statistics are generally not revealing in relation to this type of offence. Recording practices for crimes against antiquities vary across jurisdictions, and often these crimes are recorded only in the category of thefts, along with all other such property violations, with some specificity in relation to the way the theft was committed (e.g., "theft by housebreaking" or "robbery") but not in respect of the type of object stolen.

PROVENANCE

"Provenance" refers to the history of ownership of an object, and it may also include information about an object's "findspot," which in the case of an archaeological object refers to the place where it was excavated, by whom, and in what circumstances. When a buyer of antiquities asks "what's the provenance?" they might be given information about the findspot or, more likely, only about previous owners. Whether an object has had a prior owner is not always relevant to the question of whether it has been looted. The impression of 'due diligence' in a transaction can be misleading when the practice of checking provenance confuses noting some aspect of the ownership history with information about the circumstances of an object's discovery. Even when declaring ownership history there are different degrees of specificity used, and information may range from a specific collector's name to a vague reference to prior ownership by, for example, "the collection of a Belgian gentleman." Often, therefore, provenance can obscure an object's history, rather than help to trace its past. There is no accepted international approach to standards of proof in provenance, such as by way of certificates or object passports.

HOW DOES THE INTERNATIONAL MARKET IN ILLICIT ANTIQUITIES FUNCTION?

There are two streams of transnational commodity flow that constitute the illicit market in antiquities. The first stream is made up of artifacts that have been looted but that enter the publicly visible chain of supply, in the end being sold through shops or auction houses. These antiquities are "laundered" in the sense that once they have managed to enter the apparently legitimate chain of supply, each public sale gives them more provenance and provides a point of reference for future buyers to look to in determining whether they seem to be licit objects.

Prior sales or ownership history can be faked, and there have been high-profile cases where phantom "collections" have been invented for this laundering purpose. Confusion over the country where an artifact was discovered and extracted can also be exploited so as to suggest that contraband items are in fact legitimate exports from neighboring regions. This tactic has been known for some time (Gilgan, 2001), and it is currently causing problems for the attempted prohibition in dealing in items of Syrian cultural heritage. Cultural objects are appearing on the market with narratives suggesting origins in plausible nearby jurisdictions, or having been out of Syria prior to the date of the ban.

Some places function as transit ports for art and antiquities. Hong Kong has for a long time been a transit port for material illegally coming out of the Far East, and it is also able to service the currently increasing flow of antiquities back into China as collecting power and wealth grows there (Yates et al., 2017). In China, as with most source countries, it is generally illegal to dig or export antiquities. However, they can be smuggled out to Hong Kong, and then exported worldwide.

The second stream of antiquities is what has come to be called "the invisible market." This is constituted by off-the-record or nonpublic sales between individuals, and, as the name suggests, it is very hard to research. Therefore, we have little knowledge of the size or importance of the invisible market, although it is widely believed that a high number of illicit transactions are conducted in this market. The growth of Internet sales presents an ongoing challenge to policy here, as an ephemeral and only semi-visible market has emerged where relatively anonymous sellers can now easily connect with buyers worldwide.

THE LEGAL AND POLICY CONTEXT: HOW THE PROBLEM IS ADDRESSED

International Treaties

Two main treaties provide the framework for international approaches to regulation in the antiquities market: the UNESCO Convention on the Means of Prohibiting and Preventing the Illicit Import, Export and Transfer of Ownership of Cultural Property of 1970, and the UNIDROIT Convention on Stolen or Illegally Exported Cultural Objects of 1995. Of these, the UNIDROIT Convention provides the more stringent guidelines in relation to obligations on buyers of antiquities and rules for the return of looted objects to their rightful owners. Unfortunately only a small fraction of the number of countries that have signed up to the UNESCO Convention have chosen to take on the obligations in the UNIDROIT Convention. None of the major market countries have done so, which currently neutralizes much of the practical value of the 1995 Convention.

Domestic Laws

As well as restricting export, most source countries have passed laws that attempt to combat the problem of looting through vesting ownership in undiscovered antiquities in the state. A finder of an antiquity who keeps it will therefore be guilty of a theft; this is intended to discourage those who deliberately dig to look for objects. It also helps in claims for repatriation of looted artifacts once they have traveled to market countries, and in charging dealers in market countries with crimes involving the handling of stolen goods.

Nonlegal Prevention Measures

Registers of stolen objects exist, which allow buyers to check whether what they are being offered has been stolen. The main ones are the Art Loss Register, and the INTERPOL database of stolen works of art. Objects will only be listed on these databases, however, if they are known by their owners to have been stolen (and even then the owner might not choose to list the object). Antiquities that are illicitly excavated and that were unknown prior to their finding will not appear on a stolen art database. Other practical prevention measures include improving security at archaeological sites (although it is usually far too costly to effectively guard such sites), and education campaigns aimed at tourists and buyers in market countries (see O'Keefe, 1997, for a review of commonly discussed crime prevention and reduction measures in this field). Claims from source countries for repatriation of looted antiquities are becoming increasingly prevalent. The extent to which they constitute crime prevention is questionable but when these claims are made against major museums and auction houses they may play a part in influencing the climate of risk that those acquiring antiquities in the marketplace experience.

FACTORS THAT FACILITATE ANTIQUITIES TRAFFICKING

Trade Culture

Most antiquities dealers are willing to buy looted antiquities, although as with other stolen goods markets, they use techniques of neutralization to play down their role in creating a market for criminal activity (Mackenzie, 2005). They think, for example, that people would loot antiquities whether or not there are willing buyers, and that they are saving antiquities, preserving them for future generations to enjoy. Some dealers simply do not ask where the objects they buy have come from, and in such circumstances criminal prosecution can be challenging.

There are also dealers who are closer to our conventional understanding of criminals. In 2002, prominent New York dealer Fred Schultz was sentenced to 33 months in federal prison, with a fine of US$50,000, for his part in a scam to disguise his sale of antiquities looted from Egypt by manufacturing fake provenance for them. In 2009, an appellate court in Italy upheld the conviction of the infamous antiquities trafficker Giacomo Medici, who was sentenced to eight years in prison and received a €10 million fine for conspiracy to traffic in antiquities. In 1995, Medici's storage warehouse in Switzerland had been raided by police, revealing looted Italian artifacts and other evidence that led to successful claims for repatriation of objects from major museums worldwide, which had bought some of the looted objects. Medici was also in possession of Polaroid photos of objects *in situ*, suggesting that he would organize the looting of these artifacts on demand once interest was expressed by a buyer.

Limitation Periods

Antiquities that have been in circulation for some time will invariably have been "legitimized" through the operation of statutes of limitation that bar legal action against unchallenged owners of property after a number of years. The timescales for these differ depending on jurisdiction. Often a short timescale (three to five years is usual) is available for a "good faith" buyer. The formal approaches to checking provenance mentioned above are therefore important, as they can support an argument that a purchase was in good faith, and if the object was in fact stolen then only a few years later the buyer will own it, or (depending on the local rules) the original owner will be time-barred from reclaiming it even if the law does not consider the buyer the owner.

Corruption

Antiquities trafficking is made easier by corrupt officials. Sometimes these officials have a direct financial interest in the practice, such as where the military is involved in looting (Thosarat, 2001; Davis & Mackenzie, 2015). Sometimes it is simply customs agents who are bribed so as to avoid inspection of a shipment. Corruption is tied to the relative poverty experienced in many of the countries that are the major sources of antiquities, but there have also been scandals in the antiquities market that show that unethical practice is not limited to officials in source countries. Perhaps the most famous of these scandals was revealed by the journalist Peter Watson, who showed that professionals in a major international auction house were knowingly dealing in looted cultural objects (Watson, 1997).

SUMMARY AND CONCLUSIONS

We can conclude by summarizing the main characteristics of the transnational crime problem of looted and smuggled cultural heritage as follows:

- a crime problem in poorer source countries that provides an income for local populations.
- ineffective enforcement of local laws in source countries due to resource issues in policing and other public service jobs, and corruption
- a ready market for looted objects in richer countries providing a driver for the international transportation of looted objects
- difficulty in telling illicit objects apart from licit ones once they are mixed together in the chain of supply – compounded by buyers' reluctance to ask too many searching questions about provenance
- a lackluster law enforcement and policy response to the issue in market countries, since the main harm is perceived to be done to foreign states, and dealers form a reasonably powerful trade lobby group
- techniques of neutralization and other rationalizations used by dealers and collectors in the market to justify their continuing participation in a destructive activity
- high-level international treaties that receive much lip service in international policy circles but do not effectively regulate the problem at hand
- criminal laws in market countries that result in the occasional, and often quite spectacular, conviction of a prominent art world figure, but, again, do not provide much in the way of day-to-day regulation of the market
- professional associations that promulgate codes of ethics for their members – but with no real penalties for failing to abide by these codes.

REFERENCES

Brodie, N., Doole, J., & Renfrew, C. (Eds.). (2001). *Trade in illicit antiquities: The destruction of the world's archaeological heritage.* Cambridge: McDonald Institute for Archaeological Research.

Coggins, C. (1969). Illicit traffic of pre-Columbian antiquities. *Art Journal,* 29(1), 94–98.

Contreras, D. & Brodie, N. (2010). Quantifying destruction: An evaluation of the utility of publicly available satellite imagery for investigating looting of archaeological sites in Jordan. *Journal of Field Archaeology,* 35(1), 101–114.

Davis, T. & Mackenzie, S. (2015). Crime and conflict: Temple looting in Cambodia. In J. Kila and M. Balcells (Eds.), *Cultural property crime.* Leiden: Brill.

Gilgan, E. (2001). Looting and the market for Maya objects: A Belizean perspective. In N. Brodie, J. Doole, and C. Renfrew (Eds.), *Trade in illicit antiquities: The destruction of the world's archaeological heritage.* Cambridge: McDonald Institute for Archaeological Research.

Gill, D. J. W. & Chippindale, C. (1993). Material and intellectual consequences of esteem for cycladic figures. *American Journal of Archaeology*, 97(3), 602–673.

Mackenzie, S. (2005). *Going, going, gone: Regulating the market in illicit antiquities*. Leicester: Institute of Art and Law.

O'Keefe, P. J. (1997). *Trade in antiquities: Reducing destruction and theft*. London: Archetype.

Parcak, S., Gathings, D., Childs, C., Mumford, G., & Cline, C. (2016). Satellite evidence of archaeological site looting in Egypt: 2002–2013. *Antiquity*, 90, 188–205.

Polk, K. (2000). The antiquities trade viewed as a criminal market. *Hong Kong Lawyer*, September, 82–92.

Thosarat, R. (2001). The destruction of the cultural heritage of Thailand and Cambodia. In N. Brodie, J. Doole, and C. Renfrew (Eds.), *Trade in illicit antiquities: The destruction of the world's archaeological heritage*. Cambridge: McDonald Institute for Archaeological Research.

Watson, P. (1997). *Sotheby's: The inside story*. Hardback edn. London: Bloomsbury.

Yates, D., Mackenzie, S., & Smith, E. (2017). The cultural capitalists: Notes on the ongoing reconfiguration of trafficking culture in Asia. *Crime, Media, Culture*, 13(2), 245–254.

8 The Illegal Cigarette Trade

Klaus von Lampe

INTRODUCTION

The smuggling and illegal distribution of cigarettes is a global phenomenon in a dual sense. It can be observed in some form or other on every continent, and there are some schemes that span the globe, connecting distant places such as a clandestine factory in China producing counterfeit cigarettes with a street corner in London where these cigarettes are eventually sold to consumers.

Cigarettes are essentially a legal good. What makes the trade in cigarettes illegal is the evasion of excise and customs duties. Excise duties are taxes levied on certain goods produced or sold within the country. Customs duties are charged on goods imported from another country. Cigarettes are among the highest-taxed commodities and provide a significant source of revenue for governments. While the level of taxation varies across jurisdictions, in many countries taxes account for as much as 70 to 80 percent of the price smokers have to pay for a pack at a legal retail outlet store. Through a number of different schemes, suppliers and customers circumvent the taxation of cigarettes. As a result, cigarettes are being made available at a cost below legal retail prices, providing both lucrative profit margins for suppliers and significant savings for consumers, while causing substantial losses of revenue to governments, estimated at around US$40 billion globally in 2007, and at the same time undermining public health policies that aim to discourage smokers through high tobacco taxation (Joossens et al., 2009).

The illegal cigarette trade shows similarities but also some notable differences to other illegal markets. Illegal markets are characterized by the exchange of goods or services in violation of the law. Some goods are illegal under all circumstances, such as child pornography, some goods are illegal when they are handled without official permission or license, such as arms and pharmaceutical drugs, and some goods, such as cigarettes and gasoline, are illegal when duties are not paid. The peculiarity of the latter category is that, parallel to the black market, the same commodity is widely available through legal channels. In most countries, the legal market for cigarettes is much larger than the illegal market. It has been estimated that the global illicit cigarette trade accounted for 11.6 percent (or 657 billion cigarettes) of all cigarettes sold worldwide in 2007 (Joossens et al., 2009). In some countries like Libya and Guinea-Bissau, however, allegedly most (around 80 percent) of the cigarettes are sold illegally (United Nations Office on Drugs and Crime, 2009). One consequence of the parallel existence of legal and illegal markets seems to be that there is no stigma of illegality attached to the commodity as such and perhaps for that reason the cigarette black market has a higher chance of social acceptance than other illegal markets. Another characteristic of the cigarette black market is the uniformity of the commodity. While there are special kinds of cigarettes deviating from the norm, most cigarettes are similar in shape, size, consistency, and weight, and they are usually packed in packs of 20 sticks and cartons of ten-packs (200 sticks). This means that the handling of cigarettes poses the same challenges for illegal traders irrespective of place and time. Yet, there are significant variations in the manifestation of the cigarette black market internationally and nationally, and there are, as indicated, differences in the schemes used for procurement and distribution of illegal cigarettes that deserve closer examination.

THE ANATOMY OF THE ILLEGAL CIGARETTE TRADE

The term "illegal cigarette trade" as understood here is broader than the often-used term "cigarette smuggling" and encompasses three levels: the procurement level, an intermediate level where cigarettes are moved in the direction of the consumer, and the level of retail distribution.

Procurement Schemes

Cigarettes are procured for distribution on the black market in different ways, with different degrees of illegality and different levels of complicity of those involved. Three main schemes can be distinguished: bootlegging, large-scale smuggling, and counterfeiting.

BOOTLEGGING

Bootlegging involves the purchase of cigarettes in low-tax countries for resale in high-tax countries, taking advantage of cross-border differentials in legal retail prices. In these cases taxes on cigarettes are paid, though not in the country of consumption (see, e.g., Hornsby & Hobbs, 2007).

LARGE-SCALE SMUGGLING

Large-scale smuggling takes advantage of the temporary suspension of customs duties, excise, and other taxes on goods destined for export to a third country. Cigarettes destined for markets abroad are not subject to taxation in the country of origin, nor any transit country along the way for that matter, as long as certain procedures for storage and transport are followed. These untaxed cigarettes either never leave the country and are directly diverted to the black market, or, far more commonly, they are properly exported and disappear on the black market abroad or are illegally re-imported (see, e.g., Joossens & Raw, 2008). While this phenomenon has historically pertained to premium-brand cigarettes, since the mid-2000s large-scale smuggling has increasingly involved so-called cheap whites. These cigarettes are legally produced under unique brand names or with no branding at all and, given that they are largely absent from legal distribution channels, appear to be purposefully produced for the black market (Ross, Vellios, Smith, Ferguson, & Cohen, 2016).

COUNTERFEITING

While in cases of both bootlegging and large-scale smuggling, cigarettes are procured from originally legitimate sources, counterfeiting involves the production of fake-brand cigarettes, including packaging and, on occasion, fiscal marks made by unauthorized manufacturers. In addition to tax evasion, the trade in counterfeit cigarettes constitutes a violation of brand property rights. Most counterfeit cigarettes are said to be produced in illegal factories and tend to differ in every respect from their legal counterparts, including tobacco, paper, filter tips, and packaging. China, also the largest manufacturer of legal cigarettes, is believed to be the main source of counterfeit cigarettes (von Lampe, Kurti, Shen, & Antonopoulos, 2012).

Smuggling and Wholesale Distribution Schemes

The second major element of the illegal cigarette trade, following the initial procurement of cigarettes for the black market, comprises the smuggling of cigarettes, or their clandestine transport across borders without the payment of taxes and customs duties. However, the border crossing is only a small part of the overall handling of cigarettes between procurement and retail selling. In fact, there are schemes where the crossing of international borders is not required and all illicit activities take place within one country. In the USA, for example, cigarettes are brought from states with low taxes to states with high taxes (Reuter & Majmundar, 2015). Another constellation pertains to cigarettes destined for export. These untaxed cigarettes may be diverted to the black market without ever leaving the country.

The cigarettes that are procured for illegal distribution may go through similar and, at times, identical channels on the lower levels of the black market, as is true for the illegal cross-border transport of cigarettes. Smuggling modes, it seems, vary not so much according to the source of the cigarettes but rather with the size of the consignments that are being moved. Large loads of about 1 million sticks and more are typically transported while concealed in or behind legal goods under the guise of legal cross-border commerce.

The smuggling of smaller loads is typically embedded in the flow of noncommercial cross-border traffic, although smuggling across unregulated land and sea borders has also been reported. Common methods include the use of hidden compartments in cars and vans, for example, in the form of false bottoms or modified gas tanks. Another method, connected especially to the illicit sale of cigarettes over the Internet, is the use of parcel post services.

Cigarettes may be passed on directly to consumers. However, in most cases there seems to be a separate pattern of activities linking procurement and retail distribution. On this intermediate level cigarettes may be stored, reconfigured, and typically broken up into a number of smaller consignments, which are then passed on to buyers positioned further down in the distribution chain.

RETAIL DISTRIBUTION SCHEMES

A variety of patterns have also emerged by which contraband cigarettes are sold to consumers. These patterns can be grouped into three broad categories by the type of setting: public places, semipublic places, and private settings.

At public places like street corners or flea markets, the opportunity to purchase illegal cigarettes is advertised by vendors to passers-by. In semipublic places like bars and kiosks, the illegal cigarettes can be purchased under the counter as an alternative to legal cigarettes. Sometimes, consumers are defrauded when counterfeit (or stolen) cigarettes are sold as legitimate merchandise. Finally, illegal cigarettes may be passed on to consumers in private settings through social network relations.

Interestingly, the dominant distribution scheme varies geographically within and across countries. One striking example is Germany, where street vending of illegal cigarettes has been widespread in the Eastern parts of the country but virtually absent elsewhere (von Lampe, 2006).

WHO IS INVOLVED IN THE ILLEGAL CIGARETTE TRADE?

Criminal Groups and Terrorist Groups

One of the reasons why the illegal cigarette trade provides an interesting object of study is the diversity of the players involved in illicit activities. Three aspects have received particular attention: the level of involvement of criminal groups, the involvement of terrorist groups, and the complicity of the tobacco industry. It has often been alleged that the illegal cigarette trade is the domain of well-organized criminal groups who have previously been active in other areas of crime like drug trafficking. However, research in Europe has found that the illegal cigarette trade is primarily run not by known criminals but by individuals without a previous criminal record (see, e.g., van Duyne, 2003). Likewise, the involvement of terrorist groups who trade in illegal cigarettes to raise funds (see Shelley & Melzer, 2008) seems to be the exception rather than the rule (Reuter & Majmundar, 2015).

The Tobacco Industry

The involvement of tobacco manufacturers in the illegal cigarette trade appears to have been a more common occurrence in the past. There are several well-documented cases of complicity between major tobacco companies and cigarette smugglers (e.g., Joossens & Raw, 2008). In other cases, tobacco companies have at least turned a blind eye to the fact that their cigarettes are being funneled into illicit channels, typically through small countries with no significant domestic cigarette market. More recently, however, tobacco companies, under pressure from governments, have significantly reduced or entirely ceased their exports to such countries. This has apparently resulted in a sharp decline in the availability of major brands on the black market (Jossens & Raw, 2012). In fact, the emergence of counterfeit cigarettes and cheap whites may well be connected to stricter sales policies adopted by the large tobacco companies in the early 2000s.

COUNTERMEASURES

There is a heated debate over the best approaches to tackle the illegal trade in cigarettes. While anti-smoking lobbyists place the major blame on the tobacco industry, the tobacco industry itself argues that the high taxation of tobacco products more or less automatically creates a black market. From the available evidence it seems that, although there would not be an illegal cigarette trade without excise and customs duties, high taxes do not automatically lead to the emergence of a black market of significant size. Black markets for cigarettes are not necessarily most prevalent in high-tax countries and least prevalent in low-tax countries (Joossens & Raw, 2002, pp. 5–6). Likewise, there are substantial regional variations in black market prevalence within particular countries despite uniform tax rates nationwide (Calderoni, 2014). It appears to be at least as important that supply of and demand for untaxed cigarettes are linked up in an efficient way and that illegal transactions can take place in a relatively non-hostile environment. This, in turn, depends on the strength or weakness of law enforcement and civil society in a community (see, e.g., Yürekli & Sayginsoy, 2010). In this context it should be noted that through a number of countermeasures, mirroring efforts against drug trafficking, the illegal cigarette trade has become riskier in recent years. Most notably, through the introduction of stationary and mobile scanners and the use of tobacco sniffing dogs the control of international cargo has been made substantially more effective.

CONCLUSIONS

The illegal cigarette trade is essentially a form of tax evasion. Different schemes have developed to circumvent taxation to supply cigarettes to consumers below legal retail prices. Cigarettes are either diverted from legal channels, or they are produced specifically for distribution on the black market.

REFERENCES

Calderoni, F. (2014). A new method for estimating the illicit cigarette market at the subnational level and its application to Italy. *Global Crime*, 15, 51–76.

Hornsby, R. & Hobbs, D. (2007). A zone of ambiguity: The political economy of cigarette bootlegging. *British Journal of Criminology*, 47, 551–571.

Joossens, L., Merriman, D., Ross, H., & Raw, M. (2009). *How eliminating the global illicit cigarette trade would increase tax revenue and save lives*. Paris: International Union Against Tuberculosis and Lung Disease, 10. Retrieved August 30, 2009, from www.fctc.org/dmdocuments/INB3_report_ illicit_trade_save_revenue_lives.pdf.

Joossens, L. & Raw, M. (2002). *Turning off the tap: An update on cigarette smuggling in the UK and Sweden, with recommendations to control smuggling*. London: Cancer Research UK.

 (2008). Progress in combating cigarette smuggling: Controlling the supply chain. *Tobacco Control*, 17, 399–404.

 (2012). From cigarette smuggling to illicit tobacco trade. *Tobacco Control*, 21, 230–234.

Reuter, P. & Majmundar, M. (Ed.). (2015). *Understanding the U.S. illicit tobacco market: Characteristics, policy context, and lessons from international experiences*. Washington, DC: National Academy of Sciences.

Ross, H., Vellios, N., Clegg Smith, K., Ferguson, J., & Cohen, J. E. (2016). A closer look at "Cheap White" cigarettes. *Tobacco Control*, 25, 527–531.

Shelley, L. & Melzer, S. (2008). The nexus of organized crime and terrorism: Two case studies in cigarette smuggling. *The International Journal of Comparative and Applied Criminal Justice*, 32, 43–63.

United Nations Office on Drugs and Crime. (2009, July). *Transnational trafficking and the rule of law in West Africa: A threat assessment*. Vienna: UNODC. Retrieved August 28, 2009, from www.unodc .org/documents/data-and-analysis/Studies/West_Africa_Report_2009.pdf.

Van Duyne, P. C. (2003). Organizing cigarette smuggling and policy making ending up in smoke. *Crime, Law and Social Change*, 39, 285–317.

Von Lampe, K. (2006). The cigarette black market in Germany and in the United Kingdom. *Journal of Financial Crime*, 13, 235–254.

Von Lampe, K., Kurti, M., Shen, A., & Antonopoulos, G. (2012). The changing role of China in the global illegal cigarette trade. *International Criminal Justice Review*, 22, 43–67.

Yürekli, A. & Saygınsoy, Ö. (2010). Worldwide organized cigarette smuggling: An empirical analysis. *Applied Economics*, 42, 545–561.

WEBSITES

Framework Convention Alliance (for a Framework Convention on Tobacco Control). www.ftct.org.

Action on Smoking and Health (anti-smoking NGO). www.ash.org.

The Center for Public Integrity (investigative journalists on the "Tobacco Underground"). www.publicintegrity.org/health/public-health/tobacco.

Tobacco Control (journal). http://tobaccocontrol.bmj.com.

Philip Morris International (tobacco manufacturer). www.philipmorrisinternational.com.

9 · Wildlife Trafficking

The Problem, Patterns, and a Promising Path Toward Prevention

Justin Kurland

INTRODUCTION

Over the past decade wildlife trafficking has become increasingly recognized as both a specialized area of transnational organized crime as well as a significant threat to numerous species of flora and fauna. The severity of this problem is undeniable, with recent UN estimates suggesting wildlife trafficking ranks among the five most lucrative illegal trades in the world – costing approximately US$23 billion annually. However, the economic implications associated with the illicit trade in wildlife only begin to scratch the surface of this incredibly complex problem, which is markedly different to other forms of transnational crime.

For starters, the local wildlife in many places throughout the developing world is an essential community resource. More specifically, wild animals often provide the only viable source of protein required for nourishment, native trees provide a source of fuel, and some combination of these two are used as natural remedies for common ailments. Consequently, the removal of these plants and animals from many of these rural societies alters livelihoods and ultimately undermines security.

Further, the effect associated with the illegal exchange of animals and plants (or their constituent parts) has consequences that extend beyond merely robbing present and future generations from enjoying the majesty and wonder of the natural world; it also negatively impacts biodiversity and ecosystems. That is, the overexploitation of species in combination with the introduction of non-native species through illegal trade causes imbalances that can (and have already) led to the introduction of pathogens that threaten both public health and agricultural productivity (Smith et al., 2009).

Despite the severity of the wildlife trafficking problem described above, some from the conservation community, and certainly those from the criminological community interested in wildlife crime, would likely agree that a proportion of research relating to the illicit trade often offers little insight into how the immediate situation in which these crimes take place can be altered to reduce and prevent crime. Notwithstanding the dearth of empirical evidence, the prevailing wisdom amongst a large portion of the conservation community suggests that – not unlike the other forms of transnational crime in Part I of this volume – *demand* in combination with high profit margins is the primary cause of wildlife trafficking.

Thus, it should come as no surprise that this same group favors a market demand reduction approach for curbing wildlife trafficking. However, given the breadth and complexity of the wildlife trade, such an approach may be of limited practical value. It should be noted that not all in the conservation community are in agreement with those advocating for bans on legal trade, law enforcement, and interdiction-based approaches; others prefer interventions that allow legal supply from hunting or farming; still others recommend alternative livelihood methods and even money-laundering efforts for wildlife trafficking prevention (for a review, see Brown, 2017).

Lessons gleaned from criminological research that focuses on opportunity reduction may be better suited to addressing wildlife trafficking; this will require 1) greater attention by criminologists interested in crime prevention and 2) buy-in from conservationists towards action-based research that favors a situational approach toward increasing the associated *effort* and *risk of* engaging in some aspect of the illicit wildlife trade, and/or reducing the *reward* and *provocations*, and removing *excuses* for engaging in it.

BACKGROUND

Wildlife trafficking has been broadly defined by Reuter and O'Regan (2016) "to include all international transactions involving the movement of species that are protected by law in either the source or destination country, whether dead or alive." Wildlife trafficking can range in scale from a solitary item exchanged locally to multi-ton shipments transported to locations around the world. Contraband could include: live pets, pelts and skins, meat for human consumption, fashion accessories, cultural artifacts, ingredients for traditional medicines, and various other products. Timber and fisheries are typically not included in the measurement of wildlife trafficking, but it could be argued that they should be.

Both domestic and international laws attempt to prevent: 1) the extinction of species that have been identified as threatened; 2) the importation of non-native species that may damage local environments; 3) the introduction of species that have the potential to spread diseases harmful to humans, animals, or plants; 4) the inhumane transportation of wildlife; and 5) the disruption of legal trade in wildlife products (Wyler & Sheikh, 2008).

In response to the problem defined above, the International Consortium on Combating Wildlife Crime (ICCWC) in collaboration with the United Nations Office on Drug and Crimes (UNODC) constructed the World Wildlife Seizure database (World WISE) in 2015. Patterns of identified illicit wildlife trafficking were utilized to generate the first ever World Wildlife Crime Report on the Trafficking in Protected Species.

A brief accounting of trends from this report suggests that there were nearly 7,000 different species accounted for in over 164,000 seizures that took place in 120 countries (for the full report, see the link at the end of the chapter). The following are a few other statistics worth mentioning.

- No single species represents more than 6 percent of seizure incidents.
- No single country is a source of more than 15 percent of the seized shipments.
- Traffickers were identified from 80 different countries.
- All regions of the world play a role as a source, transit hub, or destination for wildlife contraband.

DISCUSSION

Current Wildlife Trafficking Research Gaps

What is clear from the extant literature on wildlife trafficking is that governments from across the world, nongovernmental organizations (NGOs) devoted to conservation, researchers from a multitude of disciplines, and practitioners alike all recognize the growing severity of this problem. Yet what is equally clear is that the work within this field is relatively uncoordinated, and robust monitoring and systematic evaluation is limited (Kurland et al., 2017).

Indeed, scant scientific evidence exists that: 1) assesses both domestic and international market characteristics and teases apart how they operate for a particular species or group of species; 2) investigates the role (if any) they serve in tangentially related illegal commodity markets such as human, arms, and drug trafficking, as has been suggested in countless reports and declarations by the media and politicians; 3) measures the relative success of domestic and/or international legislation set out to prevent trafficking; and 4) analyzes micro- and macro-level trends about those places, times, type of species or products, routes, and facilities where wildlife trafficking clusters (Schneider, 2008).

Recent Criminological Research on Wildlife Trafficking

Thankfully, over the past several years, what appears to be a growing body of research conducted primarily by criminologists interested in the prevention of wildlife crime has begun to partially fill these existing knowledge gaps. For example, Pires and Clarke (2011) conducted a study that assessed domestic markets in Bolivia involved in the illicit trade of parrots and found that risk is not evenly distributed across species of parrots native to Bolivia. Instead, those parrots considered more enjoyable as pets, more abundant in the wild, and having a range within 50 miles of the markets were at greater risk.

Reuter and O'Regan (2016) conducted a review of academic literature, popular accounts, and government reports on wildlife trafficking in an attempt to identify the scope and methods associated with the problem in the Americas and any potential links to "organized crime." Findings suggested no connections to organized crime and what appears to be small-scale activity associated with legitimate business that operates in a low-risk and technologically narrow environment.

A study by Lemieux and Clarke (2009) measured the relative success of the 1989 ban on the international trade of elephant ivory among members of the Convention on International Trade in Endangered Species (CITES), intended to reverse the sharp decline in the African elephant population that resulted from widespread poaching in the previous decade. Results from the analysis were mixed with some evidence demonstrating an overall increase in elephant population across the African continent, but also found that some of the 37 countries in Africa with elephants continued to lose substantial numbers due to the presence of unregulated domestic markets in and near countries with declines were ultimately to blame for the loss.

In a study that sought to uncover wildlife trafficking patterns, Kurland and Pires (2017) took advantage of the Law Enforcement Management Information System (LEMIS) database, which tracks all wildlife seizures made in the USA with detailed information on each incident. Findings indicated that a disproportionate share of export countries, ports of entry, times, and species accounted for a majority of incidents. Similar research conducted by Sina et al. (2016) that took advantage of the EU-TWIX database (the EU analog to LEMIS) found similar trends. Most notably for the period between 2007 and 2014, the UK, Germany, and the Netherlands were responsible for more than 70 percent of seizures.

A New Way Forward for Tackling Wildlife Trafficking

Critically, these studies also set a new precedent for research in this area and spawned a growing number of similar empirical studies. For example, prior to Pires and Clarke's (2011) formative analysis of the illicit parrot trade in Bolivia, the majority of market-based studies were conducted by NGOs such as TRAFFIC and typically captured basic details on the type and volume of particular species in a given market, which are of limited value to those interested in prevention. However, since then related research on the illicit trade of parrots in Mexico and Peru have been conducted, in addition to a number of studies on what is driving the illicit trade in fish and timber, which provide valuable insight into what might be done to reduce harm.

The work of Lemieux and Clarke (2009) highlighted to criminologists, conservationists, and policy makers alike the potential shortcomings associated with prevention-intended legislation that only acts on a single level. Moving forward, those involved in advocating (or crafting) legislation to curb the illicit trade in wildlife would be wise to consider more fully the mechanisms, costs-benefits, context, and outcomes of implementing comparable regulations.

Similarly, Reuter and O'Regan (2016) have laid to rest (at least in the Americas) the mischaracterization of wildlife trafficking as being tied to "organized crime" syndicates who also deal in human, drug, and arms trafficking. This is an important distinction to have made because the techniques utilized for preventing wildlife trafficking for organized crime syndicates and a series of "crimes that are organized" by largely legitimate businesses that take advantage of opportunities that arise in day-to-day operations to make some additional money will differ.

Last, but certainly not least, the work of Kurland and Pires (2017) highlighted the need for more rigorous analysis of data accessible to criminologists interested in wildlife trafficking. Databases such as LEMIS and EU-TWIX provide an opportunity for researchers and analysts to tease apart patterns about the where, when, who, what, and how of the illicit wildlife trade that can: 1) aid law enforcement and customs officials in the allocation of their often very limited resources; 2) provide useful intelligence to international counterparts who may be in the dark about export problems; and 3) help devise interventions that will stifle wildlife trafficking in the future.

These studies represent a few of the recent, but seminal, criminological studies on wildlife trafficking that have begun to fill knowledge gaps about the problem. They are important precisely because they address the kind of research questions required to craft interventions meant to curb specific crime problems, formulate more comprehensive legislation, and better allocate the limited resources available to help combat the wildlife trafficking problem.

CONCLUSION

While the scourge of wildlife trafficking is a growing problem, so too is the interest of those who share the common aim of helping prevent it. That said, if there is going to be genuine progress made in dealing with the illicit trade in wildlife, then those concerned must consider a multitude of interventions that operate at the local, national, and international levels. One of the primary challenges we face relates to convincing those in the conservation community, who do genuinely want to stop the problem, that greater specificity is required when examining a particular wildlife trafficking problem so that a more empirically grounded approach – namely situational crime prevention – can be adopted. It provides a more comprehensive framework that assists with the identification, implementation, and development of techniques for the reduction of specific forms of crime.

At the local, national, or international levels, if such an approach is going to be adopted, greater specificity regarding the dynamics of the particular illicit wildlife trade is required – where does the illicit trade occur, when does it occur, who is involved, what did they do, why did they do it, and how did they go about doing it? Further questions regarding specific aspects of a particular species of interest and associated patterns will also help shape measures to deal with the problem at different levels.

In theory this might work at the local level by identifying the location in a legal market where illicit wildlife trading occurs, when it occurs most frequently, if there is a particular seller or group of sellers who are involved, and so on. In this instance one could envisage a subtle but forcible change in the location of a particular vendor's (or group of sellers') stall in a market, at specific times, leading to a reduction because the proposition of making an illicit transaction would become riskier as a result of a reduced ability to conceal illicit items. Such an approach is not limited to local markets, but instead can be done at greater levels of aggregations such as at the domestic or international level if the above-mentioned questions are properly addressed.

In practice, at any of these levels, implementing interventions can be challenging. One potentially fruitful strategy might be the development of a "What Works" repository for wildlife trafficking. Such a resource, used in combination with rapid-appraisal techniques, could provide a more expedient method for seeking out what has been successful at reducing a particular type of wildlife trafficking problem in the past in order to quickly address specific wildlife trafficking problems before it is too late (Natarajan, 2016)!

REFERENCES

Brown, V. F. (2017). *The extinction market: Wildlife trafficking and how to counter it.* Oxford: Oxford University Press.

Kurland, J. & Pires, S. F. (2017). Assessing US wildlife trafficking patterns: How criminology and conservation science can guide strategies to reduce the illegal wildlife trade. *Deviant Behavior,* 38(4), 375–391.

Kurland, J., Pires, S. F., McFann, S. C., & Moreto, W. D. (2017). Wildlife crime: A conceptual integration, literature review, and methodological critique. *Crime Science,* 6(1), 4.

Lemieux, A. M. & Clarke, R. V. (2009). The international ban on ivory sales and its effects on elephant poaching in Africa. *The British Journal of Criminology,* 49(4), 451–471.

Natarajan, M. (2016) Crime in developing countries: The contribution of crime science. *Crime Science,* 5(8), 1–5.

Pires, S. F. & Clarke, R. V. (2011). Sequential foraging, itinerant fences and parrot poaching in Bolivia. *The British Journal of Criminology*, 51(2), 314–335.

Reuter, P. & O'Regan, D. (2016). Smuggling wildlife in the Americas: scale, methods, and links to other organised crimes. *Global Crime*, 18(2), 77–99.

Schneider, J. L. (2008). Reducing the illicit trade in endangered wildlife: the market reduction approach. *Journal of Contemporary Criminal Justice*, 24(3), 274–295.

Sina, S., Gerstetter, C., Porsch, L., Roberts, E., Smith, L., Klaas, K., & Fajardo, T. (2016). *Wildlife crime (IP/A/ENVI/2015-10)*. Brussels: European Parliament.

Smith, K. F., Behrens, M., Schloegel, L. M., Marano, N., Burgiel, S., & Daszak, P. (2009). Reducing the risks of the wildlife trade. *Science*, 324(5927), 594–595.

Wyler, L. S. & Sheikh, P. A. (2008). *International illegal trade in wildlife: Threats and US policy*. Washington, DC: Library of Congress Congressional Research Service.

WEBSITES

UNODC World Wildlife Crime Report 2016. www.unodc.org/documents/data-and-analysis/wildlife/World_Wildlife_Crime_Report_2016_final.pdf.

Centre for Conservation Criminology and Ecology. www.c3e.rutgers.edu.

TRAFFIC. www.traffic.org.

10 Cybercrime

Alex Alexandrou

In the twentieth century, oil was our most valuable commodity. Today, the most valuable commodity is data (*The Economist*, 2017). If data had no value, there would be no cybercrime.

Cybercrime is a computer-based criminal act utilizing a computing device and a network. This act transcends national and international borders and raises jurisdiction issues that one nation alone cannot address. Figure 10.1 demonstrates the evolution of cybercrime.

While cybercrimes encompass a broad category of offenses, the underlying technologies cybercriminals exploit remain the same. Cybercrimes are the unwelcome consequences of a data-driven and techno-centric society. Data, information, hacking tools, and instructions for using them are available to anyone, with or without computer training or experience. Most cybercriminals make money by selling or trading these tools. However, not all cybercriminals seek financial gain. A hacktivist is a person who uses unauthorized data for political and subversive goals. One of the most infamous examples is the group *Anonymous*. The purpose of hacktivism is to spread a political or social message and cause a social change.

When a cybercrime is political or social in nature, the entire world may only understand what has happened in retrospect. In the 2016 US presidential election (Trautman, 2016), we saw cybercrime as a tool of influence, and ultimately an attack against a country's infrastructure.

THE DEVELOPMENT OF CYBERCRIME

Phase I, the beginning of cybercrime, dates from the late 1970s, with the first computer worm, the "Creeper." It caused infected systems to display the message: "I'M THE CREEPER: CATCH ME IF YOU CAN" (Chen & Robert, 2004).

Phase I is characterized by direct attacks against systems and networks, with the goal of flaunting institutions by crashing systems or causing physical damage (*You can build it, but I can break it*). Some tools used in Phase I include malicious code, Trojans, and advanced worms and viruses. Targets of this phase are limited to hardware and institutions, not individuals.

In 1986, Markus Hess, a German citizen, hacked the Lawrence Berkeley Laboratory computer network, selling much of the information he obtained to the KGB.

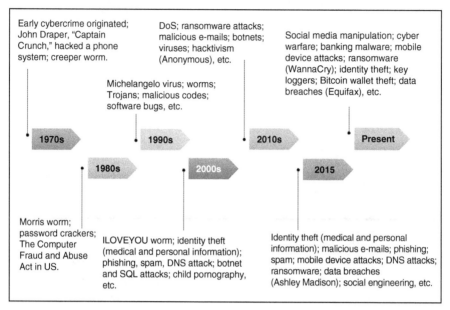

Figure 10.1. The evolution of cybercrime.

Robert Morris, a college student, was prosecuted and convicted of violating Title 18 USC 1030 – Fraud and related activity in connection with computers. Morris embedded a computer worm in a Cornell University UNIX system in 1988.

Phase II takes advantage of the same weaknesses of system and networks security, but for a different purpose – the exploitation of specific individuals. These cybercrimes target specific victims. Beginning in the early 2000s, this phase saw cybercrime become a profitable enterprise (*I can steal and use your personal information*). We saw the proliferation of financial crime, identity theft, credit card fraud, phishing, DNS attacks, botnets, ransomware and spyware, and, at times, crimes of personal revenge.

Cybercriminals quickly understood that the Internet allowed them to reach the entire planet, ignoring physical and geographical boundaries (Maras, 2017). They evaded justice by using secure software and hidden servers to conceal themselves. When attackers were identified, conflicting international laws made it difficult or impossible to gather evidence and punish them.

Every device connected to the Internet is vulnerable to cybercrime. The "Internet of Things" (IoT) includes computer-based devices that transmit data over the Internet autonomously. These include smart home devices and products like smart thermostats, smart lightbulbs, smart TVs, and wearable sensors like heart rate and respiratory rate monitors. These small devices, used by billions, are vulnerable to hacking. The "Mirai" malware attack, in 2016, targeted IoT devices, opening home networks to cybercriminals, with costly results.

WannaCry, a ransomware attack, exploited a weakness in Windows computers in a 2017 worldwide cyberattack. Attackers were able to encrypt data and then lock out users, making it impossible for them to access their own information, demanding ransom payments in Bitcoin cryptocurrency.

Ransomware also had a devastating effect on the United Kingdom's National Health Service (NHS), bringing down its medical records and other systems. As a result, medical personnel could not register patients, access medical records, or prescribe medications, delaying crucial procedures, and creating chaos (Clarke & Youngstein, 2017).

In late 2014, Sony Pictures Entertainment (SPE) detected extensive network intrusions, followed by demands that Sony refrain from releasing its film *The Interview*. The film was a satire about Americans sent to North Korea to assassinate its president, Kim Jong-Un. Sony employees were threatened with physical harm if they did not sign a denunciation of the film. It was later determined that the government of North Korea was responsible (Haggard & Lindsay, 2015).

Crime-as-a-Service (CaaS) is a criminal marketplace on the Dark Web, providing services such as password cracking, cloud cracking, distributed denial-of-service, and malware (Manky, 2013). A 2017 Internet Organized Crime Threat Assessment by EUROPOL reports that attackers used CaaS to distribute material detailing acts of sexual abuse (EUROPOL, 2017).

Cybercriminals also engage in cyberbullying, pedophilia, and sexual exploitation. The Internet has exponentially increased the production, distribution, and possession of child pornography images and child sexual abuse material (CSAM). The USA addresses online child pornography with the Child Pornography Prevention Act of 1996 (CPPA) and the PROTECT Act of 2003. In addition, the Council of Europe (COE) criminalized online activities related to child pornography, and classified such behaviors as cybercrimes in its Convention on Cybercrime.

Artificial intelligence tools like Google's TensorFlow can track us as we view online videos, making sophisticated video manipulation available to everyone. Deepfake video clips, created using TensorFlow, use Google's image search feature to locate and then almost flawlessly replace faces in videos. The program does not need human supervision after the initial machine learning process; its algorithm improves the process autonomously. Anyone can switch the faces in X-rated videos so that they feature celebrities, politicians, friends, and enemies. Individuals use the results for revenge porn, bullying, video evidence, political sabotage, propaganda, fake news video, or blackmail.

In Phase II, the cybercriminal is an opportunist who looks for easy targets to satisfy his goals. Advantages such as speed, convenience, anonymity, and the lack of physical or virtual borders make cybercrime difficult for law enforcement to police and control in jurisdictions around the globe. More collaboration and effective information sharing with INTERPOL can help address cybercrime that is progressively becoming more complex and sophisticated.

The most important weapons used by cybercriminals in Phase II are summarized in Table 10.1.

Phase III is the most recent phase in the development of cybercrime – political cybercrime, characterized by the *manipulation of social media and the theft or purchase of personal profiles*. In this phase, cybercriminals choose targets based on their political orientation, education, opinions, and other factors that make them persuadable and vulnerable. The victims are attacked with ads and fake social media, leading to increased social unrest, election upsets, changes in the power structure of nations, and ultimately a changed balance of international dominance.

Table 10.1. Cybercrime weapons summarized

Malware: Malware is short for malicious software, including computer viruses, worms, Trojan horses, ransomware, spyware, and other types of intrusive software. Malware infiltrates a computing device or system without the user's knowledge to execute specific destructive tasks.

Crime-as-a-Service (CaaS): An on-demand marketplace where one can purchase cybercrime services and attack tools.

Cyberterrorism: The use of the Internet to promote propaganda, cause fear, provide training, and disseminate advice on making bombs, promoting radicalization, and planning international terror attacks.

Cyberwarfare: A nation-state-sponsored cyberattack on another nation-state in an attempt to harm, alter, destroy, or steal information, or to conduct espionage and sabotage a computer network.

Denial of service (DoS): An attack that occurs when a hacker makes computer resources inaccessible to its users by flooding the network with information, causing a network to crash. DoS uses a single computer in the attack.

Distributed denial-of-service (DDoS): More complex attacks that occur when a hacker exploits security vulnerabilities to take control of multiple computers, using them to attack other computers or networks. DDoS attacks are frequently worldwide.

Fraud and financial crime: A form of network-based theft that involves funds or property. These online crimes include online purchase scams, auction fraud, mortgage fraud, sales fraud, embezzlement, Ponzi and pyramid schemes, credit and debit card fraud, money laundering, health care fraud, etc.

Hacking: An individual accessing a computer device or a computer system without the user's knowledge and authorization.

Hacktivist: An individual hacker driven by an ideology or politically inspired motivation.

Identity theft: A broad range of crimes, including theft of personal or medical information, accessing a victim's bank accounts, credit cards, tax refunds, impersonating another individual when apprehended for a crime, etc. Finally, the theft of personal and medical data, sold to marketing firms worldwide, for targeted marketing of a drug or other product.

Ransomware: Use of malicious software to extort victims by locking and encrypting their data unless a ransom is paid.

Spam: Any unrequested electronic message sent in bulk. Spam can be an advertising campaign, or a malicious worm or virus with a primary mission to infect.

Since the majority of American adults (62 percent) get news on social media, a large number of those who see these accounts believe they are true (Allcott & Gentzkow, 2017). The attacks present an alternative reality to the victims, and influence them through a strategy of persuasion through repetition. Individuals will believe anything they hear often enough.

We saw this in the United States presidential election of 2016 (Persily, 2017), and in European elections and referenda as well (Sunstein, 2018). In addition, we have seen Russian hackers target critical infrastructure, like electrical grids in Europe and the USA (Kshetri et al., 2017). In Phase III, cybercrime has grown into a sophisticated and subtle global threat, *a silent worldwide war*. This menace knows no boundaries and poses danger to every nation on the planet.

Fake news and advertisements have been a great source of revenue for social media like Facebook and Twitter. Disinformation is a social condition that requires government supervision, education, and continuous monitoring. As of now, the word "*truth*" has lost its meaning and instead we have "*alternative truth or facts.*" We are no longer consumers of social media; we are its products, for sale to the highest bidder. The economic impact of cybercrime globally is increasing exponentially; in 2014, cybercrime cost almost US$500 billion, while in 2017 the cost rose to US$608 billion (Lewis, 2018).

How can we understand what makes cybercriminals act as they do? A range of theories across criminology, psychology, and computer information systems provides explanations of the factors influencing cybercriminal behavior.

- The Rational Choice Theory explains that it is human nature to base decisions on reason, calculating the statistical probabilities and potential risks prior to committing a crime. When benefits outweigh costs, the cybercriminal commits the crime (Maras, 2017).
- The General Theory of Crime tells us that criminal opportunities and a lack of individual self-control may in combination have an impact on criminal behavior (Moon et al., 2010; Donner et al., 2014). Therefore, lack of regulations, the ability to function anonymously, and the increase in antisocial behavior may influence online criminality.
- The Theory of Reasoned Action considers beliefs and motivation as forecasters of behavior (Fishbein & Ajzen, 1975). Both the cybercriminal's personal judgments and what others think about the criminal act will influence behavior.
- The Deterrence Theory discourages criminal behavior through disincentives and severity of sanctions (Xu et al., 2013). If the punishment exceeds the benefits, the cybercriminal will think twice before engaging in a cyberattack.

CONCLUSION

While cybercrime is a complex global problem, understanding the human element, along with adequate deterrence, can prevent or reduce cybercrime. This requires collaboration among nations, and response at the global level. In addition to improving security efforts and learning more about the behaviors of cybercriminals, the behavior and vulnerabilities of their victims must be studied and understood as well.

So far, while cybercriminals continue to develop their methods and targets of attack, their opponents, whose job it is to defend our computer systems and networks, are not keeping pace. Attackers may come from anywhere, and may be looking for money, influence, power, or all three. Cybercriminals, like other businesspersons, supply customers' wants, and evolve and adapt to meet the needs of an increasingly complex and bitterly divided world. To control and defeat them, we must do the same.

REFERENCES

Allcott, H. & Gentzkow, M. (2017). Social media and fake news in the 2016 election. *Journal of Economic Perspectives*, 31(2), 211–236.

Chen, T. M. & Robert, J. M. (2004). The evolution of viruses and worms. In W. S. Chen (Ed.), *Statistical methods in computer security* (pp. 265). New York: Marcel Dekker.

Clarke, R. & Youngstein, T. (2017). Cyberattack on Britain's National Health Service: A wake-up call for modern medicine. *New England Journal of Medicine*, 377(5), 409–411.

Donner, C. M., Marcum, C. D., Jennings, W. G., Higgins, G. E., & Banfield, J. (2014). Low self-control and cybercrime: Exploring the utility of the general theory of crime beyond digital piracy. *Computers in Human Behavior*, 34, 165–172.

Europol Report (2017). Internet organized crime threat assessment by EUROPOL (IOCTA 2017). Retrieved from www.europol.europa.eu/iocta/2017/index.html.

Fishbein, M. & Ajzen, I. (1975). *Belief, attitude, intention and behavior: An introduction to theory and research*. Boston, MA: Addison-Wesley.

Haggard, S. & Lindsay, J. R. (2015). North Korea and the Sony Hack: Exporting instability through cyberspace. *Asia Pacific Issues*, 117, 1–8.

Kshetri, N. & Voas, J. (2017). Hacking power grids: A current problem. *Computer*, 50(12), 91–95.

Lewis J. (2018). *McAfee – Economic impact of cybercrime*. Retrieved from www.mcafee.com/us/resources/reports/restricted/economic-impact-cybercrime.pdf.

Manky, D. (2013). Cybercrime as a service: A very modern business. *Computer Fraud & Security*, 2013(6), 9–13.

Maras, M. H. (2017). *Cybercriminology*. New York: Oxford University Press.

Moon, B., McCluskey, J. D., & McCluskey, C. P. (2010). A general theory of crime and computer crime: An empirical test. *Journal of Criminal Justice*, 38(4), 767–772.

Persily, N. (2017). Can democracy survive the Internet? *Journal of Democracy*, 28(2), 63–76.

Steinmetz, K. F. & Nobles, M. R. (2017). Introduction. In *Technocrime and criminological theory* (pp. 17–26). New York: Routledge Taylor and Francis Group.

Sunstein, C. R. (2018). *Republic: Divided democracy in the age of social media*. Princeton, NJ: Princeton University Press.

The Economist. (2017). The world's most valuable resource is no longer oil, but data. Retrieved from www.economist.com/news/leaders/21721656-data-economy-demands-new-approach-antitrust-rules-worlds-most-valuable-resource.

Trautman, L. J. (2016). Is cyberattack the next Pearl Harbor? *North Carolina Journal of Law & Technology*, 18, 233.

Xu, Z., Hu, Q., & Zhang, C. (2013). Why computer talents become computer hackers. *Communications of the ACM*, 56(4), 64–74.

11 Crime and Online Anonymous Markets

Pieter Hartel and Rolf van Wegberg

INTRODUCTION

Online anonymous markets have been around since early 2011 and are a prominent part of today's cybercrime ecosystem. Their popularity as markets in illicit goods has steadily grown over the years (Soska & Christin, 2015). With the rise of markets like Silk Road, similar marketplaces came into existence where, next to drugs, supply and demand of other products and services could meet – ranging from physical goods, like passports and weapons, to digital goods and services, like carding and cybercrime software (Aldridge & Décary-Hétu, 2014; Thomas et al., 2015). As a result, we can witness an increasing supply of criminal products and services on standardized digital trading platforms in the underground economy (Thomas et al., 2015).

The general public has become aware of online anonymous markets and their underlying technologies, such as The Onion Router (TOR) and Bitcoin, by their practical application. Bitcoin handles transactions "anonymously" and the TOR-protocol supports "anonymous" browsing. We use inverted commas to indicate that both these technologies offer a degree of anonymity that, given enough effort, can always be broken. The perception of anonymity has attracted a large number of vendors and buyers to online anonymous markets. Over the last few years, these have further matured in business continuity management, in consumer-oriented operations, and in turnover. A single top-tier market can turn over around US$200,000 daily (Soska & Christin, 2015). But how do these online anonymous markets change criminal behavior and what type of criminal justice approach suits this development?

The focus of traditional law enforcement interventions lies primarily in arresting, prosecuting, and seizing drugs on anonymous online markets. According to international agencies such as INTERPOL, these strategies have only limited success and traditional interventions may actually promote innovation and evolution of the online anonymous markets. On top of that, widely publicized court cases provide online anonymous markets with free advertisement (Décary-Hétu & Giommoni, 2017). Ironically, the anonymous or pseudonymous nature of these markets – provided by technologies such as TOR and Bitcoin – creates a high level of transparency of the entire ecosystem of markets, giving LEA the opportunity to shift their policing efforts based on ecosystem insights. Hence, interventions can focus on disrupting the ecosystem and the business models behind the online anonymous markets. As the current criminal justice interventions have proven to be relatively ineffective, we look at how the criminal justice approach to crime on online markets can lever these technical components in novel interventions – making use of the transparent ecosystem.

We begin by defining a few key concepts. Then we describe the two key technologies (TOR, Bitcoin) that made online anonymous markets possible. We also discuss the genesis of one of the early online anonymous markets (Silk Road). Then, we discuss some of the mistakes that have been made in operating dark markets that could be leveraged for effective police interventions.

DEFINITIONS

We begin by giving some definitions.

- An anonymity network is network overlaid on the Internet that supports reasonably anonymous communication between parties.
- A cryptocurrency is a cryptographic software-based currency that can be traded reasonably anonymously.
- The surface web is the portion of the web that is readily available to the general public and searchable with standard web search engines.
- The deep web is the portion of the web whose contents are not indexed by standard web search engines for any reason.
- An online anonymous market is a marketplace where anonymous parties trade goods and services online.

THE TOR NETWORK

TOR is one of the most popular anonymity networks (Li et al., 2013). Clients and services can interact whilst enjoying strong anonymity. TOR anonymity protects political activists and embedded journalists but also terrorists and pedophiles.

The TOR network is accessed via a special browser (The TOR browser) that can be downloaded free on the Internet. The web servers on the TOR network are so-called hidden servers that can only be accessed using the TOR browser.

A few thousand volunteers, mostly in the USA and Western Europe, make their computers and network connections available to run the TOR network (Li et al., 2013). These volunteers are essential to provide the anonymity on the TOR network because every connection is routed via the computers of a number of randomly chosen volunteers. If the "volunteers" decide to collude, the anonymity of the TOR network is completely compromised.

An in-depth analysis (Guitton, 2013) of the offerings of three hidden service directories covering 1,171 hidden services shows that the largest category, with 18 percent of the offerings, is devoted to child pornography, and that one of the smallest categories is devoted to politics, with 1 percent. About half of the bandwidth processed by the TOR network is used for BitTorrent traffic, which is typically used to circumvent anti-piracy laws.

There are some publicly available alternatives to TOR, for example, the I2P anonymity network, which has a similar design to TOR, as well as a similar user base, and Anonymizer (Li et al., 2013). Botnets can also be used as anonymity networks. There are many more and much larger Botnets than the TOR network.

THE BITCOIN NETWORK

Cryptocurrencies, such as Bitcoin (BTC), rely on public and private keys, and digitally signed transactions. Every signed transaction is recorded in a data structure called the blockchain. This is a public ledger, which everyone can check. A network of mutually distrustful volunteers maintains the safety and integrity of this public ledger.

The first open-source Bitcoin client software was released in 2009. Initially only used by a small community, the knowledge and use of Bitcoin is now widespread, with several services such as ATM machines accepting BTC both online and offline. Bitcoin is legal tender in some countries.

Bitcoin supports pseudonymous payment, but not anonymous payment. Compared with numbered Swiss bank accounts, the Bitcoin address itself acts as a unique identifier and the account is only accessible by the owner who has the private key. Hence, Bitcoin addresses are not registered to individuals. Yet, all historic information on any Bitcoin address and transactional information is logged in the blockchain. In that sense, a Bitcoin address becomes a traceable pseudonym of its owner.

There are hundreds of cryptocurrencies but Bitcoin has the largest market capitalization. Bitcoin can be bought and sold for fiat currency at exchanges. Many hold Bitcoin to speculate on exchange rate fluctuations, but Bitcoin is also used for illicit purposes. For example, ransomware demands are usually paid in Bitcoin. Some major corporations even hold Bitcoin to be able to give in to ransom demands.

ONLINE ANONYMOUS MARKETS

Different researchers have studied how online anonymous markets support the evolution of criminal activity in the underground economy. The first studies focused on underground forums, e.g., carding forums revolving around the (re)selling of stolen credit card details (Motoyama et al., 2011). After the first standardized market came into existence, i.e., Silk Road, mostly computer scientists started to shift focus to look at these online anonymous markets (Soska & Christin, 2015). Most existing studies include (or even focus on) drugs and physical goods, which represent a large share of the products offered on the markets. Furthermore, social scientists investigated the increase in online drugs trade, specifically the wholesale side of Silk Road 1 drugs offerings, and what factors determine vendor success (Aldridge & Décary-Hétu, 2014). In addition to large-scale quantitative studies into the evolution of online anonymous markets, we can point to qualitative studies on buyers and sellers (vendors) on markets and forums. For instance, Van Buskirk et al. (2016) specifically focused on the motivation of drug buyers in Australia to turn to online anonymous markets instead of street dealers. They found that a lower risk and higher quality of drug are important.

Silk Road was one of the first online anonymous markets operating as a hidden service on the TOR network. It was the brainchild of a visionary libertarian entrepreneur who went astray. Ross Ulbricht created Silk Road as a platform where libertarian thoughts could be exchanged anonymously. Others, however, saw a vast business opportunity. From the start, Silk Road became a place where not only libertarians shared ideas, but also where people would buy and sell illegal goods and services, mostly drugs. Knowing or unknowingly, Ulbricht kickstarted an underground market in illegal goods and services.

In 2012, Silk Road had hundreds of sellers, mostly located in the USA (Christin, 2013). During its existence, Silk Road was used by hundreds of thousands of customers from across the world.

Silk Road mandated the use of Bitcoins for all financial transactions, thus providing relatively anonymous payment services. Today, other cryptocurrencies, like Monero, only have a marginal presence on anonymous online markets. For example, an investigation into the payment options of 2017 market-leader AlphaBay shows that only 4 percent of all offerings accept another cryptocurrency than Bitcoin.

Silk Road used self-regulation mechanisms similar to those in use by most online markets to "keep honest people honest." For example, Silk Road used a rating system for the buyers and an escrow facility for payments (Christin, 2013). These self-regulation mechanisms ensured that the quality of the products was higher than those available "on the street" and that the risk of non-delivery or non-payment was lower than on the street. Physical goods would be delivered via the postal system. The absence of physical contact between buyer and seller also meant that there was less violence than on the street. This meant that the user may have been better off buying drugs from Silk Road 1 than from the street (van Hout & Bingham, 2014).

Silk Road is often described as a market for consumers, with a better range of products, better quality, and less risk of violence than on the street. However, a detailed analysis of the prices and quantities sold suggests that about half the revenue on Silk Road is generated by business-to-business transactions (Aldridge & Décary-Hétu, 2014).

Silk Road was taken down by the FBI in October 2013 and replaced within 37 days by new services, including Silk Road 2. Vendors are now trading on several markets simultaneously to improve their business continuity.

CRIMINAL JUSTICE APPROACH TO ONLINE ANONYMOUS MARKETS

Being confronted with new aspects of digital innovations in crime, law enforcement had to come up with at least the same level of innovation in their actions against these online anonymous markets. And they did. Law enforcement agencies around the world have intervened on online anonymous markets in three different ways. First, they set-up interventions focusing on the ecosystem, such as affecting confidence in anonymous markets – creating distrust by infiltrating the market. Second, they aimed for interventions on specific markets, such as making them unavailable by seizing computer servers. Third, they tried to intervene on a personal level by unmasking the administrators, such as Ross Ulbricht. He is now serving a life sentence.

Policing the Ecosystem

Recently, during Operation Bayonet, two leading online anonymous markets on the dark web took center stage in a joint policing effort of the Federal Bureau of Investigation (FBI) and the National High Tech Crime and Dark Web unit of the Dutch Police. In a coordinated sweep, the FBI succeeded in the takeover and subsequent take-down of AlphaBay, while the Dutch Police took over, briefly managed, and then shut down Hansa Market. By planning these actions sequentially, the police agencies expected criminals active on AlphaBay to make their way to Hansa Market – which at that moment was operated by the Dutch Police. This put the police agencies in a perfect position to not only disrupt the ecosystem, but also to collect valuable data on thousands of users. This led to a string of arrests of large-scale vendors.

Pulling the Plug

Operation Onymous was a EUROPOL-coordinated operation between police forces from 17 countries in 2014. It resulted in the take-down of over 50 sites (reporters claim the true number lies closer to 27 different sites). Amongst others, Operation Onymous shut down the online anonymous markets Cloud 9, Hydra, and Silk Road 2. Law enforcement arrested 17 persons, of which only one name has been made public: Blake Benthall, known on Silk Road 2 as the main administrator, under the pseudonym "DEFCON."

Making it Personal

Next to interventions aimed at either the ecosystem or specific markets, there have been interventions at the personal level. These included interventions that actively informed people of the fact that, despite their assumption of being anonymous, they were identifiable by law enforcement. In three different ways, these users were informed. First, lists of identified usernames and parts of real names and residences were published on a website that is managed by the police on the dark web. Second, a so-called "love letter" informed identified persons. Third, "knock-and-talk" actions were carried out, in which the police personally informed the persons behind certain usernames and identities.

Measuring Intervention Effects

Whether these interventions have actually yielded any significant results remains unknown. Yet, it is possible to retrospectively see if and how these interventions affect the individual behavior of users on online anonymous markets (Van Wegberg & Verburgh, 2018).

CONCLUSIONS

In conclusion, we can state that both the TOR-protocol and cryptocurrencies have potential disrupting effects in the illegal economy. The criminal justice approach to tackling crime in relation to online anonymous markets still faces many challenges, both in science and in policing. That being said, although we see that the level of the criminal innovation on these platforms is greater than in traditional crime, criminal activity on online anonymous markets is of incomparable proportions.

Internet technology is changing rapidly, and much of what we have written is therefore likely to change in the future.

REFERENCES

Aldridge, J. & Décary-Hétu, D. (2014). Not an "eBay for drugs": The cryptomarket "Silk Road" as a paradigm shifting criminal innovation (Working paper). University of Manchester. http://doi.org/10.2139/ssrn.2436643.

Christin, N. (2013). Traveling the Silk Road: A measurement analysis of a large anonymous online marketplace. In *ACM Int. Conf. on World Wide Web (WWW)*, pp. 213–224. Rio de Janeiro, May 2013.

Décary-Hétu, D. & Giommoni, L. (2017). Do police crackdowns disrupt drug cryptomarkets? A longitudinal analysis of the effects of operation Onymous. *Crime, Law & Social Change*, 67(1), 55–75.

Guitton, C. (2013). A review of the available content on Tor hidden services: The case against further development. *Computers in Human Behavior*, 29(6), 2805–2815.

Li, B., Erdin, E., Gunes, M. H., Bebis, B., & Shipley, T. (2013). An overview of anonymity technology usage. *Computer Communications*, 36, 1269–1283.

Motoyama, M., McCoy, D., Levchenko, K., Savage, S., & Voelker, G. M. (2011). An analysis of underground forums. In *ACM SIGCOMM Conf. on Internet measurement (IMC)*, pp. 71–80. Berlin, November 2011.

Soska, K. & Christin, N. (2015). Measuring the longitudinal evolution of the online anonymous marketplace ecosystem. In *24th USENIX Security Symp.*, pp. 33–48. Washington, DC, August 2015. Retrieved from www.usenix.org/conference/usenixsecurity15/technical-sessions/presentation/soska.

Thomas, K., Huang, D., Wang, D., Bursztein, E., Grier, C., Holt, T. J., Kruegel, C., McCoy, D., Savage, S., & Vigna, G. (2015). Framing dependencies introduced by underground commoditization. In *Workshop on the Economics of Information Security (WEIS)*, Article 15, Delft, June 2015: Econinfosec.org. Retrieved from http://weis2015.econinfosec.org/papers/WEIS_2015_thomas.pdf.

Van Buskirk, J., Naicker, S., Roxburgh, A., Bruno, R., & Burnsa, L. (2016). Who sells what? country specific differences in substance availability on the agora cryptomarket. *International Journal of Drug Policy*, 35, 16–23.

Van Hout, M. C. & Bingham, T. (2014). Responsible vendors, intelligent consumers: Silk Road, the online revolution in drug trading. *International Journal of Drug Policy*, 25(2), 183–189.

Van Wegberg, R. S. & Verburgh, T. (2018). Lost in the dream? Measuring the effects of Operation Bayonet on vendors migrating to dream marke. Websci conference paper.

WEBSITES

Bitcoin blockchain explorer. blockchain.info.
Bitcoin wallet explorer. www.walletexplorer.com.
Dark web blogs. www.deepdotweb.com.
TNO dark web solutions. dws.pm.
TOR project. www.torproject.org.

12 Cryptocurrencies and Money Laundering Opportunities

Sarah Durrant and Mangai Natarajan

INTRODUCTION

Cryptocurrencies are private, digital forms of cash that operate under a decentralized setting with no regulations to monitor or block the flow of transactions. This provides opportunities for criminals to take advantage of cryptocurrencies in hiding the profits of illicit goods and services, such as illegal drugs, firearms, child pornography, and prostitution, as well as providing efficient and easy ways to avoid detection and arrest. Moreover, because many of the exchanges do not require face-to-face interactions, online environments give criminals the opportunity to build a diverse set of consumers and partners globally and maintain their relationships in a secured manner.

Cryptocurrencies therefore allow drug trafficking organizations, terrorists, and other organized crime groups to launder their profits utilizing a digital wallet. As criminologists have predicted, the growth of the Internet has provided a myriad of opportunities for criminals to undertake their illicit activities online (Wall, 2005). Virtual transactions that transcend borders also make it challenging for law enforcement agencies to determine jurisdiction(s), especially when dealing with darknet markets. Based on a review of the literature and of 49 court cases on crypto laundering, the purpose of this chapter is to describe and discuss the evolving nature of cryptocurrencies and how they fuel transnational crimes – especially money laundering.

CRYPTOCURRENCIES AND CRIME OPPORTUNITIES

While there are many types of cryptocurrencies, the most common is Bitcoin[1]. Bitcoin uses a peer-to-peer network, maintained by a public ledger, known as the blockchain, which contains a record of all Bitcoin transactions. Each user must download the Bitcoin client software, known as Bitcoin wallet, that connects to the decentralized network where the user can purchase Bitcoins from a Bitcoin exchange, or sell goods and services to other users, and accept Bitcoins as payment. Bitcoin holders have a public Bitcoin key, similar to a bank account number, that is given out to receive a payment and is published on the blockchain

---

[1] With Bitcoin as the most popular, there are six other common forms of cryptocurrency that are widely used: Litecoin (LTC); Ethereum (ETH); Zcash (ZEC); Dash (DASH); Ripple (XRP); Monero (XMR).

when transactions are made. They also have a private key that is linked to their public key which allows the owner of the wallet to access his or her funds. Though unique identifiers are assigned to a Bitcoin wallet, they are not linked to any personal information, thus making Bitcoin transactions pseudo-anonymous.

Some features of cryptocurrencies are highly attractive to criminals for money laundering. First, cryptocurrencies make transactions easier and allow criminals to move money faster, without the intrusion of financial banking systems. With the elimination of trusted third parties or middlemen, most commonly banks, criminals can bypass detection because there are no regulations requiring the reporting of suspicious account activity. Second, as mentioned earlier, cryptocurrency accounts are not linked to personal identifiers. Third, cryptocurrencies like Bitcoin have an all-time-high value. Hence, keeping illicit funds as Bitcoins helps criminals further their profit.

REVIEW OF CRYPTO MONEY LAUNDERING SCRIPT

Similar to traditional money laundering, crypto money laundering script consists of three stages: placement, layering, and integration (see Table 12.1). At the placement stage, criminals would exchange their cash for Bitcoin using a local Bitcoin exchange, particularly one that is criminal-friendly. Criminals could also begin their illicit business by utilizing the darknet to exchange cryptocurrencies for goods and services. Placing the fiat currency in Bitcoin or conducting business in Bitcoin allows criminals to store their money outside of legal banking systems (Christopher, 2014). This is similar to traditional money laundering, where criminals would convert the proceeds of crime into financial instruments such as bank deposits or cashier's checks. Criminals usually split up their proceeds into smaller amounts and have multiple individuals deposit these cash amounts into a variety accounts, which they can later transfer back into a personal account after the money is "cleaned." This is known as smurfing and structuring. The criminals only need to keep track of the accounts and layer the money in such a way that all the money gets back into their personal accounts (Irwin, Choo, & Liu, 2012).

At the layering stage, criminals save a lot of time and resources to layer their money using multiple Bitcoin accounts. They do not need to find individuals to deposit smaller amounts of cash into multiple accounts and to pay them for their services. They only need to create several Bitcoin wallets and layer the transactions in such a way that it would be hard for anyone looking at the blockchain to figure out if these wallets all belong to the same person or a group of people (Christopher, 2014).

At the integration stage, since there are no anti-money laundering regulations on Bitcoin, if criminals wish to "cash out," it is as simple as exchanging euros to US dollars or vice versa. However, smart criminals would still take various precautions to make sure that their Bitcoin transactions cannot be easily traced by law enforcement. For example, drug traffickers can sell drugs on the darknet and receive compensation in Bitcoins. Because their proceeds are already in Bitcoin, they could then create and use several accounts to make multiple transactions to further conceal their identities and disguise the origin of the money. Also, the traffickers could either keep their money as Bitcoin and make more transactions on the darknet, or they could "cash out" and use Bitcoin exchanges to receive their compensation in whichever fiat currency they choose. This is also particularly practical and useful if a drug trafficking ring employs multiple individuals residing in multiple countries (Christopher, 2014).

Table 12.1. Comparison of traditional money laundering and crypto laundering

Traditional Money Laundering	Crypto Laundering
Stage 1: Placement – criminals deposit illicit money into legal financial systems	
• Exchange "dirty" cash for foreign currency. • Invest in cash-intensive businesses. • Smurf and structure: divide up deposits into smaller amounts spread across several accounts to avoid detection.	• Fiat to digital currency: deposit cash into Bitcoin using local Bitcoin exchanges that will accept large amounts of cash.
Stage 2: Layering – criminals conceal the illicit origins of the money	
• Deposit and transact among multiple accounts, both domestic and foreign. • Falsify documents and/or bribe law enforcement or bank officials to verify large cash deposits. • Use front companies or cash-intensive businesses to funnel money through.	• Create several Bitcoin accounts – Bitcoin mixing. • Basic exchange to advance exchanges – primary coins to privacy coins.
Stage 3: Integration – criminals integrate illegally obtained money with legal money	
• Purchase real estate or luxurious items that are normally purchased with cash. • Mix illicit proceeds with legal proceeds through cash-intensive businesses such as restaurants and casinos.	• Keep illicit proceeds as Bitcoin to make further transactions. • "Cash out" at a local Bitcoin exchange.

Our comparison (see Table 12.1) shows that crypto laundering does not use as many techniques at each stage of the laundering process. By operating completely outside of all governmental jurisdictions, Bitcoin transactions not only facilitate money laundering but also conceal the identities of criminals and their illicit businesses.

CRYPTO MONEY LAUNDERING CASE ANALYSIS

As part of our larger study on cryptocurrencies, we were able to gather data on 49 cases where cryptocurrencies were used for money laundering, including links to drug trafficking. The 49 cases were derived from various online sources, including BBC News, USA Today, and CNN, online magazines, including *Time*, *Deep Dot Web*, and *Wired*, and press releases from government agencies regarding active court cases, such as the Department of Justice, the Federal Bureau of Investigation, and the Securities and Exchange Commission.

Though the data has limitations, it enabled us to undertake a simple descriptive quantitative and qualitative data analysis to infer the characteristic features of those involved and the patterns of market transactions, including the types of darknet market places, and the type of services (front companies and middlemen services) used and the other associated cybercrimes such as hacking and identify theft.

Characteristic Features of Crypto Laundering Cases

Our analysis of the 49 cases found that crypto laundering is generally committed by males aged between 20 and 60 years, who operate either as teams or individuals. The sums involved

Table 12.2. Crypto money laundering cases (N = 49)

Variables	N	%
Age		
15 to 19	1	2%
20 to 29	12	24.5%
30 to 39	16	32.7%
40 to 39	10	20.4%
50 to 59	7	14.3%
Unknown	3	6.1%
Gender		
Male	48	98.0%
Female	1	2.0%
Type of crime		
Money laundering	29	59.2%
Money laundering and drug trafficking	20	40.8%
Cryptocurrency type		
Bitcoin	38	77.6%
Other	11	22.4%
Type of market		
Single market	14	28.6%
Multiple markets	5	10.2%
Money laundering services	16	32.7%
No affiliation	14	28.6%

from US$100,000 to beyond US$1 billion, and the launderers used darknets (n = 19), money laundering services (n = 16), and some unknown means (n = 14). While the majority of cases were North American, European and Asian cases were also represented. In most cases, the cryptocurrencies were traded for cash and/or services (n = 36) and in 13 cases they were stolen by hacking with intent to launder.

Though there were no significant differences between Bitcoin and the use of other cryptocurrencies in terms of age group, amount of money involved, and how the cryptocurrencies were used in the laundering process, one noticeable difference concerned the predominant use of Bitcoins in darknets (Chi square < .002). This may be due to the fact that 29 of the sample cases relate to drug dealing, which mostly makes use of Bitcoins in darknet transactions.

The Darknet and Bitcoin Exchanges

A variety of darknet marketplaces and websites use Bitcoin as their primary form of currency for transactions. These sites include Silk Road, AlphaBay, Silk Road 2, Sheep Marketplace, Agora, Hansa, Nucleus, Pandora, Abraxas, Shiny Flakes, Black Bank, and Evolution. While each site is unique, their general purpose is to facilitate the trafficking of illegal goods, particularly illegal drugs. These darknet marketplaces and sites allow drug vendors to have a broader consumer base that assists shipments of their illegal drugs, both domestically and internationally. The darknet also allows these vendors to evade detection, especially when the sellers use Bitcoin in their transactions.

Regardless of the number of darknet markets used, there is a need to clean the illegal proceeds for the criminals, particularly drug traffickers. They look for Bitcoin exchanges to facilitate their "cashing out" of Bitcoins into tangible cash. On the other hand, there are also consumers looking to "cash in" for a chance to shop on the darknet marketplaces, which creates an ideal platform for exchanging currencies. For example, Charlie Shrem and Robert Faiella operated a Bitcoin exchange known as BitInstant where they exchanged Bitcoins for Silk Road vendors and consumers, for a generous commission, and also assisted vendors in laundering their money. Their business flourished because they were linked with the Silk Road, a site that only accepted Bitcoins, and they targeted both vendors and consumers to cash in and out. While there were several exchanges at the time, BitInstant was the most convenient because it was advertised on the Silk Road site. They laundered over US$1 million for their clients and were caught and sentenced to prison for their operation (USAO, 2014).

Front Companies

Like traditional money laundering, crypto money laundering also uses front companies, which fuse illicit proceeds with legitimate proceeds from a business. For example, Anthony Murgio created a phony front company called the "Collectibles Club" that was reported as a site for members to exchange collectibles. But the members were really logging into Murgio's Bitcoin exchange, called CoinMx, through which Murgio facilitated numerous domestic and international transactions laundering for his clients. From the start of his scheme to his arrest, Murgio made about US$10 million as part of his commission from his clients using this front company (US Attorney's Office [USAO], 2014).

Middleman Operations: Money Laundering Services

Not all criminals are crafty in making up phony front companies and some use other ways, including money laundering services. As described by Consumer News and Business Channel (CNBC), Vadim Vassilenko used his exchange, the Western Express International, to launder money for criminals by converting the cash into a cryptocurrency called e-gold, layering transactions on his money exchange site, and then "cashing out" and delivering the cash to the recipient. Vassilenko was a middleman doing business for criminals by cleaning their money using his cryptocurrency exchange (Pohlman & Day, 2013).

Hacking

According to a recent CipherTrace report, criminals stole US$1.21 billion in cryptocurrency from exchanges in 2017. Because Bitcoin is an unregulated form of currency, hackers will attempt to steal Bitcoins from a victim's wallet since there is no outlet to retrieve the lost money. Though Bitcoin technology makes it hard to hack into the wallets, it is not impossible. For example, Theodore Price developed his own software that would hack and skim Bitcoins out of his victims' wallets, walking away with nearly US$40 million in proceeds. The software would skim Bitcoins out of victims' wallets with no indication that their coins were missing. The stolen money could then be funneled through Bitcoin exchanges (Swenson, 2017).

In another case, Joseph Willner and his co-conspirators hacked several brokerage accounts of clients in order to profit from a short sale scheme. Willner sold stocks using his own account but made unauthorized trades using victims' hacked account information to raise the asking price of the stock. Willner exchanged the proceeds for Bitcoin and laundered the "cash out" and deposited the money into his bank account. The Securities and Exchange Commission estimate a loss of over US$2 million from his victims (SEC, 2017).

CONCLUSION

While the advent of cryptocurrencies has benefitted worldwide financial transactions, the review of the literature and the analysis of crypto laundering cases reported above suggest that the decentralized virtual system in which they operate provides crime opportunities for transnational criminal organizations, particularly drug trafficking networks. Crypto laundering allows illicit proceeds to move with ease and minimal effort. It is attractive to criminals due to the global availability, easy accessibility and convertibility, and, more importantly, the pseudo-anonymity of cryptocurrency transactions that assists in evading detection.

Law enforcement and financial institutions have been finding ways to deal with traditional money laundering, for example, through the Financial Action Task Force (FATF). They should also include crypto laundering in their agenda. Since national laws cannot effectively combat virtual money laundering, international efforts to regulate the cyber environment are needed. Jacobs (2018) suggests removing the anonymity associated with cryptocurrency transactions or simply banning those that are not linked to bank accounts in countries, which could be accomplished under the authority of the IMF, Bank of International Settlements, Basel Committee on Banking Supervision, the Financial Stability Board, and Financial Action Task Force on Money Laundering, or an entirely new agency established specifically for that purpose. Criminologists can play their part by employing situational crime prevention (Clarke, 1995) to find ways of making crypto laundering more difficult, riskier, and less rewarding, and by limiting excuses for engaging in this crime.

REFERENCES

Christopher, C. M. (2014). Wack-a-mole: Why prosecuting digital currency exchanges won't stop online money laundering. *Lewis and Clarke Review*, 18(1), 1.

Clarke, R. V. (1995). Situational crime prevention. *Crime and Justice*, 19, 91–150.

Irwin, A. S. M., Choo, K. K. R., & Liu, L. (2012). An analysis of money laundering and terrorism financing typologies. *Journal of Money Laundering Control*, 15(1), 85–111.

Jacobs, G. (2018). Cryptocurrencies & the challenge of global governance. *Cadmus*, 3(4), 109–123.

Pohlman, J. & Day, A. (2013, September 12). Busted! Inside one massive cybercrime ring. *CNBC*. Retrieved from www.cnbc.com/id/101029866.

Securities and Exchange Commission (SEC). (2017, October 30). Day trader charged in brokerage account takeover scheme [press release]. Retrieved from www.sec.gov/news/press-release/2017-202.

Swenson, K. (2017, July 24). Pennsylvania police, hunting for stolen laptops, say they stumbled on $40 million bitcoin scam. *Washington Post*. Retrieved from www.washingtonpost.com/news/morning-mix/wp/2017/07/24/pennsylvania-police-hunting-for-stolen-laptops-say-they-stumbled-on-40-million-bitcoin-scam/?utm_term=.511503eb502f.

United States Attorney's Office (USAO) – Southern District of New York. (2014, January 27). Manhattan U.S. Attorney announces charges against bitcoin exchangers, including CEO of bitcoin exchange company, for scheme to sell and launder over $1 million in bitcoins related to Silk Road drug trafficking [press release]. Retrieved from www.justice.gov/usao-sdny/pr/manhattan-us-attorney-announces-charges-against-bitcoin-exchangers-including-ceo.

United States Attorney's Office (USAO) – Southern District of New York. (2017, June 27). Operator of unlawful bitcoin exchange sentenced to more than 5 years in prison for leading multimillion dollar money laundering and fraud scheme [press release]. Retrieved from www.justice.gov/usao-sdny/pr/operator-unlawful-bitcoin-exchange-sentenced-more-5-years-prison-leading-multimillion.

Wall, D. S. (2005). The Internet as a conduit for criminals. In A. Pattavina (Ed.), *Information technology and the criminal justice system* (pp. 77–98). Thousand Oaks, CA: Sage Publications, Inc.

13 Money Laundering

David C. Hicks and Adam Graycar

INTRODUCTION

This chapter offers a selective review of international standards and definitions, the global scope and traditional stages of money laundering, and available evidence surrounding the effectiveness of the regimes and the respective implementation in the United States of America (USA) and United Kingdom (UK).

The United Nations Convention against Illicit Traffic in Narcotic Drugs and Psychotropic Substances (Vienna Convention, 1988) signaled the beginning of the international drive, and parallel national responses, to target money laundering. Early efforts focused on laundering linked to drugs and designated offences. From the turn of the century, international conventions and much national legislation has tended to include laundering related to all serious crimes (punishable by four or more years imprisonment) and virtually any interaction with the proceeds of crime.

The United Nations Convention against Transnational Organized Crime (Palermo Convention, 2000) established the generic and interactive categories of prevention and enforcement for international and parallel domestic responses to money laundering. Prevention activities focus on know-your-customer policies, the reporting of suspicious and other financial transactions, and the regulation and supervision of financial institutions with various sanctions for noncompliance. Enforcement activities focus on the underlying offences that generate the proceeds of crime and the associated investigation, prosecution, and punishment as well as criminal and civil asset recovery.

BACKGROUND

International Definition

There is a common-sense definition that focuses on turning "dirty money" into "clean money" or hiding the origins of the proceeds of crime. It is what people typically understand as the definition of money laundering. This general understanding should be contrasted with the Palermo Convention (2000). It established the international standard for states to criminalize when committed intentionally: (a) conversion or concealment of the proceeds of crime inclusive of the "financial" benefit; (b) acquisition, possession or use of property knowing that it is the proceeds of crime; and (c) conspiracy or participation in facilitating or counseling the commission of offences. Although a cross-national review of efforts to implement the international standards is beyond the scope of the present chapter, a selective comparison of the USA and the UK is instructive.

US Definition

In the USA, the three core offences focus on: (a) conducting a transaction using the proceeds of crime, with the intent to disguise its origins, avoiding a transaction report, or committing another offence; (b) transporting the proceeds of crime into, out of, or through the country with the intent to disguise its origins; and (c) conducting transactions with funds represented as the proceeds of crime. Conducting transactions in illicit funds to the value of US$10,000 or more is also criminalized using a statute commonly known as the "spending statute." The federal definition does not extend the definition of money laundering to any offence, but instead provides a focus on specified unlawful activity (SUA) as outlined under Title 18 USC § 1956(c)(7).

The list of SUA is extensive and includes crimes such as racketeering, controlled substance offences, bribery and offences against public funds, extradition or prosecution responsibilities under multi-lateral treaties, trafficking in persons, sexual exploitation of children, and any act or acts constituting a continuing criminal enterprise. It also includes computer fraud and abuse, trafficking in counterfeit goods and services, child pornography, and international terrorist acts and the financing of terrorism, among other items. The identification of each category of specified unlawful activity appears to demonstrate US legislative intent to highlight the most serious offences that should warrant the application of money laundering powers and prosecution.

UK Definition

In the UK the core money laundering offences under sections 327, 328, and 329 of the Proceeds of Crime Act 2002 include: (a) concealing, disguising, converting, transferring criminal property, and removing criminal property from the country; (b) entering into or becoming involved in an arrangement known, or suspected, to facilitate the acquisition, retention, use or control of criminal property by another person; and (c) acquiring, using, or possessing criminal property. Rather than attempting to specify offences, the UK definition is very broad and criminalizes virtually any direct or indirect interaction with the proceeds of crime or the proceeds for crime.

Under section 326 of the Proceeds of Crime Act 2002, criminal conduct is defined as "an offence" in any part of the UK or if it occurred in another jurisdiction. It is thus applicable to any offence, whether criminal, regulatory, or otherwise. It is applicable to any person who benefits in whole or in part, directly or indirectly, from criminal conduct. The targeting of criminal property is very broad and inclusive of money as well as intangible, real, and all forms of property relating to criminal conduct. This demonstrates UK legislative intent to advance a generalized crime reduction program by tackling the proceeds of crime and the proceeds for crime.

Whether the above definitions offer a specific or general focus, the consistent themes appear to be a broad approach to criminalizing virtually any interaction with the proceeds of crime as well as the intent to convert or conceal the proceeds of crime. There also seems to be a recognition that money laundering may not be a single act in many instances but may often reflect an ongoing process of continuing criminality. The complexity of that process relates to offender circumstances, in addition to the nature of their interaction with financial and related service providers, and the regulatory and control architecture in a given jurisdiction.

DISCUSSION

Global Scope and the Stages of Money Laundering

The United Nations Office on Drugs and Crime (UNODC, 2011) offered an overall best estimate that criminal proceeds of crime are approximately 3.6 percent of international gross domestic product (GDP), which was equivalent to US$2.1 trillion in 2009. The volume of criminal proceeds involved in money laundering were estimated at nearly 2.7 percent of worldwide GDP, which was equivalent to US$1.6 trillion in 2009. Readers should note that these approximations exclude tax and customs-related money laundering. Their inclusion would result in meeting or exceeding the upper band of the International Monetary Fund (IMF) estimate that 2–5 percent of global GDP involves money laundering (Quirk, 1996). Once the proceeds of crime are generated through the course of committing an underlying offence(s), a common description of the (illicit drug-related) money laundering process is as follows.

- *Placement* refers to converting the proceeds of crime into financial instruments such as bank deposits or cashier's cheques.
- *Layering* refers to supplementary transactions such as wire transfers to move the funds around and obscure their criminal origins.
- *Integration* refers to the purchase or investment into legal assets such as real estate in order to enjoy the proceeds of crime and give them the appearance of legitimacy.

We should not be surprised to see similarities and differences between jurisdictions in terms of the underlying offences and volumes of money laundering. The traditional decades-long emphasis on illicit drugs may increasingly be eclipsed by other categories such as fraud, cybercrime, and tax- and customs-related offences (Hicks, 2010; Reuter & Truman, 2004; UNODC, 2011). Those involved in illicit drug offences may conform most closely to the typical stages of money laundering, but it should be clear to the reader that fraud and online offences may skip the placement stage. The layering stage may also (potentially) be skipped where it is integral to the underlying offence(s) such as malfeasance relating to corporate accounts. Readers who wish to explore money laundering examples or case studies should refer to the methods and trends section of the Financial Action Task Force (FATF) website as well as the following sources (Hicks, 2010; Reuter & Truman, 2004; UNODC, 2011).

One of the key outcomes of the availability and use of money laundering powers and controls is forfeiture or confiscation. In simple terms, the proceeds of/for crime should be recoverable assets that can be taken away from offenders. Forfeited or confiscated assets can then revert to the state and be shared amongst government and law enforcement agencies and victims, as well as being used for crime prevention and community safety initiatives.

Forfeiture in the USA

According to the US Government Accountability Office (USGAO, 2012), in 2011 the value of US$9.4 billion was held in the combined Assets Forfeiture Fund (AFF) of the Department of Justice and the Treasury Forfeiture Fund (TFF). The primary goals of the programs are: 1) to punish and deter criminal activity and deprive offenders of criminal property; 2) to enhance law enforcement agency cooperation and sharing of recovered assets; and 3) to generate revenue in support of enforcement and forfeiture activities. Data revealed that the development and maintenance costs of the multiple Justice and Treasury asset tracking systems amounted to US$26.6 million in 2011. The auditors found duplication of systems and processes between the two funds in terms of physically separate holding facilities and different information communication systems for tracking.

The USGAO (2016) found that from 2009 through 2015, nearly US$12 billion was imposed in fines, penalties, and forfeitures against financial institutions relating to bank secrecy/anti-money laundering regulations, foreign corrupt practices, and sanctions programs. The above amount was deposited into the AFF and TFF accounts respectively with less than 1 percent of the assessments not collected. The funds distributed US$1.1 billion to law enforcement up to December 2015, about US$2 billion was to be distributed to victims, and the remainder to support forfeiture programs or other enforcement expenses.

Confiscation in the UK

According to the UK National Audit Office (UKNAO, 2013), since 1987 a total of £1 billion was collected from confiscation orders with £1.46 billion in outstanding confiscation order debt. It was estimated that 26 pence were confiscated for every £100 of proceeds of crime, and £133 million were collected in 2012–2013 at an estimated annual cost of £102 million for the confiscation order process. The audit report concluded that the process for confiscating criminal assets was "not working well enough" with the lack of a coherent overall strategy. Further problems included a flawed incentive program for participating agencies with weak accountability for confiscation enforcement, the absence of good performance data and benchmarks, insufficient awareness of proceeds-of-crime legislation, and outdated information technology systems as well as a lack of joined-up systems.

The response to the audit report largely focused on revisits for outstanding confiscation orders. The UK Government initiated a review of all outstanding files and efforts to assess and enforce existing confiscation orders against offenders. The UKNAO (2016) revisited the issue and found only some progress against recommendations and no transformation of the confiscation system. The auditors noted that £155 million was collected in 2014–2015, demonstrating better enforcement of existing confiscation orders, but they remained concerned about the lack of awareness of proceeds-of-crime legislation and its application to restrain the proceeds of crime early in investigations toward confiscation upon conviction. The joining-up of information communication technology and process appears to remain an ongoing problem.

CONCLUSION

This chapter provided a discussion of international standards and definitions, the global scope, and the traditional stages of money laundering, and available evidence surrounding the effectiveness of the regimes and the respective implementation in two selected jurisdictions. The USA and UK have advanced systems to conform to international standards to tackle money laundering, disrupt and deter criminality, and to deny offenders from enjoying the benefits of the proceeds of crime. The two countries appear to share similar problems of the lack of joined-up approaches to information communication technologies to track asset recovery goals. This should not be understood in isolation as an end-product. The product inevitably reflects the end-to-end process of the extent to which financial investigation is an embedded component in law enforcement. This embeddedness includes (but is not limited to) investigative strategy and tactics for pre-seizure planning, post-seizure activities to restrain and maintain the value of assets, and post-conviction management of assets (USGAO, 2012, 2016; UKNAO, 2013, 2016).

The amounts subject to successful confiscation in the UK, after adjusting for population size differences, appear to be significantly lower than the US forfeiture amounts. This discrepancy needs deeper examination than is possible in the context of this brief chapter. The UK legislative intent to apply money laundering powers and controls to any offence seems not to have occurred, and often appears limited to established targets of risk and threat such as organized crime (Brown et al., 2012). Despite the introduction of the Criminal Finances Act 2017, which offers new and adapted provisions to UK law enforcement, there appear to be continuing calls for new legislation and powers. Hopefully, the present chapter has clarified to the reader that there is still much work to do to implement existing legislation and powers. The challenge is to systematically embed financial investigation and money laundering powers to disrupt and deter those who benefit from the proceeds of/for crime.

REFERENCES

Brown, R., Evans, E., Webb S., Holdaway, S., Berry, G., Chenery, S., Gresty. B., & Jones, M. (2012). The contribution of financial investigation to tackling organised crime: A qualitative study. *Research Report 65. Key implications.* Retrieved from www.gov.uk/government/uploads/system/uploads/attachment_data/file/116518/horr65.pdf.

Hicks, D. C. (2010). Money laundering. In F. Brookman et al. (Eds.), *Handbook of crime* (pp. 712–725). Cullompton, Devon: Willan.

Quirk, P. J. (1996). *Macroeconomic implications of money laundering* (Working Paper 96/66). Washington, DC: International Monetary Fund (IMF).

Reuter, P. & Truman, E. M. (2004). *Chasing dirty money: The fight against money laundering.* Washington, DC: Institute for International Economics.

UK National Audit Office (UKNAO). (2013, December 13). *Confiscation orders.* London: Stationery Office Limited. Retrieved from www.nao.org.uk/wp-content/uploads/2013/12/10318-001-Confiscation-Book.pdf.

(2016). *Confiscation orders: Progress review.* London: Stationery Office Limited. Retrieved from www.nao.org.uk/wp-content/uploads/2016/03/Confiscation-orders-progress-review.pdf.

United Nations Office on Drugs and Crime. (2011). *Estimating illicit financial flows resulting from drug trafficking and other transnational organized crimes.* Retrieved from www.unodc.org/documents/data-and-analysis/Studies/Illicit_financial_flows_2011_web.pdf.

US Government Accountability Office (USGAO). (2012). Asset forfeiture programs: Justice and Treasury should determine costs and benefits of potential consolidation (Highlights of GAO-12–972). Retrieved from www.gao.gov/assets/650/648097.pdf.

    (2016). Financial institutions: Fines, penalties, and forfeitures for violations of financial crimes and sanctions requirements (Highlights of GAO-16–297). Retrieved from www.gao.gov/assets/680/675987.pdf.

WEBSITES

Financial Action Task Force. www.fatf-gafi.org.

International Monetary Fund. www.imf.org.

United Nations International Money Laundering Information Network (IMoLIN). www.imolin.org.

United Nations Office of Drugs and Crime (UNODC). www.unodc.org/unodc/en/money-laundering/index.html.

World Bank. www.worldbank.org.

14   International Fraud

Michael Levi

INTRODUCTION

In essence, fraud is the obtaining of goods or money by deception. Systematic socioeconomic or organizational status data are available only from research studies rather than from official offender statistics. However, deception is widespread and (more often than theft) can readily be committed by the more powerful against the less powerful, as well as by the poor and by professional/"organized" criminals against those with many assets to lose. Thus, fraud comprises a spectrum of social statuses of offenders and of victims (for a typology of fraud, see Box 14.1).

Box 14.1. Types of Economic Crime

1. Crime that harms government/taxpayer interests.
2. Crime that harms all corporate as well as social interests – that is, systemic risk frauds that undermine public confidence in the system as a whole; domestic and motor insurance frauds; maritime insurance frauds; payment card and other credit frauds; pyramid selling of money schemes; high-yield investment frauds.
3. Crime that harms social and some corporate interests but benefits other "mainly legitimate" ones, such as some cartels, transnational corruption (by companies with business interests in the country paying the bribe), forms of intellectual property theft – sometimes called "piracy" – especially those using higher-quality digital media.
4. Crime that harms corporate interests but benefits mostly illegitimate ones, such as several forms of intellectual property theft – sometimes called "piracy" – especially those using higher-quality digital media.

The boundary between fraud, organized crime, and money laundering can be hard to discern. Properly analyzed, money laundering is a subcategory of both, being proceeds of crimes that are saved and sometimes reinvested with their criminal origins concealed (see Hicks and Graycar, Chapter 13, this volume). Influenced as we are by profound cultural images of the Sicilian Mafia and the Italian-American Mafia that have brought *The Godfather*, *The Sopranos*, and *Narcos* to our screens, it is difficult not to be seduced by the assumption that this hierarchical, deeply embedded cultural and family mode of organization is the natural evolution of all serious crime (Glenny, 2008): the general public, criminals, and even the police are all subjected to (and sometimes entranced by) these images of power and "threat to society." However, it is dangerous to transplant models derived from the peculiar historical conditions of Italy before the collapse of communism – or even of some northeastern US cities – to other countries and regions (Varese, 2011). As the major scams of the twenty-first century – from Enron to Madoff – demonstrate, fraud and other "white-collar crimes" may be committed as part of a transnational "serious crime community" (Block & Weaver, 2005; Glenny, 2008; May & Bhardwa, 2018) who largely outwit the forces of criminal justice control anywhere in the world, but they are capable of functioning unconnected to "organized crime" as commonly conceptualized in intelligence-led policing.

What might we mean by international fraud (or international crime generally)? The immediate assumption might be that people in one country are defrauding people in another, but this is only part of the story. One helpful way of thinking about this is by placing it within the context of a process map of crime for gain (see Box 14.2 and Levi, 2012, 2015). We may deduce from this that criminal finance, as well as some or all criminal personnel and the "tools of crime" (which include anonymous corporations from US states like Delaware as well as "offshore havens") may come from or go to another country at some stage of the planning and aftermath processes, and constitute international crime. In the case of fraud, offenders may start with differential access to international resources, but the exploitation of international regulatory and criminal justice asymmetries – for example, different levels and competencies of enforcement in the countries in which the fraudsters operate – represents an advantage for the criminal.

Box 14.2. The Process of Crime for Gain

- Obtain finance.
- Find people willing and able to offend (whether specific to the crimes contemplated and/or if already part of a "criminal organization").
- Obtain any tools/data needed to offend.
- Neutralize immediate enforcement/operational risks.
- Carry out offences in domestic and/or overseas locations with or without physical presence in jurisdiction(s).
- Launder or hide *safely* unspent funds (at home and/or overseas).
- Decide in which country you want to live afterwards, taking into account extradition and proceeds of crime confiscation/civil suit risks.

One important difference between fraud and most traditional crimes that have victims is that at the time (sometimes over many years) when the offence is committed, the fraudster can be, but does not normally need to be, in the same place or even on the same continent as the victims or their property. However, some fraudsters (like gangsters) have their geographic comfort zones, and operate locally or in places with which they are familiar. Fraudsters, like other "organized criminals," may be part of ethnic or national diasporas operating globally, of whom Nigerians are the most prominent, but Nigerians have variable family, regional, and religious affiliations and should not be seen as a homogeneous group (Levi, 2008a; Smith, 2008). Since almost all fraud on Americans involves some electronic or paper cross-US state movement, or victimizes federally insured institutions or the government, almost all of it constitutes "wire fraud," founding federal jurisdiction within the US. However, national boundaries – the formal unit for police powers and crime statistics – are poor indicators of travel time and fraud opportunities. For example, it is quicker for a credit card fraudster or telemarketer to fly or drive from New York to Toronto than from New York to Miami or Los Angeles, and that can be important when the rate of fraud upon a stolen or counterfeited card is time-critical. Romance scammers are seldom where their victims think they are – they may be a different age and ethnicity also. Cross-border frauds generate problems for police jurisdictions everywhere, requiring referral via national mutual legal assistance units, consuming time and financial resource. Fraudsters crossing international borders to and from the USA with large quantities of cash or monetary instruments (like checks) run the risk of asset forfeiture and of conviction for nondeclaration of international transfers, but unless they are under surveillance they are not often caught.

HOW SIGNIFICANT A PROBLEM IS FRAUD?

There are a number of different dimensions of harm: economic damage (perhaps best seen in terms of the effects on individual and corporate victims' abilities to restore themselves to their pre-crime economic welfare level), and psychological and health damage (including disruption of expectations about future security and welfare). White-collar crimes in general and frauds/transnational procurement bribes in particular exceed the costs of other crimes (Benson et al., 2016; Cohen, 2016; Levi & Burrows, 2008). However, another dimension of harm is the sense of equal justice and social fairness that is offended by the non-prosecution of serious fraud, especially when committed by social elites.

People buying counterfeit products almost invariably know that they are fake because of the price and context, though sometimes stores sell counterfeit products as genuine. Comprehensively collated or critically assessed cost information is not available for fraud in the USA (though for some weak American evidence, see Association of Certified Fraud Examiners, 2016; Cohen, 2016). Fraud levels in different countries depend on motivations, opportunities, and (in)capable guardianship by the private sector, regulators, and the police.

Such studies do not normally examine the international components of those costs, but even when frauds are not international in their execution, they are often international in their storage or laundering (see Box 14.2). However, this international component increases the social problem of fraud by placing obstacles in the way of enforcement, not just because of problems in assigning jurisdiction (e.g., whose law, if any, applies to this conduct?), but also because law enforcement agencies are more motivated to act when they consider – on their own initiative or under political or media pressure – that the conduct harms the people they are paid to protect. The USA has the most political power and energy to expend on international investigations and prosecutions.

SOME TYPES OF INTERNATIONAL FRAUD

Fraudulent Investment Schemes

There are many types of investment fraud, varying from the simple "419" frauds (named after the relevant section of the Nigerian Penal Code) that many of us older people used to receive through the post and nowadays receive mainly via e-mail – offering us the opportunity to share the unclaimed billion-dollar wealth of whichever African kleptocrat has most recently been in the news if only we will give them our bank details – to the sort of high-yield investment fraud detailed in Box 14.3, committed over many years by Bernie Madoff, or Box 14.4, prosecuted by the UK Serious Fraud Office, to far more ambiguous schemes in which the victims may never realize that they have been swindled at all but rather think either: (a) that their investments have failed legitimately; or (b) that they have made less money than they hoped. In some of these schemes, the victims are innocent dupes, but in others – like some "419" schemes – they may be viewed as, or even charged as, attempted conspirators in transnational frauds and corruption. Many international "romance scams" have victims who may never be convinced that they are actually fraud victims (Whitty, 2013), and unpacking the geography of mass marketing may be complex (Edwards et al., 2018). The role of accountants and lawyers in creating the "tools" of fraud and money laundering is important.

Box 14.3. The Bernie Madoff Ponzi Scheme

The Madoff investment funds allegedly grew from around US$7 billion in 2000 to as much as US$50 billion by the end of 2005. What had started decades before as a small-time recruiting effort by Madoff agents networking at country clubs had gone global. Major international institutions such as Grupo Santander, Fortis Bank, and Union Bancaire Privée were all funneling billions – sometimes through intermediaries – to Madoff, lured by steady 10- to 12-percent returns. The Abu Dhabi Investment Authority sank tens of millions of dollars into the Ponzi scheme via its investment in one of the big feeder funds. Japanese people put money in a Swiss bank account held by a private Scottish bank that sent the money to an offshore firm investing in Madoff through Fairfield Greenwich funds. So did New York University. But no one really understood how he was producing those returns, and we now know he just robbed Peter to pay Paul.

Box 14.4. US$16 Million Stolen in High-Yield Investment Fraud

Thomas Pilz, Richard Walker, and Dariusz Maruzsak promoted a high-yield investment scheme that attracted US$16 million. The money was placed in an account at Swepstone Walsh, a London firm of solicitors, with investors believing it would be pooled for investment in a lucrative and exclusive banking trading program not available to private investors. However, the money was instead transferred to a New York attorney's account, to the benefit of Pilz and Walker, under the guise of funds to set up a commercial venture in the USA. Pilz and Walker pleaded guilty to theft and were sentenced on October 11, 2002 to terms of imprisonment of four-and-half years and three years, respectively. Pilz was ordered to pay nearly £1.29 million as confiscation of crime proceeds.

The investigation into the consortium led the UK authorities to another suspect investment scheme. The five defendants were charged with offenses relating to money laundering of US$11.5 million. The trial opened on October 7, 2003. Part-way through the trial, the judge expressed a view that the prosecution case depended heavily on the evidence of a solicitor who had acted for Maruszak's business affairs and who had been prosecuted separately for stealing client funds. After a review, the judge concluded that the SFO case was not sustainable and the defendants were acquitted by order of the court.

Bankruptcy and Other Credit Frauds

A popular enduring theme holds that frauds that do not obtain money directly but rather obtain goods on credit for which they do not pay either: (a) disappear altogether, having given false identities; or (b) give false explanations for nonpayment and false valuations of assets, sometimes in league with dishonest company liquidators. In some cases, professional fraudsters or gangsters set new businesses up, building up credit with the intention of fraud, but in other cases, they find businesspeople in trouble and either persuade them or threaten them into turning their businesses into fraudulent ones; and in still others, the business just carries on ordering goods for which there is no reasonable chance of payment, hoping that "something will turn up" (Levi, 2008b). The Internet has enabled "phishing" and "pharming" of corporate identities, enabling some to simulate the legitimate businesses when ordering goods or getting financial intelligence from the public – a corporate form of identity fraud. In the second half of 2008, there were at least 56,959 phishing attacks worldwide; a decade later, there were ten times as many (Anti-phishing Working Group, 2018). The entire model of phishing has been transformed by social media and other technological changes (Piscitello, n.d.). Again, there is no need for these frauds to be international, but some goods usually are ordered from overseas. In a variant, the company may make up artificial sales of, say, computers, using credit card details taken from elsewhere and defraud the card companies by getting reimbursed for the card vouchers before the cardholders get their statements and realize they have been defrauded.

CONCLUSION

Opportunity reduction takes many forms – social, technological, and targeted on individuals perceived to be particularly high-risk. For volume frauds such as payment card frauds, until everyone adopts PINs with chip cards to replace magnetic stripes (almost universal now in Europe and around the globe), people in key positions (hotel receptionists, car hire businesses, stores) may copy card details electronically and send them to their confederates overseas, who may make up good counterfeits or simply encode them onto unembossed "white plastic" to defraud the individual or, more commonly since innocent consumers are reimbursed in most countries, the card issuer. For these credit card and insurance frauds, aggregated databases for the industry as a whole, plus software that hunts for connections, can help to combat organized fraud. For telemarketing and "romance" frauds, transnational cooperation and proactive intervention by regulators and police is essential, as is better consumer education – especially focused on repeat victims – to get people to recognize the signs of online and offline scams. However, for the larger frauds committed by elites, vigilance by the media, by internal and external auditors, and by other professionals may be necessary to cut down the scale of frauds as well as to stop them happening. Keeping out "bad people" by bans on directorships and the sale of financial services will reduce only part of the problem.

In sum, fraud has become democratized in terms of both victims and offenders and, as individuals and corporations expect to trade with transnational businesses, it has become normal for both legitimate trades and scams to be international. This creates significant problems for regulation and criminal justice enforcement mechanisms that are still largely premised upon the nation-state and the locality.

REFERENCES

Anti-phishing Working Group. (2018). *Phishing activity trends report: 3rd quarter 2017*. Retrieved from http://docs.apwg.org/reports/apwg_trends_report_q3_2017.pdf.

Association of Certified Fraud Examiners (ACFE). (2016). *Report to the nations: On occupational fraud and abuse. 2016 Global Fraud Study*. Retrieved from www.acfe.com/rttn2016/docs/2016-report-to-the-nations.pdf.

Benson, M., Kennedy, J., & Logan, M. (2016). White-collar and corporate crime. In B. Huebner & T. Bynum (Eds.), *The handbook of measurement issues in criminology and criminal justice*. New York: John Wiley and Sons.

Block, A. & Weaver, C. (2005). *All is clouded by desire*. New York: Praeger.

Cohen, M. (2016). The costs of white-collar crime. In S. van Slyke, M. Benson, & F. Cullen (Eds.), *Oxford handbook of white-collar crime* (pp. 74–98). New York: Oxford University Press.

Edwards, M., Suarez-Tangil, G., Peersman, C., Stringhini, G., Rashid, A., & Whitty, M. (2018, May). The geography of online dating fraud. In *Workshop on technology and consumer protection*. IEEE.

Glenny, M. (2008). *McMafia: A journey through the global criminal underworld*. New York: Alfred Knopf.

Levi, M. (2008a). Organised fraud: Unpacking research on networks and organisation. *Criminology and Criminal Justice*, 8(4), 389–420.

(2008b). *The phantom capitalists: The organisation and control of long-firm fraud* (second edition). Aldershot: Ashgate.

(2012). Organised crime and terrorism. In M. Maguire, R. Morgan, & R. Reiner (Eds.), *The Oxford handbook of criminology* (fifth edition). Oxford: Oxford University Press.

(2015). Money for crime and money from crime: Financing crime and laundering crime proceeds. *European Journal on Criminal Policy and Research*, 21(2), 1–23.

Levi, M. & Burrows, J. (2008). Measuring the impact of fraud: a conceptual and empirical journey. *British Journal of Criminology*, 48(3), 293–318.

May, T. & Bhardwa, B. (2018). *Organised crime groups involved in fraud*. London: Palgrave Macmillan.

Piscitello, D. (n.d.). The new face of phishing. Retrieved from www.antiphishing.org/apwg-news-center/newfaceofphishing.

Smith, D. J. (2008). *A culture of corruption: Everyday deception and popular discontent in Nigeria*. Princeton, NJ: Princeton University Press.

Varese, F. (2011). *Mafias on the move: How organized crime conquers new territories*. Princeton, NJ: Princeton University Press

Whitty, M. T. (2013). The scammers persuasive techniques model: Development of a stage model to explain the online dating romance scam. *British Journal of Criminology*, 53(4), 665–684.

15 Ransom Kidnapping

A Global Concern

Stephen Pires and Rob Guerette

INTRODUCTION

Perhaps never before has kidnapping for ransom (K&R) been as prolific or lucrative. By some estimates, the taking of a person against their will and the negotiation of their safe return in exchange for payment is an estimated US$1.5-billion industry. In many countries around the world the K&R crime problem has reached seemingly epidemic[1] proportions based on global reports of risk. That is, Colombia, Brazil, Mexico, the Philippines, Venezuela, India, Nigeria, Iraq, and Ecuador have consistently experienced a disproportionate share of incidents at the global level (Moor & Remijnse, 2008; Velez et al., 2014). Such concentrations occur largely in certain regions of the world, namely Latin America, the Middle East, North Africa, and South Asia. Identification of high-risk countries is largely based on non-public intelligence reports and insurance company claims on ransom payments, which in turn are used to assess high- and low-risk countries for K&R. Consequently, systematically collected data on the exact frequency of the problem at the global level is unavailable primarily because K&R incidents are often not reported to the police, though estimates suggest anywhere between 25,000 and 100,000 incidents occur per year (Pires, Guerette, & Stubbert, 2014).

Kidnapping is often undertaken for various purposes, not all of which entail the pursuit of payment. This includes the kidnapping and killing of individuals by organized crime and terror groups to protect and enforce organized crime activities or further some political motive. Yet even kidnapping incidents that are increasingly carried out by "violent nonstate actors" in the name of terrorist motivations also commonly engage in ransom requests in order to fund their organizations' activities. For instance, it has been reported that the well-known terror groups affiliated with Al Qaeda made at least US$105 million between 2010 and 2013 from K&R activities and that the average amount paid to the group per hostage was US$5.4 million. In fact, a recent terrorism-based study finds that K&R is increasing and more likely to be committed by Muslim extremists now (Forest, 2012).

Kidnapping for ransom is a growing problem that plagues many underdeveloped countries throughout the world for a variety of reasons. This chapter will give a brief history of the problem, the types of kidnappings that exist, the conditions that are associated with its frequency, and some of the responses that could potentially reduce it.

---

[1] The term "epidemic" is widely used in the literature to refer to high-risk countries.

A BRIEF HISTORY OF KIDNAPPING FOR RANSOM

Until the latter half of the twentieth century, instances of K&R were largely isolated events in the world and were not organized as a business enterprise (Phillips, 2009). That began to change by the late 1970s as it became increasingly common to be kidnapped for ransom in Colombia and Italy, where an industry took root. In Colombia, illegal armed groups (IAGs), such as the Revolutionary Armed Forces of Colombia (FARC) and the National Liberation Army (ELN), continuously abducted wealthy city-dwellers in rural areas as they traveled between urban centers or visited their country estates. Such groups made a business out of routinely kidnapping and collecting ransom payments to fund their political cause until very recently. As a result of the profitability and ease of kidnapping individuals in Colombia, K&R became a popular crime committed by organized and common criminals in other Latin America nations such as Venezuela, Argentina, and Brazil.

Unlike the problem in Colombia, K&R perpetrators in Italy were a mix of ordinary and organized criminals operating in a politically stable and developed country. At first, the K&R problem in Italy was mostly contained and concentrated on the island of Sardinia where evidence of the first kidnappings date to the fifteenth century. By 1977, however, the K&R problem had spread to the rest of Italy and began to target children of wealthy parents (Marongiu & Clarke, 1993). While Italy and Colombia are no longer labeled as the riskiest countries for K&R, many other countries around the world are. More recent global rankings identify the top five riskiest countries for K&R as Mexico, India, Nigeria, Pakistan, and Venezuela (Perlberg, 2013). Mexico in particular is thought to be the new "kidnapping capital of the world." A combination of drug trafficking, cartel violence and the inability of the Mexican Government to effectively manage crime and criminal groups has drawn comparisons to the conditions in Colombia in the late twentieth century that produced a similar K&R epidemic.

BACKGROUND

Typically, the process of kidnapping individuals is divided into five separate stages that include: "(1) planning, (2) hostage seizing and transfer, (3) custody, (4) contacts and negotiation, and (5) outcome" (Marongiu & Clarke, 1993). According to Colombian data, most K&R events last less than ten days, but can stretch to well over 1,000 days (Pires et al., 2014). The time it takes between taking a hostage and a particular outcome will depend on the type of victim, offender, and region the incident takes place in. For example, affluent hostages are thought to remain in captivity for longer periods in order for offenders to maximize the ransom payment. Some offending groups may settle for quicker and lower ransom payments, as they are inexperienced negotiators. Finally, urban kidnappings often result in less time in captivity for hostages as it may be more difficult to keep a hostage in custody without detection in cities as compared to rural areas (Guerette, Pires, & Shariati, 2018).

By several accounts the practice of K&R is largely rational and "business like" and because of this there is often greater incentive for victims to be returned alive rather than killed. For example, kidnappings carried out off the Somali coast by so-called "pirates" are reported to be organized in a very entrepreneur-like fashion complete with pay scales and outside investors. Moreover, in response to chronic kidnapping risks the private insurance industry provides K&R insurance policies to individuals and they facilitate negotiations for the successful release of their kidnapped clients and the delivery of ransoms. In order for this market system to be sustained, there must be stability and predictability in the outcomes, which means victims are killed in only a minority of cases. Research indicates that deaths only occur among 5 to 15 percent of kidnapped victims (Guerette et al., 2018).

Types

Kidnappings for ransom can be broadly categorized as either politically or economically motivated. Perpetrators that are politically motivated typically demand the release of a prisoner (Briggs, 2001). Economically motivated K&R is far more popular in the world with a goal of transferring cash or assets to the kidnappers in exchange for a hostage. According to Moor and Remijnse (2008), there are four major types of economically motivated K&R that have become prevalent around the world: 1) traditional; 2) express; 3) group; and 4) virtual kidnappings. Traditional kidnappings involve one victim, whereby the victim may have been premeditatedly or opportunistically targeted and is kept hostage until a negotiated ransom is given to the perpetrators, unless the victim escapes, dies, or law enforcement apprehends the perpetrators beforehand. Express kidnappings became popular in the early 2000s in Latin America where kidnappers would quickly take a hostage to multiple ATMs to withdraw as much cash as possible. Such incidents would last anywhere between a few hours and a day or two. Group kidnappings became an epidemic in rural Colombia in the 1990s and 2000s where perpetrators set up illegal road-blocks and indiscriminately kidnapped individuals in cars to maximize profit. A more recent example would include maritime piracy that targets commercial cargo ships and the personnel on board. Finally, virtual kidnappings involve perpetrators randomly calling individuals and falsely notifying them their loved one has been kidnapped in the hopes of extorting money easily and without much risk (Moor & Remijnse, 2008).

Offenders of K&R are usually common criminals, organized crime syndicates, or terrorist or rebel groups. For common criminals and organized crime, the economic benefit of ransoming individuals is the primary and only motive. For example, drug cartels or organized groups that tax drug trafficking are associated with conducting K&R in Mexico as a supplementary form of generating income. However, for terrorist and rebel groups, economic motives to fund their operations may be their primary motivation, but there are secondary benefits that instill fear at the local and regional area and may be used as leverage to negotiate peace agreements with the state (Pires et al., 2017; Keijzer, 2017).

Patterns Associated with K&R

With regard to what drives and explains K&R at the national level, much of the literature suggests countries experiencing a K&R epidemic are often failing states or on the verge of failing (Pires et al., 2014). However, most failed states around the world do not experience a kidnapping epidemic. The first study to examine the socioeconomic, sociopolitical, and security conditions that potentially relate to K&R epidemics at the global level found that countries experiencing K&R epidemics – as compared to nearby countries experiencing no such epidemic – were associated with less security, less peace (i.e., sociopolitical), and unevenly developed based on socioeconomic factors (Pires et al., 2017). Importantly, security-based factors had the strongest relationship to countries experiencing K&R epidemics. This suggests that in countries that experience far more crime and where the government has less control over its territories, K&R flourishes more often.

At the more *local level*, K&R incidents are partly a consequence of the uneven distribution of criminal opportunities. Some areas may have more potential targets or more opportunities for targeting. For example, many Colombian individuals were kidnapped in areas occupied by Colombian IAGs as the national government did not have any presence in such areas (Pires et al., 2014; Moor & Remijnse, 2008). In Italy in the 1970s, one region on the island of Sardinia disproportionately experienced incidents during the vacation season because this area was frequented by wealthy tourists (Marongiu & Clarke, 1993). Such opportunities affect the distribution of K&R incidents within countries, making some areas far more likely to experience K&R. In 2002, for example, 20 percent of Colombian municipalities experienced 88 percent of all kidnapped victims. According to a recent Mexican report, similar spatial concentrations appear to hold consistent within Mexico as well (Velez et al., 2014). Altogether, where spatial analysis has been conducted, K&R has been found to be highly concentrated within Colombia, Italy, and Mexico, suggesting an uneven spatial distribution of opportunities to kidnap.

RESPONSES

In response to kidnapping problems, most efforts tend to be reactive rather than proactive. A specialized insurance industry has evolved that provides policy coverages to individuals at risk of being kidnapped. These policies provide negotiation services and ransoms to be paid to kidnappers. Policing components of governments also tend to operate reactively once victims have been reported missing. Other efforts to respond to kidnapping problems include increased penalties such as execution of offenders if caught, prohibitions against citizens paying ransoms, creation of specialized anti-kidnapping police units, targeted government operations to dismantle organized criminal groups who are responsible for kidnappings, and freezing bank accounts of victims and their family members. The latter tactic appeared to be an effective way of deterring potential offenders from kidnapping individuals in Italy by removing the rewards of the crime (Detotto et al., 2015).

Yet it is also known that kidnapping incidents tend to concentrate in space, time, and among offenders and victims, making them somewhat predictable behavior (Pires et al., 2014; Marongiu & Clarke, 1993). These concentrations are very much in line with the sorts of patterns found among domestic crime types and, consequently, this means much more could be done to proactively prevent kidnapping from occurring rather than responding to it after the fact. As a result of these patterns, many recent papers have suggested situational crime prevention (SCP) would be an appropriate framework to curtail K&R incidents by focusing on the opportunity structures that facilitate such crimes. More specifically, increasing the effort and risk and removing the rewards of committing K&R can potentially prevent K&R from occurring. Some of the proactive measures that *could* be employed through the systematic application of prevention efforts include targeting high-risk places and roads with heightened patrols, implementing citizen educational and roadway alert systems, collaborating with community and nongovernmental groups to mobilize prevention activities and alter daily operations to minimize risks, and establishing citizen-based tip line and notification systems in high-risk areas, among others (Pires et al., 2014). Perhaps the greatest example of successfully implementing SCP measures has been in response to the Somali piracy kidnapping epidemic that began in 2011. By introducing proactive techniques that increased both the effort and risk of maritime piracy, there were no more incidents by 2015 (Shane & Magnuson, 2016).

SUMMARY OF HIGHLIGHTS

Though K&R was originally somewhat isolated in its occurrence, it has now flourished into a businesslike illicit market concentrating in many countries around the world. Increasingly, ransom kidnappings have been carried out by organized crime and terrorist groups who utilize the proceeds to support their organizations' operations. Because ransoms will only be paid in exchange for victims who are kept alive, most kidnapping victims survive the ordeal. One final implication of the rational, businesslike features of ransom kidnapping markets is that it makes them highly susceptible to preventive action. In other words, since kidnapping groups are able to calculate their actions, reducing the opportunities for kidnappings by increasing penalties and risks and removing the rewards is very likely to reduce the problem.

REFERENCES

Briggs, R. (2001). *The kidnapping business*. London: The Foreign Policy Centre Diplomatic Forum.

Detotto, C., McCannon, B., & Vannini M. (2015). Evidence of marginal deterrence: Kidnapping and murder in Italy. *International Review of Law and Economics*, 41, 63–67.

Forest, J. J. (2012). Kidnapping by terrorist groups, 1970–2010. Is ideological orientation relevant? *Crime & Delinquency*, 58(5), 769–797.

Guerette, R. T., Pires, S. F., & Shariati, A. (2018). Detecting the determinants and trajectories of homicide among ransom kidnappings: A research note. *Homicide Studies*, 22(2), 214–229.

Keijzer, S. (2017). An end to Colombia's never ending conflict?: A MA thesis on the peace process between President Santos and the FARC and the role of kidnappings in the Colombian Conflict between 1982–2017 (Master's thesis). Universiteit Leiden, the Netherlands.

Marongiu, P. & Clarke, R. V. (1993). Ransom kidnapping in Sardinia: Subcultural theory and rational choice. In R. V. Clarke & M. Felson (Eds.), *Routine activity and rational choice* (pp. 179–199). New Brunswick, NJ: Transaction Publishers.

Moor, M. & Remijnse, S. (2008). *Kidnapping is a booming business*. Utrecht: IKV PAX Christi.

Perlberg, S. (2013, December 12). The 20 countries where people get kidnapped the most. *Business Insider*. Retrieved from www.businessinsider.com/top-20-countries-by-kidnapping-2013-12.

Phillips, E. M. (2009). The business of kidnap for ransom. In D. Canter (Ed.), *The faces of terrorism: Multidisciplinary perspectives* (pp. 189–207). West Sussex: Wiley.

Pires, S. F., Guerette, R. T., & Shariati, A. (2017). Specifying kidnapping for ransom epidemics at the global level: A matched-case control design. *Studies in Conflict & Terrorism*, 40(2), 139–156.

Pires, S. F., Guerette, R. T., & Stubbert, C. H. (2014). The crime triangle of kidnapping for ransom incidents in Colombia, South America: A 'litmus' test for situational crime prevention. *British Journal of Criminology*, 54(5), 784–808.

Shane, J. M. & Magnuson, S. (2016). Successful and unsuccessful pirate attacks worldwide: A situational analysis. *Justice Quarterly*, 33(4), 682–707.

Vélez, D. M., Vélez, M. A., López, J. A., Díaz, C. E., Cendejas, M. G., Rivas, F. J., … & Pérez, V. (2014). Análisis integral del secuestro en México. *Cómo entender esta problemática, México: Observatorio Nacional Ciudadano Seguridad, Justicia y Legalidad.*

16 Child Pornography

Richard Wortley

OVERVIEW OF CHILD PORNOGRAPHY

There is a long history of erotic literature and drawings involving children, but child pornography in the modern sense began with the invention of the camera in the early nineteenth century (Wortley & Smallbone, 2012). For most of the nineteenth and twentieth centuries, child pornography was generally difficult to come by. It typically comprised poor-quality photographs, magazines, and films that were traded in hard-copy form among small bands of dedicated consumers. However, the advent of the Internet in the 1980s dramatically changed the situation by increasing the amount of material that was available, the efficiency of its distribution, and the ease by which it could be accessed. The number of users grew exponentially and child pornography became a truly international enterprise.

The idea of protecting children from sexual exploitation is relatively modern. For example, as late as 1880s in the USA, the age of consent for girls was just ten years old and the use of children in obscene material was not specifically outlawed by the US federal government until 1978. Today, law enforcement agencies are faced with the challenge of controlling a flood of child pornography generated by an increasingly sophisticated technology. This is a global problem that crosses state and national borders and requires an international response.

WHAT IS CHILD PORNOGRAPHY?

Legal definitions of both "child" and "pornography" vary among jurisdictions (Wortley & Smallbone, 2012). Eighteen years of age is a commonly used legal cut-off to appear in pornography but this is not universal. Also, in some jurisdictions age is defined chronologically, while in others it is illegal to use models who appear to be underage irrespective of their actual age. In many countries the age at which a person can appear in pornographic images is higher than the age of consent, and this can lead to situations in which young people can legally engage in sexual behavior but be guilty of an offence if they send each other nude images. Similarly, judgments about what is pornographic are typically made against local community standards, and the portrayal of sexual acts that are illegal in one country may be lawful in another. In the USA, for example, child pornography can include obscene behavior that does not involve nudity. In some jurisdictions, child pornography can include virtual (computer-generated) images of children while in others such images are legal.

For the purpose of this chapter, child pornography is defined as any record of sexual activity involving a prepubescent child or young adolescent. Pornographic records include still photographs, videos, and audio recordings. In terms of content, Taylor, Quayle, and Holland (2001) identified ten levels of image severity, ranging from non-sexualized pictures of children collected from legitimate sources such as magazines, to graphic depictions of children engaging in sexual acts with other children, adults, and even animals.

It should be noted that, internationally, many researchers, law enforcement agencies, and advocacy groups working in the field strongly object to the term "child pornography," believing it to trivialize the severity of the problem. Alternative terms commonly used include child exploitation material (CEM), child abuse images, and indecent images of children.

TRENDS AND STATISTICS

Today, child pornography invariably involves the Internet. The Internet greatly enhances the capacity of individuals to create, distribute, and access child pornography (Calder, 2004). Electronic recording devices such as digital cameras, web cameras, and multi-media messaging (MMR) cell phones permit individuals to create high-quality, "home-made" child pornography images, and to upload them to the Internet from anywhere in the world. Once uploaded, these images are instantly available and may be conveniently accessed anonymously and in private, and at any time or place. The pornographic images downloaded from the Internet are inexpensive, do not deteriorate, and can be conveniently stored and catalogued on the computer's hard drive or on a removable disk (e.g., CD-ROM). The Internet provides for a variety of pornography formats (pictures, videos, sound), as well as the potential for real-time and interactive experiences. If desired, images may be modified to create composite or virtual images (i.e., "morphing"). In addition to providing access to pornography websites, the Internet provides for direct communication among users, allowing for the sharing of images and the mutual support of one another's belief systems.

It is difficult to be precise about the extent of Internet child pornography, but all the available evidence points to it being a major and growing problem (Wortley & Smallbone, 2012). In 1980, before the Internet, the largest-selling child pornography magazine in the USA was reckoned to have just 800 customers; 20 years later one Internet child pornography company (Landslide Productions) was closed down and found to have more than 250,000 customers from around the world. Law enforcement officials typically estimate the number of active users worldwide in the millions. Offenders are regularly arrested with more than a million pornographic images of children.

Child pornography can be found in open areas of the Internet (e.g., the world-wide web), but increasingly images are uploaded and traded on less public platforms such as chat rooms and peer-to-peer (P2P) networks (connections that allow direct communication between computers and facilitate file sharing) in an effort to elude detection. The newest emerging threat is that posed by the so-called "darknet" (Bartlett, 2014), the collection of encrypted communication networks that exist outside of the observable Internet. On the darknet, a user is able to transmit encrypted data that cannot be intercepted or read by unauthorized third parties, making the user anonymous and untraceable and posing special challenges for law enforcement.

PROFILE OF USERS

There is no one type of Internet child pornography user, nor is there any easy way to recognize an offender. People can behave very differently on the Internet than they do in other areas of their life. Interacting anonymously with a computer in the safety of one's own home is a disinhibiting experience and encourages people to express hidden thoughts and desires. The Internet has allowed many individuals who in the pre-Internet era would not have accessed child pornography to now do so. Many offenders have few distinguishing sociodemographic and psychological features. They can come from all walks of life and show few obvious warning signs. Those arrested for downloading online child pornography have included judges, dentists, soldiers, teachers, rock stars, and police officers. Child pornography offenders tend to be white, male, and between the ages of 26 and 39 years (Wolak, Finkelhor, & Mitchell, 2005), while in comparison to contact child sex offenders, they are more likely to be better educated, to be professionally employed, and to have fewer criminal convictions, but to engage in more pedophilic fantasies (Elliott et al., 2008; Sheldon & Howitt, 2007). Calder (2004) suggested the following categories of Internet pornography users.

1. Recreational users. They access pornography sites on impulse, out of curiosity, or for short-term entertainment. They are not seen to have long-term problems associated with pornography use.
2. At-risk users. They are vulnerable individuals who have developed an interest in pornography, but may not have done so had it not been for the Internet.
3. Sexual compulsive users. They seek out pornography to satisfy existing pathological sexual interests.

The overlap between child pornography use and contact child sex offending is contentious, with estimates varying widely from study to study. Seto, Hanson, and Babchisin (2011) conducted a meta-analysis of the available research. They found that 12 percent (range 0–43 percent) of convicted child pornography offenders also had convictions for contact child sex offending. The figure was higher for self-reported offending, with 55 percent (range 32–85 percent) of offenders admitting contact offences. Seto et al. also examined recidivism rates, finding that 3.4 percent of child pornography offenders were reconvicted for another child pornography offence and 2 percent for a contact sexual offence. However, some caution needs to be exercised when interpreting these results. The findings are based on research involving convicted offenders, who are probably at the more serious end of the offending spectrum. It would not be surprising if the degree of overlap between online and contact offenders was at the lower end of the estimates, while reoffending rates that take in self-report may be higher.

INVESTIGATING AND CONTROLLING CHILD PORNOGRAPHY

The structure and reach of the Internet makes the control of child pornography very difficult. The Internet is an international communication tool that crosses jurisdictional boundaries. Local citizens may access child pornography images that were produced or are stored on another continent. Different countries have different laws and levels of permissiveness pertaining to child pornography. Moreover, the Internet is a decentralized system with no single controlling agency or storage facility, making it difficult to enforce legislation or to electronically screen content even when there is agreement between jurisdictions. Because it is a network of networks, even if one pathway is blocked there are many alternative pathways that can be taken to reach the same destination. In addition, rapid technological developments, such as file encryption (methods of hiding or scrambling data), exacerbate the control problem (Wortley & Smallbone, 2012).

Despite the difficulties involved in policing the Internet, computers and their associated services retain a considerable amount of evidence of the uses to which they have been put (Ferraro & Casey, 2005). While determined, computer-savvy offenders may take precautions to cover their tracks, many offenders will have neither the foresight nor the necessary expertise to do so, and will leave a trail of incriminating evidence. The most obvious evidence of pornography use is actual downloaded images on the computer's hard drive. However, there are also more subtle records that specialist forensic technicians can locate during examination of a suspect's computer. For example, files on the computer can reveal when a computer was connected to the Internet and what websites were visited. Similarly, servers used to connect a computer to the Internet or to store pornographic images retain records of customer account details (the Internet Protocol or IP address), which can then be used to identify users.

Considerable law enforcement resources are now dedicated to tackling the child pornography problem on an ongoing basis, with many police forces establishing dedicated investigative units (Wortley & Smallbone 2012). A technological arms race has developed between offenders and law enforcement agencies, with increasing use by investigators of image recognition software, surveillance software, and data-linking software. Police routinely take down illegal images that they uncover or that are reported to them by other agencies and public tiplines. Many investigations involve undercover operations in which officers infiltrate forums in which offenders may be exchanging images, or child-oriented chat rooms in which offenders are seeking to groom potential victims. There have been a number of major interagency and international investigations of Internet child pornography. For example, in 2003 a classic "honey-pot" operation (Operation Pin) was carried out involving collaboration among UK, US, Australian, and Canadian policing agencies. The operation involved setting up a fake website that purported to offer child pornography. When offenders visited the site their credit card details were captured, allowing them to be traced and arrested.

Despite such efforts, it is apparent that the sheer volume of offenders is overwhelming police resources, and in reality only a tiny fraction of offenders are arrested. Thus, there is increasing interest in preventing child pornography offending before it occurs (Smallbone & Wortley, 2017). These efforts involve making it more difficult and less anonymous for potential offenders to access child pornography. One example of a prevention strategy is the work of the Financial Coalition Against Child Pornography (FCACP), a grouping of 35 Internet Service Providers (ISPs), credit card companies, banks, and other companies providing online payment services. These companies track the flow of money in child pornography transactions and block payments for illegal downloads. This strategy has made it more difficult for offenders to purchase child pornography and increased the price of images, leading to a significant drop in commercial child pornography activity. As this example demonstrates, effective prevention of child pornography requires partnerships between law enforcement agencies and a range of other stakeholders.

SUMMARY

The scale of the child pornography problem has increased dramatically with the introduction and rapid growth of the Internet. There are now estimated to be millions of pornographic images of children available online. The Internet has also made the problem of child pornography a truly international one. Almost all investigations that begin in one jurisdiction will need to cross state and even international borders to be effective. Perhaps more than any other offence, the fight against child pornography requires international cooperation and coordination among law enforcement bodies and other agencies.

REFERENCES

Bartlett, J. (2014). *The dark net: Inside the digital underworld*. London: William Heinemann.
Calder, M. C. (2004). The Internet: Potential, problems and pathways to hands-on sexual offending. In M. C. Calder (Ed.), *Child sexual abuse and the Internet: Tackling the new frontier*. Lyme Regis: Russell House Publishing.
Elliott, I. A. et al. (2008). Psychological profiles of Internet sexual offenders. *Sexual Abuse: A Journal of Research and Treatment*, 21, 76–92.
Ferraro, M. M. & Casey E. (2005). *Investigating child exploitation and pornography: The Internet, the law and forensic science*. San Diego, CA: Elsevier.
Seto, M. C., Hanson, R. K., & Babchishin, K. M. (2011). Contact sexual offending by men with online sexual offenses. *Sexual Abuse: A Journal of Research and Treatment*, 23(1), 124–145.
Sheldon, K. & Howitt, D. (2007). *Sex offenders and the Internet*. Chichester: John Wiley.
Smallbone, S. W. & Wortley R. (2017). Preventing child sexual abuse online. In J. Brown (Ed.), *Online risk to children: Impact, protection and prevention*. Chichester: Wiley Blackwell.
Taylor, M., Quayle, E., & Holland G. (2001). Typology of pedophile picture collections. *The Police Journal*, 74, 97–107.
Wolak, J., Finkelhor, D., & Mitchell K. J. (2005). *Child pornography possessors arrested in Internet-related crimes*. Alexandria, VA: Department of Justice, National Center for Missing and Exploited Children.
Wortley, R. & Smallbone S. (2012). *Internet child pornography: Causes, investigation and prevention*. Santa Barbara, CA: Praeger.

WEBSITES

International Center for Missing and Exploited Children. www.icmec.org/.
Internet Watch Foundation. www.iwf.org.uk/.
INTERPOL: Crime Against Children. www.interpol.int/Crime-areas/Crimes-against-children/Crimes-against-children.
US Financial Coalition Against Child Pornography. www.icmec.org/fcacp/.

17 Transnational Environmental Crime

Rob White

INTRODUCTION

Transnational environmental crime is one of the key reasons why our planet is in peril. Such crimes include the dumping of toxic waste, the pollution of land, air, and water, and the illegal trade of plants and animals, in ways that cross borders and, in many instances, have a global dimension. Most environmental harm is intrinsically transnational since it is by nature mobile and easily subject to transference. Analysis of transnational environmental crime therefore requires a sense of scale, and of the essential interconnectedness of issues, events, people, and places.

BACKGROUND

Transnational environmental crime, as defined in conventional legal terms, includes:

- unauthorized acts or omissions that are *against the law* and therefore subject to criminal prosecution and criminal sanctions;
- crimes that involve some kind of *cross-border transference* and an international or *global dimension*; and
- crimes related to *pollution* (of air, water, and land) and *crimes against wildlife* (including illegal trade in ivory as well as live animals).

These are the key focus of national and international laws relating to environmental matters, and are the main task areas of agencies such as INTERPOL, which has four working groups that focus on fisheries crime, forestry crime, pollution crime, and wildlife crime.

In its more expansive definition, as used by green criminologists, for example, transnational environmental crime also extends to *harms* (White, 2011). It therefore includes:

- transgressions that are *harmful to humans, environments, and non-human animals*, regardless of legality per se; and
- environmental-related harms that are facilitated by *the state*, as well as *corporations and other powerful actors*, insofar as these institutions have the capacity to shape official definitions of environmental crime in ways that allow or condone environmentally harmful practices.

The definition of transnational environmental crime is contentious to the extent that extra-legal definitions apply in addition to existing legal definitions. The necessity for the former is dictated by the actions and omissions of nation-states that may well allow harmful environmental activity to occur without it being criminalized (i.e., constructed as a crime and subject to criminal law). Perceived national and business interests do not always coincide with the best environmental outcome or ecological sustainability, although this is of major concern to green criminologists (South & Brisman, 2013).

CONCEPTUALIZING TRANSNATIONAL ENVIRONMENTAL CRIME AND HARM

In recent years there has been major growth in the number of treaties, agreements, protocols, and conventions relating to environmental protection. Nation-states have been more interested in taking governmental action on environmental matters, since much of this pertains to national economic interests. Moreover, the transboundary nature of environmental harm is evident in a variety of international protocols and conventions that deal with such matters as the illegal trade in ozone-depleting substances, the dumping and illegal transport of hazardous waste, the illegal trade in chemicals such as persistent organic pollutants, and the illegal dumping of oil and other wastes in oceans.

A key international instrument of relevance to wildlife protection is the Convention on International Trade in Endangered Species (CITES), which has the aim of ensuring that international trade in specimens of wild animals and plants does not threaten their survival.

Through these various international instruments certain kinds of activities are either being banned or highly regulated. Breach of these rules, laws, and regulations constitutes an environmental crime. The laws and rules guiding action on environmental crime vary greatly at the local, regional, and national levels, and there are overarching conventions and laws that likewise have different legal purchase depending upon how they are translated into action in each specific local jurisdiction. In part, differences in law-in-practice and conceptions of what is an environmental crime stem from the shifting nature of what is deemed harmful or not.

Those who study transnational environmental crime from a social scientific perspective argue that "harm" needs to be measured and assessed, but in doing so the study of crime has to go beyond existing legal definitions and criteria. This is because, first, wrongdoing is perpetrated by states themselves, yet it is the nation-state that defines what is criminal, corrupt, or unjust. There is a need therefore for the development of criteria and definitions of crime that are not restricted to a specific state's laws but that are more universal in nature (for example, the concept of "ecocide").

Second, harms perpetrated by powerful groups and organizations, such as transnational corporations, are frequently dealt with by the state as civil rather than criminal matters. This reflects the capacity of the powerful to shape laws in ways that do not criminalize their activities, even when these are ecologically disastrous.

Third, there are extra-legal concepts and factors that need to be studied if we are to fully appreciate the nature of environmental harm, and this requires a different way of framing the issues. An ecology-based analysis of activity may well provide quite a different picture of "harm" than an economics-based analysis. Green criminologists argue that action is needed now to prevent harms associated with global warming, pollution and waste generation, and threats to biodiversity. From this perspective, the imperative is ecological, not legal, and the outcome, ultimately, is human survival.

Critical analysis of transnational environmental crime incorporates different conceptions of harm (to environments, to animals) and different types of crime (involving nation-states and corporations, and multiple criminal activities) within an overarching harm perspective (see Box 17.1).

Box 17.1. Concepts Important to the Study of Transnational Environmental Harm

Ecocide refers to the destruction, degradation, and demolishment of ecosystems and specific environments, with harmful consequences for the living creatures within these (Higgins, 2012). When this happens due to particular types of human activity, then ecocide as a crime has occurred. Ecocide affects basic human rights to ecosystem services as well as the health and well-being of non-human environmental entities such as animals, plants, and rivers.

Theriocide refers to diverse human actions that cause the deaths of animals. Examples include intensive rearing regimes, hunting and fishing, and legal and illegal wildlife trafficking (Beirne, 2014). Animals are killed and maimed for a wide variety of reasons and in different contexts including, for example, for food (e.g., factory farming) and for collection (e.g., private trafficking of exotic animals).

State-corporate crime refers to illegal or socially injurious actions that result from a mutually reinforcing interaction between nation-states and corporations (Kramer & Michalowski, 2012). It relates to both *acts* (e.g., support for polluting industries) and *omissions* (e.g., failure to regulate carbon emissions). Inactivity around global warming, for example, can be considered criminal given the evidence base and foreknowledge of its consequences.

Cross-over crime refers to interlinked crimes that include environmental offences. An example of this is human trafficking and persons being forced into virtual slavery on illegal fishing boats. Environmental crimes such as wildlife trafficking occur alongside other serious offences, including theft, fraud, corruption, drugs and human trafficking, counterfeiting, firearms smuggling, and money laundering (South & Wyatt 2011).

DIFFERENT TYPES OF TRANSNATIONAL ENVIRONMENTAL CRIME

The most common environmental crimes fall into two broad categories: natural resources crimes (e.g., trees and animals) and pollution crimes (e.g., contamination and toxic waste).

In regards the first, deforestation provides a case in point. Most deforestation is occurring in tropical forests with net losses especially significant in South America and Africa. Reduction in species because of this includes both animals and plants. The causes of deforestation and reduction in forest biodiversity include unsustainable harvesting of forest products for industrial use, agriculture, severe drought and forest fires, and land clearance due to cattle farming, mining, oil and gas installations, and hydroelectric dams. There is also the phenomenon of "conflict timber," in which deforestation is linked to the funding of civil wars and armed conflicts (Brisman, South, & White 2014).

The motivations, objectives, and practices of deforestation vary depending upon the social context and specific industry interests, but the result is further depletion of many different kinds of trees and a variety of forests. Illegal logging occurs with the involvement of corrupt government officials, including law enforcement officers, financial institutions and backers, and business people who import timber or wood-base products (Bisschop, 2015). Deforestation not only involves the cutting down of trees but also frequently the burning of forests as part of converting land for other uses such as agriculture and biofuel plantations. This also contributes to global warming.

The second category of transnational environmental crimes relates to air, land, and water pollution, which negatively affects all exposed to it. Air pollution, for example, impacts upon humans in ways that fundamentally undermine their health and well-being, and is associated with millions of premature deaths worldwide each year (Walters, 2010). It stems from the release of chemicals and particulates into the atmosphere, including such substances as carbon monoxide and sulfur dioxide, and is clearly evident in the form of city smog. Land pollution occurs when chemicals are released into the soil, including heavy metals such as lead and cadmium and pesticides, which can kill living bacteria in the earth or contaminate all life within the soil (including plants and non-plant creatures). Water pollution occurs when contaminants, such as untreated sewerage waste and agricultural runoff containing chemical fertilizers, alter and poison existing surface and ground waters.

Agriculture and mining stand out as two of the most polluting activities, along with the burgeoning extractive and resources industries and the use of chemicals. The emergence of electronic waste (e.g., computers, mobile phones) has only added to existing waste management problems, among which has included criminal engagement in the waste industry (Bisschop, 2015). E-waste contains toxins such as lead and mercury or other chemicals that can poison waterways if buried, or release toxins into the air if burned. Much of this waste ends up as transfers from rich countries to the poor, sometimes under the guise of "recycling."

RESPONDING TO TRANSNATIONAL ENVIRONMENTAL CRIME

Many different international instruments deal with the protection of biodiversity, pollution prevention, and transfer of hazardous waste. However, the transnational nature of illegal environmental activity makes it distinctive and difficult to combat, as does the status of some environmentally harmful acts as legal (such as clearfelling of old-growth forests).

Recent years have seen a range of international collaborations emerge around specific types of commodity, and in relation to specific enforcement and regulatory bodies (Pink & White, 2016). For example, the International Consortium Combating Wildlife Crime (ICCWC) is comprised of five intergovernmental organizations: CITES, INTERPOL, the UN Office on Drugs and Crime, the World Bank, and the World Customs Organization. More broadly, the International Network for Environmental Compliance and Enforcement (INECE) brings together approximately 4,000 individual members from more than 150 countries with a view to improving policy and practice in this area.

In 2012, INTERPOL established the National Environmental Security Taskforce (NEST) model. The NEST is a conceptual framework where various representatives from a range of agencies come together to contribute and leverage from the groups' collective skill sets in order to more effectively develop, coordinate, and implement response measures (see Box 17.2).

Box 17.2. The National Environmental Security Taskforce Model

At its most basic level, a NEST is a task force of an established team of experts – comprised of senior criminal investigators through to representatives from customs, environmental, and other specialized enforcement agencies – who work together to address specific issues. NESTs are presently utilized across various project areas.

- *Project Leaf* (Law Enforcement Assistance for Forests) is an initiative that is directed against illegal logging and related crimes.
- *Project Scale* is an initiative to detect, suppress, and combat fisheries crime.
- *Project Wisdom* is an initiative to improve wildlife law enforcement in Africa, specifically targeting the illegal trade in elephant ivory and rhinoceros horn.
- *Project Predator* is an initiative to support and enhance the governance and law enforcement capacity for the conservation of Asian big cats.
- *Project Eden* is an initiative to detect and counter the illegal international trade and disposal of waste.

Environmental crime poses particular challenges for environmental law enforcement, especially from the point of view of police interagency collaborations, the nature of investigative techniques and approaches, and the different types of knowledge required for dealing with specific kinds of environmental harm. Moreover, many of the operational matters pertaining to environmental crimes are inherently international in scope and substance.

CONCLUSION: THE IMPORTANCE OF AN ECO-GLOBAL CRIMINOLOGY

To appreciate fully the nature of transnational environmental crime it is essential to consider the particular geographical contexts of harm. For instance, transnational environmental harm is always located somewhere in terms of causes and consequences. Environmental threats originate in particular factories, farms, firms, industries, and localities. What happens at the local and regional level counts at the international level. Conversely, global problems such as climate change are multi-level in nature, with harmful (and criminal) impacts at the local level.

The question of *scale* is at the heart of contemporary efforts to study transnational environmental crime. "Eco-global criminology" refers to a criminological approach informed by ecological considerations and by a critical analysis that is worldwide in its perspective (White, 2011). It is based upon eco-justice conceptions of harm that include consideration of transgressions against environments, non-human species, and humans. The barriers to and prospects of a more ecologically balanced world are interwoven with powerful social interests and the contestation of what matters when it comes to change and transformation. The differences in conceptualizations of environmental harm are located in radically different paradigmatic understandings of nature and human interests (e.g., ecology-centered versus human-centered). An adequate policy response to transnational environmental crime will require both ongoing dialogue about the nature and definition of such harms, and the cooperation of environmental law enforcement officials across different jurisdictions.

For the eco-global criminologist the biggest threat to environmental rights, ecological justice, and non-human animal well-being are system-level structures and pressures that commodify all aspects of social existence, are based upon the exploitation of humans, non-human animals, and natural resources, and privilege powerful minority interests over the vast majority. Those who determine and shape the law are very often those whose activities ought to be criminalized. Dealing with transnational environmental crime will thus always be fraught with controversy and conflict to the extent that fundamental interests clash and questions of justice come to the fore.

REFERENCES

Beirne, P. (2014). Theriocide: Naming animal killing. *International Journal for Crime, Justice and Social Democracy*, 4(3), 50–67.

Bisschop, L. (2015). *Governance of the illegal trade in e-waste and tropical timber: Case studies on transnational environmental crime*. Surrey: Ashgate.

Brisman, A., South, N., & White, R. (Eds.). (2014). *Environmental crime and social conflict*. Surrey: Ashgate.

Higgins, P. (2012). *Earth is our business: Changing the rules of the game*. London: Shepheard-Walwyn Publishers Ltd.

Kramer, R. & Michalowski, R. (2012). Is global warming a state-corporate crime? In R. White (Ed.), *Climate change from a criminological perspective* (pp. 71–88). New York: Springer.

Pink, G. & White, R. (Eds.). (2016). *Environmental crime and collaborative state intervention*. Basingstoke: Palgrave Macmillan.

South, N. & Brisman, A. (Eds.). (2013). *The Routledge international handbook of green criminology*. London: Routledge.

South, N. & Wyatt, T. (2011). Comparing illicit trades in wildlife and drugs: An exploratory study. *Deviant Behaviour*, 32, 538–561.

Walters, R. (2010). Toxic atmospheres: Air pollution, trade and the politics of regulation. *Critical Criminology*, 18, 307–323.

White, R. (2011). *Transnational environmental crime: Toward an eco-global criminology*. London: Routledge.

WEBSITES

Convention on the Illegal Trade in Endangered Species (CITES). www.cites.org/.
Global Witness. www.globalwitness.org.
Intergovernmental Panel on Climate Change. www.ipcc.ch/.
INTERPOL. www.interpol.int/.
United Nations Interregional Crime and Justice Research Institute. www.unicri.it/.
United Nations Office on Drugs and Crime. www.unodc.org/.
United Nations Environment Programme. www.unenvironment.org/.
World Health Organization. www.who.int/.

18 Multinational Corporate Criminal Negligence

A Case Study of the Bhopal Disaster, India

G. S. Bajpai and Bir Pal Singh

INTRODUCTION

One of the worst disasters of human history has been the Bhopal industrial disaster. This disaster has affected millions of people in Bhopal, the capital city of the state of Madhya Pradesh in India, due to gas leakage at a Union Carbide pesticide plant on the night of December 3, 1984. The Union Carbide Corporation technical team reported that a large volume of water was introduced into the methyl isocyanate (MIC) tank and triggered a reaction that resulted in the gas release (Lapierre & Moro, 1997). In 1969, the Union Carbide Corporation (UCC), a US company, set up a plant in Bhopal in a joint venture with the Indian Government. The plant was intended to produce pesticides for use in India's huge agricultural sector. The decision to manufacture the pesticide in India, as opposed to relying on imports, was based on India's goal of preserving foreign exchange and its policy of industrialization (Cassels, 1994).

FACTORS CAUSING LEAKAGE OF GAS

Many factors have been cited for the leakage of the gas in official and independent probes, the foremost being huge and unsafe storage of lethal chemical tanks – in which UCC stored more than the permitted quantities. Several vital safety arrangements were violated, wherein UCC was accused of having double standards for safety when planning factories in developing countries (Chouhan et al., 1994). Negligence on the part of UCC included general safety and environmental standards without a sound system of warning and monitoring the chemical levels. The large-scale devastation was the result of the densely populated area in which the plant was situated, without many effective health care and disaster management system facilities in place. Also, the staff lacked knowledge of the sensitive task of maintaining the storage and upkeep of the plant. It was also found that the gas scrubber designed to neutralize any escaping MIC had been shut off for maintenance. Even had it been operative, post-disaster inquiries revealed that the maximum pressure it could have handled was only one-quarter of that actually reached in the accident (Weir, 1987).

MAGNITUDE OF CALAMITY

The gas leakage was so intensive and engulfing that it took a massive toll of lives of people who were sleeping in their dwellings in a radius of about ten kilometers and beyond. The exact number of casualties is unknown due to mass burials, cremations, and conflicting medical opinions. In the beginning, the death toll was said to be 2,259. By 1987, it was reported as about 3,500 and by 1992 it was more than 4,000. Victims' organizations placed the figure many thousands higher. In addition, 30,000 to 40,000 people were maimed and seriously injured and 200,000 were otherwise affected through minor injury, death of a family member, and economic and social dislocation (Cassels, 1994).

SOME CONSEQUENCES

The true impact of the tragedy cannot be measured just by the number of deaths. There was also a toll in serious physiological disorders, which emerged either immediately after the incident, or developed even after many weeks. The range of disorders was extremely crippling. In the longer term, the majority of survivors developed chronic respiratory illnesses. Several surveys found the prevalence of respiratory disorders to the extent of 96 percent among those exposed to gases. A survey by the Indian Council of Medical Research (ICMR, 1994) found the gases caused serious eye irritations, corneal erosions, and cataracts, a phenomenon termed the "Bhopal eye syndrome." According to the Madhya Pradesh Gas Relief and Rehabilitation Department, the gas leak also caused damage to the immune system. Nearly 25 years after exposure, severely exposed people were four times more likely to suffer from common illnesses, five times more likely to suffer from lung ailments, three times more likely to suffer from eye problems, and more than twice as likely to suffer from stomach ailments.

ENVIRONMENTAL HARMS

A report produced by The Indian Council of Agricultural Research on damage to crops, vegetables, animals, and fish from the accident stated that as many as 4,000 cattle as well as dogs, cats, and birds were killed. Plant life was also severely damaged by exposure to the gas. There was also widespread defoliation of trees, especially in low-lying areas. The Environment Protection Act 1986 and the Hazardous Waste (Management and Handling) Rules for Management, Storage and Import of Hazardous Chemicals in 1989 were some of the developments after the tragedy. However, implementation of these laws remains futile in the sense that the chemical debris left after the tragedy has not been attended until now.

LEGAL ACTIONS

The Chairman and CEO of Union Carbide, Warren Anderson, was arrested and released on bail by the Madhya Pradesh Police in Bhopal on December 7, 1984. In 1987, the Indian Government summoned Warren Anderson, eight other executives, and two company affiliates to appear on homicide charges in an Indian court. Union Carbide resisted this on grounds of jurisdiction. Warren Anderson was charged in 1991 with manslaughter, a crime that carries a maximum penalty of ten years of imprisonment, by a local court in Bhopal. The Government of India sought Anderson's extradition from the USA, with whom India had an extradition treaty in place, but repeated attempts did not succeed. Meanwhile, very paltry sums of money from the settlement reached the survivors, and people in the area felt betrayed not only by Union Carbide, but also by their own politicians. On the anniversary of the tragedy, effigies of Anderson and politicians are regularly burned. To provide greater protection of victim rights, the Government of India enacted the Bhopal Gas Leak Disaster (Processing of Claims) Act in March 1985. The Act was amended in 1992 and authorizes the Government of India, as *parens patriae*, exclusively to represent the Bhopal gas victims so that interests of those victims of the disaster are fully protected, and that claims for compensation are pursued speedily, effectively, equitably, and to the best advantage of the claimants. In normal circumstances, *parens patriae* refers to the inherent power and authority of a legislature to provide protection to the person, and property of persons, who are *non sui juris* – such as minors, the insane, and the incompetent (Das, 1995).

In July 2004, the Indian Supreme Court ordered the Indian Government to release any remaining settlement funds to victims. The fund is believed to amount to US$500 million after earning interest "from money remaining after all claims had been paid." August 2006 saw the Second Circuit Court of Appeals in New York City uphold the dismissal of remaining claims in the case of *Bano v Union Carbide Corporation*. This move blocked plaintiffs' motions for class certification and claims for property damages and remediation. In the view of Union Carbide, "the ruling reaffirms UCC's long-held positions and finally puts to rest – both procedurally and substantively – the issues raised in the class action complaint first filed against Union Carbide in 1999." In September 2006, the Welfare Commission for Bhopal Gas Victims announced that all original compensation claims and revised petitions had been "cleared."

Criminal charges are proceeding against former senior officers of Union Carbide India Limited and federal class action litigation (*Sahu v Union Carbide et al.*) was pending on appeal before the Second Circuit Court of Appeals in New York City for a long period of time. The litigation seeks damages for personal injury, medical monitoring, and injunctive relief in the form of clean-up of the drinking water supplies for residential areas near the Bhopal plant. A related complaint seeking similar relief for property damage claimants is stayed, pending the outcome of the *Sahu* appeal before the federal district court in the Southern District of New York. In February 2009, the US Federal Court in New York declined to declare mediation in the *Sahu* case. In June 2012, the court ruled in favor of the defendants, dismissing claims of their participation and liability in the incident on the ground of insufficient evidence. It was held that Warren Anderson was not liable for environmental pollution or remediation-related claims by the victims of the tragedy. In January 2014, new evidence was submitted in the case, *Sahu II v Union Carbide Corporation* in the Southern District Court of New York. Another hurdle came when, 17 years after the tragedy, the company was bought by Dow Chemicals, which refused to clean up the site, stating that the former Indian subsidiary, i.e., Union Carbide India Limited, bore sole responsibility. Thus, litigation of the Bhopal gas disaster has become an ever-increasing process and, ultimately, has only given more pain to the living of the affected people. This painful, lengthy legal process adds to the list of basic human rights violations.

On June 7, 2010, 26 years after the occurrence of the Bhopal accident, a local court in Bhopal convicted former Union Carbide India Chairman Keshub Mahindra and seven others in the Bhopal gas tragedy case and awarded them a maximum of two years' imprisonment for acting rashly and negligently. This has triggered country-wide outrage. The main controversy is that the punishment is disproportionate to the enormity of their offense. Campaigners were quoted saying that the judgment was too little, too late. Apart from that, the accused immediately were released on bail, after which an appeal was filed in session court, to no development so far.

Since 2013, pending petitions were transferred to Madhya Pradesh High Court to supervise relief and rehabilitation of the victims of the Bhopal gas tragedy. In February 2018, Bhopal Gas Peedith Mahila Udhyog Sangathan approached the Supreme Court saying that the High Court was not able to discharge its duties because of the transfer and elevation of judges. The case is generally listed before the senior-most judge of the court and within a year-or-so, when the judge is either transferred or elevated, the case starts afresh. The Chief Justice of India, Justice Deepak Mishra, responded by requesting the Madhya Pradesh High Court to constitute a bench of such judges who have reasonable tenure. Currently, a bench headed by Justice R. S. Jha is hearing the petitions.

One of the recent developments that show some hope in rehabilitating victims of the tragedy came in March 2018, when Bhopal increased the allocation of funds to the relief and rehabilitation department by 30 crore. Also, keeping in view the deteriorating conditions of the internal organs of the victims of the tragedy and also effects of genetic degradation of organs that the incident has had on the children of the victims, the Madhya Pradesh state cabinet has decided to provide for liver and kidney transplant facilities to such victims.

PRESENT CONDITION OF THE SITE

The disaster site is becoming further contaminated owing to the massive chemical vestiges that remain because the area around the plant was used as a dumping ground area for hazardous chemicals. Between 1969 and 1977, all effluents were dumped in an open pit. From then on, neutralization with hydrochloric acid was undertaken. The effluents went to two evaporation ponds. In the rainy season, the effluents used to overflow. By 1982, tube wells near the UCC factory had to be abandoned. In 1991, the municipal authorities declared water from more than 100 tube wells to be unfit for drinking.

Studies made by Greenpeace and others of soil, ground water, well water, and vegetables from the residential areas around the factory show considerable contamination. A sample of drinking water from a well near the site had levels of contamination 500 times higher than the maximum limits recommended by the World Health Organization.

Over a period of time, the chemicals have reacted with the environment, causing irreplaceable damage. Twenty-five years after the tragedy, the Central Pollution Control Board and Centre for Science and Environment found the soil and ground water to be contaminated by heavy metals and chemicals in a joint study in 2009. A Beilstein test conducted in 2015 revealed that water from 240-feet bore wells was contaminated. This contamination is spreading due to further degradation and reaction of the chemicals with the environment, affecting human life severely in that area.

SUMMARY AND CONCLUSION

The Bhopal incident was not only an industrial disaster, but was also a fundamental violation of human rights. It is the leading example of a corporate violation of human rights. It is also a classical example of reckless negligence constituting what could be termed as "corporate deviance." Such views find mention in the Amnesty Report (2004, p. 2): "Governments have the primary responsibility for protecting the human rights of communities endangered by the activities of the corporations, such as those employing hazardous technology. However, as the influence and the reach of companies have grown, there has been a developing consensus that they must be brought within the framework of international human rights standards." In 2005, the UN Secretary-General Kofi Annan appointed Professor John Ruggie as UN Special Representative on business and human rights. In 2008, a report (the Ruggie Report) was submitted by him on "The issue of human rights and transnational corporations and other business enterprises." The Ruggie Report created an effective framework and started a significant debate about the responsibility of the corporations for violation of human rights. A substantial amount of work is still left in order to operationalize such a framework effectively. Nevertheless, it was a welcoming step taken in the right direction, which could provide relief to catastrophes like the Bhopal gas tragedy of 1984.

REFERENCES

Amnesty International. (2004). *Clouds of injustice – Bhopal disaster 20 years on*. Retrieved from www.amnesty.org/en/library/info/ASA20/015/2004.

Cassels, J. (1994). *The uncertain promise of law – Lessons from Bhopal*. Toronto: University of Toronto Press.

Chouhan, T. R. (1994). *Bhopal: The inside story. Carbide workers speak out on the world's worst industrial disaster*. New York: Apex Press.

Das, V. (1995). *Critical events: An anthropological perspective on contemporary India*. Oxford: Oxford University Press.

Indian Council of Medical Research (ICMR). (1994). Health effects of the toxic gas leak from the Union Carbide methyl isocyanate plant in Bhopal. New Delhi.

Lapierre, D. & Moro, J. (1997). *Five past midnight in Bhopal: The epic story of the world's deadliest industrial disaster*. New York: Simon & Schuster.

Weir, D. (1987). *The Bhopal syndrome: Pesticides, environment, and health*. San Francisco, CA: Sierra Club Books.

19 Maritime Crimes

An Overview

Gisela Bichler

GENERAL OVERVIEW

Maritime crime refers to a broad class of criminal and quasi-criminal behavior that is connected to recreational and commercial transportation involving ships (and excluding aircraft). This includes conventional crimes (e.g., murder), special crimes (e.g., piracy), and other quasi-criminal acts involving regulatory and public welfare offences under admiralty law (e.g., trade violations). Admiralty law consists of a body of common law rules, precepts, and practices that govern all transactions having a direct relationship with navigation or commerce on water.

Geographically, maritime crime can be divided into: (a) prohibitions involving local, recreational, and commercial sailing on internal waters; (b) illicit activity affecting navigation on the territorial sea; and, (c) illegalities that concern international seafaring on the high seas or foreign waters (see Box 19.1). This chapter examines maritime crime affecting international commercial seafaring because such crimes involve 80 percent of world trade. Generally, most maritime crime involves the exploitation of legal and legislative weakness in the transportation system.

Box 19.1. Maritime Jurisdictional Zones

Maritime jurisdiction extends up to 200 nautical miles (nm) from the low-water mark of the shoreline (a line drawn along irregular parts of the coastline). Jurisdictional zones include:

internal waters zone – which extends from the territorial sea baseline landward
territorial sea zone – which extends from baseline 12 nm seaward
contiguous zone – for which states may take limited enforcement action related to customs, immigration, and pollution 12-24 nm from the shore
exclusive economic zone – which extends from 12-200 nm seaward, wherein the state can explore and exploit resources providing that they protect and conserve the marine environment
continental shelf zone – which may extend beyond the 200-nm limit and is subject to the same jurisdiction as the exclusive economic zone.

Beyond these zones are the *high seas*, which are public waters.

THE MARITIME TRANSPORTATION SYSTEM

To understand how the system can be exploited, it is necessary to consider the legal authority of flag states and enforcement that creates opportunities for maritime crime.

Legal Authority of Flag States

Ships, like people, must have a single, documented nationality in order to call on foreign ports and to travel the high seas. Seagoing vessels acquire a flag or nationality by registering with a country that is then referred to as the "flag state." Registration brings the vessel under the legal authority of the country of registration. To attract a large merchant fleet (and the tax base provided by these ships), countries offer economic incentives (i.e., increased profitability by avoiding labor laws) and administrative conveniences (i.e., rapid registration with few inspection requirements).

A vessel is said to be flying a flag of convenience (FOC registry) when it is registered with a nation that permits foreign-owned or -controlled vessels to fly its flag when it is convenient and opportune. With no "genuine link" between flag state and vessel operations, it is thought that the registry is unable to regulate the administrative, technical, and social matters of its fleet as specified in Article 91 of the Law of the Sea (1982). Honduras, Liberia, Malta, Netherlands Antilles, and Panama are generally considered FOC registries.

Classification societies (comprised of ship owners, builders, and marine underwriters) focus on ensuring the structural integrity of vessels; in exchange for a fee, they issue certificates of compliance following inspection of the hull structure, engine, and other critical components. Large classification societies (e.g., Lloyd's Register of Shipping) locate offices at key ports around the world. This accessibility leads nations to "hire" classification societies to inspect vessels, thereby delegating statutory responsibility to private interests to ensure that the fleet is in compliance.

Competition enables owners to "shop around" to find the cheapest classification society willing to certify the vessel, and typically this is the one that enforces the least stringent standards. With a certificate of compliance, the vessel may be insured by underwriters. Distributing liability amongst multiple insurance agents reduces the risk for loss and increases the opportunity for operators to run substandard ships.

MARITIME LAW ENFORCEMENT

Law enforcement on the world's waterways is a challenging endeavor for all coast guard fleets. Generally, jurisdiction is related to three factors:

1) the nationality of the vessel in question (flag states have full jurisdiction over their own vessels)
2) the physical location of a foreign vessel in question (if the vessel is within the territorial sea there are internationally sanctioned boarding and inspection rights)
3) the status of the vessel in question (i.e., a warship can be used to board a vessel when there are reasonable grounds to suspect that a foreign vessel is engaged in piracy, engaged in the slave trade, or if the ship refuses to show its flag)

Coast guard fleets have the combined functions of a state highway patrol and customs and border inspection; as such, the coast guard is responsible for vessel safety inspection, waterways management, enforcement of immigration law, drug trafficking interdiction, and homeland security in ports, harbors, and along the coastline. The immense area (about 6 million square miles with 9,500 miles of coastline containing hundreds of ports) of the Marine Transportation System (MTS) falling within the United States Coast Guard's (USCG) jurisdiction exemplifies the geographic challenges facing all coast guard operations.

Due to the size and complexity of the global MTS, much of the system remains a self-policing environment with economic incentives not to comply with shipping conventions. The International Maritime Organization (IMO) is the only international body that negotiates with flag states to set shipping standards – standards that include antipiracy equipment, crew training, and vessel integrity. The IMO relies on flag nations to enforce standards, and flag nations may, in turn, rely on classifications societies. Generally, coast guard fleets are expected to police all activity within territorial waters, but not all fleets are equally equipped to handle this daunting task. It is these system weaknesses that are exploited by maritime criminals.

MARITIME CRIMES

Trafficking

Maritime trafficking involves the illicit transport of legal goods, illicit substances, and people from origin nations to land-based distribution networks located in transitory or primary consuming countries. Materials and humans can be smuggled in a variety of ways:

- hidden in shipping containers, goods, or vessel compartments
- transferred at sea from "mother ships" to smaller accomplice vessels (i.e., trawlers)
- dropped from airplanes to small boats

Human smuggling. Between 2016 and 2018, the Mediterranean migrant crisis captured media attention around the world. Assessing the crisis across this period, the International Organization for Migration, the UN migration agency, found evidence that the crisis was beginning to ebb. Estimates suggest that during the first 16 weeks of 2018, 18,939 migrants and refugees entered Europe by sea, with most people arriving in Italy (42 percent), Greece (38 percent), and Spain (20 percent). This compares with 44,058 arrivals across the region through the same period last year, and 205,613 at this time in 2016.

Access to Western Europe is often gained through Italy's 7,600-kilometer coastline. Launched from Libya, many of these small vessels, painted blue to avoid detection by searchlights, are unable to safely cross 660 miles to the coast; estimates suggest that more than 20,000 people have drowned en route as many attempt the crossing in small fishing vessels ill-equipped for the voyage.

Importantly, human smuggling is not a new issue for maritime authorities. For instance, a report by the IMO states that between 1999 and 2008, member countries investigated 1,667 maritime incidents involving 61,413 illegal migrants. Given the poor mechanisms for developing a global figure, this number is thought to grossly underestimate the magnitude of the human smuggling problem.

Drug smuggling. The estimated volume of the illicit drug trade is staggering; estimates by the non-profit research and advisory organization Global Financial Integrity suggest that the global market in drug trafficking has an estimated value of between US$426 billion and US$652 billion (May, 2017). Much of this trade moves through the MTS. For example, during the 2017 fiscal year, the USCG and its interagency partners seized over 455,000 pounds of cocaine, worth more than US$6 billion wholesale – a US record for most cocaine seized in a single year. But this is not all of the cocaine removed from the market. The USCG estimates that due to its interdiction actions, 223.8 metric tons, about 8.2 percent of the flow headed toward the USA, was prevented from entering the illicit drug market.

Creativity increases in response to tightening border controls on land. Recently, cocaine was found: dissolved in diesel fuel; loaded in self-propelled, semi-submersible (SPSS) vessels; and, strapped, unbeknown to the vessels' crews, to the hulls of commercial ships (this practice is called "torpedoing").

To combat illicit trafficking, many US Coast Guard operations are working to secure funds to modernize their fleets. In addition, many join forces with the US Navy to supplement patrol resources. For example, through the Posse Comitatus Act (18 USC 1385) and provisions under 10 USC 371–78, the USCG can use US Navy vessels to board and inspect ships. This joint action has been useful in combating the flow of illicit goods and illegal migration.

PIRACY AND ARMED ROBBERY

Piracy and armed robbery have plagued maritime transportation for centuries. The legal distinction between these crimes is geographically based. "Piracy" refers to international crimes involving acts of violence, vessel detention, or depredation by the crew or passengers of a private ship on international waters against another ship, persons, or property aboard. When the same actions occur within the jurisdiction of the flag state – in other words, while the vessel is at the home port – then the crime is labeled an armed robbery.

During the first quarter of 2018, pirates were most active off the coast of Nigeria, and on the waters near Indonesia. But this is a new trend. Political, social, and economic factors exacerbate piracy levels, causing regional flare-ups. For example, while Nigeria and Indonesia were hotspots during the first quarter of 2018, of the 240 reported cases between January and June in 2009, 41.7 percent occurred in the Gulf of Aden and 18.3 percent occurred near Somalia.

Examining the 927 incidents occurring January 1, 2014 to March 31, 2018 reveals that, on average, 215 attacks are reported annually. Most of these attacks involve boarding of the vessel (73.5 percent), which often results in the crew being taken hostage or kidnapped. Statistics collected by the IMB suggest that 50 percent of attacks on merchant vessels occur when the vessel is anchored in port or is berthed, and that the other half of attacks occur when vessels are underway. This marks a notable shift in attack status – previously, most vessels were attacked while berthed. Pirates typically fire automatic weapons and rocket-propelled grenades (RPGs) in their effort to board and hijack vessels. In some situations, pirates hijack fishing vessels and other ocean-going vessels, monitor radio frequencies, and launch attacks on steaming vessels.

The underreporting problem makes it difficult to ascertain the full extent of this crime. Manufacturers that own the cargo (shippers), companies that own the vessels (carriers), and the insurers of the vessels and cargo (underwriters) all have a vested interest in preventing piracy and armed robbery; however, as with other forms of business victimization, many corporate interests often decide not to report incidents, electing to absorb losses rather than face increased insurance costs for placing claims or incurring investigation related delays (i.e., operators can lose thousands of dollars each day in port costs). It is likely that the actual costs are in the billions annually.

To combat piracy, some carriers employ armed guards, while others turn to technological enhancements such as nonlethal electrified fences to deter boarding attempts, and satellite ship-tracking systems with emergency silent alarm buttons to automatically alert owners and authorities of attack. The IMO Regulation SOLAS XI-2/6 adopted in December of 2002 requires all vessels weighing more than 500 gross tons to be equipped with silent alarm systems by July 2004.

Cooperative military action between Southeast Asian nations has improved the situation in recent years. Since February 2009, an Internationally Recognized Transit Corridor (IRTC) has been established; strategic deployment of military assets (naval and air) along this corridor has augmented the private security precautions many shipmasters must adopt to secure transport through these areas.

BUILDING LAW ENFORCEMENT CAPACITY OF PORT STATES

Despite significant efforts on the part of the IMO and classification societies to establish shipping standards, as well as by flag states to police their fleets through coast guard operations, there is a critical need for multinational, cooperative law enforcement efforts. Enhancing port state control of maritime traffic is probably the most effective method of improving law enforcement capacity to combat many forms of fraud, illegal immigration, drug trafficking, and piracy. This is likely the case because all ships must dock to both unload cargo and take on supplies.

Proponents of "harmonized inspection" programs argue that cooperative enforcement strengthens international conventions; vessels failing to adhere to international standards or to carry the necessary documentation face a blanket ban from all ports in the region. Inspections check for compliance with various IMO conventions, such as the International Convention for the Safety of Life at Sea (SOLAS 74/78/88). Vessels are targeted when they enter a port for the first time or after an extended absence, if a flag state has a high detention rate, or if the vessel carries dangerous or polluting goods.

When detained, all costs incurred by the port state are charged to the owner or operator of the ship. Detentions are not lifted until payment is made in full. Of the five regional organizations, Paris MOU is the oldest (originated in 1982). Member nations inspect at least 25 percent of the foreign merchant ships entering their ports and share the information, which produces a regional coverage averaging between 85 and 95 percent. The Democratic People's Republic of Korea, Bolivia, Albania, Moldova, and Dominica are the poorest-performing flags.

Consolidated inspection information is publicly available; it typically includes access to an inspection database and access to a list of flag states with consistently poor safety records, names ships with poor safety records, lists ships with multiple detentions, provides details about banned ships, and contains detailed reports of "rust buckets."

Cyber technology affects all aspects of governance, and presently coast guard organizations worldwide are focused on building the necessary infrastructure and capacity to deal with cyber security threats launched against ports and other critical features of maritime transportation systems. With about 360 sea and river ports, handling more than US$1.3 trillion in annual cargo, the US economy is dependent on a secure and efficient MTS. Consequently, the USCG works with partner organizations to maintain a complex, globally networked system of cyber technology.

CONCLUSIONS

Commercial operations span the globe and while every nation has the right to maintain a merchant fleet, the MTS cannot adequately monitor all vessels.

(1) Legal authority does not rest with a single body; rather, law enforcement relies upon a mosaic of coast guard operations with varying capacities and resources, voluntary compliance with international conventions set, and the vigilance of flag nations.

(2) The self-policing apparatus of the maritime transportation industry developed various circular spheres of influence.

(3) Economic incentives to violate international shipping conventions, violate laws, and "cheat" the system are abundant, particularly given the disjointed nature of operations spanning across several nations and thousands of miles.

(4) Geographic and resource challenges impact on the ability of coast guard operations to effectively patrol and control ship movement.

Harmonized port inspection programs, in conjunction with joint enforcement efforts of navy and coast guard operations, can strengthen enforcement efforts aimed at suppressing maritime crime. If met with similar efforts by private interests – shippers (manufacturers that own the cargo), carriers (vessel owners and operators), and insurers – to harden soft targets, inroads can be made to improve the safety and efficiency of the MTS while reducing crime.

REFERENCE

May, C. (2017). *Transnational crime and the developing world*. Washington, DC: Global Financial Integrity.

WEBSITES

International Transport Workers' Federation (ITF). www.itfglobal.org/index.cfm.
International Maritime Organization (IMO). www.imo.org.
Paris MOU, the model cooperative port state inspection program. www.parismou.org.
ICC International Maritime Bureau (IMB). www.icc-ccs.org.
World Maritime News. www.worldmaritimenews.com.

20 Worldwide Maritime Piracy and the Implications for Situational Crime Prevention

Jon M. Shane and Shannon Magnuson

INTRODUCTION

Water covers nearly 75 percent of the earth's surface, so why should anyone believe crime is exclusive to land? There is a long and colorful history of victims and offenders of piracy on the high seas. Many believe Julius Caesar was an early victim of pirates, captured on a voyage across the Aegean Sea. Before pillaging coastal villages, the Norse Vikings first attacked ships at sea. However, seventeenth-century buccaneers who reigned across Caribbean waters and captured the imagination of Hollywood are far from reality. In the modern context, pirates are well armed and well resourced, more akin to state-sponsored terrorists. The 1985 hijacking of the *Achille Lauro* and the 2009 (Halberstam, 1988) hijacking of the *Alabama Maersk* are classic examples of modern piracy, where crew or passengers are killed and/or taken hostage and held for ransom. While these might appear as isolated cases ripe for a movie plot, hundreds of ships and their crew experience piracy each year. This is largely a result of increasing reliance on international trade in both developed and emerging nations; nearly 90 percent of the world's trade travels by sea, increasing maritime traffic and creating opportunities for maritime crime (Ho, 2006).

Traditional criminal justice approaches are limited in their effectiveness and are complicated in the maritime setting by conflicting definitions of piracy, jurisdictional issues, complex international law, slow-moving diplomatic relations, uncooperative governments, corruption in failed states, and weak judicial systems that are ill-equipped for the job. A better approach is to focus on the opportunity structure that enables piracy, including the interplay between victims, offenders, and environmental conditions. Situational crime prevention (SCP) is a method that accounts for this interconnectedness and is effective across a wide variety of crime conditions, including piracy, with little or no evidence of displacement (Clarke, 1997).

BACKGROUND

Limitations on the Definition of Piracy

Identifying the nature and scope of any crime problem depends on its definition. Slight variations in behavior can change the reporting, classification, and sanctioning structure.

Different definitions of piracy from the 1958 Geneva Convention on the High Seas[1] and the 1982 United Nations Convention on the Law of the Sea[2] complicate how the industry captures the scope of the problem. As such, the full extent of piracy and its cost to the global economy remains unknown.[3] For example, burglary and theft are not mentioned in the Geneva Convention, or the United Nations Convention. Therefore, it may not be accurate or legally appropriate to classify theft, burglary, or robbery – in certain circumstances – as an act of piracy when it occurs inside territorial waters or port facilities. Whether these crimes should be considered acts of piracy when they do not occur in international waters is subject to debate; however, including these definitions as part of maritime piracy changes the nature and scope of the problem, the prevention measures used to protect ships against attacks, and the processes for prosecution.

Piracy-Prone Regions Worldwide

Despite these definitional issues, the International Maritime Bureau (IMB) documents the number of attempted and successful piracy attacks across the globe. The IMB notes the height of modern piracy occurred in 2000, with a 400-percent increase from the onset of official reporting in 1990 (IMB, 2000) (Figure 20.1). Across IMB reporting years, there is an uneven distribution of attacks globally; in the 1990s, Southeast Asia experienced nearly 50 percent of global attacks, and in recent years piracy has been concentrated off the coast of Africa (IMB, 2017). Specifically, attacks cluster along the coast of Somalia, Nigeria, and the Gulf of Aden, as well as other parts of the world, including the Gulf of Guinea, the coast of Sri Lanka, and Indonesia. Analyzing clusters of attacks suggests these regions are hotbeds of piracy, where risk of attack at the same location or nearby is temporarily elevated following the first incident, a concept known as near-repeat offending (Marchione & Johnson, 2013). Similar to land-based crime such as burglary and robbery, where criminals return to certain locations based on the success they have had, pirates do the same. Once pirates perceive an area as conducive to successful attacks, they are likely to strike again in the near future, but repeated attacks in the exact same location may lead shipping companies to avoid those routes or increase the risk that pirates will be captured.

Although Figure 20.1 indicates piracy is on the decline from its height in 2000, attacks are increasingly violent. Pirates armed with guns and knives only represented 3 percent of total attacks in 1991 compared to 53 percent in 2017 (IMB, 2017), with guns as the favored weapon. Moreover, piracy for ransom continues to yield considerable financial sums, and from 2013 to 2017, 78 percent of all attacks involved a hostage situation (IMB, 2017). These figures may be a conservative estimate since reporting hijacking and hostage situations are voluntary. Shipping companies may elect not to report to avoid increases to their insurance rates, delays to their ship's itinerary, added expenses, and threats to their company's reputation.

---

[1] Retrieved from www.gc.noaa.gov/documents/8_1_1958_high_seas.pdf.

[2] Retrieved from www.un.org/depts/los/convention_agreements/texts/unclos/unclos_e.pdf.

[3] The IMB Piracy Reporting Centre follows the definition of "Piracy" codified by Article 101 of the 1982 United Nations Convention on the Law of the Sea. The IMB follows the definition of "Armed Robbery" as codified by Resolution A.1025 (26) adopted December 2, 2009 at the 26th Assembly Session of the International Maritime Organization (IMO). Retrieved from www.icc-ccs.org/piracy-reporting-centre.

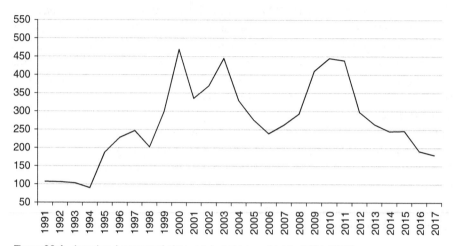

Figure 20.1. Actual and attempted piracy against ships worldwide, 1991–2017.
Source: 1991–2017 IMB Piracy and Armed Robbery Against Ships Annual Report

Economic Implications

Piracy exacts a dreadful economic toll, especially for ransom. Some insurance underwriters require shippers to carry war-risk insurance when traveling in certain waters around Africa and Indonesia; in some instances, insurance rates have increased nearly tenfold when traveling through these waters (Lansing & Peterson, 2011). Rerouting vessels to avoid the risk and high insurance premiums can add time and costs to a ship's journey, and require additional vessels to maintain frequency of delivery due to the extended trade routes (Lansing & Peterson, 2011).

Other direct costs include using private armed security and union agreements for double compensation to workers traveling in vulnerable areas. Some researchers estimate that these issues, coupled with increasing ransom payments, cost the global community between US$7 and US$12 billion annually (Bowden, 2010).[4] These costs are often absorbed into higher insurance premiums and considered the "cost of business" by the shipping industry. In reality this translates into higher prices for consumer goods. As a result, many nations have a stake in reducing maritime piracy and participating in anti-piracy agreements through traditional policing efforts and legal mechanisms.

Gaps, Inadequacies, and Current Antipiracy Efforts

To deter piracy and ransom, the global community largely turned its attention to international cooperation through naval support such as the Cooperation and Readiness Afloat and Training (CARAT) program conducted by the US Pacific Fleet and several member nations in Southeast Asia. The intent is to enhance regional cooperation while developing

---

[4] Estimates are in US dollars.

international relations. Following escalating piracy around the Horn of Africa in 2005 – specifically attacks against United Nations (UN) aid ships – the USA played a major role in adopting a resolution urging states with naval support assets in the area to actively engage in combating piracy. The Combined Task Force 151, a multinational naval task force operating under the North Atlantic Treaty Organization (NATO) and the European Union (UN), provided legal authority to any country's naval fleet to pursue pirates in Somali waters and encouraged an international effort against piracy (Roach, 2010). However, participating fleets are principally employed in reactive capacities and responsible for 2.5 million square miles of water (Shortland & Vothknecht, 2011), an exceptionally large jurisdiction keeping systematic law enforcement at bay. Naval peacekeeping efforts are extraordinarily expensive, consume precious resources, and their effectiveness for combating piracy is not fully known.

To complicate matters, the apprehending naval fleet, the flag of the vessel, the company chartering the ship, the insurance carrier, and the pirates' country of origin may be from different nations. This creates jurisdictional confusion, and makes prosecution cumbersome and, in some cases, impossible. Furthermore, international sanctions for piracy do not mandate that nations take a universal jurisdiction approach to prosecution (Roach, 2010). The interjurisdictional complexity enables states to disengage from prosecuting pirates without fear of legal consequence. For example, maritime prosecutions from 1998 to 2009 indicate only 17 instances of pirate attacks in international waters, and less than 1.5 percent resulted in prosecution by universal jurisdiction laws (Kontorovich & Art, 2010). The low prosecution rate may be the result of differing legal definitions needed to prosecute pirates, but nonetheless highlights the difficulty in reducing piracy through legal mechanisms. Moreover, in 2008, a UN sanction and US presidential order banned ransom payments to known maritime criminals. The directives threatened imprisonment and fines to private companies and individuals who knowingly pay ransom (Shortland & Vothknecht, 2010), effectively criminalizing how companies react to piracy. The shipping industry and countries that rely on maritime commerce have voiced their opposition, fearing increased risks to crew and cargo, and argue that paying ransom is the only option for securing safe release of their crew (Shortland & Vothknecht, 2010).

While these efforts are commendable, they are expensive, reactive, and cumbersome. As such, maritime piracy is likely to remain stable without greater emphasis on *prevention* techniques that shipping crews can use locally, such as SCP (Fu, Ng & Lau, 2010).

AN EMERGING APPROACH TO CONTROLLING AND PREVENTING PIRACY

Shane and Magnuson (2014) conducted the first successful test of SCP theory in a worldwide piracy context. Their study used publicly available data from the IMB Piracy Reporting Center (2000–2012). They classified how ships employed various defense maneuvers to understand how principles of SCP may affect successful or unsuccessful attacks. These maneuvers were classified according to the SCP framework and include: 1) ships increasing pirates' perceived effort (vessel performed evasive maneuvers, increased speed; employed an electric perimeter fence); 2) ships increasing the perceived risk to pirates (raised the alarm; watchman were present; anti-piracy watch in effect; private security embarked; increased lighting); and 3) ships reducing rewards (crew mustered to a central location). The analyses showed that when ships used any of these local prevention efforts, unsuccessful attacks were more likely, and explained 41.5 percent of the variability in successful and unsuccessful attacks. Other research found similar results for SCP and piracy. Keeping watch and enhanced vigilance (i.e., watchmen and anti-piracy watch) combined with at least two other protective measures substantially increased the likelihood of an unsuccessful attack (Bryant, Townsley, & Leclerc, 2014).

Following Shane and Magnuson's study, researchers again used SCP principles and IMB data (2000–2013) to test whether the global effect of SCP was consistent across individual continents. A series of mixed-effects logistic regression models and follow-up likelihood ratio tests showed that SCP techniques were associated with increases in unsuccessful piracy attacks on a global scale. When examined individually, SCP techniques were equally effective on each continent, except employing multiple techniques classified within the *increased effort* technique of SCP was associated with an increased likelihood of unsuccessful attacks in only three (Southeast Asia, the Far East, and Rest of the World) of the six regions in the study (Shane, Piza, & Mandalla, 2015). This may reflect the varied sophistication of piracy on each continent, but it also highlights the limitations of SCP techniques. The effectiveness of SCP at increasing unsuccessful pirate attacks worldwide led researchers to believe the technique may be capable of reducing violent ransom hijackings. The findings revealed that SCP was a useful strategy for reducing hijackings for ransom and injuries, again highlighting how SCP can be adapted in unique environments when other traditional crime control resources are not available (Shane, Piza, & Silva, 2017).

Although a ship's crew can employ SCP at the individual level to control piracy, one recent advancement in research revealed how "super controllers" (those responsible for creating incentives for controllers – handlers, place managers, and guardians – to prevent crime) can exert their influence to control piracy (Townsley, Leclerc, & Tatham, 2015, p. 537). Introducing super controllers such as Combined Task Force 151 and Operation Ocean Shield (place manager interventions), the Trust Fund to Support the Initiatives of States Countering Piracy off the Coast of Somalia (handler interventions), and armed security aboard ships (guardian interventions) coincided with sudden declines in piracy in 2009, 2010, and 2011 as each was implemented (Townsley et al., 2015).

CONCLUSION

Increased globalization highlights the dependency on maritime trade. Relying on the shipping industry to move goods increases vulnerability to pirates motivated by the potential for high financial gain and low risk of apprehension and prosecution. Although recent reports indicate a decline in the total number of pirate attacks since 2000, it is clear modern piracy is increasingly violent and costly to maritime companies compared to earlier decades. As such, situational crime prevention offers more promise as a long-term sustainable solution to crime than traditional arrest and prosecution. Despite its limitations, SCP is appealing because merchant vessels can become more self-reliant and avoid implementation issues associated with crime prevention techniques that involve multiple agencies and nation-states. Adopting deliberate SCP techniques holds promise to significantly reduce successful pirate attacks and improve maritime safety across the globe.

REFERENCES

Bowden, A. (2010). The economic cost of maritime piracy. *One Earth Future Working Paper*. Broomfield, CO: One Earth.

Bryant, W., Townsley, M., & Leclerc, B. (2014). Preventing maritime pirate attacks: A conjunctive analysis of the effectiveness of ship protection measures recommended by the international maritime organisation. *Journal of Transportation Security*, 7(1), 69–82.

Clarke, R. V. (Ed.). (1997). *Situational crime prevention*. Monsey, NY: Criminal Justice Press.

Fu, X., Ng, A. K., & Lau, Y. Y. (2010). The impacts of maritime piracy on global economic development: The case of Somalia. *Maritime Policy & Management*, 37(7), 677–697.

Halberstam, M. (1988). Terrorism on the high seas: The Achille Lauro, piracy and the IMO convention on maritime safety. *American Journal of International Law*, 82(2), 269–310.

Ho, J. (2006). The security of sea lanes in Southeast Asia. *Asian Survey*, 46(4), 558–574.

International Maritime Bureau. (2000). *Piracy and armed robbery against ships annual report*. London: IMB.

(2017). *Piracy and armed robbery against ships annual report*. London: IMB.

Kontorovich, E. & Art, S. (2010). An empirical examination of universal jurisdiction for piracy. *The American Journal of International Law*, 104(3), 436–453.

Lansing, P. & Peterson, M. (2011). Ship-owners and the twenty first century Somali pirate: The business ethics of ransom payment. *Journal of Business Ethics*, 102, 507–516.

Marchione, E. & Johnson, S. (2013). Spatial, temporal & spatio-temporal patterns of maritime piracy. *Journal of Research in Crime and Delinquency*, 50(4), 504–524.

Roach, J. (2010). Countering piracy off Somalia: International law and international institutions. *The American Journal of International Law*, 104(3), 397–416.

Shane, J. M. & Magnuson, S. (2014). Successful and unsuccessful pirate attacks worldwide: A situational analysis. *Justice Quarterly*, 33(4), 682–707.

Shane, J. M., Piza, E. L., & Mandala, M. (2015). Situational crime prevention and worldwide piracy: a cross-continent analysis. *Crime Science*, 4(1), 21.

Shane, J. M., Piza, E. L., & Silva, J. R. (2017). Piracy for ransom: The implications for situational crime prevention. *Security Journal*, 1–22.

Shortland, A. & Vothknecht, M. (2010). *Discussion papers combating "maritime terrorism" off the coast of Somalia*. Berlin: German Institute for Economic Research.

(2011). *Combating "maritime terrorism" off the coast of Somalia*. Economics of Security Working Paper 47. Berlin: Economics of Security.

Townsley, M., Leclerc, B., & Tatham, P. H. (2015). How super controllers prevent crimes: Learning from modern maritime piracy. *British Journal of Criminology*, 56(3), 537–557.

WEBSITES

International Maritime Bureau, Piracy Reporting Center. www.icc-ccs.org/piracy-reporting-centre.

Regional Cooperation Agreement on Combating Piracy and Armed Robbery against Ships in Asia (ReCAAP). www.recaap.org/.

Maritime Security Centre, Horn of Africa. www.mschoa.org/on-shore/home.

Center for Problem-Oriented Policing. popcenter.asu.edu/.

21 Poaching of Terrestrial Wild Animals and Plants

Lauren Wilson and Ronald V. Clarke

INTRODUCTION

Poaching, the illegal taking of protected wild animals or plants, is often the first step in the trafficking of wildlife and, broadly defined, it also includes illegal commercial fishing. Kurland deals with wildlife trafficking in his chapter for this volume (Chapter 9) and Petrossian and Clarke cover illegal fishing in theirs (Chapter 22). This chapter therefore focuses exclusively on the poaching of land-dwelling plants and animals. While not a new crime – poaching was widespread in the royal forests of medieval Britain – recent times have seen a vast increase in the international attention it has attracted.

Poaching threatens thousands of species and ecosystems worldwide – from North American cacti to tropical rainforests, from Venus fly traps to African elephants. Conservation biologists often focus on biodiversity hotspots (areas with extreme diversity of life under heavy threat from human activities), and the media have generally focused on charismatic megafauna (e.g., elephants, tigers, and rhinos). Criminologists, on the other hand, are interested in poaching because, in common with other crimes, it is concentrated spatially, temporally, by product (species), and by the nature of the offender (poacher) (Kurland et al., 2017).

THE DIVERSITY OF POACHING

Poaching includes any of a broad range of prohibited acts (though not retaliatory killings of wild animals that have killed livestock), which are summarized below.

- The targeted species is illegal to hunt or take at any time.
- The activity occurs in a protected area (e.g., a forest reserve or protected migratory habitat).
- The activity occurs outside of a legal hunting, fishing, or harvesting season.
- The activity uses banned equipment (e.g., unpermitted firearms, prohibited baiting of animals with food).
- Plants or animals below the legal age or size limit are taken.

Within this diversity, poaching serves a variety of purposes. Rare orchids are stolen from the wild to sell to collectors, and illegal logging meets the global demand for timber

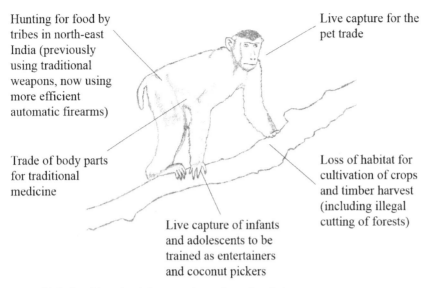

Hunting for food by tribes in north-east India (previously using traditional weapons, now using more efficient automatic firearms)

Live capture for the pet trade

Trade of body parts for traditional medicine

Loss of habitat for cultivation of crops and timber harvest (including illegal cutting of forests)

Live capture of infants and adolescents to be trained as entertainers and coconut pickers

Figure 21.1. Poaching-related threats to the northern pig-tailed macaque.
Source: Based on an original photograph by Mike Prince

resources. Wildlife may be targeted for both local and international markets. Pires and Clarke (2011) found that the natural ranges of most parrots sold in an illegal market in Santa Cruz, Bolivia began within 50 miles of the market. On the other hand, African elephant tusks comprise most of the ivory traded in Asia. Poachers' methods are also highly variable, even for one species or location. For example, within a single protected area some poachers might use vines and bicycle brake wires to construct snares for small and medium-sized animals, while other poachers might shoot animals of any size that they happen upon.

Some animals may be eaten, enjoyed as a pet or tourist attraction, used for cultural practices, and hunted for recreation. The northern pig-tailed macaque, for example, is subject to multiple crimes, not just poaching for various uses, but also illegal encroachment into protected areas and felling of trees in the protected areas in which it dwells (Boonratana et al., 2008). (See Figure 21.1.)

WHY IS POACHING DIFFICULT TO STUDY?

Poaching is difficult to study because of its many manifestations and because it is difficult to measure. Official data on poaching often do not exist or are unreliable, resulting in wide ranges of estimates, forcing researchers to use different methods of estimation. For example, INTERPOL reports that annual losses to illegal logging are anywhere from US$30 to US$100 billion (Nellemann et al., 2016). Additionally, much of the data collected by government agencies or conservation organizations is not made public or shared privately with researchers, creating barriers to research and evidence-based prevention strategies.

WHAT ARE THE HARMS OF POACHING?

Environmental and Economic

The basic premise of ecology is that life is interdependent on its environment; when a population or species is lost, perhaps to over-hunting, its entire ecosystem is affected. Some conservationists support a conservation ethic that emphasizes the intrinsic value of nature and they argue that humans have a responsibility to prevent extinction due to their activities. According to this perspective, the harms of poaching are obvious.

Naidoo et al. (2016) offer one example of the direct economic impacts of poaching; they estimate that the ecotourism industry in Africa suffers annual losses of US$25 million as a result of elephant poaching. Indirect effects of poaching include damage to resources on which communities rely and the loss of ecosystem services (e.g., air and water purification and mitigation of flood and drought damage). Illegal logging can harm local and regional economies by weakening or even eliminating some of these services, and it is known to pollute local drinking water with contaminants such as toxic metals. Because illegally logged timber is thought to represent 15–30 percent of the global market (Nellemann et al., 2016), and because it is relatively inexpensive, it depresses the global price of timber, producing an estimated US$10 billion lost from the global market yearly, plus an additional US$5 billion in lost tax revenue (The World Bank, 2006).

Political and Social

Poaching disproportionately affects developing nations. It results in losses of billions of dollars in potential tax revenue, incentivizes government corruption, and in extreme cases creates security concerns, all of which further exacerbate political fragility and economic challenges (Nellemann et al., 2016). Consider the entrenchment of armed poachers in the Democratic Republic of Congo's Salonga National Park, which exceeded the capacity of enforcement staff and required a coordinated sweep of the park by the Congolese military in 2011. This example illustrates how a local poaching problem can escalate into more serious conflict that can disrupt local communities and prevent economic investment and development.

Another example of harm to developing countries is the Gibson Guitar Corporation's exploitation of political instability in Madagascar for the procurement of protected ebony. The company was heavily fined under the US Lacey Act for importing wood products from Madagascar knowing that the wood had been illegally extracted (US Department of Justice, 2012). Severe political instability in Madagascar throughout the 2000s provided an opportunity for logging operators to illegally extract timber resources with minimal risk and for international buyers to procure this illicitly sourced commodity.

Human fatalities represent an extreme potentiality of poaching. The International Union for the Conservation of Nature (IUCN, 2014) reported that in 2013 poachers and militias killed 69 park rangers. Less is known about the number of poachers killed by park rangers. Some park authorities have empowered park rangers to use lethal force against suspected poachers. For example, rangers in India's Kaziranga National Park have been given the authority to shoot anyone in the park at night, though the director claims considerable action is taken before lethal outcomes to apprehend trespassers (Sputnik, 2017). Nonetheless,

23 suspected poachers (including two boys who accidentally wandered into the park) were killed in 2015, more than the number of greater one-horned rhinoceroses poached in the same park that year.

WHY IS POACHING DIFFICULT TO REDUCE?

As mentioned previously, limited poaching data precludes a comprehensive understanding of poaching and the problems specific to particular species or places. Without this understanding, neither short- nor long-term prevention strategies can be expected to yield strong results. Furthermore, political and economic realities challenge enforcement; particularly in poor countries, a small number of park rangers may be tasked with monitoring huge expanses of land with inadequate equipment and sometimes lacking basic necessities such as good-quality boots. Limited economic opportunities incentivize local people to poach and low ranger pay can incentivize bribery.

In many places, hunting was once commonplace and has only recently been criminalized. A study that documented hunting practices and meat preferences in a remote town in the Philippines found that even local law enforcement officials engaged in poaching, which was not regarded as a risky or criminal behavior (Scheffers et al., 2012).

WHAT HAS BEEN DONE?

The main response to poaching from conservationists has been to call for tougher penalties for wildlife offenses as well as increases for enforcement budgets or staff. Many countries have been influenced by this pressure, including, for example, Zimbabwe, which amended its Parks and Wildlife Act in 2011 to change the three-year mandatory maximum prison sentence for wildlife offenses to a nine-year mandatory minimum.

Increasingly, as poaching levels do not respond to these punitive interventions, a militarized approach to conservation has been adopted (Duffy, 2014), as exemplified by the aforementioned ranger policies in Kaziranga National Park, India. Militarized conservation portrays poachers as combatants, uses military technologies and weaponry, employs former military personnel, and uses rhetoric that depicts national parks as battlefields. These extreme measures may alienate local people whose help is needed to prevent poaching.

Programs in Caribbean nations that strive to stimulate national pride in their rare parrots have worked to protect these birds. An alternative approach is ecotourism, which provides an economic incentive for locals to stop poaching. Ecotourist lodges throughout the world attract tourists to see wildlife close-up and can to contribute to the local economy. Munn (1992) has suggested that the clay-licks in Peru, which attract large flocks of macaws, could support ecotourism, but only if the local population were given ownership of the clay-licks and could reap the profits of the tourism. This is a key point: ecotourism fails to achieve local support and meet conservation goals if it fails to provide local economic benefit, as is the case when the industry is primarily owned by foreigners or wealthy nationals and when it is not staffed by members of local communities.

Regulated sport hunting operations carry similar risks of alienating local communities but can have similar beneficial effects if locals are integrated. Sport hunting can provide very large returns to state governments through permits costing hundreds to thousands of dollars. Assuming corruption is low, these funds can be used to assist conservation.

Some conservationists propose regulating the supply of wildlife products rather than attempting to ban the trade. Cooney and Jepson (2006) propose managed off-take, *in situ* breeding assistance with nest boxes, or *ex situ* (captive) breeding in range states. They cite a successful program of this kind managed by the Argentine Government that replaced a high-volume, poorly regulated trade in blue-fronted Amazon parrots with a much lower-volume trade that provides about 20 percent of family income for peasant landowners.

Demand reduction strategies are also frequently advocated. These can be successful in shifting norms and attitudes, though this tends to be a long-term approach. For example, demand for shark fin soup appears to have declined in China as result of celebrity-led campaigns, but the effects have not yet been empirically assessed.

HOW CAN CRIMINOLOGY CONTRIBUTE TO PREVENTING POACHING?

Criminology's preventive approaches focus on three distinct levels: primary prevention, which attempts to modify criminogenic conditions of physical and social environments; secondary prevention, which attempts to understand dispositional and background factors that foster criminality and intervene in the lives of those individuals or groups who are exposed to these factors; and tertiary prevention, which attempts to reduce recidivism. One primary prevention approach is situational crime prevention (SCP), which has a record of many published successes. Specificity is a key premise of SCP, which in the present context means that each of the many varieties of poaching would need to be studied separately if feasible preventive measures are to be identified. A short-cut to identifying these measures frequently consists of analyzing how that specific form of poaching is concentrated, for example, spatially, temporally (by season, time of day, etc.), or by species and by the kind of poacher involved. Species victimization studies, such as that conducted by Pires and Clarke (2011), approach poaching similarly to theft by identifying the features of the animal or plant that make it a common or popular choice for poachers. Place-based approaches may identify poaching hot-spots (Eloff & Lemieux, 2014; Kurland et al., 2018), exploring how interventions such as road blocks could impede poachers. Poachers dependent on vehicles could also be deterred by using automatic license plate readers at protected area entry/exits points. Behavioral modeling may elucidate poacher decision making and inform enforcement strategies (Hill et al., 2014). Studying park rangers may also provide key insights into challenges and opportunities for improved prevention (Moreto & Lemieux, 2015).

CONCLUSION

Poaching is a complex crime consisting of a huge variety of acts affecting innumerable species and countless ecosystems. Much has been proposed and much has been done to reduce the harms of poaching, but evaluation of the effectiveness of these remedies has lagged. Many disciplines have a role to play in dealing with poaching, but criminology offers the most immediate prospects for effective prevention.

REFERENCES

Boonratana, R., Das, J., Yongcheng, L., Htun, S. & Timmins, R. J. (2008). *Macaca leonina. The IUCN Red List of Threatened Species.* e.T39792A10257933.

Cooney, R. & Jepson, P. (2006). The international wild bird trade: What's wrong with blanket bans? *Oryx*, 40(1), 18–23.

US Department of Justice. (2012). *Gibson Guitar Corp. agrees to resolve investigation into Lacey Act violations.* Washington, DC: US Department of Justice, Office of Public Affairs. Retrieved from www.justice.gov/opa/pr/gibson-guitar-corp-agrees-resolve-investigation-lacey-act-violations.

Duffy R. (2014). Waging a war to save biodiversity: The rise of militarized conservation. *International Affairs*, 90(4), 819–834.

Eloff, C. & Lemieux, A. M. (2014). Rhino poaching in Kruger National Park, South Africa. In *Situational prevention of poaching* (pp. 18–43). London and New York: Routledge.

Hill, J. F., Johnson, S. D., & Borrion, H. (2014). Potential uses of computer agent-based simulation modelling in the evaluation of wildlife poaching. In *Situational prevention of poaching* (pp. 120–153). London and New York: Routledge.

International Union for the Conservation of Nature (IUCN). (2014). Rising murder toll of park rangers calls for tougher laws. Retrieved from www.iucn.org/content/rising-murder-toll-park-rangers-calls-tougher-laws.

Kurland, J., Pires, S. F., McFann, S. C., & Moreto, W. D. (2017). Wildlife crime: A conceptual integration, literature review, and methodological critique. *Crime Science*, 6(1), 4.

Kurland, J., Pires, S. F., & Marteache, N. (2018). The spatial pattern of redwood burl poaching and implications for prevention. *Forest Policy and Economics*, 94, 46–54.

Moreto, W. D. & Lemieux, A. M. (2015). Poaching in Uganda: Perspectives of law enforcement rangers. *Deviant Behavior*, 36(11), 853–873.

Munn, C. A. (1992). Macaw biology and ecotourism, or "when a bird in the bush is worth two in the hand". In S. R. Beissinger & N. F. R. Snyder (Eds.), *New world parrots in crisis: Solutions from conservation biology* (pp. 47–72). Washington, DC: Smithsonian Institution.

Naidoo, R., Fisher, B., Manica, A., & Balmford, A. (2016). Estimating economic losses to tourism in Africa from the illegal killing of elephants. *Nature Communications*, 7. Retrieved from https://doi.org/10.1038/ncomms13379.

Nellemann, C., Henriksen, R., Kreilhuber, A., Stewart, D., Kotsovou, M., Raxter, P., … Barrat, S. (Eds.). (2016). *The rise of environmental crime: A growing threat to natural resources, peace, development and security.* Nairobi, Kenya: United Nations Environment Programme.

Pires, S. F. & Clarke, R. V. (2011). Sequential foraging, itinerant fences and parrot poaching in Bolivia. *British Journal of Criminology*, 51(2), 314–335.

Scheffers, B. R., Corlett, R. T., Diesmos, A., & Laurance, W. F. (2012). Local demand drives a bushmeat industry in a Philippine forest preserve. *Tropical Conservation Science*, 5(2), 133–141.

Sputnik News. (2017). Indian park rangers protect rhinos by shooting poachers. Retrieved from https://sputniknews.com/environment/201702131050643653-india-national-park-shoot-poachers/.

The World Bank. (2006). *Strengthening forest law enforcement and governance* (No. 36638 – GLB) (p. 93). Washington, DC: The World Bank.

22 Illegal Commercial Fishing

Gohar Petrossian and Ronald V. Clarke

INTRODUCTION

Illegal commercial fishing is one of the world's most serious and complex environmental crimes. More broadly defined as IUU fishing (illegal, unreported, and unregulated), it covers a wide range of activities including: (a) using prohibited gear or methods; (b) taking prohibited species; (c) fishing in prohibited areas, such as no-take Marine Protected Areas; and (c) fishing within a country's Exclusive Economic Zone (EEZ) without its permission. Whether these activities are illegal can crucially depend on local or regional laws and regulations.

THE HARMS OF ILLEGAL FISHING

Economic

Almost all fishing grounds ("fisheries") in the world, large or small, suffer from illegal fishing, due not only to their geographic location, but also to the species coveted by illegal fishers found there. It has been estimated that global fisheries collectively lose about 100,000 pounds of wild-caught fish every minute to illegal fishing (Pew Charitable Trusts, 2013), which makes up US$10–23.5 billion in annual losses. Because more than 90 percent of all commercial fishing occurs within the EEZs of coastal countries, these countries bear the direct impact of these losses. Most of them are economically deprived countries, of which most are in Southeast Asia and Western Africa.

Social

The social impact of illegal fishing on the coastal communities in these countries is much harder to quantify. Illegal fishers, seeking to maximize profit, often hire crews from impoverished countries with lax labor laws and minimal controls on working conditions. This can result in various human rights abuses aboard these vessels, which include withholding food and water, subjecting the crew to sexual, physical, and verbal abuse, and forced labor under dangerous conditions that can last 18 hours a day (EJF, 2010). It has been documented that illegal fishers recruit children, exposing them to the danger of drowning by being forced to dive so that they can guide fish into specialized, encircling nets (ITF, 2006).

Environmental

To minimize costs and maximize their catch, illegal fishers may employ destructive methods, such as bottom trawling, which damages seafloor habitats and kills thousands of tons of fish and other animals living there. They may also use illegal fishing methods, such as blast fishing, and poison and cyanide fishing. Blast fishing involves the use of dynamite set to explode under water and is used in over 30 countries (Chevallier, 2017). This harms not only coral reefs, which are among the most endangered habitats on earth, but it also harms plankton that many reef fish feed on, leading to a significant imbalance in the marine food web system (White et al., 2000). The various poisoning methods also affect the balance in the marine ecosystem. They kill countless small fish or invertebrates and discolor coral colonies. Illegal fishing also leads to overfishing and depletion of fish stocks, making fishing unsustainable.

Illegal fishing also harms many other ocean species not targeted for commercial purposes. Collectively known as "by-catch," these species are incidentally caught and thrown back into the ocean. Many by-catch species, such as turtles, sharks, porpoises, and albatrosses, are critically endangered. When dumped into the oceans in large numbers, they putrefy, creating sterile areas and dead zones (Doughty & Carmichael, 2011).

WHICH COMMERCIAL SPECIES ARE TARGETED?

Tuna, swordfish, cod, hake, herring, orange roughy, and Patagonian toothfish that are directly consumed are among the fish most frequently targeted by illegal commercial fishers. These species are not only relatively more "valuable," but they are also easily "disposable," "available," and more "enjoyable" (Petrossian & Clarke, 2014). Other species, such as the totoaba fish, various sharks, and the Beluga sturgeon, are caught for their parts, which are more prized than their meat. Shark fin is preferred over its meat, the sturgeon is caught for its row (caviar), and the totoaba's swim bladder, dubbed as "aquatic cocaine," is a highly prized delicacy in China.

IS ORGANIZED CRIME INVOLVED IN ILLEGAL COMMERCIAL FISHING?

Organized crime groups have been involved in various specialized fisheries around the world, such as the abalone, rock lobster, and shark fisheries in Australia, the abalone fishery in South Africa, the Beluga sturgeon fishery in the Caspian Sea, and the Patagonian toothfish fishery in the Antarctic. These organized criminal groups use many different strategies to avoid detection, such as modifying fishing boats to create concealed spaces for laundering the illegally caught species, using lookouts and guards to counter surveillance, working in groups to transport and distribute the illegally caught fish, and using fraudulent documents to launder the fish.

Scholars have agreed that acknowledging these groups' activities in the illegal commercial fishing business has the advantage of treating illegal fishing as a "serious crime," rather than simply as a fishery management issue (Telesetsky, 2015).

WHAT FACILITATES ILLEGAL COMMERCIAL FISHING?

Flags of Non-Compliance

According to the United Nations Law of the Sea, every merchant ship must have a flag, i.e., a single documented nationality, so that it can travel the high seas, and, importantly, leave or arrive into a port. Once registered, the vessel is subject to the flag country's regulatory controls and must operate under its laws. These countries, in turn, must maintain a register of the vessels flying their flags, so that they can exercise jurisdiction over these vessels and their crew if any legal issues arise. Importantly, it is the flag country's responsibility to ensure that the vessels not only comply by the domestic but also by international maritime laws.

Many vessels engaged in illegal fishing fly "flags of convenience" (FoC), that is, flags of countries that allow foreign-owned vessels to fly their flags. This is often a way to make money, because some FoC countries do not have the resources, or are unwilling, to monitor and control the activities of vessels flying their flags. Furthermore, they might impede efforts to deal with illegal fishing when called on to deal with the violations of their flagged vessels, either by countries where these vessels are found to be fishing illegally or by regional fisheries management organizations. They simply ignore the calls or impede boarding, inspecting, or penalizing their vessels (which can only be done with their permission) (Behnam & Faust, 2003).

If these FoC countries show any willingness to investigate and penalize the vessel engaged in illegal activity, a vessel's owners may respond by changing the vessel's flag registration, a practice known as "flag hopping." This can easily be done by fax or the Internet in a few minutes and for only a few hundred dollars. It has also been observed that illegal fishing vessels might leave the port with one flag and change their flag to an FoC flag while still at sea, making it extremely difficult to identify and penalize the owners of the vessel.

Ports of Convenience

Once a fishing vessel arrives in a port, it either offloads its catch or transships the fish into another vessel. These activities are generally closely monitored by port inspectors, but some countries do not have the resources to do this and identify either illegally caught fish, or possible other violations (such as illegal gear onboard the vessel). Many ports, collectively referred to as "ports of convenience," are particularly attractive to illegal fishing vessels because they not only offer favorable customs advantages, but also have no transshipment regulations in place. Researchers have found that the ports that have large harbors and experience high vessel traffic, as well as ports located in countries with lax regulations and enforcement, are preferred by illegal fishing vessel owners, because they offer the "concealability" and enforcement avoidance not available elsewhere (Petrossian et al., 2015).

Transshipment at Sea

Another way for illegal fishing vessels to avoid detection is transshipping their catch into refrigerated cargo vessels, where legally and illegally caught fish are mixed and become almost indistinguishable. The transshipping activity, which takes places both in the high seas outside the jurisdiction of coastal countries, and within countries' EEZs, not only allows the fishers to hide their illegal cargo, but also lets them continue fishing for long periods of time, maximizing their return for effort made.

Corruption

Impoverished coastal countries that have to deal with corruption and other governance issues are especially vulnerable to illegal fishing. Examples of the loopholes exploited by corrupt public officials in these countries include:

- fisheries' observers who take bribes to overlook illegal catches onboard fishing vessels
- port inspectors who turn a blind eye to infractions while inspecting vessels' logbooks at landing
- fisheries' secretaries who divert license fees into personal overseas bank accounts
- military, police, and fisheries' officers engaging in "pirate" attacks of foreign vessels
- those in the highest government positions who embezzle funds, for example, Senegal's then-president Abdoulaye Wade is believed to have embezzled millions of dollars received from Russian fishers to make favorable licensing arrangements to finance elections and buy votes in 2009 (Standing, 2015)

Subsidies

Government subsidies to build new fishing vessels or improve the capacity and reach of existing industrial fleets significantly contribute to fishing vessel overcapacity. This overcapacity leads to illegal fishing because of the unbalanced and inappropriate allocation of fishing rights to domestic fleets (Le Gallic & Cox, 2006).

WHAT MEASURES HAVE BEEN TAKEN TO DEAL WITH ILLEGAL FISHING?

Regulatory Measures

To reduce the likelihood of importing illegally caught fish into the European Union, the EU introduced the EU-IUU Regulation in 2010 with three major provisions. First, all EU states are required to verify the origin and legality of the fish before allowing any landings at their ports. Second, a vessel flagged to an EU member state is substantially penalized if it is found to have engaged in illegal fishing; a first-time offender is fined five times the value of the illegally caught fish, while a repeat offender faces substantially greater fines. Third, the EU uses a third-country carding process to evaluate the adequacy of non-EU control and surveillance efforts in curbing illegal fishing in their waters. Based on EU's assessments, third countries receive green (good), yellow (warning), or red (failed) cards by the EU, with the latter resulting in a temporary trade ban on the imports of their fisheries products into the

EU until the carded country demonstrates sufficient improvement in its efforts to address the problem.

Regional Fisheries Management Organizations (RFMOs), which are intergovernmental organizations that deal with the management of marine resources, create and maintain blacklists of vessels engaged in, or assisting IUU fishing in their convention areas. This information is shared publicly so that the ports receiving these blacklisted vessels can refuse entry. Also, countries that are members to these RFMOs are prohibited from engaging in any type of commercial activity, as well as transshipping, with these blacklisted vessels.

The 2009 UN-FAO Agreement on Port State Measures to Prevent, Deter and Eliminate IUU fishing legally binds signatory countries to take preventive measures at their ports of entry when inspecting arriving fishing, support, and refrigerated cargo vessels. These measures require that arriving vessels provide prior notice for port access about catches, fishing trips, and locations where fished. They also require that the ports deny entry to IUU fishing vessels, including those blacklisted by RFMOs.

Trade-Related and Other Measures

Many nongovernmental organizations, such as Greenpeace, Oceana, and Sea Shepherd, seek to raise awareness about illegal fishing around the world. Other programs, such as the Marine Stewardship Council (MSC), promote sustainable fishery practices by eco-labeling fishery products. To achieve this goal, MCS's scientists make an assessment of a given fishery, taking account of the status of the target fish, the impact of the fishery on the ecosystem, and the performance of the management measures. Dependent on a satisfactory assessment, the MSC labels fish caught at the fishery, attesting to the legality of the catch and certifying that the fish can be traced from the point of capture to the point of landing and sale. Many retailers in Europe and the USA purchase MSC-certified fish only.

In order to raise awareness about the impact consumers have on the environment and to guide their seafood choices, many organizations have issued sustainable seafood guides on "fish to eat" and "fish to avoid." The organizations include Greenpeace, the UK's Marine Conservation Society, OceanWise in Canada, and the Seafood Watch and Monterey Bay Aquarium in the USA. The guides are accessible through the organizations' websites, as well as via smartphone applications, and as in-pocket paper brochures.

CONCLUSION

Illegal fishing has a devastating impact on the world's fisheries, on coastal countries dependent on fish, and on some of the planet's critical habitats. It requires international agreements to deal with the conditions that facilitate its occurrence, such as FoC, ports of convenience, illegal transshipments, and government subsidies of fishing fleets. However, international agreements are not enough on their own – they need to be reinforced by remedial actions taken not just by the countries facilitating illegal fishing, but also by those countries most involved in undertaking it. There seems little immediate prospect of these actions being taken. Those countries that facilitate illegal fishing are unlikely to surrender a valuable source of income and might lack the resources to take any effective remedial action. Those countries that are most involved in illegal fishing would be hard-pressed to rein in their fleets, given their dependency on illegal fishing and the profits made. Meanwhile, work should proceed in refining existing preventive measures and identifying new ones not relying on international agreements. Criminologists who until recently have shown little interest in illegal fishing, partly because of its bafflingly complex nature, can contribute to this vital work. They could take advantage of the enormous data sources assembled by marine biologists to assist study of the problem, such as the Sea Around Us project (Sea Around Us, 2018), Global Fishing Watch (www.fishbase.org), and of other data established to assist the work of the commercial fishing industry, to study the problem of illegal commercial fishing.

REFERENCES

Behnam, A. & Faust, P. (2003). Twilight of flag state control. *Ocean yearbook*, 17, 167–192.

Chevallier, R. (2017). Safeguarding Tanzania's coral reefs: The case of illegal blast fishing. *South African Institute of International Affairs, Policy Insights,* 46.

Doughty, R. W. & Carmichael, V. (2011). *The albatross and the fish: Linked lives in the open seas.* Austin, TX: University of Texas Press.

Environmental Justice Foundation (EJF). (2010). *All at sea: The abuse of human rights aboard illegal fishing vessels.* London: Environmental Justice Foundation.

International Transport Workers' Federation (ITF). (2006). *Out of sight, out of mind: Seafarers, fishers & human rights.* Retrieved from www.itfseafarers.org/files/extranet/-1/2259/HumanRights.pdf.

Le Gallic, B. & Cox, A. (2006). An economic analysis of illegal, unreported and unregulated (IUU) fishing: Key drivers and possible solutions. *Marine Policy,* 30, 689–695.

Petrossian, G. & Clarke, R. V. (2014). Explaining and controlling illegal commercial fishing: An application of the CRAVED theft model. *British Journal of Criminology,* 54(1), 73–90.

Petrossian, G., Marteache, N., & Viollaz, J. (2015). Where do "undocumented" fish land? An empirical assessment of port characteristics for IUU fishing. *European Journal on Criminal Policy and Research*, 21(3), 337–351.

Pew Charitable Trusts. (2013). How to end illegal fishing. PEW, December 10, 2013. Retrieved from http://pewenvironment.org/news-room/reports/how-to-end-illega-fishing-85899522612.

Sea Around Us. (2018). Sea Around Us. Fisheries, ecosystems and biodiversity. Retrieved from www.seaaroundus.org.

Standing, A. (2015). Corruption and state-corporate crime in fisheries. U4 Issue. Retrieved from www.u4.no/publications/corruption-and-state-corporate-crime-in-fisheries/.

Telesetsky, A. (2015). Laundering fish in the global undercurrents: Illegal, unreported, and unregulated fishing and transnational organized crime. *Ecology Law Quarterly*, 41(4), 939–996.

White, A. T., Vogt, H. P., & Arin, T. (2000). The Philippine coral reefs under threat: The economic losses caused by reef destruction. *Marine Pollution Bulletin*, 40, 598–605.

23 Corruption

Adam Graycar

INTRODUCTION: A GENERAL OVERVIEW OF THE TOPIC

Surveys conducted in 49 countries revealed that corruption was the topic most frequently discussed by the public, ahead of unemployment, climate change, terrorism, or poverty (reported in Holmes, 2016, p. xiii). Corruption is not always criminal. Like criminal behavior, corruption hurts people and it causes outrage to victims and those who value civil society. Like criminal behavior, corruption is unethical.

Corruption does not feature prominently in the criminal justice literature, and to learn about it students turn to literature in psychology, philosophy, development economics, public administration, law, anthropology, political science, and business studies. The criminal nature of corruption should be studied so that offender, opportunity, and target can be understood, in order that controls can be put in place.

Corruption can and does occur in all spheres of activity, and in all countries. In many countries the criminal justice system is badly corrupted. In others criminal justice activities are at the forefront of dealing with corruption. Corruption is costly and devastating. The World Economic Forum has estimated that the cost of corruption equals more than 5 percent of global GDP (about US$2.6 trillion). The World Bank has estimated that about US$1 trillion per year is paid in bribes, while about US$40 billion per year is looted by corrupt political leaders.

BACKGROUND

Definitions of corruption abound, but certain behaviors are broadly agreed to be corrupt, and these include bribery; theft, embezzlement, or fraud by an individual whose position or employment provides access or opportunity; extortion, again by virtue of position; abuse of discretion; creating or exploiting a conflict of interest; and nepotism, clientelism, and favoritism. The common characteristic in all these instances is the abuse of formal position that involves a situation of trust.

Transparency International (TI), the world's leading anti-corruption NGO, defines corruption as "the abuse of entrusted power for private gain" (TI, 2018).

The abuse of position for personal gain has occurred throughout history, and has often been tied into culture and relationships. In ancient market societies, being allowed to have a stall in the bazaar depended on whether one was favorably viewed by the ruler. In modern societies, if one wants to operate a stall in a market, one buys a permit from an authority and/or pays an agreed rent. There are rules and procedures, and the process is usually regulated, orderly, and simple. However, there are occasions when buying the permit might involve currying favor with an official, or giving a gift, or paying a consideration to achieve an inexpensive permit to carry out a routine activity.

Corruption can be grand or petty. Grand corruption involves those at the highest level of government who loot the Treasury and improperly and dishonestly manipulate and control the institutions of power. "Grand corruption" describes the activities of former presidents like Suharto of Indonesia, Marcos of the Philippines, Mobutu of Zaire, Milosevic of Yugoslavia, all of whom were reported to have looted billions while in power. Grand corruption also describes "state capture," the manipulation by those not formally in power, of the institutions of the state and its economic direction.

Petty corruption involves relatively small amounts of money changing hands to obtain some basic service or a permit, or to prevent something like a small fine or a parking or speeding ticket. It also covers lots of contracts and purchases in procurement and in development aid programs – everything from medical equipment, bribes for medical services, purchase of textbooks in educational programs, and licenses for land clearing.

The corrupt behavior may be active or passive – one party actively offers a bribe or inducement, the other passively receives it. This can be complicated if the passive recipient solicits the bribe.

In some countries where corruption is all pervasive and endemic, combating corruption is a monumental and overwhelming task. It goes to the very heart of culture and relationships, and involves a major change in the way people do business.

There are a number of behaviors that all agree are corrupt behaviors. They include the following.

Bribery, where money changes hands to obtain or to facilitate a satisfactory outcome, that might not have happened without the money, or might not have happened as quickly. The inducement might be in cash, but it could also be in the form of inside information, meals and entertainment, holidays, employment, sexual favors, etc. It can involve getting somebody to do, or not to do, something, or to overlook something. It can flow in either direction. It can be offered by the principal, or it can be solicited by the agent.

Extortion involves the use of force or other forms of intimidation to extract payments.

Theft and **fraud** have a place in corruption studies when they involve entrusted power, in contrast to base criminal activity. This can be on a huge scale, as we saw with our kleptocrats, or can involve an official selling food from a relief aid shipment, or medical supplies that find their way into private practice when they have been donated for community health programs.

Abuse of discretion is very common. It happens in issuing of permits and licenses, procurement, real estate developments, and often in the judicial system in some countries.

Self-dealing involves hiring one's own company, or a company belonging to close associates or relatives to provide public services.

Patronage, nepotism, or favoritism occurs when one hires somebody because of who they are related to or who they are, rather than what they can do. It may provide benefits to somebody in the family or a close associate. There are also numerous examples of creating "no show" jobs – a corrupt pay-off where salaries are paid for people who never or rarely turn up.

Conflict of interest occurs when somebody is in a position to make a decision, and when they have an interest (real or perceived) that could benefit from that decision. There may be no actual impropriety, but the appearance of a conflict can undermine confidence. This is the subject of considerable debate, as very different standards are often brought to bear.

Political corruption and campaign financing irregularities are huge fields that strike at the very heart of democratic activities.

Each of these phenomena and more occur in different activities and different sectors of any society. Most commonly these apply in buying things (procurement processes, issuing contracts); or in appointing personnel; or delivering programs or services; making things (road construction, major capital works, housing developments); controlling activities (such as licensing, regulation, or the issuing of permits, etc.); and many forms of administering (such as the administration of justice, or health, or environmental services, etc.) (see Graycar & Prenzler, 2013, for further analysis of these themes).

MEASURING CORRUPTION

Unlike many crimes, corruption does not lend itself easily to measurement. What we measure depends on how we describe the specific activity, and how it is defined, if it is, in criminal codes. Even where the activity is codified, asking "how much corruption is there in a society?" does not yield a clear and unambiguous number.

The unit of analysis is often the nation-state, but it does not aid our understanding to confirm that Denmark or Sweden are less corrupt than Somalia or Zimbabwe. A secondary layer of measurement could focus on events or places (such as workplaces or local regions).

The normal empirical tools of measurement are not always useful as significant transactions are hidden and not reported, and any survey is unlikely to elicit a valid and reliable response. ("Do you take bribes? From whom? How often? What is the value? What do you have to do in return?")

While it might be good to measure types of corruption, occurrence of corrupt behavior, or costs and effects, the most common measurement is of *perceptions* of corruption.

Transparency International publishes an annual corruption perception index in which it ranks 180 nations, as well as a "bribe payers index" of 30 countries. The methodology is explained in each publication, and one criticism of this approach is that it is not a measure of how much there is, or what effect it has, but rather what a group of well-placed experts think is the state of play. Their publication *Global Corruption Barometer* does, however, survey people's experiences of corrupt transactions in many countries.

Those studying corruption do often undertake desk reviews, surveys, focus groups, case studies, field observations, and professional assessments. Of course, these will yield results that may be applicable in a specific study rather than an overall assessment.

DISCUSSION OF MAJOR CONCEPTS

In some countries it is said that corruption is a response to need. Civil service salaries may be so very low that in order to survive people working in government offices depend on bribes as part of their income. Those who have dealings with the public, such as police officers, or customs officials, or tax collectors, or health or building inspectors, can extort money from those with whom they are dealing by threatening not to allow a transaction, or prohibiting an import, or closing down a business or activity if no extortionary payment is forthcoming.

Need is no excuse for illegal or corrupt behavior. More often, however, the motivating factor is greed. For those so inclined, greed drives people in official positions to undertake activities that are both unprofessional and illegal.

Several strategies for combating corruption can be implemented.

Criminalization, Investigation, Prosecution, Sanctions

In most countries corruption has been criminalized, that is, it is illegal for a public official to solicit or accept a bribe or behave corruptly. However, investigation, enforcement, prosecution, and imposing sanctions can be challenging. These may not always be pursued with sufficient independence, nor sufficiently resourced, nor rigorously implemented.

Anti-Corruption Agencies

Many countries also have anti-corruption agencies – and some work wonderfully well, such as those in Singapore and Hong Kong, while in some other countries they have become part of the problem rather than the solution.

Structural Reform

Solutions sometimes lie in structural reform – making the civil service more accountable, merit-based, formally organized, and, very importantly, better paid. This needs to occur within a context of strong institutions of integrity – a legislature and executive that have and are seen to have integrity, a clean and functioning judiciary, an auditor general, watchdog agencies like an ombudsman, or an anti-corruption agency, whistleblower protection, etc.

Education, Integrity-Building Mobilization of the Public

A strong civic culture, vocal advocacy groups, civic education, information and education campaigns aimed at young children, an open media, and mobilization of the public are all factors that contribute to this set of strategies.

THE UNITED NATIONS CONVENTION AGAINST CORRUPTION

The most comprehensive response is the United Nations Convention against Corruption. This is a global response to a global problem. By 2018, 183 countries had ratified this treaty, which came into effect at the end of 2005.

The Convention introduces an extensive set of standards, measures, and rules that all countries can apply in order to strengthen their legal and regulatory regimes to fight corruption. It calls for preventive measures and the criminalization of the most prevalent forms of corruption in both public and private sectors. And it makes a major breakthrough by requiring member states to return assets obtained through corruption, to the country from which they were stolen. As Kofi Annan, the former UN Secretary-General, said when introducing the Convention, "Corrupt officials will in future find fewer ways to hide their illicit gains."

The Convention commits signatory countries to developing preventive anti-corruption policies and practices that properly manage public affairs and public property, and reflect the rule of law, integrity, transparency, and accountability. States are to establish anti-corruption bodies and disseminate knowledge about the prevention of corruption.

The big task in the Convention is to strengthen the public sector by having open systems of recruiting, hiring, retention, and promotion of civil servants, plus decent pay, as well as education programs. There are to be codes of conduct for public servants, proper systems for public procurement and management of public finances, as well as open public reporting. The judiciary and prosecution services are to follow standards of integrity, and the public is to have access to information. In addition, there are to be measures for preventing money laundering.

To develop specific mechanisms to combat corruption it is necessary to identify opportunities that are available and that facilitate corrupt behavior. Opportunities for corruption occur in societies or organizations where:

- there is a lack of a culture of integrity, especially among leaders
- ethical codes do not exist, or are not enforced
- patronage and nepotism are accepted
- there is complexity of regulations/complexity of systems
- there are weak financial controls
- there are weak institutions of governance

In specific and localized activities, opportunities for corruption occur where:

- supervision and oversight are not taken seriously, or are remote from the activity (e.g., a police officer patrolling a highway)
- specialized knowledge and high discretion both operate
- decisions affect costs and benefits of activities
- there is no capable guardian
- there is low decision monitoring
- whistleblowers are silenced
- there is low risk of being caught

Although there are no quick fixes, one way forward may be to examine some of the crime prevention approaches elsewhere in this volume and work creatively to apply them to the control of corruption.

SUMMARY OF HIGHLIGHTS

- Corruption occurs in rich and poor countries alike. It is sometimes a response to need, sometimes a response to greed. The dynamics of corruption are very different in, say, Denmark and Somalia.
- Corruption can be classified as grand corruption or petty corruption.

- Defining corruption leads to long and convoluted debates, but defining the component parts (e.g., bribery, self-dealing, extortion, etc.) can be useful.
- The impacts of corruption disproportionally affect the poorest and most vulnerable in any society and, when widespread, corruption deters investment and weakens economic growth. If system integrity is dubious then the rule of law cannot be maintained.
- Combating corruption has had mixed success. Criminalization has not always worked. Global approaches include the United Nations Convention against Corruption, while local approaches include statutes, codes of conduct, investigation, and prosecution.
- Another likely approach is to develop situational responses in response to opportunities that may arise for corruption behavior. The first step here is to understand the opportunity structure for corruption.

REFERENCES

Graycar, A. & Prenzler, T. (2013). *Understanding and preventing corruption*. Basingstoke and New York: Palgrave Macmillan.
Holmes, L. (2016). *Corruption: A very short introduction*. New York: Oxford University Press.
Transparency International (TI). (2018). *Frequently asked questions about corruption*. Retrieved from www.transparency.org/whoweare/organisation/faqs_on_corruption.

WEBSITES

Transparency International. www.transparency.org/.
World Bank. www.worldbank.org.
United Nations Office on Drugs and Crime. www.unodc.org/unodc/en/corruption/index.html.
United Nations Convention against Corruption. www.unodc.org/pdf/corruption/publications_unodc_convention-e.pdf.
OECD Fighting Corruption. www.oecd.org/corruption.
Council of Europe GRECO (Group of States against Corruption). www.coe.int/t/dghl/monitoring/greco/default_en.asp.
U4 Anti-Corruption Resource Center. www.U4.no.

24 Tourist and Visitor Crime

A. M. Lemieux and Marcus Felson

Many nations depend on tourism for their prosperity, yet tourists are very vulnerable to crime. This chapter puts tourist crime in a larger visitor perspective with concepts that can apply within and between nations, for those who travel both long and short distances from home. This chapter delineates tourist crime as part of a larger category, "visitor crime." Not only do visitors fall victim to crime, but they also often participate in other ways, such as committing offenses when they visit. In addition, many people work or engage in recreation outside their residential area, even if they return home in the evening. Visitors are a diverse population, including: a) seasonal visitors; b) overnight visitors; c) day visitors; and d) night visitors. Overnight visitors include foreign tourists, tourists within nations, and short-term visitors for pleasure and business purposes. Each of these subpopulations contributes to crime opportunity in their own way. We present a typology of visitor crime to assist officials and researchers who study crime events that involve one or more visitors.

TOURISTS AND VISITORS

Visitors are often crime victims. For example, Chesney-Lind and Lind (1986) studied mean annual crime rates per 100,000 in Honolulu, finding that robbery rates were 256 for visitors and 157 for residents. In Barbados, de Albuquerque and McElroy (1999) report burglary rates in 1989 of 2,173 for visitors compared to only 847 for residents. Although these ratios were somewhat lower in subsequent years, the same general conclusion remains. Stangeland (1995) investigated tourist victimization in an interesting way, interviewing tourists in the Malaga, Spain airport as they waited to leave the country. Despite visiting only a week or so, a very high percentage of visitors had been victimized.

In the studies just cited, the words "visitor" and "tourist" are used synonymously. Taking a deeper look, many visitors are not tourists in the normal sense. Residents of surrounding towns and suburbs visit a city for recreation and work. Some people visit overnight and others just for the day. For this reason, we define "visitor crime" as the larger category, then treat "tourist crime" as one part of visitor crime. We further distinguish the different roles that tourists play in crime. However, much of our discussion is about tourist crime rather than other forms of visitor crime. Our main purpose in using the larger category here is to make readers aware of the theoretical link to a larger literature than the tourist crime literature alone. Indeed, the purpose of this paper is to embed tourist crime within a larger body of information about visitors – who are more likely to be offenders or victims and less likely to be guardians against crime.

We do not assume that visitors are only victims, since some visitors commit crimes and others witness crimes in which they are neither victim nor offender. When offender and victim come from different nations, this can create tensions between those nations or interfere with the tourist industries. It can also create local hostility toward outsiders. Within nations, visitor crime involvement can raise internal tensions and interfere with industries that depend on visitors.

PUBLIC OPINION AND TOURIST-RELATED CRIME

The economic dependence on tourism provides an incentive to hide or deny tourist crime. Such evasions may lead to a failure to face up to crime's realities and the need to change them. On the other hand, some people blame their crime on outsiders without considering the contribution of locals – a point to which we will return in a moment.

We do not assume that tourist crime is significant everywhere. To quote John M. Knox's (2004) study of tourist crime in Hawaii, "The relationship between serious crime and tourism varies from place to place and time to time. It is a matter of local circumstances." Yet in some places, tourist crime is a very serious component of the crime situation. A vast influx of tourists can enhance the crime rate of a given city or region. That influx often adds numbers to the numerator, without being included in the denominator. As a consequence, tourist crime appears even greater than its reality, creating an image problem for the area into which tourists flow. Information about tourist victimization can generate bad publicity, impair future tourism, and, as a result, harm local and regional economies. Even false reports and media exaggerations of tourist crime can have major economic consequences. In addition, as offenders tourists or victims can generate new conflicts or enhance old conflicts among nations involved.

Exaggeration of tourist crime can also have negative consequences by giving the false impression that local crime is not locally generated. When tourists are victimized, local residents are still participants in many of these crimes. When tourists join with local residents in crime, the latter are not necessarily innocent parties. We can argue whether the local prostitutes or the tourist customers are more at fault, but the fact remains that the influx of tourists contributes to a local problem of social control.

THEORETICAL IMPORTANCE OF TOURIST-RELATED CRIME

Social control reminds us that tourist and visitor crime have theoretical importance. During the period 1920–1940, the "Chicago School of Sociology" conceptualized urban life (including crime) as influenced by the mix of locals and strangers. At the very foundation of crime theory, cities were seen as generating the anonymity that facilitated crime. Visitors could engage in activities that would be disapproved on their home turf, avoiding recognition. In addition, normative obligations are sometimes relaxed when strangers meet. At the very heart of urban theory and urban studies is the notion that a city assembles large numbers of people who are, in some sense, visitors. This point was central in the work of Robert Ezra Park, Ernest W. Burgess, Roderick D. McKenzie, and other participants and followers of the

"Chicago School." Arguably, the mixture of populations brings with it more opportunity for crime than either population would produce alone.

Brantingham and Brantingham (1993) distinguish between crime attractors and crime generators. A given place can generate crime because its local routines afford sufficient crime opportunities. In time a place rich in crime opportunities can become a crime attractor, where offenders go with crime in mind before they depart their prior locations. If a tourist location builds up a reputation for illicit behavior, it may in time attract offenders with that in mind. An established crime attractor may draw tourists from abroad and internally, as well as routine crime participants from within. Thus, some nations have developed a widespread reputation for prostitution or even child prostitution, drawing their own citizens to provide services and consumers from elsewhere.

Some criminal acts are very simple: a tourist arrives; someone steals his wallet and uses the money. Others are more complex: a tourist arrives, buys illicit drugs, representing the endpoint of a chain of illicit events, including the production and transport of those drugs. Many hands may be involved. In addition, a local economy can become dependent or at least reliant upon a chain of illicit activities, with tourists from abroad playing a part in fueling the entire system. In addition, some visitors purchase drugs to take home, thus linking two or more sets of illicit complexity. Moreover, tourists are but one type of visitor whose presence can be linked to crime.

TYPES OF VISITOR CRIME

Once we have dichotomized visitors and locals, we have seven types of crime combination (with examples).

- Visitor against local: a visitor steals something from a local person.
- Local against visitor: a local person robs a visitor.
- Visitor against visitor: a visitor assaults another visitor.
- Local against local: a local person steals from another local person.
- Visitor with local: a visitor joins a local in exchanging illegal drugs or sex.
- Visitor with visitor: one visitor sells illicit drugs to another visitor.
- Local with local: a local person purchases illicit sex from another local person.

By distinguishing foreign visitors from domestic visitors, and by allowing more complex combinations of offenders, these categories are easily extended. For example, some crimes involve mixes of locals and foreigners, and some involve offender networks across several nations.

Tourism is especially interesting because some offenders pose as tourists when their real purposes are to carry out illicit activities, not tourism. A strong influx of tourists makes possible the entry and exit of people with crime in mind. A vast population crossing borders provides camouflage for illicit activities. And so, on many dimensions, tourism is linked to transnational crime.

TOURISM, VISITOR CRIME, AND ROUTINE ACTIVITIES

Understanding tourist crime requires us to consider how tourism alters or clashes with the routine activities of the receiving nation, region, or city. Tourists often arrive in particular seasons, producing major shifts in activities. Those dependent on tourism for their livelihood prosper most during the tourist season and they spend more money at that time. In addition, tourism may produce an influx of workers to serve the tourists. Thus, tourism produces a multiplier of community activity beyond the number of tourists. This multiplier further enhances the impact of tourism upon the volume of crime in the area.

The significance of tourist crime also brings situational prevention to the fore. Better prevention related to tourist areas and activities can have a major payoff for crime control in general and the security of the tourist industry in particular. Tourist areas can be given extra policing, and pose a challenge for problem-oriented policing. Yet improved design of environmental settings used by tourists and better management of the public places they frequent offer potential for low-cost crime reduction without depending on arrests. Hotel security and situational prevention within hotels play an important role in reducing tourist crime. Bar and tavern management and design are especially likely to assist in reducing crime involving tourists.

Tourist activities have a major impact on the nighttime economy, both in leisure and work activities. Indeed, tourism has a major impact upon the distribution of crime over the hours of the day, days of the week, and months of the year. Moreover, the ebb and flow of tourist volume from year to year is significant for local crime rates. Tourist crimes not only impact local areas that receive tourists, but tourist acquisition of illicit substances away from home allows import of those substances to their local area. Therefore, tourist crime is linked to local crime in the areas from which tourists originate. We can readily see that tourist crime is a tale of localism as well as transnationalism, helping us understand how crime grows and flows in space and time.

In addition, visitor crime involving non-tourists is dependent on commuting to work, weekend visits, leisure activities outside of one's own area of residence, and more. We can readily see that visitor crime is a very complex topic indeed. Tourist participation in crime is just one part of this larger field of inquiry. This larger field has theoretical and empirical significance. In general, nonlocal participation in crime is part of a system of events and relationships that will require future research and theoretical effort to understand and assimilate.

REFERENCES

Brantingham, P. & Brantingham, P. (1993). Nodes, paths and edges: Considerations on the complexity of crime and physical environment. *Journal of Environmental Psychology*, 13, 3–28.

Chesney-Lind, M. & Lind, I. Y. (1986). Visitors as victims: Crimes against tourists in Hawaii. *Annals of Tourism Research*, 13, 167–191.

De Albuquerque, K. & McElroy, J. L. (1999). Tourism and crime in the Caribbean. *Annals of Tourism Research*, 26(4), 968–984.

Knox, M. J. (2004). *Socio-cultural impacts of tourism in Hawaii (general population). Part IV of Planning for Sustainable Tourism.* Prepared for Hawaii State Dept. of Business, Economic Development, & Tourism. John M. Knox & Associates, Inc.

Robert, E. P., Burgess, E. W., & McKenzie, R. D. (1925). *The city: Suggestions for the study of human nature in the urban environment.* Chicago: University of Chicago Press.

Stangeland, P. (1995). *The crime puzzle: Crime patterns and crime displacement in southern Spain.* Malaga: Instituo Andaluz Interunversario de Criminologia and Miguel Gómez Ediciones.

25 Terrorism

Graeme Newman and Ronald V. Clarke

Criminology and criminal justice programs were late in recognizing the relevance of terrorism to international criminology because it was thought that terrorism was completely different from crime, the province of political scientists. But it was also because the traditional approaches of criminology have remained preoccupied with root causes of crime and have been only secondarily interested in how to prevent it. The 9/11 attack demanded immediate action to make sure that nothing like it ever happened again. Applying the perspective of situational crime prevention, this chapter will demonstrate that it is possible to explain terrorism and develop a systematic way to prevent it without necessarily studying its "root causes."

DEFINING TERRORISM

There have been many attempts to define terrorism, and the definition of the FBI states that:

> "Terrorism is the unlawful use of force or violence against persons or property to intimidate or coerce a government, the civilian population, or any segment thereof, in furtherance of political or social objectives."

This definition states clearly that terrorism is unlawful, but, as might be expected in an "official" government definition, it leaves open the problem of "freedom fighters" acting against an unlawful government. Like other definitions the FBI makes force and violence central to a description of terrorism. While the majority of terrorist attacks are obviously violent (some are not, such as cyberterrorism), focusing on the violence itself ignores the conditions and behaviors that make for the successful completion of terrorist attacks. These are the opportunities of which terrorists take advantage. Research in situational crime prevention has shown that offenders develop many techniques and procedures as they carry out different kinds of crimes, from car theft to credit card fraud. It is necessary to identify these crime-specific conditions and environmental situations in which they occur in order to identify points of intervention. Generally, these conditions reveal the opportunities that make criminal behavior possible.

In applying this approach to terrorism, the precise definition of terrorism becomes of secondary importance and we may simply say that terrorism is crime with a political motive. This is also an unsatisfactory definition, not because it calls terrorism crime, but because it uses two highly abstract words, "political" and "crime," which hide vastly different kinds of acts. For example, successfully carrying out a suicide bombing in a restaurant requires a completely different sequence of acts (in terms of preparation, planning, and operations) than hijacking an airliner and holding the passengers and crew for ransom. And each act requires that a completely different set of actions be taken to prevent them. This is the central lesson also of decades of research on situational prevention.

In sum, from a situational crime prevention point of view, there is no essential difference between crime and terrorism. As with crime, in order to design ways to prevent terrorism we need to identify the opportunities in society and the physical environment that terrorists exploit in order to carry out the specific kinds of attacks they are planning, whether these are airliner hijackings, political assassinations, suicide bombings, bombings of buildings, mass shooting of civilians, roadside bombs, etc. This approach addresses squarely the immediate and urgent need of taking steps to prevent terrorist attacks like 9/11 from happening again. It focuses on reducing opportunities by manipulating or altering the conditions that surround the immediate environment in which the terrorist operates. The path or journey taken by the offender to the completion of his or her terrorist act is blocked or even removed. In other words, we ask not why they do it, but how they do it.

THE "ROOT CAUSES" OF TERRORISM

Critics of situational prevention insist that one cannot prevent terrorism unless one eradicates its root causes. They argue terrorists are different from criminals because terrorists are motivated by a "higher cause." Terrorists are motivated by their ideology, while criminals are motivated by greed or some other base human trait. That Islamic extremists, far-right militias, or Marxist guerillas inflict violence in the service of their "higher" cause, is better seen as: a) justifications or excuses (rather than explanations) for what they do and: b) expressions of their belief that violence is the most effective means of achieving their distant goal, which is usually toppling a government, or forcing an opponent to stop what it is doing (e.g., getting the USA to leave Iraq, or getting researchers to stop using animals for experimentation, or bringing about a caliphate).

Ideology does not predict which targets will be attacked. Routine suicide bombing attacks in the Palestine territories, for example, do not primarily target synagogues or places of worship, but rather restaurants and places where many people gather. When places of worship are attacked, this is usually for tactical or strategic reasons (e.g., to inflame interethnic violence in Iraq) rather than ideological ones.

One characteristic of terrorism that sets it apart from other kinds of crime is that most terrorists depend on publicity to magnify the impact of their attacks. This means that they must make their attacks a media affair but at the same time keep their organizations and actions secret. Even though the publicity of terrorist acts is usually accompanied by ideological justifications, it is essentially tactical since it makes up for terrorists' lack of firepower compared to the usual overwhelming weaponry possessed by any given government that may be its enemy (hence the concept of "asymmetrical warfare"). Unprotected targets, therefore, that produce the most media coverage are ideal.

In sum, the operational demands of terrorists to maximize the successful completion of their attacks will almost always outweigh whatever ideologies they claim are the reasons for their attacks.

INTERNATIONAL AND DOMESTIC TERRORISM

Terrorism is generally divided into two kinds: domestic and international. However, globalization continues to blur the boundaries between domestic and international because:

- globalization makes it much easier for terrorist groups, domestic or foreign, to purchase weapons;
- international drug dealing and human trafficking, which always have a domestic source and destination, is a ready source of finance to terrorists;
- terrorist groups that are well established within particular countries depend on foreign sources for financial and other kinds of support.

The IRA in Northern Ireland is a typical example. Before 9/11 it received financial support from sympathizers in the USA and was able to purchase Semtex explosives from Muammar Kaddafi of Libya. These kinds of supply chains have made it possible for groups such as the IRA and the various terrorist groups in Palestine (e.g., Hamas) to conduct frequent attacks within countries on a routine basis. The appearance of suicide bombings in Paris in November 2015 were made possible by new supply chains established by means of the uncontrolled migration from the centers of suicide bombing operations in North Africa.

In the USA, domestic terrorism has been mostly limited to acts by single-issue terrorists such as the right-to-life or environmentalist extremists, or isolated hate crimes by individuals or militia groups. Vastly more attacks carried out against the USA occur not on US soil, but at US embassies and other establishments in foreign countries. The explanation for this is simple: terrorists find it operationally much easier to carry out attacks in locations close to home (the same goes for burglars). Iraq was much closer to home for Al Qaeda than the North American continent. Thus, the presence of many US personnel and structures in the Middle East made them the most attractive and easiest targets compared to the extensive organizational demands needed to carry out similar attacks in the continental USA. This is why that to date there have been no suicide bombings in New York City's restaurants.

HOW MUCH TERRORISM IS THERE?

Counting terrorist acts is very difficult, not least because of definitional problems but also because many of these acts take place in countries that are not accustomed to keeping good statistical records. One widely used way to count terrorist acts is through newspaper and media reports. This method is used by the Global Terrorism Database (GTD), which shows that, worldwide, terrorist incidents rose from less than 200in 1970, to some 5,000 in the 1990s and early 2000s. By 2012 a sharp rise in incidents began, driven by exceptional levels of violence attributed to the growing Islamic State and allied groups around the world. This rise peaked in 2014 followed by significant declines in 2015 and 2016. The lethality of these attacks has also increased greatly, with dramatic increases in injuries and a noticeable increase in deaths. This is no doubt because of the ready availability throughout the world of greatly enhanced conventional weapons of many kinds, including easy-to-use plastic explosives (e.g., Semtex, C2, C3, C4), add-on devices to single-shot rifles that make them repeaters, such as used in the Las Vegas mass shooting (2017), and the easily upgradable AR-15 used in the Sandy Hook Elementary School shooting (2012) and the Marjory Stoneman Douglas High School shooting in Florida (2018).

PREVENTING TERRORISM

Given their premise of violence, terrorists will do what is, generally speaking, the easiest. This means that terrorists will survey the immediate environment in which they operate, taking advantage of opportunities that will make their job easier. These opportunities may be classified into four kinds.

1. *Targets.* Targets differ widely in their attractiveness: how easy they are to reach, how much impact their destruction will bring, whether they are occupied by many people, whether government or businesses, whether their destruction would be symbolic of victory.
2. *Weapons.* The range of weapons available and how appropriate they are for reaching the target are important considerations. Suicide bombers are used, not because of some fanatical Islamic ideology, but because they offer clear advantages such as removing the necessity of planning an escape route, increasing the chances of reaching the specific target, or even a substitute target if thwarted. Semtex explosive is used because it is small and easy to conceal under clothing. Terrorists, in fact, prefer weapons they know. Thus, they prefer conventional weapons, not weapons of mass destruction.
3. *Tools available for conducting the mission.* These are tangible products that are used in the course of an attack. Among these important and essential (depending on the mission) products for conducting terrorism are: vehicles, rented or stolen; cell phones, cash, and credit cards (it is difficult to rent a car in most places without a credit card, and buying a plane ticket with cash is viewed as suspicious); false documents such as passports, driving licenses; and information about targets such as maps, timetables, and schedules. All these tools that terrorists use are also tools that ordinary offenders use: stolen cars, stolen cell phones, false or stolen identities.
4. *Facilitating conditions.* These are the social and physical arrangements of modern society that make specific acts of terrorism possible.

Conditions that facilitate terrorist acts include:

- a local community that is sympathetic to the terrorists, or that can be used as cover by foreign terrorists
- an accessible arms market
- banking and market conditions that permit money laundering for obtaining financial support for terrorist operations
- lax or nonexistent security procedures by government agencies or businesses

Situational crime prevention research developed four principles of crime prevention that are aimed at making the successful completion of crime difficult for offenders. These are: increase the effort, increase the risks, reduce the rewards, and reduce provocations and excuses for the offender. If we put these together with the four pillars of opportunity, a quick guide to planning prevention and protection against terrorist attacks may be constructed as in Table 25.1. A prime example of the successful prevention of suicide bombings and reduction

Table 25.1. Four principles of situational prevention and the four pillars of opportunity for terrorism

	Targets	Weapons	Tools	Facilitating Conditions
Increase the Effort	Prioritize targets for protection; close streets, build walls and barriers.	Restrict sale of weapons; hold contractors liable for stolen explosives.	Eliminate high-value bank notes; make banks liable for money laundering.	High-tech passports, visas, driving licenses; national ID cards.
Increase the Risks	Strengthen surveillance through CCTV, citizen vigilance, hotlines.	RFIDs to track weapons; increase Internet surveillance of terrorist groups.	Make cars more difficult to steal, parts marking on all tools.	Tighten identity authentication procedures; tighten border controls.
Reduce the Rewards	Bomb-proof buildings, Kevlar vests; swift cleanup of attack site.	Locks and immobilizers to make weapons difficult to use.	Make cell phones and other tools unusable without ID to unlock.	Publicity to portray hypocrisy and cruelty of terrorist acts.
Reduce Provocations and Excuses	Unobtrusive public buildings at home and abroad.	Avoid use of controversial weapons such as phosphorous bombs.	Maintain positive relations with local communities.	Avoid maltreatment of prisoners; clear rules for interrogation.

of terrorist attacks generally in specific locations was the introduction of the West Bank barrier in Israel, which made it much harder (increased the effort and risk) for terrorists to reach their targets (Perry et al., 2016).

COLLECTING INTELLIGENCE

The popular view of almost all law enforcement approaches to terrorism is that intelligence is needed in order to identify, arrest, or otherwise "take out" the terrorists. While important, the take-them-out approach cannot provide all the protection that society needs because there are many other individuals ready to take the places of the terrorists arrested or killed. Instead, the collection of intelligence should be informed by the four main sources of terrorist opportunity and the four techniques of situational crime prevention as depicted in Table 25.1. Local police are in the best position to collect such intelligence. They must know their communities better than the terrorists, who depend on local knowledge to search out targets, gain access, and resources. It also follows that the interrogation of suspects should be focused on finding out how they carry out their acts rather than trying to extract names of other terrorists through coercive interrogation. The latter rests on an often-mistaken preconception that all terrorist acts are the result of some highly organized terrorist group with tentacles stretching around the world. Generally, this is not supported, even in the case of Al Qaeda.

SUMMARY AND CONCLUSION

Approaching terrorism from the point of view of situational crime prevention reveals many practical and policy choices that will help to prevent future terrorist attacks and to protect targets within communities. Identifying the specific opportunities within the four pillars of terrorist opportunity available for terrorists is the first step, followed by identifying and protecting potential targets and collecting intelligence at the local level. Finally, responses to terrorism must be forward-looking, applying interventions that aim at making life harder for terrorists: increasing the efforts they must make, increasing their risks, reducing their rewards, and reducing provocations and excuses for their attacks.

REFERENCE

Perry, S., Apel, R., Newman, G., & Clarke, R. (2016). The situational prevention of terrorism: An evaluation of the Israeli West Bank barrier. *Journal of Quantitative Criminology*, 33(4), 727–751.

26 Political Assassinations

A Global Perspective

Marissa Mandala

INTRODUCTION

Few events can prove as disruptive as a political assassination. History contains endless examples of how such incidents inflict severe consequences on countries that experience attacks. World wars, civil wars, and genocides have been precipitated by successful assassination events, including World War I and the Rwandan Genocide. While there are many different actors involved in political assassinations, the focus of this chapter is on those carried out by terrorists and mentally ill individuals, as most political assassination research is concentrated in these two sub-categories. This chapter begins by defining assassination and identifying the different actors responsible for attacks. Next, a brief overview of the assassination literature is provided, and the role of terrorists and the mentally ill is discussed. Global trends of political assassinations by terrorists are then highlighted. Finally, prevention measures and the use of threat assessment groups by law enforcement agencies are reviewed.

ASSASSINATION BACKGROUND

Defining Assassination

Due to the different actors responsible for conducting political assassinations, the definition of a political assassination can be complex. Since this chapter provides an analysis of political assassination data from the Global Terrorism Database (GTD), it is fitting to focus on the assassination definition used by the GTD.

The GTD defines an assassination as the murder of a specific and prominent individual or individuals that is politically motivated. Individuals are usually targeted because they are affiliated with the government and thus representative of a country's political, economic, or social institutions. An attack is not an assassination if members of a group are killed but not specifically targeted. Attacks that target judges are thus not considered assassinations, while an attack on a particular judge is categorized as an assassination because the target is identified. Since the GTD does not distinguish between political and non-political assassinations, political assassinations must be extracted by filtering the data by the target type. The target type variable contains 22 different categories, which can be condensed into a binary variable indicating political vs. non-political targets. For the purpose of the descriptive analysis discussed below, political assassinations can be operationalized as those that target individuals affiliated with the government. For example, attacks can be considered political assassinations if the targets are diplomats, politicians, judges, or police or military personnel. Non-political assassinations can be defined as attacks on individuals unaffiliated with the government, such as civilians, tourists, and journalists.

Although many political assassinations are ideologically motivated, psychologically unstable individuals are also responsible for many attacks. Thus, with slight modification, the GTD's definition can be applied to assassinations carried out by mentally ill individuals. This can be done by removing the political motivation component of the definition and replacing it with a psychological motivation. However, a challenge inherent in assassination research is that it can be difficult for scholars to determine the true motivation behind an attack and the extent to which it was either political, psychological, or a combination of both. This challenge is aggravated when government or open sources provide sparse information on an incident. This is an issue researchers must recognize and acknowledge when conducting studies on political assassinations.

Types of Assassinations

As previously noted, political assassinations have been conducted by a variety of actors, including: organized terrorist groups, lone actors influenced by terrorist ideology, criminal organizations, individuals plagued by mental illness, states, and corporations. Organized terrorist groups and lone-actor terrorists have been responsible for many successful assassinations, including the 1914 assassination of the Archduke Franz Ferdinand, the 1984 assassination of Indian Prime Minister Indira Gandhi, and the 1995 assassination of Israeli Prime Minister Yitzhak Rabin. Criminal organizations have also used assassinations to eliminate their rivals for political purposes. This is exemplified by the Italian Mafia's murder of two prominent anti-Mafia judges in 1992, Giovanni Falconi and Paolo Borsellino. Psychologically unstable individuals have played a central role in many famous assassination events, including presidential assassinations in the USA (Freedman, 1984). In fact, law enforcement agencies worldwide have created threat assessment groups in an effort to connect these individuals with mental health services and ultimately prevent attacks on public figures (James & Farnham, 2016). State-sponsored assassinations aim to eliminate individuals that a country perceives to be a threat. For instance, the USA has used assassination as a tool to eliminate terrorists abroad, particularly through its use of drone strikes. One state-sponsored assassination event recently received much attention in the media when the leader of North Korea, Kim Jong-un, apparently ordered his uncle and rival, Kim Jong-nam, to be killed in a Malaysian airport in February 2017. Corporations can also play a role in political assassinations. There are reportedly a growing number of attacks on human rights activists who challenge big corporations (Kelly, 2018).

LITERATURE SUMMARY

Despite the various actors that can be responsible for political assassinations, terrorists and the mentally ill are arguably responsible for some of the most well-known political assassinations, especially those carried out against heads of government and heads of state (see Table 26.2). By comparison, there is scant literature on assassinations conducted by corporations, and a smaller body of work exists that analyzes political assassinations by organized crime groups. Research on state-sponsored assassinations is growing, but it is still not as extensive as the work on assassinations by terrorists or the mentally ill. There are also methodological challenges in studying political assassinations by other actors, particularly with regards to data collection and analysis. For example, the collection of data on state-sponsored assassinations can be difficult, especially considering the covert nature of such events. Researchers are especially limited in their ability to gather information on assassinations conducted by autocratic countries. Governments, democratic and autocratic alike, are unlikely to provide information to researchers to verify whether or not an attack was state-sponsored.

The scholarly work on political assassinations is interdisciplinary. Mandala and Freilich (2017) empirically examine assassinations by terrorists through a crime prevention framework. There are also some studies that analyze the macro-level political, social, and economic conditions associated with political assassinations. Nice (1994) discovers that certain political conditions contribute to assassination attempts on US presidents, finding that periods of partisan realignments and war are associated with these attacks. In their examination of assassinations of heads of state between 1946 and 2000, Iqbal and Zorn (2006) find that attacks are related to how a leader takes and stays in office, the amount of power they exert, and the degree of repressiveness that characterizes their rule.

Researchers have examined the psychological impact of assassinations on citizens as well as the role of mental illness in motivating assassins to carry out attacks. For instance, Meloy et al. (2004) find that the majority of assassins responsible for attacking US government officials were mentally ill. Interestingly, Corner and Gill (2015) discover that while members of terrorist organizations typically do not suffer from mental illness, lone-actor terrorists are more likely to have a mental illness. Childers (2013) explains how an assassination can have a traumatizing impact on the citizens of a country attacked. Similarly, Freedman (1984) highlights the psychological effect President Kennedy's assassination had on the American public.

GLOBAL TRENDS

The Global Terrorism Database (GTD) is one of the most comprehensive sources for studying terrorism, as it attempts to record every terrorist attack that has occurred worldwide since 1970. The GTD contains over 100 different variables, and codes for various attack types, including assassination[1]. While there is no single database that records all types of assassination events, the comprehensive nature of the GTD makes it a useful source for studying political assassinations by terrorists.

Using the GTD, Table 26.1 displays the global political assassination trends from 1970 to 2014. As seen in this table, about 17,000 political and non-political assassinations have occurred globally. Government targets are attacked more often than targets unaffiliated with the government, with a total of 9,169 political assassinations occurring during this

---

[1] See Global Terrorism Database. National Consortium for the Study of Terrorism and Responses to Terrorism (START). (2016). Retrieved from www.start.umd.edu/gtd.

Table 26.1. Political assassination trends, 1970–2014

	Total	%
Political assassinations	9,169	55
Non-political assassinations	7,489	45
All assassinations (political and non-political)	16,658	100
Political Assassination Success		
Successful	6,673	73
Unsuccessful	2,496	27
Political Assassination Weapon Type		
Firearms	6,467	71
Explosives	1,744	27
Top Ten Countries Experiencing Political Assassinations		
1. Iraq	796	9
2. Colombia	720	8
3. United Kingdom	711	8
4. Peru	618	7
5. Philippines	546	6
6. India	508	6
7. Spain	431	5
8. Afghanistan	424	5
9. Pakistan	363	4
10. El Salvador	254	3
Total	5,371	58.6

Source: Global Terrorism Database (2016)

time period compared to 7,489 assassinations of non-political targets. The majority of political assassinations are successful (i.e., the target is killed). Firearms are used in political assassinations far more frequently than explosives, indicating that firearms are the most effective weapon type for eliminating specific targets. Table 26.1 also shows the top ten countries that have experienced political assassinations. Together, these ten nations account for almost 60 percent of the political assassinations that have occurred between 1970 and 2014.

Graph 26.1 displays the yearly totals of political assassinations. A notable spike in activity occurred during the late 1980s and early 1990s. Beginning in the late 1990s, political assassinations declined drastically until around 2009, when they increased sharply.

Of all the different types of political assassinations, the murder of a head of state/head of government can have particularly destabilizing repercussions. This is illustrated by the 1994 assassinations of the President of Rwanda (Juvenal Habyarimana) and the President of Burundi (Cyprien Ntaryamira), which precipitated the Rwandan Genocide. Table 26.2 presents a list of significant assassinations of government leaders that have occurred since 1980. As seen in Table 26.2, most of these incidents have occurred in the Middle East and India. It can be inferred from this table that terrorist groups operating in other regions are less concerned with assassinating heads of government to accomplish their goals. For example, the Earth Liberation Front (ELF) and Animal Liberation Front (ALF) are two far-left extremist groups active in the USA. These groups primarily seek to damage property to

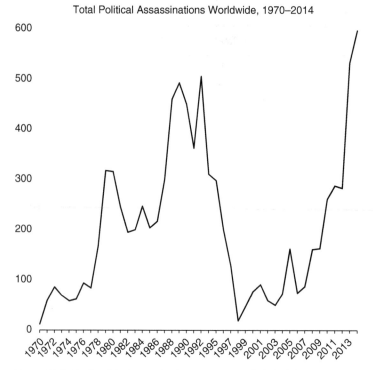

Figure 26.1. Total political assassinations worldwide, 1970–2014.
Source: Global Terrorism Database (2016)

convey their political messages as opposed to inflicting death or injury, which may explain why they carry out few assassinations.

As illustrated above, the GTD is a valuable source for examining global trends in political assassinations by terrorists. Future research could benefit from the compilation of a similar database containing assassination events carried out by other actors, including the mentally ill, organized crime groups, states, and corporations.

PREVENTION MEASURES AND THREAT ASSESSMENT

To prevent against political assassinations by both terrorists and mentally ill individuals, countries can implement a variety of prevention measures. The framework of situational crime prevention (SCP) is particularly useful for developing these measures. A central tenet of SCP is that measures that alter a crime's physical environment can help disrupt the opportunities that facilitate a crime's occurrence. Clarke and Newman (2006) pioneered the application of SCP to terrorism, and they argue that prevention measures should: increase terrorists' efforts, increase terrorists' risks, reduce the rewards or satisfaction that terrorists get from attacks, and reduce the provocations and excuses used by terrorists to justify their attacks. Examples of SCP-based assassination prevention measures include: armed security personnel, security checkpoints, entry and exit restrictions, electronic surveillance, target hardening measures like bullet-proof vehicles and vests, barriers in front of relevant buildings, traffic restrictions and road barriers, and having targets alter their daily travel routes.

Table 26.2. Important political assassinations

Name	Year
Anwar Sadat (president, Egypt)	1981
Mohammad-Ali Rajai (president, Iran)	1981
Mohammad-Javad Bahonar (prime minister, Iran)	1981
Maurice Bishop (prime minister, Grenada)	1983
Indira Gandhi (prime minister, India)	1984
Olof Palme (prime minister, Sweden)	1986
Rene Moawad (president, Lebanon)	1989
Samuel Doe (president, Liberia)	1990
Rajiv Gandhi (former prime minister, India)	1991
Melchior Ndadaye (president, Burundi)	1993
Ranasinghe Premadasa (president, Sri Lanka)	1993
Juvenal Habyarimana (president, Rwanda)	1994
Cyprien Ntaryamira (president, Burundi)	1994
Yitzhak Rabin (prime minister, Israel)	1995
Vazgen Sarkisian (prime minister, Armenia)	1999
Rafic Hariri (former prime minister, Lebanon)	2005
Benazir Bhutto (former prime minister, Pakistan)	2007

Source: Global Terrorism Database (2016); Iqbal and Zorn (2006)

Along with these prevention measures that are directed towards disrupting attack opportunities, the utilization of threat assessment units within law enforcement agencies is useful for investigating the dangers posed to public figures, particularly with regards to threats made by individuals suffering from mental illness. Threat assessment groups have been successfully formed in law enforcement agencies worldwide, effectively connecting individuals who threaten public officials with mental health services. In the USA, threat assessment groups exist in the Capitol Police, the Secret Service, and the Los Angeles Police Department (LAPD). The Fixated Threat Assessment Centre (FTAC) was formed to address threats in the United Kingdom, and the Threat Assessment Unit of the Netherlands National Police Agency was formed to investigate threats to government officials (James & Farnham, 2016).

CONCLUSION

This chapter concludes that, in order to protect public officials, prevention measures based on SCP can be implemented to disrupt opportunities for attacks. In addition, law enforcement agencies should utilize threat assessment centers to proactively investigate and respond to threats made against public officials. In some cases, mentally ill individuals who threaten public figures may have no history of receiving any medical treatment for their mental health condition. Threat assessment centers therefore serve an important intervention role by connecting these individuals with relevant services before their threats escalate into more serious behavior.

REFERENCES

Childers, J. P. (2013). The democratic balance: President McKinley's assassination as domestic trauma. *Quarterly Journal of Speech*, 99(2), 156–179.

Clarke, R. V. & Newman, G. R. (2006). *Outsmarting the terrorists*. New York: Praeger.

Corner, E. & Gill, P. (2015). A false dichotomy? Mental illness and lone-actor terrorism. *Law and Human Behavior*, 39(1), 23.

Freedman, L. Z. (1984). Social impact of attack on a president: Its public reverberations. *Behavioral Sciences & the Law*, 2(2), 195–206.

Iqbal, Z. & Zorn, C. (2006). Sic semper tyrannis? Power, repression, and assassination since the Second World War. *The Journal of Politics*, 68(3), 489–501.

James, D. V. & Farnham, F. R. (2016). Outcome and efficacy of interventions by a public figure threat assessment and management unit: A mirrored study of concerning behaviors and police contacts before and after intervention. *Behavioral Sciences & the Law*, 34(5), 660–680.

Kelly, A. (2018, March 9). "Attacks and killings": human rights activists at growing risk, study claims. *Guardian*. Retrieved from www.theguardian.com/global-development/2018/mar/09/human-rights-activists-growing-risk-attacks-and-killings-study-claims.

Mandala, M. & Freilich, J. D. (2017). Preventing successful assassination attacks by terrorists: An environmental criminology approach. *Journal of Criminological Research, Policy and Practice*, 3(3), 173–191.

Meloy, J. R., James, D. V., Farnham, F. R., Mullen, P. E., Pathé, M., Darnley, B., & Preston, L. (2004). A research review of public figure threats, approaches, attacks, and assassinations in the United States. *Journal of Forensic Sciences*, 49(5), 1–8.

Nice, D. C. (1994). Partisan realignment, the modern presidency, and presidential assassination. *Social Science Journal*, 31(3), 293–305.

Transnational Organized Crime

Organized crime is usually thought of as being committed by highly organized, professional criminals operating at domestic levels. The current researchers are now suggesting that organized crime consists of a much larger number of small, criminal enterprises, often transitory in nature, that develop to exploit opportunities for illegal profit. This new picture of organized crime is reinforced by the results of research on transnational crime such as money laundering, trafficking in women and stolen cars, and counterfeiting of currency and high-value products. Consistent with routine activity theory, these new forms of organized crime have emerged in response to new opportunities for criminal profit resulting from increased globalization and technological development. Globalization has led to increased migration, legal and illegal, which in turn has increased the opportunities for transnational crimes. Recent immigrants still have ties in their home countries, which enable them to find the partners needed for transnational crime. So, connectivity is a key factor leading directly to increased opportunity for transnational organized crime (see Albanese, Chapter 27). The "transnational" nature of organized crime (see von Lampe, Chapter 28) has become a serious global security threat that exhilarating corruption, infiltrating business and politics, and obstructing development beyond borders.

But it is unclear which kinds of organizations are most dominant, the hierarchical mafia-type or loosely linked criminal entrepreneurs. The recent definitions of organized crime promulgated by the UN and EU, which require only that only two or three offenders are acting in concert, have complicated the issue. If accepted, almost by definition, or at least by the laws of statistics, these definitions would mean that the vast majority of organized crime groups are small groups of criminal entrepreneurs. On the other hand, a survey of 40 organized crime groups in 16 countries conducted in 2000 by the UN Office on Drugs and Crime gives a quite different picture. It found that two-thirds of the groups had a classical, hierarchical structure, while one-third of them were more loosely organized. Furthermore, most of the groups were of moderate size (20–50 members), engaged in only one primary criminal activity, but operated in several countries (see Calderoni, Chapter 29). This is not the place to sort out this apparent confusion about the nature of organized crime and the organizations involved, but it does provide an important challenge for future research.

In Chapter 30, Vincenzo Ruggiero provides description of the Italian Mafia, generally portrayed as being involved in a wide variety of different criminal enterprises, such as drug dealing, smuggling, extortion (see Savona and Zanella, Chapter 31), prostitution, and so forth. Chapters in this section provide a wealth of information about criminal organizations from the various regions of the world, including Russian organized crime (Sukharenko and Lesneskie, Chapter 32), Balkan organized crime groups (Arsovska, Chapter 33), Asian organized crime groups (Lee, Chapter 34) and America's drug cartels (Arias, Chapter 35).

To date, there is a growing recognition of the organized crime-terrorism nexus that could create powerful synergies to cause enormous threat to world peace and security. Transnational organized crime (TOC) groups and terrorist groups operate under similar crime opportunities in space and time, warranting an understanding of varied relationships between them. In Chapter 36, Theodore Leggett provides an account of the "nexus" between organized crime and terrorism with an interesting perspective for further research.

27 Transnational Organized Crime

Jay S. Albanese

In 2018, both the founder of Backpage.com and its associated companies pleaded guilty to conspiracy to facilitate prostitution in interstate and foreign commerce and also money laundering. Backpage.com was a website with "personal" ads that were found to be a cover for prostitution and sex trafficking (US Department of Justice, Office of Public Affairs, 2018). In another case, a multi-jurisdiction investigation into the illegal trafficking of American eels resulted in 11 individuals charged with the illegal trafficking of more than US$2.75 million-worth of elvers (young eels). Eels are highly valued in Asia for human consumption, but overfishing has led to a decline in the eel population there. Harvesters and exporters of American eels in the USA can sell elvers to east Asia for more than US$2,000 per pound (US Department of Justice, Office of Public Affairs, 2017).

These scenarios show how organized criminal conduct occurs across national borders, but these are not traditional forms of criminal activity. What are the essential elements of transnational organized crime?

WHAT IS ORGANIZED CRIME?

The most obvious distinction between organized crime and other forms of criminal conduct is that it is "organized." In general terms, organized crime is any continuing criminal enterprise that rationally works to profit from illicit activities that are often in great public demand. Its continuing existence is maintained through the use of force, threats, monopoly control, and/or the corruption of public officials (Albanese, 2015). It is distinguished from other forms of criminal behavior in the following four primary ways.

(1) It emanates from a continuing enterprise to profit from criminal activity.
(2) Its crimes are rationally planned.
(3) It requires force, threats, monopoly control, or corruption to insulate itself from prosecution.
(4) It often caters to public demand for illicit goods and services.

Organized crime does not require a formal hierarchy or continuity in membership, and the group may be large or only a few people. Transnational organized crime has the added requirement that the crimes are planned, executed, or have impacts across national borders.

Table 27.1. Typology of organized crime activities

Type of Activity	Nature of Activity (Specific Crimes)	Harm
Provision of illicit goods Provision of illicit services	Gambling, lending, sex, narcotics, stolen property (examples of offenses: trafficking in drugs, stolen property, counterfeit goods).	• Consensual activities. • Usually no inherent violence in the activity (but possibly in protecting it). • Economic harm.
Infiltration of legitimate business or government	Coercive use or insider abuse of legal businesses or government agencies for purposes of exploitation (examples of offenses: extortion, corruption, money laundering).	• Usually nonconsensual activities. • Threats, violence, extortion are endemic. • Economic harm.

TYPES OF ACTIVITIES OF ORGANIZED CRIME

Organized crime involves two general types of activity: provision of illicit goods and services and infiltration of legitimate business or government (see Table 27.1).

The provision of illicit goods and services involves consensual activities between the organized crime group and the customer, involving no inherent violence in the activity itself, although economic harm is produced to legitimate society. On the other hand, the infiltration of legitimate business and government is inherently non-consensual, because organized crime elements push the business or government agency from their lawful purposes by: a) forcing themselves on legal businesses or government entities to illegally extort funds or obtain unjust financial advantage; or b) criminally motivated business or government insiders misuse their positions to exploit the business or government agency for criminal purposes.

Because agreements to provide illegal products cannot be enforced in court, organized crime groups must enforce agreements on their own with threats and sometimes actual violence. The use or threat of violence has several objectives. It intimidates outsiders, terrorizes would-be informers, discourages competition, and encourages quick settlement of disputes. Therefore, threats and violence enforce contracts, and also perform symbolic functions, similar to the use of force by legal governments in discouraging undesirable behaviors in conventional society.

ORGANIZING TO COMMIT CRIMES

The offenses of conspiracy and criminal association create criminal liability for those participating in the criminal activities of organized criminal groups. These offenses criminalize acts that involve participation in an organized criminal group.

In simple terms, conspiracy is an offense that is based on an agreement of two or more persons to commit crime, whereas criminal association is an offense for participating in the activities of an organized criminal group. Conspiracy is used in common-law countries, such as the UK, the USA, and Canada, and criminal association is the principle used in civil-law countries, such as Germany, Spain, France, and Italy. Several countries have implemented both conspiracy and criminal association (Hauck & Peterke, 2016; Okoth, 2014; Sergi, 2014).

Racketeering is a newer kind of law with an objective similar to conspiracy and criminal association, but it has a broader scope. The crime of racketeering was established in the USA in 1970, providing for extended penalties for crimes committed as part of an ongoing criminal enterprise. The Act is called Racketeer Influenced and Corrupt Organizations (RICO) and makes it unlawful to acquire, operate, or receive income from an enterprise through a pattern of racketeering activity. Several other countries have laws with similar intent, and the scope of these laws varies (Ayling & Broadhurst, 2014). In sum, conspiracy focuses on *planning* crime, criminal association on *participating* in organized crime groups, while racketeering focuses on the criminal *enterprise*.

Systematic extortion on a regular basis has also been called extortion racketeering. Although both extortion and racketeering imply planned intimidation, violence, corruption, and duress, extortion racketeering connotes the goal of organized crime not only to sell illegal goods and services, but also to create criminal monopolies by extorting and controlling those who provide illegal goods and services (Transcrime, 2012).

"Protection racket" is an analogous term to extortion racketeering, describing a situation where money is extracted from a victim in exchange for not doing damage to a business, construction site, or their employees and customers. When a victim refuses to pay, damage occurs and the victim often relents and pays under duress. There are many documented accounts of organized crime groups that have infiltrated construction unions, hotels, restaurants, and waste disposal businesses, or crime groups around the world systematically demanding kickbacks to avoid property damage, harassment of customers, or work stoppages.

SCOPE OF ORGANIZED CRIME

The range and scope of the objects of transnational organized crime vary by location and opportunity. Because it is profit-driven activity, the offenses correspond with the ability to exploit an illicit economic opportunity. Common examples include:

- drug production and trafficking
- firearms trafficking
- environmental crime and wildlife trafficking
- counterfeit products trafficking
- arts and antiquities trafficking
- human trafficking and migrant smuggling
- illegal gambling businesses
- cybercrime (hacking, ransomware, malware attacks)

Table 27.2 illustrates how the manifestations of these basic forms of organized crime have changed over the years. There has been an evolution from fencing stolen televisions and stereos to theft of intellectual property, such as software codes and pirated copies of movies. A shift has occurred from traditional prostitution to trafficking in human beings, where victims are moved using fraud or coercion to force them into sexual slavery. In analogous fashion, simple business scams have moved toward more sophisticated (and harder to detect) frauds.

Table 27.2. Shifts in the nature of organized crime activity

Original Activity	Modern Version
Local numbers gambling	Internet gambling at international sites
Heroin, cocaine trafficking	Synthetic drugs, less vulnerable to supply interruption
Street prostitution	Sex trafficking via the Internet or forced migration
Extortion of local businesses for protection	Extortion via cybercrime ransomware or malware
Fencing of stolen property	Misuse and theft of intellectual property

TYPES OF ORGANIZED CRIME GROUPS

There have been hundreds of cases and studies of organized crime groups with many interesting findings. It is impossible to summarize all of them across time, location, and crime types, but four different types of organized crime groups are characterized in a large number of empirical studies. These four types include hierarchical, local cultural, enterprise, and networked organized crime structures.

Some organized crime groups rely on hierarchical structure, as large, centrally controlled, highly organized entities that form the basis for the hierarchical model of organized crime. Sometimes there is a "family" structure (not necessarily related by blood) with military-style ranks from the boss down to soldiers. Bosses control the activities of the family. A second kind of organized crime group relies on local cultural ties. In these groups, the importance of heritage (i.e., racial, ethnic, or other cultural ties) forms the basis for trust in working criminal relationships. In these groups, organized crime members often obtain relatively little direction or supervision in their day-to-day activities. The third type, the business enterprise model of organized crime, focuses on how economic considerations, rather than hierarchical or cultural considerations, lie at the base of the formation and success of organized crime groups. The enterprise model labels economic concerns as the primary cause of organized criminal behavior and the relationships among the group as based in business considerations, rather than hierarchy or culture. A fourth type of structure of organized crime often occurs in the virtual world of cyberspace. Cyberspace is the electronic marketplace in which illicit goods and services are sold, and businesses sometimes infiltrated, without physical contact between the supplier and customer. Networks of convenience emerge in which criminals associate, perhaps temporarily, and only when it is necessary to do so. These circumstances might involve the need to find members with certain skills or access to supply, customers, or competitors.

It can be seen that four types of organized crime structures have been found to exist when examining specific types of organized crime activity. Organized crime groups exist in all cultures and nations, and are interethnic in nature (Albanese, 2015). Table 27.3 summarizes the different kinds of organized crime groups and networks.

RESPONDING TO TRANSNATIONAL ORGANIZED CRIME

In a world of nearly 200 sovereign countries with their own legal systems and rule-of-law capacities, it is difficult to address crimes that have impacts across borders with single-country solutions. Improving the legal or crime prevention capacity of a single country cannot be

Table 27.3. Typology of organized crime groups

Type of Group or Network	Nature of Activity	Examples
1. Hierarchical groups with a family structure and lines of authority	Bosses oversee the activities of members.	Mafia groups in Italy and the USA; Yakuza in Japan.
2. Ethnic or culturally based groups that associate in both criminal and non-criminal social activity	Groups perform social functions apart from just criminal activity. Groups define relationships among members, inspire loyalty and trust, and have an ongoing structure.	Many local groups involved in trafficking and extortion in different cities and larger areas.
3. Enterprise groups arising to exploit an economic opportunity	Operate like a business, exploiting available opportunities for profit, not ethnically exclusive or hierarchical.	Some groups involved in counterfeiting and trafficking in arts and antiquities or firearms, among other products.
4. Groups or networks that emerge to exploit a specific criminal opportunity	Groups act as a network where members come together because of access, connections, or expertise needed to carry out a particular criminal scheme, but there is no ongoing group structure.	Smaller networks involved in specific enterprises, such as cybercrime, human trafficking, counterfeiting, or fraud, as seen in recent cases emanating from Eastern Europe, Asia, and Africa.

effective against crimes that by definition are transnational. If the findings of a EUROPOL report hold true for the rest of the world, 70 percent of organized crime groups operating on an international level were found to be active in more than three countries (EUROPOL, 2017).

Multi-jurisdictional crimes require international cooperation, so that crimes, offenders, and criminal assets can be pursed across national borders. The United Nations Convention against Transnational Organized Crime was adopted in 2000 following several years of drafting and negotiations. It entered into force in 2003 after the first 30 nations ratified, and it is now ratified by 98 percent of the 193 UN member states.

Specific measures are included in the binding UN Convention to require an enhanced transnational response. These measures include mutual legal assistance, extradition, joint investigations, international cooperation for transfer of criminal proceedings, and transfer of sentenced persons. A Conference of Parties to the Convention meets every two years to monitor compliance with its provisions (UN Office on Drugs and Crime, 2018).

THE SCOPE AND FUTURE OF TRANSNATIONAL ORGANIZED CRIME

Organized crime was originally a local or regional phenomenon, but it has become an international problem for reasons that include globalization, the opening of borders to more trade and travel, and a growing ease of communication via the Internet, worldwide e-mail, and access to mobile phones. These changes have been promoted by social and technological changes that include the collapse of the Soviet Union, a large number of emerging states experiencing conflict, increased migration worldwide, and advances in technology that facilitate the movement of illegal goods, services, money, and people. These global changes have had the effect of "shrinking" the world, making possible the shift from local, neighborhood enterprises to national and international schemes linking illicit supply with illicit demand. The time lag between the supply and consumption of illegal goods has decreased as they can now be moved very quickly from source to destination.

As noted earlier in Table 27.2, the forms of organized crime have become more sophisticated, transnational forms in response to these global changes. Intervention and prevention efforts must keep pace, reducing the opportunities for organized crime networks to form and be successful.

What were once localized organized crime problems have become manifestations of transnational organized crime, as criminal networks exploit suppliers and markets for the provision and consumption of illicit goods and services.

CONCLUSIONS

It remains to be seen whether nations can reduce their high demand for illicit products and services, secure their borders from those interested in trafficking in these products, and successfully prosecute those organized crime networks already present. The long-term solution to transnational organized crime will be a reduction in demand for the products and services that fund transnational organized crime, but in the short term greater efforts toward detection and prosecution are necessary to disrupt organized crime operations. Also, crime prevention efforts are needed to reduce the supply of vulnerable victims and available markets through pressures placed on motivated offenders and their products, as well as greater economic development and anticorruption efforts to reduce the temptations of illicit organized criminal activity around the world.

REFERENCES

Albanese, J. S. (2015). *Organized crime: From the Mob to transnational organized crime*. London and New York: Routledge.

Ayling, J. & Broadhurst, R. (2014). Organized crime control in Australia and New Zealand. In L. Paoli (Ed.), *The Oxford handbook of organized crime*. Oxford: Oxford University Press.

EUROPOL. (2017). *Serious and organised crime threat assessment*. Brussels: European Union.

Hauck, P. & Peterke, S. (Eds). (2016). *International law and transnational organised crime*. Oxford: Oxford University Press.

Okoth, J. R. A. (2014). *The crime of conspiracy in international criminal law*. New York: Springer.

Sergi, A. (2014). Organised crime in criminal law: Conspiracy and membership offences in Italian, English and international frameworks. *King's Law Journal*, 25, 185–200.

Transcrime. (2012). *Study on extortion and racketeering: The need for an instrument to combat activities*. Brussels: European Commission.

US Department of Justice, Office of Public Affairs. (2018, April 12). *Backpage's co-founder and CEO, as well as several Backpage-related corporate entities, enter guilty pleas* [press release]. Retrieved from www.justice.gov/opa/pr/backpage-s-co-founder-and-ceo-well-several-backpage-related-corporate-entities-enter-guilty.

(2017, April 5). *Brooklyn seafood dealer pleads guilty for illegally trafficking American eels* [press release]. Retrieved from www.justice.gov/opa/pr/brooklyn-seafood-dealer-pleads-guilty-illegally-trafficking-american-eels.

UN Office on Drugs and Crime. (2018). *Organized crime*. Retrieved from www.unodc.org/unodc/en/organized-crime/intro.html.

28 Transnational Crime

Patterns and Trends

Klaus von Lampe

INTRODUCTION

The concept of transnational crime encompasses criminal activities that somehow transcend international borders. At the core of transnational criminal activity is the exploitation of crime opportunities that do not exist or are not as lucrative in a local or national context. A wide range of predatory and market-based crimes fall into this category (Albanese, 2011). For example, agriculturally based drugs like cocaine or heroin are produced in certain countries because of climatic conditions, but are marketed in other countries where demand and profits are higher; or predatory criminals located in a country with a low standard of living seek out victims in wealthier countries. The purpose of this chapter is to outline some significant patterns in the commission and geographical distribution of transnational crime and to hint at how the pertinent phenomena have been developing over recent decades.

WHAT CROSSES BORDERS?

In order to adequately capture the complexity of transnational crimes it is important to make some crucial differentiations. Transnational crime involves (separately or in combination) the cross-border movement of persons, goods, and information. Persons cross borders, for example, in the case of human smuggling and human trafficking, and goods are brought across borders in the smuggling of contraband like drugs or weapons. Information, in the form of digital images, is what crosses borders in the distribution of child pornography over the Internet, and in transnational fraud schemes where victims, through deceptive emails or social-media messages, are enticed to transfer money electronically to a foreign country. An example for a combination of the cross-border movement of goods and information would be the distribution of illegal drugs through the darknet (where the seller is located in one country, and the buyer in another). The communication between buyer and seller involves the cross-border flow of information while the drugs are physically transported across the border, for example, by mail.

It is important to emphasize that offenders do not necessarily cross borders when they carry out transnational crimes. In fact, the only type of transnational crime where the cross-border movement of offenders is inevitable is in cases of cross-border predatory crime where perpetrators are based in one country and operate in another country, for example, to burglarize homes or rob jewelry stores (Weenink, Huisman, & Van der Laan, 2004).

THE DIRECTIONALITY OF CROSS-BORDER MOVEMENT

Apart from the question of what crosses the border, it is necessary to consider the directionality of cross-border movement. Again, this has implications for both criminals and law enforcement agencies. Certain transnational crime schemes involve the crossing of borders in only one direction, for example, when drugs are smuggled from a source country through transit countries to a destination country. Other schemes require the bidirectional crossing of borders, for example, in the case of cross-border predatory crime when the perpetrators first cross the border from their home country to the country of operation, and then, in the opposite direction, when they return to their home country. There is a third category of transnational crimes where borders are crossed many times, sometimes repeatedly, and sometimes in a circular pattern. This includes cases of subsidy fraud and tax fraud (for example, VAT carousel fraud within the European Union), where the payment of subsidies or tax refunds are linked to commodities being shipped from one country to another (Pashev, 2008).

SMUGGLING SCHEMES

The smuggling of contraband arguably makes up the bulk of transnational crime. Four main types of smuggling schemes can be distinguished with respect to how the border is crossed:

- smuggling outside of regular border crossings
- smuggling under the guise of non-commercial (tourist) travel
- smuggling under the guise of international trade
- smuggling by mail or parcel post

The mode of smuggling has implications for the volume of contraband per shipment, the means of transportation, risks of detection, and the level of complexity and sophistication of smuggling operations.

When contraband is smuggled outside of regular border crossings, smugglers seek to completely avoid the detection of cross-border movement, for example, by selecting remote, poorly monitored stretches of the border, by using low-flying aircraft that stay below the radar, or by digging tunnels underneath the border. In a mountainous terrain such as that along the Turkish-Iranian border the volume of smuggling shipments may be limited to what a donkey can carry, while sophisticated tunnels built by engineers between Mexico and the USA allow for the movement of multi-ton quantities. What smuggling schemes outside of regular border crossings have in common is that they tend to require familiarity with local conditions.

When smuggling takes place under the guise of tourist travel, contraband is hidden in the luggage, on or inside the body of the smuggler, or inside private motor vehicles such as cars and campers. Not the cross-border movement as such is hidden, but the fact that goods are brought across the border. The size of shipments in these cases is limited which means that to increase volume, the frequency of cross-border movements or the number of smugglers (often called mules) has to be increased. The main challenge for smugglers operating under the guise of tourist travel is to develop and apply effective techniques of concealment and deception.

In the case of smuggling under the guise of international trade, contraband is hidden among, or is falsely declared as, legal goods. In other words, smugglers do not seek to conceal the movement of goods as such, but merely the illegal nature of these goods. Commonly, contraband, just like legal goods, is transported in standardized 20-ft. or 40-ft. shipping containers. The volume of a smuggling shipment is limited by the dimension of these containers. Broadly speaking, smuggling embedded in legal trade allows for the largest shipments of contraband. For example, a 40-ft (12.2m) container can hold about 10 million cigarettes, compared to about 500,000 cigarettes that fit into a van, around 50,000 that fit into the trunk of a car, and around 3,000 that someone can hide under his or her clothes. The challenge for smugglers opting for shipping containers as the means of transportation is the need to function as legal businesses in the sending and the receiving country, to interact with legal businesses such as hauling companies, and to cope with the fact that the containers have to be cleared with customs.

Smuggling by mail and parcel post is similar to smuggling under the guise of tourist travel in that the volume of individual contraband shipments is limited. There can also be similarities with smuggling embedded in international trade when mailings purport to contain commercial goods. An important distinction has to be made between smuggling shipments that are sent directly to final customers, which is the typical scenario for illegal goods marketed online, and the use of mail and parcel services by smuggling enterprises higher up in the distribution chain.

THE GEOGRAPHY OF TRANSNATIONAL CRIME

Smuggling and other forms of transnational criminal activities follow certain geographical patterns (Giommoni, Aziani, & Berlusconi, 2017). With respect to smuggling, a crucial distinction has to be made between source, transit, and destination countries. With respect to cross-border predatory crime, home-base countries of offenders and countries of operation where the victimization occurs need to be distinguished.

Five main factors have been identified that help explain these patterns. At a very general level, transnational crime is shaped by "criminogenic asymmetries" (Passas, 1998), cross-national differences in social, economic, political, and legal conditions that create opportunities and incentives for crime. For example, cross-border differences in wealth may give rise to cross-border predatory crime, and tax differentials can make it lucrative to smuggle high-excise goods like gasoline and cigarettes from countries where taxes are low. Another factor is geographical proximity. For example, the role of Iran as an important transit country for heroin can be explained by the fact that it shares borders with Afghanistan and Pakistan, two important source countries for heroin (Sabatelle, 2011). Similarly, transnational crime patterns can be explained by social proximity: close social bonds that connect countries even across great geographical distances, for example, in the form of kinship ties that transcend borders as a result of migration. Smuggling routes have also been found to mirror trade routes, arguably because it is cheaper and safer to move contraband with the large flow of legal goods. Finally, countries can play a role in transnational crime because they lack the capacity to enforce the law and to protect their borders. These so-called weak states or failed states may function as safe havens for criminals and serve as transshipment centers along smuggling routes.

TRANSNATIONAL CRIMINAL STRUCTURES

By definition, the exploitation of opportunities for transnational crime requires offenders to be willing and able to either (virtually or physically) cross borders or network with other criminals across borders. This involves a wide array of offender structures. Often, transnational criminals are classified along ethnic lines given that in certain areas of transnational crime there is a disproportionate involvement of offenders of particular ethnic or national backgrounds due to, for example, social proximity between source and destination countries of illegal goods (Paoli & Reuter, 2008). Overall, however, it is more important for understanding the organization of transnational criminals by looking into aspects like the form and function of criminal structures.

In one extreme, there are cohesive criminal organizations that single-handedly cover all aspects of a cross-border crime scheme. In the other extreme, numerous individuals and small groups cooperate along smuggling routes and illegal supply chains. An example of the former type is the Cali Cartel, one of the large Colombian drug trafficking organizations of the 1980s and 1990s, which maintained a net of operatives in transit and destination countries to handle the smuggling and distribution of cocaine (Chepesiuk, 2003). Such complex transnational criminal organizations, however, appear to be more the exception than the rule. In fact, the Cali Cartel and other notorious drug cartels of the era were eventually dismantled and a large number of smaller groups took their place (Decker & Chapman, 2008). Generally speaking, research in areas such as drug trafficking, human trafficking, and alien smuggling has found chains of individual offenders, partnerships, and small groups connected in more or less temporary cooperative arrangements to be the most prevalent form of organization (see, e.g., Bruinsma & Bernasco, 2004).

Transnational criminal structures such as drug trafficking groups that are organized around the commission of profit-making crime need to be distinguished from other kinds of structures that are often discussed under the heading of 'transnational organized crime' but are only indirectly involved in illegal businesses. These structures include associations of criminals such as Italian Mafia-type groups, Chinese Triads, and outlaw motorcycle gangs that primarily serve non-economic purposes and are centered on the creation and strengthening of social bonds, mutual support, and a sense of belonging (von Lampe, 2016). They are transnational in nature because individual members or organizational sub-units are spread out across different countries. Mafiosi, Triad members, and outlaw bikers can draw on their respective network of trusted associates in a variety of ways such as laundering illegal profits or finding refuge from prosecution in their home country (Campana, 2011).

TRENDS OVER TIME

The nature and extent of transnational crime is influenced by various factors that undergo constant changes. After the end of the Cold War, transnational crime was widely considered to be on the rise with criminals roaming freely in an increasingly globalized, borderless world and facilitated by global population growth and the growth of international trade. However, there are various countervailing developments that should not be overlooked. One such development pertains to international borders. Rather than losing relevance, they have become more of an obstacle for transnational criminals as border security has tightened in the wake of 9/11 and various refugee crises. It should also be noted that since the end of the Cold War, the mere number of international borders has grown with the disintegration of the Soviet Union and Yugoslavia into a large number of smaller countries. In addition, international law enforcement cooperation has become more prevalent and more effective through various legal and institutional arrangements (Hufnagel & McCartney, 2015). Other important developments can be observed with respect to the supply and demand sides of transnational illegal markets. For example, cannabis smuggling has been impacted by the decriminalization and legalization of cannabis in some countries and by domestic cannabis cultivation in important consumer countries like the United Kingdom (European Monitoring Centre for Drugs and Drug Addiction [EMCDDA], 2017). There are also constant changes in the geography of transnational crime. For example, trafficking routes have shifted as a result of successful countermeasures and the saturation of consumer markets, such as in the case of cocaine flows from Latin America to the USA and Europe (Ellis, 2009).

CONCLUSIONS

Differences between countries create opportunities and incentives for crime, while borders create challenges for those who seek to exploit these opportunities. Transnational crime varies greatly, for example, with respect to the type of crime (market-based and predatory crime), the nature of what crosses borders (persons, goods, and information), and the direction and frequency of cross-border movement. Research suggests that networks of individual offenders and small groups are more prevalent than large, integrated criminal organizations in the commission of transnational crime.

REFERENCES

Albanese, J. S. (2011). *Transnational crime and the 21st century*. New York: Oxford University Press.
Bruinsma, G. & Bernasco, W. (2004). Criminal groups and transnational illegal markets: A more detailed examination on the basis of social network theory. *Crime, Law and Social Change*, 41, 79–94.
Campana, P. (2011). Eavesdropping on the Mob: The functional diversification of mafia activities across territories. *European Journal of Criminology*, 8, 213–228.
Chepesiuk, R. (2003). *The bullet or the bribe: Taking down Colombia's Cali drug cartel*. Westport, CT: Praeger.
Decker, S. H. & Chapman, M. T. (2008). *Drug smugglers on drug smuggling: Lessons from the inside*. Philadelphia, PA: Temple University Press.
Ellis, S. (2009). West Africa's international drug trade. *African Affairs*, 108, 171–196.
European Monitoring Centre for Drugs and Drug Addiction (EMCDDA). (2017). *European drug report*. Lisbon: EMCDDA.
Giommoni, L., Aziani, A., & Berlusconi, G. (2017). How do illicit drugs move across countries? A network analysis of the heroin supply to Europe. *Journal of Drug Issues*, 47, 217–240.
Hufnagel, S. & McCartney, C. (2015). Police cooperation against transnational criminals. In N. Boister & R. J. Currie (Eds.), *Routledge handbook of transnational criminal law* (pp. 107–120). London: Routledge.
Paoli, L. & Reuter, P. (2008). Drug trafficking and ethnic minorities in Western Europe. *European Journal of Criminology*, 5(1), 13–37.

Pashev, K. (2008). Cross-border VAT fraud in an enlarged Europe. In P. C. van Duyne, J. Harvey, A. Maljevic, M. Scheinost, & K. von Lampe (Eds.), *European crime-markets at crossroads* (pp. 237–259). Nijmegen, the Netherlands: Wolf Legal Publishers.

Passas, N. (1998). A structural analysis of corruption: The role of criminogenic asymmetries. *Transnational Organized Crime*, 4, 42–55.

Sabatelle, D. R. (2011). The scourge of opiates: The Illicit narcotics trade in the Islamic Republic of Iran. *Trends in Organized Crime*, 14, 314–331.

von Lampe, K. (2016). *Organized crime: Analyzing illegal activities, criminal structures, and extra-legal governance*. Thousand Oaks, CA: Sage.

Weenink, A. W., Huisman, S., & Van der Laan, F. J. (2004). *Crime without frontiers: Crime pattern analysis Eastern Europe 2002–2003*. Driebergen, the Netherlands: Korps Landelijke Politiediensten.

29 Transnational Organized Crime Networks

Francesco Calderoni

INTRODUCTION

The concept of a network has increasingly gained prominence in the analysis of transnational organized crime. It enables analysts to capture the dynamic and adaptive social structure of organized criminal groups, overcoming the limitations associated with previously popular perspectives such as criminal organizations and illicit enterprises (McIllwain, 1999). However, it is important to distinguish between two different approaches to criminal networks that are often confused (Morselli, 2009; von Lampe, 2003).

The first approach considers a network as a specific organizational structure, characterized by dynamic patterns of exchange among several actors (Powell, 1990). Loose and dynamic networks are opposed to highly structured and formally hierarchical organizations (von Lampe, 2003). This approach is strictly associated with the increasing awareness of the relevance of networks in our society, and with the tendency to explain social structure through a network perspective. Network-related ideas are part of our everyday life, e.g., in social network services, in the popular idea that people are individuals worldwide may be connected through "six degrees of separation," and in "networking" events. The main issue with this approach is that it may be hard to classify a set of criminals as a network or as an organization, as they may show elements of flexibility (e.g., individuals swap roles and activities according to the needs) and formal structure (e.g., decisions are taken by few senior criminals) at the same time. The choice between network and organization may ultimately rest in the observer's preferences. This growing usage of network-related concepts has sometimes resulted in unwarranted claims by public authorities that organized crime has shifted from traditional hierarchical structures (e.g., the mafias) to new network structures. In fact, these statements are likely more influenced by the popularity of this approach to networks than by actual changes in the structure of organized crime groups, for which there is scarce empirical support (Natarajan, Zanella, & Yu, 2015). In other words, it seems more plausible that the observer's perspective has changed more than the subject of analysis (von Lampe, 2009).

The second approach considers networks as a specific, comprehensive, analytical perspective. Since human relations are the "least common denominator" of organized crime (McIllwain, 1999, p. 304), any group can be examined in a network perspective, ranging from formally structured mafias to spontaneous and short-term associations among criminals

(Morselli, 2009; Waring, 2002). The criminal network is thus a separate, although complementary, dimension to the analysis of the organizational structure of a criminal group. This second approach has gained significant importance since the 2000s, when criminologist started to apply the social network analysis in organized crime research (Natarajan, 2000). The main instrument of analysis within this approach is the use of social network analysis, a method which has gained increasing popularity in criminology since the last decade. A criminal network is thus a set of individuals engaged in criminal activity and mutually connected by social relations such as acquaintance, communication, and co-offending. A transnational organized crime network is a criminal network that shows the typical features of organized crime (e.g., internal structure, continuity, violence) and whose activities are transnational, i.e., involving different countries (McIllwain, 1999).

This chapter introduces a few basic concepts about transnational organized crime networks and summarizes the main findings from research since the 2000s.

HOW TO ANALYZE TRANSNATIONAL ORGANIZED CRIME NETWORKS: SOCIAL NETWORK ANALYSIS

The empirical study of organized crime networks has significantly grown in the last decades thanks to the increasing adoption of the social network analysis, a method investigating the structure of social relations through quantitative and mathematical techniques derived from graph theory.[1] The early developments of the social network analysis are rooted in sociology (Simmel), sociometry (Moreno), and several social scientists. It is only since the 1960s that the social network analysis has transformed into a rigorous and widespread approach in the social sciences. Integration with mathematical graph theory and the expansion of computing capacities have further expanded the scope and possibilities of network analyses.

A social network is represented as a group of actors (or nodes) and to the links (or ties) among them (Figure 29.1). The social network analysis focuses on social relations as represented by the connections among the actors. The connections are instruments for the flow of material or immaterial resources. Thus, the network analysis adopts a different point of view than "standard" social research methods such as statistics. It assumes the interdependence among the actors and does not consider the nodes as autonomous units. Unlike traditional statistics, which focus on the individual attributes (e.g., on variables such as age, income, education), the social network analysis analyzes primarily relational data (e.g., friendship, collaboration, communication). Relations do not "belong" specifically to a single actor but require at least two actors (e.g., node 1 is friend of node 2). The relations between pairs of nodes combine into a larger network generating the social structure of the group.

For many years, criminology lagged behind in the adoption of the social network analysis, possibly due to limited training in this method in criminological degrees. This is particularly surprising, as many "classic" criminological theories pointed out the role of the social environment (e.g., social disorganization, strain, and differential association theories) and the peer group (subcultures and social learning theories) in the development of deviant behavior. The late adoption of the social network analysis to study organized crime is also

---

[1] Graph theory is the mathematical study of graphs, structures made of nodes connected by links.

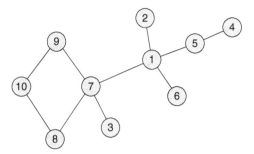

Figure 29.1. An example of a criminal network.

striking, given the importance of social relations for organized crime. Early sociological and criminological contributions had already highlighted the importance of social relations for organized crime. Whyte's classic ethnography of 1940s Italian communities in Boston showed the first attempt to represent the social relations among gang members through a graph. Research on the Italian and American Mafias (by several scholars, including Albini, Ianni, Hess, Blok) argued that mafiosi were power brokers specialized in the use of violence and in networking among different stakeholders and that – instead of a bureaucratic and hierarchical alien conspiracy – the Mafia was in fact a set of patron-client relationships, consisting in flexible networks based on kinship and friendship ties. Adler's analysis of 1970s higher-level marijuana and cocaine trafficking in California uncovered informal and flexible partnership among loosely structured groups. Starting with Natarajan (2000), a growing number of studies applied the social network analysis to criminal organizations, by systematically analyzing judicial sources to understand the internal structure of transnational organized crime. Compared to the above-mentioned and mainly qualitative works, studies relying on network analysis stimulated more quantitative analysis of criminal networks.

THE ANALYSIS OF ORGANIZED CRIME NETWORKS

Mobility of Transnational Organized Crime

Research on organized crime has generally pointed out that criminal organizations are embedded into a larger set of social relations. Criminals often rely on kinship, ethnic, and friendship ties to ensure the necessary trust to conduct criminal activities. These conclusions were supported by empirical evidence from studies on different periods and countries, ranging from Mafia families in New York to Colombian cocaine traffickers in the Netherlands, to Chinese groups smuggling migrants abroad. Studies also showed that most organized criminal groups are primarily local, since their social embeddedness often relies on strong ties within the local community. Yet, some groups may exploit the ties with ethnic diaspora communities to conduct criminal activities over longer distances or recreate criminal organizations similar to those established in the motherland in different foreign destinations.

The transnational presence and activities of organized crime networks are often debated. Some scholars (e.g., Shelley, Williams) argue that organized crime networks are illicit enterprises ready to exploit asymmetries in the regulation of goods and services across countries and can easily seize profit opportunities across the world. Transnational organized crime networks would willingly establish foreign branches and exploit global opportunities to commit crime. Other scholars (e.g., Gambetta, Varese) emphasize the local embeddedness of organized crime and suggest that these groups may face a few obstacles in expanding beyond their areas of origin. This research often argues that the mobility of criminal groups is rarely driven by rational decisions. Rather, it is often prompted by different push and pull factors that determine the movements of criminal organizations. Also, criminal groups establishing abroad often diversify their criminal activities, e.g., maintaining the core business in the home area and using foreign countries for participating in the illegal markets and laundering the illicit proceeds.

Organized Crime Networks and Illegal Markets

Research on the activities of transnational organized crime networks has examined a range of illicit markets, including smuggling of migrants, human trafficking for sexual exploit-ation, and car rigging. With the literature consistently adopting different methods, analyses of organized crime networks in illegal markets have demonstrated the flexible and dynamic structure of traffickers, suggesting that formal rules and hierarchy have a limited relevance. At the same time, studies found clear indications of a social organization, mostly driven by the characteristics of the market and the criminal environment rather than by the internal structure of specific types of transnational organized crime. Among the different markets, the drug trade is the most researched market due to its size and policy relevance (Bichler, Malm, & Cooper, 2017).

The social organization of most drug trafficking networks relies on a core set of actors densely connected among them. These individuals are often in charge of organizing major drug smuggling operations. This core set is often composed of several traffickers, individuals responsible for the organization of drug smuggling activities. They are constantly looking for opportunities to purchase illicit drugs, safely transport them to the final destination, retrieve financial resources to pay for the consignments, and distribute the loads to wholesale buyers. Other individuals participate in the trafficking in a more marginal position, e.g., by serving as couriers, enforcers, drivers, assistants, or street dealers. Other marginal subjects may grant access to specific assets and skills, further strengthening the resilience of the organization (Natarajan, 2006; Morselli, 2009; Calderoni, 2012).

For example, a study of two large-scale cocaine trafficking networks examined the network derived from the communications among the individuals mentioned in the investigations files, along with their task in the supply chain and their social status (Calderoni, 2012). The results showed the presence of a core of highly connected traffickers who constantly arranged simultaneous smuggling operations. These individuals were brokering between suppliers and buyers and ensuring that several multi-kilo consignments arrived at their Italian destinations from Spain and the Netherlands. The study pointed out that the internal hierarchy typical of the Italian Mafias had no influence on the organization of the drug-related activities. Nevertheless, individuals with higher social status successfully managed to stay far from the everyday handling of the criminal trade and limited their interventions to major moments, such as dispute settlement and strategic decisions. This internal social organization granted to the most important criminals indirect control over the illicit trade, at the same time ensuring better insulation from possible law enforcement intervention. The example shows how the analysis of the communication patterns within a criminal network can provide insight into the social structure of the group.

CONCLUSION

This chapter summarized the current knowledge on transnational organized crime networks, highlighting a few main points. First, there are two main approaches to transnational organized crime networks. The first one considers them as a specific form of structural organization, while the second one suggests that all types of criminal group are networks that can be analyzed through a social network analysis. Second, studies of criminal networks have exponentially grown since the 2000s and have improved the knowledge on the functioning of transnational organized crime groups. Third, transnational criminal networks often rely on pre-existing social relations, thus facing difficulties in moving across the world to seize opportunities for illicit profits. Nevertheless, specific factors may favor the transnational movements of criminal groups, which are likely to diversify their activities depending on specific market- and environmental factors. Fifth, studies of transnational organized crime networks pointed out the dynamics and flexible nature of these groups, which often revolve around a core of very active individuals but also rely on peripheral nodes providing specific assets.

In conclusion, it is likely that the growth of studies on criminal networks will continue in the coming years and that it will significantly improve our understanding of the internal functioning of illicit markets and groups. This development will enable researchers and policy makers to design better international and national policies and to avoid possible stereotyped and simplified narratives that have influenced the public, the media, and sometimes even the scholarly understanding of complex criminal organizations.

REFERENCES

Bichler, G., Malm, A. E., & Cooper, T. (2017). Drug supply networks: A systematic review of the organizational structure of illicit drug trade. *Crime Science*, 6, 2.

Calderoni, F. (2012). The structure of drug trafficking mafias: The 'Ndrangheta and cocaine. *Crime, Law and Social Change*, 58, 321–349.

McIllwain, J. (1999). Organized crime: A social network approach. *Crime, Law and Social Change*, 32, 301–323.

Morselli, C. (2009). *Inside criminal networks*. New York: Springer.

Natarajan, M. (2000). Understanding the structure of a drug trafficking organization: A conversational analysis. In M. Natarajan & M. Hough (Eds.), *Illegal drug markets: From research to prevention policy* (Vol. 11, pp. 273–298). Monsey: Criminal Justice Press/Willow Tree Press.

(2006). Understanding the structure of a large heroin distribution network: A quantitative analysis of qualitative data. *Journal of Quantitative Criminology*, 22, 171–192.

Natarajan, M., Zanella, M., & Yu, C. (2015). Classifying the variety of drug trafficking organizations. *Journal of Drug Issues*, 45, 409–430.

Powell, W. (1990). Neither market nor hierarchy: Network forms of organization. In B. M. Staw & L. L. Cummings (Eds.), *Research in organizational behavior* (pp. 295–336). Greenwich: JAI Press.

Von Lampe, K. (2003). Criminally exploitable ties: A network approach to organized crime. In E. C. Viano, J. Magallanes, & L. Bridel (Eds.), *Transnational organized crime: Myth, power, and profit* (pp. 9–22). Durham, NC: Carolina Academic Press.

(2009). Human capital and social capital in criminal networks: introduction to the special issue on the 7th Blankensee Colloquium. *Trends in Organized Crime, 12,* 93–100.

Waring, E. (2002). Co-offending as a network form of social organization. In D. Weisburd & E. J. Waring (Eds.), *Crime and social organization* (pp. 31–47). New Brunswick, NJ: Transaction.

30   Italian Organized Crime

Vincenzo Ruggiero

INTRODUCTION

It is widely known that the Italian Mafia, which is more appropriately termed the Sicilian Mafia, is a very specific form of organized crime – a criminal organization that may share some characteristics with its counterparts operating in other countries, while retaining some peculiar traits making it somewhat unique. In order to highlight this uniqueness, a crucial preliminary distinction should be made. According to Block (1980), there are two main types of criminal syndicate. One is the "enterprise syndicate," which operates exclusively in the arena of illicit businesses such as prostitution, gambling, contraband, and drugs. The second he calls the "power syndicate," which is predominantly engaged in extortion as a form of territorial control rather than enterprise. Territorial control is certainly one of the central objectives of the Sicilian Mafia, making it an organization of the second type in Block's classification. Its overriding aim appears to be the control over the environment and the people who are part of it (Catanzaro, 1988).

THE MILITARY MAFIA

The history of the Italian Mafia runs parallel with the history of the unitary Italian state, and though predating 1860 (the date of the unification of Italy), the Mafia is best understood against the background of the political and economic events occurring in the country in the last century-and-a-half or so. Historians have shown that landowners in Sicily employed groups affiliated to the so-called "military mafia" as their private law enforcers, entrusting them with the collection of rents, taxes, and agricultural produce. This private army also played a political role, in that it acted as a violent deterrent power against the rural labor force and its attempts to organize collective bargaining through associations of mutual aid and trade unions.

In 1876, member of parliament Leopoldo Franchetti wrote what is perhaps the most important report ever published on the Mafia. He described it as a form of political crime promoted by sectors of the ruling class, namely, official political actors and businessmen. Sectors of the elite were said to employ members of this "military mafia" and to use them as an illegal resource in their economic or political activity. The violence of the Mafia, in other words, was granted the role of discouraging economic competitors and intimidating political opponents. The management of the violent aspects of political and economic competition was, therefore, delegated to groups specializing in violence, while these groups, in exchange, were granted a relative freedom to operate in other illegal activities (mainly protection rackets and contraband). Franchetti's report, which could easily apply to the current situation, was sidelined and long neglected, and an analysis of the Italian Mafia slowly prevailed describing the organization as a glamorous group of affiliates sharing traditional cultural traits and characterized by an archaic anthropological makeup. In a recent re-writing of the history of the Mafia, however, a number of crucial events appear to corroborate the views of that old, groundbreaking report.

In 1893, Emanuele Notarbartolo, ex-mayor of Palermo and director of a leading Sicilian bank, was assassinated. Investigators discovered that the murder was the consequence of Notarbartolo's refusal to establish partnerships with fellow businessmen and politicians connected to them. Similar assassinations took place until fascism gained political power. During the 20 years of the fascist regime, Prefect Mori, also known as the "Iron Prefect," was entrusted with waging the "definitive" war against the Mafia, but he only managed to hit some elements of the "military mafia" while failing to unveil their connections with the economic and political interests they served.

After World War II the Italian Mafia was unexpectedly reinvigorated. Italy became an important strategic country in world politics because of its strong socialist party and the massive popularity of its communist party, the most powerful in the Western world. The Cold War indirectly gave the Mafia a prominent function in fighting the Soviet scare. In 1948, the very year in which the Italian Constitution was promulgated, the US National Security Council warned that "the US must use all its political, economic and, if necessary, military power to help prevent Italy falling under the influence of the USSR" (Scarpinato, 2004, p. 266). In this climate, the military mafia was again strategically used by employers and conservative politicians against opponents and competitors. In the most infamous episode of this strategy, a political rally was attacked by a Mafia gang with machine guns in Portella della Ginestra, a name that is also a scar in Italian history. The political elections held on April 20 and 21, 1947 gave the Left a significant relative majority over the Christian Democrats, the party supported by the USA. Amid growing fear of the ascent of socialism, on May Day 1947, while rural workers and their families were taking part in the traditional workers' parade, a gang led by Salvatore Giuliano opened fire, killing 12 people and injuring 27. Giuliano was hired by an alliance of conservative politicians and fearful entrepreneurs, who thought that such violent actions were part of fighting communism. Some of his associates, after being arrested, were not given a chance to denounce the officials on behalf of whom they had acted, because they were found dead in their prison cells.

The Italian Mafia has never stopped acting as a military organization, as proven by the long list of "excellent victims" of its violent action. These victims include judges, law enforcers, politicians, and intellectuals who have rebelled against the specific form of political and economic power the Mafia represents. This power system is based on a coalescence of conventional, economic, and political crime that students of different forms of organized criminality have tried to unravel in a number of ways (Antonopulos & Papanicolaou, 2018).

INTERPRETATIONS AND PERSPECTIVES

Before discussing interpretations and perspectives, it should be noted that the Mafia is not the only criminal organization operating in the Italian territory. The Calabrian 'Ndrangheta, the Neapolitan Camorra, and the Sacra Corona Unita in Apulia are deeply rooted in their respective urban contexts and, unlike the Mafia, are successful in spreading their activity beyond the local national boundaries.

In order to identify the different interpretations of these groups it is useful to refer to the concept of social organization. This concept relates to the variety of social relations that give rise to two types of networks. First, social organization can be viewed as an association, a network of relations among individuals who form some sort of culturally homogeneous group. Second, social organization can be seen as a series of transactions and a network of relations among individuals involved in a common activity, whether or not they belong to the same association, or in other words, whether or not they are socially and culturally homogeneous. Transactions range from brief encounters to elaborate, rigid, and highly coordinated undertakings. If we view social organization in terms of association, we emphasize the structure and internal cohesiveness of groups. On the contrary, if we view social organization in terms of transactions, we emphasize the structure and modality of joint activities.

Some students of Italian organized crime choose the first analytical route, thus describing the groups mentioned above as separate, cohesive entities characterized by specific cultural codes. Others opt for the second route, focusing therefore on the links these groups establish with external, mainly official actors with whom the organizations carry out joint activities. Arlacchi (1983), for example, looks at the Italian Mafia as an enterprise, viewing its criminal activity as incorporating the attributes of licit business. These attributes include an emphasis on innovation, an element of rational calculation, and an irrational and aggressive "animal spirit" incorporated in any economic enterprise. Santino and La Fiura (1990) emphasize the "power" aspect of organized crime, which is said to be guided by economic interest and, simultaneously, by the ambition to control and govern the territories in which it operates. The attempts made by the Mafia to establish forms of alliance with representatives of the local church can be regarded as part of this territorial power building (Dino, 2008). Gambetta (1992) studies the Mafia merely as a service-providing organization. Among the goods provided, trust and protection are singled out as paramount. Trust and protection, which should be supplied by the state, may under certain circumstances become the preserve of private entrepreneurs, including organized crime. This type of crime is therefore an industry for the supply of private protection and the distribution of trust to economic actors who would otherwise be unable to interact safely. In the case of the Sicilian Mafia, for example, its strength as an industry for the supply of protection and trust is deemed a consequence of the traditional popular distrust of the official agencies.

Other contributions highlight the capacity of Italian criminal organizations to polarize markets through the use of violence, thus implying that the military component of such organizations has yet to exhaust its function. Finally, observing the alliances and partnerships between organized crime and the official economic and political world, the suggestion has been made that this type of criminality combines forms of conventional delinquency with a variety of white-collar offences. This happens, in particular, when proceeds from illicit activities are invested in the official economy, where members of organized crime are said to "learn" the techniques and the rationalization of their white-collar counterparts. It has also been hypothesized that organized crime and the official world establish an exchange of services and engage in mutual entrepreneurial promotion (Ruggiero, 2017). For example, in activities such as the trafficking in weapons and the disposal of toxic waste, organized crime offers illegal transportation (or dumping) services to legitimate entrepreneurs. On the other hand, the official economy offers organized crime the opportunity to launder its profits or to invest them in some legitimate enterprise (Ruggiero, 1996). This analysis echoes recent assessments of the Mafia's current activities. It has been argued that the "military mafia" is declining, as proven by the dramatic reduction in killings and all forms of violent intimidation in Sicily. After the outrage of the 1990s, with the killings of high-profile judges such as Giovanni Falcone, the Mafia is now keeping a low profile, and violent conflict has been replaced by persuasion and cooperation. Alliances and partnerships are preferred to harsh competition leading to violence. This appears to be happening in the domain of conventional crime, in which all four organizations mentioned above are still involved, as well as in the area of legitimate economic activity. Italian criminal organizations, for example, have established good working relationships with other groups engaged in protection rackets and drugs trafficking, but also with politicians who distribute resources at the local level (Sciarrone, 2004). Groups operate with their own companies in the area of public work and service contracting, where partnerships with other legitimate companies are increasingly frequent. In this respect, it might be appropriate to talk about criminal networks, as companies owned by organized criminal groups link with other economic actors in markets where unorthodox practices and illegal behavior are widespread (Ruggiero, 2002; Gounev & Ruggiero, 2012). Criminal networks imply the existence of interdependent units linked by a wide-ranging variety of ties, including kinship, ethnicity, cultural homogeneity, social proximity, or simply business partnership. Italian organized crime may well be evolving in one such licit-illicit network (Lodato & Scarpinato, 2008).

The question has often arisen: to what extent are criminal organizations capable of expanding beyond their regional and national confines? While it is obvious that their power can be perceived outside their local context and, at times, at the national level, it is controversial whether such power can transcend the national borders and affirm itself internationally. Cases such as the "pizza connection" (international heroin trafficking) seem to prove that the Italian Mafia can establish effective working relationships with large and established communities of Sicilians resident in the USA but may find it difficult to do the same in other contexts. In this respect, as mentioned above, other criminal organizations (for example, the 'Ndrangheta, the Neapolitan Camorra, and the Sacra Corona Unita) seem to be more prone to establish international links than the Sicilian Mafia (Carnevale, Forlati, & Giolo, 2017). The international connections of the Mafia, it would appear, are the result of specific, individual initiatives of members of families setting up criminal partnerships with associates abroad, rather than a strategy driving the organization as a whole toward international expansion.

SUMMARY

This chapter provides an account of the Italian Mafia as an organization accompanying the history of united Italy, from 1860 to the present. Its uniqueness is highlighted among other forms of organized crime. Other criminal organizations are also focused upon, as is their military force. After discussing different hypotheses on the role of criminal organizations in the economy and their relationship with the official political apparatus, the chapter suggests that such organizations are now evolving into licit-illicit networks.

REFERENCES

Antonopoulos, G. A. & Papanicolaou, G. (2018). *Organized crime. A very short introduction*, Oxford: Oxford University Press.

Arlacchi, P. (1983). *La Mafia imprenditrice*. Bologna: Il Mulino.

Block, A. (1980). *East side – west side: Organizing crime in New York*. Cardiff: University of Cardiff Press.

Carnevale, S., Forlati, S., & Giolo, O. (Eds.). (2017). *Redefining organized crime*. Oxford: Hart.

Catanzaro, R. (1988). *Il delitto come impresa. Storia sociale della Mafia*. Padua: Liviana.

Dino, A. (2008). *La Mafia devota. Chiesa, religione, Cosa Noistra*. Rome/Bari: Laterza.

Gambetta, D. (1992). *La mafia siciliana. Un'industria della protezione privata*. Turin: Einaudi.

Gounev, P. & Ruggiero, V. (Eds.). (2012). *Corruption and organized crime in Europe*. London and New York: Routledge.

Lodato, S. & Scarpinato, R. (2008). *Il ritorno del principe. La criminalità dei potenti in Italia*. Milan: Charelettere.

Ruggiero, V. (1996). *Organized and corporate crime in Europe*. Aldershot: Dartmouth.

(2002). Fuzzy criminal actors. In V. Ruggiero (Ed.), *Is white collar crime organised crime?* Special issue of *Crime Law and Social Change*, 37 (3), 177–190.

(2017). *Dirty money: On financial delinquency*. Oxford: Oxford University Press.

Santino, U. & La Fiura, G. (1990). *L'impresa mafiosa*. Milan: Franco Angeli.

Scarpinato, R. (2004). La storia: Italia mafiosa e Italia civile. *Micro Mega*, 5, 259–286.

Sciarrone, R. (Ed.). (2004). *La Mafia esiste ancora*. Rome: l'Unità.

31   Extortion and Organized Crime

Ernesto U. Savona and Marco Zanella

INTRODUCTION

Extortion is "the obtaining of property from another, with his consent, induced by wrongful use of actual or threatened force, violence, or fear, or under color of official right" (The United States Code 18 USC § 1951(b)(2)). The legal definitions of extortion in other countries are similar to the US definition.

When extortion is committed on a regular basis, it turns into racketeering: "an institutionalized practice whereby tribute is collected on behalf of a criminal group that, in exchange, claims to offer [...] protection" (Volkov, 2002, p. 1).

This chapter deals with extortion, racketeering, and organized crime in Europe. The overall argument is that market opportunities for extortion driven by lack of trust in market dynamics and variations in the characteristics of organized criminal groups may give rise to two different types of extortion racketeering: systemic and casual. Extortion racketeering is systemic when it is deeply rooted and extends across a territory since it is a core part of organized crime groups' activities. Extortion racketeering is casual when it is not extended across a territory since criminal organizations do not routinely engage in such a criminal activity. These types of extortion racketeering are shaped by four interrelated variables: (1) market opportunities; (2) the organizational structure of criminal groups; (3) their presence at local level; (4) the victim/offender relationship. Put another way: on the one hand, the more organized criminal groups focus their activity on the local territory because of market opportunities, the more they develop a monopolistic position and a consequential hierarchical structure, and the more they establish parasitical and symbiotic relationships with their extortion victims, the more extortion racketeering becomes systemic (i.e., widespread and continuous). On the other hand, the more criminal market opportunities are open to transnational activities, the more criminal groups are organized in networks, and the more they establish predatory relationships with their extortion victims, the more casual extortion racketeering becomes.

Four variables and their interrelations can help us understand the nature of extortion and organized crime.

MARKET OPPORTUNITIES

Extortion is an old and simple crime committed by organized crime when the risks are low and the benefits are high. It occurs in contexts where: 1) victims do not report the crime and 2) are willing to pay the protection tax. These two conditions often arise within close-knit ethnic communities (e.g., among Italians at the beginning of the twentieth century in New York City, or among Chinese communities in the USA or in Europe). If the risk is low because of this ethnic homogeneity and the consequent control of the territory, the benefits are high only in relation to possible criminal market opportunities. Extortion is systemic when other criminal alternatives are not available or cannot be adopted because of the low expertise of the group and its organization.

ORGANIZATIONAL STRUCTURE OF CRIMINAL GROUPS

Although there is no direct relationship between the organizational structure of criminal groups and extortion, the literature and the data show that where extortion is practiced on a large scale, and is systemic, the groups that engage in it are organized hierarchically. Where extortion is more casual, their structure is more flexible (taking the form of a network).

Owing to their structure, which enables a lasting presence in a given territory, hierarchical criminal groups gain in reputation and may exercise effective threats of contingent violence against their victims. Moreover, these threats are reinforced by the fact that those threatened believe that these criminal groups "can corrupt legitimate authority or in some other way ensure that they avoid apprehension" (Reuter, 1994, p. 95) and can act as an industry which produces and sells private protection (Gambetta, 1993).

These elements of reputation – in other words, the ability to neutralize law enforcement by means of corruption, and the production and sale of protection – are closely related to the type of organized criminal group. Criminal groups with network structures "are not interested in, or capable of, exercising such a quasi-political power" (Paoli & Fijnaut, 2004, p. 608). They are too small and ephemeral to be able to carry out systemic extortion racketeering. Only in few cases are they involved in casual extortion racketeering practices. Networks may openly use violence to heighten their capacity to commit extortion, but they tend to be short-lived because they lack the necessary structure and expertise.

In sum, although it is not automatic, the relationship between hierarchical structure and systemic extortion, on the one hand, and flexible structure and casual extortion, on the other, can be explained by means of the other variables that shape extortion: the local dimension of the organized crime action, its control over the territory, and the victim/offender relationship.

OPERATIONS AT LOCAL LEVEL

Why does extortion proliferate when organized crime operates at a local level? And why is control of the territory so important? The explanation resides in the relationships between organized crime groups and local politicians, administrators, and businesses. The local level is the dimension where collusion with organized crime is easier and reciprocal exchange more profitable. Extortion racketeering is used to finance the criminal organization and its criminal activities, and to consolidate its capacity to control local resources such as property, markets, services, and votes.

Criminal groups that exercise intense control over the local territory tend to commit systemic extortion racketeering within legal markets and in the underworld. As far as the legal markets are concerned, extortion racketeering is often viewed as the key "to infiltration and baronial domination of sections of the legitimate economy" (Bell, 2000, p. 183). In regard to the underworld, it has been noted (Landesco, 1968) that extortion racketeering is often used to "protect" criminal markets. By collecting extortion money from criminals, organized criminal groups establish a form of tax levying system that facilitates the establishment of monopolistic areas and creates barriers to entry that make criminal offences less attractive.

THE VICTIM/OFFENDER RELATIONSHIP

When analyzing the victim/offender relationship in extortion racketeering cases, it should be considered that "the boundaries between victim and accomplice are often [...] blurred" (Blok, 2008, p. 8). These boundaries account for the difference between systemic and casual extortion racketeering.

When networks are involved in extortion racketeering, they establish predatory relationships with their victims. Unable to establish lasting relationships with their victims, they consequently act with the "aim or effect to destroy or bleed to death" (Passas, 2002, p. 21) their victims, exacting considerable extortive payments in a short period. This is typical of casual extortion racketeering.

By contrast, hierarchical criminal groups benefiting from their reputation and durability may establish parasitical or symbiotic relationships with their victims. This contributes to making extortion racketeering systemic.

The relationship is "parasitical when the aim is to preserve the viability of the target, such that illegal benefits can be extorted on a more or less regular basis" (Passas, 2002, p. 21). By establishing a lasting relationship with the victim, the offender "harms the host a little at a time, without killing it, or only kills it in slow motion" (Felson, 2006, p. 196). In other cases, the relationship may be symbiotic in nature, so that the victim becomes a "friend" of the extorter. The victim thus gains an advantage that is not "simply that of avoiding the likely damages that would otherwise ensue, but can extend to assistance in disposing of competitors, or protection against the threat of isolated bandits, and against the risk of being cheated in the course of business transactions" (Gambetta, 2000, p. 166).

SYSTEMIC AND CASUAL EXTORTION RACKETEERING: THE EUROPEAN CASE AND ITS EVOLUTION

The link between the presence of casual or systemic extortion racketeering and the variables indicated above has been investigated in a study on extortion and organized crime in the 27 European Union member states (Transcrime, 2009). This study analyzed the complex variety of criminal organizations present in the member states, the criminal market opportunities they exploit, differences in their organizational structures (some are hierarchical, some take the form of a network, some are permanent, some are more ephemeral), together with their differing criminal activities and control over the territory, and the various relationships that they establish with their victims.

The study has explained that extortion racketeering is casual in most of the European Union member states (EUMSs). The only exceptions are the Eastern EUMSs (Bulgaria, the Czech Republic, Estonia, Hungary, Latvia, Lithuania, Poland, Romania, Slovakia, Slovenia) and some EUMSs in the south of Europe, namely Spain and Italy.

When the geographical locations of the 27 states are divided into four regions, the following patterns emerge (see Caneppele, Gosetti, & Zanella, 2009, pp. 253–254).

1. **Northern Europe** (Denmark, Estonia, Finland, Latvia, Lithuania, Sweden). Owing to the prevalence of smuggling activities in this region, extortion racketeering is casual in Denmark, Finland, and Sweden. In fact, these countries are distinguished by the presence of criminal organizations that do not exercise control over the territory because they are transnational in their smuggling activities. Proximity to Russia and the presence of hierarchical criminal groups have generated systemic extortion racketeering in Estonia, Latvia, and Lithuania.

2. **Western Europe** (Austria, Belgium, France, Germany, Ireland, Luxembourg, the Netherlands, the United Kingdom). Owing to the structure of the organized criminal groups operating in this area and to their transnational activities, extortion racketeering is casual. Most of the countries in this area suffer from extortions carried out within close-knit ethnic communities. This is the case, for example, in Austria, Belgium, France, Germany, Luxembourg, and the United Kingdom.

3. **Central/Eastern Europe** (Bulgaria, the Czech Republic, Hungary, Poland, Slovakia, Slovenia, Romania). Because of its proximity to the Balkans, this region is an important transit area for criminal goods and services, and in particular for smuggling and trafficking activities. However, the likely hierarchical structure of the criminal organizations operating in this area, together with their strong presence at local level, make extortion racketeering systemic in countries such as Bulgaria, the Czech Republic, Hungary, Poland, Romania, Slovenia, and Slovakia.

4. **Southern Europe** (Cyprus, Greece, Italy, Malta, Portugal, Spain). This region is highly heterogeneous. Differences outweigh similarities in the structure of organized crime groups operating in these countries, and this is also reflected in the different ways in which extortion racketeering is conducted. Extortion racketeering is casual in most of the countries belonging to this cluster. In two countries – Italy and Spain – extortion racketeering is systemic. In Spain, it is systematic because it is carried out by terrorist groups belonging to ETA, which are well-structured and rooted in the territory (see Transcrime, 2009, Spain country profile). In Italy the phenomenon is mainly linked to Mafia-like organized crime, for which extortion racketeering plays a fundamental role in terms of both exercising control over the territory and financing criminal activities.

Is this geography of extortion changing? The answer is yes because of four related intervening variables: the fragmentation and decline of traditional organized crime groups with a strong control of the territory (Italian organized crime groups are one example), the development of gang model criminal organizations as a result of the process of fragmentation of traditional criminal organizations, the consolidation of traditional ethnic groups such as Mara Salvatrucha (known as MS-13 in cities of Northern Italy), and the entering of new ethnic criminal groups due to the migration flows to Europe. In these four contexts, extortion is resisting as part of the business model of traditional criminal organizations and is returning as part of the basic business model of emerging criminal organizations. It combines easy money together with control of territory. A more sophisticated form of extortion is developing inside one of the products of the transformation of traditional organized crime in direction of white-collar crime. In this framework, extortion is used for facilitating the infiltration of organized crime in the legitimate businesses (Savona et al., 2016).

CONCLUSIONS

This chapter has dealt with extortion and organized crime in Europe. Its analysis has been based on the observation that market opportunities and variations in the characteristics of organized criminal groups may give rise to two different types of extortion racketeering: systemic and casual. Four variables explain this process: (1) market opportunities; (2) the organizational structure of criminal groups; (3) their presence at the local level; and (4) the victim/offender relationship. Each of these variables interrelates with the others and continues to show the ways in which well-established criminal groups perpetrate this old and vicious crime.

Box 31.1. Definitions

Extortion racketeering. An institutionalized practice whereby tributes are collected by organized criminal groups with the intent to control legal and illegal markets and to establish territorial sovereignty.

Systemic extortion racketeering. Extortion is deeply rooted and extends across a territory. Criminal organizations routinely engage in extortion, and extortion racketeering is a core part of criminal business.

Casual extortion racketeering. Extortion is episodic and not extended across a territory. Criminal organizations do not routinely engage in extortion.

Intraethnic extortions racketeering. When, in a particular country, foreign organized criminal groups are involved in extortion racketeering and, by operating within close ethnic communities, victimize their own people.

Hierarchical structures. A group with a hierarchical structure is "characterized by a single leader and a relatively clearly defined hierarchy. Systems of internal discipline are strict. Strong social or ethnic identities can be present, although this is not always the case. There is a relatively clear allocation of tasks and often some form of internal code of conduct, although this may be implicit and not 'officially' recorded."

Network structures. A group with a network structure "is defined by the activities of key individuals who engage in illicit activity in often shifting alliances. Such individuals may not regard themselves as being members of a criminal group and may not be regarded as being a criminal group by outsiders. Nevertheless, they coalesce around a series of criminal projects [...] Networks usually consist of relatively manageable numbers of individuals [...]" (United Nations Office on Drugs And Crime [UNODC], 2002, pp. 34-35, 41).

Victim/offender relationships

Predatory. When a considerable extortive payment is demanded only once.
Parasitical. When the perpetrator demands small payments over a long period of time.
Symbiotic. When the perpetrators and the victims establish a prolonged relationship that produces illicit benefits for each of them.

REFERENCES

Bell, D. (2000). *The end of ideology: On the exhaustion of political ideas in the fifties.* New Haven, CT: Harvard University Press.

Blok, A. (2008). Reflections on the Sicilian Mafia: Peripheries and their impact on centers. In D. Siegel & A. Nelen (Eds.), *Organized crime: Culture, markets and policies.* Dordrecht: Springer.

Felson, M. (2006). *Crime and nature.* London: SAGE publications.

Gambetta, D. (1993). *The Sicilian Mafia: The business of private protection.* New Haven, CT: Harvard University Press.

(2000). Mafia: The price of distrust. In D. Gambetta (Ed.), *Trust: Making and breaking cooperative relations* (pp. 158–210). Oxford: Oxford University Press.

Landesco, J. (1968). *Organized crime in Chicago: Part III of The Illinois Crime Survey 1929.* Chicago: The University of Chicago Press.

Paoli, L. & Fijnaut, C. (2004). *Organised crime in Europe: Concepts, patterns, control policies in the European Union and beyond.* Dordrecht: Springer.

Passas, N. (2002). Cross-border crime and the interface between legal and illegal actors. In P. Van Duyne, K. von Lampe, & N. Passas (Eds.), *Upper world and underworld in cross-border crime* (pp. 11–43). The Netherlands: Wolf Legal Publishers.

Reuter, P. (1994). Research on American organized crime. In R. J. Kelly, K. Chin, & R. Schatzberg (Eds.), *Handbook of organized crime in the United States* (pp. 91–120). Santa Barbara, CA: Greenwood Press.

Savona, E. U., Berlusconi G., & Riccardi, M. (Eds.). (2016). *Organised crime in European businesses.* London:Routledge

Transcrime. (2009). *Study on extortion racketeering the need for an instrument to combat activities of organized crime.* Final Report prepared for the European Commission. Brussells (unpublished).

United Nations Office on Drugs and Crime (UNODC). (2002). *Results of a pilot survey of forty selected organized criminal groups in sixteen countries.* Vienna: UNODC.

Volkov, V. (2002). *Violent entrepreneurs: The use of force in the making of Russian capitalism.* London: Cornell University Press.

32 Russian Organized Crime

Alexander Sukharenko and Eric G. Lesneskie

INTRODUCTION

The former Soviet Union provided fruitful ground for the growth of organized crime, but the collapse of the USSR has seemingly provided even more opportunities for organized criminal networks to flourish. These modern-day Russian organized criminal groups (ROC) are more sophisticated than their predecessors and have extended their spheres of influence globally. Organized crime inflicts serious harm on Russia's economic and political development. Hundreds of companies are under criminal control. Throughout the 2000s, the leaders of some of criminal groups actively sought seats in regional and municipal power structures as well as in the national parliament. Once elected, these new officials have received procedural immunity from criminal prosecution for previously committed crimes and have continued to engage in illegal activities. In this regard, Russia's National Security Strategy, approved by the president in December 2015, included organized crime on its list of major threats to public safety.

In this discussion we want to do several things. The first is to explain which groups are defined as ROC and to provide a historical account of these groups. This history lays the foundation for the current crime situation in Russia. We will then discuss some of the current issues related to ROC and how these issues allow for ROC groups to maintain their criminal involvement. The final discussion will offer recommendations for combating organized crime in Russia.

THE HISTORY OF ROC

The type of ROC that we see today was mostly shaped by the 75-year Soviet regime, which collapsed in 1991 (see Finckenauer & Voronin, 2001). The label of ROC has been applied broadly to groups of criminals from any of the 15 former republics that made up the Soviet Union. These republics include Armenia, Georgia, Ukraine, Moldova, and others. The shortage of goods during Soviet times in these republics encouraged the emergence of a shadow economy and a black market to make up for these shortages. The shadow economy produced legal goods outside the state-mandated production quotas, which were then sold or bartered illegally, whereas the black market dealt with the sale of illegal goods, such as prohibited items from the West and drugs. Organized crime often arises to meet market demands for goods and services that are illegal, regulated, or in short supply. These shortages provided ample opportunity for organized criminal groups to thrive.

Corrupt government officials, through the abuse of their power and authority, facilitated the existence of the illegal markets and other criminal ventures. The corrupt officials received bribes in order to protect the illegal ventures of the black marketers and professional criminals. The professional criminals included the "thieves-in-law," who were products of the old Soviet prison system and lived by a rigid set of criminal rules, dedicated their life to crime, and rejected involvement with the legitimate world.

With the collapse of the Soviet Union, criminals were in the best position to exploit the opportunities when state properties and assets began to be sold to private owners (see Finckenauer & Voronin, 2001). Criminal groups and corrupt officials bought these properties and assets at low prices due to insider trading information. The level of corruption was so pervasive with the movement from socialism to privatization that it helped to contribute to the proliferation and power of organized crime that we see in Russia today.

CURRENT STATUS OF ROC

Prevalence

Despite the changing dynamics occurring in Russia, organized crime is no less pervasive today than it was during the latter stages of the Soviet régime. According to the Russian Ministry of Internal Affairs (MIA), there are 58 organized crime groups (OCGs) operating in Russia, including eight ethnic-based groups, numbering about 1,200 individuals (MIA, 2018). The majority of OCGs are concentrated in the Central, Volga, North Caucasian, and Siberian Federal Districts of Russia, which is due to socioeconomic reasons and other characteristics of the populations of these regions. However, these numbers relate only to the large OCGs that feature in the MIA records. The true numbers are certainly far larger. The extensive range of OCG activities includes extortion, assassinations, kidnapping (often of businesspersons), drug trafficking, prostitution, sales of counterfeit products (often alcohol and tobacco), vehicle theft, and a host of financial transgressions. The most common economic offenses are frauds, smuggling of strategic goods and resources (seafood, timber, antiques, wild flora, and fauna), illicit trading, counterfeiting (of currency and credit cards), illegal gambling, and money laundering.

Although the number of career criminals, so-called "thieves-in-law" (aka vory v zakone), is some 300 individuals, their ideological predisposition to crime allows them to be significant forces in the underworld. The majority of the "vory" are Georgians, who control specific criminal spheres such as thefts, robbery, extortion, illicit trade, and the trafficking in stolen goods. Further, they adjudicate disputes among OCG leaders and control the use of criminal budget, known as an "obshchak." The "obshchak" is used to support imprisoned members, bribe law enforcement and government officials, and to facilitate the advancement of criminal ventures. Thieves also forge and maintain foreign ties in order to expand criminal operations. Their connections have been documented in the USA, Italy, Spain, France, Greece, Turkey, and the United Arab Emirates (Sukharenko, 2017).

In July 2004 notorious "thief-in-law" Vyacheslav Ivankov (Little Japanese) was deported to Russia after release from American prison, where he spent nearly nine years for trying to extort $3.5 million from two Russian émigrés, who owned an investment advisory firm, and a fraudulent marriage (Birch, 2004).

To combat the ongoing threat posed by such criminals, the U.S. Department of the Treasury's Office of Foreign Assets Control (OFAC) designated seven Eurasian "thieves-in-law" pursuant to Executive Order (E.O.) 13581, which targets significant transnational criminal organizations (TCOs) and their supporters. This action generally prohibits US persons from conducting financial or other transactions with these individuals and entities, and freezes any assets they may have under US jurisdiction (US Treasury, 2017).

In 2018, the United States Attorney for the Southern District of New York announced that Russian "thief-in-law" Razden Shulaya, who was found guilty of racketeering, trafficking of stolen goods such as luxury watches and cases of contraband cigarettes, identification document fraud, and wire fraud, has been sentenced to 45-year imprisonment. In addition to the prison term, he was ordered to pay $2,169,270 in forfeiture, and restitution in the amount of $550,000. The Shulaya enterprise operated through groups of individuals, often with over-lapping members or associates, dedicated to particular criminal tasks. While many of these crews were based in New York City, his enterprise had criminal operations throughout the United States (New Jersey, Pennsylvania, Florida, and Nevada) and abroad. Shulaya oversaw and personally committed multiple acts of brutal violence in his role as a thief. He also orchestrated a scheme to defraud casinos by targeting particular models of electronic slot machines using a complicated algorithm designed to predict the behavior of those machines (US SDNY Attorney, 2018).

An Ineffective Fight Against Organized Crime

Statistical analysis shows that it has become increasingly difficult to detect the activities of OCGs. According to the MIA, over the past nine years (2008–2017), the number of recorded crimes committed by OCGs has decreased fivefold, from 30,700 to 6,055, with the number of economic offenses decreasing from 18,300 to 4,315. In the context of all nationwide recorded crimes, OCG activity dropped from 0.9 to 0.2 percent. The number of crimes listed under Article 210 of the Criminal Code, "organizing of a criminal enterprise," decreased by nine times, from 325 to 36 (MIA, 2018). This Russian law is similar to the USA's RICO statute, which allows for the prosecution of ongoing criminal enterprises.

However, this reduction of recorded crime does not indicate a decrease in the ROC's activity. Rather it demonstrates the increased ability to conceal crimes. Often this concealment is facilitated with the aid of corrupt law enforcement officials. According to the Investigative Committee (IC, 2017), for the last seven years several thousand police officers, 465 investigators, 97 prosecutors, and 26 judges were prosecuted for corruption. Some of them were convicted for protecting OCGs by concealing their crime, not initiating criminal proceedings against their members, or simply terminating the proceedings before an outcome could be reached.

To combat the "thieves-in-law," the Federal Law of 03.11.2009 No. 245-ФЗ was adopted, which supplemented Article 210 of Russia's Criminal Code with part 4. In accordance with this article, a person occupying a higher position in the criminal hierarchy is punished for a term of 15 to 20 years or life imprisonment. This amendment was adopted after familiarization with the Georgian experience (Law No. 2354 "On Organized Crime and Racket" dated

December 20, 2005). However, until now, only one Georgian thief in Altai has been convicted under this article (Sukharenko, 2017).

CURRENT ISSUES

Criminalization of Governmental Bodies

The economic strength of OCGs from their criminal ventures has provided them with the potential to gain access to political power through corruption. As the economic influence of an OCG grows, its capability to corrupt electoral processes increases. According to the Russian Central Election Commission (CEC), from 2009 to 2012, the total number of candidates with previous convictions who ran for elected office increased 3.5 times, from 132 to 469. For the same timeframe, the number of candidates convicted of more serious crimes (at least ten years of imprisonment) increased 8.8 times, from 22 to 194. In 2013, there were 227 candidates with previous convictions; of these, 150 were convicted of serious crimes (CEC, 2014).

This penetration can allow the ROC groups to use procedural immunity granted to certain categories of elected officials for protection from criminal prosecution. Additionally, by gaining electoral positions, there is the potential access to public funds and the ability to strengthen ROC's involvement with legitimate businesses.

In order to penetrate the government, leaders of the criminal groups are altering their place of residence and surnames, removing information about convictions from the regional police databases, and advancing through the electoral process as seemingly law-abiding and respectable citizens. During the electoral campaigns, these criminals are actively promoting charitable activities to gain votes, such as repairing roads, building playgrounds, distributing food to the needy, and organizing community events.

During the election process, OCGs usually engage in bribery or blackmail of key officials, the dissemination of compromising information on opponents, the bribery of voters, destruction of property (e.g., arson of a rival's private residence and/or campaign headquarters) and violence against political opponents and their families.

Factors contributing to this criminalization of governing bodies stems from the combination of the marginalization of social consciousness, legal nihilism, and political passivity of citizens. With the marginalization and legal nihilism present in Russian society, citizens are willing to overlook past criminal involvement for a favorable political agenda (*Pravda*, 2013). According to the All-Russian Center of Public Opinion poll, one-third of citizens were willing to vote for a candidate with a criminal background. Further, the Levada Center's (2016) claims that one-fourth of citizens are willing to sell their votes for trivial amounts of money.

The latest criminal cases confirm that some regional elites have an interest in including OCG leaders in schemes to manage their districts. In other words, there exists a politico-criminal symbiosis of the corporate type. Officials view their political status and available powers as an income-producing asset and their activities as a business that, in turn, is protected by the OCG they are affiliated with (Sukharenko, 2014).

Efforts have been made to try to stop this criminalization of politics. In 2014, Russia developed laws to reduce the electoral rights of citizens with criminal convictions. Depending on the seriousness of the offense, citizens convicted of certain crimes are not eligible to hold public office for a period of 10 or 15 years after the completion of their sentence. In addition to the time restriction for running for office, it is required that the election documents include information about whether an individual has ever been convicted previously of a crime.

Despite the introduction of this legislation, the number of previously convicted candidates has not decreased. According to the Russian Central Election Commission (CEC), with the election campaigns of 2014, there were 3,197 candidates who had a criminal record, or 2.8 percent of the total number of candidates. In the end, there were 520 candidates who had criminal records that were elected (CEC, 2014). A year later, in 2015, there were 6,850 candidates who had a criminal record (3.3 percent of those nominated in the elections) and 1,800 of these candidates were elected (CEC, 2015). In 2016, in the federal lists of 14 political parties that participated in parliamentary elections, 138 criminal candidates were identified, 60 of whom did not provide information about their previous convictions (CEC, 2016).

CONCLUSION AND DISCUSSION

Organized crime remains a serious menace to the economic and political well-being of Russia. Efforts to combat ROC have continued, but due to a number of reasons this fight has been ineffective. First, in an effort to reduce redundancy at the federal level, there was the retrenchment of special units of the MIA in 2008. Often these units collected the data needed to develop a true understanding of the nature and extent of organized crime. Second, in recent years, there has been reform of Russian criminal legislation. These reforms include the decriminalization of certain behaviors, the shortening of sentences, the replacement of imprisonment with fines, and the exclusion of property confiscation as a form of punishment. Third, lack of civilian cooperation with law enforcements. This is exemplified by a Russian Public Opinion Research Center opinion poll (2017) showing that 49 percent of victims did not report crime to the police because they considered them to be incapable of providing assistance.

The aforementioned shortcomings allow for the continuation of criminal activity, but this also allows for the penetration of political bodies by criminal groups. Powers of elected officials and the nature of their decisions directly influence the rights and freedoms of citizens. In this regard, the criminalization of elected bodies poses a serious threat to the functioning of a state. Clearly, organized crime is taking advantage of the opportunities present in Russia's political process to seek election and utilize their elected powers to their benefit.

In order to reduce the criminalization of the electoral processes and economy by OCGs, it is necessary for the Russian Government to adopt a long-term campaign to combat organized crime. In particular, there needs to be more focus on dismantling powerful criminal groups, particularly those with corruptive and international ties. Another part of this campaign should be to increase the punishments for offenses committed by organized groups. Stricter punishments such as longer prison terms and asset forfeitures should be implemented. It is also necessary to increase the effectiveness of the fight against corruption, which is the main catalyst for the criminalization of the socioeconomical life of Russia. The current fight against bribery and fraud, which prevails in the total volume of registered crimes, does not correspond to the scale and level of the threat since it does not affect high-ranking officials responsible for making important management decisions.

Law enforcement and legal changes are not enough to completely dismantle the foothold organized crime have in multiple realms of Russian society. It is necessary to raise the level of trust the citizens have for the legal and political processes. Part of this level of trust should include increasing citizen awareness of the negative effects of criminal involvement in politics. It appears, based upon surveys and opinion polls conducted in Russia, citizens are unaware of the seriousness of the problem. If citizens are aware that their well-being (salary, quality of education and medical care, social protection and safety) largely depends on the law-abiding and professionalism of elected officials, then this combined with the legal actions may help to reduce the sphere of influence that organized crime has on Russian society.

REFERENCES

Birch, D. (2004). U.S. prison due to free Russian mob boss. *Baltimore Sun*. Retrieved from www
.baltimoresun.com/news/bs-xpm-2004-07-08-0407080015-story.html.
Central Election Commission (CEC). (2014). *Report of the Control and Auditing Service under the CEC of Russia for 2009–2013*. Moscow.
(2015). *Report of the Control and Auditing Service under the CEC of Russia for 2014*. Moscow.
(2016). *Report of the Control and Auditing Service under the CEC of Russia for 2015*. Moscow.
(2016). *Report of the Control and Auditing Service under the CEC of Russia for 2016*. Moscow.
Finckenauer, J. O. & Voronin, Y. A. (2001). *The threat of Russian organized crime*. Washington, DC: US Department of Justice.
Investigative Committee (IC). (2017). *Annual report of the Investigative Committee activity for 2011–2016*. Moscow.
Levada. (2016). *Waiting for election abuses*. Retrieved from www.levada.ru/2016/08/22/ozhidanie-zloupotreblenij-na-vyborah/.
Levada Center. (2016). Waiting for election abuses. Retrieved from www.levada.ru/2016/08/22/ozhidanie-zloupotreblenij-na-vyborah/.
Ministry of Internal Affairs (MIA). (2018). *Form 1-OC of Ministry of Internal Affairs for 2008–2017*. Moscow.
Pravda. (2013). *Most Russians support ban on election judged authorities*. Retrieved from www.pravda.ru/news/politics/24-12-2013/1186535-opros-0/.
Russian Public Opinion Research Center. (2017, February 22). Postradavshie ot prestuplenij: v nadezhde na spravedlivost [Victims of crime: in the hope of justice]. Retrieved from https://wciom.ru/index.php?id=236&uid=116081.
Sukharenko, A. (2012). Russian organized crime and the existing measures to combat it. *Law Enforcement Executive Forum*, 12(1), 166–178.
(2014). Kriminalizatsiya regionalnikh organov vlasti: sostoyanie, tendentsii i meri protivodeistviya. Retrieved from www.nbpublish.com/library_get_pdf.php?id=32201.
(2017). Uprava na zakonnikov. Retrieved from www.index.org.ru/nevol/2017–53/11-53-suprava.html.
US Attorney South District of New York (2018). Press release, "'Thief-in-law' Razhden Shulaya sentenced in Manhattan federal court to 45 years in prison." Retrieved from www.justice.gov/usao-sdny/pr/thief-law-razhden-shulaya-sentenced-manhattan-federal-court-45-years-prison.
US Treasury (2017). Press release, "Treasury targets the 'thieves-in-law' Eurasian transnational criminal organization." Retrieved from https://home.treasury.gov/news/press-releases/sm0244.

33 The Rise of Balkan Organized Crime

Jana Arsovska

After the end of the Cold War, organized crime became a subject of grave concern for the International Community. No longer was it perceived as an American or Italian phenomenon only. In particular, organized crime groups from Southeast Europe (SEE) – frequently referred to as Balkan organized crime groups – attracted enormous international attention during the 1990s. One reason for their dramatic rise was the way the post-communist transition was initiated in SEE, compared to Central Europe or the Baltic states. In SEE, the reform process was marked by the violent dissolution of Yugoslavia.

Moreover, the emerging accommodations between corrupt SEE authorities and organized crime groups during the creation of new states fostered the development of crime-permeated societies. Balkan organized crime groups often enjoyed political support and profited from the lawlessness. They were labeled "highly dangerous," posing a serious threat to Western societies (European Council, 2003; United Nations Office on Drugs and Crime [UNODC], 2008). For the purpose of this chapter, the term "Balkan organized crime" refers to organized crime groups whose members originate mainly from Albania, Kosovo, Bosnia and Herzegovina, Bulgaria, Croatia, Macedonia, Montenegro, Romania, and Serbia. This chapter discusses the nature, structure(s), mobility, and activities of these groups.

THE EU DEFINITION OF ORGANIZED CRIME

In 2001, the European Commission and EUROPOL tried to operationalize their broad 1998 organized crime definition in order to ensure coherent action among their member states. They developed a working definition according to which 11 characteristics of criminal organizations are associated with the term "organized crime." The EU definition requires the presence of a minimum of four mandatory and two optional criteria (see Box 33.1).

Box 33.1. The EU Organized Crime Definition

Mandatory: (1) collaboration among more than two people; (2) extending over a prolonged or indefinite period; (3) suspected of committing serious criminal offences, punishable by imprisonment of at least four years or more; and (4) with the central goal of profit and/or power.

> **Optional**: (5) specialized division of labor among participants; (6) exercising measures of discipline and control; (7) employing violence or other means of intimidation; (8) employing commercial business-like structures; (9) participating in money laundering; (10) operational across national borders; and (11) exerting influence over legitimate social institutions.

However, in developing international definitions there is always a tension between those who want an all-encompassing legislation and those who want the law to be tightly drawn. Although the term "organized crime" is used to distinguish more sophisticated forms of illicit enterprise from conventional criminality, the line between the two is not clear. Organized crime encompasses a wide range of profit-motivated criminal activities, such as transnational smuggling. It can also, however, have a domestic focus, profiting from protection rackets or fraudulent acquisition of state funds.

KEY ACTIVITIES AND OPERATIONAL METHODS

From Peripheral Actors to Central Players

Until 1997, Balkan organized crime groups were regarded as peripheral actors, lacking capital to invest in high-level, criminal businesses. Initially, they were mainly involved in extortion, kidnappings, protection rackets, prostitution, and burglaries – all high-risk criminal activities – and often worked as service providers for established organized crime groups. Some were working as *scafisti*, or boatmen, for Italian criminal organizations, smuggling people from Albania to Italy. In order for Italian organized crime offenders to gain a foothold in Albania and take advantage of the Balkan criminal markets, they often allowed Albanian groups to regulate the prostitution market in southern Italy. In the 1990s, Balkan criminals also acted as drug couriers and contract killers for Italian and Turkish drug trafficking and loan sharking organizations. However, following the conflict in Kosovo (1998–1999) and the collapse of the pyramid schemes in Albania (1997), many of these Balkan criminal groups gained power and grew more international.

Since 2003 – having established themselves as prominent criminal actors in Europe and elsewhere, partly through their reputation for being violent – Balkan organized crime groups have kept a lower profile. They have ties to legitimate businesses and acquire a position of central players in international criminal networks. They still engage, however, in a full range of criminal activities, such as, arms, drugs, and human trafficking; racketeering and extortions; fraud; money laundering; and organized theft.

Transnational Smuggling

TRADE IN ARMS

One of the international community's first reactions to the Yugoslav wars (1991–1999) was the arms embargo imposed on Bosnia and Herzegovina, Croatia, Macedonia, Montenegro, Serbia (including Kosovo), and Slovenia in 1992. The UN embargo had little effect on Serbia, which maintained the control of the Yugoslav Army, but it affected the smaller Yugoslav republics. In order to push forward for their independence, Bosnia and Herzegovina, Croatia, and Kosovo established networks with foreign actors for the importation of weapons. Initially, the illegal arms trade was organized at the state level. Later, it ended up in the hands of local organized crime groups. Former secret security agents who had the "know-how" of arms trading also took part in the business (Arsovska & Kostakos, 2008).

For 41 years Albania was under the communist regime of Enver Hoxha (1944–85), who placed enormous emphasis on weapon supplies. The breakdown of the Albanian Government in 1997, however, resulted in the looting of more than 550,000 small arms, 839 million rounds of ammunition, and 16 million explosive devices from army stockpiles, in a response to a failed pyramid savings scheme (Khakee & Florquin, 2003). These weapons become available on the European black markets. Many ended up in the hands of the Kosovo Liberation Army (KLA), a militant group fighting for the independence of Kosovo, and Albanian rebel groups in Macedonia. Since the Yugoslav wars, the Balkan region has been viewed as the predominant source of Europe's illegal gun trade.

DRUG TRAFFICKING

Prior to the Yugoslav wars, most of the heroin destined for Europe went through the Balkan route (via Serbia and Croatia). The 1992–1995 wars redirected the trade through Macedonia, Kosovo, and Albania. This strengthened the position of ethnic Albanian (particularly Kosovo-Albanian) organized crime groups. For the purpose of arming the KLA, Kosovo-Albanians established connections with relatives in Europe and the USA – some known for drug trafficking (Hajdinjak, 2002).

Since 2005, ethnic Albanian traffickers have expanded their activities abroad, establishing direct links with suppliers in drug production areas (Arsovska, 2015). The heroin often travels from Turkey to Italy via Bulgaria-Macedonia-Albania or Kosovo-Montenegro-Serbia-Bosnia and Herzegovina. More frequently, Balkan organized crime groups also use women and people from their diaspora who hold legal EU or US documents as drug couriers, since they attract less police attention.

As trafficking routes are changing due to stricter antitrafficking measures, the Balkan countries are increasingly being used for the transit of cocaine from South America. Balkan groups are gaining a prominent role in this profitable business. In January 2008, the Macedonian police seized half a ton of cocaine – hidden in cans filled with rubber-tree paint and imported by a legal company. The cocaine, from Venezuela, was offloaded at a port in Montenegro. It was intended for transportation to Greece by truck, via Serbia, Kosovo, and Macedonia. Also, in the UK and the US Albanian groups began negotiating directly with the Colombian cartels. Huge cocaine shipments were arranged direct from South America while supply chains were kept in-house. In the UK, Albanian groups are also known to have lowered the price of cocaine and increased its purity to stay competitive (Townsend, 2019).

Criminal groups led by Naser Kelmendi of Kosovo and Montenegro, Darko Saric from Serbia, and Lulzim Berisha of Albania were among the Balkan drug traffickers whose names became internationally known. Also in Albania, the outlaw village Lazarat (Gjirokastra), which was reputed to be Albania's drug capital and off-limits to the police, has built a fortune from the cultivation of cannabis (Arsovska, 2015).

ILLEGAL IMMIGRATION AND HUMAN TRAFFICKING

Balkan organized crime groups are also active in facilitating illegal migration. During the 1990s, many people lost their jobs and extortions and kidnappings became common realities for ordinary citizens. This resulted in a massive exodus of refugees to Greece, Italy, and other Western destinations (UNODC, 2008, pp. 45–46). Stricter police measures made *ad hoc* border crossing difficult. As a result, Balkan crime groups saw an opportunity to make money quickly. Clients were provided with forged travel documents or were hidden in trucks. In a 2001 confidential report, one *scafisti* reported: "The border police is paid to smuggle clandestines into Albania. Then taxis drive them to Vlorë. The taxi drivers have a budget to pay the traffic police. The clandestines are put in hotels managed by the scafisti. The facilitator comes back later with the ferry."

Particularly after 2008, the Macedonian village of Lojane, which borders Serbia, has become a stop-over on the illegal migration routes to Western Europe. Immigrants from Afghanistan, Syria, and Iraq travel through Iran, Turkey, and then Greece before arriving in Macedonia. The immigrants say they heard about the village either on the Internet or through friends (Derens, 2011). Authorities, however, argue that well-organized networks wait for the immigrants along the country's southern borders. According to police, the immigrants pay approximately 3,000 euros apiece to be smuggled into Greece, and additional 800–900 euros to go on to Serbia.

Balkan criminals, particularly ethnic Albanians, are known for being notorious traffickers of women for sexual exploitation (Limanowska, 2005). They have been trafficking Albanian, Romanian, Moldovan, Ukrainian, and Bulgarian women to Western Europe via Albania and Italy. Traditionally, they recruited their victims using a "lover boy" method whereby a man seduces a girl by promising her marriage and, once abroad, either sells her or forces her into prostitution (Arsovska, 2015).

For example, Albanian Luan Plakici, who was involved in the biggest case of human trafficking for prostitution seen in the UK, deceived poor Eastern European women and trafficked them to Western Europe. He even married one teenage girl before telling her that she would be spending her wedding night working as a prostitute (BBC, 2003).

Also, from 2000 onward, some Balkan countries turned out to be major points of destination for trafficking victims. The highly paid international staff present in the Balkans due to the regional conflicts have also affected the local prostitution markets by keeping the business profitable (Stefanova, 2004).

ORGANIZED THEFT AND ROBBERIES

The rollout of automated teller machines in Western cities heralded new opportunities for Balkan organized crime groups to diversify their criminal enterprises. In particularly, ethnic Albanian groups installed cloned ATMs in small supermarkets and convenience stores in New York City, along with devices that captured personal bank account information. The groups then used the collected information to make fake ATM cards (Arsovska, 2015).

Balkan criminal groups have been also involved in numerous burglaries and robberies. One international case is that of the Pink Panther group – a name INTERPOL has given to an international network of jewel thieves responsible for some of the most audacious thefts in criminal history. The Pink Panthers have robbed at least 120 stores in 20 different countries. INTERPOL estimates that there are several hundred thieves in the group, and many come from Serbia and Montenegro as well as the broader Balkan region (Samuels, 2010).

VULNERABILITY TO ORGANIZED CRIME

Many factors contributed to the rise of Balkan organized crime. First, the transition from communism to democracy led to: (1) a diminished capacity of law enforcement agencies undergoing reform to impose order; (2) new criminal opportunities due to changes in the regulation of economic activity; and (3) sociocultural confusion, a product of globalization and rapid social change. Drifting between tradition and modernity, socialism and capitalism, many – driven by the "American Dream" – fled their homeland. There was a false romanticism about "making it" in "the West." Traditional values lost importance. Being wealthy became the most cherished cultural goal.

Second, conflict situations contribute to the rise of organized crime, too. In a war zone, social controls are loosened and criminals operate without a hindrance. Throughout the wars, Balkan organized crime groups profited by selling "protection" to their co-ethnics. Irregular combat groups in turn protected and exploited their own communities (UNODC, 2008, p. 50). Smuggling was also seen as necessary for survival. Conflicts are associated with deteriorating economy, inequalities, and a lack of legitimate opportunities as well, all leading to crime increase.

Third, the strategic location of the Balkan Peninsula has been historically an important factor for trade between the powers of the East and the West. SEE was destined to become a transit zone for a range of criminal goods since, for instance, it is placed between the world's main supply of heroin and its most lucrative destination market.

The fourth factor is the criminal-political nexus that has been flourishing in SEE since communist times. After the fall of communism, the criminal-political ties strengthened further. Members of the former communist elite that were awarded state-owned companies "teamed their clandestine skills with their criminal contacts to create [...] shady multinational conglomerates" (UNODC, 2008, p. 49). One of the reasons these criminal groups became so powerful is that, initially, they were organized by the state itself (Arsovska, 2015).

CRIMINAL STRUCTURE AND MOBILITY

Kinship and common territory have served as powerful bonding and trust-producing elements for Balkan criminal segments, particularly ethnic Albanian groups. It is, however, too simplistic to describe them as kinship-based organizations with well-defined boundaries. Each core group, often composed of three to ten members from the same ethnic background, represents a smaller, criminal subunit that is part of a larger multiethnic criminal network. Advanced groups cooperate with foreign groups in order to expand their opportunities. Members of Balkan criminal subcultures neither undergo ritual ceremonies nor sign fraternization contracts in order to become members. Balkan organized crime groups are formed more spontaneously than, for example, the Sicilian Cosa Nostra.

Although Balkan organized crime figures, particularly ethnic Albanian offenders, appear to be active in Western societies, little is known about their migration patterns. It does not appear that these groups resemble multinational corporations, or that there is a nationwide Albanian or Balkan mafia (Arsovska, 2015). Many Balkan crime figures find themselves in new markets because of forced migration, the need to escape legal proceedings and subsequent punishment, or fighting within their own criminal clans. It is not uncommon to hear stories of Balkan asylum seekers leaving their war-torn countries in hope of finding a better life in the West, but then turning to a life of crime. Yet, many "Balkan" offenders were, in fact, born and raised in Western countries (Arsovska, 2015).

CONCLUSION

Balkan organized crime groups grew rapidly over the years, partially due to the transitional and post-conflict dynamics present in post-communist SEE. Smuggling routes established to supply arms to militant factions, and escape routes for economic and political migrants became used for trafficking illicit commodities. These routes brought Balkan organized crime groups into contact with foreign groups, such as the Italian Mafia, and as their influence spread, they became important partners for Turkish and Colombian crime groups. The links with political leaders formed during times of conflict left a legacy of criminal-political symbiosis. Nowadays, Balkan organized crime is an evolving phenomenon, which does not necessarily bear the hallmarks of violence and homogeneity of the 1990s. Instead, many Balkan organized crime groups have wide connections and use legal companies as a front for their criminal activities.

REFERENCES

Arsovska, J. (2015). *Decoding Albanian organized crime.* Berkeley, CA: California University Press.
  (2009). Networking sites: Criminal group expands across the Balkans. *Jane's Intelligence Review,* 22(1), 44–47.
Arsovska, J. & Kostakos, P. (2008). Illicit arms trafficking and the limits of rational choice theory: The case of the Balkans. *Trends in Organized Crime,* 11(4), 352–387.
BBC. (2003, December 22). Prison for sex slave gang leader. Retrieved from http://news.bbc.co.uk/2/hi/uk_news/3340921.stm.
Derens, J. A. (2011, December 29). Macedonia: Europe's new hotspot for illegal immigrants. *Time.*
European Council. (2003). *A secure Europe in a better world.* France: EU Institute for Security Studies.
Hajdinjak, M. (2002). *Smuggling in Southeast Europe: The Yugoslav wars and the development of regional criminal networks in the Balkans.* Sofia: CSD.
Khakee, A. & Florquin, N. (2003). *Kosovo and the gun.* Geneva: Small Arms Survey.
Limanowska, B. (2005). *Trafficking in human beings in South Eastern Europe.* Sarajevo: UNDP.
Samuels, D. (2010). The Pink Panthers: A tale of diamonds, thieves, and the Balkans. *The New Yorker,* 86(8), 42–72.
Stefanova, R. (2004). Fighting organised crime in a UN protectorate: Difficult, possible, necessary. *Southeast European and Black Sea Studies,* 4(2), 257–279.
Townsend, M. (2019, January 13). Kings of cocaine: How the Albanian mafia seized control of the UK drugs trade. *Guardian.* Retrieved from www.theguardian.com/world/2019/jan/13/kings-of-cocaine-albanian-mafia-uk-drugs-crime.
United Nations Office on Drugs and Crime (UNODC). (2008). *Crime and its impact on the Balkans.* Vienna: UNODC.

WEBSITES

Balkan Investigative Reporting Network. www.birn.eu.com.
Center for the Study of Democracy. www.csd.bg.
RiskMonitor. www.riskmonitor.bg.

34 Organized Crime Groups in Asia

Hong Kong and Japan

Leona Lee

OVERVIEW

There are two major kinds of organized crime groups in Asia. Triads originated in China but have spread to other Southeast Asian countries (Table 34.1). Boryokudan are from Japan; their members, boryokudanin, are informally known as Yakuza. In recent decades, both groups established bases in the USA and Europe. The following section describes their origin and modern-day operation. It is important to understand the context that supports the emergence and growth of these organizations, if governments are to deal with them.

THE ORIGINS OF TRIADS

Triads emerged to fill a societal need: to provide services that were unavailable or hard to obtain from the government. Members in these groups occupied a marginal status. They were often outcasts who lost their standing due to changes in the social system. Gradually, Triads expanded and sold protection to others who needed it. Lacking legitimate means, they resorted to violence and intimidation to protect themselves and their customers. Due to the nature of their business, Triads have many opportunities to engage in illegal activities. Criminal activities are a source of power and profits that sustain them.

The word Triad, synonymous with *Tiandihui*, is said to symbolize a triangle formed by heaven, earth, and man. This interpretation, however, was absent from the early literature on Triads (Chu, 2000). A popular legend traces them to the Shoalin (young forest) Temple of China. The Ching emperor persecuted the Shoalin monks after they helped the government quell a rebellion. The monks responded by forming the Triad to overthrow the Ching Dynasty and restore the Ming Dynasty (1368–1644). After the Ching Dynasty collapsed in 1911, Triads abandoned their political mission and turned to criminal activities (Chu, 2000).

Recent studies indicate that the popular legend was erroneous, and in fact, *Tiandihui* or Triad emerged in 1674 as a mutual aid organization. It mediated conflicts in the Fujian area, provided protection to travelers, and engaged in criminal activities (Chu, 2000, p. 12). When the Fujiannese migrated to other parts of Southeast Asia (including Hong Kong and Taiwan), Triads established branches in these areas (Chu, 2000). During their early days in Hong Kong, they engaged in salt and opium smuggling, robbery, assault, and piracy (Sinn, 1989). Many migrant laborers relied on Triads for protection. Others formed their own Triads to protect

Table 34.1. Major organized crime groups in Asia

Country/City	Organized Crime Groups
China	Organized crime groups from Hong Kong
	Local crime groups
Hong Kong	Sun Yee On
	Wo Shing Wo
	14K
Japan	Yamaguchi-gumi
	Sumiyoshi-kai
	Ingawa-kai
Macau	Organized crime groups from Hong Kong
Taiwan	United Bamboo
	Heavenly Alliance
	Four Seas
Thailand	Jao Pho
	United Way Wa State Army

*See also Finckenauer & Chin (2006)

their interests. As a result, the number of Triads burgeoned. Triads from China migrated to Hong Kong and Taiwan when China fell to the communists in 1949. The various Triads in Hong Kong were consolidated into four main groups (Chu, 2000, pp. 39–40). A triad has a chief, two tiers of administrators and fighters, and ordinary members.

THE OPERATION OF TRIADS TODAY

The criminalization of triad membership is unique to Hong Kong. The Societies (Amendment) Ordinance of 1992, first enacted by the British in 1845, was a legacy from the Ching Dynasty. The Hong Kong Police track "triad related crimes," which include unlawful society offenses, aggravated assault, criminal intimidation, and serious narcotics offenses. Since first counted in 2006, this category has decreased by one-fourth (588 fewer cases) by 2017 (Hong Kong Police Force, 2018). This decline, however, has to take into account the "Organized and Serious Crime Ordinance" enacted in 1994. OSCO broadened the definition of Triad and related crimes, expanded police power to investigate these crimes and the penalties, allowing for civil forfeiture. OSCO cases almost quadrupled (266 more cases) from 2002 to 2010 (Kwok & Lo, 2013).

Triads in Hong Kong engage in legal as well as illegal businesses. The Wo Shing Wo, Sun Yee On, and 14K are the most powerful groups (Booth, 1990). Since the 1990s, triad societies have become less cohesive due to internal discord and fighting between Triads (Lo, 2010).

Many legal businesses rely on Triads for protection and debt collection (Chu, 2000). Restaurants and entertainment venues recruit Triad members to be business partners or security guards. These businesses are often victimized by gang members or customers who cause trouble or refuse to pay. While police response may be slow and ineffective, Triad protection is discreet and efficient. Triads also target construction sites, damaging or threatening expensive equipment at the site, and then offering peace or protection for a fee. Most business owners comply with such demands (Chu, 2000). People hire Triads for debt collection. Even credit card and financial companies hire Triad members to harass customers whose accounts are delinquent.

Triads nearly monopolized the movie industry in Hong Kong. During its peak (the 1980s and 1990s), film exportation from the Hong Kong movie business was second to Hollywood. Triads set up movie production companies and intimidated top stars and directors to work (often at a reduced salary) in their movies (Chu, 2000). The scare tactics included assault, kidnapping, and detention of actors and actresses, armed robbery of film negatives, and murder of an agent (Passmore, n.d.). Triads extort money from local and foreign directors when they film on location in Hong Kong. Failure to appease the Triads results in disruption of filming. They may damage sets, props, and equipment, throw objects at the crew, and make loud noise. A film crew was bombed when they refused to pay (Chu, 2000). Triads' monopoly on the distribution of pirated CDs and DVDs led to the demise of the movie business.

Triads exploited the real estate boom in Hong Kong in the 1990s. Since buying opportunities were on a first-come, first-served basis, Triad members occupied spots in the queue and sold the buying opportunities at inflated prices. In one incident, a few hundred Triad members were arrested for disrupting the queue at a sales office.

Triads are also active in drug trafficking, illegal gambling, and prostitution. Some commentators assume that Triads are international drug kingpins; Chin (1990) and Chu (2000) found that Triads are too provincial and unsophisticated for these operations. Triads may have control of *local* markets but they often lack the capital, expertise, and connections to manage *international* enterprises. Similarly, human smuggling to the USA and Europe is not monopolized by Triads. Businesses with connections to the tourist industry run these (Chu 2000; Zhang & Chin, 2003).

Handing Hong Kong over to China in 1997 led to opportunities for legal and illegal businesses. Many Hong Kong Triads expanded their business to the north, where they were welcome. In 1984, Chinese Premiere Deng said Hong Kong Triads could be patriots. In 1993, the Minister of Public Safety said Triads contributing to the prosperity of Hong Kong should be respected. Since 1978, after the Cultural Revolution, the Chinese Government has launched a series of economic reforms. China's economy evolved from state-owned to open market, allowing foreign trade, foreign direct investment, and ownership of private property and businesses. Triads and businesspeople seized the opportunities in the rapidly expanding Chinese economy to develop legal (e.g., hotels, nightclubs, film production centers) and illegal (casinos, prostitution rings) businesses in China. Illegal business growth was enabled by the corruption and bribery of Chinese Government officials. Furthermore, some Chinese Government departments (such as the Ministry of Justice) were allowed to invest in private businesses; many partnered with Triads and invested in nightclubs, brothels, and film production companies (Dannen, 1997). The casino business in Macao (its gambling revenue surpasses Las Vegas) attracts customers from Mainland China, Taiwan, and Hong Kong. Casinos, however, do not lend to customers from China. These loans are irrecoverable since China prohibits gambling and its courts do not recognize gambling debts. Consequently, Hong Kong Triads fill the void, setting up branches in Macao and China to provide banking services for casino customers.

Coupled with the increase in wealth from the expanding Chinese economy is the rising demand for consumer goods and services that cannot be met through legitimate channels. In Hong Kong, some Triads operate parking lots to routinely steal expensive cars and sell them in China. Further, anything can be smuggled, from sex workers to baby formula. In 1999, a Sun Yee On boss leaked news about fabricated business deals involving his company that was listed in the Hong Kong Stock Exchange. While manipulating the stock price with fake news, he could launder huge amounts of illicit gains by trading the stock (Lo, 2010).

Although the original Triads may have plotted to overthrow the government, Hong Kong Triads often demonstrate their loyalty to China nowadays. As the Chinese Government flexed its political muscle in response to Hong Kong public opinion and activities deemed critical of Beijing, Triads have provided hit men for Beijing (Varese & Wong, 2018). Triads arranged the kidnapping and transportation of people wanted by Beijing from Hong Kong to China. In February 2014, a newspaper ex-editor who was fired because of critical reporting of China was attacked with a meat cleaver in broad daylight, allegedly ordered by a Triad. Later in October, during the Occupy/Umbrella Movement for voting rights, peaceful and unarmed protesters were assaulted by Triad attackers (Varese & Wong, 2018).

THE OPERATION OF BORYOKUDAN TODAY

Boryokudan, i.e., violent groups, can be traced to the lord (shogun) and vassal system in twelfth-century feudal Japan (Sansom, 1943). Samurais or warriors enjoyed high status while serving the shogun. Samurais became assassins and thieves as their privileges dwindled during the Meiji Restoration (1868–1912), when Japan changed to a business economy (Hill, 2003). The displaced samurai were the origin of boryokudanin or Yakuza. They offered protection for those vulnerable to victimization.

The modern boryokudan is close-knit and adheres to ancient rituals. Strict demands for loyalty and obedience to authority are enforced with violence. A boryokudan has a chief, executives and soldiers, and trainees. Lower-level boryokudanins sometimes plead guilty and go to jail for crimes committed by high-ranking members (Hill, 2003). Disobedience and disloyalty are punishable by excommunication, severing of relations (and fingers!), fines – even death. Kaplan and Dubro (1986) reported that over 40 percent of Yakuza members had had their fingers chopped off. The major groups are Yamaguchi-gumi, Inagawa-kai, and Sumiyoshi-kai.

Boryokudan engage in legitimate and illegitimate businesses. While corporate officials hire them to intimidate shareholders, Yakuza may also blackmail those officials (Huang & Vaughn, 1992). Yakuza work as *soukaiya* (meeting goers), disrupting and blackmailing corporations. According to the National Police Agency (2005), the most common arrests for boryokudan are crimes involving stimulants, assault, larceny, extortion, and fraud. They also engage in loan sharking, gambling, pornography, and accident and bankruptcy scams. Some boryokudan have joined forces with criminal organizations in other countries to engage in the trafficking of drugs, firearms, and sex workers (Huang & Vaughn, 1992).

The police and boryokudan form a symbiotic relationship (Huang & Vaughn, 1992). While running illegal businesses, the latter maintains order in poor and disorganized neighborhoods, relieving the former of their unpleasant patrol duties. Boryokudan protects the business and power of police officers, government officials, and businesspeople (Curtis, 1983).

In recent years, the Yakuza's power has waned due to the aging of its members and tough legislations. The 1991 Anti-Boryokudan Law was amended in 2007 to target recruiting efforts, ban traditional rituals, and allow victims to file civil lawsuits against Yakuza heads. The 2012 amendment expanded police powers over organized crime (Reilly, 2014). While citizens groups mobilized against the Yakuza, the National Police Agency established the Yakuza-exclusion ordinance in 2011 (Rankin, 2012).

CONCLUSION

Fiorentini and Peltzman (1995) found that Sicilian and New York Mafia and Tongs in the USA flourish under three conditions. First, when businesses need to operate in areas deemed illegal by the government, there will be incentives for criminal organizations to emerge and establish local monopolies. Second, when fiscal and regulatory pressures are onerous, people will circumvent the regulations and operate illegally, fostering organized crime. Third, crackdowns on crime groups can backfire, leading to more violence and corruption as means of survival.

Similar factors led to the Triads and boryokudan's emergence and supported their growth. Members who formed or joined organized crime groups were disenfranchised or of marginal status. Some of their activities fill a need (often protection) in society. As business and trade prospered, merchants and businesses became vulnerable to victimization. Since protection by the government is often inadequate, organized crime groups create a monopoly to provide protection and generate demands for their services through intimidation and extortion (Hill, 2003).

Chu (2000) suggested three ways to curb the Triads. First, businesses can change their way of operation and eliminate opportunities for Triad involvement. For example, Triads exited the Hong Kong housing market when buying opportunities were awarded based on a lottery system. Second, if government protection is swift and effective, businesses will rely less on Triads. Third, legalization or decriminalization of certain trades and activities will eliminate the need for black markets and allow people to seek help from the police rather than the Triads.

REFERENCES

Booth, M. (1990). *The Triads: The Chinese criminal fraternity*. London: Grafton Books.
Chin, K. L. (1990). *Chinese subculture and criminality*. New York: Greenwood Press.
Chu, Y. K. (2000). *The Triads as business*. London: Routledge.
Curtis, G. (1983). *Election campaigning Japanese style*. Tokyo: Kodansha.
Dannen, F. (1997). Partners in crime. *The New Republic*. Retrieved from https://newrepublic.com/article/90738/partners-in-crime.
Finckenauer, J. & Chin, K. (2006). Asian transnational organized crime and its impact on the US. *Trends in Organized Crime*, 10, 18–107.
Fiorentini, G. & Peltzman, S. (Eds.). 1995. *The economics of organized crime*. Cambridge: Cambridge University Press.
Hill, P. (2003). *The Japanese Mafia*. New York: Oxford University Press.
Hong Kong Police Force. (2018). Crime statistics. Retrieved from www.police.gov.hk/ppp_en/09_statistics/csc.html.
Huang, F. & Vaughn, M. (1992). A descriptive analysis of Japanese organized crime. *International Criminal Justice Review*, 2, 19–57.
Kaplan, D. & Dubro, A. (1986). *Yakuza – The explosive account of Japan's criminal underworld*. Reading, MA: Addison-Wesley.
Kwok, I. & Lo, T. (2013). Anti-triad legislations in Hong Kong. *Trends in Organized Crime*, 16, 74–94.

Lo, T. (2010). Beyond social capital. *British Journal of Criminology*, 50, 851–872.

National Police Agency. (2005). *The Situation of violent groups in 2004*. Tokyo: National Police Agency.

Passmore, S. (n.d.). Triads and film. BBC World Service/World Agenda – Global Crime. Retrieved from www.bbc.co.uk/worldservice/specials/163_wag_globalcrime/index.shtml.

Rankin, A. (2012). Recent trends in organized crime in Japan. *The Asia-Pacific Journal*, 10. Retrieved from https://apjjf.org/2012/10/7/Andrew-Rankin/3692/article.html.

Reilly, E. Jr. (2014). Criminalizing Yakuza membership. *Washington Univ. Global Studies Law Review*, 13, 801–829.

Sansom, G. (1943). *Japan: A short cultural history*. New York: Appleton-Century-Crofts.

Sinn, E. (1989). *Power and charity: The early history of the Tung Wah Hospital, Hong Kong*. Hong Kong: Oxford University Press.

Varese, F. & Wong, R. (2018). Resurgent triads? Democratic mobilization and organized crime in Hong Kong. *Australian and New Zealand Journal of Criminology*, 5, 23–39.

Zhang, S. & Chin, K. (2003). The declining significance of triad societies in transnational illegal activities. *British Journal of Criminology*, 43, 469–488.

35 Drug Cartels

Neither Holy, Nor Roman, Nor an Empire

Enrique Desmond Arias

In the 1980s, the term "cartel" became shorthand for powerful Colombian criminal syndicates that exported narcotics, as a result of the way that it dovetailed with the wider political discourse of the war on drugs (Kenney, 2007, pp. 235–234). The two most prominent groups were based in the cities of Medellin and Cali. The Colombian groups, which achieved immense notoriety and political power, became the targets of vigorous repression efforts on the part of the US and Colombian Governments that resulted in their destruction during the 1990s. These successes have had the effect of decentralizing the Colombian drug trade and shifting control of trafficking in the region to Mexican organizations. I will begin this chapter with a historical and political background of these groups, looking at how they operated, examining them from a theoretical perspective to understand why the term "cartel" is inappropriate, and will conclude with a comparison of Colombian and similarly named Mexican trafficking groups operating today.

BACKGROUND

During the nineteenth century, Colombia experienced several civil wars culminating in the Thousand Days War. Conflict again erupted in 1948 with the assassination of Jorge Gaitan, the leader of a reformist faction of the Liberal Party (Crandall, 2002, p. 55; Bowden, 2002, pp. 7–14). His supporters rioted for days and unrest spread to the countryside where an amorphous civil war known as *La Violencia* erupted. The conflict lasted until 1957 and resulted in the deaths of between 100,000 and 300,000 Colombians. A pact to end the conflict did not resolve the rancorous national tensions over social justice that motivated many combatants (Crandall, 2002, p. 57). As a result, in the 1960s a new civil war began between leftist guerrillas and the government.

The Andes Mountains are the natural home of the coca plant, which indigenous groups have long consumed to help with the back-breaking work of high-altitude farming as well as for medicinal and ritual purposes. In 1859 a German scientist developed a process to extract the active chemicals in coca to create cocaine hydrochloride. Over the next 20 years the drug became popularized for pharmaceutical and recreational purposes (Friman, 1999, p. 84). Cocaine was legal in the USA and was sold in pharmacies around the country until 1914 when the federal government passed narcotics controls (Spillane, 1999, p. 25).

North American and European demand increased in the 1960s. Until the early 1970s Chile was the leader of the international cocaine trade. In 1973, however, a military coup took place and the new government destroyed the local drug gangs (Thoumi, 1995, p. 130). Colombia became a player in the drug market in the late 1960s when US marijuana merchants encouraged small farmers to grow the plant after a crackdown on Mexican marijuana growing. While US citizens dominated trafficking during this period, Colombians saw the economic potential and developed the international connections to engage in large-scale narcotics trafficking.

Colombia's cocaine trade exploded after 1978. In that year, the television show "60 Minutes" broadcast an alarming report that the Carter Administration had internal documents proving connections between high-ranking Colombian officials, including presidential candidate Julio Cesar Turbay, and marijuana traffickers. Turbay was elected and, to shore up his relationship with the USA, unleashed the Colombian military on marijuana growers (Chepesiuk, 2003, p. 60). This pushed Colombian criminals into cocaine since it was easier to grow and harder to interdict.

COLOMBIA'S CARTELS

Colombia and its people are divided by large rivers, high mountain ridges, and dense jungles. Economically this has led to small groups of local elites dominating business through regional conglomerates. These practices ensured the diversified regional economies at the expense of national consolidation.

The cartels built the narcotics trade on the same principals. The result was the emergence of two prominent trafficking organizations based around groups of criminals from Medellin and Cali, the country's second- and third-largest cities. Colombia's approximately 100–200 trafficking organizations generally affiliated with one of these groups.

The Medellin Cartel, led by Pablo Escobar, Carlos Lehder, José Rodriguez Gacha, and the Ochoa brothers, played a major role in the early commercialization of cocaine in the USA (Anderson & Van Atta, 1988). Strategically, the Medellin traffickers enjoyed the advantage that a large proportion of the Colombian emigrants to the USA came from Medellin, providing them with a potential distribution network (Roldan, 1999, p. 166). With Carlos Lehder's purchase of Norman Cay, an island in the Bahamas, Medellin traffickers shifted the cocaine trade away from smuggling small amounts of drugs through *mulas* (mules) who carried the contraband on their persons to large-scale shipments by small airplane and boat (Thoumi, 1995, p. 143).

Medellin criminals enjoyed notoriety and sought public acceptance (Roldan, 1999, p. 169). This group was violent and freely used cash and threats to buy off state officials. Its leaders' aspirations to political power and popular acclaim led them to provide social services in areas where they had special connections. Pablo Escobar, for example, lavished money on his native town of Envigado and was elected an alternate representative to the Colombian legislature. Carlos Lehder provided social services in his home city of Armenia where he founded a right-wing nationalist political party (Thoumi, 1995, p. 141). These efforts had the effect of buying their leaders a certain amount of popular support and protection.

The Cali Cartel had a different reputation. Led by Jose "Chepe" Santacruz Londoño, Gilberto and Miguel Rodriguez-Orejuela, and Helmer "Pacho" Herrera Buitrago, this group kept a lower profile (Clawson & Lee, 1996, p. 55). Its leaders frowned on overt violence against government officials and cooperated in state efforts to bring the Medellin Cartel to justice (Chepesiuk, 2003, p. 21). Cali traffickers put less emphasis on providing social services, instead reinvesting their money in the local economy to build support among the well-off. As Clawson and Lee (1996, pp. 58–59) write, "[i]n general, Cali's protection strategy has relied on establishing good relations with the power elite, not in cultivating a following among the poor."

In principle the two major cartels divided control over export markets with Medellin controlling Miami and Cali controlling New York, but often found themselves during the 1980s in turf conflicts. The Medellín traffickers opposed US extradition efforts, eventually leading to the assassination of Luis Carlos Galan, a charismatic presidential candidate, and Rodrigo Lara Bonilla, a young attorney general, and, among countless other atrocities, blew up a jet with 133 passengers aboard in efforts to kill Galan. Colombian police, in collaboration with US agents, executed 208 alleged cartel members and, finally, assassinated Escobar in 1993, dismantling the group by the mid-1990s (Clawson & Lee, 1996, p. 54).

Law enforcement resources only began to focus on the Cali Cartel in earnest in 1994. During the elections that year, the US Embassy received strong evidence that traffickers had donated US$3.5 million to Ernesto Samper's presidential campaign. To mollify US sentiments, Samper pursued a vigorous campaign against the Cali Cartel, leading to the arrest of the most important members of the group.

In the generation since Colombian criminal organizations have taken on multiple different structures. For the most part, Colombian criminal organizations have become significantly smaller and have ceded large portions of the international cocaine trade to Mexican crime groups. For the most part the Colombian drug trade from the 1990s forward has been dominated by criminal organizations affiliated with Colombia's right-wing paramilitaries. In 2002, the Colombian Government began a demobilization process in which these groups agreed to turn in their arms. Many of these organizations re-formed themselves into regional criminal organizations that have taken control of the drug trade in different parts of the country. Over time, most of these groups have further broken apart into still significant but nevertheless much reduced criminal organizations spread across national territory. The most significant of these post-paramilitary groups is the Autodefensas Gaitanistas de Colombia, also known as the Urabeños, Clan Usuga, and Clan del Golfo. Guerilla groups have also played an important role in the Colombian organizations in protecting cocaine growing areas. With the demobilization of some portions of the FARC in 2017 a number of FARC units have remained in the field as dissidents that have, in some cases, taken on an increasingly criminal form. The ELN and EPL remain active, especially in Choco, Norte de Santander, and Arauca. All of these organizations engage in the drug trade as well as illicit taxation, kidnapping, and extortion.

DYNAMICS OF CARTELS

From a technical perspective, a cartel is a group of economic actors who use their collective market power to fix prices. The Organization of Petroleum Exporting States (OPEC) is a classic cartel whose members set production quotas to reduce oil supply and inflate prices. DeBeers, a South African company that manages the world diamond trade on behalf of major producers, operates as a cartel by setting production quotas, purchasing stones, and limiting wholesale distribution.

Colombian criminals never had any interest in reducing the supply of cocaine since prohibition reduced supply and ensured profits. Rather, the cartels operated more along the lines of export syndicates, bringing together criminals to collectively overcome economic and political barriers to export (Thoumi, 1995, pp. 93–108).

Operating through clandestine networks to avoid arrest (Kenney, 2007, pp. 241–242), Colombia's two major criminal groups independently pooled their resources for political lobbying through bribes and violence. In these efforts the Cali Cartel preferred bribes, whereas the Medellin group was given to high-profile violence. The Cali and Medellin Cartels also worked separately to protect the interests of their organizations. After the kidnapping of the sister of a Medellin trafficker, the cartels agreed not to pay ransom and jointly formed Muerte a los Sequestradores (Death to Kidnappers), which assassinated members of the guerrilla group that organized the kidnapping (Chepesiuk, 2003, p. 64). The cartels also developed the *apuntada* system, in which traffickers built relationships with legitimate entrepreneurs, allowing them to buy into shipments of cocaine through proxies, capitalizing the cocaine trade and permitting legitimate business people to profit from it (Thoumi, 2003, p. 96).

MEXICAN CARTELS

In recent years commentators have also applied the term "cartel" to Mexican drug trafficking organizations. These groups came to international attention in the 2000s as they took control of large portions of the cocaine trade from the waning Colombian organizations. With the critical exception of the Gulf Cartel, most of Mexico's criminal organizations have their roots among families of drug traffickers that emerged in the state of Sinaloa in the 1960s and 1970s, and in the late 1970s these groups became consolidated as the Guadalajara Cartel, based in Mexico's third-largest city, several hours by car from Sinaloa. The murder of DEA agent Enrique Camarena in 1985 led to the destruction of the Guadalajara group. Its members then set up the Sinaloa, Tijuana, and Juarez Cartels. Among these the Sinaloa Cartel, led by Joaquín "El Chapo" Guzmán Loera, has emerged as the most powerful criminal organization in the country (Insight Crime, 2018). On the other side of Mexico, the Gulf Cartel arose as a result of ties in the 1980s to the Cali Cartel that stemmed from its ability to move drugs into the USA along the Caribbean coast of Mexico (Insight Crime, 2017). These groups had strong connections in the Mexican political system and eventually developed specialized units such as the Zetas and La Línea to undertake military operations (Cook, 2007, pp. 4–10).

In 2006, the Calderon Administration initiated large-scale operations against these organizations, arresting or killing many of their leaders. This had the effect of fracturing these larger organizations, generating a network of smaller criminal groups that have since competed viciously for around the country turf (Guerrero Gutiérrez, 2010). This led to the formation of second- and third-generation Mexican criminal organizations that have included the Zetas (a group that eventually separated from the Gulf Cartel), La Familia Michoacana, the Caballeros Templarios, and the Jalisco Cartel New Generation. The key factor tying these groups together is that they have emerged out of the conflict between the government and criminal groups. As old leaders have been arrested or killed, new leaders have taken over groups and pursued conflicts in order to take control of criminal turf in the country.

The Mexican drug trade is focused around *plazas*, which are drug sales locations and trafficking corridors through which drugs move toward the USA. Thus, the drug trade in Mexico is focused on controlling spaces through which narcotics are smuggled. The competition between these groups over smuggling corridors makes accommodation among them quite difficult, especially in light of state efforts to eliminate these groups' leaders. Within the spaces these groups control, they do not limit their activities to drug trafficking, often becoming involved in other criminal rackets.

CONCLUSION

Given governments' efforts to repress illegal activities, criminals have little reason to act as a cartel. Around the world other types of criminal organizations operate in different political and structural environments. Nevertheless, there is almost no evidence that these organizations collude to reduce the supplies of illegal commodities to drive up prices. Rather, these groups derive profits from undermining state-imposed scarcity of illicit goods and services.

Readers of this chapter should take away two lessons. First, the word "cartel" is a misnomer. These groups are not collectives of firms that aggregate market strength to control price. Rather, they operate as networked organizations to cooperatively assist criminal activities. Second, the Colombian cartels' vertical integration attracted governmental attention, resulting in the destruction of these organizations and their replacement with a looser set of gangs that have had just as much success delivering cocaine into North America and Europe.

REFERENCES

Anderson, J. & Van Atta, D. (1988, August 24). The kings of the Medellin Cartel. *Washington Post*. Retrieved from www.washingtonpost.com/archive/lifestyle/food/1988/08/24/the-kings-of-the-medellin-cartel/d934d1bf-887e-4fcd-8223-9673292e5199/?utm_term=.caa68f947e2c.

Bowden, M. (2002). *Killing Pablo: The hunt for the world's greatest outlaw*. New York: Penguin Books.

Chepesiuk, R. (2003). *The bullet or the bribe: Taking down Colombia's Cali Drug Cartel*. Westport, CT: Praeger Publishers.

Clawson, P. & Lee III, R. (1996). *The Andean cocaine industry*. New York: St. Martin's Gryphon.

Cook, C. W. (2007, October 16). Mexico's drug cartels, CRS report for Congress: Foreign Affairs, Defence and Trade Division. Retrieved from www.fas.org/sgp/crs/row/RL34215.pdf.

Crandall, R. (2002). *Driven by drugs: US policy toward Colombia*. Boulder, CO: Lynne Rienner Publishers.

Friman, H. R. (1999). Germany and the transformations of cocaine, 1960–1920. In P. Gootenberg (Ed.), *Cocaine: Global histories* (pp. 83–104). London: Routledge.

Guerrero Gutiérrez, E. (2010, November 1). Cómo reducir la violencia en México. *Nexos*. Retrieved from www.nexos.com.mx/?p=13997.

Insight Crime. (2018, January 24). Sinaloa Cartel. Retrieved from www.insightcrime.org/mexico-organized-crime-news/sinaloa-cartel-profile/.

(2017, March 10). Gulf Cartel. Retrieved from www.insightcrime.org/mexico-organized-crime-news/gulf-cartel-profile/.

Kenney, M. (2007). The architecture of drug trafficking: Network forms of organization in the Colombian cocaine trade. *Global Crime*, 8(3), 233–259.

Roldan, M. (1999). Cocaine and the "miracle" or modernity in Medellín. In P. Gootenberg (Ed.). *Cocaine: Global Histories.* London: Routledge.

Spillane, J. F. (1999). Making a modern drug: The manufacture, sale, and control of cocaine in the United States, 1880–1920. In P. Gootenberg (Ed.), *Cocaine: global histories* (pp. 21–45). London: Routledge.

Thoumi, F. (1995). *Political economy and illegal drugs in Colombia.* Boulder, CO: Lynne Rienner Publishers.

(2003). *Illegal drugs, economy, and society in the Andes.* Washington, DC: Woodrow Wilson Center Press.

36 Probing the "Nexus" between Organized Crime and Terrorism

Theodore Leggett

INTRODUCTION

One of the defining characteristics of organized crime is its profit-driven nature. In contrast, terrorism is generally seen as an ideological activity, in which personal material interests are set aside in pursuit of a higher goal, the most extreme manifestation of which is suicide-bombing. On the fundamental level of motivation, then, terrorists and organized criminals would appear to have little in common. Since September 11, 2001 (9/11), however, we have seen the growth of a considerable literature on the "nexus" between organized crime groups and terrorist groups. Even the United Nations Security Council (2014) has expressed concern that "terrorists benefit from transnational organized crime in some regions." Opinions on what exactly is happening have differed between analysts and across time.

At least four broad types of connection can be discerned from the literature.

1. Cooperation: organized crime and terrorist groups are increasingly working together in areas of common interest, such as the acquisition of weapons and fraudulent documentation.
2. Co-option: terrorist groups are increasingly directly involved in organized crime activities as funding device.
3. Convergence: there is no longer a sharp distinction between organized crime and terrorist groups, with many groups displaying the characteristics of both.
4. Co-hiring: terrorist groups are increasingly recruiting from the ranks of criminals.

The nexus idea is not new. Convergence and co-option were suggested as early as the 1980s, when claims of "narco-terrorism" were made in Latin America. The term "nexus" appears to have been coined by Phil Williams (1998), in an article that examined the many ways the two phenomena might interact.

After the 9/11 attacks, however, the nexus idea gained new currency. In 2004, Tamara Makarenko suggested a "crime terror continuum," in which individual groups are neither purely terrorist nor purely criminal but lie along a spectrum between these two poles. Beyond opportunistic alliances and the use of crime as funding source for terrorism in the post-Cold War world, Makarenko suggested that some groups could actually become hybrid entities or migrate from one end of the continuum to the other. Various nuances of this relationship were reviewed by Louise Shelly et al. (2005).

More recently, Basra, Neumann, and Brunner (2016) have looked at another aspect of this relationship: personnel. Both organized crime groups and terrorist groups recruit from the ranks of marginalized young men, and many foreign terrorist fighters have had prior contact with the police. Criminals may have skills useful for terrorist activities and may be seeking redemption in a higher cause. As a result, they argue, prisons could become recruitment hotspots for terrorism.

The following chapter looks at this relationship critically, exploring three broad concerns about the proposed relationship between crime and terrorism.

1. Because it is a crime to arm or fund terrorists, it becomes tautological to describe a relationship between criminal groups and terrorist groups. Separatist or revolutionary groups that control territory are invariably described as terrorists and criminals by the host state, but most of their activity becomes legal once they receive international recognition.
2. While anecdotal connections can be drawn, until these connections are quantified and deemed significant, the policy importance of making these connections is questionable.
3. The policy implications of blurring the line between criminals and enemy combatants have disturbing implications for human rights.

CRIMINAL BY DEFINITION

The United Nations does not define terrorism, and there is no universal list of terrorist groups. The individuals and groups on the United Nations 1267 sanctions list cannot be said to be a comprehensive list, as they refer only to a cluster of related Sunni Muslim groups. This leaves it to national governments to determine which groups are deemed terrorist. Once so labeled, virtually everything these groups do is considered criminal, and virtually everyone they do business with is considered criminal too.

Membership in a terrorist group is usually a crime under national law. In this sense, the "nexus" between crime and terrorism is absolute, but essentially meaningless. This taint also affects everyone who has business dealings with a group so designated. To fund, handle money for, equip, or otherwise abet such groups is against national law, and those so involved become, by definition, organized criminals.

This relationship becomes further complicated when the "terrorist" group is better described as a rebellion or insurgency, and controls significant territory. Whatever the legitimacy of their cause, armed rebellions against national governments are deemed illegal, and generally terrorist, by the host state. Most modern nation-states emerged after rebellion or conquest or both, but until they are triumphant, virtually everything rebel groups do is considered illegal.

As a result, national governments define as criminal a whole range of activities that would be considered legitimate if the rebel territory were recognized as the state it aspires to be. For example, like any emerging state, rebels controlling territory tax all commercial activity in the areas they control. Like any tax, payment is not optional. In democratic systems, accountability for this taxation is much greater, but in rebel areas, no matter how well structured or defined, or what real services are offered in return, this activity is typically described as "extortion" by the affected state.

Similarly, recognized states have the right to make use of the material resources of their sovereign territory, but rebels and those with whom they deal are said to engage in resource theft and trafficking. Likewise, any cross-border commerce in which these groups are involved is described as smuggling. All financial transactions are deemed terrorist finance, or money laundering. Should the rebel army attempt to impress locals into service, as many national armies do, this impressment is labeled human trafficking. Most importantly, armed rebellions require arms and ammunition. From what legal sources could they possibly acquire these weapons?

If these groups are successful in overthrowing a despotic government or winning international recognition for the territory they have seized, then all of these activities are retrospectively exonerated. Once victorious, leaders and organizations formerly regarded as terrorist, like the Nobel Peace Prize-winning Nelson Mandela and the ANC, are no longer regarded as criminals for their efforts at raising funds or acquiring arms, nor are the groups that supplied them. In effect, the criminality of all this activity is a matter of political, not legal, judgment.

Since these rebel groups are clearly unpopular with the states in which they occur and are often ethnically different from the group in power, information about connections to criminal or other immoral behavior should be regarded critically. Of necessity, states attempt to undermine the credibility and impugn the motives of the rebels as a form of information warfare, a fact that calls into question the reliability of reports from national law enforcement or security agencies. This is particularly true in contexts where corrupt security agencies or other corrupt elements of government may be involved in the criminal activity themselves, where rebel groups provide a convenient diversion and scapegoat.

HOW IMPORTANT IS THE NEXUS?

The financial arrangements of both terrorist and organized crime groups are necessarily obscure. While anecdotal information about connections can be marshaled, it is usually unclear how significant cooperation is to either group. Without this information, however, the policy significance of the nexus is unclear. Would undermining the criminal activity significantly impede the terrorist group? Would attacking the terrorist group have significant impact on the criminal markets in which they appear to be involved?

In the instances where estimates can be made, and excluding the pseudo-state activities outlined above, the share of terrorist financing that can be traced back to transnational organized crime activity, and the share of transnational organized activity that can be traced back to terrorists, is small. The largest transnational organized crime markets undoubtedly relate to drugs. The two highest-value transnational drug markets are those for cocaine and heroin, which are valued in the mid-tens of billions of US dollars. In both markets, drug crop production has occurred in areas controlled by groups deemed terrorist. But the share of total revenues commanded by these groups is relatively small, in the low hundreds of millions (see Box 36.1). Even as a share of national drug revenue, these groups receive a fraction of the proceeds commanded by the farmers and the drug traffickers, mainly through taxing their activity. Even in these extreme cases, drugs have represented at most one-third to one-half of the income of these groups.

The Taliban demonstrated the ability to shut down poppy production in 2001, and, at the peak of its powers, the FARC could probably have done the same. But even drug crops are not exclusive to any given country; both opium poppy and coca are produced in many other places. The removal of the Taliban from power resulted in a sharp increase in drug production, as has the demobilization of the FARC.

Box 36.1. The FARC and the Taliban: An Undeniable "Nexus"?

The most compelling examples of nexus phenomena remain the classic narco-terrorist ones: the FARC and the Taliban. Both rebellion and drug crop production tend to occur in parts of the country where state control is weak, and in both cases, the drug production emerged independently of the rebel movement. While in both cases rebel groups were undeniably taxing the production of drug crops and the trafficking of drugs through their territories, the relationship between the rebels and the traffickers was initially hostile, before an arrangement was reached in which production and trafficking were taxed like all other commercial activity. In 2001, the Taliban effectively halted production in a bid for international recognition.

In neither case did the rebel group assume control of international trafficking. Indeed, the share of total profits taken by the insurgents was a tiny fraction of the total retail value of the drug. In the case of the Taliban, UNODC (2001) estimates proceeds on the order of US$150 million, compared to a final retail market valued in the tens of billions. In Colombia, the demobilization of the FARC in 2016 has not resulted in an end to the drug trade. On the contrary, coca production soared in 2017.

Outside the world of drug crops, the evidence of significant involvement in either direction is sparse. Claims that rebel groups are involved in ivory trafficking, for example, are undermined by the fact that few elephants remain in their areas of operation. There were only about 20,000 elephants in the 11 countries with active insurgencies in 2015, out of a continental population of about 500,000. The global elephant population is not threatened by terrorists. If all these 20,000 elephants were killed by insurgents and their ivory sold for the field price they could command, then they would receive between US$10 million and US$20 million, once-off. But there are scores of rebel groups in these 11 countries competing for this ivory, with thousands of personnel to feed, so ivory does not represent a significant source of funding for terrorism either (UNODC, 2016).

Outside the world of insurgency, the more diffuse terror networks do not require criminal revenues, because network terrorism is very cheap. It is estimated that the 9/11 attacks cost less than half-a-million dollars, and all subsequent attacks have been considerably cheaper. "Self-funding," which may or may not involve minor criminal activity, appears to be the model for most terrorist attacks outside war zones.

BAD POLICY

The single greatest reason to be critical of the nexus argument is its policy implications. If it is true that organized crime and terrorist groups exist across a continuum, and that any given group can migrate from one end of the spectrum to the other, then states may be justified in treating criminals as enemy combatants. In practice, this has actually happened. For example, street gangs in parts of Latin America (Manwaring, 2005) have been likened to insurgencies, and anti-terror laws have been used against them. In the interest of maintaining civil order, the military has been used in street policing in many countries.

The criminal law and the law of war remain very different, however. The police are trained to gather evidence in order to secure a court-mandated arrest warrant, to use minimal possible force to effectuate this arrest, and to present evidence at a public trial. Soldiers are trained to use intelligence to apply maximal force to subdue or kill the enemy and captured enemy combatants may be held without process indefinitely.

Recent studies have suggested that terrorist groups are recruiting from ranks of criminals, citing the high share of foreign terrorist fighters that had been known to the police. The demographic groups involved, however, often second-generation migrant young men, generally have considerable police exposure. Using the nexus argument, these same groups may be placed under even greater police scrutiny, perpetuating a cycle of alienation and resentment.

SUMMARY

- There are several reasons to view arguments about the nexus between crime and terrorism critically.
- Since terrorism is a crime, nearly everything terrorists do is considered criminal, so the nexus is somewhat tautological.
- Even in the most extreme examples, terrorists do not control a large share of global contraband flows, and criminal revenues do not comprise an indispensable source of terror finance.
- By blurring the distinction between criminal groups and insurgents, the nexus argument can be used to undermine human rights.

REFERENCES

Basra, R., Neumann, P. R., & Brunner, C. (2016). *Criminal pasts, terrorist futures: European jihadists and the new crime-terror nexus.* London: International Centre for the Study of Radicalisation and Political Violence, King's College.

Makarenko, T. (2004). The crime–terror continuum: Tracing the interplay between transnational organised crime and terrorism. *Global Crime, 6,* 129.

Manwaring, M. G. (2005), *Street gangs: The new urban insurgency.* Carlisle: Strategic Studies Institute, US Army War College.

Shelley, L. I., Picarelli, J. T., Irby, A., Hart, D. M., Craig-Hart, P. A., Williams, P., Simon, S., Abdullaev, N., Stanislawski, B., & Covill, L. (2005). Methods and motives: Exploring links between transnational organized crime & international terrorism. *Trends in Organized Crime, 9*(2), 52–67.

United Nations Security Council Resolution S/RES/2195 (2014) on *Threats to International Peace and Security.*

UNODC. (2001). *The global Afghan opiate trade: A threat assessment.* Vienna: UNODC.

(2016). *World wildlife crime report.* Vienna: UNODC.

Williams, P., (1998) Terrorism and organized crime: Convergence, nexus or transformation? In G. Jervasm (Ed.), *FOA report on terrorism.* Stockholm: Defence Research Establishment.

Factors that Facilitate Transnational Crimes

Transnational crimes involve multiple offenders and often a string of crimes that facilitate trafficking or smuggling operations. For example, money laundering that involves converting or concealing the financial proceeds of crime cannot usually be accomplished by a single act. It typically consists of a process of sequential acts that cross the borders of two or more countries. These sequential acts often involve fraud and corruption, notoriously difficult crimes to police. Understanding the factors that promote and facilitate transnational crimes is crucial for developing effective control and prevention strategies. Traditional criminological explanations of transnational crime involve a variety of macro-level national indicators such as development and modernization, poverty and deprivation, inequality and economic dependency, discrimination and anomie. However, most transnational crimes are money-making enterprises that require some rudimentary economic understanding of the supply and demand for the goods in question. In fact, the goods and services involved in most transnational crimes are supplied by poorer countries and consumed by the citizens of wealthier ones.

Decades of study have produced considerable understanding of street crimes and delinquency, but it is unclear whether this knowledge has direct application to transnational and international crimes. Vincenzo Ruggiero (Chapter 39) argues that many standard criminological theories including positivism, functionalism, labeling theory, and conflict theory could be adapted to explain the politically motivated violence of international crimes. On the other hand, these theories, mostly developed through studies of deprived offenders, seem less able to explain transnational organized crimes, particularly their rapid growth. It is more likely that the explanations will be found in the increase of globalization (Louise Shelley, Chapter 37) with the attendant huge expansion of world trade and migration and the explosions of new technologies and electronic communications. These changes have opened up new opportunities not just for legal enterprises but also for lucrative criminal enterprises to prosper and grow.

Marcus Felson's routine activity theory (Chapter 38), which deals with the relationship between social change and the waxing and waning of crime opportunities, is one criminological theory that can be invoked to explain the effect of these changes. Indeed, as explained by Louise Shelley (Chapter 37), terrorists and transnational offenders, just like other people, take advantage of increased travel, trade, rapid money movements, telecommunications, and computer links. Globalization undoubtedly helps explain the increasing flow of people from one country to another. Many people flee harsh living conditions in their home countries, or they seek refuge from war crimes and other human rights violations. In other instances, criminal syndicates deceive or kidnap vulnerable individuals and transfer them to host countries to work in servitude or in the commercial sex trade. Migration therefore fuels transnational crime and produces the conditions for massive victimization of vulnerable people (Roberta Belli, Joshua D. Freilich, and Graeme Newman, Chapter 40). Finally, Edward Snajdr (Chapter 41) reminds us that definitions of crime are conditioned by the prevailing norms and culture of a society, and that any attempt to explain transnational and international crimes will have to address the reality and complexity of cultural variation.

37   The Globalization of Crime

Louise Shelley

Transnational crime is not a new phenomenon. The Barbary pirates that terrorized the numerous states along the Mediterranean, the trade in coolies from Macao by nineteenth-century Chinese crime groups (Seagrave, 1995), and the international movement and exchanges of Italian mafiosi for the last century illustrate that crime has always been global. Already in the 1930s, Italian organized criminals in the USA were traveling to Kobe, Japan and Shanghai, China to buy drugs, and members of US crime gangs took refuge in China in the 1930s to avoid the reach of American law enforcement (Kaplan & Dubro, 2003). Italian organized crime was renewed in the USA by new recruits from Italy, and the postwar resurgence of the Mafia in Italy was facilitated by the arrival of American mafiosi with the US military in Sicily in 1943. An active white slave trade existed between Eastern Europe and Argentina and Brazil in the early decades of the twentieth century (Vincent, 2005; Glickman, 2000).

What has changed from the earlier decades of transnational crime is the speed, the extent, and the diversity of the actors involved. Globalization has increased the opportunities for criminals, and criminals have been among the major beneficiaries of globalization. The new technology has allowed many forms of transnational crime to scale with great rapidity (Goodman, 2016; Grabosky, 2015). Fentanyl, a key part of the opioid epidemic, is imported from China and purchased over the Internet, human traffickers run large numbers of advertisements, spending US$250 million in just a two-year period to advertise sexual services (Portman & Carper, 2018; Greenmeier, 2015). Criminals' international expansion has been made possible by the increasing movement of people and goods and the increasing ease of communication that have made it possible to hide the illicit among the expanding licit movement of people and goods. More significantly, the control of crime is state-based, whereas non-state actors such as criminals and terrorists operate transnationally, exploiting the loopholes within state-based legal systems to expand their reach.

Globalization is coupled with an ideology of free markets and free trade, as well as a decline in state intervention. According to advocates of globalization, reducing international regulations and barriers to trade and investment will increase trade and development. Crime groups have exploited the enormous decline in regulations, the lessened border controls, and the greater freedom to expand their activities across borders and into new regions of the world. They travel to regions where they cannot be extradited, base their operations in countries with ineffective or corrupted law enforcement, and launder their money in countries with bank secrecy or few effective controls. By segmenting their operations, they benefit from globalization while simultaneously reducing the risks of operating.

In the 1960s, most of the growth of transnational crime was linked to the rise of drug trafficking in such regions as Asia, Latin America, Africa, and even Italy, the home of the original Mafia. By the late 1980s, the trade in drugs was already equal to that of textiles and steel (United Nations International Drug Control Programme, 1997). Though the drug trade remains the most lucrative aspect of transnational crime, the last few decades have seen an enormous rise in human trafficking and smuggling (Naím, 2006). Yet what all these transnational crimes have in common is that they are conducted primarily by actors based in developing countries who cannot compete in the legitimate economies of the world, which are dominated by multinational corporations based in the most affluent countries. Therefore, the criminals have exploited and developed the demand for illicit commodities such as drugs, people, arms, and endangered species.

Globalization has increased the economic disparities between the citizens of the developed and developing worlds. Marginalization of many rural communities, decline of small-scale agriculture, and problems of enhanced international competition have contributed to the rise of the drug trade as farmers look for valuable crops to support their families. Their financial needs are exploited by the international crime groups. The same economic and demographic forces have created pressures for emigration, yet barriers to entry into the most affluent societies have increased. Criminals have been able to exploit the demand for people for use as cheap labor and for sexual services, making human smuggling and trafficking grow rapidly.

GLOBALIZATION OF CRIME: FORMS AND METHODS

The drug trade was the first illicit sector to maximize profits in a globalized world. But as the market for drugs became more competitive and the international response to it increased, profits were reduced through competition and enhanced risk. Many other forms of crime have therefore expanded as criminals exploited the possibilities of global trade. These crimes include human trafficking and smuggling; trafficking in arms, endangered species, art, and antiquities; illegal dumping of hazardous waste; and counterfeiting and credit card frauds.

Money laundering has occurred on a mass scale because the financial system can move money rapidly through bank accounts in multiple countries. The Panama Papers revealed the large amounts of money that were moved with great facility to this offshore locale by kleptocrats, transnational criminals, and terrorists (International Consortium of Investigative Journalists [ICIJ], 2017). A transaction that might take only one hour to complete and involve banks in three different countries will take law enforcement more than a year to untangle – if they have the full cooperation of law enforcement and banks in each of these countries. With the increase in offshore banking, criminals are able to hide their money in these global safe havens without any fear of law enforcement. Moreover, banks often do not perform more than nominal due diligence (Global Witness, 2009; Sharman, 2011).

Global criminal activity has been facilitated by the possibility of speedy and secure communication. Child pornography has spread because the Internet makes it possible to distribute pornography anonymously through websites. Material can be produced in one country and distributed in another by means of the web, e-mail, and an international financial system that facilitates wire transfers. Drug traffickers can use encryption to provide security for their messages concerning their business operations. Informal financial transfers can be made without a trace, aided by instant messages on mobile phones, computers, and wire transfers made by fax or computer to offshore locales place massive amounts of funds outside of any state regulation. The development of large-scale websites on the darknet, as exemplified by Silk Road, reveal that over a billion dollars of financial transactions for drugs can occur unimpeded for a significant period (Bilton, 2017).

POLITICAL TRANSITIONS AND GLOBALIZED CRIME

The end of the Cold War has had an enormous impact on the rise of transnational crime. The most important consequences are the political and economic transition under way in the former communist states and the concomitant rise in regional conflicts. With the end of the superpower conflict, the potential for large-scale conflict has diminished, but since the late 1990s there has been a phenomenal rise in the number of regional conflicts. Although regional in nature, these conflicts have entered into the global economy because the arms and the manpower they require have often been paid for by transnational criminal activity. Drugs and diamonds are just two of the commodities that have been entered into the illicit economy to pay for the arms needed to fuel the conflicts (Nordstrom, 2007). In turn, these conflicts have produced unprecedented numbers of refugees and have destroyed the legitimate economies of their regions.

These conflicts decimate the state and divert government energy away from the social welfare of citizens. All efforts are instead devoted to the maintenance of power and the suppression of rebellions. Citizens are left without social protections or a means of financial support. The low priority attached to women and children in conflict regions has made them particularly vulnerable to traffickers in those regions. Psychologically damaged by years of conflict, they have neither the psychological nor the financial means to resist the human traffickers. They are moved along the same global routes used by the human smugglers who exploit men trying to leave economically difficult situations to find employment in more affluent societies.

DECLINE OF BORDER CONTROLS AND GLOBALIZED CRIME

The decline of border controls has proved to be an important facilitator of transnational crime. In some cases, the decline is a consequence of deliberate policy decisions, whereas in other cases it is a result of major political transitions that have followed the end of the Cold War. The introduction of the Schengen Agreement within the European Union permits individuals to travel within a significant part of Western Europe without border checks. This means that criminals can enter Europe at one point and move freely within a significant part of the continent without any passport controls. Recently, millions of migrants have entered Europe from the Balkans and from North Africa into Italy, then traveling throughout Europe (EUROPOL, 2016).

Border regions in conflict or weakened states experience an absence of effective border controls. In many Asian multi-border areas there is an absence of governmental control, where the crime groups and the smugglers have become the dominant powers. Illustrative of this is the Golden Triangle region in which drugs, women, and children trafficked from

Cambodia, Laos, Myanmar, and southern China flow into northern Thailand. In the tri-border area of Argentina, Brazil, and Paraguay, cross-border smuggling thrives. But the links between terrorism and crime also flourish in such lawless areas. For example, Hezbollah planned and financially supported its bombing of the Jewish communities in Argentina in the mid-1990s from this region.

The borders of the former Soviet Union are penetrated not only by drug traffickers from Afghanistan. With the collapse of effective controls across the 11 time zones that represent the former USSR, the borders have been rendered indefensible. Across them flow an incredible range of commodities including arms, military technology, nuclear materials, and precious metals; increasingly, there is also an illicit flow of people across these borders.

The porous border areas of Europe, particularly the large seacoasts along the Mediterranean, are the locus of significant smuggling. In Libya, for example, networks smuggle migrants from the Sahel and individuals stranded in North Africa after the Arab Spring (Tinti & Reatano, 2017).

A similar dynamic exists along the USA–Mexico border, which has large sections that are poorly policed (Andreas, 2000). This border has been the locus of smuggling for more than a century. The Mexican drug cartels have grown dramatically in the last two decades as their proximity to the loosely guarded USA–Mexican frontier has given them a competitive advantage over the Colombian cartels. The ever-present demand for cheap labor in the USA and the huge economic imbalance between the US and Mexican economies have fueled a huge illicit population flow across the US border. This movement is now being facilitated more by crime groups as the barriers to entry in the USA have been enhanced (Triandafyllidou, 2018).

GLOBALIZATION OF CRIME GROUPS

Crime groups on all continents try to globalize their activities for many of the same reasons as their legitimate counterparts. They seek to exploit valuable international markets, to run internationally integrated businesses, and to reduce risk. They obtain entry into new markets outside their regions in different ways. When organized crime is closely linked with legitimate business, for example, in the Russian and Japanese cases, the global expansion of legitimate business provides the opportunity for the criminals to globalize. For example, as Japan's large corporations globalized their business, the criminals moved with them, extorting from the corporations' foreign affiliates (Kaplan & Dubro, 2003). Therefore, the illegitimate business follows the patterns of the legitimate business.

Colombian drug organizations have been among the most successful in globalizing their business activities (Thoumi, 2003). Mexican groups have been in the ascendency (Correa-Cabrera, 2017). The Colombian and Mexican groups have far surpassed in profitability the traditional crime groups of Italy and Japan. Their success is based on many of the same principles found in the globalization of large legitimate corporations. They run network-based businesses, not top-down hierarchical structures. They integrate their businesses across continents. Drug cultivation and processing are done at low-cost production sites in Latin America, their products are marketed to the lucrative Western European and American markets, and the profits are laundered at home, in offshore locales such as Panama, and in international financial centers (Thoumi, 2003).

Specialists from different countries are hired to help with transport, money laundering, and the information technology needed to encrypt communications. Therefore, facilitators are key to the operation of transnational criminal networks (Farah, 2013).

SUMMARY AND CONCLUSION

Globalization has contributed to an enormous growth in crime across borders as criminals exploit their increased ability to move goods and people. Technologies, such as satellite and cell phones, the Internet, the darknet and the web have been used to facilitate communication among criminals. Although the narcotics trade has been international for a long time, globalization has contributed to an enormous increase in the following categories of crime: human smuggling and trafficking (Shelley, 2010), arms trafficking, trafficking in art and antiquities, credit card fraud, and counterfeiting. Money laundering has increased dramatically in the globalized economy; the illicit funds often move along with the licit funds and are frequently hidden in the numerous offshore financial havens that have proliferated in recent decades.

The problems that have caused this globalization of crime are very deep-seated. They result from the enormous disparities in wealth among countries, the rise of regional conflicts, the increasing movement of goods and people, and the increasing speed and facility of communications with limited regulation. States have little capacity to fight this transnational crime because state laws are nation-based but the criminals are operating globally.

REFERENCES

Andreas, P. (2000). *Border games: Policing the US–Mexico divide*. Ithaca, NY: Cornell University Press.
Bilton, N. (2017). *American kingpin: The epic hunt for the criminal mastermind behind the Silk Road*. New York: Portfolio/Penguin.
Correa-Cabrera, G. (2017). *Los Zetas: Criminal corporations, energy and civil war in Mexico*. Austin, TX: University Of Texas Press.
EUROPOL. (2016). Migrant smuggling in the EU. Retrieved from www.europol.europa.eu/sites/default/files/documents/migrant_smuggling__europol_report_2016.pdf.
Farah, D. (2013). Fixers, super fixers, and shadow facilitators: How networks connect. In M. Miklaucic and J. Brewer (Eds.), *Convergence: Illicit networks and national security in the age of globalization*. Washington, DC: National Defense University Press.
Glickman, N. (2000). *The Jewish white slave trade and the untold story of Raquel Liberman*. New York: Garland.
Global Witness. (2009). *Undue diligence: How banks do business with corrupt regimes*. London: Global Witness.
Goodman, M. (2016). *Future crimes: Inside the digital underground and the battle for our connected world*. New York: Penguin Books.
Grabosky, P. (2015). *Cybercrime*. Oxford: Oxford University Press.
Greenmeier, L. (2015, February 8). Human traffickers caught on hidden Internet. *Scientific American*. Retrieved from www.scientificamerican.com/article/human-traffickers-caught-on-hidden-internet/.
International Consortium of Investigative Journalists (ICIJ). (2017). The Panama Papers: Exposing the rogue offshore financial services industry. Retrieved from www.icij.org/investigations/panama-papers/.
Kaplan, D. E. & Dubro, A. (2003). *Yakuza: Japan's criminal underworld*. Berkeley, CA: University of California Press.

Naím, M. (2006) *Illicit: How smugglers, traffickers and copycats are hijacking the global economy.* New York: Anchor.

Nordstrom, C. (2007). *Global outlaws: Crime, money and power in the contemporary world.* Berkeley and Los Angeles, CA: University of California.

Portman, R. & Carper, T. (2018). Combating the opioid crisis: Exploiting vulnerabilities in international mail. United States Senate Permanent Subcommittee on Investigations. Retrieved from www.portman.senate.gov/public/index.cfm/files/serve?File_id=12F93202-C8EC-4AF1-8A66-181EE6716F37.

Seagrave, S. (1995). *Lords of the Rim: The invisible empire of the overseas Chinese.* London and New York: Bantam Press.

Sharman, J. C. (2011) *The money laundry: Regulating criminal finance in the global economy.* Ithaca, NY: Cornell University Press.

Shelley, L. (2010). *Human trafficking: A global perspective.* Cambridge and New York: Cambridge University Press.

Thoumi, F. E. (2003). *Illegal drugs, economy and society in the Andes.* Washington, DC: Woodrow Wilson Center Press.

Tinti, P. & Reitano, T. (2017). *Migrant, refugee, smuggler, savior.* Oxford: Oxford University Press.

Triandafyllidou, A. (2018). Migrant smuggling: Novel insights and implications or migrant control policies. *The Annals of the American Academy of Political and Social Science,* 676 (1), 212–221.

United Nations International Drug Control Programme. (1997). *World drug report.* Oxford: Oxford University Press.

Vincent, I. (2005). *Bodies and souls: The tragic plight of three Jewish women forced into prostitution in the Americas.* New York: William Morrow.

WEBSITES

Global Initiative on Transnational Organized Crime. http://globalinitiative.net/.

International Narcotics Control Strategy Report (issued annually). www.state.gov/j/inl/rls/nrcrpt/.

International Organization for Migration. www.iom.int.

Terrorism, Transnational Crime and Corruption Center (TraCCC). http://traccc.gmu.edu/.

United Nations Office on Drugs and Crime. www.unodc.org.

38 Routine Activities and Transnational Crime

Marcus Felson

OVERVIEW

All crime is local. That statement seems to be brusque and to conflict with the existence of transnational crime. But in this chapter, I will defend that statement and show how emphasizing it helps us understand transnational crime.

Every criminal act can be disaggregated into a sequence of events. If this sequence includes a border crossing, it is easily classified as transnational. But that classification does not tell the whole story. One or more elements in the sequence has to occur locally (see Levi & Reuter, 2006; van Duyne & Levi, 2005). Indeed, all crime requires a local focus of action at some point, perhaps at most points in its sequence. We expect that most transnational crimes include a chain of local actions that outnumber the border-crossing pieces of the chain. Indeed, local people on both sides of a border are usually involved in local aspects of transnational crimes.

This same argument applies to electronic crimes, which almost always have local requirements, such as unsupervised computers or local cooperation among offenders. Many criminal acts that eventually affect distant locations nonetheless occur initially in a much more limited setting, perhaps with several additional local requirements.

Transnational crimes are important, but they have not replaced or crowded out traditional crimes, such as direct physical theft and violence carried out in more or less the usual ways. Even electronic crimes have very local requirements. Thus, a cyberoffender needs access to local computer equipment and local ways to hide identity or evade authority. Nor should we assume that the presence of offenders born abroad proves that crime is transnational, since many of these offenders do ordinary things, such as stealing, evading, confounding, invading, attacking, or conning others.

Although all crimes are sequences of events, some criminal acts have few steps while others have many. These sequences are sometimes inter-related, so the aftermath of one crime becomes the prelude to another. In more and more cases, crimes have transnational outcomes. In some cases something stolen in one nation ends up in another through a sequence of distinct criminal acts by different offenders. Even without the transfer of property, a single criminal act might well transcend national boundaries or use telecommunications not limited to one nation. But at most stages criminal acts are local in their early stages.

SEQUENCES AND ROUTINES

Transnational consequences and transnational harm results from a sequence of local crimes. For example, a car stolen here might be resold to someone else, be taken across the border by a person residing near it, then be transported by still another person to a market for stolen cars farther from the border. This is a transnational sequence of local, illegal acts. Although the proceeds of the crime will be drawn in various places, each local offender may be paid locally for his part in the sequence.

To put this in perspective, we should begin with the "routine activity approach" to crime analysis, and then continue with its elaborations (Felson, 2002, 2006). That approach parses crime into three elements: a likely offender, a suitable target, and the absence of a capable guardian against crime. Surprisingly, for understanding the crime or sequence of crimes the offender's characteristics are not so important as the crime targets and guardians against it, and the physical nature of the various illicit transactions. An offender considers the target's suitability in terms of how easy it is to overcome, to remove without being noticed, and any other feature of the target that makes it easy for crime.

The phrase "absence of a guardian" normally refers to ordinary citizens out of range and unable to interfere with a crime. The physical placement of people and things is highly important for understanding how everyday routines produce more crime or less. This is because crime finds opportune times and places. In addition, offenders often rely on accomplices who they must find in time and space and verify or vet in one way or another whether these persons are suitable partners in crime.[1] Offenders also need a variety of local facilitators, ranging from weapons and tools to computers and software, keys, and passwords.

An offender must find the target of crime – a person to attack, property to take, or something or someone to convert to illicit purposes. Crime is historically a physical process, with goods and persons moving about in space and time to provide the convergences needed for crime to occur (Felson, 2006). Offenders historically:

1. moved along physical paths,
2. overcoming barriers,
3. using tools or weapons,
4. converging with the target of crime.

Today, most offenders work along this same sequence of events. But two other paths to crime are found in modern life.

NEWER HISTORICAL PATHS

According to the economic historian Max Weber, formal organization developed and spread in Western nations mostly in the past few centuries. Its key elements included a continuous organization of official functions bound by rules; specialization in each office, with defined spheres of competence; division of labor; a clearly defined hierarchy of offices – a

---

[1] Offenders also need to avoid those who might discourage them from crime, including parents or other family or nonfamily members who interfere with their criminal activity.

firm system of supervision based on clear levels of authority; rules of conduct; technical qualifications; impersonal, fair, and equal treatment of clients; selection and promotion based on competence; and a strict division between private lives and public responsibilities of office.

Yet personal interests do not die. In many cases organizations and professions put people in a good position to do bad things. While using their official roles inappropriately they commit crimes. Sometimes these offenses are internal to the organization and other times external. Sometimes these are white-collar crimes, but blue-collar workers can do likewise. These can be called "crimes of specialized access," because people are positioned to carry out these offenses. Although organizations are often transnational, their local outposts provide entry points for illicit action. The organizational path to crime starts locally, and its most important barriers and tools are probably local. The target of crime is sometimes transnational, but local processes remain central for organizational crime and its analysis.

Especially in the last decade, telecommunications systems have opened up tremendous additional crime opportunities. The electronic path to crime includes both electronic hardware and software, by which people send and receive information. Offenders often divert these processes for criminal purposes (Newman & Clarke, 2003). The electronic pathway helps us classify a growing variety of criminal convergences using coaxial cable, conventional telephones, cell phones, microwaves, radios, satellites, televisions, and the Internet. These media provide a means to reach crime targets beyond face-to-face contact, but also take advantage of routine activities (Williams, 2004).

More than any other, the electronic path to crime opens up a larger world to offenders. But that opening does not tell us crime is no longer local. Offenders need local access to computers and networks. Offenders need local passwords (often stolen from offices), and manuals (often found in dumpsters). Offenders need to ask local people for information and accomplices can find one another online and in different nations. But local setups from these activities are more important for defining and carrying out illicit acts. The harm is extralocal, but not the behavior itself. The offender must first escape local notice and interference.

Indeed, the question concerning cybercrime is: do computers and computer networks enable criminals to cover their tracks, or do they only help expose criminals? In either case, these criminal acts occur in specific times and places by people who must get others out of their way or get others to help them, however inadvertently. By thinking globally, crime experts divert attention from central features of the crimes in question. Even if computer crime reaches distant places, it often depends on such mundane local processes as failing to conceal passwords, whether on desks or within computer files. Media coverage of clever and ingenious offenders diverts attention from the vast majority who are not so clever. Most criminal acts are rather simple. Most crime prevention is simple, too, requiring strategies and tactics that are tangible at least in time, if not in space (Felson, 2002; Felson & Clarke, 1997; Felson & Peiser, 1998). Most of these actions against crime occur locally. Even crimes with transnational components have sufficient local components to be vulnerable to local impediments.

PUBLIC AND PRIVATE ACCESS AND CRIME

Oscar Newman (1972), a famous architect and intellectual, distinguished:

1. public space
2. semipublic space
3. semiprivate space
4. private space

This distinction does not focus on ownership. A shopping mall might be privately owned, but it allows public *access* at high rates. That makes it highly vulnerable to criminal action. A local school might be publicly owned, but it usually privatizes its space – not allowing others to enter unless they are supposed to be there.

The scale reflects the relative degree of control over space. An open street is public because it is easy to enter. A sidewalk is semipublic since it is easy to enter, but nearby residents might look over it to some extent. An apartment hallway or stairwell might be semiprivate, but the apartments themselves are private places. Outside areas have a crime problem because so much outside space is public. Crime is prevented by environmental designs that increase the share of space that is private and semiprivate in access.

Oscar Newman's concepts can be transferred to the study of electronic crime. The problem with computer systems is that they have moved from being almost totally private to totally public in a very short time. Originally, computers were not linked to the Internet at all. Later, some computers were linked, but only for expert users. In time, most computers became linked through the Internet, and hence became vulnerable to intrusion. After that, offenders moved in quickly to extend their local reach well beyond their local setting. Transnational crime became locally possible.

With the intrusions of viruses and other invasions of privacy, computer users learned to devise local barriers to intrusion. Experts developed programs and other shields to stop viruses. Vendors sold these programs. In time, many universities and companies inserted such controls into their systems. More cybernetic space became private and semiprivate. Crime risk was reduced accordingly.

Of course, offenders often learn to overcome controls. Paul Ekblom of the British Home Office (Ekblom, 1997, 1999, 2000) explains that crime contends against crime prevention in a never-ending arms race, with move and countermove driven by accelerating technological and social change. Offenders misappropriate, mistreat, or misuse new products, services, and systems as they emerge. The purpose of Ekblom's explanation is not to discourage crime prevention, but rather to encourage more foresight among those seeking to prevent crime. His point, combined with that of Oscar Newman, leads us to another conclusion, too. New technology opened up new crime opportunities by creating new public space, that is, new unsupervised areas that offenders could attack with no guardians present. Cyberspace appears to be nonphysical, but that is only part of the story. New physical space is also involved – computer labs, university computer centers, libraries, homes, schools, and other places where supervision is weak.

Yet barriers can be erected in both physical and cyberspace. Enclosures are the most significant barriers to crime access. The locks on university computers are examples, but passwords and firewalls also enclose and privatize parts of cyberspace. Not all barriers enclose fully. Impediments are often placed in paths to slow down intrusions, not to prevent them entirely. Doors and stairwells lessen outside access to company computers and information about how to use them. Many offices and homes are constructed to give a moderate sense of localism, impeding illegal access to cyberspace through physical means. Computer systems also include partial barriers to entry, some of which operate by increasing the probability that outsiders will simply get lost. Thus, they require a lot of effort to abuse the system. Only those with lots of time or expertise can do so. That is why inside knowledge is so important for illegal action using computers. Inside knowledge is extremely local – strengthening my argument that electronic crimes should be considered local rather than transnational, despite their wide consequences.

In general, the access to broad computer networks is highly local, requiring physical entry into local systems that, in turn, lead offenders beyond their local environment. Local systems can have requirements, barriers, and supervision. We are in a transition period during which these barriers are in the process of development, with offenders sometimes ahead of preventers. Those preventing electronic crime are, in effect, seeking to relocalize network usage and to isolate suitable crime targets from promiscuous incursions. This means shifting cyberspace from public and semipublic dominance toward semiprivate and private locations. It includes making public usage privately evident. It includes, also, the reduction of unsupervised public, physical locations that offenders can abuse for illicit purposes. We should think of cybercrime as requiring physical paths toward electronic paths.

CONCLUSION

Reducing unsupervised and anonymous public entry is the essential strategy for crime control. In the process, we will, of course, see conflicts between security and several other considerations: privacy of some parties, free or low-cost usage, simplicity, and more. But we will probably discover, too, that a more secure electronic world can be developed in the future.

REFERENCES

Ekblom, P. (1997). Gearing up against crime: A dynamic framework to help designers keep up with the adaptive criminal in a changing world. *International Journal of Risk, Security and Crime Prevention*, 2(4), 249–265.

    (1999). Can we make crime prevention adaptive by learning from other evolutionary struggles? *Studies on Crime and Crime Prevention*, 8(1), 27–51.

    (2000, March). *Future crime prevention – A "mindset kit" for the seriously foresighted. London: Policing and Reducing Crime Unit*. London: Home Office Research Development and Statistics Directorate. Retrieved from www.foresight.gov.uk/Crime%20Prevention/Futire_Crime_Prevention_Mindset_Kit_March_2000.

Felson, M. (2002). *Crime and everyday life*. Third Edition. Thousand Oaks, CA: Sage and Pine Forge Press.

    (2006). *Crime and nature*. Thousand Oaks, CA: Sage and Pine Forge Press.

Felson, M. & Clarke, R. V. (1997). *Business and crime prevention*. Monsey, NY: Criminal Justice Press.

Felson, M. & Peiser, R. (1998). *Reducing crime through real estate development and management*. Washington, DC: Urban Land Institute.

Levi, M. & Reuter, P. (2006). Money laundering: A review of current controls and their consequences. In M. Tonry (Ed.), *Crime and justice: An annual review of research*, Vol. 34. Chicago: Chicago University Press.

Newman, G. & Clarke, R. V. (2003). *Superhighway robbery: Preventing e-commerce crime*. Portland, OR: Willan.

Newman, O. (1972). *Defensible space: Crime prevention through urban design*. New York: Macmillan.

Van Duyne, P. & Levi, M. (2005), *Drugs and money*. London: Routledge

Williams, M. (2004). Understanding king punisher and his order: Vandalism in an online community – motives, meanings and possible solutions. *Internet Journal of Criminology*. Retrieved from www.internet-journalofcriminology.com.

39 Political Aspects of Violence

A Criminological Analysis

Vincenzo Ruggiero

When Cesare Beccaria called for an end to institutional barbarianism, invoking humanity in the treatment of offenders, he implicitly warned governments that, without the reform of penal systems, dangerous forms of "sedition" would soon arise. A few years after this warning, the French Revolution and its "excesses" proved how prophetic Beccaria's call was. Meanwhile, Jeremy Bentham revealed more impatience and less understanding for popular rebellions, which were always described uncompromisingly by him as "crimes against the state."

In brief, the two major thinkers that any criminology text would mention in its opening pages believed that political violence should be included among the issues that the new discipline was slowly identifying. It is, therefore, surprising that contemporary criminology devotes scarce attention to such a topic, leaving it to the analytical efforts of political scientists and, at times, students of social movements. And yet, terrorism, which is a specific form of political violence, has been studied by positivists, functionalists, labeling theorists, conflict theorists, and so on – namely, by most theoreticians belonging to the different schools of thought of which criminology and the sociology of deviance are composed.

A BRIEF OVERVIEW

Let us start with the founding father of "La Scuola Positiva," Cesare Lombroso (1876, pp. 258–259), who describes political offenders as individuals in need of suffering for something grand, a need produced by "an excess of passionate concentration in one single idea." As if hypnotized, political offenders are seen as "monomaniacs" who display the typical "sublime imprudence of nihilists and Christian martyrs," and turn rebellious because they are oversensitive. According to Lombroso, some of these offenders suffer from hysteria, which frequently manifests itself through excessive altruism coupled with excessive egotism; theirs is a form of "moral insanity." This formulation, antiquated though it may sound, returns in contemporary descriptions of leaders of developing countries and armed organizations, who are also connoted with variants of moral insanity.

Functionalist criminology inherits from Durkheim (1951) the notion that, under certain circumstances, "moral rules" may lose their regulatory strength, particularly when political or economic change affect the patterns of individual and group expectations and put the previous division of labor in a new, deregulated, condition. Under such circumstances, needs and desires are freed from moral constraints, so that they lose fixed points of reference. Political violence may be one consequence, as the weakening of moral constraints and the loss of points of reference may lead individuals and groups to attempt the establishment of new rules and, through violent action, to try and build a new social system.

Following Durkheim's logic, we can link criminality, including political violence, to contingent social morality, connecting it to the social structure, rather than to universal moral codes and prohibitions. As is well-known, Durkheim stresses the idea of the "normality of crime," and predicts an increase in deviant behavior as a result of growing social differentiation and individualism. Moreover, he suggests that limited levels of criminality are functional to social conservation, as they reinforce collective feelings and solidarity among law-abiding individuals. Our problem, however, is to establish where, given the normality of crime, Durkheim places the boundary between functional types and degrees of crime and unacceptable, dysfunctional, forms of political violence. In this respect, his thought becomes clear when, using the metaphor of living organisms, he distinguishes between social acts that trigger innovation and evolution, and social acts that only cause disintegration. Durkheim warns that the former bring vital forces together, whereas the latter cause morbidity, like microbes and cancer. His analysis of the French Revolution provides a precise empirical example of this distinction, a revolution in which Durkheim reads an immense effervescence of ideas, but an inability to bring about deep social change or to create new institutions.

Representatives of the Chicago School of Sociology focus on the concept of social disorganization, which incorporates an element of moral dissent. Thus, political violence is seen as marking the distinctiveness of different social worlds devoid of common understandings and meaningful communicative tools. A possible solution to the dilemmas of exclusion and impotence, political violence, in this perspective, signals the existence of shared beliefs and practices among those who deploy it, and the incapacity to establish bonds with those who are targeted.

Strain theorists would argue that political violence is an inevitable manifestation of the broken promise that everybody can rise from rags to riches. While Chicago School criminology believes that disorganization and crime are embedded predominantly in specific urban areas and affect transient groups of migrants, Robert K. Merton (1968) warns that the emphasis on status and success may turn every citizen into a deviant. Unlike Durkheimian theorists, who believe that anomic conditions mainly manifest themselves in particular periods of transition, strain theorists attribute to anomie a persistent character in developed societies. The strain experienced by those who prove unable to achieve the prescribed goal of monetary success is resolved through a number of deviant adaptations. The most relevant type, for our purpose, is the adaptation Merton describes as "rebellion," consisting of the overturning of both the official goal of success and the means to attain it. "When the institutional system is regarded as the barrier to the satisfaction of legitimized goals, the stage is set for rebellion as an adaptive response" (Merton, 1968, p. 210). Political violence, in this view, is a completely new, if illegitimate, means to pursue completely new goals, namely a radically different sociopolitical system.

Political violence can also be analyzed through a variety of "learning" theories, for example, theories recognizing basic differences between cultural norms and values between dominant and subordinate groups in society, along with theories emphasizing how deviant behavior is transmitted in social enclaves and techniques of rationalizations are learned in specific peer settings (Hagan, 1988).

Values and rationalizations relate to the celebrated "techniques of neutralizations" suggested by Sykes and Matza (1957), who argue that delinquents drift into a deviant life-style through a process of justification. There are five techniques of neutralization: the denial of responsibility, the denial of injury, the denial of the victim, the condemnation of the condemners, and the appeal to higher loyalties. Among these, the last three could apply to political violence, as political offenders would claim that their victims are wrongdoers, would regard their own as a less injurious conduct than that of those who condemn them, and, finally, would elect as sole judge of their acts the political ideology inspiring them and the social class they purport to represent.

Examples of labeling theory applied to political violence are numerous and appear to be put forward by radical and conservative criminologists alike. See, for example, the argument of Ferracuti (1982, p. 130), according to whom definitions of human behavior, including terrorism, are embedded in social and institutional processes, as tentatively exemplified in the following words: "Cynically, but perhaps truly, terrorism could be defined as 'what the other person does.' What we, or the state, do is 'anti- or counter-terrorism,' but obviously the positions can be reversed by shifting sides, or simply by the flow of history." This view is perfectly consonant with radical thinkers such as Becker (1963, p. 9), who posits that deviance is not a quality of the act performed by a person, but rather a consequence of the applications by others of definitions and rules to that person: "Deviant behavior is one to whom that label has successfully been applied; deviant behavior is behavior that people so label."

It could be argued that political violence is generated through systemic, relational processes, and that it is prevalent in contexts where control efforts eschew negotiation or accommodation, and are themselves characterized by violence (Ruggiero, 2017a). In this sense, it is not to be solely understood as violence against the establishment, but also as one of the effects of violence perpetrated by the establishment. In other words, "violence from below" and "violence from above" interact and engage in a process of mutual promotion. In this respect, some of the analytical tools offered by symbolic interactionism may be helpful.

Conflict theories might also be of help, particularly notions that people are fundamentally group-involved beings, and that social life is characterized by permanent confrontation. Individuals are said to produce associations based on common interests and to pursue them through collective action. These associations or groups engage in a permanent struggle to maintain, or to improve, the place they occupy in the interaction with other groups. Conflict is, therefore, regarded as one of the principal and essential processes in the continuous and ongoing functioning of society. The conflict between groups seeking their own interests is particularly visible in legislative politics, where definitions of acceptable and unacceptable conducts are forged. Ultimately, conflict theorists posit that the definition of political activity as criminal results from the challenge to authority through dissent, disobedience, or violence, a challenge that is deemed intolerable by the establishment (Turk, 1982).

Elements of criminological theories are used by Hamm (2007), who refers to Sutherland's notion that criminal behavior is learned through interaction and interpersonal communication. Drawing on classical sociological thought, the author also introduces the variable charisma that he applies to specific characters in the contemporary history of terrorism such as Carlos the Jackal and Osama bin Laden. Charisma, or the power of the gifted, is regarded as a quality that elicits loyalty and unquestioned action. Hamm, however, mainly looks at "terrorism as crime" from a particular angle, as he is less interested in political violence *per se* than in the crimes committed for the provision of logistical support to that violence. His analysis, therefore, focuses on crimes aimed at providing terrorists with money, training, communication systems, safe havens, and travel opportunities. This perspective has led to the development of research into "hybrids," namely groups that combine political and material objectives and that supposedly prove the growing nexus between terrorism and organized crime (Grabosky & Stohl, 2010; Ruggiero, 2017b).

Arena and Arrigo (2006, p. 3) claim that the extant literature "examines the causes of terrorism from within a psychological framework." There is, in effect, an abundance of studies addressing violent political conduct as a function of the individual's psyche, or even attempting to identify specific personality traits "that would compel a person to act violently." Arena and Arrigo suggest that the identity construct is too often deemed a contributing factor in the emergence and maintenance of extremist militant conduct, and while noting that knowledge around identity and terrorism is limited, they propose an alternative social psychological framework grounded in symbolic interactionism. The concepts utilized include symbols, a definition of the situation, roles, socialization, and role-taking.

FROM POLITICAL VIOLENCE TO TERRORISM

While there is some agreement around the definition of political violence, great difficulties are encountered when the definition of terrorism is attempted. Political violence, for example, could be described as any violent action carried out during the course of political struggle, aimed at influencing, conquering, or defending the state power. It should be noted that this definition includes both violence "from below" and violence "from above," namely violent acts carried out by a state against its internal or external enemies. As for terrorism, on the other hand, definitions appear to remain extremely controversial. The belief that a set of human acts can be described as terrorism seems today to find exclusive currency in the official political arena. Therefore, a thematic content analysis of definitions found in the international literature may lead to the conclusion that terrorism can only become a criminological or sociological object of study when filtered through the discourses of politics and the media. In this sense, it is argued, the very concept of terrorism is hollow and unworthy of specialist analytical effort.

Laqueur (1977) observes that consensus on a definition of terrorism is most difficult to be achieved, because the word is used more as an ideological weapon than as an analytical tool. At best, the author argues, terrorism serves the purpose of alluding to some mode or intensity of politically consequential violence other than spontaneous uprisings or rioting. Another definition, however, would describe terrorism as random violence targeting non-combatant civilians. Terrorism, therefore, can be equated to "pure" political violence, and consists of organized civilians, overtly or covertly, inflicting mass violence on other civilians. Political violence, in brief, becomes terrorism when political organizations using it adopt a concept of collective liability applied to the groups against which they fight (Ruggiero, 2005). Targets are not precise actors whose conduct is deemed wrongful, but general populations defined by nationality, ethnicity, or religious or political creed.

SUMMARY

This chapter argues that political violence has been a central concern for father founders of criminology such as Cesare Beccaria and Jeremy Bentham. The former warned that institutional violence exerted through penal practices would trigger violent political responses by civil society and oppositions. The latter was as aware as Beccaria of this danger but regarded all responses to institutional practices as crimes against the state. The chapter goes on to analyze the different interpretations of political violence offered by positivism, functionalism, labeling theory, conflict theory, and so on, namely the main schools of thought inspiring criminological analysis and the sociology of deviance. Finally, it focuses on terrorism as a specific form of political violence.

REFERENCES

Arena, M. P. & Arrigo, B. A. (2006). *The terrorist identity: Explaining the terrorist threat.* New York: New York University Press.

Becker, H. (1963). *Outsiders: Studies in the sociology of deviance.* New York: The Free Press.

Durkheim, E. (1951). *The division of labour.* New York: The Free Press.

Ferracuti, F. (1982). A sociopsychiatric interpretation of terrorism. *The Annals of the American Academy of Political and Social Science,* 129–140.

Grabosky, P. & Stohl, M. (2010), *Crime and terrorism.* London: Sage.

Hagan, J. (1988). *Modern criminology: Crime, criminal behaviour, and its control.* New York: McGraw-Hill.

Hamm, M. S. (2007). *Terrorism as crime.* New York: New York University Press.

Laqueur, W. (1977). *Terrorism.* Boston: Little, Brown.

Lombroso, C. (1876). *L'uomo delinquente.* Turin: Bocca.

Merton, R. K. (1968). *Social theory and social structure.* New York: The New Press.

Ruggiero, V. (2005). *Understanding political violence.* London: Open University Press.

(2017a). The radicalization of democracy. *Critical Criminology,* 25(4), 593–607.

(2017b). Hybrids: On the crime-terror nexus. *International Journal of Comparative and Applied Criminal Justice,* doi.org/10.1080/01924036.2017.1411283.

Sykes, G. & Matza D. (1957). Techniques of neutralization: A theory of delinquency. *American Sociological Review,* 22, 664–670.

Turk, A. T. (1982). *Political criminality: The defiance and defence of authority.* London: Sage.

40   Migration, Crime, and Victimization

Roberta Belli, Joshua D. Freilich, and Graeme Newman

The relationship between migration, crime, and victimization is a controversial issue that has received considerable attention from academics, media pundits, and politicians. This chapter discusses the extant literature and summarizes its major research findings. It must be noted though that some matters – in particular measurement-related issues – remain unresolved. Researchers must determine, for instance, if they wish to study legal migrants, illegal immigrants, or both. The term "migrant" may be operationalized by researchers and nations as "foreign-born" (very difficult to define, e.g., counting or not counting naturalized citizens as migrants) or noncitizens (counting native-born noncitizens as migrants). These differences make it difficult to compare studies and arrive at general conclusions, since different measurement decisions could lead to contradictory results. These difficulties are exacerbated of course when researchers examine migration cross-nationally.

In this chapter, we examine current understandings as to whether migration leads to increases in criminal offending, victimization, or both. Under this conception, migration is the independent variable – the cause – and crime is the dependent variable – the effect. We would be remiss if we did not note that the reverse occurs, unfortunately, all too often. Numerous persons migrate to host countries to flee harsh living conditions, war crimes, and other human rights violations occurring in their country of origin. In other instances, criminal syndicates deceive or kidnap vulnerable individuals and transfer them to the host country to work in servitude or to be sexually abused (Aronowitz, 2009). In these cases, crime is the independent variable – the cause – and migration is the dependent variable – the effect.

MIGRANTS AND OFFENDING

Migration is a social phenomenon that has interested all regions of the world and all periods of history. The concern over the connection between migration and crime, however, has grown exceedingly in recent years. For example, during the 1950s economic boom in Europe, the movement of workers from Southern to Northern countries was encouraged to compensate labor shortages. Migration was considered a contributing factor to the growing economy. The situation changed, however, when the guest workers, who had been recruited temporarily, became permanent residents and failed to adequately integrate within the host population. As a result, stereotypical images of foreigners and their crime-proneness started to spread (Beutin et al., 2007; Sohoni & Sohoni 2014). Today, in many countries migration issues are often considered matters of criminal justice and homeland security, at the same level as organized crime and terrorism. In this sense, the question researchers have attempted to answer is: what is the relationship between migration and offending?

Some studies suggest that first-generation immigrants usually – but not always – commit the same or lower number of crimes than the native population. Their children and grand-children, however, usually – but not always – commit more crime than nonforeigners – in some cases a lot more (Ferraro, 2016).

Some cross-national research has found that certain countries with greater diversity – including greater numbers of ethnicities, languages, and religions – have higher rates of vio-lent crime (Howard, Newman, & Freilich, 2002). There are exceptions, however, to these general statements. A study based on a sample of eighth-grade students in Italy found no evi-dence of a higher level of deviance among young "second-generation" immigrants compared to other Italians (Melossi et al., 2009). Mixed results have also been found in US studies (Bernat, 2017).

Why do second- and third-generation migrants usually commit more crime than the indi-genous population? Numerous answers have been proposed, which can be categorized into two views. One perspective emphasizes endogenous factors – in other words, the migrants' culture and attitudes – whereas the other view focuses on exogenous factors, for example, relative deprivation, and harsh living conditions in the host country.

The first perspective reflects the perception of the foreigner as the "deviant immigrant," an image that has become popular in political and media discourses in most Western countries. As Franko Aas (2007) states, "from violent asylum seekers, cynical smuggling and trafficking networks and Muslim terrorists to Nigerian and East European prostitutes, and ethnic youth gangs, the images of foreign criminals abound" (p. 78).

A common argument among proponents of this perspective is that migrant groups sub-scribe to cultural values and beliefs that may encourage criminal behaviors – that is, their ori-ginal culture is "criminogenic." According to this view, migrants "import" their criminality from their country of origin to the host country. Issues of honor and vengeance, religious and ethnic prejudices, and customary behavior that are legal or accepted in the migrant's home country may be criminalized in the host country.

Recent studies link specific migrant groups to transnational criminal activities, such as drug smuggling, weapons running, trafficking of women and children, corruption, extor-tion, and so forth. In Italy, foreign ethnic groups (primarily Albanian, Nigerian, Chinese, Russian, and Romanian) retain an almost exclusive monopoly over migrant smuggling operations and women's trafficking for sexual exploitation, although some may cooperate with local Mafia organizations (Savona et al., 2004). Colombian cartels, and more recently Mexican drug traffickers, are responsible for the constant flow of illicit drugs from Latin American countries to more than 50 nations around the world. According to Finckenauer and Voronin (2001), there are 200 Russian groups that operate in nearly 60 countries world-wide that have been involved in racketeering, fraud, tax evasion, gambling, drug trafficking, arson, robbery, and murder.

A more extreme version of the importation view claims that groups of migrants emigrate with the intention of undermining the host country's traditions from within and replacing these traditions with their own national values. Due to the terrorist attacks in the USA on

September 11, 2001 (9/11), in Spain on March 3, 2004, and continuing elsewhere through 2017, this view is enjoying increased support. It is claimed that some nations and groups (e.g., Al Qaeda) dispatch migrants or radicalize immigrants via the Internet, to attack and destroy specific host countries from within to further their religious and ideological belief systems.

The second perspective opposes the notion that the migrants' culture favors crime. Migrants are instead viewed as vulnerable individuals who are subsequently corrupted by the cultural and structural arrangements of the host country, which are viewed as conducive to crime. The living arrangements (e.g., poverty and blocked opportunities, lack of social organization, stigmatization of minorities and out-groups, and preexisting criminal subcultures) found in migrant neighborhoods are responsible for the higher migrant crime rate. Relative deprivation can also explain why second- and third-generation immigrants have higher crime rates compared to first-generation ones. While the latter may still hold on to old-country quality-of-life standards, children of immigrants are more exposed to Western values, and can therefore become more sensitive to their marginalization from mainstream society (Sampson, 2008).

Some allege that host governments unfairly imprison migrants for committing crimes that were caused by the host nation's dysfunctional structural and cultural arrangements. This problem is only compounded when host nations, like the USA, deport illegal migrants after completing their prison sentences back to their countries of origin. On occasion, these deportees subsequently form gangs and commit crimes that they learned in the host nation. Others assert that migrants do *not* commit more crime than the native population. Government statistics that demonstrate such a disparity, according to this view, are flawed. Migrants are arrested and imprisoned at higher rates not because they are committing more crime, but because the wider society in general and the criminal justice system in particular unfairly targets them (Bernat, 2017).

MIGRANTS AND VICTIMIZATION

Criminologists have also studied the victimization of migrants, although to a lesser extent compared to migration and offending. Migrants may be at a greater risk of "regular" street-crime victimization because the deprived environments in which they reside are more conducive to criminal behavior (Clarke, 2002). Migrants may also be at risk of victimization from far-right and racist groups that look upon them as inferiors. A wave of antiforeign attacks, for instance, occurred in Germany during the 1990s and continues in other parts of Europe. Illegal immigration has recently emerged as a major issue in the USA, especially in its southwest. Complaining that the government has neglected the issue, some citizens have created and joined private paramilitary organizations. One such group, the Minutemen, garnered international attention as it "patrolled" the Mexican border in Arizona to prevent drug smuggling and other crimes. Some claim that vigilantes inspired by these groups have committed hate crimes against illegal migrants.

Some criminologists argue that these anti-immigration tendencies can be explained in the perceived criminal threat that immigrants pose towards established culture of the host country (Stupi et al., 2016). This framework provides the basis for the legitimization of strict immigration policies and the use of punitive approaches, such as the criminalization of undocumented immigration (Zingher, 2014). After 9/11, many countries passed statutes that limit the rights of noncitizens as part of the global "war on terrorism."

Female migrants may face unique issues. The intersection of their national status, gender, and class position makes them vulnerable to victimization in the form of trafficking, exploitation, and abuse. According to the United Nations Population Fund, women make up nearly half of all migrants, an estimated 95 million of 191 million leaving their origin country in 2005. Female migrants confront ethnic bias from the wider society as well as patriarchal attitudes from both their own community and the larger social order. Many female migrants are thus unable to escape from or report abusive situations. Language difficulties, cultural barriers, fear of retaliation (especially in the case of abused women), fear of deportation, unfamiliarity with the host nation's laws, as well as a suspicion of police (that is sometimes due to abuse the migrants suffered in the country of origin) may cause many not to report their victimizations (Natarajan, 2005).

Some strategies have been implemented to deal with the problem of migrant victimization. In the USA, situational prevention measures, such as increased border surveillance, have been used to improve border security and monitor smuggling activities (Clarke, 2002). To prevent increased death rates among migrants who attempt to illegally cross the USA-Mexico border, harm-reduction strategies have also been implemented, including search-and-rescue operations by US Border Patrol agents specifically trained in lifesaving techniques (Guerette, 2007). Sweden has decriminalized the provision of sexual services by women and criminalized the purchase of sexual services by men as a means to counter the sexual exploitation of smuggled women. In Italy and the Netherlands, victims of human trafficking are granted access to a variety of services for their protection and safety, including the possibility to obtain a temporary residence permit if they decide to cooperate with public authorities and participate in social reintegration programs. These initiatives highlight the importance of considering the different facets of the migration-crime nexus, which include crime prevention and internal security as well as humanitarian and human rights issues.

SUMMARY

There is a tendency in the public and political discourse to blur "illegal immigrants," "asylum seekers," and "ethnic minorities" under the overarching "migration" umbrella. It is important to recognize the differences existing among various migrant types, so that policies for the prevention and prosecution of criminal activities can be tailored to them, and vulnerable subjects, like the victims of human trafficking, can be protected. Solutions to the many issues of migration and crime depend on host governments' willingness to change laws where necessary, to implement programs for cultural socialization and bicultural competence, and to improve the depressed living conditions in both host and feeder countries, where many immigrant communities reside.

REFERENCES

Aronowitz, A. A. (2009). *Human trafficking, human misery: The global trade in human beings*. Westport, CT: Praeger.

Bernat, F. (2017). Migration and crime. *Oxford Research Encyclopedia of Criminology*. Online Publication Date: April 2017. doi: 10.1093/acrefore/9780190264079.013.93.

Beutin, R., Canoy, M., Horvath, A., Hubert, A., Lerais, F., & Sochacki, M. (2007). Reassessing the link between public perception and migration policy. *European Journal of Migration & Law*, 9(4), 389–418.

Clarke, R. V. (2002). Protecting immigrants from victimization: The scope for situational crime prevention. In J. D. Freilich et al. (Eds.), *Migration, culture conflict and crime* (pp. 103–119). Burlington, VT: Ashgate.

Ferraro, V. (2016). Immigration and crime in the new destinations, 2000–2007: A test of the disorganizing effect of migration. *Journal of Quantitative Criminology*, 32, 23–45.

Finckenauer, J. & Voronin, Y. (2001). *The threat of Russian organized crime*. Washington, DC: US Department of Justice, National Institute of Justice, NCJ 187085.

Franko Aas, K. (2007). *Globalization and crime*. London: Sage Publications.

Guerette, R. T. (2007). Immigration policy, border security and migrant deaths: An impact evaluation of life saving efforts under the Border Safety Initiative. *Criminology & Public Policy*, 6(2), 201–222.

Howard, G. J., Newman, G., & Freilich, J. D. (2002). Further evidence on the relationship between population and diversity and violent crime. *International Journal of Comparative and Applied Criminal Justice*, 26(2), 203–229.

Melossi, D., de Giorgi, A., & Massa, E. (2009). The "normality" of "second generations" in Italy and the importance of legal status: A self-report delinquency study. *Sociology of Crime, Law & Deviance*, 13, 47–65.

Natarajan, M. (2005). Dealing with domestic violence in India: A problem solving model for police. In J. D. Freilich & R. Guerette (Eds.), *Migration, culture conflict, crime and terrorism*. Burlington, VT: Ashgate.

Sampson, R. J. (2008). Rethinking crime and immigration. *Contexts*, 7(1), 28–33.

Sohoni, D. & Sohoni, T. W. P. (2014). Perceptions of immigrant criminality: Crime and social boundaries. *Sociological Quarterly*, 55, 49–71.

Stupi, E. K., Chiricos, T., & Gerz, M. (2016). Perceived criminal threat from undocumented immigrants: Antecedents and consequences for policy preferences. *Justice Quarterly*, 33, 239–266.

Zingher, J. N. (2014). The ideological and electoral determinants of laws targeting undocumented migrants in the U.S. states. *State Politics & Policy Quarterly*, 14, 90–117.

41 Culture and Crime

Edward Snajdr

CULTURE, NORMS, AND TRANSGRESSIONS

This chapter explores the complex relationship between culture and crime. Social scientists define culture as a system of learned, shared ideas and behaviors. All cultural systems include basic ideas of what constitutes proper or improper actions. But not all actions interpreted to be incorrect or immoral by members of one culture may be thought of as such by another group. It is, therefore, important from the perspective of a global criminology to consider how the concept of crime is culturally constructed, that is, how ideas about what is right or wrong vary cross-culturally. Describing such variation through ethnographic field research and understanding how it may be integrated with broader systems of power are the primary tasks of cultural anthropologists.

Anthropologists broadly conceptualize the variety of acceptable and unacceptable behaviors across human societies as norms and transgressions. A norm is essentially what people expect other people to do. Most norms are informal and implicit expectations, which are so widely and consistently followed that there is no need for formal enforcement. For example, words or acts of politeness, such as saying "thank you" or shaking hands, comprise a set of exemplary customs of communication that most everyone performs. Other customs are usually repetitive behaviors, the rules of which are generally passed on orally between generations. For example, the Ju/'hoansi custom of bride service, whereby newly married males in this foraging society in the Kalahari Desert hunt for their brides' parents, is common but not formally codified (Lee, 1993). Many norms, however, are formal, written rules expressed explicitly as laws. In state-level societies, these explicit codes (including statutes, regulations, and local ordinances) are considered to be mandatory and are enforced by representatives of the state. Some rules may be so specialized that they concern only a particular subgroup within a culture. For instance, Federal Aviation Administration regulations provide an intricate set of rules for US commercial airline pilots, of which most laypersons are unaware.

Anthropologists use the term transgression to broadly conceptualize violations of norms. Like norms, transgressions may be explicitly classified and officially enforced, or they may be only casually noted by others with a frown or with gossip (Goffman, 1963). For example, in the USA there is no formal penalty for rude behavior such as butting in line. Similarly, there are no serious consequences for speaking out of turn in a moot, an informal mediation process practiced by the Kpelle, a tribal community in Liberia (Gibbs, 2001).

A crime is generally understood to be the violation of a law. But not all formal transgressions are labeled as such. In the USA, transgressions committed against individuals are known as torts, or civil violations, and are usually remedied by the victim herself. Crimes, therefore, are quite specifically characterized in the USA as violations against the political system that enacts and maintains the law. Penalties for these types of transgressions are thus pursued not by individual victims, but by people representing the government. Even societies with no formal legal system define many transgressions formally. For example, the Polynesian term *tabu* is a word for a rule that proscribes (or prohibits) certain behaviors in traditional horticultural societies of the Pacific region. A commoner in seventeenth-century Hawaii was forbidden to touch or even to look directly at a paramount chief. If this *tabu* was broken the transgressor was forced to pay tribute to the chief as a fine.

Since cultural systems vary widely, what constitutes a transgression in one society may not be the same thing in another. Thus, most anthropologists do not study "crime" *per se*, but, rather, the range and variation of norms and transgressions as constructs of a cultural system.

CULTURAL CONSTRUCTION OF CRIME

Notions of crime are commonly grounded in ideas about the supernatural. For instance, Polynesian *tabus* are reinforced by native cosmology, specifically the concept of *mana* or spirit force. A chief possesses *mana*, an essence that is dangerous to nonroyals and the intricate set of restrictions surrounding communication with the chief supports the spiritual basis of his power. Crimes in the USA such as rape or murder are also thought of as *mala in se* crimes, or inherently evil. Such a label suggests the religious origins of these crime categories, as sacred proscriptions of monotheism. For example, the Christian notion of sin, explicitly expressed in the Ten Commandments (e.g., Thou shalt not kill), corresponds to very serious crimes in the modern legal code (e.g., homicide). Less egregious transgressions are classified as *mala prohibita* crimes that, although not evil, are nevertheless violations of a law or rule.

Transgressive actions may also be shaped by political power structures that reinforce systems of religious or economic stratification. In Hindu India, for example, the caste system includes prohibitions on exogamy, or marrying outside of one's group. Thus, male members of a lower caste may not marry a woman belonging to a higher caste. Untouchables, or people in the lowest caste, are forbidden to interact in many ways with people in the system's upper levels. Other restrictions may also be integrated with notions of gender, class, and race. Sharia or Muslim law dictates certain gender practices, such as public seclusion of females, or lesser degrees of access to inheritances for women (Rosen, 1989). Similarly, upper-class urban residents routinely ignore homeless people, and the state may legally prevent panhandlers from asking for change on the street (Duneier, 2000).

In addition to religion, the way cultures conceptualize kinship also shapes certain rules and violations surrounding sexual relations. For example, incest prohibitions and rules of fidelity, which are found in all cultures, vary depending on marriage practices and descent systems. In most state-level societies sex between kin is forbidden and having more than one spouse is illegal. But cousin marriage and polygyny are common practices among small-scale tribal societies or among some Muslim elites. Divergent gender norms may also influence what types of violent behaviors may be acceptable or discouraged by a culture. Among the Abelam of New Guinea a husband may beat his wife in order to discipline her (Counts, Brown, & Campbell, 1999).

How people are punished also varies according to cultural contexts. Many cultures espouse a public approach to punishment, whereby the penalty functions retributively as both a shaming act and a deterrent against future transgression. The Muslim practice of cutting off the foot and hand of a thief, for example, fulfills both of these goals. In a utilitarian system, such as in the USA, crimes are classified by the type of punishment. For example, minor violations are labeled misdemeanors, restricting imprisonment to less than a year, and more severe crimes requiring more lengthy confinement are known as felonies.

Some non-state societies believe in supernatural forms of punishment. For example, the Kabana of New Britain, a tribal society in the South Pacific, considers illness or death by sorcery to be a justifiable penalty. Still other cultures may seek collective punishment in cases of transgression. The Kpelle, for instance, penalize not only a husband who mistreated his wife, but also extended family who may have been complicit in the abuse.

In cultures with no formal government, punishment may often be improvised. A Ju/'hoansi band once collectively killed a man who had committed the most recent murder in an ongoing blood feud. This rare communal act of homicide essentially ended a chain of lethal violence plaguing this usually peaceful community of foragers (Lee, 1993).

ETHNOCENTRISM, HUMAN RIGHTS, AND CULTURAL DEFENSE

As members of a culture, people's notions of normality and deviance are reinforced through ethnocentrism, the belief that one's culture is superior to another's and that other cultures should be judged according to one's own standards. While ethnocentrism is a universal human condition, it may be amplified when unequal power relationships exist between different cultures, such as in cases of colonialism, imperialism, and migration. For example, throughout Eurasia, North America, and the Middle East, the Romany Diaspora, more commonly known as the Gypsies, have been popularly labeled as inherently "criminal" by native populations (Fonseca, 1996). Regardless of whether some Gypsies actually engage in explicitly criminal behavior, such as pickpocketing, other Roma practices may contribute to their transgressive reputation. For example, Romany customarily share official documents between extended family members and do not have strict notions of personal property. Not surprisingly, when a Gypsy male in a Midwestern US city used his cousin's social security number to otherwise legally purchase an automobile, he was found guilty of a felony and served six months in prison (Sutherland, 2000).

Another example of a practice embraced by some people but officially criminalized by the government is *ala kachu*, or bride abduction. This Central Asian custom originating among traditionally pastoralist nomads is still followed in parts of contemporary Kazakhstan and Kyrgyzstan. Despite the fact that it is against the law, many "kidnappings" are voluntary agreements and public gender performances between future bride and groom and accepted by both of their kin networks. But other cases are non-consensual and may or may not be met with public disapproval (Werner, 2009). For example, Borbieva (2012) describes a recent case where Zura, a 16-year-old Kyrgyz woman, was kidnapped by her boyfriend, Durstan. Although Durstan appeared to abduct Zura against her will, including screams and an attempted escape from Durstan's parents' house, Borbieva learned that the couple had planned the event.

Given the ambiguities of traditional practices like bride abduction, an area where ethnocentrism presents a special challenge is with the development of a global standard of human rights. In 1946, United Nations member states signed the Universal Declaration of Human Rights, which proposes a set of rights and freedoms that should apply across all cultures. Yet there remains controversy over whether any cultural practice can be labeled as definitively criminal. One example is the debate over female circumcision, a rite of passage in some traditional communities in Africa, Asia, and even in the USA. In this rite, girls at puberty undergo genital modification, sometimes by excision of the clitoris or, more extremely, by infibulation of the vagina. In many cases, the practice is performed with the permission of the girls' parents, followed by a public celebration marking the young woman's change in status to adulthood. Human rights organizations are attempting to end this tradition, characterizing the ritual as child abuse. Proponents of the custom argue that they have a right to this practice as it is fundamental to their culture's system of norms (Walley, 1997).

Such an argument also raises the question of whether and when "culture" can provide a defensible explanation for criminal behavior in a specific legal system. The "cultural defense" is appearing more frequently in US criminal courts to justify what are perceived by the system to be acts of crime. Levine (2003) finds that this type of defense is attempted in cases of abuse, rape, and other serious crimes. She argues that these areas reflect diverse cultural perspectives on enculturation (child rearing), on sexual and marital norms, as well as on models of healing and health. For example, US authorities have pressed abuse charges against Latin American and Mediterranean immigrants for the traditional treatment of placing a heated cup over a child's open wound. More contentious are cases where defendants use culture-bound interpretations of masculine behavior to justify sexual assault (e.g., *Wisconsin vs. Curbello-Rodriguez* cited in Levine, 2003). Interestingly, culture-based defenses draw on existing legal concepts such as reasonableness, or duress, and have been somewhat successful in US courts, where although defendants are found guilty, juries or judges may reduce their punishment in light of cultural explanations for their unlawful act.

Some transgressive behavior is part of a larger context of symbolic formations and systems of meaning and thus appear to create a "culture of criminality." For example, gang activity, organized crime, and even white-collar crime often occur within social networks that, regardless of ethnic, religious, or even class affiliations, constitute specific meaning systems. Anthropologists and sociologists have studied how these subcultures develop within larger systems of inequality and domination, and produce fundamental notions of community, belonging, and loyalty. Yet understanding the social aspects of deviance also demands an awareness of how mainstream cultural institutions such as media and government can serve as moral entrepreneurs and gatekeepers who control and disseminate models of standard behavior (Ferrell, 1995). Thus, alongside the social activism of the Black Lives Matter movement, has been a growing body of research critiquing the culture of law enforcement and social control (Harris 2002; Weitzer & Tuch 2002) What impact does bias in particular institutions have on societies in which the intersections of race, class, and gender are critical and complex manifestations of daily life?

Clearly culture plays various roles in shaping notions of crime. Any attempt to formulate universal standards will have to address the reality and complexity of cultural variation.

REFERENCES

Borbieva, N. (2012). Kidnapping women. *Anthropological Quarterly*, 85(1), 141–169.

Counts, D. A., Brown, J. K., & Campbell, J. C. (Eds.). (1999). *To have and to hit: Cultural perspectives on wife beating.* Urbana, IL: University of Illinois Press.

Duneier, M. (2000). *Sidewalk.* New York: Farrar, Straus and Giroux.

Ferrell, J. (1995). Culture, crime and cultural criminology. *Journal of Criminal Justice and Popular Culture*, 3(3), 25–42.

Fonseca, I. (1996). *Bury me standing: The Gypsies and their journey.* New York: Vintage.

Gibbs, J. L. (2001). The Kpelle moot. In A. Podolefsky and P. J. Brown (Eds.), *Applying cultural anthropology* (pp. 234–241). London: Mayfield Publishing.

Goffman, E. (1963). *Behavior in public places: Notes on the social organization of gatherings.* New York: Free Press.

Harris, L. (2002). Crime and culture: Challenges facing law enforcement. *Institute for Criminal Justice Education.* Retrieved from www.icje.org/id162.htm.

Lee, R. (1993). *The Dobe Ju/'hoansi.* Fort Worth, TX: Harcourt Brace.

Levine, K. L. (2003). Negotiating the boundaries of crime and culture: A sociolegal perspective on cultural defense strategies. *Law and Social Inquiry*, 28(1), 39–86.

Rosen, L. (1989). *The anthropology of justice: Law as culture in Islamic society.* New York: Cambridge University Press.

Sutherland, A. (2000). Cross-cultural law: The case of the Gypsy offender. In J. Spradley and D. W. McCurdy (Eds.), *Conformity and conflict: Readings in cultural anthropology* (pp. 286–293). Boston: Allyn and Bacon.

Walley, C. J. (1997). Searching for "voices": Feminism, anthropology, and the global debate over female genital operations. *Cultural Anthropology*, 12, 405–438.

Weitzer, R. & Tuch, S. (2002). Perceptions of racial profiling. *Criminology*, 40(2), 435–456.

Werner, C. (2009). Bride abduction in post-Soviet Central Asia. *Journal of the Royal Anthropological Institute*, 15, 314–331.

Transnational Justice Matters

Nulla crimen sine lege – like all truisms, "no crime without law" conceals as much as it reveals. In particular, it leaves open the question of how law is defined. It is society, of course, that defines some acts or omissions as crimes, and which acts are considered tolerable or intolerable depends upon the prevailing local culture. Having said that, there are some acts that would receive almost universal condemnation – "almost," because in every case small exceptions can be adduced. This section reviews the various legal traditions and philosophies of punishment and crime control. What works for one country may or may not work for others because of deep-rooted cultural beliefs and attitudes. These cultural differences often make it difficult to achieve international agreements in dealing with international and transnational crimes.

Three major legal traditions can be found worldwide: civil law, common law, and Islamic law (though some societies follow indigenous traditions where the problems are solved informally without any prescribed codified law). Each legal tradition deals with substantive law (defining crime and specifying punishments) and procedural law (the details of the adjudicatory process and judicial review). Each of these traditions has its own merits in dealing with crime and, in the modern world, most countries incorporate elements of other legal systems into their own laws (see Chapter 42 by Matti Joutsen).

In all legal traditions, punishments for breaking the law vary according to the perceived severity of harm. Two principal punishment philosophies vie with each other – utilitarian and retributive – each of which achieves ascendancy in certain situations. The former focuses on deterrence to preserve social order, while the latter focuses on moral order, whereby the individuals are held responsible for their crimes (see Chapter 43 by Graeme Newman). In most countries, the principal punishment reserved for serious offenses has been imprisonment. Because of their increased use of incarceration, many countries have experienced prison crowding, which exacerbates conditions such as institutional violence, human rights violations, and communicable disease (see Chapter 44 by Harry Dammer).

However, as Rob Mawby reminds us (Chapter 45), the difficulties of coordinating the actions of different law enforcement entities in different countries should not be underestimated. Even data sharing among different police forces is greatly complicated by language difficulties and differences in computer technologies and recording systems. Additionally, each law enforcement agency has its own model of operations and its own organizational structures, which again might impede collaboration with other agencies. In addition to obstacles identified by Mawby, there is the lack of extradition agreements among certain states; differences in the legal definitions of crimes; asymmetry in the professionalism of the law enforcement agencies; corruption and international and domestic politics. There are some specific difficulties of coordinating the policing of borders between countries. Effective border policing performs a critical role in the control of transnational crimes such as human smuggling and drug trafficking (see Chapter 46 by Rob Guerette). In some countries, the military is given the responsibility of border policing. In others, such as the USA, border policing is performed by a distinct policing agency. In addition, the cybercrimes pose jurisdictional issues particularly when the criminal is in another country where the laws and police strategies might differ. In Chapter 47, Marie-Helen Maras describes the need for consistent laws and investigation methods to deal with cybercrimes.

It is widely assumed that if police operations close off any of these sources of income, the organization switches resources to one of its other enterprises or finds a new avenue for illegal profit. Therefore, police have tried to "take out" these organizations and the United Nations has devoted much effort to coordinating international efforts to eradicate these groups. The UN work culminated in 2000 with the adoption of the Palermo Convention, which formalized international agreements to deal with transnational crime syndicates and to harmonize the necessary legal requirements.

The growth in transnational crimes has resulted in an increasing need for international cooperation among police agencies and for new multi-lateral agreements regarding the arrest and prosecution of offenders. For many years, INTERPOL has embodied this cooperation, but many more such international organizations have been established in recent times. This is notably the case in the European Union. In 1999, the EU Council of Ministers established the European Police Office, or EUROPOL, a fully fledged, multi-purpose policing agency. It performs an intelligence and information-clearing function supported by high-level information systems, linked to each member state's security and police institutions. Subsequently, the EU established Eurojust and the European Judicial Network, which are designed to assist day-to-day cooperation between member states and to simplify extradition processes and have substantially improved the speed and efficiency of dealing with cases that span national borders in the EU. As Matti Joutsen explains (Chapters 48 and 49), mutual assistance and extradition are instruments that could assist in building a bridge to overcome the differences in their legal systems and assisting each other in law enforcement matters.

It is important to note that cooperation among non-law enforcement institutions will be needed to deal with certain crimes. For example, in dealing with money laundering and international frauds, global cooperative efforts are needed by such institutions as the World Bank, the International Monetary Fund, the African Development Bank, the Asian Development Bank, and the Financial Action Task Force (FATF) (see Chapter 50 by Adam Graycar).

The United Nations Office on Drugs and Crime Control (UNODC) was established in 1997 to assist member countries in building legislative and regulatory frameworks in line with international conventions, standards, and norms. Other notable efforts to improve the policing of transnational cases include the establishment of ASEANAPOL and international protocols established by the World Customs Organization and the G7's Experts on Transnational Crime (see Chapter 51 by Yulia Zabyelina).

Partly in response to the enormous costs of imprisonment, some countries are now giving more attention to crime prevention. In Chapter 52, Ronald Clarke discusses the different prevention approaches that vary from measures to reduce opportunities for crime, which can have an immediate effect on crime levels, to longer-term measures intended to reduce criminal dispositions, whose benefits are generally longer-term. An improved capacity to deter, detect, and respond appropriately to transnational and international crimes will bring tangible improvements in the quality of life for millions of people around the world. It is vital that these fledgling efforts to improve global cooperation are nurtured and allowed to take wing.

42   Major Legal Systems of the World

Matti Joutsen

LEGAL SYSTEMS AND LEGAL TRADITIONS

A basic distinction is made in comparative law between legal systems and legal traditions. A legal system consists of the set of legal institutions, procedures, and rules that govern the interpretation and enforcement of law. A legal tradition is a set of attitudes, values, and norms in society about the nature, role, and operation of law, and about how the law should be made. The criteria that are generally used when determining the legal system to which a legal tradition belongs are its sources of law, the historical background and development of the system, its characteristic mode of thought, and its distinctive institutions, such as the roles of judges and lawyers.

The main legal traditions are the common law legal tradition, the civil law legal tradition, the Islamic legal tradition, and the indigenous legal tradition. One major legal tradition that is not dealt with in this chapter is the socialist legal tradition, which is based on the civil law legal tradition but is politicized law that recognizes the dominance of the Communist Party. It was at one time widespread, primarily in Eastern Europe and the USSR. Today, its influence can still be seen, for example, in aspects of law in China, Cuba, Vietnam, and North Korea.

THE COMMON LAW LEGAL TRADITION

The common law legal tradition emerged in England and is generally associated with judge-made law (as opposed to statutory law) and adversarial procedure (as opposed to inquisitorial procedure). The roots of common law can be traced back to the early Middle Ages (*ca.* 500) when England was a feudal society with a relatively weak king. The "law" that was followed at that time was essentially local folk custom. Disputes were settled in assemblies of freemen in shire courts and hundred courts. William the Conqueror (King William I, 1066–1087) added a layer of royal courts. These royal courts based their decisions on custom, and often depended on juries to inform them about local custom. Since the members of the jury were part of the same small, tightly knit community, they were expected to know the people coming before them on trial, and thus have prior knowledge of the case.

A combination of feudal practices, custom, and equity produced a legal tradition that emphasized the grassroots nature of law (and of criminal justice), and the role of the judge in ascertaining custom (the law). Once a judge had established what the custom was in respect of an individual case, this decision served as a guide for other judges in subsequent cases that had similar features; the case became a precedent.

Common law also evolved in an adversarial direction. The most active participants in the trial came to be the lawyers for the two parties (in criminal trials, the defense counsel and the prosecutor), each presenting their client's position. The role of the judge was largely passive, listening to the arguments of the two sides before deciding the case.

By the 1600s, when England began to establish colonies, common law had emerged as a distinct legal tradition. As a result, this legal tradition spread to English colonies around the world, including, for example, to what is now the USA, Canada, Australia, and India. Today, roughly one-fifth of the countries in the world can be classified as belonging to the common law legal tradition.

As common law spread, it evolved in different directions. Developments in England were no longer necessarily followed in the colonies, especially after these colonies became independent. In some colonies, the common law legal tradition mixed with other legal traditions. For example, in the colonies in North America, common law blended here and there with a Puritan emphasis on Church law, as well as with an emerging "law merchant" (international trade law). In some North American colonies, Spanish and French law also had an impact. The influence of French law is most clearly visible in North America in the state of Louisiana and the province of Quebec. Although common law originally emerged through decisions made by independent judges, modern common law is based to a large extent on laws passed by a legislature (statutory law).

THE CIVIL LAW LEGAL TRADITION

The civil law legal tradition (also known as Roman law or Continental law) is often described as being based on laws passed by the legislature (statutory law). (Note: The civil law legal tradition is often referred to simply as "civil law." This short-hand term is avoided here, since the same term is widely used to refer to private law – the law of contracts, the law of property, etc. – as opposed to criminal law.)

The roots of the civil law legal tradition in Continental Europe lie in a mixture of Roman law, codification, and Church law. Ancient Rome was highly centralized, and the laws passed by the Roman Senate applied to Roman citizens throughout the Empire – essentially, much of Europe, Northern Africa, and parts of the Middle East.

Roman law evolved from roughly 450 BCE to 500 CE. With time, it became increasingly difficult even for lawyers to understand how different pieces of legislation enacted at different times fit together. This led to efforts to codify law, to bring all legislation on a certain topic together into one statute. In one important respect, codified law is the opposite of judge-made law. Instead of looking at individual cases, the codifiers try to establish basic principles, and then synthesize a comprehensive set of regulations on this basis.

The fall of the Roman Empire in 476 CE left room for another centralized power structure, the Catholic Church, which established a network of courts. These courts did not limit themselves to spiritual or religious matters, but instead took on a wide remit. At a time when nations on the continent of Europe were slowly emerging in the aftermath of the fall of Rome, Roman law had largely fallen out of use. As had been the case in England during the Middle

Ages, the law that was applied was traditional folk custom. This law was adequate in a static rural society but had difficulties in responding to economic and political developments. During the 1100s, Roman law was "rediscovered" by jurists and re-introduced into legal practice. This development was supported by the Church and the merchant class. More importantly, the re-introduction of Roman law was supported by the many kings and princes who saw Roman law as a way of centralizing power into their hands.

Over the next centuries, a mixture of Roman law and Church law came to dominate legal practice throughout Continental Europe. Nonetheless, it was mixed in with local folk custom, and the kings and princes in the different countries added their own statutes. Thus, for example, the law in France developed quite differently from that in the German states. Beginning with the so-called Napoleonic Code in France in 1804, many countries with a civil law legal tradition codified their law. Each new code replaced previous legislation.

Despite the importance of statutory law, jurisprudence also in the civil law legal tradition countries began to refer extensively to court cases. The civil law legal tradition is associated with the inquisitorial process, in which the judge is active in fact finding, for example, in collecting evidence, and in questioning the parties or the witnesses during the trial. As happened with common law, the period of colonization led to the export of the civil law legal tradition around the world. Today, roughly one-half of all countries apply the civil law legal tradition. In addition to Continental Europe, it is applied in almost all of Central and South America, in most of Africa, and in much of Asia.

THE ISLAMIC LEGAL TRADITION

While the common law and civil law legal traditions are essentially secular, the Islamic legal tradition is decidedly religious. Its basis is the law as revealed by Allah to His Prophet, Muhammad (*ca.* 570–642), written down in the Qur'an. The Qur'an, together with the Sunna (the collected statements and deeds of Muhammad), comprise the Shari'a, the "path to follow."

Muhammad lived in the Arabian Peninsula, which was then populated by many small tribes worshiping a number of gods. The divine revelations to Muhammad served to restore monotheism and unite the feuding tribes.

Islam, and with it Islamic law, spread very rapidly. Within the space of only a century its influence extended beyond the Arabian Peninsula to northwest India and Central Asia in the East, and to North Africa and the Iberian Peninsula in the West. Subsequently, it spread in particular to many countries in Southeast Asia.

The Shari'a is more than law. To Muslims, the Shari'a is a guide to what should be followed in all facets of life. There is thus no distinction between a legal system and other controls on behavior. Since the Qur'an is divinely revealed, it is also immutable. It cannot be amended by the legislator or set aside by the judge.

In order to apply Islam to changing circumstances, two additional sources of Islamic law have evolved: analogical reasoning (*qiyas*) and consensus among jurists (*ijma*). Because *qiyas* and *ijma* vary among the different denominations that have emerged in Islam (the most important of which are Sunni and Shi'a), the way in which Islamic law is applied in practice today varies considerably. Modern Islam also incorporates statutory law, allowing for even more variety from one Islamic country to the next.

During the colonial period, the Islamic legal tradition was eroded by the introduction of the common law or civil law legal traditions. Following independence, Islamic law has resurged in many countries. Today, a distinction can be made between countries where Islam provides the basis for the entire legal system (e.g., Saudi Arabia, Afghanistan, Iran, Iraq, Libya, and Sudan) and countries where Islam is one major source for the legal system, along with elements from, for example, the civil or common law legal traditions (e.g., Indonesia, Malaysia, and Pakistan).

THE INDIGENOUS LEGAL TRADITION

Traditional society has no written law, nor even a sense of law as something apart from proper standards of behavior. When a problem arises in the community, the members gather together to discuss how to resolve it. Using at times ritualized procedures, all those who believe that they can contribute to the discussion are allowed to do so. Village elders might refer to how similar problems have been dealt with before, which helps to guide the discussion and suggests a resolution. The emphasis is on participation and on restoring harmony within the society.

Despite the spread of the common law, civil law and Islamic legal traditions, as well as other more developed types of law, this indigenous legal tradition remains in wide use in many areas, alongside the "official" legal system. This is the case in many African countries as well as, for example, Indonesia, Papua New Guinea, and the Philippines. The tradition is also resurging among indigenous people in, for example, the USA, Canada, and New Zealand. Furthermore, many of the elements of the indigenous legal tradition have been used in the development of mediation and restorative justice programs in "mainstream" legal traditions.

MIXTURES OF LEGAL TRADITIONS

The development of the different legal traditions did not take place in a vacuum. Each was influenced by other traditions. For example, the common law legal tradition has adopted some inquisitorial aspects from the civil law legal tradition, and the civil law legal tradition has correspondingly been influenced by common law adversarial procedure.

In some cases, several legal traditions operate alongside one another in the same country. For example, in both Nigeria and Pakistan, common law, Islamic law, and indigenous law are applied in separate court systems. As a result, there are few "pure" examples of a legal tradition. According to one calculation, almost one-half of the legal systems in the world are hybrids that combine different legal traditions. Historical developments and structural factors help to explain why a country follows a certain legal tradition, but the differences between the traditions are not hard and fast. Table 42.1 provides an overview of the four main legal traditions. The differences are not so much of kind, as of degree.

Moreover, there is a lot of variation within legal traditions. Common law countries vary in the extent to which they use codification, jury trial, and allow judicial activism. Different civil law legal tradition countries have developed different institutions. Examples of such institutions include the investigating magistrate in French-based systems and the role of the victim as a subsidiary prosecutor in some German-based systems.

Table 42.1. Overview of the main legal traditions

	Sources of Law	Centralization	Discretion	Features	Examples
Common law	Case law and legislation.	Low.	Extensive.	Jury; rules of evidence; passive role of judge; active role of lawyer.	USA, Canada, United Kingdom.
Civil law	Legislation (synthesis; broad principles).	High.	Some.	Active role of judge.	France, Germany, Mexico.
Islamic law	Shari'a; analogical reasoning; consensus among jurists.	Low.	Religious interpretation.	Law is divinely inspired; immutability of the Shari'a.	Saudi Arabia, Iraq, Afghanistan.
Indigenous law	Local custom; primarily oral sources.	Very low.	Extensive; wide use of mediation.	Extensive informal control; search for community harmony.	Tribal courts in the USA, aboriginal communities in Australia, Maori communities in New Zealand.

SUMMARY

Studying the legal traditions helps us to understand why they differ in their use of various sources of law, and why they have developed certain specific features. However, to a surprising degree, there are few major differences in how the legal traditions operate in practice. This can be seen in the operation of the criminal justice system. The way in which each and every society responds to dangerous or harmful conduct such as stealing, fighting, and vandalism is broadly the same. A central authority (usually a democratically elected legislature, although it can also be, for example, a king, a religious leader, or a council of elders) defines what behavior is prohibited, how to determine whether or not someone has been guilty of such behavior, and what the punishment may be. The broad outlines of the criminal justice process are much the same in every country, with one or more law enforcement agencies charged with the investigation of alleged offenses; a prosecutorial service charged with presentation of the cases in court; an adjudicatory body charged with hearing the case and deciding the outcome; and a separate organization charged with the enforcement of the sentence. The main practical differences between individual criminal justice systems – and legal traditions – appear to arise not so much from the legal system, but from the political system, and in particular its approach to the question of control.

FURTHER READING

Dammer, H. R. & Albanese, J. S. (2014). *Comparative criminal justice systems*. Fifth edition. Belmont, CA: Wadsworth.

Pakes, F. (2017). *Comparative criminal justice*. Third Edition. London and New York: Routledge.

Reichel, P. (2018). *Comparative criminal justice systems: A topical approach*. New York: Pearson.

Terrill, R. J. (2013). *World criminal justice systems: A comparative review*. Boston, New York, San Diego, and San Francisco: Anderson Publishing.

43 Punishment Philosophies and Practices around the World

Graeme Newman

INTRODUCTION

While punishment is universal in all criminal justice systems, it varies in the justifications given for its administration, and the kinds of punishments employed. However, comparing or even describing the use of punishments around the world is fraught with many difficulties, as is the comparison of crime (see Aebi, Chapter 79, this volume). By far the most difficult problem is to be sure that when we compare punishment from one country to another we are in fact comparing the same thing.

DEFINING PUNISHMENT

In general, the definition of punishment in criminal justice should include the following elements (Newman, 2008).

- It must result in pain or consequences normally considered unpleasant.
- It must be for an actual or supposed offender for his offence.
- It must be administered for an offence against the law.
- It must be intentionally administered by a legal authority.
- It must be administered by someone other than the offender.

This definition has many problems, but it does serve to establish some boundaries. It eliminates, for example, wanton or indiscriminate violence against others, such as rape in war or death squads in times of insurrection. On the other hand, many countries that have Departments of Corrections aimed at rehabilitation (most do) may claim that the consequences are not intended to be painful, nor are they necessarily experienced as unpleasant.

PHILOSOPHIES OF PUNISHMENT

There are basically two philosophies of punishment – though they are perhaps better termed "justifications" for punishment – offered by governments and societies around the world. These are the utilitarian and the retributive. The modern view of the former, probably the most dominant, holds that, since social order is the supreme necessity of society, any amount of punishment used to deter offenders as an example to the offender and to others is well justified. Thus, the more crime that punishment can deter, the greater the good achieved.

In contrast, the justification based on retribution focuses on a lofty idea of justice: that social order (the utilitarian concern) is secondary to the moral order that is violated when an offender breaks the law. The retributivist holds that since morality is concerned with individual responsibility, the individual offender must be held to account; indeed, it is society's duty to punish him. Thus, the offender deserves to be punished, from which comes the common expression "just desserts." It further follows that the punishment must match the crime as closely as possible in order for the moral balance to be restored. This idea is but a sanitized version of the ancient principle of vengeance, "an eye for an eye." In almost all societies we find elements of both the utilitarian and retributive approaches. Taken to the extreme, there is no limit to the utilitarian use of punishment in order to preserve social order. Retribution provides limits by insisting that the "punishment fit the crime" and no more.

THE FUNCTIONS OF PUNISHMENT

The functions of punishment (often difficult to distinguish from justifications for punishment) are mostly characterized by social theorists as hidden in any given society (Garland, 1993). That is, the obvious functions of punishment, such as to deter criminal acts, hide the real functions. These hidden functions gain favor because it is often difficult to demonstrate, in fact, that punishment deters crime. These latent functions of punishment also lack basis in fact, are speculative, and depend in large part on the detailed analysis of the cultures and histories of particular societies. In general, a short list of the hidden functions of punishment in society advanced by scholars includes: scapegoating ("let he who is without sin cast the first stone"), boundary definition ("they must be bad because they're in prison"), catharsis ("It makes us feel good to see the guilty punished"), enhancing social solidarity ("it's us against them"), and various forms of class or ethnic conflict ("to keep the dangerous classes in their place") (Newman, 2008).

ADMINISTRATION OF PUNISHMENT

The basic factors that guide the administration of punishment are its: type, intensity, frequency, and duration. For example, whipping (a common punishment in Singapore and other countries) may be administered according to: 1) the intensity with which the lash is brought against the body, which may be a function of the strength of the punisher or the size of the lash; 2) how many strokes are administered in one session; and 3) how often they are administered (e.g., one session a day for two weeks). Depending on the type of punishment, one or another of these administrative elements of punishment may be more dominant. Obviously, for prison, duration is the most dominant feature of the punishment, but cutting off the hand of a thief is an intense punishment of very short duration and low frequency (though its long-term effects are considerable).

TYPES OF PUNISHMENT

Any classification of punishments can only be made roughly, since many actual punishments may easily fit into more than one category. The extent to which punishments also express or emphasize retributive or utilitarian philosophies is also sometimes difficult to determine. The preponderance of different types of punishment and their examples described later in this essay are derived from the exhaustive publication *Crime and Punishment Around the World* (Newman, 2010), which surveys crime and punishment in more than 230 countries, dependencies, and territories.

Economic punishments. These are expressed most simply as fines of designated amounts, varying according to the seriousness of the offense and usually, though not always, for property crimes of lesser amounts. However, fines can be complicated because their use is subject to the criticism that they punish unequally those who have the least and are felt less by those who have more. Countries with civil law systems, such as Scandinavia, calculate the amount of a fine according to the daily income of the offender (day fine). This punishment is further complicated if the offender has no income or property. In this case, many legal systems may calculate an equivalent in prison time. For example, in Finland, one day in prison equals three days of fines. In all countries surveyed in *Crime and Punishment Around the World*, fines in one form or another were universally applied. The other major form of economic punishment is that of forced labor, which may occur in a prison if the crime is a very serious one, but it may also be performed in the community. In common and civil law systems (see Joutsen, Chapter 54, this volume) the usual designation given to this economic-based punishment is "community service" in which the offender is required to perform tasks in various locations, such as helping in a hospital or charity, sweeping the streets, etc. Finally, a method of economic punishment that responds more to the retributive expression of punishment is the requirement that the offender pay back to the offended the amount that he stole, or at least return the items taken. Many systems will also add a fine on top of this punishment.

Public condemnation. This punishment may take several forms. In many countries the mass media serves to denounce the offender's crimes. In Sweden, the customers of brothels are publicized, and depending on the locality in the USA names of offenders of all kinds will be publicized in local media, and even national media. A more recent and intense form of this punishment (though strictly speaking it is an "after-punishment") is the widespread introduction in the USA and other countries of sex offender registries. Customary legal systems are also said to use shaming as a punishment, in which offenders are publicly denounced or shunned. The extreme form of this customary punishment is, of course, stoning to death. In fact, all punishments that are conducted in public assume an element of public condemnation.

Disenfranchisement. Closely related to public denunciation is the disenfranchisement of offenders, most often in the form of removal from public office, or withdrawal of license to practice a profession, such as in law or medicine. These acts of disenfranchisement are widely used throughout countries with developed service economies and are especially well developed in the criminal codes of civil law countries of Eastern Europe. The crimes for which this punishment is commonly used are corruption and bribery. Banishment or exile, an old form of punishment that combines disenfranchisement with deprivation of rights, is listed as a punishment in the codes of Uruguay, the Maldives, and Haiti, though the extent of its use is unknown. Many countries, however, may deport offenders who are illegal aliens.

Deprivation of liberty. Offenders are deprived of their liberty through the universal application of prison (see Dammer, Chapter 54, this volume). However, there are degrees in deprivation of liberty. For example, the amount of contact allowed inmates with the outside world may vary considerably according to the conditions inside the prison, such as allowing TV or radio access, allowing visitation by family and friends, allowing inmates to work outside of prison in designated businesses or factories, allowing weekend furloughs, etc. Noncustodial deprivation of liberty may take on several forms, ranging from house arrest and tracking with ankle bracelets, to probation of various intensities (e.g., reporting to the officer every day or once every few months). While probation is widely used throughout most countries, it is not universal as is prison. In addition, parole – a probationary period usually applied after release from prison – is not universally applied and tends to be most common in countries with well-established common law or civil law systems. Some critics argue that probation is not painful enough to be classified as a punishment.

Corporal punishments. These commonly include amputation of body parts (e.g., hands and feet), the lash, or caning. Eighty countries or territories use corporal punishment either as a sentence for a crime or as a disciplinary measure within prisons (Newman, 2010). Of these, 30 have Islamic or customary legal systems. Most Islamic legal systems (present in 37 countries or territories around the world) contain corporal punishment as a sentence in their written laws. Where corporal punishment is used in civil and common law systems, it is mostly used as a disciplinary method in prisons, not as a specific sentence for a crime. There are exceptions to this: the Isle of Man, for example, retains the birch as a punishment, and its system is mostly one of common law.

The death penalty. Seventy-three countries or territories still retain the death penalty. Of these, 47 also use corporal punishment. The methods of execution range from lethal injection (USA), firing squad (Ethiopia), shooting in the neck (Mongolia), hanging (Sierra Leone), beheading (Saudi Arabia), and stoning to death (Iran). Public executions are still carried out, mainly in Middle Eastern and some African countries.

Restorative punishments. These include actions required of the offender that either compensate the victim or, if possible, reconcile the offender and victim. Customary law, present in at least 62 countries or territories around the world, is most commonly identified with this approach to punishment. In many African countries, especially North Africa, customary legal systems (which may be entirely oral, without written law) operate to resolve conflicts that occur between family groups or factions. The solution is usually the payment of compensation by one family group to another for injury or damage done. However, there is a tendency to romanticize these customary legal systems and the logic of reconciliation can take on unexpected forms. For example, in Syria and the Palestine territories, when a girl is raped, the restorative solution is to have her marry her rapist. The argument is that this restores her honor – and it forces the families of the offender and victim to come together. Compensation may also be achieved through "blood money" recognized in some Islamic legal systems where an offender may settle accounts with a victim or, in the case of murder, a victim's family. In these cases, the victim may exert considerable influence over the final punishment of the offender, since, by accepting blood money or other compensation, the offender may escape the death penalty.

MATCHING PUNISHMENTS TO CRIMES

The scale by which punishments are matched to crimes remains a particularly difficult puzzle. Islamic legal systems generally give precedence to retribution in deciding the severity of punishments, but this leads to some difficulties because retribution requires that the punishment match the particular offence and only that offence. Punishing an offender more severely because he has repeated his crime (i.e., deterrence) is not found in the Qur'an. However, some Islamic scholars have argued that deterrence may be used as a "secondary principle" in punishing offenders, and this has led to the common use of imprisonment (Alizadeh, 2010) in most, if not all, Islamic countries. An additional difficulty is that, because Islamic law defines so few crimes compared to civil and common law systems, the small range of punishments available do not lend themselves to establishing a scale of punishments according to their severity. For example, the punishment for rape, murder, robbery, and adultery can all lead to the death penalty under Islamic law. In contrast, in civil and common law countries the degrees of seriousness within each of those crimes are always specified. In fact, in civil law systems (present in 164 countries and territories of the world), it is typical for there to be a long and exhaustive list of major crimes and their subdivisions, and even subdivisions within these, carefully matched to punishments that are highly classified and defined in every detail (see, for example, the codes of Georgia, the Czech Republic, Belarus, and Armenia, described in Newman, 2010).

The simple conclusion from these observations is that in order to develop and implement a system of punishment that takes into account many fine gradations of seriousness of crimes, one needs a punishment that also can be graded finely. Prison turns out to be the most adaptable punishment for this enterprise, since its frequency and amount can be easily quantified (e.g., days, months, years), as can its intensity (e.g., with or without hard labor, furloughs, conjugal visits, etc.). Among the many explanations put forward by scholars, this is the simplest and most likely explanation for the now-universal use of prison as a punishment throughout the world. Unfortunately, its side effects, particularly the destruction of local communities and families of offenders, have only recently been acknowledged, if at all, in recent revelations of "mass incarceration" in the USA and much of the Western world (Newman, in press; Alexander, 2012).

REFERENCES

Alexander, M. (2012). *The new Jim Crow: Mass incarceration in the age of colorblindness*. New York: The New Press.

Alizadeh, M. S. (2010). Iran. In G. R. Newman (Ed.), *Crime and punishment around the world. Volume 1, Africa and Middle East*. New Haven, CT: Greenwood Press.

Beccaria, C. (2009). *On crimes and punishments* (Fifth Ed). G. R. Newman and P. Marongiu (Eds. and Trans.). Piscataway, NJ: Transaction Publishers.

Garland, D. (1993). *Punishment and modern society*. Chicago: University of Chicago Press.

Newman, G. R. (2008). *The punishment response*. Second Edition. Piscataway, NJ: Transaction Publishers.

(Ed.). (2010). *Crime and punishment around the world*. Four Volumes. New Haven, CT: Greenwood Press.

(in press). *Punish me robot: Punishing criminals in the 21st century*.

44 Prisons around the World

Harry R. Dammer

This chapter will provide an overview of the key issues related to prisons around the world, including a brief historical overview of prisons, global incarceration numbers, trends, and governance, and the global concern about prison crowding.

HISTORICAL OVERVIEW OF PRISONS

Although the common use of the term "penitentiary" is credited to the USA, it is believed that a Benedictine monk named Jean Mabillon in the seventeenth century first coined the phrase. The first institution bearing that moniker appeared in France after the 1790 revolution, while the same year a variation of the penitentiary was being implemented at the Walnut Street Jail in Philadelphia. Nonetheless, the philosophical roots of the penitentiary were formed in Europe during the late 1700s through the Age of the Enlightenment and the ideas of Cesare Beccaria, Jeremy Bentham, and John Howard. The penitentiary method was seen as an advance – as opposed to the retributive view of punishment. It took an optimistic view of human nature and the belief in the possibility of change and reform. Conceived as a place where prisoners would be isolated from the bad influences of society, engaged in productive labor, and made to reflect on past misdeeds, they could be reformed and become "penitent" (sorry) for their sins – hence the term, "penitentiary" (Clear et al., 2015).

Although the earliest attempt to institute the penitentiary system failed at the Walnut Street Jail, between 1790 and 1829 numerous other states in America adopted aspects of the system. In 1829, an influential group of Pennsylvania Quakers were eventually able to open two correctional institutions with a system of solitary confinement with labor, silence, and religious instruction in Pittsburgh and Philadelphia called Western and Eastern Penitentiary, respectively. In Auburn, New York a prison opened in 1817, and, being influenced by the reported success of the Walnut Street Jail, administrators began to implement the separate and silent Pennsylvania system. But because the Pennsylvania system was found to cause mental and physical problems for the inmates, as well as being very expensive because it called for single cells for all inmates, it was abandoned in 1823. An alternative soon developed called the New York (Auburn) system. Promoted by members of the Calvinist religion, by 1833 this method was adopted by penitentiaries in ten states, the District of Columbia, and in parts of Canada. In the New York (Auburn) system, inmates were locked in separate cells at night but allowed to congregate at work and meal times, albeit in silence, during the day.

Supporters of the penitentiary hoped that a regime of solitude (i.e., the Pennsylvania system) or of silent, controlled work (the New York/Auburn system) would provide a humane way to bring about a change of disposition and lifestyle in convicted criminals. For decades, the two systems were hotly debated and by 1900 most jurisdictions adopted the New York (Auburn) method.

The American experiment rapidly became the focus of reform in other countries as well. The reformative prison spread to Russia in 1863, Brazil in 1834, Japan in 1868, and China in 1905 (Weiss, 2005). The reformative prison was undoubtedly a major topic of discussion at the first International Prison Congress, held in 1872 in London. What is interesting, however, was that the idea of American-style prison continued to grow despite evidence that it did not reform offenders or even provide them with humane conditions of incarceration. The penitentiary movement, launched with high hopes in the late eighteenth century, had not lived up to the expectations of the reformers who conceived it.

By the early twentieth century, it was obvious that prisons were not fulfilling their promise, and, in fact, they were generally seen to be as cruel and inhumane as any previous method of punishment. In response, the American Progressive Movement provided a new approach to corrections called rehabilitation. Rehabilitation calls for restoring a convicted offender to a constructive place in society through some form of vocational or educational training or therapy. These methods include probation, parole, therapeutic prison regimes, and separate juvenile justice mechanisms. Until the nineteenth century, many countries, including the USA, did not have separate institutions for males, females, and juveniles. The change to separate the females and juveniles from the adult male offenders was also part of the Progressive Movement.

However, in the early 1970s, criminal justice officials throughout the world, especially in the USA, turned to a crime-control model including increased use of incarceration and stricter forms of community supervision. As a result, in the last half of the twentieth century, mandatory sentences, longer sentences, intensive probation supervision, and detention without bail have increased jail and prison populations to record levels throughout the world. Much of the call for increasing severity of sentences has been driven by penal populism, a term used to describe crime policies that are formed by politicians in their attempt to appease the public and their call for punitiveness despite a lack of program efficacy or even a clear understanding of community opinion (Pratt, 2007).

GLOBAL INCARCERATION NUMBERS AND RATES

There are currently more than 10.35 million persons imprisoned throughout the world. Large numbers of those imprisoned are concentrated in a few countries, and about half of them are in the USA, Russia, and China (Walmsley, 2016). Although using incarceration rates (see Table 44.1) is probably superior to the use of absolute numbers for almost any purpose of analysis, they are far from flawless. Many problems exist with the use of rates and absolute numbers in terms of prisoners and because the meanings of the key terms like "prisoner" and "prison" are not uniform across nations (for more about problems with prison data, see Tonry, 2007). Although some nations, especially those in Western Europe, have turned to increasing alternatives to incarceration, such as probation, fines, community service, day fines, and other forms of intermediate sanctions, many others have remained reliant on incarceration

Table 44.1. Top ten prison population in total numbers and prisoners per 100,000 in 2016

Top Ten	Total Numbers	Rate per 100,000
1	United States of America 2,145,100	United States of America 760
2	China 1,649,804	El Salvador 614
3	Brazil 670,111	Turkmenistan 583
4	Russian Federation 602,176	Virgin Islands (USA) 542
5	India 419,623	Maldives 514
6	Thailand 325,298	Cuba 510
7	Indonesia 232,063	Thailand 483
8	Turkey 229,790	Northern Mariana Islands (USA) 482
9	Iran 225,624	Virgin Islands (UK) 470
10	Mexico 208,689	Seychelles 448

Source: Walmsley, R. World Prison Brief, Institute for Criminal Policy Research (2016)

and on a general hardening of attitudes toward offenders. According to Walmsley (2016), prison populations have grown since 2000 by at least 20 percent. The female prison population total has increased by 50 percent since about 2000, while the equivalent figure for the male prison population is 18 percent. In Table 44.1, the total number provided for the prison populations also includes female prisoners. In almost all cases (Thailand is the exceptional case) the number of females consists of less than 10 percent of total inmates incarcerated. The total number of incarcerated juveniles is inconsistently included in the total prison numbers across nations.

PRISON GOVERNANCE

All countries have some form of correctional institution that serves to incarcerate alleged or convicted criminals. In general, prisons serve to incarcerate those who have been convicted of relatively serious crimes, while facilities called jails or remand prisons are used for those awaiting trial, transfer to another institution, and for those serving time for minor offenses.

Prisons have developed classification systems that segregate inmates according to time to be served or seriousness of the offense. In the USA, for example, prisons are classified into levels of security called Minimum, Medium, Maximum, and more recently Super-Maximum or Administrative Maximum. In countries with ample financial resources, some form of rehabilitation is offered to assist offenders. In some countries, institutions called open prisons serve to incarcerate inmates during the evening but allow them much freedom to work, attend school, or visit with family during the day. Private prisons, correctional institutions operated by private firms on behalf of governments, are operating in the USA, Puerto Rico, Australia, South Africa, Canada, England, New Zealand, Scotland, and Wales.

Although many prison systems around the world share similarities, individual nations also have distinctive approaches to prison governance. For example, in England the Independent Monitoring Boards, formerly called the Boards of Visitors or Visiting Committees, represent a way to bring "outsiders" into the prisons to help with problems of administration and discipline. The Boards act as an independent watchdog on the prisons, meeting with inmates and staff to safeguard the well-being and rights of all prisoners. They visit inmates, hear complaints about prison conditions and prison officials, and report back to the prison administration and the national correctional office at the Home Office. The Boards represent a distinctly English way of involving laypersons in the criminal justice process.

In China, the underlying foundation for the correctional system is based on two ancient traditions: Confucianism and legalism. Confucianism holds that social harmony can be secured through moral education that brings out the good nature of all. Formal legal structures are not necessary for this purpose. At the same time legalism, which developed almost 200 years after Confucianism, held that only a firm application of laws and strict punishments could persuade people who are innately evil not to commit crime. Early in the first millennium AD, these two philosophies began to merge, with Confucianism serving as the primary social control mechanism and formal legalism providing support (Dikotter, 2002). China in the post-1949 Communist era has developed a correctional system that retains remnants of both the Confucian and legalist perspectives, meshing both to placate the Communists' need to reeducate the people in Socialist values. It is important to mention that this article does not specifically address the issue of female or juvenile prisons. While female and juvenile prisons do have some problems that are endemic only to their institutions, the most pressing problem of prison crowding is most often present in all kinds of correctional institutions.

PRISON CROWDING

Prison crowding is the single most pressing problem faced by major prison systems today, not only in Western countries but also in Eastern European and in many least developed countries. According to United Nations Asia and Far East Institute (UNAFEI) Report (2001), "Factors influencing prison overcrowding may vary from country to country; socioeconomic conditions, crime rates, differences in criminal justice policy, efficiency in on-going practices and functioning in criminal justice systems, public attitudes towards offenders and so on might contribute to modulate the prison population." The most crucial factor contributing to increased incarceration and prison crowding are sentencing decisions made by policy makers (Kuhn, 1996). Many countries, especially advanced nations with effective media, have greatly politicized crime and this has led to a hardening of penal control. Experts have found that in some poorer countries, like Pakistan, Malaysia, and Kenya, a lack of correctional resources is a major reason for prison crowding, along with a slow and inefficient criminal justice system and a lack of alternatives to incarceration.

Although prison crowding rates may be difficult to determine, the impact of crowding on inmates and staff are painfully clear. Prison crowding can limit the ability of correctional officials and increase the potential for violence and the spread of diseases. For example, in European prisons the incidence of tuberculosis can be up to 81 times higher than in the general population (World Health Organization [WHO], 2014). Similarly, rates of HIV infection are much higher in prisons because of high rates of drug use and needle sharing (Penal Reform International, 2018).

Another problem related to prison crowding is the increasing possibility of human rights violations. Although legal challenges to prison conditions and prisoner treatment have occurred for decades, the infusion of inmates accused of terrorism has exacerbated the issue.

The USA's involvement in the Abu Ghraib incident, which surfaced in Iraq in 2004, is one example.

The legal basis for challenges to prison conditions in the USA comes from the Eighth Amendment to the US Constitution, which states that "excessive bail shall not be required, nor excessive fines imposed, nor cruel and unusual punishments inflicted." In the international community, legal challenges arise from a number of covenants and conventions. The foundation for these documents is rooted in the UN Universal Declaration of Human Rights, which states "no one shall be subjected to torture, or cruel, inhuman or degrading treatment or punishment" (Article 5). The Declaration, originally proposed in 1948 by the United Nations and subsequently ratified by a large number of nations, was the result of the desire to combat the massive violations of human rights that occurred in World War II. Since then, other international organizations have produced documents that support Article 5, such as the European Convention on Human Rights, the African Charter on Human and People's Rights, and the Inter-American Convention on Human Rights (Dammer & Albanese, 2014).

In 1955, the United Nations developed the Standard Minimum Rules for the Treatment of Prisoners, which address a range of prisoner issues including prison living conditions, amenities and programs, methods of discipline, and the treatment of those that are unconvicted. The Rules have been modified numerous times, including in 2010 when the Bangkok Rules clarified principles for the treatment of female prisoners and females in non-custodial sanctions, and in 2015 when the Rules were renamed the Nelson Mandela Rules. At that time, they were adjusted to consolidate human rights principles with criminal justice standards into one document consisting of eight substantive areas.

SUMMARY

The purpose and form of prisons has changed considerably throughout history. In the nineteenth century a new prison model emerged called the penitentiary. The penitentiary greatly influenced prison architecture and the treatment of offenders throughout the world. Because the goals of the penitentiary were allusive, other means of dealing with offenders have surfaced such as rehabilitation, and more recently the crime-control model. Because of increased reliance on incarceration, many countries have experienced prison crowding. Prison crowding has shown to exacerbate factors that erode living conditions, such as institutional violence, human rights violations, and communicable disease. International agencies, such as the United Nations, have tried to address treatment issues through the promotion of prison standards and conventions. Although prisons primarily serve to incarcerate criminal offenders, the ways in which this is accomplished vary considerably across the globe.

ACKNOWLEDGMENTS

Dr. Dammer would like to thank his student assistant Marlene Geerinck for her assistance with this revision.

REFERENCES

Clear, T., Cole, G., Reisig, M., & Petrosino, C. (2015). *American corrections*. Eleventh Edition. Belmont, CA: Wadsworth Cengage Learning.

Dammer, H. & Albanese, J. S. (2014). *Comparative Criminal Justice Systems*. Fifth Edition. Belmont, CA: Wadsworth Cengage Learning.

Dikotter, F. (2002). The promise of repentance: Prison reform in modern China. *British Journal of Criminology*, 42, 240–249.

Kuhn, A. (1996). Incarceration rates: Europe versus the United States. *European Journal on Criminal Policy and Research*, 4(3), 46–73.

Penal Reform International. (2018). Retrieved from www.penalreform.org/priorities/prison-conditions/key-facts/health/.

Pratt, J. (2007). *Penal populism*. London: Routledge.

Tonry, M. (2007). Determinates of penal policies. In M. Tonry (Ed.), *Crime, punishment, and politics in comparative perspective* (pp. 1–48). Chicago: University of Chicago Press.

United Nations Asia and Far East Institute (UNAFEI). (2001, September). *Annual report for 1999 and resource material*, series no. 57. Fuchu, Japan: UNAFEI.

Walmsley, R. (2016). *World prison population list*. Eleventh Edition. London: International Center for Prison Studies. Retrieved from www.prisonstudies.org/sites/default/files/resources/downloads/world_prison_population_list_11th_edition_0.pdf.

Weiss, R. P. (2005). From anticolonialism to neocolonialism: A brief political-economic history of transnational concern about corrections. In P. Reichel (Ed.), *Handbook of transnational crime and justice* (pp. 346–362). Thousand Oaks, CA: Sage Publications.

World Health Organization (WHO). (2014). Retrieved from www.euro.who.int/__data/assets/pdf_file/0005/249188/Prisons-and-Health.pdf?ua=1.

45   World Policing Models

Rob Mawby

OVERVIEW

When members of the public travel abroad and experience crime and the response of the police in other countries, they take with them a common sense notion of what "the police" means. They will often draw distinctions between their own society and these "other" systems. Teasing out the similarities and the differences between police systems and their components in different societies, explaining the differences, drawing examples of good practice that might be introduced elsewhere, and learning from experiences of bad practices – these are the key features of comparative police studies. While the difficulties surrounding such endeavors may be considerable, the potential benefits make the challenge worthwhile.

The nature of "the police" varies markedly between countries and over time. For example, the public police model that emerged in the United Kingdom and USA in the nineteenth century differed from the centralized, autocratic arm of state authority that preceded it in continental European (Chapman, 1970), and while the cross-national interchange of ideas in recent years has resulted in police structures and methods from one country being imported to others, there are still stark contrasts. This chapter, therefore, begins by offering a definition of the police that incorporates variations, before moving on to consider alternative models and recent trends.

DEFINITIONS

First, it is crucial to distinguish between "policing" as a process and "the police" as an organization. "Policing," a term we might apply to the process of preventing and detecting crime and maintaining order, is an activity that is engaged in by a growing number of agencies or individuals: members of the public, the private sector, and locally based organizations like neighborhood watch (Jones & Newburn, 2006). The police as an institution, in contrast, might be responsible for many other services that are only tenuously related to maintaining order or preventing crime.

When we consider police systems in different societies we mean by the police an agency that can be distinguished in terms of its legitimacy, its structure, and its function (Mawby, 1990). Legitimacy implies that the police is granted special authority by those in power, whether this is an elite within the society, an occupying force, or the community as a whole. Structure implies that the police is organized, with some degree of specialization and with a code of practice within which, for example, the extent to which use of force is legitimate is specified. However, the extent of organization or specialization, and the types of force considered appropriate, will vary. Finally, function implies that the role of the police is concentrated on the maintenance of law and order and the prevention and detection of offences, but there might be considerable differences in the balance between these, and in the extent to which other duties are assigned to the police.

ALTERNATIVE POLICE SYSTEMS

This section considers the police systems of a wide range of countries worldwide. This endeavor can, however, be approached in a number of different ways. One is to focus on countries separately and to identify the core features of their policing systems in the context of their social and political systems, subsequently classifying them according to a typology. An alternative approach is to identify different models that apply to groups of countries. For example, we might distinguish between Anglo-American policing, policing on Continental Europe, communist/post-communist policing, colonial police and the type of policing that has emerged in the Far East. And even the religious police system evident in, particularly, Islamic countries, can be distinguished (Mawby, 2018). However, there are, arguably, as many differences between countries within a model as there are between alternative models, a point made forcefully by Anderson and Killingray (1991, 1992) in the context of a colonial police system. Equally, there are often variations within a country. For example, in Canada marked variations exist between the centralized Royal Canadian Mounted Police (RCMP) and local urban and provincial police. Therefore, there is an attempt to distinguish between two broad models of policing: a control-dominated system and a community-oriented system.

A control-dominated system is one where the main function of the police is to maintain order, where the population generally fails to recognize the legitimacy of the state and its agents, the police. In such societies, the police may carry out a range of administrative tasks on behalf of the state, but rarely provide a public service that addresses the welfare needs of the community. The police is, consequently, generally organized and managed centrally and has many paramilitary qualities. In some cases, the distinction between police and military is negligible.

In complete contrast, a community-oriented system is one where the main function of the police is to provide a public service that addresses the wider needs of the community. Maintaining order is important, but the emphasis is more on crime as symptomatic of community problems than an affront to authority. Such a model assumes that the police are accorded considerable legitimacy by local communities. The police are consequently generally organized and managed locally and barriers between police and public are minimized. Community policing and problem-oriented policing typify this approach.

The control-dominated system can be identified with traditional policing on Continental Europe, the colonies established by Britain and its European neighbors, Communist Europe, and Islamic police systems. Raymond Fosdick, for example, who worked as an administrator with the New York Police Department, toured Europe at the beginning of the twentieth century. His text, published in 1915, contrasted the centralized, militaristic, control-oriented police systems he found there with the situation in England and the USA (Mawby, 1990).

This notion of a "Police State" (Chapman, 1970) formed the basis for the development of policing in communist Russia and subsequently, its satellites in Eastern Europe. This was characterized by: a centralized and militaristic uniformed police subordinate to the secret police; an emphasis upon maintaining political order rather than tackling conventional crime; and a close link between police and the Communist Party, with minimal public or legal accountability. The other police system that has been consistently recognized in the literature as control-dominated is the colonial model. For example, the British Government allegedly created a police system for its empire that was appropriate for the control of a subjugated population where the needs of economic imperialism required a politically controlled paramilitary force prioritizing public order (Cole, 1999). The model it used was the one first established for Ireland where the police could not rely on public consent. Colonial police may be characterized as: militaristic (e.g., armed and living as units in barracks) and, in many cases, centralized; prioritizing public order tasks; and deriving their legitimacy from their colonial masters rather than the indigenous population. Additionally, given the difficulties occupying powers have had in locally recruiting loyal and reliable police officers, a common tactic was to recruit from either indigenous minorities or from other colonies, on the basis that such groups would be less likely to form allegiances with local people against the interests of the occupying power. A similar model was introduced by other colonial powers, as O'Reilly (2018) has recently discussed *vis-à-vis* the Portuguese empire.

Islamic police systems generally incorporate two police organizations: a conventional police and religious police. While both are centrally controlled, the latter operate as, in effect, morals police, with a mandate to enforce strict Islamic codes of conduct, relating *inter alia* to the behavior of women, good business practices, and drug/alcohol laws. In this sense there are marked similarities between religious and communist police systems, especially in terms of the way state ideologies underpin the principles of policing (Mawby, 2018).

However, while identifying a control-dominated model may be useful, it should not blind us to the fact that most countries associated with it differ in a number of respects. For example, although British colonial authority was centralized in London, within different countries the police system was often regionally based; and officers were not always issued with firearms. In Continental Europe, there were also considerable variations, with, for example, the Dutch system neither overtly militaristic nor excessively centralized, and although countries such as France, Spain, and Italy traditionally had control-dominated police systems, in each case the maintenance of at least two police forces allowed the rulers to ensure that no one institution achieved sufficient power to threaten government.

The task of assigning specific police systems to a community-oriented model is even more difficult. Although this may be the type of democratic policing that many of us aspire to, it is difficult to nominate any one country as even approaching achieving it (Brogden, 1999; Mawby, 1990). In England and Wales, for example, often eulogized as the home of "community policing," modern systems of policing emerged at least in part as a means of maintaining order in the midst of working-class protest, a point revisited when Margaret Thatcher's government used the police to break the miners strike in the early 1980s. And in many cases police were recruited from rural areas to work in the cities, undermining the claim that they were local citizens in uniform. In the USA, where police systems have been traditionally locally based, personnel have been recruited locally, and officers have engaged in a wide range of "non-crime" responsibilities, the image of the police as a militaristic body charged with fighting the "war" against crime is equally pervasive. Elsewhere, Bayley's (1976) early presentation of the Japanese Police as community-based and welfare-oriented has been questioned (Leishman, 1999; Miyazawa, 1992). It may, therefore, be that the key strength of specifying a community-oriented model is as an ideal type, in the Weberian sense, so as to better evaluate police systems and changes within them.

RECENT TRENDS

While traditionally, the main generators of change have been conquest and migration (Mawby, 1990), more recently two broad generators of change can be identified: external influence and internal pressure.

External influence is particularly important in postmodern societies where similar influences are prevalent across national boundaries and where examples of innovative developments in one society are readily available as examples of best practice elsewhere. The expansion of private policing is a case in point (Jones & Newburn, 2006). Formal pacts add a further impetus to change. For example, the emergence and expansion of the European Union has involved greater cross-border cooperation and, consequently, increased pressure toward the harmonization of policy. Most recently, EUROPOL was ratified in 1999 as the EU organization for cross-border coordination between national law-enforcement agencies, providing collation, analysis, and dissemination of information, and a European Police College (CEPOL) was established in 2001. Such initiatives may lead to increased cooperation, but national interests may prevent more radical change, as illustrated by conflicts over drug policies. A further source of external pressure involves postwar reconstruction. Here Fairchild (1988) has detailed the transformation of the (West) German police under allied occupation.

Internal pressures to change the structure and functions of the police are also evident, but it is sometimes difficult to identify any consistent pattern. For example, in countries such as Sweden and the Netherlands the police have become more centralized; in contrast, the traditionally centralized French system has diversified to allow the addition of local police bodies. Internal changes may, on the other hand, be predicated by regime change. This is particularly well illustrated in the case of former Eastern Bloc countries and postcolonial societies. In each case, the transformation of the traditionally control-dominated police into a community-oriented police was commonly advocated by aspiring leaders. However, in the former case a perceived threat to law and order led to a dismantling of police reform agendas (Mawby, 1999), with subsequent reforms less radical than had been anticipated (Beck, Chistyakova, & Robertson, 2006), while in the case of postcolonial societies, new governments also sometimes retained old police systems in order to establish and assert their authority (Anderson & Killingray 1992).

In many cases, of course, internal pressures for reform may combine with external influences. For example, both the USA and many Western European countries have been influential in advising former Eastern Bloc counties on reform agendas, in the former case including the funding of a police college in Budapest. However, as in the case of South Korea (Lee, 1990), the pressure toward community-oriented policing might be outweighed by foreign policy concerns, be these political or international crime-related. This point has current resonance in the context of Iraq (Pino & Wiatrowski, 2006).

SUMMARY

This chapter provides an introduction to policing in different societies, starting with a discussion of how "the police" is defined. It then considers alternative policing systems, identifying two models: control-dominated and community-oriented. Although there are numerous examples of the former, the latter is more a target than a reality. This leads into a discussion of recent changes in former colonial and communist societies. Inevitably, we can here provide only a broad sweep of policing systems across the globe and there are areas and sociopolitical systems missing from the list. What we have attempted to do is to raise questions concerning the relationship between policing and the wider context within which it takes place.

REFERENCES

Anderson, D. M. & Killingray, D. (Eds.). (1991). *Policing the empire.* Manchester: Manchester University Press.

(Eds.). (1992). *Policing and decolonisation.* Manchester: Manchester University Press.

Bayley, D. H. (1976). *Forces of order: Police behaviour in Japan and the United States.* Berkeley, CA: University of California Press.

Beck, A., Chistyakova, Y., & Robertson, A. (2006) *Police reform in post-Soviet societies.* Abingdon: Routledge.

Brogden, M. (1999). Community policing as cherry pie. In R. Mawby (Ed.), *Policing across the world: Issues for the twenty-first century* (pp. 167–186). London: UCL Press.

Chapman, B. (1970). *Police state.* London: Pall Mall Press.

Cole, B. (1999). Post-colonial systems. In R. Mawby (Ed.), *Policing across the world: Issues for the twenty-first century* (pp. 88–108). London: UCL Press.

Fairchild, E. S. (1988) *German police.* Springfield, MA: Charles C. Thomas.

Jones, T. & Newburn, T. (2006). *Policy transfer and criminal justice.* London: Open University Press.

Lee, S. Y. (1990). Morning calm, rising sun: National character and policing in South Korea and in Japan. *Police Studies,* 13, 91–110.

Leishman, F. (1999). Policing in Japan: East Asian archetype? In R. Mawby (Ed.), *Policing across the world: Issues for the twenty-first century* (pp. 109–125). London: UCL Press.

Mawby, R. I. (1990) *Comparative policing issues: The British and American experience in international perspective.* London: Routledge.

(1999). The changing face of policing in Central and Eastern Europe. *International Journal of Police Science and Management,* 2(3), 199–216.

(2018). An international comparison of police systems in a legal context. In M. Den Broer (Ed.), *Research handbook on comparative policing.* Northampton, MA: Edward Elgar.

Miyazawa, S. (1992). *Policing in Japan: A study on making crime.* New York: State University of New York Press.

O'Reilly, C. (2018) *Colonial policing and the transnational legacy.* Abingdon: Routledge.

Pino, N. & Wiatrowski, M. D. (2006). *Democratic policing in transitional and developing countries.* Aldershot: Ashgate.

46   Cross-Border Policing

Rob Guerette

INTRODUCTION

One of the primary functions of national governments is to provide security for their people. Since the earliest times this has meant protecting against cross-border invasions and infiltrations from other governments or individuals who are believed to threaten the national order or social structure (Rotberg, 2003). Establishing national security is necessary so that other government services can be delivered. These include systems for regulating the norms and mores of the society generally, as well as establishing systematic means of managing disputes, establishing and enforcing legal codes, and facilitating economic markets, among others. The ability of governments to ensure the security of the nation-state also helps to promote the sovereignty of the nation and demonstrates the competence of political leaders.

Though border guards were originally established to defend against incursion from other countries, increasingly, their role has shifted toward threats, such as smuggling and trafficking (Farer, 1999). To secure nation-states from external threats most countries have established police organizations that are responsible for managing border areas.

THE NATURE OF CROSS-BORDER POLICING[1]

In some nations, the military is given the responsibility of border policing. In others, such as the USA and some states in the European Union, border policing is performed by a distinct policing agency. Sometimes referred to as the "border guard," the primary role of these agencies is to enforce laws against illegal immigration, though they are also responsible for countering drug smuggling, human smuggling or trafficking, and safeguarding against terrorism. Policing borders presents more difficulty for destination countries compared to interior policing because nations lack authority to comprehensively address transnational crimes that originate in other countries.[2] Because of this, border police must often rely on cooperation from governments in origin and transit countries.[3]

---

[1] The terms "border" policing and "cross-border" policing are used interchangeably throughout this chapter. As used here, the reference is to any policing activity that is directed toward detecting or preventing crimes and other illicit activities that are carried out across nation-state boundaries.

[2] A "destination" country is one that goods or people are smuggled into as the final destination.

[3] An "origin" country is one where goods or people originate. A "transit" country is one that serves as a transfer point between origin and destination countries.

In some ways border police units are hybrid forms of policing agencies in that they operate similarly to local-level police organizations yet they derive their authority from the national government rather than the local municipality where they operate. They are similar because, like local police, border police engage in routine patrols and respond to calls for assistance. They differ in that border police enforce national or federal laws such as those governing immigration and the movement of illicit goods rather than laws against conventional crimes such as robbery, assault, or burglary that are the responsibility of local-level police agencies. The extent to which this is true, however, varies from country to country and largely depends on whether securing the border is the responsibility of the military or a separate border-policing agency.

During times of crisis, border police groups are sometimes used to support the nation's military against external threats. When not in times of war or international conflict, the role of border police focuses more on preventing, detecting, and responding to the illicit movement of people and products across their national borders. Most border policing agencies have increasingly relied on developing technology to detect unauthorized activity and to secure the nation-state (Andreas, 2001). These technological advancements include the use of underground motion sensors, remote surveillance cameras, and real-time satellite surveillance systems, among others.

OVERVIEW OF BORDER POLICING IN THE USA AND THE EUROPEAN UNION

There is considerable similarity across the various border police agencies in terms of their purpose and operational practice. However, many border police agencies have their own distinctive characteristics and qualities that stem from the historical geopolitical context within which the agency was founded. Some agencies have evolved into their current arrangement in response to changing conditions brought about by globalization. The following provides a brief overview of border policing in just a few places around the world.

US BORDER POLICING

There are three primary agencies responsible for securing the borders of the USA, all of which operate within the Department of Homeland Security: the US Border Patrol, Immigration and Customs Enforcement, and the US Coast Guard.

The primary role of the US Border Patrol is to secure the nearly-6,000 miles of US land border between the points of entry and 2,000 miles of water border surrounding Florida and Puerto Rico. The USBP carries out its mission through several operational strategies, including routine patrol and surveillance of international borders; tracking of unauthorized migrants and smugglers; vehicle inspections at traffic checkpoints; inspection of transportation lines entering the country; helicopter patrols of remote border areas; marine patrols along bodies of water; and bike patrols within border towns and cities. The Border Patrol also relies on technology to monitor borders, including infrared night-vision devices, seismic ground sensors, CCTV systems, modern computer information processing systems, and unmanned aerial aircraft.

The US Immigration and Customs Enforcement (ICE) agency is responsible for monitoring the flow of people and products coming into the USA at the nation's points of entry. These include those positioned in airports, land-based entrances along roadways, and maritime ports around the country. Working in collaboration with the USBP and other government agencies, ICE is responsible for enforcing a broad range of federal statutes that involve matters of visa security, illegal arms trafficking, document and identity fraud, drug trafficking, child pornography and sex tourism, immigration and customs fraud, intellectual property rights violations, financial crime, and human smuggling and trafficking, among others.

The US Coast Guard (USCG) is responsible for monitoring the US border waterways. Operating under the auspices of the US Department of Homeland Security, the USCG is divided into three operational units: aviation forces, boat forces (vessels less than 65 feet in length), and cutter forces (vessels more than 65 feet in length). The USCG undertakes a variety of tasks but those relevant to border policing center mostly on the interdiction of migrants and narcotics smugglers while they are attempting entry into the country, environmental protection, securing of the nation's maritime ports against crime and terrorist activity, and interdiction of other nation's fishing vessels within US protected zones.

THE EUROPEAN UNION

The borders of the European Union are operationally secured by the individual border police agencies of the external member states. An organization called Frontex, which derives from the French, meaning "external borders," is responsible for coordination of border security measures of the individual member nations. Formally, Frontex was known as the European Agency for the Management of Operational Cooperation at the External Borders of the Member States of the European Union. The headquarters of Frontex is located in Warsaw, Poland. Frontex is a young agency that was established by EU Council Regulation and became operational in October of 2005.

Another agency with responsibility for securing EU borders is EUROPOL. EUROPOL stands for the "European Law Enforcement Organisation," which facilitates cooperation of the policing authorities in the EU member states to prevent transnational crimes such as terrorism and drug and human trafficking. Unlike the other border police agencies, however, EUROPOL's responsibility is to gather and disseminate intelligence of transnational crime. The agency does not conduct policing operations.

Each of the EU member nations maintains its own agencies responsible for customs and border security. They operate like most border security forces in the sense that they patrol border areas and regulate flows of people and products that come into the country and the European Union. While each of the member states maintains its own sovereignty, they must all follow the rules and regulations of the European Union as a requisite for membership. The Schengen Agreement provided for the removal of systematic border controls between participating countries of the European Union. This agreement liberalized the requirements for travel between the EU member states, while security and regulatory controls along the external borders of the EU have been strengthened.

One of the most visible developments in EU border policing involves securing the southern borders. The Spanish Government has created a surveillance system of its maritime border along the African straits using the latest in available technology. Named SIVE, which stands for "External Surveillance Integrated System," the early-warning system pulls together data received from sensors deployed on the ground, in aircraft, in boats, and on satellites, to produce real-time graphical displays of the border zone. There are plans to implement a similar system, labeled EUROSUR (European Border Surveillance System), to monitor the entire border region of the European Union.

CHALLENGES AND CRITICISMS OF CROSS-BORDER POLICING

Perhaps the greatest overarching challenge faced by all border police agencies involves achieving the balance between securing the nation-state from unwanted intrusions without suffocating the efficient flow of needed goods and commerce across borders upon which the country depends. Beyond this, several other challenges face cross-border policing. First, jurisdictional issues often limit the ability of border police to fully address transnational crime issues that originate outside of their jurisdiction where they have no legal authority. As a consequence, they must rely on cooperation with neighboring countries, which often have limited resources or lack the incentive to provide meaningful assistance (Nadelmann, 1993). Transnational crime groups take advantage of this jurisdictional divide in carrying out their illicit business (Naím, 2005). Second, many border areas are comprised of vast and diverse terrain that makes it difficult to comprehensively police. Agencies must focus their limited resources on known high-traffic areas, which mean many places along border areas go unmonitored. Third, technological advancements, such as the Internet and other forms of communication, have given unprecedented abilities to smugglers, traffickers, and terrorists to conduct their business (Battacharyya, 2005; Naím, 2005). This assists them in effectively circumventing border security measures.

Criticisms of border policing in any country can be divided into two categories: those that address the function and those that address the process. The most frequent criticism of the function of border policing concerns the exclusion of migrants from opportunities in destination countries. Some argue that preventing individuals from migrating freely in search of better living conditions violates intrinsic human rights. Others see it as an intrinsic right of nations to safeguard their borders from products and people entering without permission.

The most common process criticism of border policing concerns the treatment of migrants by border police. Agents are frequently criticized for using excessive force against migrants (King, 2004; Phillips, Rodriguez, & Hagan, 2002). Though it is uncertain whether excessive force among border police is greater than among police generally, reports of its occurrence are common. Moreover, the process of border policing is sometimes cited as ineffective in distinguishing refugees with legitimate claims of political asylum from illegal immigrants. A related concern stems from ever-increasing dangers that migrants undertake in the aftermath of heightened border enforcement campaigns. Many border watchers criticize governments for displacing migrants to routes that are more remote and perilous resulting in greater fatalities among migrants. In response, some governments have stepped up life-saving operations along border areas. The US Border Patrol, for instance, adopted the Border Safety Initiative (BSI) to reduce the number of migrant deaths along the US–Mexico border (Table 46.1).

SUMMARY

The agencies responsible for securing borders use a variety of techniques including physical patrols and tracking and have increasingly employed technological innovations such as

Table 46.1. Challenges and criticisms of cross-border policing

Challenges	Nature of the Problem/Issue
Legal jurisdiction	• Limits police powers to within own country. • Unable to address transnational crime groups at their base of operations/origins (i.e., in other countries).
Vast and diverse terrain	• Limited resources mean inability to police all border areas. • Must focus on known high-traffic corridors.
Technology	• Allows transnational crime groups to rapidly access information, communicate, and orchestrate finances. • Facilitates circumvention of border security measures.
Criticisms	
Blocking opportunities	• Opportunities for gainful employment, access to healthcare, and dignified living conditions are argued to be universal human rights. • Blocking access to these violates these rights as well as the right to freedom of movement.
Treatment of migrants	• Securing borders leads migrants to ever-more treacherous methods of gaining entry, resulting in death and harm to migrants. Security is said to cause death of migrants. • Mistreatment of migrants by border police is at times criminal. Border police may fail to recognize migrants' legitimate claims of asylum. • Migrants are commonly victimized and exploited by others during their migration.

satellite surveillance and electronic monitoring systems. Border policing around the world has become more important in light of concerns about terrorism and greater immigration as global resources have been concentrated in certain regions of the world. Criticisms of border policing stem from the exclusion of individuals from opportunities in destination countries and the manner in which apprehended immigrants are treated. The greatest challenge of border policing involves finding ways to competently secure national borders while also being responsive to individual rights.

REFERENCES

Andreas, P. (2001). *Border games: Policing the U.S-Mexico divide*. Ithaca, NY: Cornell University Press.

Bhattacharyya, G. (2005). *Traffick: The illicit movement of people and things*. Ann Arbor, MI: Pluto Press.

Farer, T. (Ed.). (1999). *Transnational crime in the Americas: An inter-American dialogue book*. New York: Routledge.

King, L. (2004, September 29). The world: 5 in Israeli border police charged with abuse. *Los Angeles Times*, p. 3.

Nadelmann, E. A. (1993). *Cops across borders: The internationalization of U.S. criminal law enforcement*. University Park, PA: Penn State Press.

Naím, M. (2005). *Illicit: How smugglers, traffickers and copycats are hijacking the global economy*. New York: Doubleday.

Phillips, S., Rodriguez, N., & Hagan, J., (2002). Brutality at the border? Use of force in the arrest of immigrants in the United States. *International Journal of the Sociology of Law*, 30(4), 285–306.

Rotberg, R. I. (2003). *When states fail: Causes and consequences*. Princeton, NJ: Princeton University Press.

WEBSITES

EUROPOL Main Site. www.europol.europa.eu.
Frontex Main Site. www.frontex.europa.eu.
US Customs and Border Protection Main Site. www.cbp.gov.
US Coast Guard Main Site. www.uscg.mil.

47 Cybercrime Laws and Investigations

Marie-Helen Maras

INTRODUCTION

Cybercrime poses unique challenges to criminal justice agents by transcending traditional borders. These challenges are exacerbated when the perpetrators of these cybercrimes are located beyond the jurisdiction of national authorities. In these situations, cooperation between criminal justice agents worldwide is required to ensure that perpetrators are identified, charged, and ultimately prosecuted for their cybercrime(s). This cooperation was observed in the investigation of the infamous Infraud Organization (the largest online carding forum) by the USA, United Kingdom, Australia, France, Italy, Kosovo, and Serbia (to name a few countries) (US Department of Justice [DOJ], 2018). The US Department of Justice (2018) indicted 36 individuals and arrested 13 people for their role in the Infraud Organization, which facilitated cyberfraud that caused over US$530 million in losses to customers, companies, and financial institutions. Despite successful cooperative cybercrime investigations, barriers to international investigations still exist today. This chapter critically examines the main challenges to international cybercrime investigations, looking in particular at the manner in which cybercrime investigations are conducted, national and international cybercrime laws, formal and informal information and evidence sharing networks, and countries' national capacities to deal with cybercrime.

CONDUCTING INTERNATIONAL CYBERCRIME INVESTIGATIONS

During the initial cybercrime investigation, the investigator seeks to determine what cybercrime(s) was (were) committed, when the cybercrime(s) was (were) committed, and whether the cybercrime(s) is (are) limited to US jurisdiction. The investigator also seeks to identify the digital evidence that should be collected to prove the facts of the matter being asserted in the case; the location of this evidence; the manner in which the evidence can be preserved, obtained, and maintained for criminal proceedings; and the need for immediate access to evidence and/or its preservation (Maras, 2014). The appropriate legal order (e.g., subpoena, court order, search warrant) is needed to obtain identified evidence. The legal order needed depends on the type of evidence sought. When requesting evidence from another country, letters rogatory are used, which include "information about the case, a description of the evidence needed and why it is needed, and a promise for reciprocity in future cases" (Maras, 2016, p. 78).

In traditional offline investigations, the first step is to secure the crime scene and then to search for the evidence of the crime (Maras, 2014). With cybercrime, the crime scene is no longer limited in space. The crime scene can be spread out on multiple computer systems, digital devices, and servers in different areas of the world. The transnational nature of this form of crime requires cooperation and coordination of efforts of nations to identify, investigate, and ultimately prosecute cybercriminals. Despite this identified need, today there are obstacles to international cooperation and coordination in cybercrime investigations.

MAIN CHALLENGES IN INTERNATIONAL CYBERCRIME INVESTIGATIONS

The main challenges that cybercrime investigators face in international investigations are the lack of or inadequate national and international cybercrime laws and enforcement of them, the significant amount of time it takes to obtain information and evidence requested, and the deficit in national capacities to investigate cybercrime and respond to requests for information and evidence.

Lack of or Inadequate National and International Laws

The vast majority of countries worldwide have national laws that cover cybercrime or some facets of cybercrime (United Nations Office on Drugs and Crime [UNODC], 2015). Nevertheless, in Africa alone, many countries have no cybercrime laws in place or laws that only cover some forms of cybercrime (Lucchetti, 2018). In Namibia, for example, as of June 2018, there is no comprehensive cybercrime law and no laws that explicitly prohibit and protect children from online child sexual exploitation and abuse (Nashuuta, 2018; United Nations Children's Fund [UNICEF], 2016). The lack of and/or inadequate cybercrime laws serve as an impediment to international cybercrime investigations and create cybercrime safe havens. These cybercrime safe havens are created because a person cannot be prosecuted unless the act is considered a crime in the country from which the act was perpetrated.

National cybercrime laws facilitate international cooperation in cybercrime cases because this cooperation depends on dual criminality (i.e., the act being investigated is considered a crime in the country conducting the investigation and the country from which assistance is requested), which is needed for mutual legal assistance on cybercrime matters and the extradition of cybercriminals (Maras, 2016). Mutual legal assistance treaties (MLATs) are agreements between countries that apply to a list of crimes and delineate the type of assistance provided by each country in investigations (Maras, 2016). Understanding the changing nature of crime (and cybercrime), in some MLATs, instead of lists of crimes, parties agree to cooperate in investigations and prosecutions of all offenses proscribed under their respective national laws (Garcia & Doyle 2010). Similarly, countries with extradition treaties agree to extradite individuals who committed a crime (or crimes) to the requesting party. The existence of an extradition treaty, however, does not guarantee that a person will be extradited for their crime(s). For example, Lauri Love, a British hacker, was charged with hacking US Government systems, defacing websites, and stealing sensitive information from these systems (Parkin, 2017). Despite the existence of the UK-US Extradition Treaty 2003, Love won his appeal against his extradition to the USA in February 2018 (BBC, 2018).

International cybercrime laws in the form of multilateral and regional agreements and conventions exist of varying scope and geographic applicability. For instance, the Council of Europe Convention on Cybercrime of 2001 provides guidance to signatories on the national criminal law and criminal procedural law needed to deal with cybercrime and guidance on mutual legal assistance (Articles 29–35). In addition to this multilateral treaty, regional treaties exist, such as the Arab League's Arab Convention on Combating Information Technology Offences of 2010, which requests that member states adopt measures to strengthen cooperation on cybercrime-related matters, and the Shanghai Cooperation Organization's Agreement on Cooperation in the Field of International Information Security of 2010, which emphasizes national control over digital systems and content.

Even though national and international cybercrime laws exist, barriers to international cybercrime investigations remain. International cybercrime laws are rather broad, leaving it up to governments to decide how to criminalize the acts described in these laws. The varied definitions of cybercrime in national legislation complicates cooperative efforts. What is more, regional and multilateral agreements create clusters of nations that cooperate with each other. As a result, this cooperation does not extend to countries outside of these regions, unless there are other agreements, conventions, and treaties between the countries. Furthermore, countries are not obliged to sign, ratify, and/or accede existing regional and multilateral agreements and conventions. For these reasons, these legal instruments have a limited effect.

Slow Formal and Informal Information and Evidence Sharing Networks

Regional and multilateral cybercrime agreements and conventions and mutual legal assistance treaties serve as formal information and evidence sharing channels. These channels slow the investigation process down and prevent the timely response needed to obtain digital evidence, which is ephemeral and volatile in nature. Because there is no time restriction for the provision of information and evidence, requests can go unanswered for months (even years).

Informal information and evidence sharing networks exist between law enforcement agencies around the world. For instance, EUROPOL (the law enforcement agency of the European Union) and INTERPOL (an international police organization that facilitates cooperation between law enforcement agencies around the world) facilitate such police-to-police information and evidence sharing across countries. Other forms of informal information sharing networks exist between the private and public sectors. For example, in the USA, legislative efforts (e.g., US Cybersecurity and Information Sharing Act 2015) have focused on strengthening and supporting the private sector's efforts in sharing information about cybersecurity and cybercrime with the public sector. Like formal channels, informal channels are prone to delays.

The delays in formal and informal information and evidence sharing networks highlight the importance of a 24/7 network of professionals to provide assistance to countries when needed. The G8 24/7 High Tech Crime Network was created to expedite contact between law enforcement agencies conducting cybercrime investigations, supplement existing formal mechanisms, and enhance informal information sharing mechanisms. Moreover, INTERPOL established a National Central Bureau in each country that serves as the contact point for law enforcement agencies and includes a 24/7 network. Other countries have created their own cybercrime contact points. For example, Japan established the police-operated Cybercrime Technology Information Network System, which connects law enforcement agencies in the Asia-Pacific region. These points of contacts are familiar with domestic and international rules of evidence and procedure and provide information to assist authorities in their investigations of cybercrime. Nevertheless, these 24/7 networks are not available and/or used by all countries, ultimately impeding international investigations that involve these countries.

Deficits in National Capacities

A final barrier to cybercrime investigations is the deficit in national capacity to deal with cybercrime. Criminal justice agencies require human, financial, and technical resources and up-to-date information on cybercrime cases, training and technology used in the field in order to effectively investigate cybercrime. Countries all over the world suffer from a shortage of qualified and trained professionals, law enforcement, judges, and digital forensics experts who can work on cybercrime cases (UNODC, 2013). Where such professionals exist, the types of qualifications and the breadth of training and experience they have varies. Furthermore, some countries lack the necessary funds and resources to investigate cybercrime and provide assistance to countries requesting information and evidence in investigations (UNODC, 2013). In addition to a lack of qualifications, training, and funds, these countries struggle with inadequate technical resources and lab equipment, especially the software and tools needed to conduct cybercrime investigations and preserve digital evidence (UNODC, 2013).

Nevertheless, investigators and prosecutors that do not have the human, financial, and technical resources needed to identify and collect evidence of a cybercrime can partner with other national and/or international agencies that have these resources. To assist nations in building national capacity, international organizations (e.g., the United Nations Office on Drugs and Crime and the International Telecommunications Union), and national organizations (e.g., the US Department of Justice and US Bureau of International Narcotics and Law Enforcement Affairs), fund training programs of criminal justice agents, legislators, and customs and border agents in other countries. What is more, the UN Global Programme on Cybercrime provides technical assistance and helps build national cybercrime capacity in Central America, the Middle East and North Africa, Eastern Africa, Southeast Asia, and the Pacific (UNODC, 2017). The program is designed to improve the abilities of countries in these regions to investigate, prosecute, and adjudicate cybercrime, and strengthen national and international cooperation in combating cybercrime and communication between governments, criminal justice agents, and the private sector (UNODC, 2017). These initiatives, however, do not target all countries in need of assistance and even in the cases where such assistance can be provided, it is only short term and cannot meet the ever-expanding cybercrime cooperation and assistance needs of countries (UNODC, 2013; Maras, 2016).

CONCLUDING REMARKS

Countries can only cooperate in international cybercrime investigations when harmonized national laws, MLATs, extradition treaties, and regional and multilateral agreements exist. Human resources are also needed to continuously staff units in the criminal justice system that investigate, prosecute, and respond to requests for digital evidence and/or assist cybercrime investigators from other countries. Training is also needed to enable cybercrime professionals to locate and identify cybercriminals. Universal digital evidence and forensics standards and protocols are also required to ensure that the evidence collected, shared, and preserved by one country can be admissible in the national court of another country. Timely preservation and sharing of data between countries are further required. This can be accomplished by strengthening formal and informal information and evidence sharing mechanisms by including time restrictions for assistance and expediting the sharing of information and digital evidence. Nevertheless, even with cross-border cooperation, time restrictions, and expedited channels for cooperation, cybercrime takes time to investigate.

The current challenges to cooperation in international cybercrime investigations can only be overcome by using a multifaceted approach to deal with the current deficits in national and international laws, enforcement of these laws, investigation procedures and practices, and human, financial, and technical resources. Even if international cooperation is improved, this will not have a positive impact on the extent of cybercrime unless cybersecurity measures are implemented, which include educating the public on protective measures when utilizing the Internet and digital technologies, as well as the implementation of security measures designed to protect systems, networks, and data (e.g., firewalls, antivirus and antispyware programs, intrusion detection systems, and access controls, to name a few). These cybersecurity measures can deter cybercriminals, deny cybercriminals access to systems, data, and networks, and prevent or at the very least mitigate the harm done when a cybercrime occurs.

REFERENCES

BBC. (2018, February 19). Lauri Love case: US abandons extradition case. Retrieved from www.bbc.com/news/uk-england-suffolk-43119355.

Garcia, M. J. & Doyle, C. (2010, March 17). Extradition to and from the United States: Overview of the law and recent treaties. *Congressional Research Service* 7-5700. Retrieved from https://fas.org/sgp/crs/misc/98-958.pdf.

Lucchetti, M. (2018). Cybercrime legislation in Africa: Regional and international standards. Retrieved from https://au.int/sites/default/files/newsevents/workingdocuments/34122-wd-05.pres_cybercrime_legislation_in_africa_12apr2018_matteo_l.pdf.

Maras, M.-H. (2014). *Computer forensics: Cybercriminals, laws, and evidence*, second edition. Burlington, MA: Jones and Bartlett.

(2016). *Cybercriminology*. New York: Oxford University Press.

Nashuuta, L. (2018, February 7). Namibia a safe haven for cybercriminals. *New Era* [Namibian newspaper]. Retrieved from www.newera.com.na/2018/02/07/namibia-a-safe-haven-for-cybercriminals/.

Parkin, S. (2017, September 8). Keyboard warrior: The British hacker fighting for his life. *Guardian*. Retrieved from www.theguardian.com/news/2017/sep/08/lauri-love-british-hacker-anonymous-extradition-us.

United Nations Children's Fund (UNICEF). (2016). Increasing legal protection for children from sexual exploitation and abuse in Namibia. Retrieved from www.unicef.org/namibia/na.COP_Legal_Brief_2016_web.pdf.

United Nations Office on Drugs and Crime (UNODC). (2013, February). Comprehensive study on cybercrime. Retrieved from www.unodc.org/documents/organized-crime/UNODC_CCPCJ_EG.4_2013/CYBERCRIME_STUDY_210213.pdf.

(2015). Cybercrime repository. Retrieved from www.unodc.org/unodc/en/cybercrime/cybercrime-repository.html.

(2017). Global programme on cybercrime. Retrieved from www.unodc.org/unodc/en/cybercrime/global-programme-cybercrime.html.

US Department of Justice (DOJ). (2018, February 7). Thirty-six defendants indicted for alleged roles in transnational criminal organization responsible for more than $530 in losses from cybercrime. Retrieved from www.justice.gov/opa/pr/thirty-six-defendants-indicted-alleged-roles-transnational-criminal-organization responsible.

WEBSITES AND READINGS

African Union. (2014). Convention on Cyber Security and Personal Data Protection.

Commonwealth of Independent States. (2001). Agreement on Cooperation in Combating Offences related to Computer Information.

Council of Europe. (2001). Convention on Cybercrime.

Council of Europe. Octopus Cybercrime Community. Retrieved from www.coe.int/ka/web/octopus/country-wiki/.

League of Arab States. (2010). Arab Convention on Combating Information Technology Offences.

Shanghai Cooperation Organization. (2010). Agreement on Cooperation in the Field of International Information Security.

UNODC. Cybercrime repository. Retrieved from www.unodc.org/cld/v3/cybrepo/.

48   The European Union and Cooperation in Criminal Matters

Matti Joutsen

GENERAL OVERVIEW

The European Union represents a unique form of international cooperation. In a remarkably brief time (from 1995 to the present) the European Union has developed forms of police and judicial cooperation that are unknown or rare elsewhere, such as cross-border police powers and mutual recognition of judgments.

The European Union was originally known as the "European Communities" (or, more popularly, as the "Common Market"). The Common Market was designed to make it possible for persons, products, services, and capital to move freely from one country to another.

Such freedom of movement encourages economic growth, but it also creates opportunities for crime, and possibilities for offenders to slip from one country to another in order to evade justice. It also raises questions of security that had to be decided in a coherent manner throughout the economic bloc. For example, there had to be a coherent approach to immigration and asylum policy. If one country would be less restrictive than its neighbors, a likely outcome would be that migrants and asylum seekers would enter the EU through this country and then cross the internal borders to other countries.

The response was the 1992 Maastricht Treaty, which extended the scope of the European Union beyond internal trade issues dealt with by the "Common Market" to cooperation in law enforcement and justice. The Maastricht Treaty entered into force in 1995. (In 2009, the Maastricht Treaty was replaced by the Lisbon Treaty, which among other things sought to make the way decisions are taken on police and judicial cooperation more democratic, for example, by strengthening the role of the European Parliament.)

In the European Union, police and judicial cooperation consists primarily of measures designed to ensure that offenders cannot take advantage of differences in national law and national jurisdiction, and that those guilty of serious offenses can and will be brought to justice no matter where the offense was committed. Further stimulus came from the September 11, 2001 attacks (9/11) and the threat of terrorism. The management of borders received renewed attention from 2015 on, when the deteriorating situation in Syria and many other Near East countries led to a huge increase in the number of migrants and refugees seeking to enter the EU.

BACKGROUND

The European Union consists of a total of 28 European countries. At the time of writing, the United Kingdom is negotiating its "Brexit" from the EU, but other countries are knocking on the door. In police and judicial cooperation, Denmark has decided not to take part.

The European Union has four basic institutions: the Council of Ministers, the European Commission, the European Parliament, and the Court of Justice of the European Union. The *European Commission* proposes regulations, directives, and decisions (the main forms of legislative instruments), although a quarter of all the member states, acting together, also have the right of initiation. The Commission also supervises that member states adhere to European law.

The decisions are adopted by the *Council of Ministers* together with the *European Parliament* through a "co-decision procedure." When deciding on police and judicial cooperation, the Council of Ministers consists of the ministers of justice and internal affairs of each member state. (These ministers hold a Cabinet-level position, and their functions are broadly comparable to those of the US Attorney General and the Secretary of Homeland Security.)

In addition to participating in decision making on EU instruments, the *European Parliament* adopts resolutions. Several resolutions deal with police and judicial cooperation. One resolution led to the establishment in 2014 of the "Area of Freedom, Security and Justice" (AFSJ), which is designed to further strengthen police and judicial cooperation. The European Parliament has a role in the evaluation and monitoring of the AFSJ.

The *Court of Justice* guides the interpretation of European Union law, in particular by deciding matters referred to it by national courts through what is known as a "preliminary referral" process. If the European Commission is of the view that a member state is not following European Union law, it can initiate an infringement procedure before the Court of Justice.

The EU and the Council of Europe. All EU member states are also members of a larger intergovernmental organization, the Council of Europe. (Note the potential for confusion: the Council of Europe is not the same as the European Council.) The Council of Europe has adopted a large number of conventions, recommendations, and resolutions on judicial cooperation, including an extradition treaty and a mutual legal assistance treaty, as well as the European Convention on Human Rights. The conventions in particular form part of the bedrock for police and judicial cooperation in the European Union.

FORMS OF POLICE AND JUDICIAL COOPERATION IN THE EU

The main forms of *EU police cooperation* are the work of EUROPOL (formally known as the European Union Agency for Law Enforcement Cooperation), joint investigation teams, liaison officers, and the so-called Schengen arrangements.

EUROPOL was established in 1998, and is located in the Hague, the Netherlands. Each member state sends an officer to EUROPOL on permanent duty. EUROPOL is non-operational, in the sense that it does not investigate individual cases. Instead, it focuses on the exchange and analysis of data, and notification of member states of suspected offenses and offenders. EUROPOL also develops special expertise in key fields and provides training to national police forces.

A *joint investigation team* (JIT) is a tool used in the conduct of investigations of complex crimes that have links to two or more countries, in which coordination appears to be required. A JIT consists of representatives of law enforcement authorities (and possibly also prosecutorial and judicial authorities) from the two or more countries affected by the investigation in question, with all the members of the team sharing information on the progress of the investigation in the different countries.

Liaison officers (which correspond to the US concept of legal attachés) are police officers who have been assigned to work with law enforcement agencies in a foreign country. Although they do not have police powers in the host country, they are able to follow investigations that are of interest to their colleagues at home and can in turn help their foreign colleagues with cases that have connections to their home country.

Within the European Union, the 1985 Schengen Agreement and the 1990 Schengen Convention eliminated internal border controls among most European Union member states (all except Bulgaria, Croatia, Cyprus, Ireland, Romania, and the United Kingdom), as well as border controls with the territorially contiguous Switzerland, Liechtenstein, Norway, and Iceland. The ease with which borders can be crossed has led these so-called Schengen countries to agree on special arrangements to enable border control and law enforcement authorities to better respond to crime in a "borderless Europe." (Following the 2015 refugee crisis, a few Schengen countries have re-instituted some border controls.)

The most important form of Schengen cooperation is the *Schengen Information System* (SIS), used by border control and law enforcement authorities of the Schengen countries. Data entered into the SIS on, for example, arrest warrants, missing persons, and missing objects can be consulted by any competent law enforcement or border agent in any Schengen country.

The Schengen countries have also developed three forms of cross-border cooperation: controlled delivery, hot pursuit, and cross-border surveillance. *Controlled delivery* refers to the covert surveillance of illegal trafficking (for example in drugs or endangered species) from the beginning to the end of its route, in order to identify all the offenders, in particular the main offenders. Hot pursuit and cross-border surveillance of suspects and persons of interest are (limited) exceptions to the rule that a police officer has no police powers in another country. In *hot pursuit*, a police officer may pursue a suspect detected in the commission of a serious offense across a border into the territory of another Schengen country. In *cross-border surveillance*, if a person being kept under surveillance crosses the border to another Schengen country, the surveillance may be continued until it is taken over by the competent authorities of the latter country.

EU judicial cooperation takes many forms, including the work of two institutions, EUROJUST and the European Judicial Network; liaison magistrates; the approximation of legislation; and three unique forms of cooperation: mutual recognition of judgments, the sharing of criminal records, and the European Public Prosecutor's Office.

EUROJUST is in many ways a parallel organization to EUROPOL. It was established in 2001, and as with EUROPOL is located in the Hague. Each member state assigns a prosecutor or investigating magistrate to EUROJUST, where they coordinate the prosecution of serious cases with links to two or more member states.

The *European Judicial Network* allows practitioners responsible for extradition and mutual legal assistance to be in direct contact with their counterparts in other EU countries (instead of, as is the usual case elsewhere in the world, going through diplomatic channels). It also provides tools that prosecutors can use to prepare requests for mutual legal assistance.

As with the corresponding police concept of liaison officers, *liaison magistrates* are prosecutors or judges on permanent assignment to another country in order to assist in the prosecution of international cases.

Approximation of legislation. Each EU member state continues to have its own distinctive legal system and criminal justice system. Instruments adopted on the EU level cannot be drafted so that they would be tailored to the peculiarities of these different systems. Instead, the instruments seek to *approximate* the legal systems, adjusting them to a common minimum standard, using common definitions. For example, in respect of serious crimes with a cross-border impact, the EU instruments seek to ensure that at least the core forms are covered throughout the EU. This has been done in respect of the offenses of terrorism, participation in a criminal organization, racism and xenophobia, trafficking in persons, sexual exploitation of children and child pornography, financial crime (fraud, money laundering, corruption), cybercrime, environmental crime, and counterfeiting.

Approximation has also taken place in respect of criminal procedure. EU directives have established minimum standards in respect of the rights of victims, the right to legal counsel and to legal aid, the presumption of innocence, and the rights of a child suspect or defendant.

Mutual recognition. According to traditional judicial cooperation, each country has discretion in deciding whether or not to enforce a decision given by a foreign court. The process is long and complex. There are many grounds on which a country may (and, in some cases, must) refuse to enforce a foreign judgment.

According to the principle of mutual recognition, the courts of one member state must recognize a judgment or decision made by a court in another member state, and enforce it accordingly, with a minimum of formalities. For example, if the court in one country issues an arrest warrant, courts in any other EU member state must enforce the arrest warrant. As a result of these two decisions, once a court in any EU member state orders the arrest of a certain suspect or convicted offender, and the freezing of the accounts of a suspect, the courts in any and all other member states can enforce these immediately.

The principle of mutual recognition extends also to court orders on the freezing of assets, confiscation orders, the obtaining of evidence, and financial penalties (fines).

Sharing of criminal records. EU countries have agreed on the sharing of criminal records. Previous convictions recorded in any EU country can be taken into consideration in sentencing.

In 2017, a decision was taken to establish the *European Public Prosecutor's Office*, which in time (perhaps as of 2021) will investigate and prosecute cases of EU fraud. It is unique in that it will be an EU agency that prosecutes cases in national courts, independently from national prosecutorial authorities.

CONCLUSIONS

In the space of 20 years, the EU has significantly changed and strengthened police and judicial cooperation, developing entirely new tools such as hot pursuit and mutual recognition

Table 48.1. Comparison of ordinary international cooperation and EU cooperation in criminal matters

	"Ordinary" International Cooperation	EU Cooperation
Police cooperation	• Cooperation is based on informal contacts, relatively rare bilateral agreements, and the work of INTERPOL. • Only a few non-EU states (in particular the USA) use liaison officers (legal attachés). • Information can be exchanged through INTERPOL. Otherwise, information is exchanged through slow official channels or through informal channels.	• EUROPOL coordinates cross-border investigations and provides support for national police authorities. • Also other structures for police cooperation. • Extensive liaison officer network. • Possibility of establishing joint investigative teams. • Police cooperation is especially intensive among so-called Schengen countries (e.g., the Schengen Information System, and hot pursuit).
Prosecutorial cooperation	• Prosecutorial cooperation is based on a very few bilateral or multilateral agreements. • The International Prosecutors Association provides a loose structure for cooperation.	• EUROJUST coordinates cross-border prosecutorial cooperation. • More and more EU instruments permit direct cooperation among prosecutorial authorities. • The European Judicial Network facilitates direct cooperation between prosecutorial authorities. • Liaison magistrate network. • Also the Schengen arrangements facilitate prosecutorial cooperation. • Establishment of the European Public Prosecutor's Office is under way.
Judicial cooperation	• Judicial cooperation (primarily extradition and mutual legal assistance) is based on a few bilateral or multilateral agreements. • Requests go through central authorities or through diplomatic channels. • Often, requests are not answered, the response comes too late, or comes in a form that cannot be used in the courts of the requesting state.	• All EU member states are parties to the major multilateral agreements on judicial cooperation (Council of Europe 1957, 1959, 1990; United Nations 1988, 2000, 2003). • Mutual recognition of judicial decisions has become the basis for judicial cooperation within the EU; the first instruments on mutual recognition have entered into force (the EU arrest warrant; the freezing of property and evidence; securing of evidence; and fines). • EU standards of good practice enforced through a rigorous peer review system.
Approximation of criminal law and criminal procedure	• Approximation is based on a few rare multilateral agreements and on a number of non-binding recommendations and resolutions, all of which leave extensive discretion to the state parties.	• The EU has adopted a large number of instruments on the approximation of criminal and procedural law, and these have had an impact in practice. • Attention has also been paid to the rights of victims, and of suspects and defendants.

of judgments. The power to decide on key criminal justice issues has devolved from individual countries to the supranational, EU level. Agreement has been reached on minimum requirements in criminalizing a number of serious offenses, and on minimum standards of justice, such as the rights of suspects and victims.

At the same time, the EU has faced a number of external and internal challenges, such as an economic crisis and a refugee crisis (both easing at the time of writing), the growing threat of terrorism, the decision of the United Kingdom to withdraw from the EU, and populist policies, for example, in Hungary, Poland, and Slovakia, which are seen by other EU states and by the European Commission to endanger fundamental rights and freedoms.

How these different challenges may reshape the EU is unclear. However, the law enforcement and judicial authorities throughout the EU have by and large welcomed the ways in which EU police and judicial cooperation have been strengthened. It is therefore likely that the EU will continue to evolve new mechanisms for this cooperation.

Furthermore, EU cooperation has had an impact even beyond Europe. The EU consists of countries representing different legal traditions (the common law and the civil law traditions), and very different legal systems. Even so, the EU has found ways to bridge the differences. Several forms of EU cooperation have found their way into UN conventions, and have been replicated to a small degree or are being explored in other parts of the world (e.g., in Southern Africa and in Southeast Asia). The EU is offering a template for wider cooperation throughout the world.

RECOMMENDED READING

Banach-Gutierrez, J. B. & Harding, C. (2016). *EU criminal law and policy: Values, principles and methods*. London: Routledge.

De Ruyver, B., Vermeulen, G., & Vander Beken, T. (2002). *Strategies of the EU and the US in combating transnational organized crime*. Antwerp: Institute for International Research on Criminal Policy.

Guild, E. & Geyer, F. (Eds.). (2016) *Security versus justice? Police and judicial cooperation in the European Union*. London and New York: Routledge.

Mitsilegas, V. (2016). *EU criminal law after Lisbon: Rights, trust and the transformation of justice in Europe*. Oxford and Portland, OR: Hart Publishing.

Peers, S. (2016). *EU justice and home affairs law*. Fourth Edition. Oxford: Oxford University Press.

WEBSITES

Acquis of the European Union in the field of Justice and Home Affairs (Title IV of the TEC and title VI of the TEU). http://europa.eu.int/comm/justice_home/acquis_en.htm.

Fact Sheets on the European Union. European Parliament. www.europarl.europa.eu/atyourservice/en/displayFtu.html?ftuId=FTU_4.2.6.html.

Police and Judicial Cooperation in the EU. EUR-lex. http://eur-lex.europa.eu/TodayOJ.

49 Extradition and Mutual Legal Assistance

Matti Joutsen

INTRODUCTION

The investigation and prosecution of international or transnational crime often require that judicial measures be taken abroad; a suspect needs to be apprehended and returned to stand trial, witnesses need to be summoned and heard, documentary evidence needs to be collected and submitted, and assets need to be traced, frozen, seized, and confiscated. Under international law, states may not take such action in the territory of another country. They must rely on judicial cooperation in criminal matters.

International judicial cooperation in criminal matters can involve the recognition of a foreign judgment, the transfer of proceedings, or the transfer of convicted offenders to serve their sentences. The most common forms, however, are *extradition* and *mutual legal assistance* (also referred to as legal assistance, mutual assistance, and mutual assistance in criminal matters). The need for and the use of these forms has increased considerably, and both forms have evolved to make them more efficient and easier to use.

THE BASIS FOR EXTRADITION AND MUTUAL LEGAL ASSISTANCE

Judicial cooperation in criminal matters is largely a recent development. For centuries, extradition and mutual legal assistance were a courtesy between rulers, rarely requested and even more rarely granted. The prevailing attitude was that the courts of one country should not give effect to the criminal law of another country – and, therefore, they should not provide judicial assistance in criminal cases.

Despite this prevailing attitude, over time the tool of *letters rogatory* was developed. A letter rogatory is a formal request from the judicial authority of one state to the judicial authority of another state to perform one or more specified actions on behalf of the first judicial authority. This request would be conveyed through diplomatic channels. Whether or not the requested country would provide such assistance was entirely at its discretion. The process was lengthy and bureaucratic, and the outcome was quite uncertain. Furthermore, letters rogatory were primarily used in civil cases, not criminal cases.

It was not until the late 1800s that *bilateral* instruments (involving two countries) began to emerge, which provided a framework for judicial cooperation, and a greater expectation of success. The first *multilateral* instrument on extradition (involving several countries) did not emerge until 1933: the Convention on Extradition prepared within the framework of the Organization of American States. This was followed by the 1952 Arab Extradition Agreement, the 1957 European Convention on Extradition, and the 1966 British Commonwealth scheme for the "rendition of fugitives."

In respect of mutual assistance in criminal matters, the first multilateral instrument was not negotiated until 1959: the European Convention on Mutual Assistance in Criminal Matters. The 1986 British Commonwealth Scheme for Mutual Assistance in Criminal Matters, while not a treaty, represents an agreed set of recommendations.

The European Convention on Mutual Assistance proved to be a key factor in stimulating US interest in similar instruments (Ellis & Pisani, 1985, pp. 196–198). As a common law jurisdiction, the US has had difficulties in working with jurisdictions with different legal traditions. Evidence obtained in different procedures may not be admissible in US courts, and conversely certain measures or formalities that US courts may request or require may be unknown to foreign practitioners working under quite different laws.

Box 49.1. Differences in Admissibility of Evidence

In common law criminal procedure, the examination of witnesses in court is conducted by the prosecutor and the defense counsel, and the evidence is recorded verbatim. In many French-based civil
law jurisdictions, however, the questioning of witnesses may be conducted by an investigating judge,
who will generally summarize the testimony for inclusion in the case file (*dossier*). Such summaries
would not generally be admissible in common law jurisdictions.

The USA used the European Convention in negotiating its first mutual legal assistance treaty, with Switzerland. This was signed in 1973. Since then, the USA has negotiated some 60 such treaties, generally with countries with which the USA has traditionally had strong ties, but also with several jurisdictions that became of interest primarily because of their suspected role as centers for money laundering. The USA has been even more active in nego-tiating extradition treaties, over 100 so far (Boister, 2012, p. 335).

This growing US interest in negotiating bilateral treaties was not shared by many other countries, which preferred multilateral treaties as being less resource-intensive to negotiate, and as providing a more uniform framework for judicial cooperation with a number of coun-tries. Within the framework of the United Nations, three major conventions were negotiated on specific types of crime: illicit trafficking in narcotic drugs and psychotropic substances (1988, referred to below as the 1988 Drug Convention), transnational organized crime (2000; the Palermo Convention) and corruption (2003). These three conventions differed from earlier crime-specific instruments in one notable respect: they contained detailed provisions on extradition and mutual legal assistance.

EXTRADITION

Extradition is the process by which the competent authorities of a jurisdiction forcibly transfer a person to another jurisdiction, generally for this person to stand trial for an offense or to serve a sentence.

The requested state may refuse the request for extradition on a number of grounds, even if an extradition treaty exists between the two countries. The most common grounds are the absence of double criminality, that the person in question is a national of the requested state, or that the offense is deemed a "political offense." (Other common grounds for refusal include the danger that the suspect would be persecuted or have an unfair trial in the requesting country, that the expected punishment would be excessive, or that the person in question has already stood trial for the offense.)

Extradition treaties generally require that the offense in question is criminal in both the requesting and the requested state. Even where extradition is possible in the absence of an extradition treaty, this principle of *double criminality* is generally applied.

States are generally not willing to extradite their own citizens to stand trial abroad. This principle of the *non-extradition of nationals* is often expressly stated in treaties. The reason is a mixture of the obligation of a state to protect its citizens, doubts about due process in foreign courts, the disadvantages that defendants face when defending themselves in a foreign legal system, and the disadvantages of being in custody in a foreign state (Nadelmann, 1993, p. 427). Should the requested state refuse to extradite on these grounds, the state is seen to have a general obligation to bring the person to trial in its own courts.

The reluctance to extradite one's own nationals appears to be lessening in many states. The Palermo Convention, for example, encourages extradition of nationals, on condition that they be returned to serve out the possible sentence.

During the early 1800s, the view began to emerge that suspects should not be extradited for politically motivated offenses. Although there is no universally accepted definition of what constitutes a "political offense," reference is generally made to the motive and purpose of the offense, the circumstances in which it was committed, and the character of the offense as treason or sedition under domestic law. Largely because of the increase in terrorism, these grounds for refusal have been restricted or even abolished. The Palermo Convention, for example, does not make specific reference to political offenses as grounds for refusal.

MUTUAL LEGAL ASSISTANCE

The earliest international instruments on mutual legal assistance covered the hearing of witnesses and other taking of evidence. The scope has been constantly expanded. The Palermo Convention, for example, provides for the following forms of mutual legal assistance:

- taking evidence or statements from persons
- service of judicial documents
- execution of searches and seizures
- freezing of assets
- examination of objects and sites
- provision of information, evidence, and expert evaluations
- provision of originals or copies of government, bank, financial, corporate, or business documents or records
- identification of or tracing the proceeds of crime
- facilitation of the voluntary appearance of persons in the requesting state party
- any other type of assistance that is not contrary to the domestic law of the requested state

Most of these forms were to be found in the 1986 Harare Scheme and the 1988 Drug Convention, as well as in many bilateral instruments. The Palermo Convention, however, allows several forms of assistance that were not envisaged under these instruments, developed only a decade earlier. Examples include the freezing of assets and the use of video conferences.

Grounds for Refusal

The most common grounds for refusal are the absence of double criminality, that the offense is a political or fiscal offense, bank secrecy, and violation of vital interests of the requested state (*ordre public*).

As with extradition, a state may decline mutual legal assistance if the conduct in question is not an offense under its laws. More recent instruments, however, give the requested state the option of providing the assistance even in the absence of *double criminality*. In such cases, states would usually provide assistance that does not require so-called coercive measures, which are measures that are taken against the will of the suspect or of third parties (such as house searches).

If the offense is a *political* one, this is generally an optional reason for refusal. As with extradition, the possibility or obligation to refuse assistance in such conditions has been curtailed.

Early treaties on mutual legal assistance allowed a refusal on the grounds that the offense was a *fiscal offense*; basically, countries would not help other countries to recover money owed to the government (for example, investigations of tax fraud). Along the same lines, countries would often refuse a request if this would be contrary to *bank secrecy* (for example, requests in money laundering investigations for information on whether funds were moved into or out of an account at certain times). Also in these respects, practice has been changing, as shown by the fact that the Palermo Convention specifies that countries may *not* refuse a request on the sole ground that the offense is considered to involve fiscal matters, or that bank secrecy is involved.

One ground for refusal generally found in conventions on mutual legal assistance that can be interpreted quite expansively is that the requested state can refuse assistance that it deems might endanger its sovereignty, security, law and order, or other vital interests (*ordre public*).

THE MUTUAL LEGAL ASSISTANCE PROCEDURE

The general trend is toward broader multilateral treaties on mutual legal assistance, a wider scope of assistance, fewer grounds for refusal, and various ways of making the process more efficient and rapid.

For example, the traditional diplomatic channels are being replaced by reliance on central authorities, or even by direct contacts between courts. Increasingly, treaties require that states designate a *central authority* (generally, the ministry of justice) to which the requests can be sent directly, thus providing a quicker alternative to diplomatic channels. Today, to an increasing degree, even more direct channels are being used, in that an official in the requesting state sends the request directly to the appropriate official in the other state. The European Union, with its European Arrest Warrant and other mechanisms, has played a pioneering role in this area. (See Chapter 48, this volume, on European Union cooperation in criminal justice.)

Another trend is toward overcoming differences between the procedural laws of states, for example, when the requesting state requires special procedures (such as notarized affidavits) that are not recognized under the law of the requested state. Traditionally, the requested state always followed its own procedural law, and would refuse assistance if unknown procedures were required. Already the 1988 Drug Convention, while not *requiring* that the requested state comply with the procedural form required by the requesting state, urged the requested state to do so. A corresponding provision was taken into the Palermo Convention.

One major problem in mutual legal assistance worldwide is that the requested state is often slow in replying, as a result of which suspects must be freed due to absence of evidence. There are many understandable reasons for this slowness: a shortage of trained staff, linguistic difficulties, differences in procedure that complicate responding, and so on. Nonetheless, it can be frustrating to find that a case must be abandoned because even a simple request is not fulfilled in time.

The 1988 Drug Convention does not explicitly require that the requested state reply promptly. The Commonwealth Scheme calls for the requested state to grant the assistance requested as expeditiously as practicable. The Palermo Convention is even more emphatic by providing that the central authority should ensure speedy and prompt execution and that the requested state is to take "as full account as possible of any deadlines suggested by the requesting State Party and for which reasons are given."

RECENT TRENDS AND CONCLUSIONS

Much of the everyday practice of extradition and mutual assistance continues to be based on bilateral and multilateral instruments that were drafted many years ago. Moreover, many states that are parties to instruments on these issues still do not have the necessary legislation or resources to respond to requests for extradition or mutual assistance. As a result, in many cases requests continue to be transmitted through diplomatic channels, and the resulting delays may mean that justice cannot be done. Even if the requested state responds, it may misunderstand the formal requirements needed.

Nonetheless, some developments have taken place to strengthen judicial cooperation over the past 20 years:

- bilateral instruments are being increasingly replaced by *multilateral instruments*
- the scope of the instruments has been expanded to cover more offenses
- the grounds of refusal are being restricted
- the range of mutual legal assistance measures has expanded
- there is a trend toward granting *greater rights to the person in question* as an object (as opposed to subject) of the process and to greater consideration of how he or she would be treated or punished in the requesting state
- there is a trend toward *less rigid procedural requirements*, including the possibility of direct contacts and simplified procedure

International cooperation in responding to transnational crime has expanded and deepened. International instruments have provided the main building blocks for this development. The pace of development has clearly quickened. The 1988 Drug Convention and the Palermo Convention are signs that multilateral instruments are assuming increasing importance.

Along with the spread of transnational crime, multilateral and bilateral instruments on extradition and mutual legal assistance will assume increasing importance. Law enforcement authorities, prosecutors, defense counsels, and judges will find that cases no longer have solely domestic connections; they must turn to their colleagues in other countries for assistance. Without international instruments on extradition and mutual legal assistance, such assistance would be difficult if not impossible to obtain.

REFERENCES

Boister, N. (2012). *An introduction to transnational criminal law*. Oxford. Oxford University Press
Ellis, A. & Pisani, R. L. (1985). The United States treaties on mutual assistance in criminal matters: A comparative analysis. *The International Lawyer*, 19(1), 189–223.
Nadelmann, E. A. (1993). *Cops across borders: The internationalization of U.S. criminal law enforcement*. University Park, PA: Pennsylvania State University Press.

50 International Cooperation to Combat Money Laundering

Adam Graycar

MONEY LAUNDERING

Money laundering is a process that turns "dirty money" into "clean money." The proceeds of crime – dirty money – are disguised to hide their illicit origins, and then the money is integrated into the legitimate economy. The process washes dirty money until it appears to be clean. Often, but not always, the cleaning of dirty money involves moving it across national borders and integrating it into another economy.

In April 2016, about 11.5 million financial and legal documents, the so-called "Panama Papers," were leaked through Panamanian law firm Mossack Fonseca (Forster, 2016). These documents allegedly revealed a global system of undisclosed offshore accounts, money laundering, and other illegal activity, implicating world leaders, financiers, celebrities, criminals, and tax evaders. One of the consequences of the Panama Papers was the sharpening of the national and global focus on the risks associated with money laundering, tax evasion, and terrorist financing.

Criminals disguise the illegal origins of their wealth, and terrorist organizations try to conceal the destination and the purpose for which the money has been collected. Money laundering plays a part in corruption as corrupt public officials need to hide the kickbacks they receive and the public funds they may have misappropriated. Organized criminal groups have substantial proceeds from drug trafficking and commodity smuggling. Together these activities have profound social consequences and require cooperative international activity to combat them.

There is a great deal of international and national cooperative efforts to counter financial crime and money laundering. The evidence for success is very mixed (U4, 2017). Legislation exits in most countries to criminalize money laundering and the associated activities such as opening bank accounts in false names. Law enforcement agencies have investigated and prosecuted those accused of money laundering and prison sentences have been imposed. Money laundering is certainly big business and is significant for many economies, with estimates of over US$1 trillion being laundered every year by drug dealers, arms traffickers, tax evaders, and other criminals.

GLOBAL COOPERATIVE EFFORTS

There are numerous international agencies and collaborative networks that toil actively against money laundering and that have striven for uniform standards and cooperative development. Among them are the World Bank, the International Monetary Fund, the African Development Bank, the Asian Development Bank, INTERPOL, the United Nations Global Program against Money Laundering and the Financial Action Task Force (FATF) and its regional groups. Details on all of these can be found on their websites. In addition, several United Nations conventions have money laundering as the key.

United Nations

The 1988 United Nations Convention against the Illicit Traffic in Narcotic Drugs and Psychotropic Substances was the first international convention that criminalized money laundering. It contained legal instruments for nations to use. The International Convention for the Suppression of the Financing of Terrorism came into force in April 2002. This requires member states to take measures to protect their financial systems from being misused by persons planning or engaged in terrorist activities. This was followed by two other UN conventions, the UN Convention against Transnational Organized Crime in 2003, and in 2005 by the United Nations Convention against Corruption (UNCAC).

Together these conventions require explicit commitments against money laundering. States are to develop domestic regulatory and supervisory regimes for banks and non-bank financial institutions as well as mechanisms to deter and detect all forms of money laundering. States are also to emphasize requirements for customer identification, record keeping, and the reporting of suspicious transactions and develop an ability to cooperate and exchange information at the national and international levels. State parties, the UNCAC Convention says, shall endeavor to develop and promote global, regional, subregional, and bi-lateral cooperation among judicial, law enforcement, and financial regulatory authorities in order to combat money laundering.

Together these form the UN's Global Program against Money Laundering, Proceeds of Crime, and the Financing of Terrorism. The objective is for all states to adopt legislation for the legal instruments against money laundering and to counter the financing of terrorism. Through technical assistance programs the UN helps equip states with the knowledge, means, and expertise to lay in place legal frameworks, as well as to investigate and prosecute complex financial crimes. This is backed by information exchange and mutual legal assistance.

The Financial Action Task Force (FATF)

To complement the work of the United Nations, the Financial Action Task Force (FATF) is a policy-making body that works to bring about national reforms and to generate the political will to counter money laundering. An intergovernmental body, the FATF was established in July 1989 by a Group of Seven (G-7) Summit in Paris, initially to examine and develop measures to combat money laundering. At that time the FATF comprised 15 jurisdictions plus an international organization. It now comprises 37 members, though its standards are much more widely agreed.

"The FATF monitors members' progress in implementing necessary measures, reviews money laundering and terrorist financing techniques and counter-measures, and promotes the adoption and implementation of appropriate measures globally. In performing these activities, the FATF collaborates with other international bodies involved in combating money laundering and the financing of terrorism" (FATF website).

The four essential objectives of the FATF are to:

1. revise and clarify the global standards and measures for combating money laundering and terrorist financing
2. promote global implementation of the standards
3. identify and respond to new money laundering and terrorist financing threats
4. engage with stakeholders and partners throughout the world

The FATF has established the international standards for combating money laundering and terrorist financing, in what are known as the 40+9 Recommendations – that is, 40 initial recommendations plus nine special recommendations to deal with terrorist financing (www .fatf-gafi.org/home/).

The bulk of the recommendations relate to measures to be taken by financial institutions and non-financial businesses and professions to prevent money laundering and terrorist financing. These cover

- customer due diligence and record-keeping
- reporting of suspicious transactions and compliance
- other measures to deter money laundering and terrorist financing
- measures to be taken with respect to countries that do not or insufficiently comply with the FATF Recommendations
- regulation and supervision

The remaining recommendations relate to institutional and other measures necessary in systems for combating money laundering and terrorist financing. They cover

- competent authorities, their powers and resources
- transparency of legal persons and arrangements
- international cooperation
- mutual legal assistance and extradition
- other forms of cooperation

The FATF standards have been endorsed directly by 180 jurisdictions around the world, as well as by the boards of the International Monetary Fund and the World Bank. In addition, the United Nations Security Council, in its Resolution 1617 of July 2005, stated that it "strongly urges all Member States to implement the comprehensive international standards embodied in the FATF Forty Recommendations on Money Laundering and the FATF Nine Special Recommendations on Terrorist Financing."

The FATF works to generate the necessary political will to bring about national legislative and regulatory reforms in the areas addressed by the 40+9 Recommendations.

The FATF continues to identify additional jurisdictions, on an ongoing basis, that pose a risk to the international financial system. It identifies various jurisdictions that have strategic AML/CFT deficiencies for which they have developed an action plan with the FATF. At its February 2018 meeting, for example, it outlined reports and action plans for Ethiopia, Iraq, Serbia, Sri Lanka, and five other countries (FATF 2018). For Serbia, for example, the report outlined means for developing a better understanding of key risks; subjecting lawyers, notaries, and casinos to supervision; pursuing measures related to politically exposed persons and wire transfers in line with the FATF standards; establishing an effective mechanism for ensuring timely access to beneficial ownership information; and a number of other measures.

As part of its fourth round of mutual evaluations, the FATF and its regional bodies have committed to publish, between 2014 and 2021, more than 180 country-specific reports that will evaluate what governments are doing to fight money laundering and stop illicit financial flows (U4, 2017).

Nonprofit organizations are particularly vulnerable to terrorist organizations posing as legitimate entities, and can be used as conduits for terrorist financing, and to conceal or obscure the clandestine diversion to terrorist organizations of funds intended for legitimate purposes. We can therefore see that the issue is broader than banks and financial institutions alone.

ENFORCEMENT

The UN and the FATF are mostly concerned with developing positions and instruments for use by various countries. Enforcement has been both country-based, and when cooperation has been required, a prominent role has been played by INTERPOL, which provides information on money laundering activities to national law enforcement agencies. There has been criticism that the level of enforcement could be substantially improved (U4, 2017).

There are many players – the UN and its constituent parts, the FATF, INTERPOL, and the World Customs Organization, plus many more operators, such as the International Monetary Fund (IMF), the Commonwealth Secretariat, the Organization for Security and Cooperation in Europe (OSCE), the Asian Development Bank (ADB), the UN Counter-Terrorism Executive Directorate (CTED), the UN Counter-Terrorism Implementation Task Force (CTITF), regional development banks, the European Union, and the United Nations Commission on International Trade Law (UNCITRAL), as well as the US Department of Justice (OPDAT), the US Department of Treasury – Office of Technical Assistance (OTA), the Inter-American Drug Abuse Control Commission of the Organization of American States (OAS/CICAD), FATF-style regional bodies, and a number of individual country technical assistance providers.

Most countries have created Financial Intelligence Units (FIUs), and they operate in a wide range of different systems and use different methods. These are the people who analyze financial intelligence, and if there is sufficient evidence of unlawful activity they then pass the information on to a prosecuting authority. Formed in 1995, The Egmont Group of Financial Intelligence Units is an informal international gathering of 155 national financial intelligence units, which provides a platform for the secure exchange of expertise and financial intelligence to combat money laundering and terrorist financing. These FIUs meet regularly to find ways to cooperate, especially in the areas of information exchange, training, and the sharing of expertise (see https://egmontgroup.org/en/content/about).

Banks have always played a role in money laundering, and legendary were the Swiss banks that hid money (often ill-gotten) behind secret numbered accounts. Switzerland, however, was one of the first countries to pursue measures against money laundering. In January 2017, *The Independent* reported that new rules for Swiss banks ensured details would be shared with tax authorities of other nations and vice versa, potentially resulting in the end of the era of the secretive Swiss bank account, favored by criminals and errant politicians alike (Chapman 2017).

Switzerland has legislation for identifying, tracing, freezing, seizing, and forfeiting narcotics-related assets and its money laundering laws and regulations apply to both banks and non-bank financial institutions (NBFIs). It was reported that in 2011, one hour after Egypt's ex-president Hosni Mubarak stepped down, the Swiss Government ordered its banks to freeze his assets held in Switzerland (U4, 2017, p. 4). In 2018, Switzerland's attorney general launched criminal proceedings against banks for failing to prevent possible crimes being committed (Revill & Shields, 2018).

While Switzerland is tightening up, banks in other countries are sometimes all too willing to step into the money laundering space.

CONCLUSION

International cooperation is essential for combating money laundering. International conventions are based on the premise that if crime crosses borders, so too must law enforcement. Terrorists, criminals, drug dealers, traffickers in people, and others who undo the works of civil society take advantage of the open borders, the free markets, and the technological advances that shape modern society.

Responses to money laundering are different to responses to volume crimes such as robbery, motor vehicle theft, burglary, assault, larceny, and even homicide. Two things stand out.

First, legal and illegal activities have the same *modus operandi*. Money from legal sources is converted in the same sorts of ways and into the same sorts of assets as is money from illegal sources. The challenge for enforcers is to regulate and investigate so as not to impede or taint the movement of legitimate capital. Responding to volume crimes does not pose this dilemma for law enforcement.

Second, many of the agencies described above that work to combat money laundering do not deal in actual enforcement. The United Nations, the FATF, the Egmont Group, and the plethora of other agencies are all framework constructors and information sharers. Much of the understanding of combating money laundering lies in understanding the problem, why it is a problem, and how regulatory arrangements are circumvented, rather than doing what needs to be done to investigate and prosecute. However, the very international nature of the problem requires international cooperation. Learning about this is a necessary first step in combating money laundering.

REFERENCES

Chapman, B. (2017, January 3). Secretive Swiss bank accounts face new crackdown. *The Independent*. Retrieved from www.independent.co.uk/news/business/news/swiss-bank-accounts-not-secret-tax-avoidance-money-laundering-crackdown-a7507696.html.
Financial Action Task Force (FATF). (2006). Trade-based money laundering. Retrieved from www.fatf-gafi.org/dataoecd/60/25/37038272.pdf.
(2018). Improving global AML/CFT compliance. Retrieved from www.fatf-gafi.org/publications/high-riskandnon-cooperativejurisdictions/documents/fatf-compliance-february-2018.html.

Forster, K. (2016, November 8). Panama Papers probe. *The Independent*. Retrieved from www
    .independent.co.uk/news/uk/crime/panama-papers-22-people-tax-evasion-investigation-philip-
    hammond-government-taskforce-a7405771.html.

Halliday, T., Levi, M., & Reuter, P. (2014). Global surveillance of dirty money. Retrieved from www
    .lexglobal.org/files/Report_Global%20Surveillance%20of%20Dirty%20Money%201.30.2014.pdf.

KPMG. (2007). Global anti–money laundering survey. Retrieved from https://home.kpmg.com/xx/en/
    home/insights/2014/01/global-anti-money-laundering-survey.html.

Revill, J. & Shields, M. (2018, February 1). Swiss bank PKB broke money-laundering rules in Brazilian
    cases: FINMA. Reuters. Retrieved from www.reuters.com/article/us-swiss-pkb-petrobras/
    swiss-bank-pkb-broke-money-laundering-rules-in-brazilian-cases-finma-idUSKBN1FL6FN.

U4. (2017). International support to anti-money laundering and asset recovery: Success stories.
    Retrieved from www.u4.no/publications/international-support-to-anti-money-laundering-and-
    asset-recovery-success-stories/pdf.

US Department of Justice. (2005). US money laundering threat assessment. Retrieved from www
    .usdoj.gov/dea/pubs/pressrel/011106.pdf.

World Bank. (2006). Reference guide to anti-money laundering and combating the financing of
    terrorism. Washington, DC: World Bank. Retrieved from http://siteresources.worldbank.org/
    EXTAML/Resources/396511-1146581427871/Reference_Guide_AMLCFT_2ndSupplement.pdf.

WEBSITES

Some of the following will require readers to search within for money laundering.

Various international conventions and multi-lateral conventions can be found at https://treaties
    .un.org/Pages/Home.aspx?clang=_en.

Asia/Pacific Group on Money Laundering. www.apgml.org/.

Australian Transaction Reports and Analysis Centre (AUSTRAC). www.austrac.gov.au/.

The Egmont Group. www.egmontgroup.org/.

Financial Action Task Force (FATF). www.fatf-gafi.org.

International Monetary Fund. www.imf.org/.

INTERPOL. www.interpol.int/.

United Nations International Money Laundering Information Network (IMoLIN). www.imolin.org/.

United Nations Office of Drugs and Crime (UNODC). www.unodc.org/unodc/en/money-laundering/
    index.html.

World Bank. www.worldbank.org/.

51 The Role of Major Intergovernmental Organizations and International Agencies in Combating Transnational Crime

Yuliya Zabyelina

INTRODUCTION

States establish intergovernmental organizations (IGOs) and international agencies (IAs) to achieve the objectives that they are either unable or unwilling to accomplish alone. When creating IGOs and IAs, states consent to be bound by some rules and carry out obligations according to the principles of sovereign equality, territorial integrity, and non-intervention in the domestic affairs of other states.

IGOs are composed of sovereign states and are usually established by treaty or a formal agreement. IAs are typically smaller-sized IGOs that are subordinated to a larger political and economic body. Their non-independent status affects the mandate, administration, and scope of activities.

Some of the main functions accorded to IGOs and IAs are: (a) information gathering, sharing, and analysis; (b) regularization of cooperation among states and consensus building; (c) formulation and dissemination of internationally acceptable norms, standards, and best practices; and (d) provision of legal and technical assistance. Although these general functions apply to most international organizations, there exists a variety of IGOs and IAs. There are single- and multi-issue organizations. Some organizations allow universal membership and have a geographically balanced membership and management, while the membership of others is based on certain criteria (e.g., location in a continent or subcontinental region, a certain level of economic development, etc.).

This chapter discusses some of the most influential IGOs and IAs that participate in combating transnational crime.

AGENCIES OF THE UNITED NATIONS

In terms of membership and staff, the world's largest IGO is the United Nations (UN). It also has the widest network of IAs, including those with mandates relevant for countering transnational crime.

UN Specialized Agencies

Although the UN's specialized agencies are coordinated by the Economic and Social Council (ECOSOC) and the Chief Executives Board (CEB), they are self-managing organizations funded by both voluntary contributions and UN budget assessments and have their own process for admitting members, appointing administrative heads, and establishing policy.

At present, there are 15 specialized agencies that carry out various functions on behalf of the UN. The work that about half of them carry out contributes in important ways to preventing and responding to various forms of transnational crime. For instance, the International Labour Organization (ILO) – one of the oldest UN specialized agencies – is devoted to advancing opportunities for people to obtain decent and productive employment in conditions of freedom, equity, security, and human dignity. This mandate includes activities against human trafficking and forced servitude.

The World Tourism Organization (UNWTO) focuses on matters of child protection, including prevention of all forms of child exploitation in the tourism sector (e.g., sex tourism). Important work on child protection is also performed by the United Nations Educational, Scientific and Cultural Organization (UNESCO). This specialized agency works to raise awareness and mobilize the wider public to act against violence, exploitation, and abuse of children. Additionally, UNESCO coordinates global operations targeting the destruction of cultural sites and trafficking of cultural property.

Working within a much broader mandate of poverty eradication and economic development, the World Bank Group (WBG) provides support to UN member states in nearly every region and sector. Its role in the fight against transnational crime has expanded since the adoption of the Millennium Development Goals (MDGs) and the Sustainable Development Goals (SDGs). Whereas there is only indirect reference to transnational crime in the MDGs (2000–2015), the SDGs (2015–2030), which replaced the MDGs in 2016, vividly reflect the UN member states' concern with continuously high homicide rates in some parts of the world, global expansion of illicit trade, human exploitation, and uneven access to justice, among other pertinent issues (see Sustainable Development Goal 16, "Peace, Justice and Strong Institutions," in UN, 2015). Additionally, the International Monetary Fund (IMF) and the WBG provide financial and technical assistance to UN member states in the areas of anti-corruption and anti-money laundering/combating the financing of terrorism (AML/CFT).

UN Funds and Programs

UN funds and programs are established by UN General Assembly resolutions, which subordinate them to ECOSOC. In respect of administration and staff, they are therefore subject to UN rules and regulations. Funding for UN funds and programs is provided by governments, the private sector, and other sources, in the form of voluntary contributions.

At least six out of the 11 UN funds and programs bear relevance to the global response to transnational crime. The United Nations Children's Fund (UNICEF) provides long-term humanitarian and development assistance to children and mothers. It works in more than 190 countries and territories to help children survive and grow into happy and healthy adults. A portion of UNICEF's mission deals with protecting children from forced labor and other exploitative practices as well as with developing standards of assistance to child trafficking victims.

Although neither the issue of human trafficking nor trafficking victims fall into the mandate of the United Nations High Commissioner for Refugees (UNHCR), this organization has worked to protect refugees, internally displaced persons, and stateless persons from exploitative and degrading practices.

With their general mandate of eradicating poverty and mitigating the negative consequences of inequality, the United Nations Development Programme (UNDP) and the United Nations Industrial Development Organization (UNIDO), among other UN developmental agencies, are instrumental in responding to the driving forces behind the formation of illicit economies. Together with the UNODC (discussed immediately below), the UNIDO and the UNDP promote grassroots development in communities dependent on the cultivation of illicit crops and, among other relevant activities, respond to the corrosive effect that corruption has on development.

The United Nations Office on Drugs and Crime

The UN's leading international agency in the response to transnational crime is the United Nations Office on Drugs and Crime (UNODC). Established in 1997 through a merger between the United Nations Drug Control Programme and the Centre for International Crime Prevention, the UNODC operates in all regions of the world through an extensive network of field offices. UNODC's activities fall into five interrelated areas: (a) organized crime and trafficking; (b) corruption; (c) crime prevention and criminal justice reform; (d) drug prevention and health; and (e) terrorism prevention.

UNODC performs several important tasks. First, it conducts research and data analysis to inform policy and operational decisions. It provides countries with statistical expertise that can enable them to collect, process, analyze, and disseminate data on drugs and crime. Second, the UNODC is committed to expanding the capacity of member states to respond to crime and improve their criminal justice institutions. It provides technical cooperation to help member states counteract illicit drugs, organized crime, and terrorism, in addition to facilitating cross-border cooperation and knowledge sharing (UNODC, 2010). Third, the UNODC assists member states in the ratification, implementation, and administration of relevant international treaties. For instance, it acts as the guardian of the United Nations Convention against Transnational Organized Crime (UNTOC) and the United Nations Convention against Corruption (UNCAC). Finally, the UNODC engages in public awareness and advocacy campaigns aimed to expand the rule of law, prevent crime, and encourage universal respect for human rights.

REGIONAL POLICE ORGANIZATIONS

Since its creation in 1923, the International Criminal Police Organization (INTERPOL) has served as a model for regional police organizations. Almost all regions of the world have created regional police bodies. These include the European Union's EUROPOL, the African Union's AFRIPOL, AMERIPOL, ASEANAPOL, and the Gulf Cooperation Council's GCCPOL (Table 51.1). All these regional police organizations work to identify areas for collaboration

Table 51.1. Regional police organizations

Acronym	Full Name	Status	Creation	Secretariat	Membership
AMERIPOL	The Police Community of the Americas.	Western-hemispheric mechanism of law enforcement cooperation.	2007.	Bogotá, Colombia.	About 30 law enforcement agencies from countries in the Americas.
ASEANAPOL	n/a.	Police organization of the Association of Southeast Asian Nations (ASEAN)	1981.	Kuala Lumpur, Malaysia.	Ten ASEAN member states (Indonesia, Thailand, Vietnam, Singapore, Malaysia, Philippines, Myanmar, Cambodia, Laos, and Brunei).
AFRIPOL	The African Union Police.	The African Union's (AU) regional mechanism for police cooperation.	2017.	Algiers, Algeria.	Chiefs of Police from 55 countries of the African Union.
EUROPOL	The European Union Agency for Law Enforcement Cooperation.	Law enforcement agency of the European Union (EU).	1998.	The Hague, the Netherlands.	Liaison officers from 28 EU member states (Austria, Belgium, Bulgaria, Croatia, Cyprus, the Czech Republic, Denmark, Estonia, Finland, France, Germany, Greece, Hungary, Ireland, Italy, Latvia, Lithuania, Luxembourg, Malta, the Netherlands, Poland, Portugal, Romania, Slovakia, Slovenia, Spain, Sweden, the UK).
GCCPOL	The Gulf Cooperation Council Police (GCC).	Regional police force of the Gulf Cooperation Council (GCC).	2014.	Abu Dhabi, UAE.	Police chiefs from seven GCC member states (Bahrain, Iraq, Kuwait, Oman, Qatar, Saudi Arabia, and the UAE).

and encourage greater information exchange among their members and with other relevant international bodies. Neither INTERPOL nor regional police organizations, however, constitute supranational police agencies with far-reaching executive powers. All investigations and arrests in each member state are carried out by the national police and in accordance with national laws. The distinction between INTERPOL and regional police organizations is that the latter are smaller in size and focus on specific regional issues and needs.

Regional police organizations vary with regards to their legal status. Some regional police organizations are independent organizations of police forces. They are not based on a treaty or convention and function largely based on a constitution drawn up by their members. National police forces apply for membership, appoint delegates, and contribute to the organization's budget. For instance, the Police Community of the Americas (AMERIPOL), founded in 2007, offers a mechanism of cooperation among law enforcement in the Western

Hemisphere. It coordinates law enforcement cooperation and enhances efforts in criminal investigations in the Americas. AMERIPOL has signed partnerships with up to about 20 other organizations, including law enforcement agencies from other parts of the world (e.g., Civil Guard and National Police Corps of Spain, Italy's Guardia di Finanza and Carabinieri, etc.) and international organizations (e.g., INTERPOL and International Association of Chiefs of Police).

In contrast to AMERIPOL, some regional police organizations are embedded in larger regional political and economic bodies and do not have complete decision making and budgetary autonomy. For instance, the European Union Agency for Law Enforcement Cooperation (EUROPOL) is a law enforcement agency of the European Union (EU). It was formed in 1998 with a mandate to collect and manage criminal intelligence and respond to organized crime and terrorism threats in the region. EUROPOL is accountable to EU justice and interior ministers (the Council of the European Union), Members of the European Parliament, other EU bodies, and a EUROPOL Management Board drawn from all 28 EU member states. EUROPOL supports various EU bodies working in the area of freedom, security, and justice, such as the European Union Agency for Law Enforcement Training (CEPOL) in Budapest (Hungary) and the European Anti-Fraud Office (OLAF) in Brussels (Belgium). Its budget consists of allocations from the EU's general budget. Although EUROPOL is embedded in the EU governance architecture, it has legal personality and can enter into agreements in its own name. In 2004, for instance, EUROPOL and the UNODC signed a cooperation agreement, whereby both parties consented to work together against serious forms of crime within their field of competence and in accordance with their respective mandates.

INTERORGANIZATIONAL PARTNERSHIPS WITHIN THE UN SYSTEM AND WITH NON-UN ORGANIZATIONS

Given the partly overlapping mandates of national and international agencies, coordination is encouraged. This has been done, for example, through the signing of Memoranda of Understanding (MoU) and Action Plans (APs).

MoUs express some convergence between the cooperating parties, indicating an intended common purpose and anticipated activities. MoUs do not usually impose any legal commitment on the parties and rely primarily on their genuine interest in working together. APs are usually more detailed than MoUs and describe the course of action to be taken in order to achieve the objectives set out in MoUs. APs may also include an evaluation component, whereby the parties come together to review progress periodically.

For instance, the World Customs Organization (WCO) is not part of the UN system. Yet, it has maintained ties with the UN and its agencies. The partnership between the WCO and UNODC is based on a MoU signed in November 1996. The two organizations have been working together on a number of international projects. One of the most important joint initiatives is the UNODC-WCO Container Control Programme that has assisted UN member states in minimizing the risk of shipping containers, exploited for illicit trafficking and other forms of criminal activity since 2003.

In 2016, the UNODC and INTERPOL signed a cooperation arrangement focusing on operations against organized crime and terrorism. Having worked closely for many years, the two organizations formalized their partnership in order to provide a more strategic action against the increasingly complex nature of transnational threats. The agreement comes with the UNODC-INTERPOL Joint Action Plan, which includes an activity matrix which categorizes joint or complementary activities of the two organizations across six common thematic areas, such as terrorism, illicit trafficking and organized crime, cybercrime, maritime and border security, forensic and criminal justice capacity, and institutional capacity.

Interorganizational cooperation is also observable in anti-human trafficking responses. The UNODC maintains channels of communication with the UN's UNWTO, UNESCO, and ILO, and has occasionally joined forces with related organizations, such as the International Organization for Migration (IOM) and the Organization for Security and Cooperation in Europe (OSCE), in order to promote a global response to different forms of trafficking in persons. In 2015, the EU and the UNODC launched the Global Action to Prevent and Address Trafficking in Persons and the Smuggling of Migrants (GLO.ACT). This is a four-year (2015–2019) initiative that develops policies and strategies tackling the nexus between human trafficking and human smuggling. The World Health Organization (WHO), UN-Women, and the United Nations Population Fund (UNFPA) have joined in a number of initiatives to provide essential services to women in order to end and respond to gender-based violence.

SUMMARY

Global governance and cooperation on an international level for the containment of transnational crime is essential. Agencies of UN system foster international cooperation and harmonization of regulatory and legal regimes. They assist member states in drafting and implementing international conventions and establish norms and standards that promote outcomes for the benefit of the international community as a whole.

In addition to the activities of UN agencies, INTERPOL and regional police organizations provide improved communication for national law enforcement agencies, assist in intelligence sharing, and facilitate other activities related to the prevention and combating of all forms of transnational crime.

REFERENCES

United Nations. (2015, October 21). Transforming our world: The 2030 Agenda for Sustainable Development. A/RES/70/1.

United Nations Office on Drugs and Crime (UNODC). (2010). *UNODC services and tools: Practical solutions to global threats to justice, security and health.* Vienna: UNODC.

52 Crime Prevention in International Context

Ronald V. Clarke

INTRODUCTION

The law and the criminal justice system constitute the modern state's first line of defense against crime. These "formal" systems of control serve the dual purposes of deterring law breaking among the population at large and of apprehending, punishing, and treating those who offend. Complementing the formal systems of control are society's "informal" social controls. These include measures taken by parents, by schools, and by religious bodies to: (i) instill respect for the law among children and young people; (ii) regulate the conduct of people as they go about their daily lives; and (iii) afford protection to persons and property by routine precautions and security measures.

The formal and informal systems of control depend upon one another for their effectiveness. Without informal social controls, the criminal justice system would soon be swamped with crime and, without the threat of arrest and punishment provided by the criminal justice system, informal social controls would encounter constant challenges to their credibility.

As governments have come to recognize the costs and limitations of the formal system of crime control, they have begun to explore more direct ways of improving informal social controls. This activity falls under the general heading of "crime prevention," which can be defined as *interventions that seek to promote the security of individuals and communities without resort to formal criminal justice sanctions*. It is useful to distinguish among four general approaches as follows.

1. **Child development**. Research has documented a variety of risk factors in early childhood associated with later delinquency and crime. Interventions designed to address these factors through improved parenting skills, enriched early education, and improved physical and mental health could lead to large reductions in future crime and delinquency. Some early efforts focused on delinquency reduction, such as the famous Cambridge-Somerville project and the Headstart program in the USA, met with little success. However, recent research has identified more promising ways of preventing the development of persistently delinquent personalities (Weisburd et al., 2018).
2. **Community development**. Criminologists have long recognized that powerful forces in local communities can promote or inhibit crime. An important strand of preventive work consists of efforts to strengthen the economic viability and social cohesiveness of local communities, to provide more local services and facilities for community

enhancement, to strengthen resident ties to their local communities, to teach young people about the importance of the rule of law, and to develop local police/community relations. Sustained efforts along these lines have been made in many Western countries, most notably in France (the Bonnemaison initiatives), in Britain ("safer city" programs), in Italy (the anti-mafia education of young people in Palermo), and in the USA (neighborhood watch and community policing). Unfortunately, there is little hard evidence of success to date. Doubts have also been raised about the meaning of the local community in highly developed, modern societies and about its role in crime prevention.

3. **Social development.** This is the least advanced of the four approaches but is of great interest in an international context. It proceeds on the assumption that much crime in developing countries results from poverty, lack of paid employment, poor education, discrimination, and a variety of other social and economic deprivations. It is assumed that social development will remove these "causes" of crime. Unfortunately, there is no direct relationship between social conditions and crime. Thus, crime unexpectedly increased in Western countries in the 1960s, which was a time of increased affluence and improved social security. However, these findings may not hold for developing countries and countries in transition, where the general social and economic conditions are much less favorable.

4. **Situational crime prevention.** Unlike the other forms of crime prevention, all of which seek to reduce the motivation for crime, situational prevention seeks to reduce opportunities for crime. This has been the fastest-growing form of crime prevention in the past few decades. It has come to be associated with the spectacular rise of private policing and the private security industry in Western countries (Garland, 1996). In its government-sponsored forms it consists of: (i) crime prevention advertising campaigns; (ii) efforts to influence city planning and architectural design to promote a "crime-free" environment; (iii) focused efforts to diagnose and remove opportunities for highly specific forms of crime such as bank robbery or residential burglary; and, more recently, (iv) pressure brought to bear on business and industry to alter criminogenic products and practices.

CURRENT STATUS OF CRIME PREVENTION

It is only during the past 30 years that governments have devoted serious attention to crime prevention and that it has become a subject for concentrated academic study. Even so, considerable progress has been made, as follows.

1. National crime prevention councils and agencies have been established by governments in many countries, including in Western Europe and in Australia, Canada, and the USA. Numerous national and international meetings have been held to focus public attention on crime prevention and to explore the many issues that surround it.

2. Situational crime prevention has become an established part of government crime policy in many countries and it is also widely practiced by businesses. This has had a direct and visible effect on people's everyday lives. Examples include the adoption of "defensible space" architecture in public housing (which has contributed to the

demolition of high-rise public housing buildings), the widespread adoption of closed-circuit television (CCTV) surveillance in streets and town centers in Europe, and the wholesale use by retailers of anti-shoplifting technology.

3. Many community crime prevention programs have been implemented with government support in developed countries. Sometimes this has been in the form of "demonstration" projects such as the "safer cities" initiatives in the United Kingdom, and sometimes in the form of generally available programs such as neighborhood watch in the USA and the "Bonnemaison" community development approach in France (Bousquet, 1996).

4. Criminologists have greatly expanded writing and research on crime prevention during the past three decades. Many new concepts assisting with the design, implementation, and evaluation of crime prevention have been developed. Several specialist journals now exist and numerous textbooks on crime prevention are available (e.g., Tilley, 2012). Many university criminology departments now offer graduate courses on crime prevention. Police training in many countries also includes an introduction to crime prevention (see www.popcenter.org).

5. Evidence has recently been accumulating that crime prevention can achieve tangible reductions in crime. Indeed, sufficient numbers of evaluations have been reported so that meta-analyses (in which the results of separate evaluations are systematically compared within a common framework) can be undertaken (Sherman et al., 1997; Weisburd et al., 2018). Meta-evaluations provide a methodology for taking account of small inconsistencies among studies to reach the most reliable conclusions about the effectiveness of particular approaches.

NEW CHALLENGES

Despite the considerable progress of the past 30 years, many challenges lie ahead in developing the full potential of crime prevention. These include the following.

1. Even in countries where crime prevention is now an established component of government criminal policy, the resources devoted to it are tiny compared to those devoted to the criminal justice system. Waller (1991) found that the expenditure on prevention was less than 1 percent of that on the criminal justice system in the USA, the United Kingdom, France and, Canada.

2. Community crime prevention and situational prevention have attracted many more resources than other forms of prevention in the past few decades. More recently, crime prevention through child development has begun to attract research support from governments. The most difficult challenge will be in finding the resources to support research on crime prevention through social development, given that this form of prevention is of greatest interest to developing countries and countries in transition.

3. Crime prevention is primarily a concept recognized in the developed world and it is unclear how technical assistance about crime prevention can be delivered from the more-developed to the less-developed parts of the world. On the other side of the coin, developed countries have made little effort to learn from the methods of crime prevention already practiced in the less-developed world.

4. To date, most crime prevention has been focused on traditional forms of crime comprising the bulk of the official crime statistics – predatory property crimes such as robbery, burglary, and car theft. Many other crimes have received relatively little preventive attention, including corruption, fraud, and economic crimes, hate crimes, domestic violence, and crimes against women. Furthermore, the nature of even traditional crimes is changing with new technology. For example, in developed countries, the growth in theft involves services (such as telephone and television services) rather than products (such as telephones or TV equipment). It is unclear to what extent current preventive models can be adapted to deal with these changes in crime and with new crimes associated with the development of the Internet.

5. It is also unclear to what extent preventive approaches developed to date can be applied to transnational crimes – such as drug trafficking, trafficking in humans, and money laundering – that constitute a particular threat to developing countries. These crimes are likely to increase with increased globalization, and with the associated increase in international trade, the expansion of business and leisure travel, and the greater erosion of political borders (Williams, 1999).

6. Whether or not it operates internationally, little is known about preventing organized crime. It thrives on disadvantage, which means that social development, community development, and child development all have a part to play in prevention. However, disadvantage is only part of the explanation for organized crime; equally important is that in every society, developed or not, illegal opportunities abound to make large sums of money. It is these opportunities that permit organized crime to flourish. That being so, considerable preventive potential rests in the situational approach, adapted to deal with the more planned, complex offences characteristic of organized crime (Bullock et al., 2010).

7. Implementation difficulties are encountered in every form of crime prevention. In community development, considerable difficulties have been experienced in achieving the necessary coordination among local agencies to implement agreed measures. Leadership is crucial and in the USA most of the leadership has fallen on "community" police officers. Several European countries (including France, the Netherlands, and the United Kingdom) have decided, instead, to fund "community safety" or "crime prevention" officers to coordinate local efforts. In social development, implementation difficulties are presently focused on obtaining agreement about the necessity and feasibility of this approach to crime prevention. Subsequently, the issue of obtaining the needed resources will have to be faced. In child development, the controversies focus on resource procurement and the ways in which crime prevention goals should be combined with the other goals of child development. The main obstacle to implementation of situational prevention is that it is frequently seen as neglecting the social problems giving rise to crime and as largely a repressive approach to crime control (Clarke & Bowers, 2017).

8. Without evaluation, crime prevention practice cannot be improved. The potential afforded by the rapid development of systematic reviews of evidence was noted above. However, detailed crime data needed for measuring the outcome of crime prevention measures are frequently lacking because statistical record keeping is deficient. There is

also a lack of trained personnel competent to undertake evaluative studies, not merely in developing countries and countries in transition, but also in some developed countries without strong traditions of quantification in the social sciences. In especially short supply is expertise in undertaking cost-benefit evaluations, which attempt to assign a specific monetary value to the outcomes of prevention compared to the cost of implementation. These kinds of evaluations will become increasingly important as business assumes a greater role in crime prevention.

9. That business is already assuming this role has been suggested by Farrell et al. (2014). They credit the substantial drops in traditional crime that have occurred in many Westernized countries since the mid-1990s to an "avalanche" of security measures that businesses and other private and public agencies have taken to protect themselves against victimization. If these authors are proved right, this will greatly strengthen the appeal of prevention.

CONCLUSION

This chapter has reviewed worldwide developments in crime prevention policy during the past few decades. Crime prevention is now no longer seen as merely a way to avoid some of the social and economic costs of the criminal justice system, but as a vitally important way to deliver safety and security in a modern democracy. The increased attention being paid by governments to child development is a change of considerable significance. Equally significant is that international bodies, such as the United Nations Organization and the World Bank, are increasingly recognizing that the rule of law must precede economic and social progress. This could ultimately result in more international resources being channeled into crime prevention through social development. Current debates are focused less on the value of crime prevention than on the merits of different approaches in specific national contexts. Ways are being explored of integrating crime prevention with broader social policy concerns, and of ensuring that ethical and humanitarian values are not compromised. The next few decades promise to be as interesting as the past few have been.

REFERENCES

Bousquet, R. (1996). Social development and cities. Preventing crime in France. Paper presented at the International Conference for Crime Prevention Practitioners, Marc/April, Vancouver.

Bullock, K., Clarke, R. V., & Tilley, N. (2010). *Situational prevention of organised crimes*. Abington: Routledge.

Clarke, R. V. & Bowers, K. (2017). Seven misconceptions of situational crime prevention. In N. Tilley & A. Sidebottom (Eds.), *Handbook of crime prevention and community safety*. Second Edition. Abington: Routledge.

Farrell, G., Tilley, N., & Tseloni, M. (2014). Why the crime drop? *Crime and Justice*, 43(1), 421–490.

Garland, D. (1996). The limits of the sovereign state: Strategies of crime control in contemporary society. *British Journal of Criminology*, 36, 445–471.

Sherman, L. W., Gottfredson, D. C., Mackenzie, D. L., Eck, J., Reuter, P., & Bushway, S. (1997). *Preventing crime: What works, what doesn't, what's promising*. Office of Justice Programs Research Report. Washington, DC: US Department of Justice.

Tilley, N. (2012). *Crime prevention*. Abington: Routledge.

Waller, I. (1991). *Introductory report: Putting crime prevention on the map*. Paper presented at the II International Conference on Urban Safety, Drugs and Crime Prevention, November, Paris.

Weisburd, D., Farrington, D. P., & Gill, C. (2018). What works in crime prevention and rehabilitation: An assessment of systematic reviews. *Criminology and Public Policy*, 16(2), 415–449.

Williams, P. (1999). Emerging issues: Transnational crime and its control. In G. Newman (Ed.), *Global report on crime and justice*. United Nations Office for Drug Control and Crime Prevention. New York: Oxford University Press.

PART II

OVERVIEW: INTERNATIONAL CRIME

Core International Crimes (As Defined by the Rome Statute, 1998)

After decades of deliberation, agreement was reached among the countries signing the Rome Statute in 1998 on the definition of international crimes that would fall under the jurisdiction of the International Criminal Court. These were considered to be the gravest crimes threatening the peace, security, and well-being of the world. This definition covers specific crimes yet to be agreed upon, but it includes the following four "core" crimes: 1) the crime of genocide; 2) crimes against humanity; 3) war crimes; and 4) the crime of aggression. At the date of writing, more than half of the member states of the United Nations have signed the Rome Statute and have begun to incorporate the crimes that it identifies into domestic legislation. This section provides brief descriptions of the four core crimes as a background to understanding the challenges in enforcing the Rome Statute.

The concepts of genocide, war crimes, and crimes against humanity have undergone considerable transformation since the end of World War II. Whether one examines the main elements of each crime, or the context in which they occur (wartime or peacetime, whether international or not), there is a discernible trend toward strengthening the protection of individuals and groups at the expense of state-centric interpretations of legal obligations (see Chapter 53 by George Andreopoulos).

In respect of the four core crimes, however, there are many difficult questions to be resolved. For genocide, two of the important questions are "At what point do individual killings amount to genocide?" and "Does the crime of genocide always require it to be demonstrated that there was the intention to eradicate a particular ethnic or racial group?" In Chapter 54, Itai Sneh grapples with these and other questions while reviewing the history of genocide and considering recent advocacy and policy guidelines that are influencing emerging international law concerning intervention in acts of genocide. Douglas Irvin-Erickson, in Chapter 55, describes the role of culture in understanding the conflict situations and the various ways of preventing genocide.

War crimes are violations of a special body of criminal law triggered by an armed conflict. They were comprehensively addressed in the Geneva Conventions of 1949, which are still considered the cornerstone of contemporary international humanitarian law. They define as war crimes a wide variety of inhumane acts, including the following examples: a Congolese warlord fighting for control of diamond mines in Ituri forces local children into his army as cannon fodder; Al Qaeda operatives crash airplanes into buildings in New York City with the intention of killing innocent civilians; and American guards sexually humiliate detainees in Iraq. Weisbord and Reyes, in Chapter 56, discuss why these acts fall under the Geneva Conventions and, at least on their face, qualify as war crimes.

According to the Rome Statute, crimes against humanity involve degradation of human dignity and the infliction of violence, in the course of a widespread or systematic attack intentionally directed against a civilian population. In 1976, UN General Assembly recognized the South African Government's policy of Apartheid as a crime against humanity. In Chapter 57, Helen Capstein describes the systematic persecution of black South Africans under Apartheid and shows that this fits the definition of a crime against humanity.

What constitutes the crime of aggression, the "supreme international crime," is still under discussion. In Chapter 58, Stefan Barriga seeks to clarify the definition by considering questions such as: which instances of the use of force would qualify, by their character, gravity, and scale, as "manifest" violations of the UN Charter? Does criminal responsibility for the crime of aggression rest with leaders only? Why should it be possible to hold an individual soldier accountable for war crimes, but not the state for which he is fighting? Anamika Twyman-Ghoshal provides a contemporary criminological perspective of the crimes of the powerful on four key areas (see Chapter 59), including state crimes that constitute some elements of the Rome Statute.

53 Genocide, War Crimes, and Crimes against Humanity

George Andreopoulos

INTRODUCTION

The atrocities that have been associated with genocide, war crimes, and crimes against humanity have been witnessed throughout human history. Whether in times of war, or in times of peace, human wrongs have been committed against fellow human beings, often in a systematic or widespread manner, irrespective of existing moral and legal restraints. While each of these concepts has followed its own trajectory, there are considerable overlaps among them.

WAR CRIMES

"War crimes" refer to serious violations of treaty and customary rules applicable in situations of international and non-international armed conflict. The body of rules and customs that address issues pertaining to armed conflict situations are known as the laws of war, or international humanitarian law (IHL).

The changing nature of many modern-day conflicts (Kaldor, 2007) and the evolving jurisprudence of international tribunals have contributed to some interesting developments in IHL. Due to space limitations, two of these will be highlighted here: 1) the erosion of the distinction between international and non-international armed conflicts; and 2) the reinterpretation and further development of certain basic IHL concepts. Concerning the former, traditionally the rules and regulations covering international armed conflicts (that is, conflicts between two or more states, or between one or more states and a national liberation movement) were more fully developed, and perpetrators of abusive conduct could, and sometimes would, incur criminal responsibility. By contrast, the rules and regulations covering non-international armed conflicts were much less developed and violations committed during such conflicts were not criminalized. Part of the reason for this reconsideration was the sheer brutality exhibited in many modern-day conflicts, in which the primary targets of combatants were the civilian population, as opposed to their armed opponents (Kaldor, 2007). In this context, the international criminalization of internal atrocities, as exemplified in the 1995 appeals chamber decision of the International Criminal Tribunal for the Former Yugoslavia (ICTY) in the *Tadic* case, constituted an important development (Meron, 1998). The decade-long ICRC study on customary international humanitarian law concluded "that many rules of customary international law apply in both international and non-international armed conflicts" (Henckaerts & Doswald-Beck, 2005). Concerning the latter, the evolving jurisprudence of the *ad hoc* tribunals on key concepts like that of protected persons has demonstrated the ability of international courts to maintain conceptual relevance in light of the changing context of warfare. In particular, in the *Celebici* case, the appeals chamber of the ICTY relied on a broad and purposive interpretation of the Geneva Conventions to rule that, given the nature of the conflict, nationality should not be the defining criterion for the protected status of persons; thus Bosnian Serbs, detained in a camp by Bosnian Muslims, should be regarded as "having been in the hands of a party to the conflict [...] of which they were not nationals," and, therefore, as protected persons (*Prosecutor v. Zejnil Delalic, Zdravko Mucic, Hazim Delic, and Esad Landzo*, 2001).

In addition to key conceptual developments, international criminal tribunals have highlighted the importance of relatively neglected offenses committed in conflict situations. A prominent example here relates to the obligation of parties to a conflict to safeguard and protect cultural property as stipulated in several legal instruments, including the 1954 Convention for the Protection of Cultural Property in the Event of Armed Conflict. Individuals responsible for such violations incur international criminal responsibility under treaty and customary international law, irrespective of the nature of the conflict (international or non-international) (O' Keefe, 2006). In the *Strugar* case, the ICTY found the defendant guilty of "destruction and willful damage of cultural property," "caused by the JNA artillery attack against the Old Town of Dubrovnik" (*Prosecutor v. Pavle Strugar*, 2005), a position endorsed by the Appeals Chamber. Moreover, in the *Al Mahdi* case, the International Criminal Court (ICC) found the defendant, a member of Ansar Eddine, guilty of intentionally directing attacks against historic monuments and buildings, including nine mausoleums and one mosque in Timbuktu, Mali (*Prosecutor v. Ahmad Al Faqi Al Mahdi*, 2016).

Crimes against Humanity

Crimes against humanity refer to acts that violate fundamental tenets of human dignity (e.g., murder, extermination, enslavement, deportation); are committed as part of a widespread or systematic attack against (primarily, but not exclusively) any civilian population, which is instigated, condoned, or tolerated by a state or non-state authority; and can be committed during war or peace (Cassese, 2003). Crimes against humanity are usually divided into two categories: "murder-type" offenses, which can be perpetrated against any civilian population, and more targeted "persecution-type" offenses, which can be perpetrated against any collectivity on "political, racial, national, ethnic, cultural, religious, gender [...] or other grounds that are universally recognized as impermissible under international law," as stipulated in the statute of the ICC. The crime of genocide is an offspring of "persecution-type" offenses.

Since its appearance in the charter of the Nuremberg Tribunal, the concept has undergone a considerable evolution. In the charter, the concept was anchored to the other two crimes in the indictment, namely crimes against the peace and war crimes. This meant that only those crimes against humanity that resulted from interstate aggression would be punishable – what came to be known as the "war nexus requirement" (Van Schaack, 1999). Genocide, as noted below, was the first crime against humanity to be de-linked from the war nexus requirement. Recent jurisprudential developments indicate that such de-linking now applies to all crimes against humanity. As the ICTY appeals chamber noted in the *Tadic* case, "it is by now a settled rule of customary international law that crimes against humanity do not require a connection to international armed conflict [...] customary international law may not require a connection between crimes against humanity and any conflict at all" (*Prosecutor v. Tadic*, 1995). Moreover, the term "any" in reference to civilian population means that crimes against humanity could be committed against any civilians irrespective of their defining characteristics. As the ICTY trial chamber noted in the *Vasiljevic* and *Kunarac* cases, a crime against humanity could "in principle be committed against a state's own population if that state participates in the attack" (Mettraux, 2006). In addition, in discussing the policy element in the commission of crimes against humanity, the ICTY ruled in the *Tadic* case that state policy does not constitute any more a requirement for their commission: "In this regard the law in relation to crimes against humanity has developed to take into account forces which, although not those of the legitimate government, have de facto control over, or are able to move freely within, defined territory" (*Prosecutor v. Tadic*, 1995). Thus, crimes against humanity could be committed by non-state entities. Last, but not least, particularly noteworthy is the designation, in the Statute of the ICC, of different forms of sexual violence as crimes against humanity.

GENOCIDE

Genocide is the most heinous crime against humanity. According to the 1948 Convention on the Prevention and Punishment of the Crime of Genocide, genocide refers to "any of the following acts committed with intent to destroy, in whole or in part, a national, ethnical, racial or religious group, as such: (a) Killing members of the group; (b) Causing serious bodily or mental harm to members of the group; (c) Deliberately inflicting on the group conditions of life calculated to bring about its physical destruction in whole or in part; (d) Imposing measures intended to prevent births within the group; (e) Forcibly transferring children of the group to another group." In addition to the commission of genocide, the convention also made conspiracy, incitement, attempt, and complicity in genocide punishable under international law.

What primarily distinguishes genocide from other crimes against humanity is intentionality (Andreopoulos, 1994). Intentionality indicates, in addition to the criminal intent that accompanies the underlying offence (e.g., killing), the existence of an aggravated criminal intention (*dolus specialis*) to commit this offence in order to destroy the targeted group as such (Cassese, 2003). This definition was included, without changes, in the statute of the ICC (Schabas, 2004).

The Genocide Convention has certain noticeable strengths and weaknesses. Among its strengths (this list is by no means exhaustive) are: the delinking of this crime against humanity from the war nexus requirement. In its very first article, the Convention characterizes genocide as a crime under international law, "whether committed in time of peace or in time of war." Second, the provision for the international criminal responsibility of all individuals for the commission of this crime, irrespective of their status (i.e., whether rulers, public officials, or private individuals); third, the prospect for the use of force under international auspices for the prevention and suppression of acts of genocide. Concerning the last issue, it is worth noting that, with Article VIII of the Convention, member states "may call upon the competent organs of the United Nations to take such action under the Charter [...] as they consider appropriate" to deal with situations involving genocide. Since one of these "competent organs" is the Security Council, the international community had at its disposal, ever since the entering into force of the Convention, the option of authorizing coercive measures, including, if necessary, the use of force for humanitarian purposes (prevention and suppression of genocide) (Andreopoulos, 2002). Among its weaknesses (again, the list is not exhaustive) are: 1) the exclusion of certain groups from the list of those groups whose persecution would constitute the crime of genocide (in particular, social and political groups); and 2) its enforcement provisions. Concerning the latter, according to Article VI of the Convention, those responsible for the commission of genocide "shall be tried by a competent tribunal of the State in the territory of which the act was committed," or by an international penal tribunal. This meant that, for a long period of time, there was no credible forum for judicial enforcement. Until the creation of the ICC, the only possible legal venue would have been the courts of the country in which the crime was committed; thus, unless a regime responsible for the commission of genocide were to be overthrown and the successor regime were to embark on legal proceedings against the perpetrators of the predecessor regime (a remote possibility indeed) nothing could be done to punish those responsible for the commission of such acts.

The Genocide Convention was first used in international proceedings in 1993, when the Republic of Bosnia and Herzegovina (RBH) instituted proceedings against the then-Federal Republic of Yugoslavia (FRY) before the International Court of Justice (ICJ). The Republic of Bosnia and Herzegovina argued that former members of the Yugoslav Peoples' Army, together with Serb military and paramilitary forces, had engaged, with the assistance of FRY, in acts that amounted to breaches of the Genocide Convention. This petition was followed by RBH requests for provisional measures that would enable RBH to exercise its inherent right of individual or collective self-defense. After almost 14 years of proceedings, the ICJ eventually rendered its judgment in February 2007. In a decision that stirred great controversy, the Court found that Serbia had not committed genocide, had not conspired to commit genocide, and had not been complicit in genocide, in violation of its obligations under the Convention; however, it also ruled that Serbia had violated the obligation to prevent genocide in respect of the genocide that had occurred in Srebrenica, and had violated its obligations under the Convention by having failed to fully cooperate with the International Criminal Tribunal for the Former Yugoslavia (ICTY) (*Bosnia and Herzegovina v. Serbia and Montenegro* case; ICJ, 2007).

There was a second proceeding before the ICJ concerning the Genocide Convention. The second proceeding was initiated by Croatia in 1999 against the FRY for the alleged acts of JNA and Serb forces in the regions of Eastern Slavonia, Western Slavonia, Banovina/Banija, Kordun, Lika, and Dalmatia. This was followed by a Counter-Memorial submitted by the Republic of Serbia against Croatia for the alleged actions of Croatian forces during Operation "Storm." In a judgment delivered in February 2015, the ICJ rejected both countries' claims, having concluded that, in both cases, genocidal intent had not been demonstrated (*Croatia v. Serbia* case; ICJ, 2015).

With the establishment of the two *ad hoc* tribunals for the Former Yugoslavia (ICTY) and Rwanda (ICTR), the Genocide Convention was finally invoked before international criminal proceedings. The evolving jurisprudence of these two tribunals has been instrumental in the clarification of key elements of the crime of genocide. Concerning "the intent to destroy," for example, the ICTY ruled in the *Krstic* case that the targeting of Bosnian men of military age in Srebrenica constituted such intent, since "this selective destruction of the group would have a lasting impact upon the entire group" (*Prosecutor v. Krstic*, 2001). Moreover, the issue of "direct and public incitement to commit genocide" has received considerable attention in both tribunals due to the role of the media. The media were instrumental in creating and perpetuating a criminal mindset that legitimized the carrying out of mass killings (Mettraux, 2006). In particular, the trial chamber (ICTR) in the *Nahimana* case noted the power of the media to both create and destroy important human values; this power, the Court stated, "comes with great responsibility. Those who control such media are accountable for its consequences" (Mettraux, 2006).

While the ICC has yet to try a defendant for the crime of genocide, there is one case in which such charges are included: that of Omar Hassan Ahmad Al Bashir, president of the Republic of Sudan. The two ICC-issued arrest warrants against him include three counts of genocide allegedly committed against the ethnic groups of Fur, Masalit, and Zaghawa in Darfur. Al Bashir has remained defiant in the face of these warrants and his stance has been supported by the African Union, whose Peace and Security Council claimed that the ICC action was jeopardizing the peace process in Sudan (Rudolph, 2017).

CONCLUSION

There is no doubt that the concepts of genocide, war crimes, and crimes against humanity have undergone considerable transformation since the end of World War II. Whether one examines our understanding of the main elements of each crime, or of the context in which they occur (whether in times of international or non-international war or peace), there is a noticeable trend toward strengthening the protection of individuals and groups at the expense of state-centric interpretations of legal obligations (Andreopoulos, 2014). However, these normative developments also pose the challenge of relevance – namely, the extent to which state practice as manifested during the conduct of hostilities, as opposed to declarations before international fora or during treaty deliberations and the signing of agreements, corresponds to the relevant treaty provisions and the interpretation of these provisions by judicial organs. What is urgently needed at this stage is not further standard setting (although this remains an important task), but better implementation of already-existing standards.

REFERENCES

Andreopoulos, G. J. (Ed.). (1994). *Genocide: Conceptual and historical dimensions.* Philadelphia, PA: University of Pennsylvania Press.

(2002). On the prevention of genocide: Humanitarian intervention and the role of the United Nations. In G. J. Andreopoulos (Ed.), *Concepts and strategies in international human rights.* New York: Peter Lang.

(2014). The turn to "protection": International human rights law/international humanitarian law and the implications of their convergence. In H. F. Carey & S. M. Mitchell (Eds.), *Understanding international law through moot courts.* Lanham, MD: Lexington Books.

Cassese, A. (2003). *International criminal law.* New York: Oxford University Press.

Henckaerts, J.-M. & Doswald-Beck, L. (2005). *Customary international humanitarian law.* Volume I: Rules. Cambridge: Cambridge University Press.

International Court of Justice (ICJ). (2007). Application of the *Convention on the Prevention and Punishment of the Crime of Genocide* (*Bosnia and Herzegovina v. Serbia and Montenegro*) Judgment. (2015). Application *of the Convention on the Prevention and Punishment of the Crime of Genocide* (*Croatia v. Serbia*) Judgment.

Kaldor, M. (2007). *New & old wars: Organized violence in a global era.* Second Edition. Stanford, CA: Stanford University Press.

Meron, T. (1998). *War crimes law comes of age.* New York: Oxford University Press.

Mettraux, G. (2006). *International crimes and the ad hoc tribunals.* New York: Oxford University Press.

O' Keefe, R. (2006). *The protection of cultural property in armed conflict.* New York: Cambridge University Press.

Prosecutor v. Tadic, IT-94–1, Appeals Chamber. (1995). Decision on the defense motion for interlocutory appeal on jurisdiction.

Prosecutor v. Krstic, IT-98–33-T. (2001). Judgment.

Prosecutor v. Dragoljub Kunarac, Radomir Kovac, and Zoran Vukovic, IT-96–23-T & IT-96–23/1-T. (2001). Judgment.

Prosecutor v. Zejnil Delalic, Zdravko Mucic (aka. "Pavo"), Hazim Delic, and Esad Landzo (aka. "Zenga"). Celebici Case. IT-96–21-A. (2001).

Prosecutor v. Mitar Vasiljevic, IT-98–32-T. (2002). Judgment.

Prosecutor v. Ferdinand Nahimana, Jean-Bosco Barayagwiza, and Hassan Ngeze, ICTR-99–52-T. (2003). Judgment and Sentence.

Prosecutor v. Pavle Strugar, IT-01-42-T. (2005, January 31). Judgment.

Prosecutor v. Pavle Strugar, IT-01-42-A. (2008, July 17). Public Judgment.

Rudolph, C. (2017). *Power and principle: The politics of international criminal courts.* Ithaca, NY: Cornell University Press.

Schabas, W. (2004). *An introduction to the international criminal court.* Second Edition. New York: Cambridge University Press.

Situation In The Republic Of Mali. In The Case Of Prosecutor v Ahmad Al Faqi Al Mahdi, ICC-01/12-01/15. (2016, September 27). Public Judgment and Sentence.

Situation in Darfur, Sudan. The Prosecutor v. Omar Hassan Ahmad Al Bashir, ICC-02/05-01/09. Case Information Sheet. (2018, April).

Van Schaack, B. (1999). The definition of crimes against humanity: Resolving the incoherence. *Columbia Journal of Transnational Law*, 37(3), 787–850.

54 History of Genocide

Itai Sneh

INTRODUCTION

In the history of international human rights, "genocide" is a planned and organized attempt to destroy a group of people. Genocide mixes the Greek *genos* (race or kind) and the Latin *cide* (kill). It was coined by Raphael Lemkin (1900–1959), a Polish Jew, in his 1944 book *Axis Rule in Occupied Europe* to describe Nazi Germany's extermination policy, now known as the Holocaust.

Historical studies on the background, scope, prevention, and punishment of genocide explain how racism, the othering of minorities and individuals that do not fit conventional identities, politics, intersectionality, and hatred trigger genocide by addressing ideological, social, cultural, psychological, gender, economic, class, security, territorial, diplomatic, and logistical problems. Tracing the history of genocide, recent advocacy and policy guidelines focus on how to prevent genocide by identifying, reporting, and addressing such issues, then treating them before these problems culminate in mass killings. This chapter covers the definition and history of genocide, developments in researching the field, and its popular-culture presentations.

GENOCIDE: HISTORICAL BACKGROUND

Earlier Genocides

Acts of genocide have reoccurred throughout human history, carried out especially by empires craving territories and obedience. Examples include the Assyrians who, between the ninth and seventh centuries BCE, destroyed and exiled the Arameans, claimed their land, which became Syria, and dispersed Israel's biblical ten tribes. The Babylonians perpetrated similar genocides in the seventh and sixth centuries BCE, famously against the Judeans. The Greeks and the Romans, from the fourth century BCE until the fifth century CE, created, expanded, and preserved their vast empires – employing policy, military, and cultural structures – by committing acts of genocide against ethnic and religious groups that opposed them. Athens destroyed Melos in 416 BCE. After Alexander's conquests in the 330s BCE, Hellenism swept the Near East, assimilating by might, coercion, and will numerous local groups into Greek culture and identity. Outside the West, ancient civilizations in Africa, in the Americas, and in Asia, such as the Aztecs, the Berbers, the Chinese, the Incas, the Nataruk, the Polynesians, the Yanomami, and the Zulus were perpetrators and victims alike.

In medieval times, Muslims committed acts of genocide against nonbelievers, especially in Europe and in the Middle East. Christians reacted in kind with the Crusades, the Inquisitions, and the *Reconquista* of Spain, which also targeted Jews. The Mongols, led by Genghis Khan, perpetrated numerous acts of genocide against multiple populations in Eurasia.

Colonial European empires, especially the Spanish, the French, the British, the Portuguese, and the Belgians, have committed repeated acts of genocide since the sixteenth century against indigenous populations in Africa, the Americas, Asia-Pacific, and even in Ireland. Victims have included the Australian Aboriginals, the Catholic Irish, the Carib, the Incas, the Seminoles, the Sioux, the Mohawks, the Cherokee, the Congolese, the San (Bushmen), the Maoris, and the Tasmanians.

TWENTIETH-CENTURY GENOCIDES

The following are approximate numbers of deaths for a collection of genocides.

- Germans in Southwest Africa, 1904–1905: Avo-Herreros 65,000, and the Namaqua 10,000.
- Armenians killed by Turk Ottomans, 1914–1918: 1.2 million.
- Stalin's Soviets killings of independent farmers ("Kulaks") and Ukrainians ("Holodomor"), 1932–1935: 7 million.
- Chinese killed by Japanese, 1931–1938: 300,000 (memorably the 1937 Rape of Nanking).
- Haitians killed by Dominicans, 1937: 20,000–30,000.
- Germany's Holocaust killing of Jews, 1938–1945: 6 million.
- Stalin's Soviets killings of Chechens and Ingush, Estonians, Kalmyks, Latvians, Lithuanians, Polish, and Tartars during World War II, 1939–1945: at least 500,000 deaths and numerous others deported.
- Cambodians killed by Khmer Rouge Communists ("Killing Fields" era), 1975–1978: 2 million.
- Mostly Serb killings of Croats, and of Muslims in Bosnia-Herzegovina, but also victim groups killing Serbs, 1991–1995: 200,000.
- Mostly Hutu killings of Tootsies in Rwanda, 1994: 800,000.

CONTEMPORARY ISSUES

In the first decades of the twenty-first century, multiple sovereign states and sub-state armed organizations alike have perpetrated acts of genocide, often using social media such as Facebook and Twitter to incite violence. That pattern has prompted responses by the international community that range from attempts of preemption, prevention, and publicity of crimes to covert and overt military retaliation that are tantamount to a humanitarian intervention. The United Nations Security Council is authorized to deploy troops. In such cases, regional associations, such as the African Union, have acted to end atrocities and keep the peace. The emerging international law's duty to prevent genocide and to report and stop actions is a universal advocacy goal. Chronologically, convicted genocide dictatorial criminals of the 1980s and the 1990s, such as Guatemalan Efrain Rios Montt (1926–2018) and Bolivian Luis Garcia Meza (1929–2018), have died of natural causes.

A major area of concern is the Greater Middle East, where civilians and infrastructure are targets. There have been numerous acts of genocide in Afghanistan and Pakistan between warring tribes such as the Pashtuns and the Hazara, in Iraq, and in neighboring Syria, by extreme Muslim groups such as Al Qaeda and ISIS against Christians, Kurds, and Yazidis, but also by national armies such as the Syrian and the Turkish armies against ethnic and religious minorities. In Yemen, warring factions have been credibly accused of perpetrating acts of genocide against each other, with many civilian victims. In Burma, the junta renamed the country Myanmar in 1988. The junta was forced out of political power by the National League for Democracy in the 2015 elections. Nevertheless, the junta kept control over the armed forces. The army used social media to incite violence and perpetrated violent acts of genocide against Rohingya Muslims and Kachine Christians without reprimand from civilian leader Aung San Suu Kyi. Human rights monitors report tens of thousands of deaths, and nearly 1 million who became refugees in nearby countries, mainly Bangladesh (about 700,000), but also in Western countries such as Canada.

Large portions of Africa make it a troubled continent. In the east, the regions included are Darfur and most of South Sudan; in the Great Lakes, the Congo and the Central African Republic. In the west, acts of genocide continue in Mali and in Nigeria. In all these places, inhabitants suffer from territorial, religious, and ethnic conflicts, spurred by Muslim terrorist organizations such as Boko Haram, and heightened by divisive colonial heritage. In Liberia, Leymah Gbowee helped end a civil war in the 2000s through her organization Women of Liberia Mass Action for Peace. She won the 2011 Nobel Prize for Peace. Since 2014, Russian ethnic warfare in Ukraine, expulsions of locals, and the annexation of Crimea may qualify as acts of genocide.

The increasing interest in exploring social, gender, race, and class issues led sophisticated researchers to include in their interests from organizational structures, political leaders, and military elites, common people, the methods used to demonize opponents, and sexual assaults. This new perspective highlights the motives, roles, and reactions of victims, foot soldiers, and ordinary people that murdered, helped, warned against, resisted, or escaped acts of genocide, and responses.

Perpetrators excuse genocide by asserting their groups' right to sovereignty, ideology, or security. Official and dehumanizing terms used to justify genocide include "vigilante justice," "counter-insurgency," "transfer," "ethnic cleansing," "purification," and "decolonization." How many must die violently for "humanitarian tragedy," "mass murders," "massacres," and "atrocities," to become legally charged "war crimes," and "crimes against humanity," then "genocide"?

RESEARCH AND ADVOCACY AGENDA

Academic sensitivity to genocidal actions, and understanding of their background and impact, is growing worldwide. Books, articles, literature, art works, exhibitions, museums, workshops, conferences, lectures, courses, programs, majors, and centers educating the public about genocide are rising in quantity and in quality. Scholars confront ethical choices by translating the moral absolutes of good and bad into prescribing rehabilitation and reconstruction. Conceptual questions include: when genocide occurs, does the ultimate result indicate intention? When do individual killings amount to genocide? What are the long-term psychological results due to suffering from or witnessing acts of genocide? A new facet of genetics, known as epigenesis, inquires whether there are consequences to descendants from the pain and trauma associated with enduring genocide.

The study of genocide encompasses existing geographic designations (such as Europe), national identities (such as Ukrainian), ethnic distinctions (such as Jewish), and functional disciplines (such as law, sociology, forensic and clinical psychology, medicine, criminology, criminal justice, ethnography, cultural anthropology, gender studies, education, media and communications, political science, international relations, strategic studies, comparative literature, theology, philosophy, economics, demographics, and, regrettably, genetics, biology, and anatomy), together with emerging fields (such as human rights, transnational justice, conflict resolution, and genealogy).

Holocaust scholars reconstruct acts of genocide by analyzing personal testaments and written submissions by eyewitnesses to understand the context, probing for details, names, and numbers. They aim for humanity's collective memory, justice for dead and living victims, shaming of the culprits, warning of the potential for future atrocities, and encouragement of preventive activism. Research explored the plight of refugees, displaced persons, and their descendants. The role of Nazi allies such as Ukrainians and collaborators among the French and the Dutch were more closely scrutinized.

The collective memory and the political agenda of groups such as Native Americans, descendants of African slaves, and other forcibly removed indigenous peoples in Australia and Latin America demand exposure and cry for justice. This shows increased recognition of the connection between genocides, diasporic experience, and the human cost of large-scale displacement. Consistent coverage, with ample photos of death and destruction, by the international media of the wars and massacres in Yugoslavia, Rwanda, Central America, and East Timor increased public awareness worldwide.

The Belgian subjugation of the Congo in the nineteenth century murdered many in the Congo and led to acts of genocide in neighboring Rwanda in the twentieth century. Demands for German reparations for victims of its crimes in Namibia are growing, but are highly politicized, and divisive, in both countries.

Scholarship had focused on states during international or civil wars in the twentieth century. Three major trends inform contemporary genocide studies. One pedagogic and defensive trend stresses the stages of genocide, the responsibility to provide curricula about past and potential acts of genocide, the need to inform the public to protect vulnerable communities, and the need to educate people whose lives have been disrupted by acts of genocide by providing safe schools, to advocate for a duty or a responsibility to report, prevent, and perhaps even pre-empt, through humanitarian interventions. Another trend is the increased discussion of the aftermath of genocide, and how to reconstruct, rehabilitate, and heal societies. Should truth and reconciliation commissions be mixed with foreign guidance and international aid? Scholars continually re-evaluate the tensions between justice and legality among civilized members in the "community of nations."

Recently, personal stories and memoirs by and of family members highlight the horrors witnessed by their kin and the multiple consequences of genocides. Books include Grigoris Balakian's *Armenian Golgotha*, Daniel Mendelsohn's *The Lost: A Search for Six of Six Million*, and Louise Mushikiwabo and Jack Kramer's *Rwanda Means the Universe: A Native's Memoir of Blood and Bloodlines.*

Popular movies on genocide blend reality with fiction, pain with absurdity. In 1984, *The Killing Fields* addressed Cambodia. In 1993, *Schindler's List* comforted audiences with the saving of select Jews by a German industrialist during the Holocaust. In 1997, *Life is Beautiful* humorously celebrated survival over surrender by an Italian Jew. In 1999, *The Specialist*, on Adolph Eichman's trial in Jerusalem, caused controversy by enhancing Hannah Arendt's "banality of evil" or "cog in the machine" paradigm that arguably exculpated bureaucrats and soldiers alike. In 2004, *Hotel Rwanda* realistically portrayed survival amid horror. In 2004, the Austrian-German *Downfall* presented the Nazis' final days in a humane way. In 2008, *Valkyrie* presented elite Nazis in an anti-Hitler, positive light, and *The Reader* arguably did so for common perpetrators. In 2009, *Inglourious Basterds* used a Western science-fiction format to allow the Jews acts of revenge against their former tormentors.

CONCLUSION

After World War II, especially the Holocaust, the United Nations proclaimed the 1948 Convention on the Prevention and Punishment of the Crime of Genocide. The definition of genocide that the UN proposed included the destruction of national, ethnical, racial, and religious groups that were the traditional victims. The definition's strength is in the pioneering recognition of genocide as a crime in international law, increasing the likelihood of consequences such as prosecutions for these crimes, but its scope betrays its inadequacy.

The UN Security Council examines and confronts acts of genocide. The authoritarian states of China and Russia, former colonial empires with residual interests, namely the French and the British, and the USA, with a dubious past treatment of natives and Africans slaves, may wield veto power in the Security Council if they, or their allies, are culprits. This veto power is detrimental to intervention efforts not only by the UN but also by regional powers, continental associations, and nongovernmental organizations (NGOs), especially Genocide Watch, Human Rights Watch, Amnesty International, and Human Rights First. The Security Council veto power is also detrimental to efforts by researchers and grassroots advocates who risk their lives to prevent and to stop genocide. These individuals and groups provide the UN, policy makers, and the public with knowledge and tools for immediate and effective action, although results are mixed.

However, the danger of additional acts of genocide, and the need to draw lessons from history, persists. Scholars and NGOs repeatedly analyze past and ongoing acts of genocide. The duty to prevent or intervene during acts of genocide is emerging in international law. Growing genocide scholarship blends prevention, punishment of perpetrators, and acknowledgment of heroism. Studies have advanced beyond describing graphic details into exploring contexts and consequences.

FURTHER READING

Applebaum, A. (2017). *Red famine: Stalin's war on Ukraine.* New York: Doubleday.
Bartov, O. (2003). *Germany's war and the Holocaust: Disputed histories.* Ithaca, NY and London: Cornell University Press.

Bloxham, D. (2001). *Genocide on trial: War crimes trials and the formation of Holocaust history and memory.* Oxford: Oxford University Press.

Gellately, R. & Kiernan, B. (Eds.). (2003). *The specter of genocide: Mass murder in historical perspective.* Cambridge: Cambridge University Press.

Greenhill, K. & Krause, P. (2018). *Coercion: The power to hurt in international politics.* New York: Oxford University Press.

Hafetz, J. (2018). *Punishing atrocities through a fair trial: International criminal law from Nuremberg to the age of global terrorism.* Cambridge: Cambridge University Press.

Heberer, P & Jürgen, M. (Eds.). (2008). *Atrocities on trial: Historical perspectives on the politics of prosecuting war crimes.* Published in association with the United States Holocaust Memorial Museum. Lincoln, NE: Lincoln University of Nebraska Press.

Hornstein, S. & Florence, J. (Eds.). (2003). *Image and remembrance: Representation and the Holocaust.* Bloomington, IN: Indiana University Press.

Lang, B. (2017). *Genocide: The act as idea.* Philadelphia, PA: University of Pennsylvania Press.

Powers, S. (2002). *A problem from Hell: America and the age of genocide.* New York: Basic Books.

Stanton, G. (n.d.) The eight stages of genocide. Retrieved from www.tamilnation.org/indictment/eight_stages_of_genocide.htm.

Sarkin, J. (2009). *Colonial genocide and reparations claims in the 21st century: The socio-legal context of claims under international law by the Herero against Germany for genocide in Namibia, 1904–1908.* Westport, CT: Praeger Security International.

55 Understanding Culture and Conflict in Preventing Genocide

Douglas Irvin-Erickson

INTRODUCTION

In the late 1990s, genocide studies debated the proposition that particular cultures were inherently genocidal. This position was handily rejected, as the comparative study of genocide demonstrated that particular cultures played no significant causal role in the commission of genocide (Rummel, 1994). Still, portrayals of genocide in scholarship, the media, and popular discourses – from the Rwandan genocide in 1994 to the case of the Rohingya in Rakhine State in Myanmar in 2018 – often present genocide as something only committed by illiberal and authoritarian regimes, or that only occurs in failed or weak states or in societies overcome with atavistic fears and a culturally determined disregard for life. Indeed, there is a tendency in Western societies to view the violence of liberal democracies as "legitimate," and to not interpret such violence as genocidal, while the violence committed in the name of non-Western political ideologies is condemned (Irvin-Erickson, Hinton, & La Pointe, 2014).

All societies have the capacity for genocide; no "culture" is immune from genocide, and genocide has been closely intertwined with modernity and democracy. This is not to say that each case of genocide is not deeply symbolic and embodies a cultural patterning. While we can say that culture and cultural knowledge does not "cause" genocide, we can demonstrate that cultural knowledge structures mass violence within particular ethnohistorical contexts (Hinton, 2002). Nor should the importance of good governance and democratic values be discounted. Human rights, governance, and local peace building are important aspects of global efforts to prevent genocide and other mass atrocities. Still, in the absence of robust systems of global governance and international criminal justice, understanding the local dynamics of conflict and violence is crucial to genocide prevention efforts.

BACKGROUND: CULTURE, GENOCIDE, AND GENOCIDE PREVENTION

Racial, ethnic, national, and religious groups might be the only groups that enjoy legal protective status under the UN Genocide Convention, but there is no reason why the intentional destruction of any social group should not qualify as genocidal. For example, Genocide Watch, which operationalizes Gregory Stanton's ten stages of genocide, categorizes the Philippines as being in the seventh stage of genocide – preparation – with the regime of President Rodrigo Duterte identifying drug addicts and opponents of the government as distinct social groups, and preparing to exterminate these two groups.[1] In the case of the Holocaust, the Nazi attempt to exterminate the disabled and homosexuals was just as much an attempt to annihilate a social group that had been marked as different, racially impure, and socially parasitic as the Nazi attempt to destroy the Jews. The question for understanding the role of culture in the commission and prevention of genocide, therefore, is not whether a culture predetermines genocidal violence. Rather, the better question is: what causes a society to categorize human beings into groups whose identities are believed to be mutually exclusive, then mark a category of people as different and try to eradicate that group? And, finally, what kinds of interventions can be undertaken to prevent intergroup conflicts from escalating into genocide?

Box 55.1. Gregory Stanton's Ten Stages of Genocide

1. classification
2. symbolization
3. discrimination
4. dehumanization
5. organization
6. polarization
7. preparation
8. persecution
9. extermination
10. denial

The distinction of stages has implications for genocide prevention. When we recognize situations at an early stage, the international community can help protect civilians and vulnerable populations from atrocities before they escalate further. For a more detailed look at the operationalization of mass atrocity prevention, see Scott Straus's *Foundations of Genocide and Mass Atrocity Prevention*, published in 2016 by the United States Holocaust Memorial Museum.

Source: http://genocidewatch.net

All cases of genocide exhibit precursors, such as socioeconomic upheavals, polarized social divisions, structural social and economic changes, and ideological manipulations by elites (Fein, 1993; Harff & Gurr, 1988). These precursors increase the saliency of socially based hatred, fear, resentment, threat perceptions, group solidarity, and the desire to protect social status and social positions. Genocide becomes increasingly likely as social divisions deepen, often through segregation, differential legal statuses, and sociocultural hierarchies that are connected to efforts to dominate or monopolize access to social, political, educational, and economic opportunities for certain groups. Genocide, therefore, is not about the identity of groups, but the implications of identities in terms of access to social, political, economic, or cultural resources and opportunities. Oftentimes, regimes and elites have a vested interest in deepening or reifying these categories. In such cases, perpetrator regimes often introduce

[1] See Genocide Watch, www.genocidewatch.com/Philippines.

legislation and impose policies that further polarize divisions, or disseminate messages of hate and group vilification (Hinton, 2002). Such acts draw upon locally salient idioms and cultural models to heighten and reify "us/them" dichotomies, and legitimize acts of suppression and violence against victim groups who are characterized as subhuman, outsiders, parasitic, or dangerous to the well-being of the perpetrator group.

Leaders of genocidal programs often present the extermination of a group as a form of self-defense, as typified by genocides in Rwanda and Burundi in the 1990s. Other times, genocidal acts are committed under the guise of waging counter-insurgency, if there is an ongoing armed conflict or civil war, such as the genocides in Argentina in the late 1970s and Guatemala in the early 1980s. Political processes such as peace accords or elections that threaten the dominance of the genocidal group may trigger genocide as a way for groups to retain control of a country or preserve the social and political order from which the group derives its dominance. These dynamics reveal that ancient hatreds, primordial animosities, and identity-group incompatibilities are not the causes of intergroup conflict and violence, but are exploited to justify persecution and extermination.

Discrimination, Persecution, and the Genocidal Process

Genocide is a dynamic social process (Rosenberg, 2012). The escalation of group conflicts that leads to genocide is not linear, but genocide is predictable and preventable. This escalation begins with social classification and symbolization, as societies manufacture differences between groups, assign individuals to groups, and symbolically distinguish groups as distinct (Stanton, 2016). Deeply divided societies, or societies experiencing intractable conflicts and deeply rooted conflicts, are often bipolar societies that lack mixed categories between social groups, which makes it easier to vilify or scapegoat particular groups. Discrimination – through the law, tradition, or political power – denies the rights of people from certain groups and deprives less-powerful groups of access to resources and opportunities. Leaders who espouse exclusionary ideologies are often charismatic, expressing and fueling the social resentments of their followers, and attracting widespread social support by giving salience to, and reifying, social classifications and group symbolisms that cast the "Other" as subhuman. In addition, extremist groups often seek to polarize a society by forbidding social interaction between groups, intimidating and silencing the center, or killing or repressing moderates whose very moderation and tolerance invalidates the belief that group membership is mutually exclusive and the victims are subhuman. Acts that target the leaders of victims groups are often accompanied or followed by persecution, which in some cases involves identifying and separating populations, drawing up death lists and carrying out arbitrary arrests and executions, expropriating property, segregating victims, or confining victims and depriving them of resources (Stanton, 2016).

The prevention of genocide requires the development of universalistic institutions that transcend divisions, promote an understanding of group identities that are not mutually exclusive, and promote tolerance and understanding. Outlawing discrimination, and promoting the political and economic empowerment for all groups, are effective means for the early prevention of genocide. Hate symbols and hate speech can also be legally forbidden but must be accompanied by the social enforcement of these values. Finally, persecution often escalates in the absence of resistance or condemnation. The prevention of genocide, therefore, requires protection for moderate leaders and vulnerable communities, the strengthening of human rights, and assistance to human rights groups combating persecution (Stanton, 2016).

DISCUSSION: GENOCIDE PREVENTION AND UPSTREAMING PREVENTION

International and local condemnations, sanctions, prosecutions, and interventions are important prevention tools, and can deter individuals who are the agents of genocide. Efforts to prevent mass-atrocity crimes, including genocide and crimes against humanity (Scheffer, 2006), rely on international human rights law, which encompasses international and regional human rights treaties, specialized UN agencies, and international or regional courts. International humanitarian law is likewise an important part of the global architecture for preventing genocide, establishing obligations for states, armed groups, and individuals in times of armed conflict, and governing the treatment of civilians and noncombatants. The most important sources of international humanitarian law for genocide prevention efforts are the Geneva Conventions of 1949 and the three Optional Protocols, the case law of the International Military Tribunal at Nuremberg, the International Criminal Tribunal for Rwanda, the International Criminal Tribunal for the Former Yugoslavia, and the Rome Statute of the International Criminal Court (Straus, 2016).

The Responsibility to Protect (R2P) is the only full international policy framework for mass-atrocity prevention. A 2009 Secretary-General report, *Implementing the Responsibility to Protect*, established three pillars of R2P. The first assigned states the primary responsibility for protecting populations from mass atrocities (a crafty turn of diplomatic language, given that state actors have been the primary perpetrators of mass atrocities). The second pillar established that the UN, UN member states, and regional organizations had an obligation to help states develop the capacity to protect their populations from mass atrocities. The third pillar called on the international community to take appropriate and decisive collective action through the Security Council to protect populations, including through the use of force.

The credibility of R2P suffered in 2013 when the USA was widely viewed as invoking R2P as an excuse for a NATO intervention in Libya to overthrow the Kaddafi regime. What is more, despite a growing number of successful international prosecutions of genocide and crimes against humanity, it does not appear that international law has prevented future mass atrocities. In the last five years, the world has witnessed ISIS genocides in Syria and Iraq, the genocide against the Rohingya in Rakhine State in Myanmar, genocide in South Sudan, and crimes against humanity committed by the governments of Syria with Russian and Iranian support and by the government of Yemen with the support of Saudi Arabia and the USA, to name only a few. In all of these cases, efforts to prevent and prosecute mass-atrocity crimes fail when the states are powerful actors in international affairs, or when the governments have powerful international benefactors. Efforts to prosecute mass atrocities (in Rwanda, the former Yugoslavia, Cambodia, and Argentina) have succeeded, meanwhile, when the genocidal regime collapsed, exposing leaders to prosecution.

At the national level, within the last five years, a number of governments – such as the USA, Switzerland, Kenya, and Uganda, among others – have created national-level bodies dedicated to mass-atrocity prevention. These national-level bodies in African countries have played constructive roles in de-escalating conflicts at the local level and preventing the escalation of genocidal violence. Yet, to this point, none of the national-level atrocity prevention bodies, with the exception of Switzerland, have been permanently institutionalized, which prevents efforts to mainstream atrocity prevention across their respective governments' domestic or foreign policy (Finkel, 2018).

Given that mass atrocities occur in the context of complex domestic and international politics, where states tend to pursue their own interests above humanitarian ideals, the majority of atrocity prevention work has taken place at the local level. Genocide and mass-atrocity prevention has, therefore, seen a movement to "upstream" prevention – which refers to efforts to prevent genocide and mass atrocities before they become evident (Manojlovic, Ogata, & Bartoli, 2016). Strong arguments can be made that atrocity prevention, strictly speaking, should be concerned only with the prevention, suppression, and prosecution of imminent mass-atrocity crimes, not the de-escalation of conflict dynamics that lead to mass-atrocity crimes, which is the domain of concern for upstream prevention efforts – and that everything else should be called peace building or conflict resolution (Luck, 2018). Still, upstreaming and localizing atrocity prevention has meant that practitioners have had to engage in local conflicts, immerse themselves in the communities in which they are working, speak local languages, and familiarize themselves with local customs, politics, and governance. This has also meant that the majority of the world's genocide prevention work has been undertaken by local actors working within their own communities, sometimes with the support of IOs and NGOs, but often not. Indeed, this work looks more like the work undertaken by conflict resolution, peace building, and human rights advocacy practitioners, rather than the work of international criminal justice or international affairs.

CONCLUSION

Communities that resist violence during escalating intergroup conflicts often share several traits, namely: community cohesion, ethical leadership, and communication across identity-group divides, and a willingness and ability to engage with armed groups (Anderson & Wallace, 2013). In such communities, international involvement in conflict usually plays no significant role in the community's ability to avoid community and identity-based violence. This would suggest that, in efforts to prevent genocide, "local peacebuilding can be most effective upstream, before violence erupts, and in the aftermath and recovery to break cycles of violence," and if "external actors may need to intervene [...] they should do so [...] in ways that re-enforce local leadership for peace and strengthen local resilience against violence" (Moix, 2016, p. 64). Indeed, in the absence of a robust international criminal justice regime, international pressure, local moral resistance, global and local political and religious responses, and efforts to bridge social divides and lessen the implications of identity in terms of access to resources and opportunities are all necessary for preventing genocide (Hinton, 2002; Kuper, 1981).

REFERENCES

Anderson, M. B. & Wallace, M. (2013). *Opting out of war: Strategies to prevent violent conflict.* London: Lynne Rienner.
Fein, H. (1993). *Genocide: A sociological perspective.* London: Sage.

Finkel, J. P. (Ed.). (2018). Global approaches to atrocity prevention: Theory, practice, and the state of the field. [Special issue] *Genocide Studies and Prevention*, 11(3), 4.

Harff, B. & Gurr, T. (1988). Toward empirical theory of genocides and politicides: Identification and measurement of cases since 1945. *International Studies Quarterly*, 32(3), 359–371.

Hinton, A. L. (Ed). (2002). *Annihilating difference: The anthropology of genocide*. Berkeley, CA: University of California Press.

Irvin-Erickson, D., La Pointe, T., & Hinton, A. L. (2014). Hidden genocides: Power, knowledge, memory. In A. L. Hinton, T. La Pointe, & D. Irvin-Erickson (Eds.), *Hidden genocides: Power, knowledge, memory* (pp. 1–18). New Brunswick, NJ: Rutgers University Press.

Kuper, L. (1981). *Genocide: Its political use in the twentieth century*. New Haven, CT: Yale University Press.

Luck, E. C. (2018). Why the United Nations underperforms at preventing mass atrocities. *Genocide Studies and Prevention*, 11(3), 32–47.

Manojlovic, B., Ogata, T., & Bartoli, A. (Eds.). (2016). Towards the prevention of genocide. [Special issue] *Genocide Studies and Prevention*, 9(3), 4–12.

Moix, B. (2016) Turning atrocity prevention inside-out: Community-based approaches to preventing, protecting, and recovering from mass violence. *Genocide Studies and Prevention*, 9(3), 59–69.

Rosenberg, S. (2012). Genocide is a process, not an event. *Genocide Studies and Prevention*, 7(1), 16–24.

Rummel, R. J. (1994). *Death by government*. New Brunswick, NJ: Transaction.

Scheffer, D. (2006). Genocide and atrocity crimes. *Genocide Studies and Prevention*, 1(3), 229–250.

Stanton, G. (2016). The ten stages of genocide. *Genocide Watch*. Retrieved from http://genocidewatch.net/genocide-2/8-stages-of-genocide/.

Straus, S. (2016). *Foundations of genocide and mass atrocity prevention*. Washington, DC: The United States Holocaust Memorial Museum.

FURTHER READING

Bellamy, A. J. & Dunne, T. (Eds.). (2016). *The Oxford handbook of the responsibility to protect*. Oxford: Oxford University Press.

Waller, J. (2016). *Confronting evil: Engaging our responsibility to prevent genocide*. Oxford: Oxford University Press.

56 War Crimes

Noah Weisbord and Carla L. Reyes

INTRODUCTION

War crimes are violations of a special body of criminal law triggered by an armed conflict. The most serious violations of the patchwork of international treaties and customs that make up the laws of war – violations such as torture, rape, and pillage during wartime – have been criminalized and offenders can be prosecuted in national or international courts with jurisdiction. Humanitarian lawyers, lawyers who specialize in the laws of war, attempt to deploy laws to moderate the behavior of fighters and their leaders and to reduce human suffering. This, at least, is the ideal. The notion that law can and should permeate war is, however, intensely problematic.

Humanitarian law, which at first appears to be a principled constraint on war, is intricately entwined with it. The involvement of law and lawyers with the dominating, destructive, and coercive aims of war lends warmaking the legitimacy of the law and this has on-the-ground implications. Humanitarian law's contradictions and ambiguities, meanwhile, create opportunities for strategic lawyering. Consequently, humanitarian law exists as a humanizing influence on warfare, but also as an important zone of contestation where the courtroom, a multi-lateral treaty negotiation, or the media become the battlefield.

THE LAW OF WAR: AN INTRODUCTORY HISTORICAL OVERVIEW

Ancient History

The laws and traditions of war in ancient times are an early lesson about the moral dangers – and strategic possibilities – of entwining law and war. The Code of Manu (350–283 BC), the Hindu text that became the basis of the Indian caste system, contained rules that might be described as concerned with war crimes. For example, it instructs that noncombatants and warriors who surrender must never be killed. According to the German philosopher Friedrich Nietzsche, writing 2,000 years later, The Code of Manu was a positive manifestation of the will to power based on the "Holy Lie" of religious authority (Nietzsche, 1988, p. 239) Even today, it is difficult to know whether the law of war moderates violence, increases its efficiency, or both.

Eighteenth- and Nineteenth-Century Precursors

The modern war crimes regime is often traced to the 1859 Battle of Solferino and the legal innovation of the Swiss businessman Henry Dunant, who witnessed the carnage. In *A Memory of Solferino* (1862), Dunant proposed an international congress where sovereigns would agree to a war convention with shared rules applicable to all parties. This innovation brought the battle, metaphorically, to the halls of Geneva and The Hague, where diplomatic delegations vied to draft humanitarian rules that would offer them a military advantage over their adversaries.

As Dunant labored to finish his book, Francis Leiber, an American professor, was drafting General Orders No. 100, another precursor to the modern war crimes regime. The Leiber Code, as General Orders No. 100 came to be known, was intended to limit the destruction wrought by the armies of the USA to acts deemed strictly necessary to accomplish military goals. Confederate Secretary of War James Seddon, however, denounced the code as a tool of "military despotism [allowing] a barbarous system of warfare under the pretext of military necessity." "It is in this code of military necessity," argued Seddon, "that the acts of atrocity and violence which have been committed by the officers of the United States and have shocked the moral sense of civilized nations are to find an apology and defense" (Seddon, June 24, 1863, p. 123).

Birth of the Modern War Crimes Regime

The proposal for the first The Hague Convention in 1899, where the modern international laws of war were born, came from Russian Czar Nicholas II, who called for a legal regime "insuring to all peoples the benefits of a real and durable peace, and, above all putting an end to the progressive development of armaments." Other European leaders at the time suspected that the proposal was a "ruse to enlist public opinion to support measures that would help Russia overcome its military weakness" (Jochnick & Normand, 1994, pp. 69–70).

World War I broke out in 1914 and tested the law of war with new forms of weaponry and tactics. The war's end galvanized a fresh round of humanitarian law conventions addressing gas and bacteriological warfare, protection for the wounded and the sick, and the treatment of prisoners of war. These interwar agreements required states to enact national legislation through which individual offenders would be punished, while holding states accountable in the international realm for failure to prevent or punish violations by individuals.

The Nuremberg Trial

International humanitarian law survived the industrialized barbarity of World War II, in large part, through the judgment of the International Military Tribunal at Nuremberg. Following the Allied victory, the German leaders were held criminally accountable and punished for violations of The Hague and Geneva Conventions, with the Nuremberg court famously holding, "crimes against international law are committed by men, not by abstract entities." This decision began a transformative shift in the subject of international law of war from the state to the individual that only culminated at the end of the Cold War.

Cold War-Era Lawfare

Cold War-era (1945–1991) international law was shaped by the epochal conflict between American and Soviet superpowers to determine the ideological basis of the international system – liberal or communist. The Soviets and the Americans each supported international laws of war that, first and foremost, advanced their geo-strategic agendas.

The Soviet Union, which aimed to escalate wars of national liberation and thereby loosen the grip of the West (i.e., the USA and its allies) on its colonies, challenged the legitimacy of The Hague Conventions, asking,

> can we confine a sacred people's war against an aggressor and enslaver, a heroic struggle of millions of people for their country's independence, for its national culture, for its right to exist, can we confine this war with the strict bounds of the Hague rules, which were calculated for wars of a different type and for a totally different international situation? (Ginsburgs, 1964, pp. 934–935)

US President Ronald Reagan, for his part, refused to send Protocol I of the 1977 Geneva Conventions to the Senate for ratification, arguing that it "would give special status to 'wars of national liberation' […] [W]e must not, and need not, give recognition and protection to terrorist groups as a price for progress in humanitarian law" (Office of the President, January 29, 1987).

The Post-Cold War Moment

The 1990s was a period punctuated by internal armed conflicts occurring in the power vacuum left by the Soviet Union and not yet filled by the Western liberal democracies. Instead of preventing the massive violations of international humanitarian law arising out of sectarian conflicts in the former Yugoslavia, Rwanda, and elsewhere, the liberal democracies, through the UN Security Council, established a number of *ad hoc* international war crimes tribunals to punish them. When diplomatic delegations met in Rome in 1998 to create a permanent international criminal court with global reach, many of the great powers – Russia, China, India, the USA – chose not to subject themselves to its jurisdiction. Nonetheless, the statute establishing the International Criminal Court was adopted and the majority of the world's states have now ratified it.

The Challenge of 9/11 to the Laws of War

Debates raged in the USA and abroad over the characterization of the 9/11 attacks under the laws of war and the bounds of the legally justified response. Politicians, pundits, and legal scholars debated the legal status of Al Qaeda fighters (did they qualify for the protections offered by the Geneva Conventions?), the most appropriate forum for prosecuting terror suspects (international, military, or domestic tribunal?), and the relevance of the laws of war generally in the age of terror (were they obsolete?).

MAJOR CONCEPTS: CATEGORIES OF WAR CRIMES

War crimes are conventionally divided into four categories: use of prohibited weapons, engaging in prohibited means of combat, altering the status of particular civilians, and targeting crimes. The first category of war crimes aims to protect both combatants and noncombatants by prohibiting the use of weapons that "are of a nature to cause superfluous injury or unnecessary suffering or which are inherently indiscriminate." The ICC Statute, for example, bans poisoned weapons, asphyxiating gases, and bullets that expand when they hit.

As to the second category, the ICC Statute contains a hodgepodge list of prohibited means of combat. These proscribed means include, but are not limited to, killing or wounding a combatant who has laid down his arms, pillaging, sexual violence, and using civilians as human shields.

The third category of war crimes, altering the status of particular civilians during war, developed to prevent warring parties from using tactics that "are capable of destroying the fabric of particular nations or communities" (Bantekas & Nash, 2007, p. 120). It is a war crime, for example, to compel civilians of the enemy nation to take part in hostilities against their own country.

Targeting crimes involve violations of the principle that participants in armed conflict may only lawfully target military combatants and objects, and must refrain from targeting civilians and civilian objects. The law regulating targeting crimes is intricately linked to another key concept: collateral damage (discussed below).

Trends

SEXUAL VIOLENCE AS A WAR CRIME

Until the 1990s, rape was often explicitly absent from international war crimes treaties. According to Theodore Meron, former President of the International Criminal Tribunal for the Former Yugoslavia, the "abuse of thousands of women in the territory of former Yugoslavia was needed to shock the international community into re-thinking the prohibition of rape as a crime under the laws of war" (1993, p. 425). The ICTY, in the *Celebici*, *Furundzija*, and *Kunarac* cases, found that because rape and other sexual violence constitute torture, it amounts to a grave breach of the Geneva Conventions and is punishable as a war crime and as a crime against humanity. Although these decisions have been applauded as a step forward in international gender jurisprudence, they have also been criticized for identifying women, first and foremost, as victims of war and stripping them of political agency (Engle, 2005, p. 812).

LAWFARE

US Airforce General Charles J. Dunlap Jr. (2001) defines lawfare as "the use of law as a weapon of war," and describes it as "the newest feature of 21st century combat." He warns that, "there is disturbing evidence that the rule of law is being hijacked into just another way of fighting (lawfare), to the detriment of humanitarian values as well as the law itself" (p. 2). When insurgents in Iraq use human shields to deter law-abiding American soldiers from firing upon them, or hide weapons in mosques that are protected under the laws of war, they are using the law as a strategic weapon. The challenge to humanitarians is to protect law from being hijacked by warring parties for strategic ends and, ultimately, to ensure that it mitigates harm to civilians rather than exacerbating it.

COLLATERAL DAMAGE (NECESSITY, PROPORTIONALITY, AND DISTINCTION)

The US Department of Defense defines collateral damage as "[u]nintentional or incidental injury or damage to persons or objects that would not be lawful military targets in the circumstances ruling at the time." The term collateral damage derives from the IHL principles of necessity, proportionality, and distinction, summed up by ICC Prosecutor Luis Moreno Ocampo in his 2006 open letter responding to allegations of war crimes in Iraq.

> [T]he death of civilians during an armed conflict, no matter how grave and regrettable, does not in itself constitute a war crime. International humanitarian law and the Rome Statute permit belligerents to carry out proportionate attacks against military objectives, even when it is known that some civilian deaths or injuries will occur. A crime occurs if there is an intentional attack directed against civilians (principle of distinction) [...] or an attack is launched on a military objective in the knowledge that the incidental civilian injuries would be clearly excessive in relation to the anticipated military advantage (principle of proportionality). (International Criminal Court Office of the Prosecutor, 2006, pp. 4–5).

Legal arguments over the characterization of civilian deaths as collateral damage or war crimes arise because the terms "necessity" and "proportionality" are dynamic, changing throughout an armed conflict. The malleability of these principles creates opportunities for strategic lawyering and lawfare and recalls Confederate Secretary of War James Seddon's warning that the Leiber Code has served as "an apology and defense" for acts of atrocity.

CONCLUSIONS

The history of international humanitarian law might be – and has been (Bassiouni, 2008, pp. 269–280) – told as a story of barbarity to civilization whereby enlightened individuals recognize the awfulness of war and, against adversity, manage to curtail it with law. This history has also been presented as a tragedy where reason struggles to control violence and fails (Provost, 2002). This chapter, by contrast, has attempted to identify the tensions between proscription and prescription, humanitarianism and patriotism, and law and politics, which have run deep through the field of humanitarian law from its early inception. The following chapter questions are an opportunity to consider these historic tensions in relation to current events.

REFERENCES

Bantekas, I. & Nash, S. (2007). *International criminal law*. Third Edition. London: Routledge-Cavendish,
Bassiouni, M. C. (2008). *International criminal law: Sources, subjects & contents*. Third Edition. Leiden: Martinus Nijhoff Publishers.
Dunlap Jr., C. J. (2001). *Law and military interventions: Preserving humanitarian values in 21st century conflicts*. Humanitarian Challenges in Military Intervention Conference. Washington, DC: Carr Center for Human Rights Policy, Kennedy School of Government, Harvard University.
Engle, K. (2005). Feminism and its (dis) contents: Criminalizing wartime rape in Bosnia and Herzegovina. *American Journal of International Law*, 99, 779–815.
Ginsburgs, G. (1964) Wars of national liberation and the modern law of nations: The Soviet thesis. *Law and Contemporary Problems*, 29, 910–942.

International Criminal Court Office of the Prosecutor. (2006). Open letter from Chief Prosecutor Luis Moreno Ocampo. Retrieved from www2.icc-cpi.int/NR/rdonlyres/-F596D08D-D810–43A2–99BB-B899B9C5BCD2/277422/OTP_letter_to_senders_re-_Iraq_9_February_2006.pdf.

Jochnick, C. & Normand, R. (1994). The legitimization of violence: A critical history of the laws of war. *Harvard International Law Journal*, 35(1), 49–96.

Lieber, F. (1983). *Lieber's Code and the law of war*. Chicago: Precedent Publishing, Inc.

Meron, T. (1993). Rape as a crime under international humanitarian law. *American Journal of International Law*, 87(3), 424–428.

Office of the President. (1987, January 29). *Message to the Senate transmitting a Protocol to the 1949 Geneva Conventions*. Retrieved from www.reagan.utexas.edu/archives/sp-eeches/1987/012987B.htm.

Provost, R. (2002). *International human rights and humanitarian law*. Cambridge: Cambridge University Press.

Seddon, A. Letters to the Confederate Secretary of War, to Ould, denouncing the General Orders, No. 100 (June 24, 1863). Reprinted in Hartigan, R. S. (1983). *Lieber's Code and the law of war*. Precedent.

Apartheid

A Crime against Humanity

Helen Kapstein

INTRODUCTION

South Africa's racist apartheid regime was inaugurated in 1948 with the victory of the Afrikaner[1] National Party and technically ended in 1994 with the country's first democratic election resulting in a government led by the opposition African National Congress (ANC) and former political prisoner Nelson Mandela. However, these dates cannot be considered the actual start and endpoints of apartheid, since a long history of discrimination and segregation predates the official policy of apartheid, and a deeply embedded legacy of inequality persists today.

Apartheid, from the Afrikaans[2] for apartness, was a system of multiple laws, rules, and regulations designed to keep South Africans physically, economically, and culturally apart in order to consolidate power and wealth in the hands of the white minority. Using discredited social and scientific theories to claim differences of culture and nature, South African authorities classified people as white, black, "coloured,"[3] or Indian (in order of preference and preferential treatment), and endowed these groups with unequal rights and degrees of mobility and opportunity. A highly institutionalized structure, apartheid governed every aspect of South African life, determining everything from whether one could vote and where one could live to what sort of education one was entitled to and with whom one could interact.

This chapter offers a synopsis of apartheid and its aftermath, concentrating on the ways in which apartheid criminalized certain groups and behaviors and on how apartheid itself amounted to a crime against humanity, a crime against the citizens of South Africa.

HISTORICAL BACKGROUND

South Africa's culture of segregation dates back to its earliest days as a contact zone, that is, as a space "where cultures meet, clash, and grapple with each other, often in contexts of highly asymmetrical relations of power" (Pratt, 1991, p. 34). In 1658, only a handful of years after the

---

[1] Afrikaners, also known as Boers or Voortrekkers, are South Africans of Dutch descent.
[2] Afrikaans, a Dutch-derived language spoken only in South Africa.
[3] The term "coloured" is the vernacular for mixed-race South Africans, often descendants of former slaves.

arrival of the first Dutch settlers, two shipments of slaves were imported (Thompson, 2000, p. 36), introducing codes and practices of discrimination that would shape the area's history. Tensions over race relations marked interactions between Dutch and British settlers, who arrived to colonize in the early 1800s. After the Afrikaner loss of the Anglo-Boer War (1899–1902), the Union of South Africa (1910) amalgamated the country for the first time, but only because of compromises over racial policy. Unity initiated the institutionalization of racial discrimination, with the 1913 Natives Land Act forcing hundreds of thousands of Africans off of land they occupied. It also spurred the growth of opposition parties, including what would become the ANC, and the parallel development of the National Party, a response to Afrikaner penury and to a perceived threat from black Africans (Omond, 1985, pp. 15–16). With the 1948 election of the National Party, *de facto* racial boundaries, beliefs, and attitudes swiftly became systematized. This legislation reinforced inequities and increased the government's power to control and classify the population. It infiltrated the most personal aspects of people's lives and it restructured society in the broadest possible ways, creating, for instance, geographical divisions that designated certain areas for certain racial groups.

What these laws amounted to in the everyday lives of individuals cannot be overstated. To mention only a few: the Population Registration Act (1950) designated the racial categories of all South Africans. The Bantu Education Act (1953) gave the government control of African education to prepare blacks for "certain forms of labor," in the words of former Prime Minister Hendrik Verwoerd. The Group Areas Act (1950) divided zones for living and working by race. The Promotion of Bantu Self-Government Act (1959) created homelands, allegedly independent nations within South Africa's borders, not internationally recognized. A slew of pass laws required identification of South Africans of color, granting them permission to live or work in certain areas and limiting freedom of movement. The Prohibition of Mixed Marriages (1949) and the Immorality Act (1950) enforced color lines in private life. From every side, South Africans were pushed and pulled into obedience to the inequitable laws of the land.

THE LANGUAGE OF APARTHEID

Apartheid terminology was replete with euphemism, used highly cynically by the authorities to provide the thinnest veneer of justification for their policies, as in the case of the term homeland, where the government performed the successful prestidigitation of appearing to exchange South African citizenship for independence but in fact leaving people with no real power. Here, the appellation "home" seems like a brutal irony when applied to the remote and unusable fragments of land designated as homelands with which residents had little or no previous affiliation. Similarly, the concept of group areas cements the idea that racial groups empirically exist and that, therefore, policy built around them makes sense.

Such policies tried to petrify apartheid's racial identities as timeless, pure, and physically isolated qualities when they were really the source of constant displacement and rootlessness. The invented geography of homelands and group areas made the majority of South Africans into foreigners in their own country. Re-imported as strictly controlled labor units, they now came from places that, prior to forced removals, they had never been. In other words, apartheid relied on the illusion of fixity while operating under the need for mobility. Mobility and access were thus granted unevenly and only at the whim of the authorities. It is important to note that, considering curbs on freedom of speech, publication, and gatherings, discursive mobility was as much at stake as physical mobility.

APARTHEID'S APPARATUSES

As a strategy for control, apartheid can be read a number of ways. As a geographic strategy, even before homelands were created, various legislative acts had redistributed land into the hands of whites, leaving millions fenced in by artificial borders that they needed permission to move across, or across which they were unwillingly moved. As a primarily economic ploy, apartheid took advantage of those geographic boundaries to concentrate the vast wealth of a resource-rich land in the hands of a few and to position the rest of society at their service. Apartheid depended on the production of specifically placed laboring bodies and on the regulation of their movement so that the laboring population was both carefully contained and also available for work. Everything was organized toward this end, from the specific mechanisms that controlled mobility such as pass laws and influx control, to the state's investment in education as a workforce tool, calibrating the dispensation of education to suit different groups to different vocations. It would be a mistake, however, to read apartheid as a singular strategy and, therefore, to overlook the ways in which South Africans were radically positioned by race, class, gender, and geography simultaneously.

In order to accomplish this extreme social manipulation, the regime applied legalities illegally and immorally. That is, apartheid criminalized the legal system by developing it to support crimes committed in the name of apartheid. Among these were forced removals, detention without trial, torture, treason trials, arrests, banning, and censorship. Infamous examples of removals include Sophiatown, a township[4] near Johannesburg emptied of its black inhabitants in 1955 and rezoned for whites under the mocking moniker Triomf (Afrikaans for triumph), and District Six in Cape Town, a "coloured" community razed to the ground starting in the late 1960s. Legal grounds for the removals came from a dozen and more laws on the books. By declaring the nation under threat from a "total onslaught" of black radical and communist forces, the government allocated to itself the power of detention without trial and the right to declare states of emergency. These powers were invoked in 1960 (and not for the last time) after the police massacre of pass law protesters in Sharpeville.

These spectacularly violent forms of coercion, layered over the swaddling of everyday experience in apartheid divisions, expose the difficulties of enforcing the system. Despite the extremes of separation under apartheid, the ambiguities and complexities of keeping people segregated become apparent in such seeming contradictions as the police officer of color or the use of Afrikaans (widely perceived as the language of the oppressor) as the mother tongue of the Cape Coloured community. Apartheid produced powerful resistance movements, notably led by labor unions and student groups, which engaged millions of people and made the townships ungovernable. This resistance in turn produced a proliferation of draconian laws. In hindsight, the ultimate unsustainability of the system is evident in this snarled and to some extent unenforceable (and expensive) mass of restrictions. In the face of ever-more-organized domestic resistance (school boycotts, strikes, sabotage) and increasing global rejection of practices of this sort (via widespread decolonization, United Nations embargos,

---

[4] Townships, black urban settlements adjacent to white cities.

international disinvestment campaigns) a series of states of emergency were declared in the 1980s, illustrating anxiety about a loss of control on the part of the authorities.

THE CRIME OF APARTHEID

Apartheid resulted in the saturation of South African life and culture with normalized criminality and violence. A glance at the cultural production of apartheid shows the structuring force of crime and the persistence of the problem. The literature (for example, Nadine Gordimer's novel *The House Gun* (1999)) shows the intrusion of a culture of violence into the privileged lives of those shielded from it under apartheid. Films (such as *Mapantsula* (1988)) reveal the intersections of public and personal crime. Other artifacts, like prison memoirs, newspaper articles, and the Truth and Reconciliation Commission (TRC)[5] reports, headline the human rights violations, war crimes, and everyday acts of violence that characterized apartheid's *modus operandi*. None of these texts exaggerates and many of them underestimate the reach and result of the crimes of apartheid; apartheid-era South Africa's high crime rate probably correlated to increasing state violence, and there has been a well-documented rise in violent crime in apartheid's aftermath, attended by a growing perception of the threat of violence. Although there is clearly a split between representations of criminality and illegality during and after apartheid, there is also a great deal of overlap since apartheid leaves behind a legacy of brutality and social disarray. The system imposed illegality on black South Africa and left habits of crime as its inheritance. In order to survive under apartheid, black South Africans inevitably had to break the law, which was constructed so as to trap them in a maze of restrictions and controls that governed every aspect of behavior. By the official end of apartheid in 1994, crime was no longer the sole burden of the oppressed, but the obsession of a society unanchored from its familiar chains.

Beyond the crimes perpetrated under apartheid, beyond the post-apartheid rise in violent crime, apartheid itself was a crime against the majority of the South African population for almost 50 years, as the ANC has charged (ANC, 1987). The UN concurs, with its General Assembly declaring in 1966 that apartheid is a crime against humanity and in 1973 adopting the Convention on the Suppression and Punishment of the Crime of Apartheid, which included the following language: "the term 'the crime of apartheid,' which shall include similar policies and practices of racial segregation and discrimination as practiced in southern Africa, shall apply to […] inhuman acts committed for the purpose of establishing and maintaining domination by one racial group of persons over any other racial group of persons and systematically oppressing them." In 1977, Additional Protocol 1 to the Geneva Convention called apartheid a war crime (United Nations High Commissioner for Human Rights, UNHCHR, 1973). And we have seen in this overview the built-in contradictions of a legal system systematically enforcing crimes against its own people.

CONCLUSION

To use a now rather tired phrase a quarter-of-a-century on, the "new South Africa" does not face particularly new issues of crime and justice. Since huge social inequities persist (the

---

[5] The TRC was a post-apartheid mechanism for addressing apartheid-era human rights violations, amnesty, and reparations. Operating from 1995 to 1998, it conducted amnesty hearings on crimes by all parties.

World Bank in 2018 declared it the country with the world's worst income inequality), there has been a continuity of crime and its causes in the post-apartheid era, including police aggression, vigilantism, and gang violence. Although the TRC attempted with all good intentions after 1994 to address and redress crimes committed under apartheid, it fell far short of gaining proportionate reparations and met with criticism for its undefined notion of truth, its suggestion of a break with the past, and its risk of promoting forgiving and forgetting over remembering. Regardless, the TRC alone was always going to be an insufficient mechanism to deal with apartheid's fallout. Neither have Mandela's successors lived up to expectations, their administrations characterized by scandal, corruption, and mismanagement. To make South Africa new again, the nation needs a radical, ongoing restructuring of social and economic opportunities to follow its transition to democratic politics. Current president Cyril Ramaphosa must help decide if that includes controversial land expropriations to right the original wrong of property theft.

Post-apartheid crime has taken on some very specific forms. A rampant rape culture, xenophobic attacks, and hate crimes reflect a precariat desperately holding on to the little it has. Events like the 2012 Marikana massacre of striking miners by the police look horribly like the past repeating itself for more or less the same reason: the entrenchment of wealth and power. In addition to the headlines, though, we must pay attention to environmental and psychological harms – to toxic mining waste, squalid townships, and a failing education system – in order to see that apartheid's enduring crimes are slow[6] as well as spectacular.

REFERENCES

African National Congress (ANC). (1987, December 1–4). *The illegitimacy of the Apartheid regime, the right to struggle against it, and the status of the African National Congress*. Statement from the ANC Arusha Conference. Retrieved from www.anc.org.za/ancdocs/history/acrime.html.

Nixon, R. (2013). *Slow violence and the environmentalism of the poor*. Cambridge, MA: Harvard University Press.

Omond, R. (1985). *The Apartheid handbook*. Middlesex: Penguin.

Pratt, M. (1991). Arts of the contact zone. *Profession*, 33–40. Retrieved from www.jstor.org.ez.lib.jjay.cuny.edu/stable/25595469.

Thompson, L. (2000). *A history of South Africa*. Third Edition. New Haven, CT: Yale University Press.

United Nations High Commissioner for Human Rights (UNHCHR). (1973, November 30). *International Convention on the Suppression and Punishment of the Crime of Apartheid*. Retrieved from https://treaties.un.org/doc/Publication/UNTS/Volume%201015/volume-1015-I-14861-English.pdf.

WEBSITES

African National Congress (ANC). www.anc1912.org.za.

BBC country profile for South Africa. http://news.bbc.co.uk/2/hi/africa/country_profiles/1071886.stm.

Center for the Study of Violence and Reconciliation. www.csvr.org.za.

Mail & Guardian newspaper. www.mg.co.za.

Truth and Reconciliation Commission. www.justice.gov.za/trc/.

---

[6] To adjust Rob Nixon's idea of slow violence (2013).

58 The Crime of Aggression

Stefan Barriga

INTRODUCTION

The crime of aggression, or crime against peace, has been famously labeled as the "supreme international crime" by Robert H. Jackson, the Chief American Prosecutor at the Nuremberg Trials. Of the 22 former Nazi leaders tried in Nuremberg, 12 were convicted for crimes against peace. The International Military Tribunal for the Far East (the "Tokyo Tribunal") had an even stronger focus on aggression. It prosecuted only those military and political leaders whose crimes included aggression. Twenty-four of them were convicted of this crime.

The crime of aggression is, in essence, the crime of waging an illegal war, in other words, a war in contravention of the United Nations Charter. It is, thus, the criminal law corollary to state responsibility for the most serious cases of illegal use of armed force. The Charter prohibits the threat or use of force except in the case of self-defense or when authorized by the Security Council. But while there have been many instances of such illegal use of force since the founding of the United Nations, no international (and very few domestic) trials for a crime of aggression have been conducted since Nuremberg and Tokyo. This is due to two basic reasons: a longstanding controversy over a legally binding definition of aggression, and the lack of an international court effectively empowered to prosecute aggression. Both of these issues, however, have recently been resolved for the purpose of the Rome Statute of the International Criminal Court (ICC). In June 2010, a Review Conference held in Kampala, Uganda, adopted amendments to the Rome Statute on the crime of aggression by a consensus decision. And in December 2017, state parties decided to "activate" them as of July 17, 2018. The amendments contain a legally binding definition of the crime and the precise conditions under which the ICC is empowered to prosecute those responsible for crimes of aggression. Already prior to the Review Conference, it was generally accepted that the crime of aggression was indeed an existing crime under international law. In 2006, this view was confirmed by the British House of Lords. Furthermore, around 30 countries worldwide (including Germany and the Russian Federation) have incorporated the crime of aggression into their domestic criminal codes.

The notion of "crime" of aggression must be distinguished from the "act" of aggression. The former refers to the conduct of the individual leader who bears criminal responsibility for the state's use of force, typically without even actively participating on the battlefield. The latter refers to the act of the state, such as one state army's invasion of a neighbor state's territory.

A crime of aggression and war crimes often go hand-in-hand, though conceptually they are very different. War crimes are serious violations of the rules applicable in armed conflict (*ius in bello*), whereas a crime of aggression constitutes a serious violation of the rules that govern the use of force by a state (*ius ad bellum*). War crimes can be committed by individual soldiers on the field, whereas a crime of aggression can only be committed by a state's leadership. War crimes can be committed in both international and non-international armed conflicts, whereas a crime of aggression is by definition of international character, as it always involves at least two states.

DEFINING THE CRIME OF AGGRESSION

While the drafters of the United Nations Charter could not agree on a definition of aggression, the 1945 London Charter of the International Military Tribunal in Nuremberg referred to crimes against peace as the "planning, preparation, initiation or waging of a war of aggression, or a war in violation of international treaties, agreements or assurances, or participation in a common plan or conspiracy for the accomplishment of any of the foregoing." That rather vague definition of aggression was subsequently endorsed by the International Law Commission as part of the 1950 Nuremberg Principles.

In 1974, following decades of negotiations, the UN General Assembly agreed on a much more detailed "Definition of Aggression," contained in Resolution 3314 (XXIX). Article 1 defines aggression as "the use of armed force by a State against the sovereignty, territorial integrity or political independence of another State, or in any other manner inconsistent with the Charter of the United Nations, as set out in this Definition," and Article 3 contains an illustrative list of acts that qualify as aggression, such as an "invasion or attack by the armed forces of a State of the territory of another State, or any military occupation, however temporary, resulting from such invasion or attack." The major drawback of that definition, however, was its non-binding nature. Its primary purpose was to guide the Security Council in the determination of state acts of aggression, and it was not intended to serve as the basis for individual criminal proceedings.

At the 1998 Rome Conference establishing the ICC, there was no agreement on how to define aggression for the purpose of individual criminal justice. While the ICC Statute included aggression as one of the crimes under the jurisdiction of the Court, the Court's active exercise of jurisdiction over the crime was deferred until a provision was adopted defining the crime and setting out any further conditions for that exercise of jurisdiction, such as possibly an authorization by the UN Security Council. In February 2009, a Special Working Group on the Crime of Aggression (open to all states, not just ICC states parties) agreed on a definition of aggression, thereby concluding an important phase of the negotiations. The Working Group's proposal incorporated the definition contained in Resolution 3314, but sought to exclude some acts from the Court's jurisdiction. Only an act of aggression – as defined in Resolution 3314 – "which, by its character, gravity and scale, constitutes a manifest violation of the Charter of the United Nations" would qualify. A minor border skirmish, for example, would thus not trigger the ICC's jurisdiction. Similarly, a use of armed force whose illegal character is debatable rather than "manifest" would not end up before the ICC – arguably to protect the Court from entering highly controversial political terrain.

The 2010 Review Conference decided to include the above-mentioned definition in the Rome Statute as a new Article 8 *bis* (Box 58.1). In addition, the Conference adopted a number of "understandings" that should guide the interpretation of the definition. One such understanding states that "aggression is the most serious and dangerous form of the illegal use of force," thereby re-confirming that not every illegal use of force constitutes aggression.

Under the amended Rome Statute, criminal responsibility for crimes of aggression is limited to those in charge of the aggressor state's policies. Such leaders are defined as persons "in a position effectively to exercise control over or to direct the political or military action of a State." This leadership clause could refer to more than one single person and include, for example, cabinet-level officials or military leaders. It would, however, clearly exclude individual soldiers from criminal responsibility for aggression. The proposal does not explicitly criminalize the "participation in a common plan or conspiracy" for the accomplishment of aggression, as Nuremberg did, but it incorporates the Rome Statute's general rules on modes of participation. Secondary modes of participation, such as aiding and abetting, do therefore give rise to criminal responsibility – provided that the perpetrator fulfills the leadership requirement.

Box 58.1. Rome Statute Definition of the Crime of Aggression (Excerpt)

ARTICLE 8 BIS CRIME OF AGGRESSION

1. For the purpose of this Statute, "crime of aggression" means the planning, preparation, initiation or execution, by a person in a position effectively to exercise control over or to direct the political or military action of a State, of an act of aggression which, by its character, gravity and scale, constitutes a manifest violation of the Charter of the United Nations.

2. For the purpose of paragraph 1, "act of aggression" means the use of armed force by a State against the sovereignty, territorial integrity or political independence of another State, or in any other manner inconsistent with the Charter of the United Nations. Any of the following acts, regardless of a declaration of war, shall, in accordance with United Nations General Assembly resolution 3314 (XXIX) of December 14, 1974, qualify as an act of aggression:

   a) The invasion or attack by the armed forces of a State of the territory of another State, or any military occupation, however temporary, resulting from such invasion or attack, or any annexation by the use of force of the territory of another State or part thereof;

   b) Bombardment by the armed forces of a State against the territory of another State or the use of any weapons by a State against the territory of another State;

   c) The blockade of the ports or coasts of a State by the armed forces of another State;

   d) An attack by the armed forces of a State on the land, sea or air forces, or marine and air fleets of another State;

   e) The use of armed forces of one State which are within the territory of another State with the agreement of the receiving State, in contravention of the conditions provided for in

> the agreement or any extension of their presence in such territory beyond the termination of the agreement;
>
> f) The action of a State in allowing its territory, which it has placed at the disposal of another State, to be used by that other State for perpetrating an act of aggression against a third State;
>
> g) The sending by or on behalf of a State of armed bands, groups, irregulars or mercenaries, which carry out acts of armed force against another State of such gravity as to amount to the acts listed above, or its substantial involvement therein.

CONCLUSIONS: A COMPROMISE BASED ON LIMITED JURISDICTION

While the Special Working Group was successful in finding a definition of aggression, it could not overcome a deep division over the equally important issue of the "conditions for the exercise of jurisdiction." The central question here was whether the UN Security Council should act as a gatekeeper for the Court's exercise of jurisdiction, given the Council's primary responsibility for the maintenance of international peace and security under the Charter. Some countries argued that the ICC should only be allowed to proceed with investigations into crimes of aggression if so authorized by the Security Council, in order to prevent the Court from interfering unduly with the Council's business. Others considered such a role incompatible with the concept of equality before the law, as it would allow any single permanent member of the Security Council to shield individuals from prosecution.

The 2010 Review Conference found a compromise on this issue. First, it deferred the "activation" of the Court's exercise of jurisdiction to a decision to be taken by ICC states parties no earlier than 2017 (that decision was indeed taken in December 2017), and second, it agreed on a differentiated jurisdictional regime, based on different trigger mechanisms, through the inclusion of two new articles, Articles 15 *bis* and 15 *ter*.

Article 15 *ter* empowers the Court to investigate and prosecute crimes of aggression based on a referral by the Security Council – even where the act of aggression involves a non-state party to the Rome Statute. In other words, once a situation has been referred to the Court, it can now investigate whether any of the four core crimes has been committed – and without any further procedural conditions specific to the crime of aggression. Based on a Security Council referral, the Court can thus investigate a crime of aggression even in the absence of an explicit Security Council determination that an act of aggression has occurred. In any event, the Court would not be bound by such a determination, in order to preserve the due process rights of the accused.

Article 15 *bis* deals with *proprio motu* investigations and state referrals. When acting on the basis of these two trigger mechanisms, the Court's jurisdiction over crimes of aggression is severely restricted compared to the other three core crimes, in three ways. First, acts of aggression committed by or against non-state parties are entirely excluded. Second, when "activating" the amendments in December 2017, the Assembly of States Parties stated that the Court shall not exercise such jurisdiction over a crime of aggression when committed by a national or on the territory of a state party that has not ratified the amendments. Third, and on top of that, acts of aggression committed by state parties that have lodged an opt-out declaration are also excluded.

The limited jurisdiction, and thus limited practical relevance, of this trigger mechanism made it possible to find a compromise on the role of the Security Council in Article 15 *bis*. First, it recognizes the Security Council's primary responsibility for the maintenance of international peace and security in that it instructs the Court to inform the Council about the investigation, allowing the Council to make a determination of aggression. However, if no such determination is made within six months, the prosecutor may still proceed – provided the Pre-Trial Division authorizes him or her to do so. In other words, when acting under Article 15 *bis*, the Court is not dependent on Security Council action – and thus also not on the approval of each of its permanent members. The price of that independence, however, was the severely restricted scope of jurisdiction.

In conclusion, it seems unlikely that the Court will have many aggression cases, given its jurisdictional limitations. This can be compensated to some extent by domestic jurisdictions. So far, relatively few states have criminalized the crime of aggression domestically. Some have not done so for lack of an internationally agreed definition. This excuse no longer exists, and it is indeed to be expected that more and more states will incorporate the Kampala definition into their penal codes, thereby contributing to deterrence.

FURTHER READING

Barriga, S. & Grover, L. (2011). A historic breakthrough on the crime of aggression. *American Journal of International Law*, 105, 517–533.

Barriga, S. & Kreß, C. (2012). *The travaux préparatoires of the crime of aggression*. Cambridge: Cambridge University Press.

Ferencz, B. (1975). *Defining international aggression – the search for world peace: A documentary history and analysis*. Dobbs Ferry, NY: Oceana Publishers.

Kreß, C. & Barriga, S. (2016). *The crime of aggression – a commentary*. Cambridge: Cambridge University Press.

McDougall, C. (2013). *The crime of aggression under the Rome Statute of the International Criminal Court*. Cambridge: Cambridge University Press.

United Kingdom House of Lords. (2006). *R. v. Jones et al.*, UKHL 16. Retrieved from www.publications.parliament.uk/pa/ld200506/ldjudgmt/jd060329/jones.pdf.

United Nations Office of Legal Affairs. (2003). Historical review of developments relating to aggression. Retrieved from www.ods.un.org as Doc. Nr. PCNICC/2002/ WGCA/L.1.

59 Crimes of the Powerful

A Global Perspective

Anamika Twyman-Ghoshal

The "crimes of the powerful" label unifies into one framework, on a more systematic level, research on organizational and institutional networks of power that harm and injure people. Although the term was originally coined by Frank Pearce in 1976, it has only recently entered mainstream discourse (Friedrichs, 2015). This framework is a product of a long history of broadening criminology beyond its narrow focus on street crime.

Sutherland (1940) introduced the concept of white-collar crime in his Presidential Address to the American Sociological Association. Sutherland challenged assumptions that crime is closely correlated with poverty because data failed to "include criminal behavior of persons not in the lower class" (Sutherland, 1940, p. 2), calling for white-collar crime to be brought within the scope of criminology. Nearly 50 years later, Chambliss (1988) broadened the scope of criminology again in his Presidential Address to the American Society of Criminology, this time to include state-organized crime, identifying that governments are also susceptible to engaging in deviant behavior. In 1990, Kramer and Michalowski (1990) noted that states can collaborate with corporations in what they termed state-corporate crime, that is, "illegal and socially injurious actions that occur when one or more institutions of political governance pursue a goal in direct cooperation with one or more institutions of economic production and distribution" (p. 4). More recently, Friedrichs added "crimes of globalization" as another area of criminological research that further explored the relationships between various nodes of power. Crimes of globalization builds on the idea of state-corporate crimes by adding a third actor, international financial institutions. Together, these powerful actors can engage in projects that create serious and foreseeable social harms (Friedrichs, 2015).

Despite these attempts to develop criminology to be more inclusive of various forms of deviance, to date many criminological theories contain implicit assumptions that crime, at its core, is a problem located among the poor. The resistance to broadening criminology beyond the crimes of the powerless rests on how we define crime.

DEFINITION OF CRIME

The concept of crime is highly contested; however, much of mainstream criminology has relied on the legal definition of crime as the foundation for conducting research. The problem with using the legal definition of crime rests in the notion that crime has an inherent reality rather than being a social construct. Fundamentally, acts that are defined as crimes are dependent on the context within which they occur. It is the context, not the content of the act, that allows it to be interpreted as illicit or licit. The legal construction of behavior as criminal depends on those who create and administer the law, i.e., those in power. Criminologists, therefore, need to be cautious of using state definitions, which often exclude behaviors that are more likely to occur in locations of power. Such awareness allows criminologists to be true to their craft by including all forms of deviance in their purview.

A notable suggestion for a more inclusive definition has been a humanistic definition of crime that, instead of using national laws, uses violations of fundamental human rights and the resulting willful harm as a means of identifying crime (Schwendinger & Schwendinger, 1970). Another definition that has been built on the social harm approach includes any acts that cause willful harm to society that require state intervention and are similar to other forms of criminalized behaviors (Twyman-Ghoshal & Passas, 2015). The benefit of these inclusive definitions is that they incorporate various forms of deviance, ranging from oppressive social conditions to white-collar crimes and state-organized crimes without excluding street crimes. Moreover, these definitions incorporate legal concepts (such as the Universal Declaration of Human Rights and legal modes of criminalization) to avoid subjectivity. Criminology can remain relevant in a globalized world only if it incorporates all forms of deviance committed in the various social strata.

DEFINITION OF POWER

Sutherland referred to white-collar crime as a "violation of delegated or implied trust" (1940, p. 3). He did not distinguish between those in power and those who were relatively powerless (Friedrichs, 2015). The emphasis in "crimes of the powerful" is on analyzing power more explicitly, not merely to include individuals in privileged positions but also to understand collective responsibility and the system within which it resides. Power refers to the (potential) exercise of control, relying on a combination of authority and trust that exists due to a perceived legitimacy. Similar to crime, power is socially constructed; "power exists only through social relationships and is historically and culturally specific" (Rothe & Kauzlarich, 2016, p. 4). The following section lists four key areas of the crimes of the powerful framework.

TYPES OF CRIMES OF THE POWERFUL

The crimes of the powerful framework includes cases where power is vested in individuals, organizations, or networks, where the exercise of this power causes large-scale willful social harms. Although these may be domestic, international, and transnational crimes, due to globalization and the symbiotic nature of powerful actors, cases are often global.

State Crimes

Chambliss's original formulation of state-organized crime included "acts defined by the law as criminal and committed by state officials in the pursuit of their job as representatives of the state" (1989, p.184). The 1998 Rome Statute of the International Criminal Court has established genocide, war crimes, crimes against humanity, and crimes of aggression as forms of state crime. However, state crime also includes acts that violate other international norms. Past research has identified examples such as nuclear warfare, drone strikes, and forced eviction. One such example is the forced eviction of the Chagossians (Box 59.1).

Box 59.1. The Forced Eviction of the Chagossians

Between 1967 and 1974, the United Kingdom systematically expelled the entire population of Chagossians from the island of Diego Garcia. The Chagos Archipelago was separated from colonial Mauritius in 1965 and renamed British Indian Ocean Territory (BIOT). This was done in fulfillment of a secret agreement between the UK and the USA that the island would be used as a US military facility. The decision to separate the islands from Mauritius contravened a United Nations (UN) General Assembly declaration that mandated colonial powers to maintain the national and territorial unity of a country. The agreement was concealed from the oversight of the US Congress, the UK Parliament, and the UN Trusteeship Council. In the agreement, the US required that the island of Diego Garcia be free of any local population prior to occupancy. In order to fulfill this requirement, the UK proceeded to evict all the islanders in a series of actions including compulsory land acquisition, refusal of the right of return to any islanders who left temporarily, restricting the visitation of supply ships, the extermination of all pets on the island, and then finally the forced eviction of the remaining islanders in 1971. All of this was done in violation of provisions in the UN Charter that required colonial powers to protect the permanent inhabitants of colonies.

(Twyman-Ghoshal & Passas, 2015)

Corporate Crimes

Sutherland's initial conception of white-collar crime was not nuanced enough to explore the varieties of behaviors that would be incorporated in the umbrella term of corporate crime or occupational crime. Within the crimes of the powerful framework, the focus has been particularly on corporate crime.

Corporate crimes are deviant acts committed for the benefit of organizations. These behaviors often occur without violating any criminal laws, particularly when corporations are active in multiple jurisdictions and are able to influence the legislation through lobbying or other forms of political influence. Much of the research on corporate crime has centered on the effect of granting personhood to corporations, the conglomeration of ownership, and the diffusion of corporate power globally (Rothe & Kauzlarich, 2016). Together these processes have created an enabling structure and a criminogenic organizational culture. The externalities of corporate activity have been grouped into three types: corporations that create a product that is harmful *per se*; corporations that produce a desirable product but use a harmful production process, and corporation that are performing public functions for profit that have "predictably adverse consequences" (Passas, 2005, p. 776). The first category refers to corporations that create a product that is in itself a criminogenic commodity, such as arms or tobacco. Desirable product but harmful production process refers to companies that deliver a product or perform a service that in itself is necessary, but in the interest of maximizing profits the production process creates massive collateral damage. Examples include toxic waste disposal and intensive animal farming that cause large-scale environmental damage. Finally, privatized public functions refer to corporations that provide a service that presents a conflict of interest between the public needs and the motivation for profit. Example industries include private security, health care, and education.

State-Corporate Crimes

State-corporate crimes are joint ventures between political and economic institutions that result in grave and predictable social harms. Two types of state roles are discerned in these schemes: state-facilitated and state-initiated schemes (Rothe & Kauzlarich, 2016). State-initiated refers to an intentional and willful collaboration of government and business to engage in behaviors that are willfully harmful. This can be with direct or implicit control of the government. State-facilitated refers to instances where the government fails to regulate harmful corporate behavior due to a shared interest in the outcome of the deviant activity. Examples include the Challenger disaster (Kramer & Michalowski, 1990), Iraq war-profiteering (Rothe & Kauzlarich, 2016), and the Deepwater Horizon oil spill (see Box 59.2).

Box 59.2. The Deepwater Horizon Oil Spill

In 2010, an explosion on the Deepwater Horizon oil rig killed 11 and injured a further 17 people. In addition, an estimated 4.9 million barrels of crude oil poured into the Gulf of Mexico. A US federal court concluded that the explosion was due to willful misconduct and a series of negligent decisions driven by the pursuit of profit by British Petroleum (BP) (petroleum prospect owner), Transocean (rig owner), and Halliburton (contractor). In the aftermath of the oil spill, state and corporate actors hid the extent of the environmental damage caused by the spill by censoring the statements given by clean-up workers, coercing surviving crew members, prohibiting other offshore rig crews from contacting family and friends, and controlling images and information released to the public by the US Coast Guard. In addition, to prevent visibility of the environmental damage, the US Environmental Protection Agency, together with the Coast Guard and BP, emptied 2 million gallons of toxic chemical dispersants into the Gulf. This was followed by the enforcement of a 65-foot restriction of access to media around the clean-up area by the US Coast Guard and a 3,000-foot fly-over restriction by the Federal Aviation Administration.

(Bradshaw, 2015).

Crimes of Globalization

Building on the state-corporate model, crimes of globalization examines the policies of key international financial institutions (such as the World Bank (WB) and the International Monetary Fund (IMF)) and their interaction with states and multinational corporations. The IMF and the WB have pursued a strategy of extensive global neoliberalization, which has resulted in a transfer of control from the public to the private sector. Both the IMF and the WB have used their key position in financing development projects to ensure that free-market policies are implemented in countries receiving loans. The approach does not suggest that other economic approaches (such as communism or feudalism) are not criminogenic; rather, it is an examination of the effects of the dominant economic model of our time. In their efforts to create a global, unfettered capitalist economy, there has been little regard for the mass victimization that these policies have caused, such as a WB-financed dam in Thailand (Friedrichs, 2015) and Structural Adjustment Programs (SAPs) in Somalia (see Box 59.3).

Box 59.3. Structural Adjustments and the Mass Victimization of Somalis

Today, Somalia is known internationally for its protracted civil conflict dating back to 1991, when the country's president Siad Barre was ousted. The precursors to the conflict date back to repeated economic restructuring, gross human rights violations, and extended suffering of the Somali people. In the late 1970s, after the failed Oganden war, Barre shifted allegiance from the USSR to the USA. The USA was interested in Somalia's strategic location for its military bases and the possibility of oil exploration in the Ogaden region. The USA supported the regime's military growth (resulting in lucrative contracts with US arms suppliers) while turning a blind eye to Barre's domestic human rights violations. Simultaneously, development loans that were granted to Somalia by the IMF and WB were attached to SAPs. The SAPs required strict austerity measures, reductions in public spending, tax reform, privatization, and deregulation. The implementation of SAPs in Somalia included cutting government spending on health and education, shrinking the public sector, reducing pay for civil servants, opening the market to foreign direct investment, and selling off food and grain reserves as cash crop exports to service the national debt (the reserves had been collected and stored to cope with future droughts). As a result of these policies, in 1991–1992 Somalia suffered its first famine. Somalia's primary export, livestock, was also affected by SAPs. As publically provided veterinary services and water supplies were privatized, rangeland conservation spending was cut, and drought animal feed was sold, the livelihood of pastoralists was destroyed. The agricultural sector, which relied on trade with pastoralists, was also impacted and was then worsened when international food aid (that came from subsidized farming in developed nations) provided cheaper grain alternatives.

(Twyman-Ghoshal, 2012).

SUMMARY

This chapter traced the development of criminology away from its traditional and narrow focus on street crime and introduced the area of research known as "crimes of the powerful." The broadening of criminology has relied on abandoning the legalistic definition of crime for one that uses human rights and willful social harms as a benchmark.

The crimes of the powerful framework explores the symbiotic relationship of those in power, recognizing that power is a product of history and culture. Four key areas include:

- state crimes, which include behaviors captured by the Rome Statute as well as other human rights violations
- corporate crimes, which probe the harmful acts of corporate actors
- state-corporate crimes, which include collaborative ventures between the public and private sector that produces large-scale suffering and impoverishment
- crimes of globalization, which analyze the international policies of international financial institutions that cause victimization of large segments of the population that they are meant to serve.

REFERENCES

Bradshaw, E. (2015). Blacking out the Gulf: State-corporate environmental crime and the response to the 2010 BP oil spill. In G. Barak (Ed.), *The Routledge international handbook of the crimes of the powerful* (chapter 25). London: Routledge.

Chambliss, W. J. (1989). State-organized crime. The American Society of Criminology, 1988 Presidential Address. *Criminology*, 27(2), 183–208.

Friedrichs, D. (2015). Crimes of the powerful and the definition of crime. In G. Barak (Ed.), *The Routledge international handbook of the crimes of the powerful* (chapter 3). London: Routledge.

Kramer, R. & Michalowski, R. (1990). *Toward an integrated theory of state-corporate crime*. Paper presented at the meeting of the American Society of Criminology, Baltimore, MD.

Passas, N. (2005) Lawful but awful: "Legal Corporate Crimes". *The Journal of Socio-Economics*, 34, 771–786.

Rothe, D. L. & Kauzlarich, D. (2016). *Crimes of the powerful: An introduction*. London: Routledge.

Sutherland, E. (1940). White-collar criminality. *American Sociological Review*, 5(1), 1–12.

Schwendinger, H. & Schwendinger, J. (1970). Defenders of order or guardians of human rights? *Issues in Criminology*, 5, 123–137.

Twyman-Ghoshal, A. (2012). Understanding contemporary maritime piracy. Criminology and Justice Policy Doctoral Dissertations. Paper 7. Retrieved from http://iris.lib.neu.edu/criminology_diss/7/.

Twyman-Ghoshal, A. & Passas, N. (2015). State and corporate drivers of global dysnomie: Horrendous crimes and the law. In G. Barak (Ed.), *The Routledge international handbook of the crimes of the powerful* (chapter 6). London: Routledge.

WEBSITES

Amnesty International. www.amnesty.org/en/.

Human Rights Watch. www.hrw.org.

International State Crime Initiative. http://statecrime.org/about-isci/about-state-crime/.

International Crime and Justice for Women and Children

If traditional criminology has only little to offer to the study of international and transnational crime, this is not so for its neglected offspring – victimology. In the criminal law of Western countries, there has been little place for the victims of crime, but the needs of victims are a major preoccupation of the International Criminal Court and other international legal entities. Women and children are particularly at risk of victimization, and victimologists have consistently identified them as requiring special protections under international human rights and humanitarian law. In Chapter 60, Mangai Natarajan and Elenice Oliveira discuss the status of women as offenders, as victims, as subjects of treatment, and as employees in the criminal justice system and offer suggestions for protecting their status and their rights.

Among other forms of victimization, domestic violence is the most common form of violence against women across the globe. Domestic violence (DV) is committed by a spouse, ex-spouse, or current or former partner and can occur among heterosexual or same-sex couples. Though both men and women experience DV, the empirical literature attests to the fact that women are much more often victimized and suffer physical and psychological harm as a consequence. DV is underreported in many parts of the world, whether in economically developed or traditional countries. In developed countries, the social infrastructure and improved social status of women have gradually strengthened efforts to improve reporting of DV.

DV is a multifaceted problem, which should be addressed by various constituencies including human rights activists, and criminal justice and public health researchers and practitioners. It is crucial to understanding and responding to DV. How we measure the prevalence of DV, what we identify as the risk factors, which theories seem to provide most help in understanding and responding to DV, which preventive and treatment programs seem most effective, and the respective roles of the health and criminal justice systems are all questions of vital importance in global response to the problem (see Chapter 61 by Mangai Natarajan and Diana Rodriguez-Spahia).

There are specific forms of victimization of young women and girls, for example, honor-based violence (HBV), a collection of practices that are used to control behavior within families or other social groups to protect perceived cultural and religious beliefs and/or honor. The victims of HBV are girls and young women between the ages of 13 and 25 years and the perpetrators are parents, brothers, and close relatives, and sometimes the elders in the community. Though HBV has been prevalent in several countries in South Asia, the Middle East and some African regions, countries including the USA, Canada, the UK, the Netherlands, Germany, and Sweden have recently identified HBV as an issue that is especially problematic in first-generation immigrant communities. Popy Begum and Mangai Natarajan (see Chapter 62) provide a descriptive account of conceptualizing the types of actions by their components – nature, extent, patterns, perpetrators, victims, and countries of occurrence – and contextualizing the situations in which the HBV occurs are crucial for understanding and reducing the violence.

According to the World Health Organization (WHO), child maltreatment is a global problem that includes all types of physical and/or emotional ill-treatment, sexual abuse, neglect, negligence, and commercial or other exploitation, which has immediate and long-term repercussions. It occurs to children under 18 years of age. In Chapter 63, Emily Hurren and Anna Stewart provide an overview of child maltreatment and its components, especially in the hands of known people, and discuss the challenges associated with researching maltreatment, its causes and consequences, and the policy implications. They note that it is important to understand the context of victims and their maltreatment experiences over time and the protection of children across the globe is dependent upon evidence-based prevention and intervention, and local, national, and international policies.

At a more global level, the WHO informs that in armed conflict and refugee settings, both boys and girls are particularly vulnerable to physical and sexual violence, exploitation, and abuse by combatants, security forces, members of their communities, aid workers, and others. In Chapter 64, Cécile Van de Voorde and Rosemary Barberet state that although children have increasingly received attention from the international community in recent years, they often remain vulnerable for serious victimization. Though the creation of the ICC, *ad hoc* entities, and other conflict-specific mechanisms are assisting in promoting legislations to exercise children's rights, a rigorous enforcement and action plan is needed within the existing regulatory framework.

60 Women and International Criminal Justice

Mangai Natarajan and Elenice Oliveira

INTRODUCTION

Despite considerable progress made in the past few decades, women in the Western world still suffer discrimination and are not treated equally to men. Consider how much truer this is in the developing or traditional world, where the gap between the treatment of men and women is a yawning chasm. These facts illuminate any consideration of women's criminality, the particular nature of their criminal victimization, and their treatment by the criminal justice system. In addition, women's unequal status has repercussions for their employment in the criminal justice system as police officers, prosecution or prison staff, and court judges and magistrates. It even helps to explain the nature of their involvement in transnational and international crimes, whether as offenders or victims. These are the topics explored within this chapter.

WOMEN AS OFFENDERS

Surveys and police records of crime in Western nations show that women still constitute a small minority of offenders, but they are becoming increasingly involved in crime. Women are mostly involved in common crimes – minor thefts and frauds, low-level drug dealing, prostitution, and misdemeanor assaults against their mates or children – and are far less likely than men to be involved in serious crime. At the international level, however, women are becoming more involved in serious crimes of drug trafficking, human trafficking, terrorism, and genocide.

Drug trafficking. Analysis of 1,715 drug traffickers caught smuggling drugs through Heathrow Airport between July 1991 and September 1997 indicates that women take on a high-risk but lower-status role of courier and carry Class A drugs in large quantities (Harper, Harper, & Stockdale, 2002). This is confirmed by a recent study by Kleemans, Kruisbergen, and Kouwenberg (2014) that showed women do play a role, but a peripheral one.

Human trafficking. Women make up the largest proportion of traffickers and they are involved in all stages of the trafficking operations, including: recruitment; transportation;

escort; provision of forged documents; provision of flats; control of victims; and cashing (Kangaspunta, 2008).

Terrorism. Women have been participants in terrorist groups in Sri Lanka, Iran, West Germany, Italy, and Japan. They are increasingly involved in many terrorist organizations (in Russia, India, Colombia, Israel, Britain) and in suicide bombing and other attacks (Weinberg & Eubank, 2011).

Genocide. A substantial number of women, and even girls, were involved in the slaughter in Rwanda. They inflicted extraordinary cruelty on other women, as well as children and men (Brown, 2014).

Several competing theories explain why women are increasingly involved in criminal activities.

1. More women are motivated to commit crimes as a result of (a) impoverishment, unemployment, and a lack of educational opportunities, and (b) increases in domestic violence, divorce, and separation.

2. Steffensmeier and Allan (1996) provide an integrated model of female offending intended to assist understanding of gender differences in type and frequency of crime, criminal opportunity, motivation, and the context of offending. Their model includes gender norms, moral development and relational concerns, social control, physical strength, aggression, and sexuality.

3. The increase in female crime is a function of the greater emancipation of women in society; as women are liberated and assume more traditional male social roles, they begin to act more like males (Adler, 1975).

4. Cohen and Felson (1979) contend that the most general explanation of crime rate trends is an indicator of the dispersion of activities away from family and household settings. The increased participation of women in work outside the home provides increased opportunities for women to become both victims and criminals, just as these opportunities had for men (Anderson & Bennett, 1996).

WOMEN AS VICTIMS OF VIOLENCE

Though women are disproportionally the victims of domestic violence or family violence across societies around the world, there are many specific forms of violence against women that are related to their gender role and that represent the abuse of unequal power relations between women and men at social, cultural, and economic levels. Some of these are presented below.

Culture-Specific Violence

1. *Female genital mutilation.* FGM is a social convention that is considered a necessary part of raising a girl properly, and a way to prepare her for adulthood and marriage, linking procedures to premarital virginity and marital fidelity. It is primarily practiced in Africa (especially in Somalia, Sudan, Ethiopia, Eritrea, and Côte D'Ivoire), and in some parts of Asia and the Middle East, but also among some immigrant communities in Europe, North America, and Australia.

2. *Honor killings*. These murders are based on the cultural belief that a woman's lack of conformity to sexually prescribed norms severely undermines the honor of her family. When unmarried or married women do not abide by these rules, their fathers, husbands, or brothers may kill them to re-establish the family reputation. The majority of these incidents are documented in India, Pakistan, Afghanistan, Egypt, Jordan, Turkey, and Lebanon.
3. *Female infanticide*. This is prevalent in India and among Arabian tribes due to the preference for sons and the low value associated with the birth of females. It is also said to be common among South Asian immigrants in Britain, the USA, and Canada.
4. *Bride burning*. In the Indian subcontinent, hundreds of young brides are burned to death every year as a result of dowry disputes. The dowry is a customary practice of gift-giving by the bride's family to that of the groom during and after marriage.
5. *Fatwah*: This is a religious decree often practiced against women (relating often to marriage, sexual abuse, and adultery) issued by religious leaders, known as *moulavi* or *moulana* in Bangladesh.
6. *Bonded labor*: In many villages in Sindh (India) and Pakistan some women are virtually imprisoned and forced to labor over many years.
7. *Acid attacks*. Predominantly in the Indian subcontinent, acid is thrown on women who refuse to marry a man or turn down his sexual advances.

Armed Conflict and Sexual Violence

During wars and other armed conflicts, sexual assaults, enforced prostitution, and many forms of exploitation of women occur. Indeed, systematic violations of women's rights during wars have been the norm around the world, despite the Geneva Conventions that codify the laws of war and conflict. During the 1992 campaign of ethnic cleansing in Bosnia, 20,000 Muslim women were systematically raped and 15,000 women were raped during the 1994 genocide in Rwanda. Many of the rape victims in Rwanda were infected with AIDS. Sexual violence routinely involving mutilation, sexual slavery, gang rape, torture before being killed, and disembowelment of pregnant women has been reported in African countries involved in armed conflict between 1987 and 2007 (Bastick, Grimm, & Kunz, 2007).

Transnational Violence against Women

Trafficking of women occurs within, as well as across, national borders. Poverty and gender discrimination in many less-developed countries results in them being a disproportionate source of trafficked women. These vulnerabilities are maintained through the collusion of the market, the state, the community, and the family unit. In fact, traditional family structures, which are based on the maintenance of traditional sex roles and the division of labor that derives from such roles (for women, housekeeping, caretaking, and other unpaid or underpaid subsistence labor), frequently support the system of trafficking. Studies have shown that many trafficked women are kept in conditions of forced labor through sexual, physical, and psychological abuse. Women are threatened with violence against their families; they are kept in isolation; they are raped and forced to take drugs; and their passports and identity documents are seized.

TREATMENT OF WOMEN IN THE CRIMINAL JUSTICE SYSTEMS

According to the World Prison Brief (2017), women and girls make up only 6.9 percent of the global prison population, though this is a 50-percent increase since 2000. This is a reflection of judicial reluctance to impose custodial sentences on women due to the obligations of females in society and also to the lack of facilities to meet the specific needs of female prisoners, such as prenatal and postnatal care. This reluctance has been labeled as "chivalry."

Of particular concern in the international context is that, in a number of countries, trafficked women who are members of ethnic and racial minorities are held in prison before deportation (United Nations, 2000). While in prison these women are confronted not only with linguistic and cultural isolation, but also with racism and xenophobic violence. This is known as secondary victimization. The abuse of women in custody is a particularly urgent matter that requires a more prompt and effective response on the part of prison systems in accordance with international standards and norms.

WOMEN AS JUSTICE PROFESSIONALS

Based on 2015 data compiled by UNODC on female professionals employed in the criminal justice system in 30 countries (see Table 60.1), it can be inferred that women have the lowest representation among the police (less than one-third) and an equal, or more than equal, representation in the judiciary. While the representation of women in the prison system includes women in management, treatment, custodial, and other areas (maintenance, food service, etc.), they have still not reached equal representation. While gender equality has been promoted throughout the labor force, the under-representation of women in the police in particular has to do with organizational culture. Other reasons for the low proportion of women in the police service are the work conditions and the prevailing organizational climate (gender bias, harassment, the military model of policing, and discriminatory practices based on physical differences), which make the work unattractive to women (Natarajan, 2008).

As shown in Table 60.1, countries that employ few women in the police are generally those with higher disparities between men and women in the Gender Inequality Index (GII). The GII measures gender inequalities in three important aspects of human development – reproductive health; empowerment, and economic status. However, a correlation analysis of the three CJ sectors and GII found no significant association between them.

SUMMARY AND CONCLUSION

Seven important points can be drawn from the above discussion of the treatment of women as victims, as offenders, and as employees in criminal justice systems in Western and non-Western countries.

1. There is much wider recognition of the widespread and serious forms of victimization committed against women in many traditional societies. The 1995 UN Convention against the Elimination of All Forms of Discrimination against Women (CEDAW) requires member states to challenge those cultural beliefs and practices based on gender inequality and to eliminate those forms of victimization against women that

Table 60.1. Percentage of women professionals in the criminal justice system and the gender inequality measure (GII) scores for 30 nations

	Country	Police	Judges	Prison	GII
1	Denmark	14.43	56.45	46.39	0.041
2	Slovenia	13.3	78.26	25.07	0.053
3	Finland	16.29	54.49	36.81	0.056
4	Singapore	18.08	38.23	24.77	0.068
5	Belgium	21.75	51.6	33.05	0.073
6	Italy	7.13	52.4	16.74	0.085
7	Portugal	7.47	58.92	25.27	0.091
8	France	19.03	68.08	25.17	0.102
9	Lithuania	36.12	61.42	37.26	0.121
10	Czech Republic	15.73	59.84	24.6	0.129
11	United Kingdom	28.61	48.3	37.03	0.131
12	Poland	15.4	63.33	21.32	0.137
13	Croatia	17.62	69.77	29.82	0.141
14	Montenegro	9.34	58.18	20.7	0.156
15	Bosnia and Herzegovina	7.31	64.17	15.77	0.158
16	Slovakia	16.98	62.68	21.16	0.179
17	Serbia	23.22	69.66	25.35	0.185
18	Latvia	37.4	78.65	34.76	0.191
19	Kazakhstan	6.86	43.33	11.34	0.202
20	Malta	19.29	42.86	16.22	0.217
21	Albania	9.6	45.6	14.7	0.267
22	Barbados	16.44	54.17	38.1	0.291
23	Chile	15.12	59.07	26.84	0.322
24	Trinidad and Tobago	24.77	58.24	2.03	0.324
25	Mexico	13.56	35.69	34.36	0.345
26	El Salvador	12.78	46.78	31.29	0.384
27	Algeria	6.35	43.21	11.15	0.429
28	Honduras	10.34	52.89	21.74	0.461
29	Guyana	29.04	56.1	43.44	0.508
30	Paraguay	7.97	47.11	25.51	0.966

Source: UNODC: Criminal Justice System Resource Data and UNDP: Gender Inequality Index 2015

are culturally and country-specific. National and international efforts are leading to improvements in reporting, recording, and prosecuting crimes against women. The International Criminal Court (ICC) statutes explicitly lay down a number of sexual violence crimes unprecedented in international criminal law. Rape, sexual slavery, enforced prostitution, forced pregnancy, or any other form of sexual violence of comparable gravity are now incorporated as both crimes against humanity and war crimes (see the chapter on the ICC).

2. As more women take their full place in society and more of them make a living outside the home, it might be expected that greater proportions of them will fall victim to regular street crimes and to sexual harassment. This is already evident in some societies, such as in India, where "eve teasing" is a widespread problem. An international survey on the victimization of women is therefore an urgent research priority

3. Women are victimized because they are women. Gender-based violence is most often culturally normalized and socially accepted in most parts of the traditional world. Understanding and minimizing the harm from such violence requires a more culturally sensitive human rights approach than a criminal justice approach. The international agenda should consider ways to empower women to allow them to take charge of their own lives.

4. It is unclear whether the growing emancipation of women in developing countries will result in larger proportions of women becoming involved in crime, as occurred in industrialized and developed countries for the past three decades. At the international level, however, women are becoming more involved in serious crimes of drug trafficking, human trafficking, terrorism, and genocide, but they still play a marginal role compared to men.

5. If the number of women offenders increase, there is likely to be a concomitant increase in the number of women incarcerated. This will have important consequences for the prison system, which has signally failed, even in developed countries, to cater adequately to the special needs of women in custody, including to the need to preserve the relationship with the children and families.

6. Even in developing countries, the growing emancipation of women has resulted in large numbers of them obtaining employment in the criminal justice system in prosecution, the prisons, probation, and courts. One exception is the police, where women account for a small minority of officers even within most developed countries. There is a special need to find ways to making policing an attractive job for women, in which their special talents are employed and rewarded.

7. There is a need to develop and to pursue more comparative cross-cultural research on women offenders and criminal justice professionals. The purposes would be to improve treatment of women offenders in the criminal justice system and to find ways to increase the representation of women among criminal justice professionals.

ACKNOWLEDGMENT

The authors would like to thank Dr. Monica Ciobanu, Associate Professor of Sociology and Criminal Justice at the State University of New York Plattsburgh for her assistance with the earlier version of the chapter published in the first edition of the book.

REFERENCES

Adler, F. (1975). *Sisters in crime: The rise of the new criminal*. New York: McGraw-Hill.

Anderson, T. & Bennett, R. (1996). Development, gender and crime: The scope of the routine activities approach. *Justice Quarterly*, 19, 499–513.

Bastick, M., Grimm, K., & Kunz, R., (2007). *Sexual violence in armed conflict: A global overview and implications for the security sector*. Geneva: DCAF.

Brown, S. E. (2014). Female perpetrators of the Rwandan Genocide. *International Feminist Journal of Politics*, 16(3), 448–469.

Cohen, L. E. & Felson, M. (1979). Social change and crime rate trends: A routine activity approach. *American Sociological Review*, 44(4), 588–608.

Harper, R. L., Harper, G. C., & Stockdale, J. E., (2002). The role and sentencing of women in drug trafficking. *Legal and Criminological Psychology*, 7, 101–104.

Kangaspunta, K. (2008). *Women traffickers*. UNODC. www.ungift.org/docs/ungift/pdf/vf/traffickerworkshop/women%20traffickers.pdf.

Kleemans, E., Kruisbergen, E., & Kouwenberg, R. (2014). Women, brokerage and transnational organized crime. Empirical results from the Dutch Organized Crime Monitor. *Trends in Organized Crime*, 17(1/2), 16–30.

Natarajan, M. (2008). *Women police in a changing society: Back door to equality*. Aldershot: Ashgate.

Steffensmeier, D. & Allan, E. (1996). Gender and crime: Toward a gendered theory of female offending. *Annual Review of Sociology*, 22, 459–487.

Steffensmeier, D. & Emilie, A. (1996). Gender and crime: toward a gendered theory of female offending. *Annual Review of Sociology*, 22, 459–487.

United Nations. (2000). Women in the criminal justice system. Retrieved from www.uncjin.org/Documents/congr10/12e.pdf.

Weinberg, L. & Eubank, W. (2011). Women's involvement in terrorism. *Gender Issues*, 28(1/2), 22–49.

World Prison Brief. (2017). World female imprisonment list. Retrieved from www.prisonstudies.org/sites/default/files/resources/downloads/world_female_prison_4th_edn_v4_web.pdf.

61 Domestic Violence

A Global Concern

Mangai Natarajan and Diana Rodriguez-Spahia

INTRODUCTION

Domestic violence (DV) is a pervasive problem and the most common form of violence against women worldwide. Also called intimate partner violence, battering, or spouse abuse, in all cases it is committed by a spouse, ex-spouse, or current or former partner (Straus, 1979). It can occur among heterosexual or same-sex couples and both men and women can be victims. Thus, the term domestic violence is gender-neutral, though the empirical literature documents that women are much more often victimized and more frequently suffer physical and psychological harm.

Based on data from 79 countries, the World Health Organization (WHO, 2013) reports that 35 percent of women worldwide have experienced either physical and/or sexual intimate partner violence or sexual violence by a non-partner at some point in their lives. Forty-two percent of women who have been physically and/or sexually abused by a partner have experienced injuries and a significant portion of homicides (38 percent) and various forms of assaults (including sexual assaults) are related to DV (WHO, 2013, p. 31). The Council of Europe reports that about one-quarter of European women experience domestic violence at some point in their lives, and 6–10 percent of women suffer domestic violence in a given year. The Status of Women report from Canada estimates that gay, lesbian, or bisexual individuals are three times more likely than heterosexuals to experience violence. Transgendered people are nearly twice as likely as other people to experience intimate partner violence in their lifetimes. Women with physical and/or cognitive impairments are two to three times more likely to experience violence than women without such impairments.

Victims of domestic violence are subjected to many forms of torture and cruelty, including murder, in a supposedly "domestic" environment, and many are terrified of living in their martial/conjugal homes. According to the United Nations' Universal Declaration of Human Rights (1948), DV is a human rights violation and is a major impediment to achieving gender equality.

DV is therefore a multifaceted problem, which should be addressed by various constituencies including human rights activists, and criminal justice and public health researchers and practitioners. Research is crucial for understanding and responding to DV. How we measure the prevalence of DV, what we identify as the risk factors, which theories seem to provide most help in understanding and responding to DV, which preventive and treatment programs seem most effective, and the respective roles of the health and criminal justice systems are all questions of vital importance in society's response to the problem (Natarajan, 2007).

FACTORS CONTRIBUTING TO DV

Though many different contributory individual, interpersonal, community, and societal-level factors have been identified as predictors of DV, one factor consistently recognized is the patriarchal system that exists in many societies. The Duluth Model of Power that was developed in 1981 by the Duluth Domestic Abuse Intervention Project in Duluth, Minnesota identifies "the power control" of men over women as the central cause and it advocates a "cultural shift" to an egalitarian relationship, i.e., men and women should help develop mutual respect, trust, support, honesty, and accountability. This feminist approach of "equality" between men and women is fundamental to dealing with domestic violence, but for international responses in dealing with domestic violence it needs to include cultural and sexual contexts.

MEASUREMENT OF DOMESTIC VIOLENCE

DV is difficult to measure because it consists of so many different forms. Pushing, shoving, and grabbing are the most common types of assault, but kicking, slapping, and hitting with fists resulting in bruising, cuts, and broken bones are not uncommon. The violence may be nonphysical as when a partner threatens to harm the other, or someone close to them. The WHO (2014) report based on 133 countries points out the following impediments in developing measures. (1) *Lack of available data*. Only 57 percent of countries have conducted nationwide surveys on violence against women and depending on the region, the quality and consistency of data often varies. (2) The *varied definition* of DV from country to country. (3) *Lack of empirical support for policies*. For example, some countries are starting to discuss and develop policies against violence, though these policies are often not data-driven. (4) *Lack of coordinated effort* in developing polices. For example, multiple agencies are spearheading efforts in dealing with DV, but they don't typically communicate or collaborate with each other. This often results in uncoordinated, ineffective results and expenditures. (5) *Limited or lack of quality and availability of victim services* to reduce repeat victimization.

Johnson (1995) makes a useful distinction between two types of DV taking place in the USA and other Western nations – patriarchal violence and common couple violence. Patriarchal violence involves a systematic use of violence including economic subordination, threats, isolation, and other control tactics. In such situations, beatings by men to control their wives occur on a regular basis and escalate in seriousness over time. Common couple violence is occasional and rarely escalates to serious forms. This distinction has implications for the type of data collected to measure DV. For example, data collected from women's shelters might capture quite different kinds of violence from national surveys.

LAWS AGAINST DV

The term domestic violence is not defined by international law. However, the customary laws that obligate states to prevent and respond to acts of violence against women and ensure access to justice have been recognized by the UN Committee on the Elimination of Discrimination Against Women (CEDAW). Two overall principles guide the DV laws: offender accountability (criminal responsibility) and victim safety and protection (victim assistance). The laws are evolving and have played a part in emboldening thousands of women to exercise their legal right to leave harmful situations at home.

CRIMINAL JUSTICE RESPONSES TO DV: POLICING AND PROSECUTION

Four major policing approaches can be distinguished when responding to cases of domestic violence.

(1) *Mandatory arrest* where police officers responding to a call of domestic violence must arrest the alleged perpetrator if there is probable cause to do so (UNODC, 2010).

(2) *Pro-arrest* offers some discretion to responding officers. They are expected to evaluate the scene, examine physical injuries/evidence, and are encouraged to arrest the primary aggressor but are not required to do so.

(3) *Mediation*, which does not expect or typically result in responding officers making an arrest. Instead, officers act as intermediaries and ensure safety of both parties while deescalating the conflict. India's use of women police stations falls within this approach.

(4) *Passive or traditional approach* where police officers may only respond to a call of domestic violence because they are required to do so and may only "warn" abusers as they believe that domestic violence is a personal, not a criminal justice, matter.

While mandatory and pro arrest policies are followed in the USA, countries such as the UK and New Zealand follow pro-arrest methods. The USA also practices *dual arrest* when the police arrest both parties involved in an incident. UN Women (2015) notes that in some countries, domestic violence calls are not a priority and officers often dismiss complaints and blame the victim. In the USA, no-drop prosecution has sometimes been adopted as a counterpart of mandatory arrest, which focuses more on punishing the perpetrator than on meeting the needs of DV victims. All evidence that might suffice to convict a defendant, even where the victim is unwilling to take the stand, is considered. Mandatory arrest and no-drop prosecution policies demonstrate the fact that DV is a crime that warrants societal outrage and batterer accountability that works under the premise of "public safety" and "the public interest." However, neither is consistent with the victim empowerment model and they are unlikely to work in more traditional cultures where DV is still not recognized as a crime by wide sections of society. The UK uses pro-arrest policy with substantial victim support. It has introduced a program known as Multi-Agency Risk Assessment Conference (MARAC) which brings multi-agencies including the police, health providers, child protection, housing authorities, independent domestic violence advisors, and other specialists from the statutory and voluntary sectors to assess the risk and to develop a comprehensive safety plan for high-risk victims based on risk assessment. This is made possible by the welfare state and existence of a variety of social agencies thus paving the way for a balanced approach using both deterrence and the victim's welfare.

GLOBAL RESPONSE TO DV

Feminist Initiatives

Since the 1970s, feminist advocates of women's equality (Walker, 1979) have played an important role in creating the "battered women's movement," which has taken hold in most Western nations. Despite five decades of struggle, however, this movement has little effect on the patriarchal culture in many parts of the world that produces inequality and violence at home. However, the United Nations has now taken up the challenge of protecting women and children from violence at home.

Though knowledge of DV has increased, we have yet to find effective ways to prevent it. Since the victim's safety is the top priority of feminist agenda, the main research focus was on the mandatory arrests of perpetrators. However, the effectiveness of mandatory arrest in the longer term is still in doubt. Research also shows that many women victims do not want their spouses to be arrested and caught up in the criminal justice system. Further, even if there are laws in place, judicial bias against women often prevents effective action taken against perpetrators. In addition, there is a need for: magistrate/judge cooperation with police; resources training, funding to sensitize the criminal justice personnel (police, prosecutors, lawyers, judges, and corrections officers); clarity in DV policies; DV intelligence team for focused attention; prioritization of the DV cases; assessment of the various DV needs; understanding the limited role of police; improving diversity in the recruitment polices of the CJ system.

Women Police Stations

Some countries such as India and Brazil have introduced women police stations consisting mostly of women that are trained to handle cases of violence against women. There are 631 women police stations in India and about 500 in Brazil. According to Natarajan (2010) women police stations serve as gendered crime control agents and provide an opportunity for woman-to-woman communication. They empower women who have been culturally conditioned to be submissive and not to report DV or seek help from police. They help many families (husband, children, in-laws) to understand how harmful cultural practices can result in the abuse of women. A recent evaluation by Perova and Reynolds (2017) of women police stations in Brazil states that establishing a women's police station in a metropolitan municipality is associated with a 17-percent reduction in the female homicide rate among ages 15–49 years.

Many Asian nations including Sri Lanka, Pakistan, Nepal, and the Philippines are creating women desks, women cells, women stations, women bureaus, and women units providing opportunities for women to serve in the police, as well as to deal with the increased numbers of DV cases now being reported. Latin American countries (Argentina, Colombia, Costa Rica, El Salvador, Ecuador, Nicaragua, Peru, and Uruguay) have adopted the Brazilian model and are now introducing women police stations.

SUMMARY

DV is a crime that cannot be tolerated in the modern world – though some countries are still in denial because they still see DV as a private not a public matter. In sum, while laws

Table 61.1. Countries that have defined DV as a crime

Year	Countries
1990–1999	Puerto Rico, Niger, Bahamas, Israel, Belize, Barbados, Peru, Argentina, Chile, Finland, France, Malaysia, USA, Australia, Bolivia, New Zealand, Panama, Portugal, Saint Lucia, Saint Vincent and the Grenadines, Austria, Colombia, Costa Rica, Ecuador, El Salvador, Guatemala, Guyana, Ireland, Jamaica, Mexico, Nicaragua, Singapore, United Kingdom, Belgium, Dominica, Honduras, Korea (North and South), Mauritius, South Africa, Sweden, Venezuela, Antigua and Barbuda, Slovakia, Slovenia, Spain, Trinidad and Tobago.
2000–2009	Brunei Darussalam, Canada, Cyprus, Madagascar, Paraguay, Saint Kitts and Nevis, Seychelles, Turkey, China, Comoros, Czech Republic, Germany, Italy, Japan, Liechtenstein, Mauritania, Chad, Dominican Republic, Netherlands, Norway, Uruguay, Croatia, Hungary, Kyrgyzstan, Lesotho, Luxembourg, Namibia, Philippines, Romania, Indonesia, Laos, Macedonia, Mongolia, Montenegro, Switzerland, Bosnia and Herzegovina, Bulgaria, Cambodia, India, Poland, Serbia, Sri Lanka, Sudan, Brazil, Albania, Estonia, Georgia, Greece, Kenya, Malawi, Malta, Ghana, Moldova, Sierra Leone, Thailand, Turkmenistan, Vietnam, Zimbabwe, Botswana, Denmark, Jordan, Rwanda, San Marino, Sao Tome and Principe, Vanuatu, Burundi, Equatorial Guinea, Fiji, Kazakhstan, Mozambique, Nepal, Suriname, Timor Leste, Tuvalu, Uganda.
2010–2018	Azerbaijan, Bangladesh, Cape Verde, Central African Republic, Grenada, Angola, Lithuania, Zambia, Benin, Maldives, Palau, Bhutan, Guinea-Bissau, Pakistan, Papua New Guinea, Samoa, Saudi Arabia, Swaziland, Tajikistan, Tonga, Belarus, Kiribati, Solomon Islands, Algeria, Andorra, Bahrain, Armenia, Liberia, Nauru, Tunisia, Ukraine, Morocco.
In progress	Burkina Faso, Iraq, Myanmar.
No law	Afghanistan, Cameroon, Democratic Republic of the Congo, Côte d'Ivoire, Cuba, Djibouti, Egypt, Eritrea, Ethiopia, Gambia, Guinea, Haiti, Iceland, Iran, Kuwait, Latvia, Lebanon, Libya, Mali, Marshall Islands, Micronesia, Nigeria, Oman, Qatar, Russia, Somalia, Syria, Tanzania, Togo, United Arab Emirates, Uzbekistan, Yemen Gabon, Monaco, Senegal, South Sudan.

Sources: UN Global Database on Violence Against Women, UNHCR RefWorld, and the US Department of State

are in place (see Table 61.1), the ways in which the enforcement plan takes place in any given country depends on the culture of the society, the institutions of the society, and the agencies that in place to deal with them. Nevertheless, there are variations in the development of enforcing the DV law, all countries are still struggling to deal with diversified communities within. So, a one-size-fits-all solution does not work. The challenges lie in developing victim-centered services and dealing with diversified communities. Victims of DV continue to be harmed at unacceptable rates by their intimate partners and harm themselves by not seeking help. The most important need is to educate men and women to report the violence and seek help to protect safety and health. DV affects not only the couple involved, but also their innocent children, other family members, and their friends. Every individual is entitled to live in a violence-free environment.

REFERENCES

Johnson, M. P. (1995). Patriarchal terrorism and common couple violence: Two forms of violence against women. *Journal of Marriage and the Family*, 57, 283–294.

Straus, M. A. (1979). Measuring intrafamily conflict and violence: The Conflict Tactics (CT) Scales. *Journal of Marriage and the Family*, 41, 75–88.

Perova, E. & Reynolds, S. A. (2017). Women's police stations and intimate partner violence: Evidence from Brazil. *Social Science and Medicine*, 174, 188–196.

Natarajan, M. (Ed). (2007). *Domestic violence: The five big questions*. International Library of Criminology, Criminal Justice and Penology. Aldershot: Ashgate.

(2010). *Gendered crime prevention: The role of women police stations in India and Brazil*. Individual Expert Report, Twelfth United Nations Congress on Crime Prevention and Criminal Justice, Salvador da Bahia, Brazil, 12–19, 2010.

World Health Organization (WHO). (2013). *Global and regional estimates of violence against women: Prevalence and health effects of intimate partner violence and non-partner sexual violence*. Geneva: WHO Library.

(2014). *Global status report on violence prevention 2014* (First Edition, pp. 1–290, Reprint). Geneva: WHO Library.

United Nations Office on Drugs and Crime (UNODC). (2010). *Handbook on effective police responses to violence against women* (E.10.IV.3, pp. 1–95). New York: United Nations.

UN Women's Virtual Knowledge Centre to End Violence against Women and Girls. (2015, April). Criminal justice system response to domestic violence. Retrieved from www.stopvaw.org/criminal_justice_system_response_to_domestic_violence.

Walker, L. E. (1979). *The battered woman*. New York: Harper & Row.

62 Honor-Based Violence

A Review

Popy Begum and Mangai Natarajan

INTRODUCTION

The British Crown Prosecution Service (CPS) defines honor-based violence (HBV) as a collection of practices that are used to control behavior within families or other social groups to protect perceived cultural and religious beliefs and/or honor. Such violence can occur when perpetrators perceive that a relative has shamed the family and/or community by breaking their honor code. The victims of HBV are primarily girls and young women between the ages of 13 and 25 years and the perpetrators are typically parents, brothers, close relatives, and sometimes the elders in the community.

HBV has been prevalent in several countries in South Asia, the Middle East, and some North African regions. Countries including the USA, Canada, the UK, the Netherlands, Germany, and Sweden have recently identified HBV as an issue that is especially problematic in first-generation immigrant communities (Gill, Strange, & Roberts, 2014; Helba, Bernstein, Leonard, & Bauer, 2015). The term "honor" distinguishes HBV from other violent crimes that are direct, planned, and premeditated, with defined perpetrators. Patriarchy is widely regarded as the main culprit for HBV. While women are generally the victims, young men and LGBTQ people may also be affected. Therefore, HBV is not just violence against women but a form of gender-based violence. This chapter provides a review of what is known about HBV and what needs to be done to reduce it.

NATURE AND PREVALENCE OF HBV

An official Netherlands report (n.d.) describes various forms of HBV, including physical abuse (kicking and beating); psychological pressure (strict monitoring, humiliation, threats); forced marriage; abandonment (leaving someone in their country of origin or sending them back there); forced suicide; and murder. According to many reports, the behaviors that result in HBV include: (a) dressing in a manner unacceptable to the family or community; (b) wanting to terminate or prevent an arranged marriage or desiring to marry by own choice; (c) engaging in sexual acts outside marriage, or a nonsexual relationship perceived as inappropriate; or (d) engaging in homosexual acts.[1] Though honor killings

---

[1] Some classifications of HBV include genital mutilation, which in our view is gender-based violence, not HBV.

are the most serious form of HBV, the most common form is "forced marriage." Forced marriages are arrangements where one or both people do not freely and fully consent to the marriage and consequently are subjected to pressure and/or abuse (Begum, 2016). Western countries differ in their focus on HBV crimes. In Finland and Sweden, the focus has been on "honor-killings," whereas in Norway and Denmark the focus has been on "forced marriages" (Keskinen, 2009).

While many countries recognize HBV, the UK is the only country that has officially recorded and reported the crimes since it introduced the law to criminalize forced marriages under the Anti-Social Behavior, Crime and Policing Act of 2014. This act defines the problem and punishment that derived from the Forced Marriage (Civil Protection) Act of 2007. In 2016, the Forced Marriage Unit (FMU) claims to have given advice and/or support to 1,428 forced marriage-related cases. In the USA, the Tahirih Justice Center in 2011 reported 3,000 cases of known and suspected cases of forced marriage among diverse national, ethnic, and religious groups.

At a global level, the United Nations Population Fund (UNFPA, 2000) has provided an estimate of the number of honor killings of up to 5,000 women murdered by family members each year. Based on a comparative analysis of the number of reported cases in Western industrialized countries, Curtis et al. (2014) estimated 24–27 honor killings per year in the USA. The British police and Crown Prosecution Service estimated that 10 to 12 women are victims of HBV murder each year in the UK. According to the Indo-Canadian Association, Canada experienced 13 cases of honor-based murders between 2002 and 2010. The Max-Planck Institute estimate about 12 per year in Germany, but only three were considered to be HBV killings.

In many countries, no reliable estimate can be made of HBV because there are no specific laws to record the offense. For example, in India, a sizable number of HBV murders occur, but there is no special category to record the offenses, which are simply registered as murders. Based on UNICEF data, Reuters reported (Srivastava, 2018) that, "India constitutes more than 20 percent of the world's adolescent population and accounts for the highest number of child marriages in South Asia given its size and population." However, there has recently been a sharp decline in marriages below 18 years, which is likely to be the result of the Prohibition of Child Marriage Act, enacted in 2006. Specific legislation of this kind is needed to permit recording of these crimes and the development of preventive strategies and victim assistance programs.

One area that needs special attention when estimating levels of HBV in India and elsewhere is self-immolation or suicides that are the outcome of HBV. Studies have shown that many homicides of young women in India are covered up under the categories of suicide or accidental deaths (Natarajan, 2014) because the perpetrators camouflage any evidence of homicide. Again, even when the victims do survive, they frequently will not identify the perpetrators due to fear or to safeguard their family honor.

HBV CASES

Media sources have provided snapshots of high-profile cases that illustrate acts of "honor" that end in violence. Below we provide samples of cases of HBV in various parts of the world (see the end of this chapter for references for each case).

Case 1. Fadime Şahindal, a 26-year-old Kurdish woman, who moved to Sweden when she was seven years old, was shot by her father in January 2002 for refusing to accept Kurdish traditions of arranged marriages and instead had chosen a relationship with a Swedish man. Her father was an uneducated Kurdish farmer who moved to Sweden in 1980. She grew up under the control of her father and younger brother, who physically abused her. She moved to another town to get away from her parents – for four years the father threatened to kill her, but Fadime took a chance to visit her mother and sisters before she left for Africa to study, which is when her father killed her (Hildebrand, 2002).

Case 2. In 2007, Manoj, a 23-year-old man, married a 19-year-old woman, Babli, against the wishes of her family. The village elders Khap Panchayat (a village informal judiciary) accused the couple of violating the code of conduct related to marriage. For that reason, they were murdered by her family members. But Manoj's mother fought for justice and in March 2010, the Karnal district court sentenced the five perpetrators, including Babli's family members – her brother, uncles, and cousins – to death. This is the first time an Indian court had done so in an honor killing case. The Khap leader, who ordered and orchestrated the killings but did not take part in the killings, was given a life sentence (Singh, 2011).

Case 3. On January 1, 2009, 22-year-old Amandeep was fatally stabbed in the basement of a Mississauga grocery store in Canada by her father-in-law, who justified the killing because she was going to dishonor their family by leaving his son for another man. He was sentenced to life imprisonment with no chance of parole for 15 years (Government of Canada, 2016).

Case 4. In October 2009, 20-year-old Noor al-Maleki from Phoenix, Arizona was killed when her father ran her over with his Jeep in a parking lot, crushing her body beneath its wheels. According to police her father believed she had become "too Westernized" and refused to submit to the marriage her father had arranged for her to an Iraqi man who needed a green card (Ali, 2015).

Case 5. June 2, 2016. An 18-year-old schoolteacher Maria Abbasi died from injuries (85 percent body burns) after her body was set on fire for refusing a marriage proposal in Islamabad, Pakistan. The perpetrators beat her up, then drenched her in petrol and set her body ablaze before leaving her for dead. Three people were arrested in connection with this killing (Ansari & Saifi, 2016).

CONCEPTUALIZING AND CONTEXTUALIZING HBV

HBV is a recently defined phenomenon, and research to date consists mostly of qualitative analyses of cases that are reported in the media and a few interview studies of offenders (Doğan, 2016) or victims and survivors (Mulvihill et al., 2018). The most discussed causal hypothesis is that the patriarchal system, which differentiates and stratifies people based on sex and/or gender, is responsible for HBV. This system marginalizes women through norms that are constructed and maintained to foster male domination that become part and parcel of everyday life. This subcultural collectivism leads to a culture that valorizes honor, any violation of which brings shame, admonition, and eventually punishment. The behaviors of HBV are crimes under mainstream culture (but not defined as such), and criminology offers

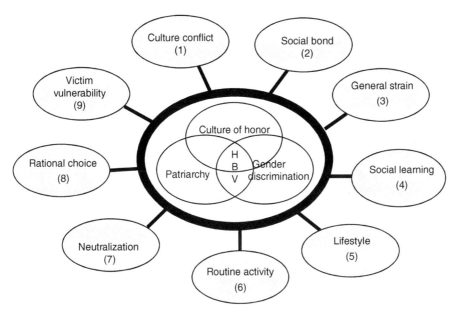

Figure 62.1. Contextualizing the criminology of honor-based violence.

nine theories that could help to explain these crimes, as summarized in the outermost rings of Figure 62.1.

1. Thorsten Sellin's (1938) culture conflict theory can help explain how immigrants who move to countries with their own norms and behaviors will have conflict with the host culture or mainstream prevailing culture.
2. Hirschi's social bond theory's (1969) four elements of involvement, commitment, belief, and attachment can help explain the perpetrator's act of HBV.
3. Agnew's general strain theory (1985) focuses on the emotional strains that push family members to take drastic measures against those members of the family that violate their codes.
4. Sutherland's social learning and differential association (1947) can help explain how honor and gender codes are transmitted through generations.
5. Hindelang, Gottfredson, and Garofalo's lifestyle theory (1978) helps to understand the effect of changing societal environments on individuals who migrate from their own countries.
6. Cohen and Felson's routine activity theory (1979) deals with the convergence in space and time of the motivated offender and suitable target in the absence of guardianship, in this case the absence of "law" to control HBV.
7. Sykes and Matza's (1957) five techniques of neutralization, including denial of responsibility, denial of injury, denial of victims, condemnation of condemner's, and appeal to higher loyalties can help to justify the perpetrators' behaviors to themselves.

8. Cornish and Clarke's rational choice theory (1986) explains how adherence to honor-based gender codes brings benefits to the perpetrators of HBV.
9. Culturally legitimate victim (Weiss & Borges, 1973) theory posits that social processes prepare women as vulnerable or potential victims and makes them socially approved victims. Young girls and women become vulnerable to victimization for violation of honor codes in the isolated home environments in which they are they are socialized.

CONCLUSION: PREVENTING HBV

Each type of HBV has specific characteristics and therefore should be dealt with differently. For example, forced marriage and murder are completely different due to the perpetrators' motives, severity of the harm, and the victim's needs. Specific policies and procedures to effectively address each category of violence are therefore needed. Conceptualizing the types of actions by their components – nature, extent, patterns, perpetrators, victims, and countries of occurrence – and contextualizing the situations in which the HBV occurs, are crucial for understanding and reducing the violence.

While murder, torture, and verbal and psychological abuse are HBV strategies employed by family members, the "intent" or "purpose" of HBV is different from other forms of violence against women. Scholars debate whether HBV is domestic violence (DV) or even hate crime (Chesler, 2010; Hayes et al., 2018). However, many risk factors for DV identified by WHO and CDC do not fully explain HBV. HBV is committed not just by husbands, as in intimate partner violence, but also by other family members and relatives. The cultural norms and scripts associated with HBV distinguish it from DV. While research to inform policy is underway, immediate responses are needed to prevent HBV. In the UK, HBV is included informally under the category of DV to help victims. Under the umbrella of the "Multi-Agency Risk Assessment Conference" (MARAC), representatives from various statutory and voluntary organizations (police, independent DV advisors, health, child care services, mental health and substance abuse treatment services, religious representatives, and other specialists) convene to assist DV victims who are identified as high-risk using the "Domestic Abuse, Stalking, Harassment and Honor-based Violence" (DASH) tool. MARAC serves to protect high-risk HBV victims from repeat victimization.

Another problem is that perpetrators flee back to the countries where they come from. There is an urgent need for extradition treaties that are forcefully implemented so that the perpetrators can be held accountable.

HBV is a serious form of gender-based violence, independent of religion, which requires empirical investigation (including scientific estimation of its prevalence) to find ways of reducing harm inflicted on vulnerable young people. Accurately identifying risk factors of HBV will help in generating appropriate solutions to end it (Payton, 2014).

Finally, a considerable obstacle to the prevention of HBV is the hidden nature of these crimes. Families are quick to disguise such killings as accidents or suicides, and usually have little remorse about what they did to their own kin. Many victims of HBV will not seek help from anyone because they are socialized to safeguard family honor and culturally expected to suffer in silence.

Honor-based violence has its roots in non-Western nations, where these crimes have been paid scant attention, and indeed are often not seen or recorded as crimes. Now that

HBV-related crimes are mushrooming in Western nations due to globalization and the attendant patterns of migration, it is time for criminologists to think about this issue independent of DV-related crimes. Regardless of whether they live in Western or non-Western countries, unless HBV victims come to public notice, little can be done to protect them. Empowering girls and boys in schools and sensitizing the public through social media could help. Criminologists could play an important part in identifying effective measures to control and prevent HBV.

REFERENCES

Begum, P. (2016). *Should "forced marriage" be criminalised?* London: Howard League for Penal Reform.

Agnew, R. (1985). A revised strain theory of delinquency. *Social Forces*, 64, 151–167.

Chesler, P. (2010). Are honour killings simply domestic violence? *Middle East Quarterly*, 16(2), 61–69.

Cohen, E. L. & Felson, M. (1979). Social change and crime rate trends: A routine activity approach. *American Sociological Review*, 44(4), 588–608.

Cornish, B. D & Clarke, V.G. R. (1986). *The reasoning criminal: Rational choice perspectives on offending.* New York: Springer.

Curtis, R., Delgado, S., Misshula, E., Henninger, A., Alsabahi, L., Hanna, E., Robbins-Stathas, L., Begum, P., & Marcus, A. (2014). *A comparative approach to estimating the annual number of honor killings in the United States among people from North African, Middle Eastern and Southeast Asian (MENASA) countries.* New York: AHA Foundation.

Doğan, R. (2016). The dynamics of honor killings and the perpetrators' experiences. *Homicide Studies*, 20(1), 53–79.

Gill, A. K., Strange, C., & Roberts, K. (2014). *Honour killing and violence.* London: Palgrave Macmillan.

Hayes, B. E. Mills, C. E, Freilich, J. D., & Chermak, S. M. (2018). Are honor killings unique? A comparison of honor killings, domestic violence homicides, and hate homicides by far-right extremists. *Homicide Studies*, 22(1), 70–93.

Helba, C., Bernstein. M., Leonard, M., & Bauer, E. (2015). *Report on exploratory study into honor violence measurement methods.* Washington, DC: US Department of Justice.

Hindelang, M. J., Gottfredson, M. R., & Garofalo, J. (1978). *Victims of personal crime: An empirical foundation for a theory of personal victimization.* Cambridge, MA: Ballinger.

Hirschi, T. (1969 [1998]). A control theory of delinquency. In F. P. Williams & Marilyn D. McShane (Eds.), *Criminology theory: Selected classic readings* (pp. 289–305). Cincinnati, OH: Anderson.

Keskinen, S. (2009). "Honour-related violence" and Nordic nation-building. In S. Keskinen, S. Tuori, S. Imi, & D. Mulinari (Eds.), *Complying with colonialism: Gender, race and ethnicity in the nordic region* (pp. 257–272). Farnham: Ashgate.

Mulvihill, N., Gangoli, G., Gill, A. K., & Hester, M. (2018). The experience of interactional justice for victims of "honour"-based violence and abuse reporting to the police in England and Wales. *Policing and Society*. doi:10.1080/10439463.2018.1427745.

Natarajan, M. (2014). Differences between intentional and non-intentional burn injuries in India: Implications for prevention. *Burns*, 40, 1033–1039.

Netherlands Report. (n.d). Retrieved from www.government.nl/topics/honour-based-violence/question-and-answer/what-forms-of-honour-based-violence-are-there.

Payton, J. (2014). "Honor," collectivity, and agnation: emerging risk factors in "honor"-based violence. *Journal of Interpersonal Violence*, 29(16), 2863–2883.

Sellin, T. (1938). Culture conflict and crime. *American Journal of Sociology*, 44(1), 97–103.

Srivastava, R. (2018). *India's child marriage numbers drop sharply, driving down global rate.* UNICEF. Retrieved from www.reuters.com/article/us-india-gender-child-marriage/indias-child-marriage-numbers-drop-sharply-driving-down-global-rate-unicef-idUSKBN1GI03F.

Sutherland, E. H. (1947). *Principles of criminology*. Fourth Edition. Philadelphia, PA: Lippincott.

Sykes, G. M. & Matza, D. (1957). Techniques of neutralization: A theory of delinquency. *American Sociological Review*, 22(6), 664–670.

Tahirih Justice Center. (2011). Forced marriage in immigrant communities in the United States 2011 National Survey Results. Retrieved from www.tahirih.org/wpcontent/uploads/2015/03/REPORT.

United Nations Population Fund (UNFPA). (2000). Annual report UNFPA. Retrieved from www .unfpa.org/sites/default/files/pub-pdf/annual_report00_eng.pdf.

Weis, K. & Borges, S. S. (1973). Victimology and rape: The case of the legitimate victim. *Issues in Criminology*, 8(2), 71–115.

Details of case stories can be obtained from the following references listed below:

Case 1. Hildebrand, J. (2002, January 31). "Honour" killing in Sweden silences courageous voice on ethnic integration. *Guardian*. Retrieved from www.theguardian.com/theguardian/2002/jan/31/guardianweekly.guardianweekly1.

Case 2. Singh, A. (2011, September 3). Manoj-Babli honour killing. *The Times of India*. Retrieved from https://timesofindia.indiatimes.com/india/Manoj-Babli-honour-killing-SC-allows-plea-against-acquittal-of-accused/articleshow/9844060.cms.

Case 3. Government of Canada. (2016, December 30). *Preliminary examination of so-called "honour killings" in Canada*. US Department of Justice. Retrieved from www.justice.gc.ca/eng/rp-pr/cj-jp/fv-vf/hk-ch/p2.html.

Case 4. Ali, A. (2015, April 30). Honor killings in America. *The Atlantic*. Retrieved from www .theatlantic.com/politics/archive/2015/04/honor-killings-in-america/391760/.

Case 5. Ansari, A. & Saifi, S. (2016, June 2). Pakistani woman dies after being set on fire for rejecting marriage proposal. *CNN*. Retrieved from www.cnn.com/2016/06/01/asia/pakistan-woman-fire-death/index.html.

63 International Perspectives on Child Maltreatment

Emily Hurren and Anna Stewart

INTRODUCTION

Child maltreatment is a global social problem affecting a concerning proportion of children and young people in all jurisdictions. Many assume that victimization of children primarily occurs at the hands of strangers outside of the home, but this is not the case. In addition to violating the rights of the child, maltreatment is associated with a range of negative biopsychosocial outcomes and economic costs.

In this chapter we provide an overview of child maltreatment and its components. We discuss the challenges associated with researching maltreatment, its causes and consequences, and the policy implications of this knowledge. We note that protection of children across the globe is dependent upon evidence-based prevention and intervention, and local, national, and international policies.

DEFINITION AND PREVALENCE OF CHILD MALTREATMENT

Child maltreatment is a broad concept, incorporating both abuse and neglect. Definitions vary widely across research, legislation, and jurisdictions, but typically include four subtypes: physical abuse, emotional or psychological abuse, sexual abuse or exploitation, and neglect (Institute of Medicine [IOM] and National Research Council [NRC], 2014). Some jurisdictions distinguish between subcategories of neglect, such as physical and emotional neglect. Likewise, in some jurisdictions exposure to domestic violence is considered an additional subtype of child maltreatment; others consider this a subcategory of emotional or psychological abuse, or neglect (IOM & NRC, 2014).

Variations in definitions of child maltreatment and its subtypes can be attributed to a range of factors (for a review, see NRC, 1993). Cultural differences impact definitions, particularly due to diverse perspectives of appropriate parenting, normative behavior, and child needs (Manly, 2005; NRC, 1993). Additionally, sources vary in consideration of the maltreater's identity (some exclude those who are not the child's parent or guardian), the maltreater's responsibilities, capabilities, and intentions, incorporation of risk of harm versus experienced harm, assessment of severity, and incorporation of commissions (actions) versus omissions (failure to act). The intended purpose of the definition (i.e., research, legislation, or treatment) may also affect inclusion of certain factors.

Definitional variations make global prevalence estimations challenging; different data sources yield different estimations (IOM & NRC, 2014). A recent review of meta-analyses produced an estimated global prevalence of maltreatment subtypes. Across self-report studies in particular, the estimated prevalence rate was 226/1000 for physical abuse, 127/1000 for sexual abuse, 363/1000 for emotional abuse, 163/1000 for physical neglect, and 184/1000 for emotional neglect (Stoltenborgh et al., 2015). Prevalence estimations varied across data sources, regions, and genders. Regardless, it is apparent that child maltreatment is an entrenched and significant problem across the globe.

CHILD MALTREATMENT RESEARCH CHALLENGES

Child maltreatment is inherently difficult to research, as families are typically private, and victims of maltreatment are vulnerable (Manly, 2005). There are two main types of data used in maltreatment research – self-report and official data – and there are advantages and disadvantages associated with each (for an overview, see IOM & NRC, 2014).

Due to ethical challenges most self-report data are collected from the parents of maltreated children, or from adolescents or adults who were previously maltreated. This data can be biased, or affected by interpretation, memory, trauma, or the passage of time. Nonetheless, self-report data can improve understanding of the lived experience of maltreatment, and the impact on the child's development.

The alternative to self-report data are official data (for an overview of literature, see Hurren, Stewart, & Dennison, 2017). Agencies responsible for responding to maltreatment keep records regarding the individuals they service; these administrative records form the basis of official data. Researchers are increasingly using administrative data and data-linkage, allowing records of maltreatment to be linked with records from justice, health, and education agencies. This improves understanding of maltreatment, mental health, and criminal offending links. Problematically, official records of maltreatment provide an underestimation of prevalence, as maltreatment often goes unrecognized and unreported. Importantly, discrepancies between self-report and official data are noted, particularly in estimations of the prevalence and outcomes of maltreatment. Both data sources should be incorporated in research efforts and policy development (Stoltenborgh et al., 2015).

CAUSES OF CHILD MALTREATMENT

There is no single cause of child maltreatment. A variety of risk and protective factors have been linked to child maltreatment, including factors relating to children, their parents, families, and context, including communities and macrosystems. Some risk factors considered important include parental substance/alcohol abuse or mental illness, limited social support, poor relationship quality, stressful living environment, low socioeconomic status/poverty, unemployment, young parental age, child disability or difficult temperament, and a parent's own childhood history of victimization (for a review, see IOM & NRC, 2014).

Intergenerational child maltreatment explores links between a parent's history of maltreatment and their child's maltreatment. A recent prospective, matched-comparisons study indicated that the observed extent of intergenerational transmission varied by data source (i.e., parent reports, child reports, and official data). While there was evidence of increased risk of neglect and sexual abuse among children of previously maltreated parents, detection/surveillance bias played a role in this relationship when official data were used (Widom et al., 2015). Methodological limitations and inconsistent results in this area of study necessitate further research (Thornberry, Knight, & Lovegood, 2012).

Overall, it is acknowledged there are a large number of individual, parent, family, community, and macrosystem factors associated with child maltreatment. To understand the causes of maltreatment and guide prevention and intervention efforts it is important to consider this range of risk factors, and their interactions (IOM & NRC, 2014).

CONSEQUENCES AND ECONOMIC BURDEN OF CHILD MALTREATMENT

Early research examining the consequences of child maltreatment compared children who experienced maltreatment with those who did not experience maltreatment. This research demonstrated that maltreated children were at an elevated risk of negative outcomes. These negative outcomes include criminal offending, mental illness, poor short- and long-term physical health and well-being, poor educational outcomes, alcohol and substance abuse, and risky behavior, including risky sexual behaviors (for a review, see IOM & NRC, 2014).

Work on the "cycle of violence" (Widom, 1989) led to greater recognition that while both abused and neglected children are at increased risk of violence perpetration, this relationship is not deterministic. Further, earlier research indicates different outcomes for different types of maltreatment. Current research indicates that a significant proportion of maltreated children experience multiple types and events of maltreatment across the life-course (IOM & NRC, 2014). Maltreatment dimensions or typologies have been proposed to understand the complexity of the maltreatment experience and outcomes. The Maltreatment Classification System (MCS; Barnett, Manly, & Cicchetti, 1993) is one of the earliest and most widely recognized structured frameworks, and assists conceptualization of child maltreatment and its consequences. The MCS incorporates maltreatment subtype, frequency/chronicity, developmental period, and severity, as well as identity of the perpetrator, and child separations/placements.

Fry, McCoy, and Swales' (2012) systematic review confirmed many of the previously identified links between child maltreatment and mental health, physical health, risky sexual behavior, and future violence (including intimate partner violence perpetration and victimization), but noted that level of risk varied relative to maltreatment types. However, complex relationships exist among individual, social, and contextual factors. For example, adolescent and persistent maltreatment appear to share stronger links with youth offending than early childhood maltreatment (Malvaso, Delfabro, & Day, 2016).

Finally, maltreated children are at increased risk of other types of victimization. Poly-victimization is when children and adolescents experience multiple categories of victimization, such as child maltreatment, conventional crime, witnessing and indirect victimization, and peer/sibling victimization. Risk of negative developmental outcomes appears greatest among those who experience poly-victimization (Finkelhor, Ormrod, & Turner, 2007). Clearly, it is important to consider the accumulation of risk.

In addition to negative outcomes for individuals, child maltreatment produces enormous economic costs for communities. Fang, Brown, Florence, and Mercy (2012) estimated an average lifetime cost of over US$210,000 per victim of nonfatal child maltreatment in the

USA. They considered costs of short- and long-term health care, child welfare, criminal justice, and special education, as well as productivity losses, to reach this estimation. For new cases in 2008, the estimated total lifetime burden for the USA was approximately US$124 billion.

CHILD MALTREATMENT PREVENTION AND INTERVENTION

In many jurisdictions, the social and economic burden of child maltreatment is unsustainable. Prevention is better than cure, but depends on an understanding of child maltreatment, its associated risk and protective factors, and consequences. Adequate investment in preventative programs, particularly those with a solid evidence base, is crucial.

Mikton and Butchart (2009) performed a systematic review of reviews, focusing on the effectiveness of seven main types of child maltreatment prevention approaches, including early childhood home visitation, parent education programs, child sex abuse prevention programs, abusive head trauma prevention, media-based interventions/campaigns, support and mutual aid groups, and multi-component interventions including family support, pre-school education, parenting skills, and childcare. Home-visiting, parent education, abusive head trauma prevention, and multi-component interventions showed the greatest promise for preventing maltreatment, while home-visiting, parent education, and child sexual abuse prevention appeared effective in reducing maltreatment risk factors. Importantly, their conclusions were "tentative," due to methodological limitations across studies and the fact that most studies occurred in high-income countries. Prevention and intervention efforts need to be tailored to the needs of the jurisdiction or population of interest and rigorously evaluated.

More recent literature has focused on the value of a public health approach to child maltreatment, meaning the incorporation of primary (universal prevention of future cases of child maltreatment), secondary (targeted preventions for specific at-risk groups focusing on risk factors), and tertiary (detection and intervention for existing cases of maltreatment to prevent long-term harms) responses (Scott, Lonne, & Higgins, 2016). These approaches target the individual, family/parent, and environmental (including community and societal) levels, and require a systematic approach to investment across multiple sectors, including health, justice, education, and social services, and quality research and evaluation. For recent work on this topic see Herrenkohl, Leeb, and Higgins (2016).

Based on increasing evidence of the short- and long-term consequences of maltreatment, and the likelihood that maltreated individuals will have contact with a variety of agencies and services across their life-course, it is imperative that different sectors work together to ensure coordinated responses to prevent and intervene in child maltreatment (for example, see Fallon, Filippelli, Black, Trocme, & Esposito, 2017). Likewise, intervention and prevention should address both maltreatment victimization and perpetration.

CONCLUSION

Child maltreatment is a complex social problem associated with a range of biopsychosocial and economic costs. Protection of children is dependent upon effective policies at the local, national, and international levels. Effective policies are dependent upon a solid evidence base regarding the causes, short- and long-term consequences, and prevalence of maltreatment. Investment in quality data, and evidence-based prevention and intervention, is crucial, as is methodologically sound evaluation.

It is important to understand the context of victims and their maltreatment experiences over time. We must consider the complex lived experiences of victims, guided by knowledge of maltreatment dimensions/typologies and the accumulation of risk over the life-course. In addition to addressing short-term consequences associated with child maltreatment, long-term consequences and opportunities for prevention and intervention across the life-course should be considered. Intervention based on early identification and effective responses to perpetrators is also important. Researchers and policy makers must consider the likelihood that multifaceted processes underlie the links between child maltreatment and a range of developmental outcomes. Funding, as well as collaboration between researchers, policy makers, and practitioners, and cross-sector and interagency cooperation, are essential to prevent child maltreatment.

REFERENCES

Barnett, D., Manly, J. T., & Cicchetti, D. (1993). Defining child maltreatment: The interface between policy and research. In D. Cicchetti & S. L. Toth (Eds.), *Advances in applied developmental psychology: Child abuse, child development, and social policy* (pp. 7–74). Norwood, NY: Ablex.

Fallon, B., Filippelli, J., Black, T., Trocme, N., & Esposito, T. (2017). How can data drive policy and practice in child welfare? Making the link in Canada. *International Journal of Environmental Research and Public Health*, 14, 1223.

Fang, X., Brown, D. S., Florence, C. S., & Mercy, J. A. (2012). The economic burden of child maltreatment in the United States and implications for prevention. *Child Abuse & Neglect*, 36, 156–165.

Finkelhor, D., Ormrod, R. K., & Turner, H. A. (2007). Polyvictimization and trauma in a national longitudinal cohort. *Development and Psychopathology*, 19, 149–166.

Fry, D., McCoy, A., & Swales, D. (2012). The consequences of maltreatment on children's lives: A systematic review of data from the East Asia and Pacific Region. *Trauma, Violence & Abuse*, 13(4), 209–233.

Herrenkohl., T. I., Leeb, R. T., & Higgins, D. (2016). The public health model of child maltreatment prevention. *Trauma, Violence and Abuse*, 17(4), 363–365.

Hurren, E., Stewart, A., & Dennison, S. (2017). New methods to address old challenges: The use of administrative data for longitudinal replication studies of child maltreatment. *International Journal of Environmental Research and Public Health*, 14, 1066.

Institute of Medicine (IOM) and National Research Council (NRC). (2014). *New directions in child abuse and neglect research*. Washington, DC: The National Academies Press.

Malvaso, C. G., Delfabbro, P. H., & Day, A. (2016). Risk factors that influence the maltreatment-offending association: A systematic review of prospective and longitudinal studies. *Aggression and Violent Behavior*, 31, 1–15.

Manly, J. T. (2005). Advances in research definitions of child maltreatment. *Child Abuse & Neglect*, 29, 425–439.

Mikton, C. & Butchart, A. (2009). Child maltreatment prevention: A systematic review of reviews. *Bulletin of the World Health Organization*, 87, 353–361.

National Research Council (NRC). (1993). *Understanding child abuse and neglect*. Washington, DC: National Academy Press.

Scott, D., Lonne, B., & Higgins, D. (2016). Public health models for preventing child maltreat-ment: Applications from the field of injury prevention. *Trauma, Violence and Abuse*, 17(4), 408–419.

Stoltenborgh, M., Bakermans-Kranenburg, M. J., Alink, L. R. A., & van IJzendoorn, M. H. (2015). The prevalence of child maltreatment across the globe: Review of a series of meta-analyses. *Child Abuse Review*, 24, 37–50.

Thornberry, T. P., Knight, K. E., & Lovegrove, P. J. (2012). Does maltreatment beget maltreatment? A systematic review of the intergenerational literature. *Trauma, Violence and Abuse*, 13(3), 135–152.

Widom, C. S. (1989). The cycle of violence. *Science*, 244, 160–166.

Widom, C. S., Czaja, S. J., & DuMont, K. A. (2015). Intergenerational transmission of child abuse and neglect: Real or detection bias? *Science*, 347(6229), 1480–1485.

WEBSITES

International Society for the Prevention of Child Abuse and Neglect. www.ispcan.org/.

UN Human Rights Office of the High Commissioner – Convention on the Rights of the Child. www.ohchr.org/EN/ProfessionalInterest/Pages/CRC.aspx.

WHO. www.who.int/news-room/fact-sheets/detail/child-maltreatment.

64 Children and International Criminal Justice

Cécile Van de Voorde and Rosemary Barberet

INTRODUCTION

Considering children as perpetrators, victims, and witnesses within the framework of international criminal justice, this chapter highlights special protections for children as a highly vulnerable population and focuses on key issues of criminal responsibility under international criminal law. Impunity negatively impacts current and future generations of children by hindering their growth and the formation of their identity, values, and beliefs. Similarly, the harsh treatment of juvenile offenders is not conducive to their social development or reintegration. It is, therefore, crucial to study children within the broader and highly nuanced context of conflict resolution, restoration, and effective justice.

INTERNATIONAL CHILD PROTECTION INSTRUMENTS

The 1924 Geneva Declaration on the Rights of the Child provided an international framework for the protection of children. After World War II, the UN General Assembly created the United Nations Children's Fund, known today as UNICEF. Progressively thereafter, children's rights became enshrined in major human rights instruments: the 1948 Universal Declaration of Human Rights, the 1959 Declaration on the Rights of the Child, the 1966 International Covenant on Civil and Political Rights and the International Covenant on Economic, Social and Cultural Rights, and the 1979 Convention on the Elimination of All Forms of Discrimination Against Women.

The landmark 1989 Convention on the Rights of the Child (CRC) entitles children to protection by others and the state, and to basic rights: life, health care, education, and protection from harm and exploitation. It defines children as "those under 18 years of age unless, under the law applicable to the child, majority is attained earlier." The Optional Protocol on the Involvement of Children in Armed Conflict establishes 18 as the minimum age for mandatory recruitment and mandates states to prevent minors from taking a direct part in armed conflict. The Optional Protocol on the Sale of Children, Child Prostitution and Child Pornography further mandates the criminalization of these activities. The United States is the only country in the world that has not ratified the CRC.

VIOLENCE AGAINST CHILDREN

Currently, 535 million children live in countries impacted by armed conflict or (often man-made) disaster, typically without access to protection, education, medical assistance, or proper nutrition. Of these, 393 million are located in Sub-Saharan Africa; most of the other minors are in the Middle East and North Africa. These children are at increased risk of violence, ranging from abuse, forced conscription, or sexual slavery to death, and expended as disposable resources in increasingly asymmetric conflicts (UNICEF, 2017).

In 2017, the UN Secretary-General reported grave concerns about "the increasing disrespect of international law" and "the use of abhorrent tactics of warfare" by numerous parties to conflict across the globe, and their lasting, devastating impact on children (p. 2). Also decried were the denial of humanitarian access to children, the use of children as human shields, the presence of explosive remnants of war in areas frequented by children, the deprivation of liberty of children in areas formerly held by armed groups, and the lack of protection for refugee and internally displaced children.

UNICEF has relentlessly condemned the pervasiveness of violence against children and advocated to engage and galvanize civil society and to mobilize citizens, policy makers, governments, and international stakeholders for local, national, and global collective action (UNICEF, 2014). It has urged states to provide safe and legal pathways to protection and to share the responsibility of protecting children, especially where they are displaced due to conflict and therefore even more likely to fall prey to dangerous people in violent or exploitative situations (UNICEF, 2017).

Underreported and often undetected, violence against children is also gendered; societies with a historical or cultural preference for boys perpetuate practices like sex-specific abortion or female infanticide that markedly alter national sex ratios. In most countries, girls are also at higher risk for sexual exploitation and abuse, educational and nutritional neglect (including differential access to food and services), child marriage, domestic and intimate partner violence, honor killing, sexual harassment, and female genital mutilation (UN General Assembly, 2017; UNICEF, 2017, 2018).

CHILD-SENSITIVE JUSTICE AT THE ICC

The International Criminal Court (ICC) was established by the Rome Statute of 1998. As of February 2019, 123 states are parties to it. The Statute and accompanying documents include multiple child-related provisions: crimes against children within the jurisdiction of the ICC, special measures to protect children during investigations and prosecutions, and requirements for ICC staff with expertise in children's issues. The ICC has jurisdiction over individuals accused of these crimes, either those directly responsible or those liable by aiding, abetting, or assisting with the crimes.

Crimes against Children

Children can be victims of any crimes within the ICC jurisdiction. The Rome Statute also includes crimes that can only be committed against children and crimes that are particularly relevant to children.

"Using, conscripting or enlisting children under 15 as soldiers" (Article 8(2)(b)(xxvi)) or using them to participate actively in hostilities is a war crime within the jurisdiction of the ICC. "Forcibly transferring persons under the age of 18" belonging to a national, ethnic, racial, or religious group intentionally targeted for whole or partial destruction constitutes genocide (Article 6(e)). "Crimes of sexual violence" can be tools or outcomes of conflict. The ICC has jurisdiction over rape, sexual slavery, enforced prostitution, forced pregnancy, enforced sterilization, and other forms of sexual violence of comparable gravity. When such acts are committed during an international or non-international armed conflict, they are war crimes, under Article 8. If they are committed against civilians as part of a widespread or systematic attack and pursuant to or in furtherance of a state or organizational policy, in peacetime or wartime, they may be prosecuted as crimes against humanity, under Article 7. "Intentionally attacking schools" is a war crime (Article 8(2)(e)(iv)). "Attacks on humanitarian staff and objects" can directly affect children and also constitute a war crime (Article 8(2)(e)(iii)).

Children as Perpetrators, Victims, and Witnesses before the ICC

In 2016, the ICC launched its Policy on Children to vigorously address atrocity crimes against and affecting children and to strengthen its preliminary examinations, investigations, and prosecutions against the danger of impunity. Opting for a child-sensitive approach to reparations, it recognized that "in a given context, a child may be vulnerable, capable, or both" (ICC Office of the Prosecutor, 2016, p. 3), and reasserted the need to evaluate the best interests of each child depending on his or her circumstances, views, influences, and rights. Emphasis was also placed on "any other factors, including legal and operational issues, that require a careful balancing of the various interests" (2016, p. 3).

To prevent children from re-experiencing trauma in court, special measures are available at the request of the prosecutor, the defense, the victim or witness, and his or her legal representative. The chamber involved may also order measures to facilitate the testimony of a traumatized child. The goal is to mitigate the risk of psychological harm and accommodate a vulnerable witness with in-court assistance or a modified, context-specific and age-appropriate line of questioning. Moreover, if a witness is the child of the accused, he or she shall not be required to make any statement that might incriminate the accused parent.

The prosecution of children has become a hot topic given the increased media coverage of high-profile cases involving child soldiers. Entertaining the concept of the criminal accountability of children at the international level is not easy; not only is it problematic to establish intent with certainty when the psychological development of a child varies from case to case, but the international legal community has also failed to agree upon a minimum age for criminal liability (Leveau, 2013, p. 38). Furthermore, international criminal law appears to be uneasy with the ambiguities inherent in a debate it has traditionally approached as a series of simplistic dichotomies: adult vs. child, victim vs. perpetrator, capacity vs. incapacity, and guilt vs. innocence (Drumbl, 2012).

Setting ICC Legal Precedents for Children

The Lubanga case is a cornerstone of the ICC's jurisprudence on children in armed conflict. Thomas Lubanga Dyilo, a national of the Democratic Republic of the Congo (DRC), was the first person ever arrested under an ICC arrest warrant. The Congolese warlord went on trial at the ICC in January 2009 as a co-perpetrator of war crimes, including enlisting and conscripting children under the age of 15 into the Patriotic Forces for the Liberation of Congo (FPLC) and using them to actively participate in hostilities within the context of an international armed conflict and a non-international armed conflict. In March 2012, the first permanent ICC found Lubanga guilty; he was sentenced to 14 years in prison.

A key outcome of the Lubanga trial is that former child soldiers now benefit from an official reparations plan covering restitution, compensation, and rehabilitation. Established under the Rome Statute in an unprecedented effort to promote restorative and retributive justice for children, the Trust Fund for Victims (TFV) is mandated to support and implement ICC-ordered reparations awarded individually, collectively, or both. It also provides medical, psychological, and material support to victims and their families via voluntary contributions from state and non-state donors. The TFV has helped more than 120,000 victims in countries where the ICC is investigating cases, such as the DRC and Uganda (Coalition for the ICC, 2015–2016).

The prosecution of Dominic Ongwen further illustrates how convoluted and divisive cases involving children may become, and how deeply the victim-perpetrator status of former child soldiers challenges accepted modalities of accountability within the ICC framework. Ongwen was abducted by Joseph Kony's Lord's Resistance Army in northern Uganda when he was nine years old. Trained as a child soldier, he grew up to be a senior LRA commander. He was apprehended in the Central African Republic in January 2015 and transferred to the ICC. Whereas some argued he should have been granted amnesty, as other child combatants have, many maintained that he had to be prosecuted to stop the culture of impunity. He stands accused of 67 counts of war crimes and crimes against humanity; 2026 victims are set to take part in the proceedings.

SUPPLEMENTARY MECHANISMS OF JUSTICE FOR CHILDREN

Judicial Mechanisms

The International Criminal Tribunal for Rwanda (ICTR) and the International Criminal Tribunal for the Former Yugoslavia (ICTY) were *ad hoc* international tribunals that had jurisdiction over natural persons without any reference to age, although no minor was ever indicted or prosecuted for crimes within their jurisdiction. Child-sensitive practices were in place and children could testify or be used as witnesses without taking an oath, provided they were capable of reporting the facts within their knowledge and understand the duty to tell the truth.

In cases involving prosecution by national courts, children had to receive special protection given their age and other special circumstances. Depriving a child of his or her liberty could only be used as a last resort and for the shortest possible time.

Nonjudicial Mechanisms

Human rights abuses can be addressed through truth commissions investigating pervasive human rights violations after armed conflict within the framework of transitional justice. Truth commissions seek to establish accountability and accurate historical records of atrocities by collecting testimonies and publicly acknowledging previously undisclosed crimes.

International child rights and juvenile justice standards guide all proceedings and policies. The South African Truth and Reconciliation Commission has been most efficient at reintegrating children by focusing explicitly on crimes committed against children or adolescents and by organizing separate hearings to encourage children to come forward.

Traditional justice measures, so long as they uphold international standards of justice, provide another reliable system of accountability within informal, culture-specific systems based on indigenous or customary practices. Local communities resort to such people-centered mechanisms to resolve localized disputes and promote safe access to justice for all. Traditional justice for child perpetrators underscores the importance of rehabilitation, reintegration, and respect for the rights of others, as well as reparation to the community that suffered harm (Coalition for the ICC, 2015–2016; Drumbl, 2012).

CONCLUSION

Although children have increasingly received attention from the international community in recent years, they often remain invisible, potential, but silent political actors in world events. Given their vulnerability and underrepresentation, adults still bear the responsibility of monitoring and guaranteeing their protection and safety. With the creation of the ICC, *ad hoc* entities, and other conflict-specific mechanisms, it is possible to promote children's rights more compellingly than before. Still, more action is needed within the existing regulatory framework.

Civil society has lofty justice and accountability expectations when it comes to crimes against or affecting children. The ICC is being scrutinized as refugee crises intensify and multiply around the world. Ongoing reforms are aiming to bolster investigations and prosecutions, shorten trials, explicitly tackle sexual and gender-based violence, simplify bureaucratic processes, but also foster trust and deliver restorative and retributive justice in affected communities. Yet, the most vulnerable populations, notably children, continue to be systematically targeted in countries where atrocities are committed by governments and non-state armed groups alike.

It is imperative to reinforce child protection systems and develop community growth initiatives, comprehensive policy reforms, and strategic partnerships that foster protective environments and prevent discrimination. This requires a deeper understanding of effective justice and sustainable peace as corollaries of shared responsibility. Reparations programs shed light on the importance of rehabilitating children and the shared duty to help former child soldiers reintegrate society by providing them with proper tools to durably reengage with their communities. They also show why stronger support from state and non-state entities is crucial to efficiently promote wider campaigns against stigmatization and discrimination. Likewise, sexual and gender-based violence cases involving children, especially girls, illustrate the dire need for transformative gender justice and anti-discrimination campaigns to collectively empower and sustainably restore communities.

REFERENCES

Coalition for the International Criminal Court. (2015–2016). Balancing redress in eastern Congo. *The Global Justice Monitor*, 47, 10.

Drumbl, M. A. (2012). *Reimagining child soldiers in international law and policy*. Oxford: Oxford University Press.

International Criminal Court (ICC) Office of the Prosecutor. (2016). *Policy on children*. The Hague: International Criminal Court.

Leveau, F. (2013). Liability of child soldiers under international criminal law. *Osgoode Hall Review of Law and Policy*, 4(1), 36–66.

United Nations Children's Fund (UNICEF). (2009). *Progress for children: A report card on child protection*. New York: UNICEF.

(2014). *Ending violence against children: Six strategies for action | #ENDviolence*. New York: UNICEF.

(2017). *A child is a child: Protecting children on the move from violence, abuse, and exploitation*. New York: UNICEF.

(2018). *Gender-based violence in emergencies*. New York: UNICEF.

United Nations General Assembly. (2006). *Rights of the child*. New York: United Nations Organization.

(2017). *Children and armed conflict – report of the Secretary-General*. New York: United Nations Organization.

International Justice

As explained in the introductory chapter, the Rome Statute defines international crimes as the gravest crimes that threaten the peace, security, and well-being of the world. Because these crimes are of such gravity the statute declares that "it is the duty of every State to exercise its criminal jurisdiction over those responsible for international crimes." This provides the foundation for international criminal law and for the institutions required to uphold and deliver that law. The United Nations has long been concerned with the development of international laws and standards. This work falls into two basic categories: 1) the formation of international obligations by treaty to criminalize, at the national and international level, activities of fundamental concern to the international community; and 2) the development of "norms and standards" in criminal justice, which are desirable or even obligatory practices (see Chapter 65 by Roger S. Clark).

This section of the book is concerned with the various legal instruments, international treaties (see Chapter 66 by Gloria J. Browne-Marshall), charters, protocols, and understandings that have contributed to the development of international criminal law and it deals with the criminal tribunals, commissions, and courts that are playing a part in administering the law. It describes the important role of the United Nations in these developments and it provides several chapters describing the International Criminal Court, its short history, and key aspects of its work.

The Rome Statute led to the creation of the permanent International Criminal Court. The statute sought the commitment of signatory nations to apply and enforce the rule of law in their own territory, but also their commitment to support the work of the ICC in processing the cases brought to its attention. This marks the beginning of truly global criminal justice (see Chapter 67 by Mangai Natarajan and Antigona Kukaj). Since its inception in 2002, the ICC has handled four major "situations." One of these situations, referred by the Security Council, concerns Darfur, Sudan, a non-state party to the ICC. The account of this situation in Chapter 68 by Xabier Agirre Aranburu and Roberta Belli exposes the complexities inherent in the investigation of international crimes where the primary purpose may be to restore a sense of justice to victims and bring international condemnation of the suffering inflicted upon them. In fact, the proceedings of the International Criminal Court (ICC) include an unprecedented role for victims' rights in three important respects: 1) protection, 2) participation, and 3) reparations (see Chapter 69 by David Donat Cattin).

In addition to the ICC, *ad hoc* international criminal tribunals have been created for prosecuting individuals responsible for the grossest violations of international humanitarian law (see Chapter 70 by Gloria J. Browne-Marshall) Non-judicial forums have also been established that allow victims to seek resolution and redress. These include regional and global human rights commissions (see Chapter 71 by Jose Morin) and the remarkable Truth Commissions that have sought to promote reconciliation in South Africa (see Chapter 72 by Stephan Parmentier and Elmar Weitekamp), and in Guatemala (see Chapter 73 by Marcia Esparza). Truth commissions are especially important when societies are in transition – moving from an autocratic regime towards more democratic forms of government. Finally, nongovernmental organizations play an important role in the delivery of international criminal justice, both through their relationship with the United Nations and as grassroots movements that are promoting social change with the goals of achieving global peace, justice, and security (see Chapter 74 by Rosemary Barberet).

The concept of justice relies on morality and ethical principles that drive three models of justice, namely: retributive justice, restorative justice, and reparation. While retributive justice is based on the rule of law and widely applicable, the countries in transition need other approaches since they are in the process of restoring peace and repairing their social and political systems. The international justice apparatus such as the ICC help punish perpetrators and deter them from committing mass atrocities. By and large, this is needed; however, the countries need much beyond this retributive approach. John Braithwaite's well-known model of restorative justice is primarily victim-centered, at the same time being a collective process in restoring relationships between victim and perpetrator and reintegrating them in societal structure. The dialogue among the victim, perpetrator, and the community lead to reparative justice in the form of restitution and apology, which may well assist many victims in the rebuilding process within the local cultural settings. In Chapter 75, Kerry Clamp describes the process of transforming restorative justice for transitional settings.

65 The Role of the United Nations

Roger S. Clark

UN work in this area is rooted in the UN Charter. In the preamble to that treaty, "we the peoples of the United Nations" are said to be "determined to save succeeding generations from the scourge of war, which twice in our lifetime has brought untold sorrow to mankind." The Charter contemplates not only coercive power against aggressors but also efforts to build a just world to secure peace. Thus, Article 55 of the Charter exhorts the organization (especially through the General Assembly and the Economic and Social Council) to promote:

a. higher standards of living, full employment, and conditions of economic and social progress and development
b. solutions of international economic, social, health, and related problems; and international cultural and educational cooperation
c. universal respect for and observance of, human rights and fundamental freedoms for all without distinction as to race, sex, language, or religion

The UN has no standing body with criminal jurisdiction over particular crimes. Its court, the International Court of Justice (ICJ), deals with states and international organizations, not individuals. The ICJ's judgments have sometimes clarified the obligations of states in the criminal justice area, such as the prevention of genocide, immunity of senior officials from prosecution in other countries, and the duty to prosecute or extradite persons charged with offenses against international law. Occasionally, on an *ad hoc* basis, the UN has taken on some features of a law enforcement agency, as in the Security Council's creation of the International Tribunals for the Former Yugoslavia and Rwanda, whose work is now concluded. Those tribunals were designed to enforce international law relating to genocide, crimes against humanity, and war crimes against individual perpetrators in the particular instances of the former Yugoslavia and Rwanda. But the Security Council chose not to create international tribunals for situations that were arguably as egregious. The UN was, however, involved in the creation of several "hybrid" courts, having a mixture of local and foreign judges. These were formed in, for example, Cambodia, Sierra Leone, Timor-Leste, and Lebanon.

Against this backdrop of selectivity, the UN provided the forum for negotiations to create the International Criminal Court (ICC) at a diplomatic conference in 1998. The ICC is a separate legal entity from the UN but has a close working relationship with it. Proponents of the ICC hope that in due course it will have power to deal with the most egregious of international crimes in all countries of the globe where the states most closely involved are unwilling or unable to prosecute. It currently can deal with acts occurring on the territory of, or perpetrated by the nationals of, the 123 states that are parties to the Rome Statute of 1998, the treaty setting up the Court. It has subject-matter jurisdiction over genocide, crimes against humanity, war crimes, and the crime of aggression. It has achieved several convictions and is fine-tuning its principles of sentencing and the reparation of victims.

These concrete efforts at law enforcement are exceptional. Mostly, the UN's work on international crime and international justice has been concerned with the development of international laws and standards. This work falls into two basic categories: 1) the formation of international obligations by treaty to criminalize, at the national and international level, activities of fundamental concern to the international community; and 2) the development of "norms and standards" in criminal justice, desirable or even obligatory practices.

THE OBLIGATION TO MAKE CERTAIN ACTIVITIES CRIMINAL

The UN first used the treaty suppression approach in the 1948 Genocide Convention. State parties to that treaty undertake to make it criminal to take part in genocide on their territory. This model was expanded in later instances, notably in the areas of terrorism, torture, trafficking in drugs, transnational organized crime, trafficking in human beings, and corruption. UN work in such areas builds on pioneering efforts in the nineteenth century to suppress the slave trade by means of treaties. In treaties of this kind, states promise to make the actions in question criminal under their domestic laws. The object of the treaties is to get as many states as possible with power to prosecute (not only the territorial state where the events occurred or the state of which the accused is a national). This reduces the odds that there will be "safe havens." The trend is for states to agree by treaty either to prosecute suspects who come on their territory (regardless of where the crime occurred or whose citizens they are) or to extradite them to someone else who will undertake a genuine prosecution (such as the state where an aircraft was registered, or from where it began its journey). This is known as *aut dedere aut judicare* (extradite or bring before a legal process – see also Podgor, Clark, & Dervan, 2016).

The success of these law-making efforts relies on painstaking treaty negotiation followed by ratification or acceptance – state by state. The UN General Assembly, where most of these treaties gained approval, has never been regarded as a legislator in this. It is merely the midwife who makes the process happen. After the events of September 11, 2001, however, the Security Council (as opposed to the General Assembly) entered into new waters in SC Resolution 1373. The Council, purporting to act under its compulsory powers in Chapter VII of the UN Charter dealing with the maintenance of international peace and security, required states to give effect to obligations that track those in the 1999 Convention against Terrorist Financing, even for states not party to that treaty. It created a Council Committee to ensure that states take appropriate action. Those enforcement efforts continue. The Council thus began acting as a legislator and making efforts to see that its legislation is enforced.

PROMULGATION OF UN NORMS AND STANDARDS IN CRIMINAL JUSTICE

Formulating standards in criminal justice has occurred in two main parts of the UN structure: that part dealing with the broad field of human rights (operating primarily through the office of the United Nations High Commissioner for Human Rights in Geneva and the Human Rights Council, which was created by the General Assembly in 2006) and that dealing specifically with crime prevention and criminal justice (operating primarily through the Office of Drugs and Crime in Vienna (UNODC)). The Vienna office, the most significant part of the UN system for this chapter, combines longstanding programs in crime prevention and criminal justice and in drug control with more recent efforts to combat terrorism and corruption. Standards dealing with crime prevention have been developed primarily under the auspices of the Commission on Crime Prevention and Criminal Justice and the UN "Congresses" (see infra). In the drug area, the Commission on Narcotic Drugs and the International Narcotic Control Board are the significant focal points. The work of the UNODC is augmented by a network of criminal justice institutes loosely affiliated in the International Scientific and Professional Advisory Council for the program (ISPAC). Notable among the institutes are the United Nations Interregional Crime and Justice Research Institute (UNICRI), in Turin, Italy, the European Institute for Crime Prevention and Control (HEUNI), in Helsinki, Finland, the National Institute of Justice (NIJ), in Washington, DC, and the International Centre for Criminal Law Reform and Criminal Justice Policy (ICCLR&CJP), in Vancouver, Canada.

A feature of the UN program specific to criminal justice has, since 1955, been the holding of five-yearly Congresses on Crime Prevention and Criminal Justice, attended by most states, by individual experts, and by numerous representatives of civil society. Numerous instruments setting forth criminal justice standards and model treaties were finalized at the congresses up to 1990 and then endorsed by ECOSOC or the General Assembly (Clark, 1994).

Space constraints preclude detailed discussion of these documents, but a brief mention of the most significant will suggest what has seemed important internationally. The First Congress in 1955 adopted the Standard Minimum Rules for the Treatment of Prisoners. (These Rules were revised in 2015 as "The Nelson Mandela Rules.") The 1975 Congress produced the Declaration on the Protection of All Persons from Being Subjected to Torture and Other Cruel, Inhuman or Degrading Treatment or Punishment. In 1982, the General Assembly followed up the Torture Declaration by adopting Principles of Medical Ethics designed to preclude doctors from assisting torture. The 1985 Congress produced, notably, the Declaration of Basic Principles of Justice for Victims of Crime and Abuse of Power, the Beijing Rules for the Administration of Juvenile Justice, a Model Agreement on the Transfer of Foreign Prisoners, and a very important statement on judicial integrity, the Basic Principles on the Independence of the Judiciary. It also triggered the organization's ongoing work on violence against women. The 1990 Havana Congress added several standards about human rights in the administration of justice.

Since the 1990s, partly in response to criticisms of the sheer volume of material being produced, standard-setting has taken place mainly under the auspices of the Commission on Crime Prevention and Criminal Justice rather than the Congresses. As before, final endorsement comes either from ECOSOC or the General Assembly.

An important recent affirmation of the significance of criminal justice issues is contained in Goal 16 of the Sustainable Development Goals adopted at a UN Summit in 2015 as objectives for the next 15 years. Goal 16 seeks the promotion of peaceful and inclusive societies for sustainable development, provision of access to justice for all, and the building of effective, accountable, and inclusive institutions at all levels. It is especially significant in encouraging efforts to deal with human trafficking and other organized crime as well as discriminatory laws or practices.

While some of the criminal justice provisions are in treaties like the Covenant on Civil and Political Rights, most of the instruments are in the form of recommendations to states. Neither the General Assembly nor ECOSOC is given a direct power to "legislate" under the Charter. It is widely accepted, however, that such resolutions may contribute to the development of general international law, by codifying past developments, by providing an authoritative interpretation of treaty obligations, or by providing a basis for new (customary) law. For customary law to develop there must be both some relevant state practice and some *opinio juris*, a notion that what is done is done from a sense of legal obligation. In modern international law both the practice and the *opinio juris* may be inferred from what states do in international organizations. The strongest candidates for international law are resolutions called "Declarations." Note that the Universal Declaration of Human Rights and the 1975 instrument on torture, for example, are in the form of General Assembly Declarations. On the other hand, the titles and adopting language of many of the others are peppered with words like "guidelines," "standards," and "principles," which suggest something much softer and more aspirational rather than "legal."

The soft nature of such standards and norms does not mean that most states, as members of the United Nations club, do not feel some obligation to make an effort to comply – or to rationalize reasons for not complying. Nor does it mean that the organization is powerless to try to encourage the implementation of the instruments, starting with disseminating the material as widely as possible. Particularly by asking for reports of what states are doing and making some effort to discuss responses, the UN seeks to invoke the principles in the abstract if not in concrete cases. In the human rights part of the system there are also several "treaty bodies," such as the Human Rights Committee established under the Covenant on Civil and Political Rights. These bodies try to give effect to the specific treaty materials. Increasingly, they have been referring to the Standard Minimum Rules for the Treatment of Prisoners and to other non-treaty instruments as a way to interpret the general provisions of the treaties. A number of "theme mechanisms" such as Special Rapporteurs and Committees have been put in place in particular areas to encourage states, sometimes quietly, sometimes by shaming in the glare of publicity, to give effect to the material. Examples are torture, extrajudicial killings, and the independence of lawyers and judges.

Moreover, non-treaty material has a habit of creeping into later treaties. Much of the material in the Universal Declaration Human Rights found itself in the two 1966 Covenants on Human Rights. Substantial parts of the 1985 Declaration concerning victims appear in the Rome Statute of the International Criminal Court, the 2000 Convention against Transnational Organized Crime, and its Protocol to Prevent, Suppress and Punish Trafficking in Persons, Especially Women and Children.

There is a very large body of norms and standards covering all the basic fields of criminal justice. The challenge now is to make it operational on a global basis.

SUMMARY

Generally, the UN is not a law enforcement agency. Its main function in criminal justice is to formulate international laws and standards. They are twofold: those creating international treaty obligations to make certain heinous activities criminal under the criminal justice system of nation-states; and those developing "norms and standards" – desirable and sometimes obligatory practices that are applicable domestically within states and internationally when the UN itself or some other international organization operates.

REFERENCES

Clark, R. S. (1994). *The United Nations Crime Prevention and Criminal Justice Program: Formulation of standards and efforts at their implementation* (Vol. 20). Philadelphia, PA: University of Pennsylvania.

Podgor, E. S., Clark, R. S., & Dervan, L.E. (2016). *International criminal law: Cases and materials, fourth edition*. Durham, NC: Carolina Academic Press.

United Nations. (2006). *Compendium of United Nations standards and norms in crime prevention and criminal justice*. New York: United Nations. Retrieved from www.unodc.org/pdf/compendium/compendium_2006_cover.pdf.

WEBSITES

Crime Prevention and Criminal Justice Programme (ISPAC). ispac.cnpds.org.
International Scientific and Professional Advisory Council of the UN
Office of United Nations High Commissioner for Human Rights. www.ohchr.org.
United Nations Office on Drugs and Crime. www.unodc.org.

66 Treaties and International Law

Gloria J. Browne-Marshall

INTRODUCTION

In 1815, the Treaty of Vienna was negotiated after the Napoleonic Wars to punish the defeat of Napoleon Bonaparte I and act as a preventive measure against such future aggression. It was precedent for the treatment of Wilhelm II of Hohenzollern, the Kaiser of Germany (1859–1941), who was accused of committing horrific acts against civilians during World War I (Cabanes, 2014). The Treaty of Versailles, signed in 1919, established a tribunal guided by international policy and international morality of that era to try Wilhelm II for committing crimes against the laws and customs of war. Kaiser Wilhelm argued that he was a victim of *ex post facto*, or acts made criminal after the fact, and fled. The Netherlands, where he took refuge, refused to extradite Wilhelm. Despite the failure to directly punish Kaiser Wilhelm, the Treaty of Versailles was evidence that under certain circumstances members of the world community would limit the sovereignty of an individual state by international agreement (Cabanes, 2014).

The 1969 Vienna Convention defines a treaty as "an international agreement concluded between States in written form and governed by international law, whether embodied in a single instrument or in two or more related instruments and whatever its particular designation." The 1986 Vienna Convention extends the definition of treaties to include international agreements involving international organizations as parties. Treaties are binding bi-lateral agreements, as between two states, or multi-lateral agreements, as between several states. These agreements represent one area within the complex system of courts, agreements, customs, principles, and national laws that comprise international law. International criminal law involves agreements between states to criminalize certain conduct with an internationally accepted response even if that conduct is outside of a particular state's jurisdiction or national authority. States entering as signatories to an agreement are not bound by its terms until the government of that state ratifies the treaty. The state may limit the application of certain terms prior to ratification by adding reservations or declarations to clarify the manner in which the treaty will be applied in that state. Once ratified, enforcement of treaty terms is defined by the compliance provisions within the particular treaty. This chapter examines the characteristic features of international treaties and international law, including multi-lateral, bi-lateral, interpretation, enforcement, and comparison with customary international law.

INTERNATIONAL CRIMINAL LAW AND SCOPE OF TREATIES

International criminal treaties were developed to prevent, protect, and punish. Criminal law covers a myriad of crimes and may be addressed by treaty, national law, or conventions of the United Nations. States may enter into bi-lateral or multi-lateral treaties covering specific crimes unique to that region. A treaty may set forth extradition, the place of trial, and due process rights. The United Nations Office on Drugs and Crime (UNODC) includes combating transnational organized crime, illicit traffic in narcotic drugs as well as money laundering, seizure of aircrafts, and the trafficking of human beings. Regional organizations such as the Arab League and North Atlantic Treaty Organization (NATO) can draft counterterrorism treaties. The Convention against Torture and Other Cruel, Inhuman or Degrading Treatment or Punishment aims to prevent acts of cruelty against human beings. The United Nations, European Union, African Union, and United Nations Economic Commission for Europe are among international organizations criminalizing offences against the environment.

A treaty has a specific scope. International law has jurisdictional limits. Jurisdiction may be the territorial boundaries of a state. In international criminal law, it is the authority to prosecute. A treaty may provide the terms for jurisdiction, or power, over a suspected criminal, the criminal activity itself, or the persons victimized by the crime. Extraterritorial crimes involve criminal activity outside of state borders that may be prosecuted under the jurisdiction of national laws because the crimes affect that state, such as drug trafficking (Hauck & Peterke, 2016).

The League of Nations and International Law

The initial laws governing war crimes were enforceable only by the national government. After the devastating magnitude of World War I, national leaders created a society of states called the "League of Nations." The League of Nations had as its mandate the codification of international values, the resolution of disputes, and, above all, the prevention of war (Cabanes, 2014). The League of Nations was the first truly international forum. Formed by covenant, or constitution, in 1919, "to promote international cooperation and to achieve peace and security," the original members of the League of Nations were the victors of World War I.

Twenty-eight countries were permanent members of the League. More than 30 nations joined and withdrew during its existence; the USA never ratified the Treaty of Versailles to join the League of Nations. Although the League of Nations failed to prevent World War II, it provided the basis for a forum in which states could work out their differences peacefully and create legal contracts and consequences for international disputes. With little international support and limited resources, this historic institution dissolved itself in 1946. That same year, the League's Geneva property was transferred to a new organization – the United Nations. Many of the treaties ratified by members of the League of Nations remained enforceable international law under the United Nations (Cabanes, 2014).

The UN Security Council, the organ of the United Nations charged with the maintenance of international peace and security, is instrumental to the fight against breaches of international criminal law. The Council has 15 member states, five of whom are permanent members, with ten being elected by the General Assembly for two-year terms. The Security Council may undertake an investigation and mediation of nations. The Council can issue ceasefire directives, sanctions, or send peacekeeping forces to help reduce tensions in troubled regions (Mertus, 2018). The Council may authorize regional organizations such as the North Atlantic Treaty Organization (NATO), the Economic Community of West African States, or coalitions of willing countries to implement certain peacekeeping or peace enforcement functions. Most important to this analysis is that the UN Security Council can establish international criminal tribunals to adjudicate international crimes following war or armed conflict.

The need for international criminal law to address drug trafficking was recognized as early as 1908. The International Opium Convention of 1912 resulted in a treaty to internationally control the distribution of narcotics. The United Nations adopted the Convention against Illicit Traffic in Narcotic Drugs and Psychotropic Substances in 1988. In 2000, the United Nations developed a Protocol to Prevent, Suppress and Punish Trafficking in Persons, Especially Women and Children, supplementing the United Nations Convention against Transnational Organized Crime. The United Nations Convention against Transnational Organized Crime and its Protocols to stem the laundering of illicit funds from drugs, prostitution, or governmental corruption.

Suppression Treaties

Treaties may be created to suppress or limit the actions of another state. During the Atlantic Slave Trade, millions of persons were kidnapped from Africa, forced onto ships, and enslaved in far regions of the world. After centuries of involvement in the slave trade, England, France, Russia, Austria, and Prussia abolished slavery and entered into the Quintuple Treaty of 1841 intended to suppress the continued slave trade among other European nations by seizing their ships on the high seas (Browne-Marshall, 2013).

Modern suppression treaties include the Treaty on the Non-Proliferation of Nuclear Weapons, which attempts to contain the spread of nuclear weapons among states. States in possession of nuclear weapons agree not to transfer nuclear weapons, and states without nuclear weapons agree not to receive nuclear weapons. Suppression treaties are often created to reach international crimes. But, reliance on national criminal justice systems is needed (Nollkaemper, 2012). Treaties to limit the manufacture or trade in illicit drugs represent an agreement intended to suppress criminal activity such as growing and transporting opium plants from which the narcotic drug heroin is manufactured.

Extradition Treaties

Extradition is the removal and delivery of an accused or convicted person, by request of a state or domestic jurisdiction, for prosecution. A state's refusal to extradite, or surrender, an alleged violator of international law is an obstacle to international justice. Extradition is controlled by treaty or custom between states (Kittichaisaree, 2018). Law enforcement agencies can be stymied by a lack of cooperation between states. Extradition of suspects depends on the cooperation of national governments while enforcement of international law relies on cooperation and international clearinghouses of informational resources (Kittichairsaree, 2018). International law has evolved into treaties of mutual assistance, the effectiveness of which depends upon mutual goals of peace, protection, and prevention.

Humanitarian Treaties

Humanitarian law is based on human need (Cabanes, 2014). Humanitarian treaties restrict the methods and manner of warfare. International humanitarian treaties arose after the appalling treatment of soldiers wounded in the Battle of Solferino (1859) as chronicled by Henry Dunant (Crawford & Pert, 2015). The Geneva Convention of 1864 was created as the first multi-lateral humanitarian treaty. The Convention for the Amelioration of the Condition of the Wounded in Armies in the Field of 1865 and the establishment of the International Red Cross followed. Humanitarian treaties restricted the type of warfare as well as the proximity of battle to civilian residences, places of worship, hospitals, and other nonstrategic buildings. The Geneva Convention of 1949 and its Protocols provide the legal standards for the treatment of prisoners of war or armed conflict.

The brutality of war led to the League of Nations of 1919 and the United Nations, World War I, and World War II respectively. A forum was needed for states to resolve differences through treaties and international cooperation (Cabanes, 2014). In 1948, members of the United Nations adopted the Convention on the Prevention and Punishment of the Crime of Genocide. The Universal Declaration of Human Rights adopted in 1948 is not a treaty. Signatory states to the Universal Declaration aspire to recognition of the need for human rights and provide the basic human rights that form the basis of international humanitarian law (Crawford & Pert, 2015).

As the world community recognized the need to protect human rights, the need to punish crimes against humanity evolved as well. The UN Security Council, charged with maintenance of international peace and security, is instrumental in the fight against crimes against humanity and thus breaches of international criminal law. The Council investigates, issues ceasefire directives, sanctions, and can send peacekeeping forces to help reduce tensions in troubled regions (Bassiouni, 2014). The UN Security Council can establish international criminal tribunals to adjudicate international crimes following war or armed conflict. Tribunals are *ad hoc* or temporary with limited jurisdiction, venue, and scope (Crawford & Pert, 2015).

Treaties can require states to assist refugees entering their borders when violence, natural disaster, and food shortages cause mass migration. The Office of the UN High Commissioner of Refugees is the leading organization aiding and protecting people forced to migrate. However, there is limited punishment for refusal. States are co-dependent entities with porous borders subject to mass migration. In addition to humanitarian reasons, assistance can be a mutual investment in own future need.

The Rome Treaty

The tribunals created by the UN Security Council led to treaty creating the international criminal court. In 1993, the UN Security Council established the International Criminal Tribunal for the Former Yugoslavia (ICTY) for the Prosecution of Persons Responsible for Serious Violations of International Humanitarian Law Committed in the Territory of the Former Yugoslavia and, in 1994, the International Criminal Tribunal for Rwanda (ICTR) for the Prosecution of Persons Responsible for Genocide or Other Serious Violations of International Humanitarian Law Committed in the Territory of Rwanda, and Rwandan Citizens Responsible for Genocide and Other Such Violations Committed in the Territory of Neighboring States (Crawford & Pert, 2015). However, these tribunals and others that followed are limited in jurisdiction and scope.

The United Nations Diplomatic Conference of Plenipotentiaries convened in Rome, Italy, from June 15 to July 17, 1998, to finalize a draft statute for the establishment of the International Criminal Court. In 2002, the Rome Treaty established the International Criminal Court. It became the first permanent international criminal court with the jurisdiction to adjudicate crimes of genocide, crimes against humanity, crimes of aggression, and war crimes; its jurisdiction is complementary to national criminal courts. The creation of the International Criminal Court provides the international community, both military and civilian, with a legal standard for moral conduct during war and civil conflict (Bassiouni, 2014). Only states that have ratified the Rome Treaty are bound by the jurisdiction of the International Criminal Court.

SUMMARY AND CONCLUSION

States are highly interdependent. Treaties are formal agreements requiring expertise and time to negotiate. They may protect the vulnerable and punish criminals or encourage a state to negotiate more for its citizens. A treaty may be bi-lateral, as between two states, or multi-lateral, as between several states. Treaties are a part of a complex system of courts, agreements, customs, principles, and national laws that comprise international law. Suppression treaties may be created to limit the criminal trafficking within or between states. International criminal law covers a myriad of crimes and may be addressed by treaty, national law, or the United Nations. States may enter into bi-lateral or multi-lateral treaties covering specific crimes unique to that region and requiring extradition by treaty or custom. States can be obligated to feed and house migrants fleeing persecution or violence. As the world community recognized the need to protect human rights, the need to punish crimes against humanity evolved, as well. The Rome Treaty established the International Criminal Court. The application and interpretation of the Rome Statute presents the next phase in the development of international criminal law. Treaties of mutual assistance, extradition, and the sharing of information between states will assist in the effectiveness of international criminal law.

REFERENCES

Bassiouni, M. C. (2014). *Crimes against humanity: Historical evolution and contemporary application.* New York: Cambridge University Press.
Browne-Marshall, G. (2013). *Race, law, and American society: 1607 to present.* Second Edition. New York: Routledge.
Cabanes, B. (2014). *The Great War and the origins of humanitarianism: 1918–1924.* New York: Cambridge University Press.
Crawford, E. & Pert, A. (2015). *International humanitarian law.* New York: Cambridge University Press.
Hauck, P. & Peterke, S. (2016). *International law and transnational organized crime.* New York: Oxford University Press.
Kittichaisaree, K. (2018). *The obligation to extradite or prosecute.* New York: Oxford University Press.

Mertus, J. (2018). *The United Nations and human rights: A guide for a new era*. Third Edition. New York: Routledge.

Nollkaemper, A. (2012). *National courts and the international rule of law*. New York: Oxford University Press.

WEBSITE

United Nations Treaty Collection. https://treaties.un.org/Pages/Home.aspx?lang=en.

67   The International Criminal Court

Mangai Natarajan and Antigona Kukaj

"In the prospect of an international criminal court lies the promise of universal justice."

– Kofi Annan, United Nations Secretary-General

For many years, the United Nations held a series of meetings to establish an independent and permanent structure – the International Criminal Court (ICC) – to deal with the gravest international crimes and gross violations of international humanitarian law. This dream became a reality on July 17, 1998, when the Rome Statute was agreed upon by 120 nations. Some four years later, on July 1, 2002, the ICC was established and, of 2018, 123 states have ratified the Rome Statute. The ICC is thus a product of a multi-lateral treaty whereas the *ad hoc* International Criminal Tribunal for the Former Yugoslavia (ICTY) and the International Criminal Tribunal for Rwanda (ICTR) were created by decision of the UN Security Council.

The ICC, a permanent entity situated in The Hague, Netherlands, offers a new paradigm of accountability, equality, and justice in dealing with the most serious crimes of concern to the international community. This chapter provides a brief account of its structure and functioning, of its ongoing investigations and trials, as well as the challenges inherent in executing the mission of Rome Statute.

THE ROME STATUTE IS THE ICC

The Rome Statute is a unique legal apparatus that takes into account both the adversarial and inquisitorial models of criminal procedure in seeking to provide protection for all global citizens (Kress, 2003). It directs and governs the ICC, which has jurisdiction over the following: international crimes, genocide (Article 6), crimes against humanity (Article 7) and war crimes (Article 8). It was also intended to cover the crime of aggression (Article 5), but this has not yet been brought into effect due to the lack of consensus about its definition. In June 2010, a Review Conference was held in Kampala, Uganda, to further clarify the crime of aggression (for details, see Chapter 58 on crimes of aggression).

Under the Rome Statute, the ICC can act only when a country is "unwilling" or "unable" to take up the case. In essence, domestic and national courts have supremacy over the jurisdiction of cases before they are referred to the ICC. This complementary nature of the Statute is a symbol of a symbiotic relationship between national and international judiciaries in dealing with the gravest crimes of the world order.

Since there is no international police force or enforcement mechanism to apprehend war criminals, states must cooperate with the court in the investigation, arrest, and transfer of suspects. The maximum term of imprisonment is 30 years, but if the crime is of extreme gravity then life imprisonment can be imposed. In addition to imprisonment, fines can also be imposed. The prisoner serves the sentence at a volunteering state party or otherwise in the Netherlands. ICC has its detention center located in Scheveningen, a suburb of The Hague.

The ICC has jurisdiction over crimes committed only after July 1, 2002; in other words, the Court can only address crimes committed after the entry into force of the Statute and the establishment of the court.

STRUCTURE OF THE ICC

The ICC is comprised of four main parts: presidency, judiciary, office of the prosecutor, and registry.

- The presidency manages all administrative concerns of the court, with the exception of the prosecutor's office. It makes decisions regarding the full-time status of the judges (Sadat, 2002).
- The judiciary consists of pre-trial, trial, and appeals divisions made up of 18 judges elected by the Assembly of State Parties (ASP), the Court's management oversight and legislative body that is composed of representatives of the States which have ratified or acceded to the Rome Statute.
- The pre-trial division is a unique element of the Court in that it maintains oversight over the activities of the prosecutor. As expressed in the Rome Statute, the trial chamber must adopt all the necessary procedures to ensure that a trial is fair and expeditious, while fully respecting the rights of the accused with consideration for the protection of victims and witnesses. The Appeals chamber may decide to reverse or amend a decision, judgment, or sentence and may also order a new trial.
- The office of the prosecutor (OTP) "acts independently as a separate organ of the court" (Article 42(1)) and is responsible for receiving and investigating referrals made to the ICC. In June 2003, Mr. Luis Moreno-Ocampo of Argentina was appointed as the first Prosecutor of the court. In December 2011, Ms. Fatou Bensouda of Gambia was appointed as prosecutor. As per Article 53 (initiation of an investigation), the prosecutor shall initiate an investigation unless he or she determines that there is no reasonable basis to proceed under this Statute.
- The registry handles nonjudicial matters, such as maintaining the ICC's records and serving as a depository of notifications and providing channel for communication with states. The registry is also responsible for the development and operation of the Victims and Witness Unit, as well as for supervising and facilitating the assignment of a defense counsel. The Registry is headed by the Registrar, who is the principal administrative officer of the court.

FUNCTIONING OF THE ICC

The referral of a case to the prosecutor of the ICC may occur under the following circumstances.

1. A state that has ratified the Rome Statute can refer the case if crimes within the jurisdiction of the Court appear to have been committed.

2. The UN Security Council can refer the case by acting under Chapter VII of the UN Charter. Under these circumstances, no state consent is required.

3. The prosecutor can initiate investigations *proprio motu* on his or her own behalf.

Except where the Security Council makes the reference, the "preconditions" to the court's jurisdiction require that the accused must be a national of a state party or that the alleged crime was committed on the territory of a state party. A country may also voluntarily accept the ICC's jurisdiction over a crime by formal agreement.

In order for ICC to function effectively, two things must be in place: the necessary finance to pursue the case and the cooperation of affected nations. Article 116 stipulates that the ICC is permitted to receive and make use of any voluntary contributions from governments, international organizations, individuals, corporations, and other entities. It also requires that member states to the Assembly of States Parties (ASP), the body responsible for adopting the Financial Regulations and Rules, must match their political commitment with the financial resources necessary for the operation of the Court. The estimated ICC budget for 2017 is a total of €144.59 million (US$169.5 million), which is just a fraction of the proposed US Judiciary budget of $ US$7.582 billion for 2017.

ICC CASE PROCESSING

To proceed with an investigation, the OTP must establish: 1) jurisdiction; 2) admissibility (including complementarity and gravity); and 3) the interests of justice. In the course of its investigation and prosecution, the OTP must protect the rights and interests of victims and the rights of the accused, including investigation of exonerating circumstances. The prosecutor targets the main leaders and the main criminals (Wouters, Verhoeven, & Demeyere, 2008). See Box 67.1 for steps in case processing.

Box 67.1. Steps in ICC Case Processing

Investigation *(Prosecution)*
- Preliminary analysis of the situation; investigation of situation; collating evidence for seeking arrest warrants for cases.

Pre-trial *(Pre-Trial Chamber)*
- Evaluation of evidence for executing the arrest warrant.
- Authorization to bring the named individuals before the court.
- First appearance of suspects before the Pre-Trial Chamber for public hearing.
- Confirmation of charges and detention.

Adjudication *(Trial Chamber)*
- Trial begins.
- Determination of the innocence or guilt of the accused.
- Sentencing – imprisonment and or fine; monetary compensation, restitution or rehabilitation for victims.

Post-trial *(Appeals Division)*
- Appeal by prosecutor or convicted persons.
- Revision of sentences.
- Review of sentence after the person has served two-thirds of sentence.

To date, there are 11 situations (26 cases) referred by state parties to the Rome Statute, security council and prosecutor *proprio motu* (See Box 67.2).

Box 67.2. Situations under Investigation

I. Referred by State Parties

1. Uganda (January 2004) for alleged war crimes and crimes against humanity.
2. The Democratic Republic of the Congo (April 2004) for alleged war crimes and crimes against humanity.
3. The Central African Republic (CAR) I (April 2004) for alleged war crimes and crimes against humanity.
4. The Central African Republic II (May 2014) for alleged war crimes and crimes against humanity committed in the context of renewed violence –Throughout the CAR.
5. Mali (July 2012) for war crimes.

II. Referred by the Security Council

6. Darfur, Sudan (March 2005) for alleged genocide, war crimes, and crimes against humanity.
7. Libya (February 2011) for alleged crimes against humanity.

III. Prosecution *proprio motu*

8. Kenya (March 2010) for alleged crimes against humanity – post-election.
9. Côte d'Ivoire (October 2011) for alleged crimes against humanity.
10. Georgia (2016) for alleged crimes against humanity and war crimes – armed conflict in 2008.
11. Barundi (October 2017) for alleged crimes against humanity.

SPECIAL FEATURES OF THE ICC

Deterrence

In principle, the ICC has enormous power to deter the gravest crimes against world peace, law, and order. It is too early yet to determine whether the ICC serves that deterrent function, but this should be a research priority when it has been in existence for a sufficient period of time.

Victim Rights and Support

According to the Rome Statute, victims can intervene before the Pre-trial Chamber when the prosecutor is seeking authorization to proceed with an investigation. Victims can also intervene at the trial stage and may be represented by counsel in the presentation of their views and concerns. This confirms that the ICC Statute and Rules of Procedure and Evidence offer important protections for victims and witnesses, particularly those who suffered sexual or gender violence. This provides avenues for scholars of victimology to undertake empirical and policy research concerning the Rome Statute and victim concerns.

Checks and Balances

The prosecutor must seek authorization from the Pre-Trial Chamber to initiate an investigation. If the prosecutor is not given this authorization, the appeals division can overrule the Pre-Trial Chamber in order to allow the prosecutor to proceed. The interaction of these chambers exemplifies the court's system of checks and balances where the pre-trial division has oversight over the prosecutor, and the decisions of the Pre-Trial and Trial Chambers are subject to checks by the appeals division.

Gender-Sensitive Justice

The ICC statute governs a number of sexual violence crimes unprecedented in international criminal law. For the first time, rape, sexual slavery, enforced prostitution, forced pregnancy, enforced sterilization, or any other form of sexual violence are explicitly incorporated as both crimes against humanity and war crimes. Sexual violence crimes can also be prosecuted under the crime against humanity of persecution based on gender (Pillay, 2008).

Role of Nongovernmental Organizations

The ICC is supported by the Coalition for the International Criminal Court, comprised of 2,500 nongovernmental organizations (NGOs) from 150 countries. These serve: 1) to ensure that the ICC is fair, effective, and independent; 2) to make justice both visible and universal; and 3) to advance stronger national laws that deliver justice to victims of international crimes.

Opportunity for Jobs, Internships, and Visiting Professionals

The ICC seeks to raise awareness about the role of the Court through internships, employment opportunities, and visiting programs. These provide avenues for many young people and scholars to contribute to research and to develop professional careers in dealing with international crimes.

CHALLENGES

One of the major political challenges is that the USA, China, and India, all major powers, are not parties to the ICC, although the United Kingdom, France, Germany, and Japan are. The

USA played a leading role in the establishment of the Rome Statute, but it strongly opposes the ICC on grounds that it will be used as a tool for politically motivated trials against the USA (Bradley, 2002). The lack of endorsement by the USA and other major powers has important repercussions on the substantive law that dictates the procedures of ICC.

The lack of international police and prisons poses a major problem for the ICC because it has to depend on volunteering state parties to supply the criminal justice services in executing the arrest warrants and imprisoning the prisoners. The need to negotiate these services contributes significantly to delays.

There is a danger that the state parties that provide a disproportionate amount of funding for the ICC might expect to have a commensurate influence in its proceedings.

While the ICC makes strenuous and real efforts to involve victims in the proceedings and to provide them with assistance in terms of counseling and financial help, it is impossible for ICC to recover their lives and heal their wounds. Ways must be found of retaining and strengthening the focus on victims without leading them to expect unrealistic outcomes. More needs to be done to educate state parties and the public about the unavoidable reasons for the lengthy investigations and trial processes so as to forestall criticism of the court.

The fact that all of the cases so far under trial relate to countries in Africa might suggest that ICC is only able to intervene in cases where governments are weak or disorganized.

SUMMARY AND CONCLUSIONS

Despite the many obstacles confronting the ICC, including the criticisms of ICC's investigations being mainly into African states, its establishment represents the dawning of a new era in international criminal justice. Its key purpose is to ensure that war criminals are subject to individual criminal liability in cases of serious human rights violations. As one of the first permanent international institutions to challenge threats to international order, the ICC is intended to contribute to the prevention and deterrence of the Rome Statute's core crimes. As stated by Clark (2005), what is important is "getting the best possible judges and Prosecutor and making proper provision for the defense; legislative implementation at the national level; fostering a culture of boldness on the part of States Parties and civil society in bringing well-documented situations to the attention of the Prosecutor; making operational the Statute's many provisions dealing with victims; responding to the chilling effect of the United States' efforts, in the Security Council and through a complicated series of bilateral negotiations, to chip away at the edges of the Statutory regime; and finally, the unfinished business of Rome and the Preparatory Commission, the crime of aggression."

REFERENCES

Bradley, C. A. (2002, May). US announces intent not to ratify International Criminal Court treaty. *The American Society of International Law Insights*. Retrieved from www.asil.org/insights/insigh87 .htm.

Clark, R. (2005). Challenges confronting the assembly of states parties of the International Criminal Court. In E. Vetere & P. David (Eds.), *Victims of crime and abuse of power: Festschrift in honour of Irene Melup* (p. 141). Bangkok: 11th UN Congress on Crime Prevention and Criminal Justice.

Kress, C. (2003). Symposium. The procedural law of the International Criminal Court in outline: Anatomy of a unique compromise. *Journal of International Criminal Justice*, 1(3), 603–617.

Pillay, N. (2008). *Gender justice at the ICC.* Plenary Speech at the John Jays' Eighth International Conference, Puerto Rico.

Sadat, L. (2002). *The International Criminal Court and the transformation of international law: Justice for the new millennium.* New York: Transnational Publishers, Inc.

Wouters, J., Verhoeven, S., & Demeyere, B. (2008). The International Criminal Court's Office of the Prosecutor: Navigating between independence and accountability? *International Criminal Law Review*, 8(1/2), 273–317.

WEBSITES

Coalition for the ICC. www.iccnow.org.

ICC Preparatory commission work. www.un.org/law/icc/prepcomm/prepfra.htm or at www.jus.unitn. it/icct82/home.html.

International Criminal Court. www.icc-cpi.int/iccdocs/asp_docs/ASP8/OR/OR-ASP8-Vol.II-ENG-Part.A.pdf.

68 The ICC and the Darfur Investigation

Progress and Challenges

Xabier Agirre Aranburu and Roberta Belli

INTRODUCTION

The investigation in the Darfur region of Sudan has been especially challenging for the newly founded International Criminal Court (ICC). The Prosecutor of the ICC has succeeded to complete the investigation of four cases against senior leaders in Darfur in spite of the huge and complex nature of the crimes, lack of cooperation, security threats, and open armed conflict. This chapter will provide a brief introduction on the Darfur investigation with a timeline of legal precedents, and focus on the cases brought before the ICC judges, the methods and evidence utilized for this investigation, and the issues that still need be resolved to ensure prospects of justice for the victims of Darfur.

BACKGROUND

In February 2003, fighting erupted between Sudanese military troops and Darfur rebels, who were accusing the government of purposefully marginalizing the western region of Darfur from the economic and political agenda, and of discriminating against the local tribes of the Fur, Zaghawa, and Masalit. The government responded with a brutal counterinsurgency campaign (assisted by the *Janjaweeds,* militias from Arab tribes), which quickly escalated to widespread and indiscriminate violence. A large part of the civilian population fled to eastern Chad, and hundreds of thousands of civilians were internally displaced within Sudan (Prunier, 2005).

In July 2004, the US State Department, in cooperation with the US Agency for International Development's Office of Transitional Initiatives (USAID OTI) and the Coalition for International Justice (CIJ), established the "Darfur Atrocities Documentation Team" (ADT), a multinational team of investigators who traveled along the Chad/Sudanese border to interview refugees and collect data on the magnitude of the crisis. Based on the results of this survey, on September 9, 2004, US Secretary of State Colin Powell declared that the violence perpetrated in Darfur amounted to genocide. This was the first time in history

The views contained in this chapter are those of the authors and do not represent necessarily the views of the Office of the Prosecutor of the International Criminal Court. The information contained in this chapter has been updated as of June 2018.

that a sovereign state accused another one of genocide during an ongoing conflict (Totten & Markusen, 2006).

The US Government referred the matter to the UN Security Council, who passed Resolution 1564 on September 18, 2004, establishing a "Commission of Inquiry," composed of five prominent international justice and human rights experts, to investigate into the genocide allegations. In January 2005, the UN Commission of Inquiry released its final report concluding that several violations of international humanitarian law had been committed in Darfur, including crimes against humanity and war crimes. The Commission of Inquiry additionally recommended that the situation be referred to the International Criminal Court for a proper criminal investigation.

On March 31, 2005, the UN Security Council passed Resolution 1593, which referred the situation in Darfur to the ICC, with 11 votes in favor of the Resolution and four abstentions (the USA, Algeria, Brazil, and China). The ICC Office of the Prosecutor (OTP) received several thousands of evidence items collected by the Commission and other organizations, including statements from victims and experts, pictures, videos, documents, maps, and forensic reports. On June 6, 2005, Prosecutor Luis Moreno-Ocampo publicly announced his decision to start an official investigation into the atrocities committed in Darfur after determining there was sufficient evidence to proceed.

CASES UNDER INVESTIGATION

Between 2005 and 2012, the ICC-OTP completed the investigation of four cases comprising seven individuals who were identified as bearing the greatest responsibility for crimes committed in Darfur (see details in the reference section for the ICC court cases).

On February 27, 2007, the Prosecutor filed an Application for a Warrant of Arrest (AWA) against Ahmed Harun and Ali Kushayb for war crimes and crimes against humanity committed mainly in West Darfur. The corresponding Warrants of Arrests were issued by the Pre-Trial Chamber I on May 2, 2007. The evidence gathered by the Prosecutor showed that the Sudanese Government launched a counterinsurgency campaign starting in 2003 against the areas of activity of the Darfur rebel groups. While counterinsurgency warfare as such is not a crime under international law, the Sudanese forces conducted their campaign in full disregard of the principle of distinction (the duty under international humanitarian law to distinguish between civilians and military), and systematically destroyed hundreds of villages throughout the three states of Darfur (North, South, and West Darfur), with the result of tens of thousands of civilians killed, raped, and tortured, and hundreds of thousands forcibly expelled. Unable to target the elusive guerrilla units, the government decided to punish and destroy the civilian fabric from which the rebels were gathering their recruits and supplies. The military operations were planned from the top level of the government in Khartoum and they were carried out jointly by the military, air force, police, intelligence, and the local *Janjaweed* militias.

Ahmed Harun, a devoted member of the ruling National Congress Party, was identified by multiple documents and witnesses as the senior officer in the Ministry of Interior who was in charge of financing, mobilizing, and coordinating operations with the *Janjaweed*. In 2003–2004, at the height of the military campaign, Harun traveled in numerous occasions from Khartoum to Darfur to transmit instructions and to deliver money and weapons to the militias that carried out the most murderous attacks. This kind of senior civilian bureaucrat is typically used by the top level of authority to develop a shorter and more secretive chain of command that may be more suitable than the conventional army for clandestine criminal operations. His profile resembles that of Jovica Stanisic, the senior civilian officer that worked directly for Milosevic in mobilizing Serbian paramilitary groups to carry out massive ethnic cleansing in former Yugoslavia in the 1990s.[1] Ali Kushayb was identified as a militia leader that acted as field commander in a series of deadly attacks on villages in West Darfur in 2002–2003.

The second case was a progression from the first one, focusing on the same scenario of violence but covering the whole geographical scope, a longer period up to 2008, charges of genocide in addition to war crimes and crimes against humanity and the highest authority of the President of the Republic Omar Hassan Ahmad Al Bashir. The Prosecutor filed the AWA against Bashir on July 14, 2008, and Pre-Trial Chamber I issued the corresponding Warrant of Arrest for crimes against humanity and war crimes on March 4, 2009.

On July 12, 2010 the judges issued a second Warrant of Arrest, including a charge of genocide, which is the only instance so far in the history of the ICC when the Prosecutor has pursued a charge of genocide. The Prosecutor had included the charge of genocide in the first AWA, but the Pre-Trial Chamber dismissed it. Then the Prosecutor appealed that decision, and finally the Appeals Chamber agreed with the Prosecutor and instructed the Pre-Trial Chamber to issue the genocide charge.

The evidence gathered by the Prosecutor showed that, the Republic of Sudan being a presidential system, President Bashir directed all branches of the state that were involved in the criminal campaign against the civilians of Darfur. The Statute of the ICC establishes that "official capacity as a Head of State or Government […] shall in no case exempt a person from criminal responsibility under this Statute" (Article 27.1). Bashir joined the list of heads of state indicted for crimes under international law with Pinochet (Chile), Habre (Chad), Milosevic (Serbia), Mengistu (Ethiopia), and Taylor (Liberia).

The third case deals with an attack and destruction by a rebel group against an African Union peacekeeping base in Haskanita in September 2007, in which 12 peacekeepers were killed. The Prosecutor considered the attack particularly grave because of the broader impact on the civilian population that benefited from the protection of the peacekeepers, and filed charges of war crimes against three rebel commanders. Further to the Prosecutor's application, on May 7, 2009, Pre-Trial Chamber I issued a Summons to Appear for Bahr Idriss Abu Garda, the leader of the United Resistance Front and former commander of the Justice and Equality Movement. The Application for the summonses for the other two rebel commanders is pending.

The fourth case is a continuation from the first and second cases, alleging responsibility for the same pattern of crimes against Abdel Raheem Muhammad Hussein, who was at the relevant time Minister of Interior and Sudanese President's Special Representative in Darfur. In this case the Prosecutor pursued and obtained from the judges charges of crimes against humanity and war crimes, but not genocide.

---

[1] Jovica Stanisic was indicted by ICTY IN 2003; see related documentation at the ICTY official site www.icty.org/case/ stanisic_simatovic/4.

THE ICC INVESTIGATIVE STRATEGY

According to the Rome Statute, the ICC Warrants of Arrest or Summons to Appear are based on the evidence collected by the Office of the Prosecutor and reviewed independently by the judges of the Pre-Trial Chamber. Investigating Darfur was particularly challenging because of the ongoing armed conflict in the areas of the crime and the lack of access to the scene of the crime (unlike the precedents of international investigations in the former Yugoslavia or Rwanda).

The Prosecutor overcame these difficulties with a creative investigative strategy that included the following: 1) recruiting investigators and analysts with field experience in Darfur; 2) interviewing victims in third countries that had received them as refugees around the world; 3) interviewing qualified international observers that gained an overview of the violence and interacted with key leaders; 4) conducting systematic open-source searches, including video records and public statements by the suspects; 5) using satellite imagery and remote sensing data; 6) analyzing military and other official documents provided by the Sudanese Government and the African Union; and 7) using the evidence collected by the UN Commission of Inquiry.

From an early stage of the investigation, the OTP Analysis Section developed a crime database to integrate multiple sources of evidence and analyze the patterns of violence, including their geographical and chronological distribution (e.g., to find "hot-spots" and "peaks" of crime), statistics and correlations with key actions of the suspects and their military forces. The results of the investigative strategy persuaded the judges, who issued arrest warrants or summons to appear against four of the six leading individuals requested by the Prosecutor, with the two pending requests expected to be decided shortly.

PROCEDURAL AND INVESTIGATIVE ISSUES

The Darfur investigations have been innovative for international criminal justice in a number of ways. For example, in the case against Abu Garda, the ICC judges issued for the first time a Summons to Appear, under Article 58 of the ICC Statute, instead of a Warrant of Arrest. Upon suggestion from the Prosecutor, the judges found that the arrest of Abu Garda was not necessary because he had cooperated with the Court and committed himself to appear before the judges. Mr. Abu Garda honored his commitment and had his first appearance before the ICC judges on May 18, 2009. His collaboration stands in sharp contrast with the other suspects in the Darfur situation and it should serve as an example to promote further cooperation by individuals subject to international investigations.

Whether genocide was committed in Darfur has been the subject of controversy. In the first Darfur case, the evidence collected by the Prosecutor sufficed to obtain Warrants of Arrest for multiple war crimes and crimes against humanity, including murder, rape, and expulsions at a massive scale. In the second case, against President Bashir, the AWA included additional charges of genocide because a holistic understanding of the case, in its full geographical extent and chronological duration, convinced the Prosecutor that such massive mortality and destruction must have followed from the specific intent of Bashir to destroy the ethnic groups perceived as harboring the rebellion. The judges confirmed unanimously the charge of extermination as a crime against humanity (Article 7(1)(b) of the Rome Statute), which is an extraordinarily grave charge, but they were divided in their assessment of the genocide allegations because of the very strict requirements to establish the mental element for this crime under the ICC Statute.

Quantitative estimates about mortality in armed conflicts are often controversial because of problems of data quality and sampling over areas and periods with sharp pattern variations. Since 2005, social scientists and activists have engaged in a controversy about the figures of mortality in Darfur, with estimates ranging from some 10,000 (as alleged by the government of Sudan) up to 400,000 (as reported by some NGOs; see also Hagan & Rymond-Richmond, 2009). Such wide-ranging discrepancies have even led the US Government Accountability Office (GAO) to take the unusual step of conducting an expert review of the statistical estimates produced by different agencies. The ICC Prosecutor avoided this controversy, focusing on the consensus among all reliable sources about the massive scale of the violence and quoting conservative estimates of 30,000 direct killings, a larger number of deaths caused by the hardship of the expulsions and destruction, and up to 2 million civilians forcibly displaced.

Finally, the ICC Statute does not allow trials *in absentia*, so that the development of actual prosecutions depends on the arrest or voluntary appearance of the accused. The ICC does not have the mandate to carry out the arrests, which must be trusted to the cooperation of national and international authorities. Additionally, since the first arrest warrants were issued the Sudanese Government has refused to cooperate with the Court. Despite these problems, the ICC Prosecutor continues monitoring the activities of the accused and is actively engaged in seeking the necessary cooperation so that international fugitives are brought to justice. INTERPOL has issued Red Notices for some of those still sought by the ICC, and international cooperation has so far led to the arrest of four ICC accused from other situations and their transfer to the Detention Unit in Scheveningen (The Hague, the Netherlands), where they should be soon joined by those responsible for the crimes in Darfur.

Further to the UNSC referral from 2005, the Prosecutor is invited to report every six months on the progress of the Darfur investigation. In June 2018, Prosecutor Fatou Bensouda presented the "Twenty-seventh report of the Prosecutor of the ICC to the UN Security Council pursuant to USCR 1593 (2005)." She reiterated that "Regrettably all the suspects in the Darfur situation remain at large" and requested the cooperation of the states to arrest the suspects. Her report included details of the travel of Mr Al Bashir to different states that failed to arrest him, including Jordan, Uganda, Chad, Ethiopia, Turkey, Egypt, Rwanda, and Saudi Arabia. She concluded stating that "The support of the Council for this mandate, triggered by its own resolution, remains essential, now more than ever."[2]

CONCLUSION

The mission of the ICC to put an end to impunity for the perpetrators of the gravest crimes of concern to the international community is as paramount and crucial as it is hard to achieve.

[2] See "Twenty-seventh report of the Prosecutor of the ICC to the UN Security Council pursuant to USCR 1593 (2005)" at www.icc-cpi.int/itemsDocuments/20180620-27-rep-UNSCR-1593-ENG.pdf.

The Darfur investigation provides an example of the many problems and obstacles an international prosecutor must deal with compared to a national prosecutor. Despite the many challenges, however, significant steps have been made, and the international justice system can greatly benefit from the efforts of the ICC investigators.

REFERENCES

Hagan, J. & Rymond-Richmond, W. (2009). *Darfur and the crime of genocide.* New York: Cambridge University Press.

Prosecutor v. Ahmad Muhammad Harun ("Ahmad Harun") and Ali Muhammad Ali Abd-Al-Rahman ("Ali Kushayb") (Pre-Trial Chamber I), ICC-02/05-01/07-3, International Criminal Court (ICC) (2007, April 27). Available at www.icc-cpi.int/iccdocs/doc/doc279858.PDF.

Prosecutor v. Ahmad Muhammad Harun ("Ahmad Harun") and Ali Muhammad Ali Abd-Al-Rahman ("Ali Kushayb") (Pre-Trial Chamber I), ICC-02/05-01/07-2, International Criminal Court (ICC) (2007, April 28). Available at www.icc-cpi.int/CourtRecords/CR2007_02902.PDF.

Prosecutor v. Omar Hassan Ahmad Al Bashir (Pre-Trial Chamber I), ICC-02/05-01/09-1, International Criminal Court (ICC) (2009, March 4). Available at www.icc-cpi.int/iccdocs/doc/doc639078.pdf.

Prosecutor v. Bahr Idriss Abu Garda (Pre-Trial Chamber I), ICC-02/05-02/09-15-AnxA, International Criminal Court (ICC) (2009, May 7). Available at www.icc-cpi.int/iccdocs/doc/doc689342.pdf.

Prunier, G. (2005). *Darfur: The ambiguous genocide.* Ithaca, NY: Cornell University Press.

Totten, S. & Markusen, E. (2006). *Genocide in Darfur: Investigating the atrocities in the Sudan.* New York: Routledge.

69 Victims' Rights in the International Criminal Court

David Donat Cattin

INTRODUCTION: GOALS OF THE ICC

The unprecedented role for victims in the International Criminal Court (ICC) proceedings is an important feature of the ICC, a judicial institution that should fulfill – at the same time – the criminal justice goals of prevention and retribution as well as truth telling and reparation. Hence, it is very important to understand that such goals are present in the innovative legal framework of the ICC, which is the first international penal jurisdiction where victims' rights are recognized and enforced. This chapter provides an introduction on victims' rights in the law and practice of the ICC and identifies core principles in three areas of victims' rights: 1) protection, 2) participation, and 3) reparations. These are crosscutting elements in the ICC procedural law and are regulated by principles that serve one another and may not be separated when defining the elements of the victim's right to justice, which is an inalienable human right attributed to victims of crime or abuse of power under international law.

THE CORE PRINCIPLES OF VICTIMS' RIGHTS

Protection

To protect victims and witnesses is an absolute duty for all the organs of the Court that may not be derogated even if there is express consent of the relevant victim(s) or witness(es). Such a legal principle, which is present throughout the entire Statute and the Rules of Procedure and Evidence (the Rules), is expressly defined at Article 68, paragraph 1 and entails the unconditioned right to be protected for victim(s) and witness(es) relevant to the ICC at any stage of its proceedings. The extreme consequence of this principle is that in case the production of a certain piece of evidence in Court, or outside Court, would cause risks for a given victim or witness, and those risks could not be effectively minimized by measures of protection available to the ICC or state parties to the Statute, the relevant Chamber and the Prosecutor shall abstain from admitting or producing such evidence. The reasoning behind the principle is to be found in the doctrine against secondary victimization (retraumatization), which does not occur as a direct result of the criminal act but is caused by the response of institutions or individuals to the victim's demand to access to justice (United Nations Commission on Crime Prevention and Criminal Justice [UNODC], 1999). In no way shall criminal proceedings before the ICC or complementary national jurisdictions result in the secondary victimization of a victim or the victimization of a witness. Protective measures taken by all appropriate ICC organs and by relevant organs and agencies of states must be targeted to the prevention of this phenomenon. The practice of the Court has been generally in line with this normative requirement of Article 68(1) of the Rome Statute, which regards not only the *safety* and *security* of persons at risk on account of their interaction with ICC organs, but also their *privacy* and *well-being*. However, in the situation regarding the post-electoral violence in Kenya and the attempted prosecutions of two leading policy makers (Mr. Kenyatta and Mr. Ruto, who decided to create a presidential ticket after the commencement of proceedings against them for crimes against humanity before the ICC, and eventually won by a small margin the 2013 presidential elections), numerous reports indicated that witnesses, including victims, were subjected to retaliatory violence and other coercive actions. This led the Office of the Prosecutor to re-assess the effectiveness of protective measures, and to expand the use of "sealed" proceedings, given that the publicity of certain proceedings might endanger the safety, security, privacy, and well-being of victims and witnesses, even if the policy of public announcement of preliminary examinations or investigations may still need to be re-evaluated in light the vulnerability of persons on the ground – who could be "eliminated" by the potential accused persons who are put on alert by the publicity of proceedings that could end up in establishing their individual criminal responsibility.

Participation

"Justice must be done and must be seen to be done." This appeared to be the favorite motto of victims' rights advocates before, during, and after the Rome Diplomatic Conference. But how can justice be seen to be done if victims are not entitled to access to the justice process and contribute, in one way or another, to its effective and fair development? This question finds its ICC-related answer in Article 68, paragraph 3 of the Statute, which mirrors Section 6(b) of the Declaration of Basic Principles of Justice for Victims of Crime and Abuse of Power (UNGA Res. 40/35 1985). Victims are entitled to participate in ICC proceedings and to express their views and concerns at appropriate stages of the proceedings to be identified by the relevant Chamber. Victims' interventions shall be appropriate vis-à-vis the rights of the accused and the "fair and impartial trial." Such interventions may, therefore, appropriately be done through a third person (a legal representative) who has the legal skills to interact with the judges and the parties in open court and *ex parte*, within the complex framework of principles, rules, and regulations of international criminal jurisdiction.

Victims who decide to participate in ICC trials may take the courageous decision to expose themselves to the public scrutiny and to the potential retaliation of the accused and his or her accomplices, who may still be at large (e.g., under an ICC or a national arrest warrant, not yet executed) or may have been spared from prosecution by the selective practice of the ICC Office of the Prosecutor[1] and by the failure of states' authorities to effectively

---

[1] It is of particular concern for this author that the ICC Prosecutor has so far followed a policy to restrict the ICC's prosecutions to very few individuals (44 publicly known defendants in almost 16 years of operations), namely, those allegedly "bearing the greatest responsibility for the most serious crimes" of concern to the international community as a whole (www.icc-cpi.int/NR/rdonlyres/1FA7C4C6-DE5F-42B7-8B25-60AA962ED8B6/143594/030905_Policy_Paper. pdf). While this policy appears reasonable *in abstracto*, it may lead to significant negative repercussions *in concreto* (e.g.,

exercise their complementary national jurisdiction. Even though protective measures may be put in place for these victims, the fact that they formally participate in ICC public hearings make them known to the accused and, in one way or another, to the wider public. However, it has been demonstrated that in several circumstances the best way to be "protected" is to go public and openly declare one's personal status. Protective measures shall be tailored to such victims without frustrating their aspiration to intervene in ICC proceedings when they believe that this is the best way to give effect to their "right to justice."

In the first 16 years of ICC practice, public sources of information indicate that approximately 25,000 victims applied to participate in the Court's proceedings. Approximately 11,000 have been granted the right to participate in the relevant situation and/or case under investigation and/or prosecution before the ICC, hence obtaining recognition of their status and allowing them to start a process of reparative justice.

Reparations

Remedying wrongs is always difficult when such wrongs entail the violation of criminal law(s). Redress for victims of ordinary crimes is often not available in national legal orders. It is, therefore, even more difficult to provide redress for victims of crimes under international law in the ICC system, which consists of the complementary jurisdictions of state parties and of the ICC itself.

An important attempt in the right direction is made in Articles 75 and 79 of the Statute and related provisions in the Rules, which affirm the right of victims to obtain reparations on the basis of "principles relating to reparation" that shall be established by the Court in each and every case before it. Other important features of the discipline of reparations in the ICC framework will not be commented here. Appropriate reparations will have to be tailored to the individual case as a result of the assessment of concrete victimization of individuals and groups of individuals. The jurisprudence will, thus, play a crucial role in applying and shaping the development of standards fulfilling the victims' right to see their wrongs remedied to a degree that, while aiming at restoring the situation(s) preexisting the commission of the crimes, will inevitably have a symbolic and only partially restitutive nature, due to the irreparable damage caused by atrocities like extermination, murder, enslavement, rape, or torture. Legal concepts such as restitution, compensation, and rehabilitation (which includes guarantees of non-repetition and may include satisfaction and "memorialization") will assist the judges while performing their decision making duties, together with the factual representations and submissions made by victims or groups of victims who will apply to the Court for reparations. The experience of national jurisdictions of civil law countries may provide the ICC with interesting ways and means to implement the statutory norms on reparations.

---

inability of the OTP to prove certain crimes committed by the "commanders-in-chief" in the absence of *res judicata* against other leaders or mid-level commanders, a too-wide impunity gap that states' authorities may be unable to tackle, a perception that the OTP policy is too heavily restricted and guided by states' policies to limit the budget and size of the OTP itself, thus infringing upon its independence and effectiveness). In 2016, the second Prosecutor of the ICC has partially rectified this policy of case selection and prioritization (cf. www.icc-cpi.int/itemsDocuments/20160915_OTP-Policy_Case-Selection_Eng.pdf).

VICTIMS' PARTICIPATION AND ICC COURTROOM

The courtrooms of the *ad hoc* International Criminal Tribunals for the Former Yugoslavia and for Rwanda (ICTY and ICTR) have not been conceived to accommodate the presence of victims, since victims were not recognized as intervenient parties in the *ad hoc* tribunals' procedural law. To overcome this problem and – above all – to fulfill the requirements of the procedural law of the ICC, within which a precise role is attributed to victims, the courtroom of the ICC permanent premises should have been designed in a different way, thus rectifying the mistake made in the interim headquarters of the Court in The Hague, where the bench of the judges was facing the public gallery and a stand for witnesses while the benches of the prosecution and of victims were placed on the left of the judges, and the benches of the accused and of potentially intervenient state(s) were placed on the right of the judges. Regretfully, the same model of courtroom has been made in the permanent premises of the ICC in The Hague.

The organization of the space in the courtroom has a symbolic and important meaning to the victims, since the recognition of their role in the justice process and, consequently, their position in open court can make them understand how an institution representing the international society recognizes and respects them. An effective access to victims or groups of victims to ICC proceedings shall in no way reduce the space and time allocated in such proceedings to its fundamental parties, the prosecution and the defense. But since the role of the prosecution is not that of bringing charges and winning a case, but of establishing the truth and searching and disclosing all incriminating and exonerating circumstances equally, it must be understood that the Prosecutor is not just a party in the proceedings. While the Prosecutor seems to play the role of party in an apparently adversarial framework, the goal of the Prosecutor is to be impartial and search for the truth. In this respect, the Prosecutor is the first defense counsel of the accused, since he/she is under the unconditioned duty to search and present exculpatory evidence in all cases such evidence is found. And if the Prosecutor fails, the judges "shall have the authority to request the submission of all evidence that it considers necessary for the determination of the truth."

The combined reading of these and many other provisions of the Rules of Procedure and Evidence make clear that the ICC proceedings are not simply adversarial, but they draw prominent inspiration from the civil law systems. In those systems, Prosecutors are magistrates, who are members of the judiciary together with the judges. The ICC Prosecutor is an organ of the court and a magistrate. Even though she appears to be a party to the proceedings, she is not – and she cannot be – an "advocate of the prosecution." The Prosecutor is, instead, an impartial player who has a functional role in investigating and prosecuting with the ultimate goal of achieving a judicial truth, namely the truth pertaining to the individual criminal responsibility in a concrete case under the law.

Victims have an inalienable right to know the truth. They are, therefore, not interested in convictions of innocent individuals, who have the right to acquittal. If the Prosecutor does not genuinely fulfill her duties, victims will act as guardians of the interest of justice and express their views and concerns in accordance with Article 68(3) of the Statute. At the same time, the emotions, and often trauma, afflicting victims shall not produce uncontrolled interventions against the accused and consequent disruption of the proceedings. The power of the judges in regulating victims' interventions is designed to avoid these situations, and the almost necessary presence of a legal representative is aimed at ensuring that statements and questioning on behalf of victims take place in respect of the court procedure and the fair trial. Hence, the correct organization of the space in the ICC courtroom should have entailed the separation of victims from the prosecution and from the accused and should have avoided the current scheme in which the victims have a confronting position vis-à-vis the accused and side position vis-à-vis the prosecution; all parties should have faced the judges, who are in control of the proceedings. This organization of courtroom's space would have created a more conducive environment for the search of the judicial truth.

PROCEDURE FOR THE APPLICATION OF VICTIMS TO APPEAR IN ICC PROCEEDINGS

Public information and outreach are crucial in ensuring that victims and groups of victims are aware of the possibility to participate in ICC proceedings. Definition of victims under Rule 85 reads as follows.

"For the purposes of the Statute and the Rules of Procedure and Evidence:

a. Victims mean natural persons who have suffered harm as a result of the commission of any crime within the jurisdiction of the Court
b. Victims may include organizations or institutions that have sustained direct harm to any of their property which is dedicated to religion, education, art or science or charitable purposes, and to their historic monuments, hospitals and other places and objects for humanitarian purposes."

It is up to the judges to assess whether a victim who applies to participate in a given ICC proceeding is a victim under Rule 85. In its first 16 years of practice, the Court has recognized that the crucial test for recognition of the procedural status of victim before the ICC is the nexus between the conduct for which the accused is brought before the Court (i.e., the charges) and the harm suffered by the victim, whether a survivor (e.g., a child soldier) or a family member of a murdered victim. The most critical issue for the applicant-victims is, therefore, to make sure that a link between their actual victimization ("the harm suffered") and the concrete situation or crime under investigation is established. Victims' applications are directed to the Court's registrar, who has the task under Rule 16.3 to maintain "a special register of victims who have expressed their intention to participate in relation to a specific case."

CONCLUSION: PRACTICAL CHALLENGES FOR ICC IN VICTIM SUPPORT AND ASSISTANCE

Some states' representatives and a few observers to the ICC decision making process expressed the concern that the innovative role of the ICC in promoting the respect of victims' rights cannot imply the realization of a victims' support system at the international level in the framework of the Court. In their view, the limited resources of the ICC should not be directed towards the care of victims while the Court's fundamental aim is to fight impunity and thus contribute to the prevention and repression of crimes. This concern is having a true bearing on the budgetary allocations on and development of ICC structures such as the Victims and Witnesses Unit and the Victims Participation and Reparations Section within the Court's Registry. However, this concern should be addressed in the wider framework of the ICC system, and not be confined to the Court as such. The ICC system comprises of the primary role of jurisdictions (and related agencies) of member states and the complementary role of ICC organs in protecting victims' rights. It goes without saying that the application of the principle of complementarity to victims' assistance would make it possible for the ICC to concentrate only on situations in which victims may not have access to a remedy. In these situations, a key role that the ICC should be able to play is the one of coordination and, as appropriate, cooperation with international organizations and other entities that may assist victims.

Another role that the ICC plays, in the context of its outreach efforts, relates to the management of the expectations of victims and their communities. While explaining that victims have rights under the Rome Statute and international law, the ICC outreach program may provide information on the necessity for victims to first approach national agencies, if available, and international organizations operating in the field to verify the availability of assistance as well as access to justice and procedures to obtain reparations. But once such avenues are *de facto* exhausted, victims are entitled to find an answer to their questions before the ICC. And the Court itself, in the absence of available national programs, should be able to recommend to relevant national and international institutions the action to be undertaken to fulfill the rights of victims.

REFERENCES TO THE INITIAL PRACTICE OF THE ICC

Pre-Trial Decision on Victims' Protection: Authorization of an Investigation into the Situation in the Republic of Burundi, November 9, 2017. www.icc-cpi.int/CourtRecords/CR2017_06720.PDF.

Trial Decision and Dissenting Opinion on Halting Ruto case (due to tampering of witnesses and victims), April 5, 2016. www.icc-cpi.int/Pages/record.aspx?docNo=ICC-01/09-01/11-2027-Red.

Trial Decision on Victims' Protection: Decision on the withdrawal of charges against Mr Kenyatta, March 13, 2015. www.icc-cpi.int/CourtRecords/CR2015_02842.PDF.

Trial Decisions on Victims' Participation: Katanga and Ngudjolo case, January 22, 2010. www.icc-cpi.int/iccdocs/doc/doc810967.pdf; Lubanga case, January 18, 2008. www.icc-cpi.int/iccdocs/doc/doc409168.PDF.

Pre-Trial Decision on Victims' Participation: Kony et al. case, August 10, 2007. www.worldcourts.com/icc/eng/decisions/2007.08.10_Prosecutor_v_Kony.pdf; Lubanga case, January 17, 2006. www.icc-cpi.int/iccdocs/doc/doc183441.PDF.

Appeals Judgements on Certain Aspects of Victims' Participation: Lubanga Case, July 11, 2008. www2.icc-cpi.int/iccdocs/doc/doc529076.PDF; February 13, 2007. www.icc-cpi.int/iccdocs/doc/doc248155.PDF (with dissenting opinion of Judge Song).

Pre-Trial Decision on Protective Measures and Victims' Rights: Lubanga case, February 10, 2006. http://145.7.218.139/iccdocs/doc/doc236260.PDF.

Assembly of States Parties Web site on ICC permanent premises. www.icc-architectural-competition.com.

REFERENCE

United Nations Commission on Crime Prevention and Criminal Justice (UNODC). (1999). *Handbook on justice for victims on the use and application of the United Nations Declaration of basic principles of justice for victims of crime and abuse of power.* U.N. Doc. E/CN.15/1998/1.

70 International Criminal Tribunals and Hybrid Courts

Gloria J. Browne-Marshall

INTRODUCTION

International criminal tribunals were created for prosecuting individuals responsible for shockingly horrific mass violence. These violations of international humanitarian law are embodied in the Universal Declaration of Human Rights, the International Covenant on Civil and Political Rights, The Hague Conventions, the Geneva Conventions, the Genocide Convention, and the Convention against Torture and Cruel, Inhuman and Degrading Treatment and Punishment. This chapter examines the continued development of international tribunals from the Nuremberg and Tokyo Trials to the Criminal Tribunal for the Former Yugoslavia, the Criminal Tribunal for Rwanda, and the hybrid courts including the Special Panel for Serious Crimes in East Timor, the Special Court for Sierra Leone, and the Cambodian Extraordinary Chambers.

THE NUREMBERG TRIBUNAL

The lives of more than 60 million persons, primarily civilians, were lost during World War II. The German military was accused of the premeditated murder of civilian populations. After the war, leaders of the Allied nations – the USA, France, Great Britain, and the USSR – drafted the Nuremberg Charter creating the International Military Tribunal (the Tribunal) for the "just and prompt trial and punishment of the major war criminals of the European Axis" powers (Bassiouni, 2014). The Chief Prosecutor was Robert H. Jackson, Associate Justice of the United States Supreme Court. The trial was conducted in Nuremberg, Germany.

The Tribunal had jurisdiction or authority to adjudicate crimes against peace, war crimes, and crimes against humanity (Bassiouni, 2014). Jurisdiction allows a court or legal authority to have power over a person, subject area, or thing. Crimes against humanity are massive acts of cruelty and destruction taking place during war or strife, usually against civilians. Acts of genocide were subsumed within crimes against humanity. These German defendants were provided counsel, due process rights, and translators. They argued that their actions were not crimes and, alternatively, that they were following the orders of the government; thus, as individual soldiers, they should not be held responsible for war crimes. The Nuremberg Tribunal established *in personam* jurisdiction or jurisdiction over the person leading to the indictment of 24 individuals (Bassiouni, 2014). Sentences ranged from imprisonment to death by hanging.

An individual's responsibility for military acts of barbarism during wartime or conflict was established during the Nuremberg Tribunal. It remains an important part of international criminal law because it further established limits to the actions of states during war.

THE TOKYO TRIBUNAL

The lesser-known Tokyo Tribunal was created to prosecute the Japanese accused of brutally murdering civilians, torturing prisoners, and utilizing the bubonic plague against Chinese cities during World War II. Japanese wartime terror campaigns called for soldiers to "kill all, burn all, destroy all" (Browne-Marshall, 2013). In 1946, the Tokyo Tribunal was created to adjudicate and punish war crimes committed by the Japanese in the Far East (von Lingen, 2018).

Defendants were represented by counsel, given translators, and provided due process rights. Prime Minister Tojo Hideki, was indicted. However, Emperor of Japan Hirohito was not charged with any crimes. Arguments of non-responsibility similar to those of the Nuremberg defendants were defeated in similar fashion. Upon convictions, sentences ranged from imprisonment to execution. Although verdicts of the Nuremberg and Tokyo Tribunals were condemned by some as "victors' justice," the creation of these historic tribunals drew attention to the need for a permanent court to address crimes of massive brutality taking place during times of war and peace.

In 1948, the United Nations adopted the Convention on the Prevention and Punishment of the Crime of Genocide. The Charter of the United Nations gives the UN Security Council the power and responsibility to take collective action to maintain international peace and security when a war-torn nation's infrastructure and court system makes it unable to provide proper adjudication of accused war criminals (Mertus, 2018).

AD HOC INTERNATIONAL CRIMINAL TRIBUNALS AND COURTS

International Criminal Tribunal for the Former Yugoslavia

Yugoslavia was a federation comprised of different ethnic and religious groups, generally Croats, Serbs, and Muslims. In 1991, systemic acts of government-led violence by Serbs against Muslims and Croats led to the deaths of hundreds of thousands of persons and the displacement of millions. Civil war ensued with vicious exchanges of violence. An investigation revealed violations of the Geneva Conventions and humanitarian laws with allegations of mass graves, concentration camps, torture, rape, and genocide (Bassouni, 2014).

In 1993, the UN Security Council established the International Criminal Tribunal for the Former Yugoslavia (ICTY) in response to serious violations of international humanitarian law committed in the territory of the former Yugoslavia since 1991, the first international war crimes tribunal since the Nuremberg and Tokyo Tribunals. Located in The Hague, the Netherlands, the ICTY is financed with contributions from the UN and its member states. All cases, including appeals, were concluded by December 21, 2017. The ICTY is significant because it recognizes rape as a war crime and as genocide. Military as well as governmental leaders can be found individually liable for war crimes committed against civilian populations. ICTY established enslavement as a crime against humanity. Working with domestic courts of the region, defendants are provided counsel and due process while thousands of victims have been provided the opportunity to testify. The death penalty is prohibited. International humanitarian law and international criminal law have been expanded by the work of the ICTY (Crawford & Pert, 2015).

International Criminal Tribunal for Rwanda

In 1994, conflicts stoked by outside influences brought animosities between Rwanda's majority Hutu and minority Tutsi to unprecedented violence. Between April and July, more than 800,000 Tutsis were murdered by Hutu civilians and military personnel. The Hutu-led government is accused of inciting Hutu civilians to rape, torture, murder, and utilize biological warfare in the form of HIV patients against Tutsi civilians. In 1994, the Security Council of the United Nations established the International Criminal Tribunal for Rwanda (ICTR).

Unlike the ICTY, the Rwandan Tribunal violations are not war-related. Located in Arusha, Tanzania, the ICTR is an *ad hoc* tribunal for the prosecution of persons responsible for genocide or other serious violations of international humanitarian law committed in the territory of Rwanda and Rwandan citizens responsible for genocide and other such violations committed in the territory of neighboring states, between January 1, 1994 and December 31, 1994. Significantly, the ICTR has the authority to prosecute and adjudicate charges of genocide, crimes against humanity, and breaches of Common Article 3 of the Geneva Conventions. The Tribunal became operational in 1996. Unlike the ICTY, a defendant may receive a prison term or a capital sentence. The ICTR recognizes rape as both a war crime and as genocide (Crawford & Pert, 2015).

Unlike the ICTY, the Rwanda genocide involved tens of thousands of civilians committing brutal acts led by members of the military. The ICTR is based largely on the ICTY sharing its Appeals Chamber and the Chief Prosecutor with the ICTR. The military defendants are tried separately. Civilians may be tried in tribunals by an appointed panel of respected members of the community or prosecuted in official courtrooms. The ICTR is financed through the UN General Assembly, which requests voluntary contributions from UN member states in the form of financial support, services, and supplies. In sum, despite obstacles, the ICTR played a very important role in the evolution of international criminal law in that it established international standards of conduct for the military as well as civilians who commit such crimes during civil unrest. Armed conflict in any form must have restrictions (Solis, 2016).

HYBRID COURTS

Hybrid courts share jurisdiction, funding, and staff with the United Nations and the domestic courts of the state wherein the criminal acts occurred. The hybrid courts allow the state to have more input in the development of cases and the outcome. However, these courts have also come under criticism due to the influence states have over the legal process, selection of witnesses, pursuit of defendants, and application of law (Nollkaemper, 2012). A hybrid court system was established in the following cases.

East Timor Special Panels

In 2000, the United Nations Security Council established the UN Transitional Authority for East Timor (UNTAET) to adjudicate crimes against humanity in the form of murder, rape, property loss, and displacement following election results in East Timor in 1999. UNTAET has jurisdiction over genocide war crimes, crimes against humanity, murder, rape, and torture committed in East Timor between January 1 and October 25, 1999. For the Timorese, it was critical for the UN to provide security, rule of law, and a credible judiciary and police force (Bull, 2008). The obstacles to justice in East Timor are an underfunded court system, a lack of cooperation by the government, a well-funded defense, and a lack of witness protection. Indonesia's lack of cooperation plays a key role in the events of East Timor. High-level officials and witnesses with important evidence concerning the crimes are located in Indonesia. Their refusal to testify continues to undermine justice in East Timor.

The Special Court for Sierra Leone

In 1991, an attempted coup supported by paramilitary forces from Liberia led to attacks on civilians and soldiers who supported the standing government in Sierra Leone. Crimes of murder, torture, mutilation, and burned villages were committed against tens of thousands of civilians during this civil war. In 2002, the United Nations assisted in the creation of the Special Court for Sierra Leone to adjudicate crimes against humanity taking place in Sierra Leone from 1996. Significantly, in addition to violations against humanity, violations under Common Article 3 of the Geneva Conventions and Additional Protocol II, the Special Court for Sierra Leone will adjudicate crimes against peacekeepers, the crime of recruitment of child as soldiers, as well as violations of local Sierra Leone laws (Jalloh, 2015). Rape does not fall within its jurisdiction. A defendant may receive a prison sentence or the death penalty for participating in crimes against humanity for reasons of political expediency and revenge allegedly fomented by former president Charles Taylor. Financed through voluntary contributions raised by a management committee of the United Nations, obstacles include a lack of infrastructure, resources, and trained personnel. The case was moved to The Hague in the Netherlands in 2006. Despite these obstacles, in 2012, Charles Taylor, the former president of Liberia, was found guilty of aiding and abetting in war crimes in neighboring Sierra Leone. Taylor is serving a sentence of 50 years in prison. An estimated 50,000 people lost their lives due to this armed conflict.

Extraordinary Chambers in the Courts of Cambodia

During the final battles of the Vietnam War, the Khmer Rouge, a political and military movement, rose to power in Cambodia. Led by Pol Pot, the Khmer Rouge executed elites, intellectuals, and certain ethnic groups using murder, scientific experimentation, forced labor, and torture. Between 1975 and 1978, more than 1 million lives were lost and millions were displaced. Evidence of these crimes against humanity was received as early as 1979. Decades passed. Given the lapse of time, there was uncertainty as to whether the Khmer Rouge would ever be brought to justice. Pol Pot was finally tried by a national court and condemned to death. Pol Pot was sentenced to life in prison after a subsequent, which that was viewed by many as procedurally flawed, thus renewing efforts for an international tribunal. He died in 1998.

In 2003, after years of negotiation, the United Nations and Cambodia signed an agreement establishing the Extraordinary Chambers in the Courts of Cambodia for Prosecution of Crimes Committed during the Period of Democratic Kampuchea. The Extraordinary Chambers are a national tribunal financed by pledges from UN member states placed in a trust fund. Due process is based on the Cambodian system, which has a death penalty. In 2006, the Extraordinary Chambers with Cambodian (ECCC) and UN justices began trials of senior personnel accused of genocide. The effectiveness of this tribunal largely depends on the abilities of the Cambodian jurists, prosecutors, and investigators, as well as the cooperation of the Cambodian Government. Cambodia's policy of reconciliation with former members of the Khmer Rouge may undermine the necessary governmental cooperation required to fully adjudicate high-level officials and others who participated in war crimes against civilians. After spending US$200 million and hearing 3,500 witnesses, the ECCC convicted two high-level members of the Khmer Rouge and a prison warden, giving life sentences for crimes against humanity committed between 1975 and 1979. About 1.7 million people lost their lives due to forced labor, starvation, torture, and murder.

Special Tribunal for Lebanon

A special tribunal was requested by the Lebanese Government. In 2007, the Special Tribunal for Lebanon (STL) was established to prosecute persons responsible for the attack of February 14, 2005 resulting in the death of Lebanese Prime Minister Rafiz Hariri and in the death or injury of 22 other persons. Although the Tribunal is located in the Netherlands, members of the Special Tribunal seek to create dialogue and a high level of cooperation with Lebanese civil society as trial preparation proceeds. The main trial is ongoing and involves defendants Salim Jamil Ayyash et al., charged with conspiracy to commit a terrorist act, along with other charges. Two media companies were charged with contempt and given fines for the first time in the history of international tribunals.

SUMMARY AND CONCLUSION

Armed conflicted must have limits and punishments for abuses. The Nuremberg Tribunal was created in 1945 to address premeditated crimes against civilian populations by the German military during World War II. Created in 1946, the Tokyo Tribunal adjudicated war crimes and crimes against humanity committed by Japanese soldiers during World War II. In 1993, the UN Security Council formed ICTY to adjudicate crimes against humanity within the former Yugoslavia in the 1990s. In 1994, the Security Council created the ICTR to adjudicate crimes by the Rwandan Government and Hutu civilians against Tutsi civilians. The hybrid courts of Cambodia, East Timor, Sierra Leone, and Lebanon provide states with shared jurisdiction resulting in possible political influence and delays.

Each international criminal tribunal, or special court, plays a significant role in the evolution of international criminal law. Tribunals were formed to prosecute military personnel accused of crimes against civilians. Hybrid courts use both domestic and international law established to adjudicate cases involving military, government, as well as civilians accused of mass crimes committed during wartime or civil unrest. They are criticized as slow-moving and expensive. International criminal courts and tribunals can provide victims with a degree of justice and reconciliation.

REFERENCES

Bassiouni, M. C. (2014). *Crimes against humanity: Historical evolution and contemporary application.* New York: Cambridge University Press.

Browne-Marshall, G. (2013). *Race, law, and American society: 1607 to present.* Second Edition. New York: Routledge.

Bull, C. (2008). *No entry without strategy: Building the rule of law under UN transitional administration.* New York: United Nations University Press.

Cabanes, B. (2014) *The Great War and the origins of humanitarianism: 1918–1924.* New York: Cambridge University Press.

Crawford, E. & Pert, A. (2015). *International humanitarian law.* New York: Cambridge University Press.

Jalloh, C. C. (2015) *The Sierra Leone Special Court and its legacy: The impact for Africa and international criminal law.* New York: Cambridge University Press.

Mertus, J. (2018). *The United Nations and human rights: A guide for a new era.* Third Edition. New York: Routledge.

Nollkaemper, A. (2012). *National courts and the international rule of law.* New York: Oxford University Press.

Solis, G. (2016) *The law of armed conflict.* New York: Cambridge University Press.

von Lingen, K. (2018). *Transcultural justice at the Tokyo Tribunal: the Allied struggle for justice, 1946–48.* Leiden: Brill.

WEBSITES

East Timor Hybrid Court. www.eastwestcenter.org/stored/pdfs/api061.pdf.
International Criminal Tribunal for the Former Yugoslavia. www.icty.org.
International Criminal Tribunal for Rwanda. www.ictr.org.
www.sc-sl.org.
Special Tribunal for Lebanon. stl-tsl.org.
United Nations Treaty Collection. https://treaties.un.org/Pages/Home.aspx?lang=en.

71 Global and Regional Human Rights Commissions

José Luis Morín

INTRODUCTION

The United Nations established the UN Commission on Human Rights – now the Human Rights Council – to provide a forum for addressing human rights violations on a global scale consistent with the UN Charter of 1945. Regional organizations – such as the Organization of American States (OAS), the Council of Europe, and the Organization of African Unity (now the African Union) – have created their own commissions to promote human rights and provide redress for human rights victims in their respective regions of the world (Alston & Goodman, 2013). This chapter presents a brief overview of global and regional human rights commissions and their evolution, shortcomings, and achievements. The commissions that are the subject of this chapter function as ongoing standing human rights entities of the United Nations or regional organizations, not commissions created for temporary, specific purposes, such as the Truth and Reconciliation Commission in South Africa.

THE UNITED NATIONS: FROM COMMISSION TO HUMAN RIGHTS COUNCIL

Pursuant to Article 68 of the UN Charter requiring that the Economic and Social Council (ECOSOC) create "commissions in economic and social fields and for the promotion of human rights," the United Nations Commission on Human Rights was founded in 1946 as a "charter-based" or "non-treaty-based" human rights mechanism. By 1948, the UN Commission on Human Rights produced the Universal Declaration on Human Rights, adopted that same year by the UN General Assembly.

From its inception, the UN Commission on Human Rights' work encompassed developing new international human rights standard-setting instruments; monitoring and securing compliance with human rights norms, principles, and laws; and playing a key role in many UN human rights programs and activities in coordination with the Office of the UN High Commissioner for Human Rights. The Commission investigated the human rights situation in numerous countries utilizing a variety of fact-finding approaches, including working groups, rapporteurs, observer delegations, special envoys, and representatives – as in the case of the 1967 Ad Hoc Working Group of Experts on southern Africa – and it issued its findings annually and publicly. The Commission's work also integrated two complaint procedures to address human rights claims – one that offered public debate of human rights cases in accordance with ECOSOC Resolution 1235 (XLII) of 1967, and a second that authorized the Commission to conduct confidential investigations on complaints or "communications" in keeping with ECOSOC Resolution 1503 (XLVIII) of 1970, commonly referred to as the 1503 Complaint Procedure (Buergenthal et al., 2009; Alston & Goodman, 2013).

Over the years, criticism, primarily by Western nations, was levied on the UN Commission on Human Rights that the Commission's agenda was too heavily influenced by states with disreputable human rights records (Fasulo, 2009; Ramcharan, 2007). Often cited was the example of the election of the representative from Libya as chair of the Commission in 2003 (Hanhimäki, 2008).

Dissatisfaction with the Commission eventually led to the passage of General Assembly Resolution 60/251 of March 15, 2006, creating a 47-member Human Rights Council to replace the 53-member Commission on Human Rights. The resolution – which passed overwhelmingly, with 170 out of 191 UN member states in favor and only four opposed (the USA, the Marshall Islands, Palau, and Israel) – called for an equitable regional distribution of seats, with 13 seats for Africa, 13 for Asia, six for Europe, eight for Latin America and the Caribbean, and seven for Western Europe and other states (Hanhimäki, 2008).

In 2007, the Council adopted an "Institution-building package" to guide its work. Changes made by the Council included the implementation of a "Universal Periodic Review" mechanism to assess the human rights situations in all UN member states on a rotating basis; a new "Advisory Committee" to provide expertise and advice on thematic human rights issues; and an updated "Complaints Procedure" to improve on the former 1503 Complaint Procedure and allow individuals and organizations to file complaints in a more efficient and unbiased manner. The Human Rights Council also continues to avail itself of "Special Procedures" established by the previous Commission on Human Rights. Special Procedures make available a range of options, such as the appointment of special rapporteurs to examine specific countries or themes (e.g., terrorism and torture) and the creation of working groups to address particular topics (e.g., arbitrary detentions and enforced or involuntary disappearances).

The Council, designed to pacify criticism of the Commission, quickly drew another round of disapproval from certain member states. Similar to the Commission, the Council's members sit as representatives of UN member states, and certain states, most notably the USA, denounced the Council for seating representatives from countries notorious for human rights violations (Fasulo, 2009; Ramcharan, 2007). In a change of course from the Bush administration, which railed against the Council, especially over its scrutiny of Israel's treatment of Palestinians, the Obama administration decided to work for change from within, which allowed the USA to be voted in as a member of the Council in 2009 (MacFarquhar, 2009). The Trump administration, however, has changed course, asserting claims that the UN Human Rights Council is biased against Israel, and in June of 2018, the United States withdrew from the Council (Kelemen, 2018).

Among its achievements, the UN Charter-based human rights machinery has been vital in setting international standards for the human rights observance and enforcement. As one international human rights scholar notes, the Commission on Human Rights' "initial vision of an international bill of human rights – consisting of a declaration, one or more covenants, and measures of implementation – has inspired the human rights movement throughout the UN's history" (Ramcharan, 2007). Criticisms that its actions are too political or selective notwithstanding, the Human Rights Council's utility, like its predecessor, is that it serves as a vehicle for human rights progress through the development of a substantial agenda and legal parameters for the promotion of human rights worldwide.

In contrast to the Human Rights Council, the UN human rights system also includes "treaty-based" mechanisms for human rights oversight and enforcement provided under treaties ratified by member states. For instance, Part IV of the 1966 International Covenant on Civil and Political Rights establishes the Human Rights Committee, a body of independent experts that monitor the treaty's implementation. Under the First Optional Protocol to the International Covenant on Civil and Political Rights of 1996, the Human Rights Committee can also receive complaints concerning states that have ratified the Protocol. Other treaties contain similar individual complaint procedures, such as the Convention on the Elimination of All Forms of Discrimination against Women, and some require periodic compliance reports, as with the Convention on the Rights of the Child (Bayefsky, 2002; Lewis-Anthony & Scheinin, 2004).

REGIONAL HUMAN RIGHTS COMMISSIONS

Presently, three regional human rights systems operate in the world today – the Inter-American, the European, and the African. An Arab system is mostly inactive, and a system for Asia has been proposed. While concerns about the efficacy of "regional" versus "universalist" approaches have been raised, no significant conflict between regional systems and the UN human rights scheme has occurred (Alston & Goodman, 2013, pp. 889–890). The following is a brief description of the three functioning systems.

The Organization of American States: The Inter-American Commission on Human Rights

The Organization of American States (OAS) is a regional organization comprised of the 35 sovereign nations of the Americas. The Inter-American Commission on Human Rights was established by amendment to the OAS Charter of 1948, which entered into force in 1970 and is guided by the American Declaration of the Rights and Duties of Man of 1948, a normative and authoritative instrument protecting fundamental rights, such as the right to life, the right to equality before the law, among others. The Inter-American Commission plays a key role in the procedures found in the 1969 American Convention on Human Rights.

The Inter-American Commission's quasi-judicial functions include the ability to receive and render opinions on individual cases. Unlike the UN Human Rights Council, its members are not governmental representatives, but experts chosen by the OAS General Assembly. Petitioners before the Inter-American Commission may also request hearings. Before the merits of a petition to the Inter-American Commission are heard, a petition undergoes an admissibility phase in which the petition may be rejected for not complying with admissibility rules. Although lacking the power to enforce its decisions, the Inter-American Commission can pursue settlements and bring cases to the attention of the OAS General Assembly.

Under the American Convention on Human Rights, the Inter-American Commission can refer cases to the Inter-American Court of Human Rights against a state that has ratified the Convention. The Court, in turn, can issue orders to enforce its rulings. Among its other responsibilities, the Inter-American Commission conducts country studies and on-site investigations of the human rights situation in various OAS member states (Buergenthal & Stewart, 2009; Shelton, 2004; Alston & Goodman, 2013).

Council of Europe: From European Commission to European Court of Human Rights

The Council of Europe, established in 1949, created a system for the protection of human rights that has adopted numerous human rights treaties, including the European Convention on Human Rights, signed in 1950, which entered into force in 1953. Article 19 of the European Convention originally provided for the creation of a European Commission of Human Rights and a European Court of Human Rights, but both were replaced by a permanent human rights court under Protocol No. 11, which entered into force in 1998. This change now allows individuals to submit complaints directly to the Court. From 1959 to 2017, "the Court has decided on the examination of around 798,600 applications through a judgment or decision, or by being struck out of the list" (European Court of Human Rights, 2018, p. 4).

Prior to its elimination, the European Commission sought settlements, issued non-binding opinions, or referred cases to the Court. The current European Court of Human Rights provides a more rigorous human rights enforcement mechanism for cases addressing individual and interstate complaints (Boyle, 2004; Buergenthal & Stewart, 2009) and guarantees certain basic rights, such as the right to life, freedom of expression, and the prohibition against torture and arbitrary and unlawful detentions.

The African Union's African Commission on Human and Peoples' Rights

In 1981, the Organization of African Unity – now the African Union – adopted the African Charter on Human and Peoples' Rights (the African Charter), which entered into force in 1986. Compared to the European and American conventions on human rights, the African Charter has a distinct focus on duties as well as individual rights. For instance, it establishes a duty "to preserve and strengthen the national independence and territorial integrity" (Article 29(5)), in addition to protecting individual liberty and security (Article 6). Africa's experience with colonialism is reflected in the document's adherence to securing the rights of all peoples to self-determination (Article 20). Two other important human rights instruments of the African human rights system are the African Charter on the Rights and Welfare of the Child of 1990 and the Protocol to the African Charter on Human and Peoples' Rights on the Rights of Women in Africa of 2003.

The African Charter calls for the creation of an African Commission on Human and Peoples' Rights to promote human rights and act in a quasi-judicial capacity to address interstate and individual communications. The African Commission also has the authority to refer cases to the African Court on Human Rights, established under the Protocol to the African Charter on the Establishment of an African Court on Human and Peoples' Rights, adopted in 1998. Under the Protocol, the African Commission retains an important role in hearing cases, as the Court could also transfer cases to the Commission for resolution (Alston & Goodman, 2013).

CONCLUSION

As imperfect and controversial they may appear at times, global and regional human rights commissions have made significant contributions in setting human rights standards, as evidenced by the Universal Declaration on Human Rights, and in providing mechanisms to address violations. Human rights commissions and courts have proven effective in addressing human rights issues, as in the case of *Tyrer v. United Kingdom*, 26 Eur. Ct. H.R. (ser. A) (1978), which held that the judicial corporal punishment inflicted on a juvenile violated the prohibition of torture, or inhuman or degrading treatment. Commissions, in contrast to courts, may be limited in their enforcement capacity; yet, in many instances, they have afforded meaningful relief for victims. Regional human rights commissions have been effective especially when given the authority to refer cases to a court with enforcement powers, as in the case of the *Velasquez Rodriguez Case* [Compensatory Damages], I.A. Court H.R., Series C: Decision and Judgments, No. 7 (1988), in which the Honduran Government was found to have engaged in the disappearance of one of its citizens and was ordered to pay monetary compensation. Hence, global and regional human rights commissions can be a force for advancing, promoting, and protecting human rights.

REFERENCES

Alston, P. & Goodman, R. (2013). *International human rights: The successor to international human rights in context.* New York: Oxford University Press.

Bayefsky, A. F. (2002). *How to complain to the UN human rights treaty system.* Ardsley, NY: Transnational Publishers.

Boyle, K. (2004). Council of Europe, OSCE, and European Union. In H. Hannum (Ed.), *Guide to international human rights practice.* Fourth Edition (pp. 143–170). Ardsley, NY: Transnational Publishers.

Buergenthal, S. T. D. & Stewart, D. P. (2009). *International human rights in a nutshell.* Fourth Edition. St. Paul, MN: West.

European Court of Human Rights. (2018). *European Court of Human Rights: Overview, 1959–2017.* Retrieved from www.echr.coe.int/Documents/Overview_19592017_ENG.pdf.

Fasulo, L. (2009). *An insider's guide to the UN.* Second Edition. New Haven, CT: Yale University Press.

Hanhimäki, J. M. (2008). *The United Nations: A very short introduction.* Oxford: Oxford University Press.

Kelemen, M. (2018, June 20). U.S. pulls out of U.N. Human Rights Council. *National Public Radio.* Retrieved from www.npr.org/2018/06/20/621726939/u-s-pulls-out-of-u-n-human-rights-council.

Lewis-Anthony, S. & Scheinin, M. (2004). Treaty-based procedures for making human rights complaints within the UN system. In H. Hannum (Ed.), *Guide to international human rights practice.* Fourth Edition (pp. 43–64). Ardsley, NY: Transnational Publishers.

MacFarquhar, N. (2009, May 13). U.S. joins rights panel after a vote at the U.N. *The New York Times*, p. A5.

Ramcharan, B. G. (2007). Norms and machinery. In T. G. Weiss & S. Daws (Eds.), *The Oxford handbook on the United Nations* (pp. 439–462). Oxford: Oxford University Press.

Shelton, D. (2004). The Inter-American human rights system. In H. Hannum (Ed.), *Guide to international human rights practice.* Fourth Edition (pp. 127–142). Ardsley, NY: Transnational Publishers.

WEBSITES

African Charter on Human and Peoples' Rights. https://au.int/en/treaties/african-charter-human-and-peoples-rights.

African Union. https://au.int/en/history/oau-and-au.

European Court of Human Rights, information documents. www.echr.coe.int/Pages/home.aspx?p=court&c=#newComponent_1346149514608_pointer.

Organization of American States human rights webpage. www.oas.org/en/topics/human_rights.asp.

UN Human Rights Council. www.ohchr.org/EN/HRBodies/HRC/Pages/AboutCouncil.aspx.

72 The Truth and Reconciliation Commission in South Africa in Perspective

Origins and Achievements

Stephan Parmentier and Elmar Weitekamp

INTRODUCTION

Debates over what to do about previous gross and systematic violations of human rights often arise during times of transition, i.e., when societies are moving away from an autocratic regime toward more democratic forms of government, or from war to peace. In the crimological literature, many of these acts are considered "political crimes," meaning crimes committed by people against the state, designed to protest, change, or oust the existing establishment, as well as crimes committed by the state against people to sanction the acts that threaten that same establishment (Parmentier, 2001; Ross, 2003). The problem is one of "dealing with the past" (Huyse, 1995; Boraine, Levy, & Scheffer, 1997), "transitional justice" (Kritz, 1995), or "post-conflict justice" (Bassiouni, 2002).

Over the last decades various transitional justice mechanisms have been developed to deal with the legacy of a dark past (Parmentier, 2016; www.ictj.org, 2018): 1) criminal prosecutions of the perpetrators, by national courts, courts in a third country, hybrid courts, or international tribunals and courts; 2) truth commissions, i.e., non-judicial bodies of enquiry to document the crimes and violations committed and operating out of any court setting; 3) victim reparations for the several types of harm inflicted upon direct and indirect victims, through a variety of procedures and institutions; and 4) reforms of various institutions involved in the crimes and violations with a view of preventing similar ones to occur in the future. Each of these mechanisms may be used independently or as complementary mechanisms operating alongside others.

A truth commission is a non-judicial body of enquiry with the following five characteristics (Hayner, 2011): 1) it is concerned with past events, not present ones; 2) it is investigating patterns of events, rather than individual events, over a certain period of time; 3) it engages in a direct and broad manner with the people that are affected, and collects information about their perceptions and needs; 4) it is not a permanent but a temporary body that is supposed to produce a final report; 5) and it enjoys the support and/or the powers provided by the state being investigated. The truth commission process has been described as a "third way" – in other words, as a mechanism that lies between total impunity (e.g., as a result of amnesty laws) and formal criminal prosecutions.

Truth commissions were created in Latin America in the 1980s and early 1990s (in, e.g., Argentina, Chile, and El Salvador) and later were adopted in other parts of the world as well (e.g., in East Timor, Sierra Leone, and Morocco). In recent years some truth commissions were established in mature democracies (like the USA and Canada) to deal with the legacy of racism directed toward African-Americans and indigenous peoples.

This chapter discusses a prime example of a truth commission, the one that operated in South Africa following the first democratic elections of 1994. We will take a closer look at its background, its mandate, and its institutional framework, and discuss its legacy.

THE TRUTH AND RECONCILIATION COMMISSION IN SOUTH AFRICA

The Historical Background: A "Third Way"

The idea to set up a commission of enquiry was formulated as early as the fall of 1992, by Kader Asmal, a prominent intellectual and member of the African National Congress (ANC), with a view of investigating allegations of human rights violations in some of its training camps organized in neighboring African countries. When it became clear that the Apartheid government wanted to introduce far-reaching amnesty provisions for members of the outgoing elites, the ANC launched an appeal for a commission to investigate both its own abuses and those of the government. It was a strong and deliberate attempt to ensure that the serious human rights abuses of the past would not go unacknowledged and that some form of accountability be installed, though of a non-judicial nature (Boraine, Levy, & Scheffer, 1997; Kritz, 1995).

Next to the installment of the Truth and Reconciliation Commission, after the 1994 elections several criminal trials were instituted against high-ranking officials of the former regime, although most led to acquittals (Hayner, 2011). Some commentators have argued that the determination of the criminal courts to prosecute certain crimes of the past prompted more people to cooperate with the TRC and avoid criminal prosecutions, thus constituting a policy of "carrots and sticks" (Sarkin, 2004).

The Mandate: Seeking Truth and Promoting Reconciliation

The TRC was set up with five tasks (Articles 3,1 and 3,2): 1) to establish a picture of the gross human rights violations covered; 2) to facilitate the granting of amnesty for specific acts and under specific conditions; 3) to grant victims an opportunity to relate their own accounts and to recommend reparation measures for them; 4) to compile a comprehensive report; and 5) to make whatever recommendations in view of the overarching objective.

The Commission's two essential tasks were to seek truth and to promote reconciliation (Villa-Vicencio & Verwoerd, 2000). The final Report distinguished between four forms of "truth" (Truth and Reconciliation Commission of South Africa, 1998): 1) factual or forensic truth, meaning the evidence obtained and corroborated through reliable procedures normally used in court; 2) personal and narrative truth, meaning the many stories that individuals told about their experiences under Apartheid; 3) social or dialogue truth, established through interaction, discussion, and debate; and 4) healing and restorative truth, or the truth that places facts and their meaning within the context of human relationships. Also the concept of reconciliation was subdivided in four different levels (Report, vol. 1, pp. 106–110; Bloomfield et al., 2003): 1) the intrapersonal level of coming to terms with painful truth; for example, after exhumations and reburials of beloved ones; 2) the interpersonal level of specific victims and perpetrators; 3) the community level, when addressing the internal conflicts inside and between local communities; and 4) the national level, by focusing on the role of the state and non-state institutions. The Commission tried to clarify the relationship between these various notions by consistently repeating that truth constituted "the road to reconciliation." It also made the link with the notion of restorative justice, interpreted in the Report as "restoring civil and human dignity" for all South Africans (Report, vol. 1, pp. 125–131; Parmentier, 2001). This restorative process was first of all directed to the victims, who were given extensive possibilities to tell their stories and who received recognition for their severe victimization, and also to the perpetrators, by trying to understand their motives and the social and political structures they operated in, without excusing the violations they committed. The impact of this restorative discourse on popular perceptions and political discourses has been heralded by some, and severely criticized by others (Wilson, 2001).

The Institutional Framework: One Commission, Three Committees

The TRC was given the authority to investigate several serious violations of human rights expressly mentioned in the Act (Section 1(1)). These violations included the killing, abduction, torture, or severe ill-treatment of persons, in the period between March 1, 1960 and May 10, 1994. It investigated the activities of all parties – the former Apartheid regime and its paramilitary sections, as well as the former "freedom fighters" and other resisters – including those violations committed in neighboring countries (like Mozambique and Zimbabwe) and in other parts of the world but attributable to one of the conflicting parties.

The Commission was composed of 17 members, appointed by the President of the Republic based on their expertise in the field of democracy and human rights, and following a public debate allowing public institutions and nongovernmental organizations to propose concrete names of possible commissioners. One of the unique features of the TRC lay in its interdisciplinary composition, as it was not limited to lawyers but also included medical doctors, educators, theologians, and other professions, under the charismatic leadership of Archbishop Desmond Tutu. While the Commission assumed its responsibility as a plenary body most of its actual work took place in three separate Committees.

Best known is the Human Rights Violations Committee (HRVC), entrusted with all investigative aspects (Report, vol. 1, pp. 140–151). The Committee gathered more than 21,000 written statements from victims all over South Africa, relating to more than 37,000 violations of human rights. Among the most innovative aspects of its work, in comparison with previous truth commissions in other parts of the world, were the more than 75 public hearings organized by this Committee all over the country (Hayner, 2011). Finally, the Committee held "institutional hearings" about specific sectors of society, such as the legal and medical professions, the media, and business, in order to hear their views about the crimes committed under the Apartheid regime. Sometimes, the Committee used its legal powers of subpoena, search, and seizure, to oblige certain witnesses and perpetrators to be questioned, as well as to produce probative evidence. The combined results of all hearings were published in the five-volume final Report of 1998, which, for the first time, detailed a specific part of South Africa's horrendous past and thus enabled the construction of a collective memory of mass victimization that could be shared by various sectors of society.

A unique feature of the TRC was its Amnesty Committee (AC), in charge of dealing with individual applications for amnesty and chaired by a magistrate (Report, vol. 1, 1998, pp 153–157). The "carrot" of amnesty was included to elicit information from offenders about political crimes that would otherwise have remained in the dark (Sarkin, 2004). Amnesty could only be granted under very strict conditions: 1) it was limited to political crimes committed within a specific period of reference; and 2) it required the full disclosure of all relevant facts. The South African version of amnesty thus differed substantially from amnesty provisions in other parts of the world, notably in Latin America, where amnesty was mostly introduced to serve specific groups, such as the military and the police, and came about by enacting "blanket" amnesties through legislation. The Amnesty Committee continued its work until 2003 and in that period dealt with more than 7,100 applications in total, of which a good 1,300 received full or partial amnesty (Report, vol. 6, 2003, p. 36). The decision to grant amnesty precluded any further criminal or civil action in court against the person concerned. Less clear proved the situation of those who were denied amnesty and against some of whom criminal investigations have been initiated by the prosecutors.

Finally, the Reparation and Rehabilitation Committee (RRC) made recommendations on reparation and rehabilitation matters to the government (Report, vol. 5, 1998, pp. 170–195). It recommended measures at various levels: individual reparations; symbolic reparations, and legal and administrative matters; community rehabilitation programs; and institutional reforms. While it did not possess any legal authority to order the restitution of property, to impose community service, or to organize programs for the reintegration of victims or offenders, it did grant urgent and interim reparations to some persons in need of medical, psychological, or material help.

LEGACY OF THE TRUTH AND RECONCILIATION COMMISSION

Few truth and reconciliation commissions possess a stronger legacy than the South African one. Its composition, mandate, working methods, and strong publicity have constituted several benchmarks for commissions worldwide since to position themselves (Parmentier & Aciru, 2016).

Yet, in South Africa itself many have criticized almost all aspects of the TRC's work. Critiques related to the limited mandate, the limited number of victims involved, the limited accountability for perpetrators, etc. They continue to relate to the limited victim reparations provided by the government following the TRC recommendations, resulting from its prime choice for development instead of reparations.

Reconciliation remains a difficult concept and an even more difficult reality. Since 2003 the South African Reconciliation Barometer has generated a representative measure of people's attitudes to national reconciliation, democratic governance, social cohesion, and transformation. The 2017 Report (Potgieter, 2017) clearly demonstrates that for many South Africans the TRC provided a good foundation for reconciliation in the country. It also highlights that just over half of the population see any progress in terms of reconciliation, and the same share indicate not having experienced reconciliation themselves. About 60 percent consider poverty a major obstacle to reconciliation, as viewed from a perspective of forgiveness, moving on, and peace building.

CONCLUSION

The South African Truth and Reconciliation Commission has attracted worldwide attention for its dealing with the horrendous legacy of Apartheid. As the result of a political compromise and in a context of a "negotiated transition" to democracy, the TRC was set up as a non-judicial body with the objectives to seek the truth and to promote reconciliation outside of court. It displayed some unique features, such as the legal authority to grant amnesty on an individual basis, and its own decision to hold public hearings with a view of reaching out to communities, the nation, and the world.

The truth commission process was not completely detached from the criminal justice system in South Africa. It has been argued that the ongoing criminal trials of the mid-1990s were threatening enough to many South Africans to encourage them to cooperate with the TRC. The information obtained through the Commission's written submissions, public hearings, and amnesty proceedings have to a limited extent also been used afterwards to institute criminal proceedings.

On a more general level the South African TRC has provided an innovative model to deal with specific crimes of a very dark past, notwithstanding some critiques. Some have argued that this model can be transferred to other countries and other contexts. Given the uniqueness of the South African case, however, this is subject to ongoing debate. It seems that every transitional justice experience is unique and thus context-specific, although it remains possible to draw important lessons from and for different experiences across the globe.

REFERENCES

Bassiouni, C. (Ed.). (2002). *Post-conflict justice*. New York: Transnational Publishers.

Boraine, A., Levy, J., & Scheffer, R. (Eds.). (1997). *Dealing with the past: Truth and reconciliation in South Africa*. Cape Town: Institute for Democracy in South Africa (idasa).

Bloomfield, D., Barnes, T., & Huyse, L. (Eds.). (2003). *Reconciliation after violent conflict: A handbook*. Stockholm: International Idea.

Hayner, P. (2011). *Unspeakable truths: Confronting state terror and atrocity*. Second Edition. New York: Routledge.

Huyse, L. (1995). Justice after transition: On the choices successor elites make in dealing with the past. In N. Kritz (Ed.), *Transitional justice: How emerging democracies reckon with former regimes*, vol. I: *General considerations* (3 vols. in total, pp. 337–349). Washington, DC: United States Institute of Peace.

Parmentier, S. (2016). Transitional justice. In W. Schabas (Ed.), *The Cambridge companion to international criminal law* (pp. 52–72). Cambridge: Cambridge University Press.

(2001). The South African Truth and Reconciliation Commission: Towards restorative justice in the field of human rights. In E. Fattah & S. Parmentier (Eds.), *Victim policies and criminal justice on the road to restorative justice* (pp. 401–428). Leuven: Leuven University Press.

Parmentier, S. & Aciru, M. (2016). The whole truth and nothing but the truth? On the role of truth commissions in facing the past. In P. Malcontent (Ed.), *Facing the past: Amending historical injustices through instruments of transitional justice* (pp. 225–246). Cambridge/Antwerp: Intersentia Publishers.

Potgieter, E. (2017). *SA Reconciliation Barometer Survey. 2017 report.* Cape Town: Institute for Justice and Reconciliation.

Ross, J. (2003). *The dynamics of political crime.* New York: Sage.

Sarkin, J. (2004). *Carrots and sticks: The TRC and the South African amnesty process.* Antwerp/Oxford: Intersentia/Hart.

Truth and Reconciliation Commission of South Africa. (1998). *Report 1,* 110–114 (7 Vols in total). Cape Town: Juta & Co.

   (1998 and 2003). *Report.* (5, 6, 7 Vols.). Cape Town: Juta & Co.

Villa-Vicencio, C. & Verwoerd W. (Eds.). (2000). *Looking back, reaching forward: Reflections on the Truth and Reconciliation Commission of South Africa.* Cape Town: University of Cape Town Press.

Wilson, R. (2001). *The politics of truth and reconciliation in South Africa: Legitimizing the post-Apartheid state.* Cambridge: Cambridge University Press.

WEBSITES

Centre for the Study of Violence and Reconciliation. www.csvr.org.za.

International Centre for Transitional Justice. www.ictj.org.

International Institute for Democracy and Electoral Assistance. www.idea.int.

Program on Negotiation, Harvard Law School, and European Centre for Common Ground. www.truthcommission.org.

Truth and Reconciliation Commission. www.doj.gov.za/trc.

United States Institute of Peace. www.usip.org/library/truth.html.

73 The Guatemalan Truth Commission

Genocide Through the Lens of Transitional Justice

Marcia Esparza

INTRODUCTION

More than 30 truth commissions have been set up throughout the world since the 1970s, in Latin America, Africa, and Europe, in particular. Truth commissions are not-state entities typically created either by presidential decrees, as they were in Chile and Peru, or through agreements negotiated between governments and guerrilla forces, as in Guatemala, to investigate human rights crimes. They are considered in the field of transitional justice as pivotal mechanisms to be used to bring societies together, remember the victims, and foster a culture of peace, tolerance, and human rights. Truth commissions are one of the mechanisms of transitional justice many countries use to shift away from an authoritarian toward a more democratic form of government. They rarely name individual perpetrators or try them in courts. More than 20 truth and reconciliation commissions have been set up throughout the world since the 1970s.

The overall purposes of truth commissions are to reach a universal truth about past human rights crimes, to provide a safe forum for testimonies, to write reports of their findings, to reconcile opposing groups in war-torn societies, and to make recommendations. Truth commissions seek to discover what really happened to people who were forcibly "disappeared," and to discover where people are buried. They provide a safe forum in which victims and survivors can openly and publicly attest to human rights crimes they have experienced.

A standard characteristic of truth commissions is that they do not have the power to prosecute or to grant perpetrators amnesty for their crimes, except in the case of the Truth and Reconciliation Commission in South Africa (1996–1998). They contain recommendations for steps governments can take to prevent political violence from recurring. In Chile, for example, the Commission recommended that the state provide victims and families with special health programs recognizing and helping to heal their sufferings.

Using primary data collected from the victims of the massacres committed against impoverished Indigenous Mayans in Guatemala, this chapter aims to provide details of the Guatemalan Truth Commission in terms of its history and nature, the processes of reaching the truth, and the recommendations of the "Memory of Silence" report.

GUATEMALA: ETERNAL SPRING, ETERNAL BLOODSHED

Guatemala borders the North Pacific Ocean. It is located between El Salvador, Mexico, Honduras, and Belize in Central America, on the Gulf of Honduras in the Caribbean Sea.

Today, 23 different Maya groups live mainly in the northwestern part of the country. Large sectors of the population eke out their livings in a subsistence economy, relying on the harvests of *milpas* (corn fields) on tiny plots of land. Indigenous people make up the majority of those whom the landed oligarchy use as cheap laborers, employing them as they have for centuries as seasonal migrants who work in large coffee, sugar, and banana plantations located in the lowlands, or southern coastal areas. Guatemala is characterized by its precapitalist agrarian socioeconomic and political structure, as well as by extreme social polarization. Unlike other commissions, the Guatemalan Truth Commission traced the exclusion and exploitation of Indigenous peoples back to colonial times (Grandin, 2005). It was also unique in that it provided a comprehensive historical account of the sociopolitical economic structure that maintains Indigenous communities as slaves in coffee or palm oil plantations.

Historical Background

In Guatemala, starting in the 1960s, rural Indigenous communities organized a vibrant social movement demanding economic, political, cultural, and social rights. The movement threatened the power of the authoritarian government. In the late 1970s, heightening the conflict, sectors of the Indigenous population supported a growing left-wing guerrilla movement called the National Revolutionary Unity of Guatemala, or *Unidad Revolucionaria Nacional Guatemalteca* (URNG). The government responded by launching bloody counterinsurgency campaigns, to quell the growing resistance. Under the rules of Generals Romeo Lucas Garcia (1978–1982) and Efrain Rios Montt (June 1982 to August 1983), brutal campaigns of genocide were perpetrated against four Mayan groups: Maya-Q'anjob'al, Maya-Chuj, Maya-Ixil, Maya-K'ich'e, and Maya Achi.

In the 1990s, peace negotiations between the guerrillas, the Guatemalan Government, and sectors of civil society gave rise to the Oslo Peace Accord of June 1994, which created the Guatemalan Truth Commission, called the Commission to Clarify Past Human Rights Violations and Acts of Violence That Have Caused the Guatemalan People to Suffer (HCCG), or *Comisión de Esclarecimiento Histórico* (CEH). Its specific aims were: 1) to clarify with objectivity and impartiality the human rights violations and acts of violence causing people suffering during the war; 2) to prepare a report of the findings of the investigation; and 3) to recommend ways the government could promote peace and reconciliation (HCCG, 1999, Conclusions, pp. 47–69).

Negotiating Truth and Silences

Initially, the commission was mandated to work for only six months, with a staff of approximately 200 people, assigned to 14 offices across the country; six more months were then added. German professor Christian Tomulschat, Guatemalan teacher Otilia Lux de Coti, and Guatemalan lawyer Alfredo Balsells Tojo led the Commission. Chilean lawyer Jaime Esponda was head of the Investigative Unit, responsible for the analysis of the testimonies. This unit determined whether the daunting violence besieged upon people as described in the testimonies the staff collected should be considered human rights crimes under international law.

The author of this chapter was assigned to conduct interviews and record testimonies in the Department of El Quiché, where half of the 669 massacres took place. In this capacity, I conducted face-to-face interviews with survivors and victims and took their heartwrenching testimonies recounting the great suffering imposed on them by the state.

One example of a testimony collected is an account I gathered from a Catholic priest. He told me that civilians collaborating with the Guatemalan Army, called Civil Defense Patrols (PACs), served as the "eyes" and "ears" of the military, controlling frequently traveled roads, checking villagers' identification cards, and spying on neighbors, local groups, and associations. With the help of hooded guides, PACs often swept roads and hills searching for and rounding up villagers the army accused of being communists. These hunts often concluded with the public execution of the so-called communists, in gruesome spectacles in which their bodies were hacked to pieces. The priest asserted,

> At first, to avoid murdering family members and neighbors, some PAC members would strike the ground rather than their victims. To make them show their loyalty, the Army began forcing them to stain their machetes with blood every time when they hacked their victims. (Author interview, El Quiché, Guatemala, 1999)

The Guatemalan Truth Commission set in motion an extraordinary recollection of testimonies. Many victims and survivors had already organized grassroots organizations and the Truth Commission reached out to groups such as the Widows National Association, or *Asociación de Viudas de Guatemala* (CONAVIGUA), which had formed during the war to pressure the government to account for the whereabouts of relatives who had been "disappeared," and to provide reparations for their losses. The Commission interacted with 20,000 people, and received more than 7,000 testimonies (CEH, 1999, Vol. I, p. 33).

The Commission launched a nationwide media campaign calling on everyone who had information about human rights crimes to come forward. Often, we, field researchers, had to walk, hike, ride horses, and even fly by helicopter to reach remote communities in the mountains, where testimonies were often collectively recorded as community members gathered to recollect their memories of the war. As a fieldworker, I visited families in their communities up in the mountains since many didn't have the time and money to travel to the offices in the centers of their towns to give their testimony, even for one day. For thousands of these women, the Commission's researchers were the only people they had met who would listen to them as they told of their horrific experiences.

In addition to direct oral testimonies, the Commission sought information from historical documents provided by the parties involved in the armed conflict – the government and its armed forces, the URNG guerillas, and other parties involved in the war, including the USA. The Commission also used data the Catholic Church had collected during its own initiative, which was called the Recovery of Historical Memory Project (REMHI), conducted from 1995 to 1998 through its Human Rights Office (ODHAG). The Truth Commission was valuable in two ways. One was that it gave people who had not been heard the chance to tell about grievous wrongs Guatemalan soldiers and collaborators, and in some cases guerrillas, perpetrated against them and members of their families and communities. Another was that it made these stories part of the official, permanent public record. Among its shortcomings are two problems. One, the findings the government disseminated were written mainly in Spanish, though most Mayans can barely read or write in Spanish. More detrimentally, no perpetrator has yet been held responsible for his crimes. It is important to note that while survivors' testimonies have played a key role in exposing the dynamics of state violence, truth commissions are now recognized as limited (Daly, 2008) in their accounts of what moves people to become torturers, killers, or accomplices.

"Guatemala: Memory of Silence" – What it Found

"Guatemala: Memory of Silence" was the title of the final report. The Guatemalan Truth corroborated REMHI's report, "Guatemala Never Again," or *Guatemala Nunca Más*, which showed that the Guatemalan state had committed genocide against Indigenous Mayan groups.

Released to the public on February 25, 1999, "Guatemala: Memory of Silence" consisted of 12 volumes. It was submitted to the then-United Nations Secretary-General Kofi Annan and many sectors of Guatemalan society, and the international human rights community embraced it as the official authoritative record of human rights crimes of some of the darkest years the country had lived through, at the end of the last century.

"Guatemala: Memory of Silence" established that the Guatemalan Government bore responsibility for 93 percent, and the URNG left-wing guerillas for only 3 percent, of all murders, disappearances, and torturing committed between 1962 and 1996. Eighty-three percent of all the victims of the conflict were identified as Mayan (CEH, 1999, Conclusions, p. 85). Testimony after testimony told of how the army slaughtered civilians the government falsely accused of being members of, or of supporting, the URNG. The following is an account the Commission collected in the Department of Huehuetenango, where an estimated 350 people were killed:

> On that morning soldiers from the army base #19 arrived in the Finca. First, they called all members of the community to a public meeting: women, children, men, young and old. They separated the men and locked them up in the courthouse. Then they rounded up the women and locked them up at another location. They killed the women first by burning them alive. Then they killed the children. Informants could see through a hole in the window. They watched the soldiers cut the children's stomachs with knives and grabbed their legs smashing their heads against heavy sticks. A few survivors escaped walking and crawling all night long until they reached the border with México. (Illustrative case #18, July 17, 1982. Massacre in San Francisco Nentón, CEH, 1999, Vol. VI, p. 345)

The Recommendations: Have they Been Fulfilled?

The Truth Commission was mandated by the United Nations to recommend measures the state could take to "preserve the memory of the victims, to foster a culture of mutual respect and observance of human rights, and to strengthen the democratic process" (HCCG, 1999, Conclusions, p. 47). The CEH's recommendations "[were] fundamentally designed to facilitate unity in Guatemala and banish the centuries-old divisions suffered" (HCCG, 1999,

Conclusions, p. 48). For example, the Commission recommended that a day of victims' remembrance be designated to safeguard victims' memories.

Unfortunately, while "Guatemala: Memory of Silence" accomplished some important goals, it fell short of its objective of bringing about reconciliation. Retrospectively, I realized that it was too "naïve" to assign the lofty task of bringing peace to this war-torn country to a commission of inquiry. First, the government did little to disseminate the Truth Commission's findings among the populace. Second, the findings the government did disseminate were written mainly in Spanish, and only minimally in Mayan languages, though Mayans, for the most part, can barely read or write in Spanish. The most serious shortcoming is the fact that the report did not lead to even one perpetrator being held responsible for his crimes (see Esparza et al., 2009).

CONCLUSION

The work of truth commissions is an important first step in uncovering human rights crimes and crimes against humanity, as established in the Universal Declaration of Human Rights and in the Geneva Conventions protecting the rights of civilians and combatants involved in armed conflicts. The Guatemalan Truth Commission concluded that the Guatemalan state had committed genocide against the Mayan population during the administrations of Generals Lucas Garcia and Efrain Rios Montt.

FURTHER *IN SITU* MATERIAL, READINGS, AND WEBSITES

For a visual understanding of the Guatemalan genocide, visit the Historical Memory Project's website: www.historicalmemoryproject.com. This project's archival material includes ten photographs of the Guatemalan genocide by acclaimed photographer, Jonathan Moller.

REFERENCES

Commission for Historical Clarification (HCCG). (1999). *Guatemala, memory of silence: Conclusions and recommendations.* Guatemala: Oficina de Servicios para Proyectos de las Naciones Unidas (UNOPS).

Comisión para el Esclarecimiento Histórico (CEH). (1999). *Guatemala: Memoria del Silencio* (Vols. 1–12). Guatemala: Oficina de Servicios para Proyectos de las Naciones Unidas (UNOPS).

Daly, E. (2008). Truth skepticism: An inquiry into the value of truth in times of transition. *The International Journal of Transitional Justice*, 2(1), 23–41.

Esparza, M., Feierstein, D., & Huttenbach, H. (Eds.). (2009). *State violence and genocide in Latin America: The Cold War years.* London: Routledge.

Grandin, G. (2005). The instruction of great catastrophe: Truth commissions, national history, and state formation in Argentina, Chile, and Guatemala. *The American Historical Review*. Retrieved from www.history-cooperative.org/journals/ahr/110.1/grandin.html.

74 Nongovernmental Organizations and International Criminal Justice

Rosemary Barberet

INTRODUCTION: THE ROLE OF CIVIL SOCIETY AND THE HISTORY OF NGOS IN INTERNATIONAL CRIMINAL JUSTICE

It has long been recognized that private citizens working together are effective pressure groups for social change. With globalization, social movements have become transnational and activists have learned to work together across borders to achieve social justice. In the study of international criminal justice, students are often introduced to the work of national, intergovernmental, or supranational bodies that enforce and interpret national and international law, but rarely to the work of nongovernmental organizations. This chapter aims to fill that gap by presenting an overview of the work of nongovernmental organizations that is relevant to international criminal justice.

WHAT IS A NONGOVERNMENTAL ORGANIZATION?

NGO, an abbreviation for nongovernmental organization, is an international term used to denote formally registered organizations that are neither part of the state or otherwise governmental apparatus, nor part of the profit-making sector of the economy. They are commonly referred to as "civil society," and in various contexts are also called "nonprofit" or "voluntary" organizations. Of course, there are many such organizations in the world, and not all are directly relevant to international criminal justice. The civil society database of the UN Department of Economic and Social Affairs lists more than 24,000 organizations with international interests, and more than 5,000 who have been granted consultative status with the United Nations. Those NGOs that aim to influence international criminal justice policy because their main mission, aims, or activities are directed at policy or intervention arenas in international criminal justice are those that are of interest to this chapter. In both Vienna (the headquarters of the United Nations Office on Drugs and Crime, and the annual meeting place of the UN Commission on Crime Prevention and Criminal Justice) and New York, there is an Alliance of NGOs on Crime Prevention and Criminal Justice, which serves to coordinate the work of NGOs active in the area of international criminal justice. These alliances are evidence that the NGO community, originally conceived as local, grassroots activism, is increasingly transnational in scope. Apart from activism at the United Nations, NGOs are formed at different levels. While some NGOs are only active at the local level, others are national, regional, and international in scope. When the problems that NGOs seek to prevent are transnational, it is not surprising to find NGOs that work at all levels.

HOW ARE NGOS RELEVANT TO ICJ?

NGOs are relevant to international criminal justice (ICJ) through their areas of expertise and the ways in which they use their expertise in their relations with external organizations. ICJ-oriented NGOs are those that are related to criminal justice improvement or reform, to the denouncement of human rights violations, and to offender rehabilitation, victim support, and the prevention of crime or human rights violations. NGOs work generally alongside or outside authority structures to hold them accountable to their mandates, or to change them, their laws, or their policies. They work to change attitudes and raise awareness of certain issues. Sometimes, NGOs work to change the status quo; other times, they work to stop change to the status quo. NGOs organize and mobilize people so as to draw attention to social problems or injustices. They protes and hold rallies, sit-ins, marches, and boycotts. They observe, bear witness, and gather testimony. They research, monitor, and fact check. They educate and train. They also provide alternative services to those provided for by governments or the private for-profit sector (Barberet, 2014).

Human rights NGOs, such as Amnesty International or Human Rights Watch, focus their efforts on preventing, denouncing, and documenting human rights violations. Other large NGOs may have a broad mission, of which the international criminal justice component may only be a part. Save the Children, for example, works in the area of children's rights worldwide (see Van de Voorde and Barberet, Chapter 64, this volume), and devotes part of its energies to help children who are the victims of violence, abuse, neglect, and exploitation, including child soldiers and trafficked children. Soroptimist, an international organization of business and professional women who work toward the empowerment of women and gender equality, devotes a part of its activities to combating domestic and sexual violence worldwide, the trafficking of women, female infanticide, and female genital mutilation. Smaller NGOs often have more limited missions. The World Society of Victimology, whose membership includes victim assistance practitioners, academics, social workers, physicians, lawyers, and students, works to further research on victims and foster victim-oriented practices. Criminologists without Borders seeks to provide research input to the United Nations Commission on Crime Prevention and Criminal Justice. The websites for these organizations are listed at the end of this chapter. In sum, these organizations are examples of how, by developing an area of expertise, NGOs can deliver services, provide information, and influence policy, as we shall see now.

NGOS AND THE UNITED NATIONS

Some NGOs choose to be active in the United Nations system. The participation of NGOs in the UN system varies greatly, but most NGOs whose work is relevant to international criminal justice apply for consultative status with the Economic and Social Council of the United Nations (ECOSOC). Currently, there are more than 5,000 NGOs "in status" and among those more and more are from developing countries; however, there is no easy way to estimate how many of these NGOs tackle issues of international criminal justice because, while some

NGOs tackle these issues exclusively, many NGOs tackle criminal justice issues along with other social issues.

NGOs with consultative status are expected to support the mission and activities of the United Nations by providing input into decision making. In other words, NGOs that receive consultative status are not supposed to be anti-United Nations. Every four years, NGOs must submit reports of what they have done to contribute to the work of the United Nations. Most NGOs attend and observe United Nations meetings and disseminate information, including research findings and their own fact-finding missions, to the United Nations community. Some NGOs organize ancillary or parallel events alongside United Nations meetings, and still others actively advocate for certain policies or positions, often via specific wording in resolutions, declarations, and treaties. NGOs bear witness to violations of international law, and appeal to the implementation and enforcement of international law in their local communities. Still other NGOs partner with the UN in its operational role. In the 1970s, the United Nations asked the World Wide Fund for Nature for help in monitoring the CITES Convention (Convention on International Trade in Endangered Species of Wild Fauna and Flora), and in partnership they created TRAFFIC, a network of offices around the world that monitors compliance with CITES (Wapner, 2007, p. 260).

STRENGTHS AND LIMITATIONS OF NGOS

The work of NGOs is generally praised by the press and United Nations officials and is considered key to good decision making. This is because NGOs are often the only groups to bring expertise to the decision making process. The diplomatic community, as well as many United Nations staff, are not trained in specific policy issues, nor are they given the resources to undertake detailed research before every decision is made. NGOs are also assumed to be the sounding board of civil society. As Wapner explains (2007, p. 254), "[t]here has always been a tension between the UN's state-centered character and its aspiration to represent 'We the peoples of the United Nations,' the opening words of the organization's Charter." UN Secretary-General Antonio Guterres, shortly before taking office, stressed that "civil society is a key instrument for the success of today's UN," particularly in a global political climate "where governments are finding it more and more difficult to do their job." He observed that civil society had emerged as a key instrument in relation to development and other UN activities, from preventing conflicts to promoting human rights, and concluded: "Dialogue and cooperation with civil society will, I'm sure, be a central aspect of the activities of the UN in the next few years, not only because of my own activities, but because of the concerns that all the UN bodies have, making sure that partnership becomes a key element in solving global problems" (www.1for7billion.org/news/2016/10/21/ antonio-guterres-civil-society-is-key-instrument-in-solving-global-problems).

However, NGOs also have their critics. Some argue that NGOs are not really representative of civil society, but are rather interest groups that are as biased as some private lobbies could be. Others argue that most NGOs are based in the global North, and thus do not represent the developing countries of the world (see Smith, 2004, p. 313). The proliferation of NGOs suggests to many that NGOs are not truly effective and cannot be counted on as voices of authority. The transparency procedures applied to NGOs with status at the United Nations are minimal; NGOs are scrutinized formally only when they apply for consultative status and every four years thereafter.

EXAMPLES OF NGOS IN INTERNATIONAL CRIMINAL JUSTICE

One of the more successful examples of the effectiveness of nongovernmental organizations is the case of the NGO Coalition for an International Criminal Court (CICC), established in 1995. Many attribute the creation of the ICC to the pressure exercised by the Coalition. Cakmak (2009) analyzed this process in detail. CICC was present at the 1998 Rome Conference and helped create a more wide-reaching institution than that originally proposed by the International Law Commission report of 1994. For example, it ensured that gender-based violence would be taken seriously, and that victims and witnesses would be guaranteed safeguards. It also conducted a global ratification campaign that led to the rapid entry into force of the Rome Statute and thus the creation of the Court. It continues to promote the Court as well as to encourage its visibility and transparency. The CICC was founded with 25 NGOs (Cakmak, 2009). Today, there are more than 2,500 member organizations in 150 countries. The Coalition Secretariat is headquartered in New York and The Hague, with regional offices in Benin, Belgium, Peru, and Thailand.

Human Rights abuses and torture have been traditionally denounced by global NGOs such as Amnesty International (AI) and Human Rights Watch (HRW). Both of these organizations conduct research on human rights violations around the globe and engage in advocacy to prevent these violations and to hold perpetrators (including states) accountable. Amnesty International's headquarters are in London. AI engages in research, advocacy and lobbying, education, and mobilization through campaigns, petitions, and action. Human Rights Watch is headquartered in New York City. Each year, Human Rights Watch publishes more than 100 reports and briefings on human rights conditions in more than 90 countries, garnering local and international media coverage. Human Rights Watch meets with governments, the United Nations, regional groups like the African Union and the European Union, financial institutions, and corporations to press for changes in policy and practice that promote human rights.

Women Living Under Muslim Laws (WLUML) is headquartered in London with an Africa and Middle East Coordination Office in Senegal and an Asia Coordination Office in Pakistan. WLUML is an "international solidarity network that provides information, support and a collective space for women whose lives are shaped, conditioned or governed by laws and customs said to derive from Islam." It aims to strengthen women's individual and collective struggles for equality and their rights, especially in Muslim contexts. WLUML puts out alerts for action, provides networking opportunities, publishes reports, and organizes collective projects among its network.

In the area of prisons, Penal Reform International (PRI) is a global NGO that works to make prisons more rehabilitative and humane, and in compliance with international laws and standards. It also works to abolish the death penalty and encourage countries to consider alternatives to incarceration and fair and proportionate sentencing. PRI has headquarters in London with staff in regional offices in sub-Saharan Africa, the South Caucasus, South Asia, the Middle East and North Africa, and Central Asia. Penal Reform International has been instrumental in assisting the United Nations in implementing the UN Rules for the Treatment of Women Prisoners and Non-Custodial Sanctions for Women Offenders (the Bangkok Rules).

The most well-known NGO in corruption monitoring is Transparency International. Transparency International has a secretariat in Berlin and chapters in more than 100 countries. Since 1995, drawing on expert analysis, Transparency International has compiled the Corruption Perceptions Index, which rates countries and territories according to their perceived level of public-sector corruption. Transparency International has worked for the adoption of global conventions against corruption, most notably the UN Convention against Corruption in 2003. It denounces corruption around the globe and works for better oversight of public and private funds.

The International Rescue Committee (IRC) is a humanitarian organization that helps people who are affected by conflict and disaster to survive, recover, and plan for the future. With headquarters in New York City, the IRC works in Africa, the Middle East, Asia, Europe, and the USA. IRB works in a variety of areas, including health, safety, education, economic well-being, and the empowerment of displaced people.

Promundo, founded in Brazil, works globally for gender equality and violence prevention by working with men and boys in partnership with women and girls. Promundo conducts research and runs intervention programs to prevent violence against women and foster non-violent attitudes and behavior among men and boys.

SUMMARY AND CONCLUSION

Nongovernmental organizations are a growing influence in international criminal justice, both through their relationship with the United Nations and as grassroots movements that are becoming increasingly transnational. Through these organizations, citizens organize and work together to promote social change and achieve global peace, justice, and security. Their work is different from that of intergovernmental organizations; ideally, the two complement each other, but it is also true that the conflict that ensues from different points of view serves to enhance the democratic process of global governance.

REFERENCES

Barberet, R. (2014). *Women, crime and criminal justice: A global enquiry.* London: Routledge.
Cakmak, C. (2009). Transnational activism in world politics and effectiveness of a loosely organized principled global network: The case of the NGO Coalition for an International Criminal Court. *The International Journal of Human Rights,* 12, 373–393.
Smith, J. (2004). Transnational processes and movements. In D. Snow, S. Soule, & H. Kries (Eds.), *The Blackwell companion to social movements.* Malden, MA: Blackwell.
Wapner, P. (2008). Civil society. In T. G. Weiss & S. Daws (Eds.), *The Oxford handbook on the United Nations.* Oxford: Oxford University Press.

WEBSITES

Amnesty International. www.amnesty.org.
Coalition for the International Criminal Court (CICC). www.coalitionfortheicc.org.

The Conference of NGOs in Consultative Relationship with the United Nations. www.ngocongo.org.
Criminologists without Borders. www.criminologistswithoutborders.org.
Human Rights Watch. www.hrw.org.
International Rescue Committee. www.rescue.org.
New York Alliance of NGOs on Crime Prevention and Criminal Justice. www.cpcjalliance.org.
NGO Branch, UN Department of Economic and Social Affairs. http://csonet.org/.
Penal Reform International. www.penalreform.org.
Promundo. https://promundoglobal.org.
Save the Children. www.savethechildren.net/.
Soroptimist. www.soroptimist.org/.
Transparency International. www.transparency.org/.
Women Living Under Muslim Laws. www.wluml.org.
World Society of Victimology. www.worldsocietyofvictimology.org.

Kerry Clamp

INTRODUCTION

In criminal justice, it is common for restorative justice activists to say, "Because crime hurts, justice should heal." In the context of transitional justice, this restorative vision becomes "Because war hurts, justice should heal." Transitional justice broadly seeks to respond to the harms endured because of conflict, human rights abuses, persecution, and violence on a systematic scale. There are two conventional approaches: retributive approaches, broadly defined as anything that is court-based, and restorative approaches, broadly defined as all "efforts to locate an appropriate normative role for victims and reparation in the labyrinth of transitional justice theory" (Clamp & Doak 2012, p. 339). In democratic settings, where restorative justice theory and practice first emerged, it has been conceptualized as a micro-level theory concerned with the *relationships between individuals*. In transitional settings, however, the remit of restorative justice has expanded from repairing the harm of single incidents between individuals to responding to the *needs of a harmed society*.

While many embrace this development as an important step in attempts to transform protracted conflict and the limitations of the retributive approach, there are a number of conceptual challenges in transporting restorative justice from democratic settings to those affected by mass victimization and/or civil war (Clamp & Doak, 2012). Currently no consensus exists within the extensive literature about the conceptual meaning of restorative justice, the suitability of its application in response to human rights abuses, or what the objectives of restorative justice should be (Clamp, 2014). These contentious issues reduce the ability of both proponents and critics to engage in meaningful conversation with each other (Daly, 2012) and to produce meaningful restorative outcomes of the caliber that restorative justice scholars would expect.

A central tenet is that our conventional conceptions and approaches to restorative "justice" need developing further within transitional contexts. In particular, these settings require us to engage with the often "blurred boundaries" between individuals and groups who may at once be considered both "victims" and "perpetrators." This reality has consequences for our justice approaches that often seek to locate blame and accountability with one party (individuals or groups) and innocence and reparation with another. These settings also require the necessary inclusion of the state as an actor in the justice complex given its central role in the "conflict." Furthermore, there is a question of scale. The sheer numbers of people involved in atrocities means that a number of compromises are needed; resources (time, human, financial) mean that often justice is a selective process. In short, the strategies employed in responding to "normal" crime guided by a restorative framework in advanced democracies need revising within emerging democracies. This chapter offers an overview of how we might strive for a more inclusive and just approach.

A BRIEF OVERVIEW

Restorative justice first gained currency in transitional contexts with the establishment of the South African Truth and Reconciliation Commission in 1997. Since then, restorative justice has been associated with a number of transitional justice *institutions*. These have included the Gacaca courts/hearings in Rwanda; the International Criminal Court in The Hague; the Community Reconciliation Program in Timor-Leste; community-based alternatives to paramilitary punishment violence in Northern Ireland; efforts to confront atrocities committed by paramilitary groups in Colombia; and community-based approaches to deal with the violent conflict in Sierra Leone.

Beyond institutions, restorative justice has been conceptualized as a *form* of truth telling, accountability, apology and reparation, and reconciliation. It has also been conceptualized as a *mechanism* through which to: devolve power down to communities, increase the participation of victims, transform long-standing colonial abuses, produce meaningful outcomes for victims and communities, and achieve collective responsibility (see, for example, chapters in Clamp, 2016).

Clamp (2014) has categorized restorative justice at three different levels in the post-transition milieu. At a *conceptual* level, restorative justice has become associated with highly visible state-funded macro-level transitional justice mechanisms (such as truth commissions) aimed at nation building (e.g., the South African Truth and Reconciliation Commission). These institutions have a normative value in that they communicate new values for an inclusive and democratic society. At a *strategic* level, restorative justice has been integrated as a catalyst for institutional reform (e.g., in the Czech Republic, Northern Ireland, and South Africa). By promoting a legal culture based on participative deliberative democracy, it signals a radical departure from the oppressive criminal justice agencies of the previous undemocratic regime. At a *practical* level, restorative justice has been used to plug a justice gap within communities where criminal justice institutions have no reach or legitimacy (e.g., Northern Ireland Alternatives and Community Restorative Justice Ireland). One particular limitation of these trends is the dearth of interaction that occurs between these different levels of implementation.

CHARTING A WAY FORWARD: "LENGTHENING THE RESTORATIVE JUSTICE LENS"

In this section, adopting Howard Zehr's metaphor of a "lens," a framework is provided to move beyond the confines of current restorative justice praxis in transitional settings (see further Clamp, 2016). Despite restorative justice embracing both backward- and forward-facing concerns, the former has often received the most attention in the field. While it is important to respond to what individuals have done and experienced in transitional settings, it is imperative that we create tangible opportunities to break down barriers between former adversaries and to reintegrate ex-combatants. Without this latter focus, long-lasting peace is unlikely. As such, the elements that make up the proposed framework involve a deliberate attempt for inclusivity, cultural relevance, and a future orientation.

Restorative Justice Should be Inclusive

Despite a broad desire for stakeholders to be actively involved in the response to the atrocities of the past and the reconstruction of a peaceful society, current "restorative" transitional justice mechanisms have been criticized for *dis*empowering rather than empowering citizens. Part of the reason for this is that (often legal) "elites" determine who is involved, how they are involved, what the format will be, and when and where processes occur. This form of passive (or directed) participation is detrimental to the project of peace building precisely because it lacks stakeholder engagement.

In the pursuit of sustainable peace, it is important that all factions play an active role in dealing with the past and shaping the future. The transitional context, therefore, encourages us to stop thinking of restorative justice as a "one-incident encounter," and to consider it rather as a framework to discuss, debate, and uncover the "chain of causation that has nurtured and intensified conflict" (Froestad & Shearing 2007, p. 535). The restorative potential of this interaction, underpinned by the values of "respectful dialogue" and "non-domination" (Braithwaite, 2002), should be based primarily on how local stakeholders experience and conceive the conflict. For this reason, Froestad and Shearing (2007) argue, processes that are reliant on "experts" will always be less "restorative" than those led by local people. Where all parties to the conflict are able to claim ownership over the process, we can say that they have been empowered – an important quality for long-lasting peace.

Restorative Justice Should be Culturally Relevant

Local justice institutions are often overlooked as legitimate sites for conflict management and resolution because of the dominance of legalism in transitional justice. However, research has demonstrated that those for whom conventional transitional justice mechanisms (such as trials and truth commissions) are meaningful is limited. Critics have argued that not only might Western approaches to dealing with conflict be "foreign" to some local actors, but also others may actually hold quite a negative perception of it based on personal experience (both criminal justice and restorative justice processes often benefit ethnic minorities the least).

As such, justice approaches should be rooted in local understandings of justice that often combine restorative and retributive practices in their response to crime, rather than the Western tendency to uncouple each approach. According to Findlay (2000, p. 187), "restorative justice has, in some instances, failed to respect the limitations of the model that it promotes, as well as the tensions with the systems it replaces." In order to avoid what he refers to as "a new wave of colonialism in the current domain of social control," restorative scholars need to move away from clearly prescribed processes and outcomes of restorative justice to *values* that allow more culturally relevant processes and priorities to emerge. The goal of any intervention or assistance should be to help to facilitate the transformation of conflict into peace.

Restorative Justice Needs to be Forward-Looking

There are two arguments for adopting more forward-looking orientation for restorative justice within transitional settings. First, there is a gap within current praxis in transitional settings in addressing the underlying causes of the conflict and therefore creating the conditions for sustainable peace. Second, there is a lack of attention on the ongoing social, cultural, and political consequences of the previous regime, which may perpetuate victimization in the new democratic order. A number of empirical studies confirm that more importance is attached to creating a sustainable future than to focusing on what has happened in the past, and that neither retributive justice nor truth telling on their own is perceived as "justice" (e.g., Millar, 2011; Pells, 2009; Robins, 2011; Vinck & Pham, 2008).

Millar (2011, p. 530) argues that if we can accept that groups are also capable of being victimized and perpetrators, it is important that we "expand the definition of infringement to include collective infringements on rights to social and collective needs, and, by extension, to see society itself as an actor, both a victim and a perpetrator." Addressing this means that our starting point should not be seeking accountability, but rather addressing needs within transitional justice settings.

There is no reason why addressing immediate needs cannot become the first step in our justice response. By harnessing community-based mechanisms, government relief and local strategies to build networks and services could be devised. Once immediate needs have been responded to, it would then be possible for the past to be addressed at the local level and for the key themes and findings that emerge to be fed up into macro-level processes. In an acknowledgment that the needs of individuals living in societies emerging from conflict evolve over time, restorative justice mechanisms at the local level could continue to exist and respond to the changing needs of the community by drawing attention to new priorities and providing a forum through which resources can be harnessed to address those priorities.

CONCLUSION

Given the complex nature of the underlying causes of conflict in transitional settings, it is essential that we embrace broader conceptions of restorative justice and think more creatively about the manner in which we design and deliver justice. The first suggestion is that we have to devolve power down to communities by harnessing local institutions to allow stakeholders – victims, offenders, communities, and the state – to feed into macro-level processes. The second is that we must pay attention to notions of restorative accountability that prioritize the restoration of the victim and reintegration of offenders. This involves a shift away from an emphasis on establishing individual responsibility and, instead, an increased focus on collective responsibility.

Finally, we need to increase the time and space for all involved to share their experiences through living memorials. In other words, transitional justice harnessing a restorative framework should be something that evolves over time rather than being time-bound. The restricted nature of much transitional justice means that it excludes those who are not yet ready to deal with the past in the initial transitional justice period. There is growing currency in the perception that both restorative justice and transitional justice are too limited to deal with the complex and historical causes of protracted periods of violence (Arthur, 2009; Mani,

2014; Millar, 2011). For the most part, this is based on allegations that these approaches are too focused on the past on the one hand, and that they are too transient on the other.

If restorative justice is conceived in a much more expansive way than it currently is, it can have a much more significant impact in the lives of those affected by conflict. If restorative justice is about increasing contact between individuals and providing a safe space through which to increase dialogue, then there is no reason why restorative justice cannot be harnessed as a framework through which to create institutions and to set the agendas of those institutions so that they are responsive to the needs of all stakeholders. Conflict occurs because of inequality (perceived or otherwise) and it is this injustice that needs to be addressed if further conflict is to be avoided. Restorative justice can play an important role in allowing perceived and actual injustices to come to the fore and for strategies to respond to those injustices to be challenged.

REFERENCES

Arthur, P. (2009). How "transitions" reshaped human rights: A conceptual history of transitional justice. *Human Rights Quarterly*, 32(2), 321–367.

Braithwaite, J. (2002). Setting standards for restorative justice. *British Journal of Criminology*, 42, 563–577.

Clamp, K. (2014). *Restorative justice in transition*. Oxon/New York: Routledge.

  (2016). *Restorative justice in transitional settings*. Oxon/New York: Routledge.

Clamp, K. & Doak, J. (2012) More than words: Restorative justice concepts in transitional justice settings. *International Criminal Law Review*, 12(3), 339–360.

Daly, K. (2012) *Victimisation and justice: Concepts, contexts, and assessment of justice mechanisms*, paper presented at the 14th International Symposium of the World Society of Victimology, The Hague, May.

Findlay, M. (2000). Decolonising restoration and justice in transitional cultures. In H. Strang & J. Bathwater (Eds.), *Restorative justice: Philosophy to practice*. Aldershot: Dartmouth Publishing Company Limited.

Froestad J. & Shearing, C. (2007). Conflict resolution in South Africa: A case study. In G. Johnstone & D. Van Ness (Eds.), *Handbook of restorative justice*. Cullompton, Devon: Willan Publishing.

Mani, R. (2014). Integral justice for victims. In I. Vanfraechem, A. Pemberton, & F. Ndahinda (Eds.), *Justice for victims: Perspectives on rights, transition and reconciliation*. London: Routledge.

Millar, G. (2011). Local evaluations of justice through truth telling in Sierra Leone: Postwar needs and transitional justice. *Human Rights Review*, 12(4), 515–535.

Pells, K. (2009) We've got used to the genocide; it's daily life that's the problem. *Peace Review: A Journal of Social Justice*, 21(3), 339–346.

Robins, S. (2011). Towards victim-centred transitional justice: Understanding the needs of families of the disappeared in post conflict Nepal. *International Journal of Transitional Justice*, 5(1), 75–98.

Vinck, P. & Pham, P. (2008). Ownership and participation in transitional justice mechanisms: A sustainable human development perspective from Eastern DRC. *International Journal of Transitional Justice*, 2(3), 398–411.

WEBSITES

International Centre for Transitional Justice. www.ictj.org/search-results?search=re.

John Braithwaite: War, Crime and Regulation. http://johnbraithwaite.com/?s=restorative+justice.

PART III

OVERVIEW: INTERNATIONAL AND TRANSNATIONAL CRIME RESEARCH

A fundamental requirement of science is measurement. Without measurement there is no possibility of advancing understanding about the phenomena in question, beyond anecdote and impressionistic accounts or of testing and developing theories to build the discipline. In criminology and criminal justice, a great deal of effort has been devoted to developing reliable measures of crime as well as comprehensive measures of criminal justice processes and outcomes.

At the national level, there now exist three main sources of data about crime: 1) official crime reports based on police records; 2) crime victimization surveys; and 3) self-reports of criminal offending. These data sources each have their strengths and limitations, which make them suitable for use in different contexts and for different purposes. Concerning the first of these sources, some countries have for many years published routine compilations of police records of crime, which are used as social indicators as well as to measure the workload of the criminal justice system. An excellent example is the Uniform Crime Reports (UCR), an assemblage of crimes reported to the thousands of independent law enforcement agencies in the USA. Because police records do not include the substantial numbers of crimes not reported by victims, some countries have more recently begun to conduct victimization surveys of sample of the general population. The best-known of these surveys is the National Crime Victimization Survey (NCVS) conducted each year with thousands of households throughout the USA. Chapter 76 by Steven Block and Michael G. Maxfield describes both the UCR and NCVS. Until recently, self-report surveys of offending crime have mostly been used in research studies, but a national-level self-report survey, the Offending Crime and Justice Survey, has now been initiated in the United Kingdom.

Two extremely innovative and important cross-national surveys of crime have also been created, the International Crime Victim Survey (ICVS), described in Chapter 77 by Jan J. M. Van Dijk, and the International Self Reports of Delinquency, described in Chapter 78 by Ineke Haen Marshall and Katharina Neissl. These have produced valuable findings, but there is still a great deal of research to be done in developing comparative measures. This presents many opportunities for creative research including research that is qualitative in nature (see Chapter 79 by Gregory J. Howard, Martin Gottschalk, and Graeme Newman).

The difficulties of compiling reliable measures of crime at the national level are multiplied many times when these measures are developed for use at the international level. A fundamental problem is the lack of international agreement over definitions of crime. However, a variety of different data sources are available, which, if carefully interpreted, can assist international comparisons of crime (see Chapter 80 by Marcelo F. Aebi for a discussion of the difficulties of international comparisons). Principal among these data sources are the International Criminal Police Organization's (INTERPOL) International Crime Statistics; the United Nations (UN) Surveys on Crime Trends and the Operations of Criminal Justice Systems; the European Sourcebook on Crime and Criminal Justice Statistics; and the World Health Organization's (WHO) data on homicide and purposely inflicted injuries.

While a country's rate of imprisonment is often taken as measure of its "punitiveness," there are many components that contribute to a high incarceration rate other than a desire for punishment. These can include more crime, greater police effectiveness in solving crimes, and more aggressive prosecution (see Chapter 81 by Alfred Blumstein).

The information revolution of the past 20 years has helped to create and disseminate vast stores of data on every imaginable topic. While this has benefited every field of research, it may have particularly helped those studying crime occurring in distant parts of the world. From the relative comfort of their offices they can travel to the far reaches of the planet at the click of a keyboard and gather critical items of information about crimes committed, offenders arrested, and punishments administered. On a personal note, this almost makes me wish that I was starting my research career now, rather than 30 years ago when, as a young student, I had to traverse half the Indian subcontinent from my university in Madras (now Chennai) to the Tata Institute of Social Sciences Library in Bombay (now Mumbai) to compile the literature review for my research on women policing.

No doubt the Tata Institute library still holds a vast store of books, journals, government reports, and newspapers, which are all of great value for researchers. There is also no doubt that the library, just as all other research libraries, has been transformed by the Internet, which provides electronic access to many of the paper materials held on their shelves. Even in the libraries themselves it is easy to see the results of this revolution. Rarely do students and professors wander among the stacks, searching for that elusive book or journal. Instead, they will be found interrogating the library computers, which have grown exponentially in number from the time, less than 20 years ago, when they held access only to the library catalog.

The need for human links as well as electronic coordination was recognized by the founders of the World Criminal Justice Library Network (WCJLN). This consists of a group of librarians and information specialists drawn from more than 30 countries, who work in universities and colleges and in government and nongovernment organizations and research institutes (see Chapter 82 by Phyllis A. Schultze). They are of great help to one another, when a researcher cannot gain access to an important paper published in another country – something that occurs with great regularity. To fulfill its purpose, the Network does not rely simply on electronic communications among the members, but the bonds between them are cemented at biannual meetings, held in different parts of the world, where matters of mutual concern are discussed and developed. Librarians, like everyone else, are much more likely to help each other when they personally know and like one another. Perhaps there is wider lesson here for the field of international crime and justice.

While the libraries of modern educational institutions strive to expand their collections and to find ways to connect to new e-resources, it is of little use if they cannot help their users to find the information they need. The multidisciplinary nature of international crime and justice makes it practically impossible to provide students and researchers with a definitive list of resources. However, Maria Kiriakova, a librarian at John Jay College of Criminal Justice, lists the best of these resources and provides a guide to accessing them (Chapter 83). Her work shows how the new electronic world of libraries still depends on the knowledge and energy of well-trained librarians to make their resources accessible.

While scholarly journals relating to international and transnational crime research are on the increase recently, a wealth of quality information that could provide a comprehensive picture of crime and justice issues can be found in published or unpublished government and nongovernment reports on line and in libraries around the world. The students and scholars of international crime and justice must include such gray literature when undertaking a systematic review. In Chapter 84, Phyllis A. Schultze and Estee Marchi describe the importance of gray literature and how to search it.

76 The US Uniform Crime Reports and the National Crime Victimization Survey

Steven Block and Michael G. Maxfield

INTRODUCTION

Measuring national crime rates reflects two fundamental activities of government: to protect public safety and to document social indicators. Governments report data on crime in the same way that national statistics are collected for population, employment, education, income, consumer prices, and birth and mortality rates, along with countless other measures. Just as consumer prices are measured by an index based on the sorts of things people routinely purchase, an index of national crime is measured.

This chapter describes two national measures of crime in the USA. Uniform Crime Reports (UCR) are police-collected measures of crime compiled by the thousands of independent law enforcement agencies throughout the country. Largely because police-based measures have built-in limits, victim-based measures of crime have been collected for more than 45 years. Each measures slightly different dimensions of crime.

UNIFORM CRIME REPORTS: CRIMES KNOWN TO POLICE

Begun in 1929, the Uniform Crime Reports, administered by the Federal Bureau of Investigation (FBI), serve several purposes. First, they provide national estimates of serious crime in the USA each year. Second, UCR data estimate annual arrests for serious crime and a variety of lesser offenses. Third, UCR data are reported for individual law enforcement agencies, in addition to totals for each state and the nation, which facilitates analysis below the national level. Fourth, the relatively long time period for UCR data makes it possible to examine short- and long-term trends in crime. Fifth, detailed data on individual homicide incidents have been reported since 1976; this makes it possible to examine features of individual victims, offenders, and homicide characteristics.

These basic goals are embodied in the *uniform* part of the UCR name – the data series was begun to provide consistent records of crime across law enforcement agencies. This is important because criminal justice in the USA is a highly decentralized endeavor. Each state maintains its own system of courts, and within states most municipalities and counties maintain their own law enforcement agencies. In 2016, nearly 18,000 agencies reported summary

UCR data (FBI, 2017). The number of participating agencies has increased substantially in recent years, probably due to efforts by individual states to improve crime data.

Types of UCR Data

UCR Part 1 offenses are commonly referred to as "crimes known to police," which means these numbers reflect crimes reported to police, recorded by police, and reported to the FBI. The UCR also presents totals of persons arrested for a variety of other Part 2 offenses. These include less-serious assaults, drug offenses, fraud, public order offenses, weapons violations, and juvenile status offenses. These crimes are tabulated only if someone is arrested because such offenses are often not reported to police and are thus difficult to estimate.

UCR Part 1 and Part 2 offenses are reported as summary-based data. This means that data are available as summary totals for each reporting jurisdiction – city, county, zero-population agency, and aggregations of these. Summary-based data are useful for obtaining national- and subnational-level estimates of crime, but cannot be used to analyze individual incidents or groups of incidents. For example, total reported Part 1 offenses are available for Chicago (and other cities with a population of 10,000 or more) for each reporting year. But in the summary-based UCR, no information is available about any of the individual incidents that were reported in Chicago, or about any of the individual people arrested in Chicago.

In contrast, incident-level data are available for all homicides reported to the UCR program. Known as Supplementary Homicide Reports (SHR), these data provide information about individual homicide incidents, such as characteristics of victims and offenders (if known), weapons used, and other features of homicide incidents. This means that researchers can analyze data about each homicide incident.

Limits of UCR Data

Counts of UCR offenses do not include certain types of crime in all cases and provide selective data in other instances. Most prominent in the first group are crimes not reported to police. Research has found that personal crimes not involving injury and property crimes involving small monetary losses are frequently not reported to police.

A source of inconsistency across reporting agencies stems from the fact that crime definitions vary in different states (Maltz, 1999). These differences present reliability problems that should be considered in making comparisons in crime levels or rates across jurisdictions. However, research focusing on national-level crime rates, especially trends over time, would be less affected by variation in cross-jurisdictional practices. Uniform Crime Report definitions rarely change, but one notable exception is the broadening of the previous "Forcible Rape" definition. The new definition of "Rape," effective January 1, 2013, includes gender-neutral language and a wider array of sexual acts.

NATIONAL CRIME VICTIMIZATION SURVEY

The National Crime Victimization Survey (NCVS) is an alternate measure of national-level crime based on interviews with residents in a large nationally representative sample of US

Table 78.1. Comparison of UCR and NCVS

Uniform Crime Reports	National Crime Victimization Survey
• Count serious crimes known to police, and arrests for other crimes.	• Counts personal and household victimizations, including crimes not reported to police.
• Collected by thousands of local and state law enforcement agencies in the USA; reported to the FBI, usually through state-level agencies.	• Is based on a large nationally representative sample of households.
• Participation in the UCR is voluntary, though many states require participation; over 90 percent of agencies participate.	• Household representatives are interviewed twice each year to increase the accuracy of recall and crime estimates.
• Except for homicide, UCR data are summary-based – data are available at the agency level. Incident-based homicide data are available, providing details on each homicide incident.	• Permits analysis of individual incident details. • Uses more uniform collection procedures. • Produces incident-based data that can be used to estimate national-level victimization rates.
• Some variation in definitions and collection procedures exist across agencies; cross-agency comparisons must be made with caution.	• Best for measuring crimes less often reported to police.
• Produces summary-based data that can be used to estimate national, state, and local crime rates.	• Does not count commercial victimizations, or victimization of children under age 12.
• Best for assessing long-term trends, nationwide and within individual agencies.	
• Do not include crimes not reported to police.	

households (see Table 78.1 for a comparative account of UCR and NCVS). Regular national crime surveys were first conducted in 1972 in an effort to measure crime and support analysis in ways that are not possible with summary-based police data. The NCVS is administered by the Bureau of Justice Statistics; interviews are conducted by the Census Bureau.

One of the chief differences between survey-based measures of victimization and police-based counts of crime is that surveys include crimes not reported to police. Victimization surveys made it possible to measure the so-called dark figure of unreported crime. The NCVS has evolved into its current form to become the world's longest-running annual victimization survey.

Overview of NCVS Procedures

The NCVS is a household-based sample. Using a complex multistage cluster design, a nationally representative sample of about 135,000 households is drawn, yielding interviews with about 225,000 individuals (Morgan & Kena, 2017). Households are retained in the NCVS sample for three years; individuals in the sampled households are interviewed twice each year, usually by telephone.

These basic procedures reflect the primary purpose of the NCVS – to estimate national levels of victimization. Because some crimes are relatively rare, a large sample is drawn so that adequate numbers of victims will be selected. In each interview respondents are asked about incidents for the previous six months. People are interviewed every six months to minimize the recall period between interviews, and thus increase the accuracy of annual estimates.

The NCVS has been conducted largely in its present form since 1972 and, therefore, offers a long, uniform series that can be used to trace patterns of change in victimization. A major redesign of questions to screen for possible victimization was implemented in 1993. Screening questions became more explicit in an effort to detect violent offenses, especially sexual assaults and crimes involving intimate partners or family members. More recently, changes have been put in place to increase the survey's sample size and allow for state and local estimates of victimization.

In addition, the NCVS has occasionally served as a research platform. This means questions, or batteries of questions, are temporarily added to supplement standard items. For example, in 2011 NCVS respondents answered a series of questions about traffic and street stops with police (Langton & Durose, 2013).

Limits of NCVS Data

Although the NCVS offers better estimates of certain offenses, survey data are deficient in important ways. Some limits are due to NCVS sample and survey design; others are consequences of survey methods in general.

Because the NCVS uses a household-based sample, individuals not living in households are excluded. Homeless persons are obvious examples. Another consequence of the household-based sample design is that the NCVS does not count commercial victimizations such as burglary of a business. Finally, the NCVS does not collect information about victimizations of individuals under age 12. This excludes child abuse, assaults, and theft of personal property that targets young children.

Other problems stem from difficulties of collecting information about crime by interviewing victims. People tend to forget distant events or things they might view as minor problems. Although NCVS interviews are conducted every six months, respondents might forget some incidents that occurred between interviews. This is more likely to be true for minor incidents or individuals victimized more than once; in the latter case, victims may not be able to distinguish individual incidents.

Collecting data through surveys also tends to underestimate sensitive events or conditions – things people might be embarrassed to talk about (Cantor & Lynch, 2000). Domestic violence and sexual assaults are examples of incidents that are difficult to measure in general-purpose crime surveys. Other general-purpose surveys, such as the British Crime Survey (Mirrlees-Black, 1999) and specialized efforts like the National Violence Against Women Survey (Tjaden & Thoennes, 2000), have revealed higher rates for sexual offenses and intimate-partner violence compared to those estimated by the NCVS.

SUMMARY AND CONCLUSION

The US experience illustrates that developing data series to count crime at the national level is complex. Comparisons of the UCR and NCVS are the focus of edited books (Lynch & Addington, 2007) and numerous recent peer-reviewed publications. Even these two data sources fail to capture some offenses. For instance, self-report offending surveys provide crucial information on behaviors that are rarely reported to police and have no direct victims, such as illicit drug use.

REFERENCES

Cantor, D. & Lynch, J. P. (2000). Self-report surveys as measures of crime and criminal victimization. In D. Duffee (Ed.), *Measurement and analysis of crime and justice*. Vol. 4. Washington, DC: US Department of Justice, Office of Justice Programs, National Institute of Justice.

Federal Bureau of Investigation (FBI). (2017). Crime in the United States 2016. US Department of Justice, Federal Bureau of Investigation. Retrieved from https://ucr.fbi.gov/crime-in-the-u.s/2016/crime-in-the-u.s.-2016.

Langton, L. & Durose, M. (2013, September). *Police behavior during traffic and street stops, 2011*. Washington, DC: US Department of Justice, Office of Justice Programs, Bureau of Justice Statistics. NCJ 242937.

Lynch, J. P. & Addington, L. A. (Eds.). (2007). *Understanding crime statistics: Revisiting the divergence of the NCVS and UCR*. New York: Cambridge University Press.

Maltz, M. D. (1999, September). *Bridging gaps: Estimating crime rate from police data*. A discussion paper from the BJS Fellows Program. Washington, DC: US Department of Justice, Office of Justice Programs, Bureau of Justice Statistics.

Mirrlees-Black, C. (1999). *Domestic violence: Findings from a new British crime survey self-completion questionnaire*. London: Home Office Research, Development, and Statistics Directorate.

Morgan, R. E. & Kena, G. (2017, December). *Criminal victimization, 2016*. US Department of Justice, Office of Justice Programs, Bureau of Justice Statistics. NCJ 251150.

Tjaden, P. & Thoennes, N. (2000, November). *Full report of the prevalence, incidence, and consequences of violence against women*. Washington, DC: US Department of Justice, Office of Justice Programs, National Institute of Justice.

WEBSITES

Detailed tables containing data from the UCR for each year can be found at https://ucr.fbi.gov/crime-in-the-u.s.

Information about methodology and published reports using NCVS data are available at www.bjs.gov/index.cfm?ty=dcdetail&iid=245.

Original data files for the UCR, NCVS, Supplementary Homicide Reports, and the National Incident-Based Reporting System can be obtained from the National Archive of Criminal Justice Data at www.icpsr.umich.edu/NACJD/index.html.

Highlights of the International Crime Victim Survey

Jan J. M. Van Dijk

BACKGROUND TO THE INTERNATIONAL CRIME VICTIM SURVEYS

Over the years, an increasing number of countries have undertaken "victimization surveys," sample surveys among the general population about experiences of crime, such as the National Crime Victim Surveys. These surveys provide a source of data on crime independent of crime statistics recorded by police (Maxfield, Hough, & Mayhew, 2007). They also provide important additional information on crime, including rates of reporting crimes to the police, victims' experiences with the police, fear of crime, and the use of crime prevention measures. If the research methodology used is standardized, the surveys also offer a new opportunity for the collection of crime statistics, which can be used for comparative purposes. This allows crime problems to be analyzed from a truly international perspective.

The first ICVS took place in 1989 in a dozen countries. Since its initiation, surveys have been carried out one or more times in over 80 countries, including all 27 member states of the European Union, Australia, Canada, Japan, and the USA (Van Dijk, Van Kesteren, & Smit, 2007). More than 400,000 citizens have been interviewed to date in the course of the ICVS with the same questionnaire, translated into 30 or more languages (Van Kesteren, Van Dijk, & Mayhew, 2014). This process has resulted in a body of victim survey data across a variety of countries covering a period of 30 years. The full dataset is available for consultation and secondary analyses (http://wp.unil.ch/icvs).

METHODOLOGY

The ICVS targets samples of households in which only one respondent is selected, aged 16 or above. National samples include at least 2,000 respondents who are generally interviewed with the CATI (computer-assisted telephone interview) technique. In the countries where this method is not applicable because of insufficient distribution of telephones, face-to-face interviews are conducted in the main cities, generally with samples of 1,000 to 1,500 respondents.

The questionnaire includes sections on ten types of "conventional" crime, of which each question provides a standard definition. The ICVS provides an overall measure of victimization in the previous year by any of the "conventional" crimes included in the questionnaire. Among the "conventional" crimes, some are "household crimes," in other words, those which can be seen as affecting the household at large, and respondents report on all incidents known to them. A first group of household crimes deals with the vehicles owned by the respondent or his or her household:

- theft of car
- theft from car
- theft of bicycle
- theft of motorcycle

A second group refers to breaking and entering at the home address:

- burglary
- attempted burglary

A third group of crimes refers to victimization experienced by the respondent personally:

- robbery
- theft of personal property
- assaults and threats
- sexual incidents

Besides rates of victimization per country, one of the most important findings of the ICVS deals with the reporting of victimizations by victims to the police and their reasons for not reporting crimes, thus to provide comparative information on why police statistics often do not reflect the full crime picture. Those who have reported a victimization to the police are asked to assess the way the police have handled their report. Furthermore, all respondents are asked about their feelings of safety, their assessment of police performance, their reception of victim support, and the use of crime prevention measures.

SOME MAJOR FINDINGS ON LEVELS OF CRIME

The results of the ICVS 1996–2005 show that, on average, approximately 25 percent of citizens living in urban areas suffered at least one form of victimization over the 12 months preceding the interview. In Africa and Latin America significantly higher levels of victimization were observed (33 percent and 34 percent, respectively).

Globally, over a five-year period, two out of three inhabitants of big cities were victimized by crime at least once. Criminal victimization has evidently become a statistically normal feature of urban life across countries of both the developed and developing world. Almost no citizens anywhere in the world can feel immune from these threats to their personal security.

Figure 77.1 shows one-year victimization rates for any of the ten crimes included in the ICVS for the countries participating in the ICVS 2004/2005. In most of the surveys carried out in 2004/2005 booster samples of 1,000 were drawn from the capital cities. This allows the calculation of special capital city rates.

Figure 77.1 confirms that levels of victimization by common crime are universally higher among capital-city populations than among national populations, with Lisbon as the only exception to this rule. The mean victimization rate of the participating cities is 21.7 percent, whereas the mean national rate was 15.7 percent. In almost all countries, risks to be criminally victimized are one-quarter to one-third higher for capital-city inhabitants than for

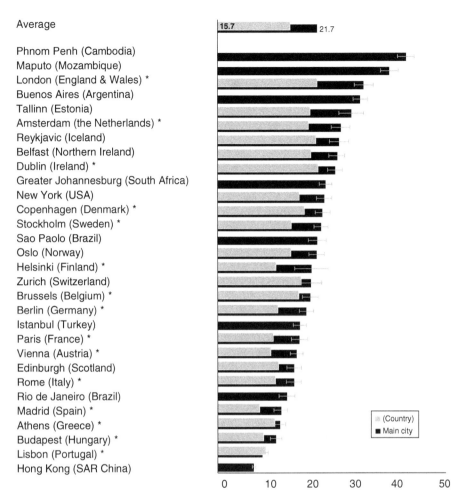

Figure 77.1. Overall victimization for ten crimes; one-year prevalence rates (percentages) of capital cities and national populations in 28 countries in 2005.

* *Source*: The European Survey of Crime and Safety (EUICS 2005). Gallup-Europe, Brussels; ICVS, 2005

others. Differences between the ten top countries and the ten at the bottom are statistically significant at the 90-percent confidence level.

The ranking of cities in terms of crime puts Phnom Penh (Cambodia) and Maputo (Mozambique) on top. Relatively high rates are also found in London, Buenos Aires, Tallinn, Amsterdam, Reykjavik, Belfast, Dublin, and Johannesburg. Victimization rates near the global city average of 21.7 percent are found in New York, Copenhagen, Stockholm, Sao Paulo, and Oslo. The five safest capital cities of those participating are Hong Kong, Lisbon, Budapest, Athens, and Madrid.

High-crime countries include both relatively affluent countries (Ireland, Denmark, and Iceland) and some of the least affluent (Estonia and Mexico). The category of low-crime countries is equally diverse. It includes both relatively affluent countries, such as Austria, and less-prosperous ones, such as Hungary, Spain, and Portugal. Macro factors known to be consistently associated with levels of common crime are urbanization and the proportion of

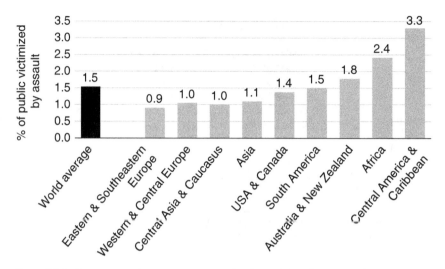

Figure 77.2. One-year prevalence rates among national populations for assault/threat.
Source: ICVS 1996–2015

young adolescents in the population. Together, these factors can explain some of the variation in overall levels of crime across countries.

The crime category of assault and threat is defined in the ICVS as personal attacks or threats, either by a stranger or a relative or friend, without the purpose of stealing. Figure 77.2 shows results from the ICVS surveys carried out between 1995 and 2015, including surveys in five Caribbean countries.

Assaults on women are more likely to be domestic in nature than assaults on men. In one-third of the cases of violence against women, the offender was known at least by name to the victim. In one-fifth of the cases the crime was committed in the victim's own home. The level of violence against women across countries is inversely related to the position of women in society, with most developing countries showing much higher rates (Van Dijk, 2008).

VICTIM EMPOWERMENT: POLICE RESPONSES AND VICTIM SUPPORT

Reporting to the Police

The ICVS shows that victims in Western Europe, North America (the USA and Canada), and Oceania (Australia and New Zealand) are more likely to report their victimization to the police than those in other regions (see Figure 77.3). The picture of regional reporting rates is the reverse of that of victimization rates. In the regions where more crimes occur, fewer of those crimes are reported to the police. This general pattern introduces a fatal flaw into international police figures of crime by systematically deflating crime in developing countries.

In general, burglary is the most frequently reported crime (apart from car theft, which is almost universally reported). Burglary was most frequently reported in Western Europe, North America, and Australia. Important factors determining reporting are insurance

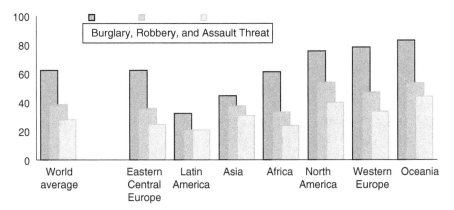

Figure 77.3. Percentage of assaults, robberies, and burglaries, respectively, reported to the police, by region. *Source*: ICVS, 2005

coverage (the requirement for making a claim for compensation being dependent on reporting the incident to the police) and the ease of reporting (determined by factors such as access to the local police, availability of telephones, etc.).

Robbery was also frequently reported in Western Europe, but much less in the remaining regions, with a minimum in Latin America, where only one victim of robbery out of five reported to the police. In places where robberies are rampant, victims are less likely to report. In the case of robberies, reporting seems to be dependent on confidence in the police. Those refraining from reporting often have no trust in their local police. This is borne out by the finding that more than 50 percent of the Latin American victims of robbery who did not report to the police said they did so because "the police would not do anything" and approximately 25 percent said that they feared or disliked the police.

Finally, assaults and threats were the least frequently reported crime. Globally less than half of violence victims report to the police. Less than one in three of the female victims of threat and assault had filed a complaint with the police. Reporting rates are again lowest in Africa, Latin America, Eastern Europe, and Asia (one in five). As a general rule, the most vulnerable categories of victims – such as women in developing countries – are the least likely to seek assistance from the police, and thus those most in need of services are least likely to receive it.

Victim Satisfaction and Trust Levels

Among those who reported, less than half were satisfied with the way the police dealt with their case. Those least satisfied were the respondents from Africa, Asia, Latin America, and Central-Eastern Europe. Only in Western Europe, North America, and Australia more than 60 percent of victims who reported to the police positively evaluated the treatment received. The most common reason for dissatisfaction was that the police "did not do enough" or "were not interested." Around 10 percent said the police had been impolite or incorrect. This reason was given most often by victims of violence against women, especially by those from Latin America. Another common complaint is that the police failed to provide information about the case.

A special section of the ICVS deals with the assessment of police performance by respondents. The results suggest that in many developing countries the public remains skeptical about the capacity of the police to control local crime. At the country level, lack of trust in the police appears to be strongly related to low rates of reporting of crimes to the police.

Ironically, then, low levels of police-recorded crime in a country should not necessarily be seen as a good sign. Rather than as evidence for low levels of crime, low police figures may actually point to poor performance of the police and a resulting low trust level among the public, limiting the proportion of crimes reported to the police.

Victim Support Services

Victims of more serious crimes who had reported to the police were specifically asked whether they had received support from a specialized agency. In most countries, few victims had received such help. The figures are variable across offence type. Of those who reported burglaries to the police, 4 percent had received help. The level of support was the highest in the Western European countries, especially in the United Kingdom, Sweden, Denmark, and the Netherlands, where victim support for such victims is indeed institutionally most developed.

Approximately 16 percent of women victims of sexual offences who had reported to the police had received specialized support in North America, Western Europe, and Africa. Elsewhere the percentages were even lower.

STRENGTHS AND WEAKNESSES OF THE ICVS

The ICVS has over the years proven to be a reliable source of information on the level and trends of crimes that directly affect ordinary citizens on a large scale (so-called volume crime) (Lynch, 2006). It has over the years also improved its measurement of street-level corruption and of sexual violence, although for the latter type of crime the use of specialized survey instruments such as the International Violence Against Women Survey (IVAWS) seems preferable (Johnson, Ollus, & Nevala, 2007). No information is provided by the ICVS on the most serious violent crimes such as homicides and kidnappings, or on crimes victimizing businesses or society at large (racketeering, grand corruption, environmental pollution). In these areas, ICVS data must be supplemented by data on police-recorded crimes or from other sources. Global information on homicides and on convictions for human trafficking can be consulted at the website of UNODC (www.unodc.org/gsh/en/data.html). A comprehensive overview of available international data on crime and justice is given in Van Dijk (2008).

THE WAY AHEAD

By disclosing important aspects of crime and victimization at the international level, the ICVS has become an important source of information for researchers, policy makers, and the international community. In 2015 the United Nations adopted the 2030 Global Agenda defining Sustainable Development Goals, including Goal 16 on Security and Access to Justice. Among the performance indicators chosen for Goal 16 are several items of the ICVS such as rates of women victimized by violence, of victims of assault/threats who have reported to the police, and of perceptions of safety in one's neighborhood. In recent years ICVS-type surveys have been conducted in a dozen Latin American and Caribbean countries under the supervision of UNODC. These are likely to be repeated regularly. New surveys will also be executed in the Caucasian region with funding from the EU. Partly because of much-reduced levels of common crime in the region, interest in crime surveying has somewhat waned across the Western world. In the absence of updated information from the ICVS, progress in the attainment of Sustainable Development Goal 16 will be hard to assess in Europe and North America.

REFERENCES

Johnson, H., Ollus, N., & Nevala, S. (2007). *Violence against women: An international perspective.* New York: Springer.

Lynch, J. P. (2006). Problems and promises of victimization surveys for cross-national research. *Crime and Justice*, 34(1), 229–287.

Maxfield, M., Hough, M., & Mayhew, P. (2007). Surveying crime in the 21st century: Summary and recommendations. In M. Hough & M. Maxfield (Eds.), *Surveying crime in the 21st century.* Monsey, NY: Criminal Justice Press.

Van Dijk, J. J. M. (2008). *The world of crime: Breaking the silence on problems of crime, justice and development across the world.* Thousand Oaks, CA: SAGE.

Van Dijk, J. J. M., Van Kesteren, J., & Smit, P. (2007). *Criminal victimisation in an international perspective: Key findings from the 2004–2005 ICVS and EU ICS.* The Hague: Ministry of Justice/WODC (www.WODC.nl/publicaties).

Van Kesteren, J., Van Dijk, J. J. M., & Mayhew, P. (2014). The international crime victims survey: A retrospective. *International Review of Victimology*, 20(1), 49–69.

78 The International Self-Report Delinquency Study (ISRD)

Ineke Haen Marshall and Katharina Neissl

BACKGROUND

The International Self-Report Delinquency Study (ISRD) is an ongoing large internationally collaborative self-report study of delinquency, victimization, and substance use of young adolescents (12- to 15-year-old pupils in grades seven, eight, and nine). The ISRD project was initially developed to respond to the need for standardized, internationally comparable data on the prevalence and incidence of offending and victimization among youth, but its main focus was and continues to be on testing theories about offending and victimization. This ambitious project started on a modest scale over 25 years ago and has now matured into a respected continuing survey. Indeed, "the long-term impact of the ISRD is difficult to over-estimate" (Gottfredson, 2018, p. vi). The first ISRD study (1991–1992) pioneered the cross-national use of standardized international self-report methodology on youth in 13 countries (Junger-Tas et al., 1994, 2003); 15 years later, the study was repeated, this time with a larger number of countries and an expanded questionnaire (ISRD2) (Junger-Tas et al., 2010; Junger-Tas et al., 2012). The third wave of data collection (ISRD3) started in 2012 and continues through 2019, with about 40 countries participating. At the time of this writing, planning has started for the fourth sweep (ISRD4), slated to begin in 2020. This chapter reports primarily on the experiences and results of ISRD3.[1]

METHODOLOGY

Through the use of surveys, ISRD estimates the prevalence and incidence of youthful offending, substance use, and victimization, examines the correlates of youth crime, and tests different explanations of crime in countries across the globe. The main objectives of the ISRD project are to study cross-national variability as well as international trends in juvenile delinquency, substance use, and victimization over time; to improve standardized self-report methodology for comparative purposes; and to generally advance comparative criminological research beyond the constraints of officially recorded crime. Official crime rates do not lead to valid international comparison, due to variations in crime definitions

---

[1] For more information, please refer to Enzmann et al. (2018) and to the ISRD website (https://web.northeastern.edu/isrd/).

and in prosecution policies. Moreover, unlike official data, self-reports provide background information needed to test criminological theory (Junger-Tas & Marshall, 1999).

The ISRD has an explicitly comparative design. The standardization of methodology demands that all countries adopt the core ISRD module and survey procedures, use comparable sampling designs, and coordinated data management and analysis. That is a challenge, since ISRD3 includes a large number of countries, including Armenia, Australia, Austria, Belgium, Bosnia and Herzegovina, Brazil, Cape Verde, China, Croatia, the Czech Republic, Denmark, Estonia, Finland, France, Germany, Georgia, Greece, India, Indonesia, Italy, Japan, Kosovo, Lithuania, Macedonia, the Netherlands, Poland, Portugal, Russia, Serbia, Slovakia, South Korea, Spain, Sweden, Switzerland, Taiwan, Turkey, the United Kingdom (England, Scotland), Ukraine, the USA, and Venezuela. As of summer 2018, data collection for ISRD3 has been completed in 33 of these countries. Selection of countries was not based on a random sampling of the nations in the world, but on the shared interest from researchers working in universities, research institutes, and government agencies in these countries (Junger-Tas et al., 2010).

Questionnaire

The original ISRD questionnaire was collectively produced by the participants in a number of workshops. The questionnaire has undergone some modifications in the different sweeps, but in order to maintain comparability with ISRD2 and ISRD1, the changes to the core instrument and the research design have been kept to a minimum for ISRD3. The ISRD questionnaire has a modular structure with a core set of fixed questions, and a flexible part which will vary from sweep to sweep. This flexibility allows one to respond to the most recent relevant developments in the nature of delinquency and victimization, as well as theoretical advances. The ISRD3 questionnaire includes items to test social bonding and social control theory, self-control, routine activity/opportunity theory, and social disorganization/collective efficacy (comparable to ISRD2), as well as procedural justice theory, institutional anomie theory, and situational action theory. Offending is measured by asking about carrying a weapon, group fights, assault, extortion, theft from a person, vandalism, graffiti, shoplifting, illegal downloads, theft from car, bicycle theft, car/motorcycle theft, burglary, and drug dealing (lifetime and last year prevalence and incidence). Questions on substance use (alcohol and drugs) are asked but are not treated as measures of delinquency. ISRD3 has expanded the number of questions on victimization to include: extortion, assault, theft, hate crime, cyberbullying, and parental use of physical violence. An important addition is an item asking about willingness to be open about delinquent behavior (see Findings section). Some countries have decided to add country-level optional modules, located at the end of the questionnaire, about country-specific areas of interest, such as stop-and-frisk, gang membership, grooming, or neighborhood context. The core ISRD questionnaire is in the English language, but each country translates the questionnaire as needed.

Data Collection

Whereas for ISRD1 and ISRD2 the questionnaires were usually completed using pencil and paper, the majority of the ISRD3 surveys were completed electronically. Several countries used a mixed-method approach (paper and pencil, as well as electronically, depending on circumstances), and a small number of countries still solely relied on paper-and-pencil questionnaires. Regardless of the method of administration, the ISRD3 protocol demands that the questionnaires are completed in a classroom setting. Parental consent was required in all countries, with the majority consisting of the parental "opt out" procedure (i.e., students are allowed to participate unless their parents opt out of the survey), with a few countries (the USA, Italy, Croatia) using the more demanding "opt in" process (i.e., students are only allowed to participate in the survey if parents give explicit permission). In some but not all countries, teachers were present during data collection. (For more detailed information, see Enzmann et al., 2018, Table 2.1.)

Sampling

The ISRD project is a school-based study, with random samples drawn at the city level. A few countries (e.g., Switzerland and the Czech Republic) opted for a national sample, with oversampling one or two cities. Clearly, city-based and national samples have different advantages and disadvantages, and may not be directly compared. Strictly speaking, international comparisons of ISRD3 prevalence rates should be limited to only those respondents who live in cities. Other reasons to be very cautious when making direct international comparisons of prevalence rates of offending are related to the cross-national variability in the validity of self-report responses (Rodríguez et al., 2015; Enzmann et al., 2018, chapter 3), which will be briefly discussed in the Findings section. The data for a total of 62,636 students are available for analysis and presentation at the time of this writing (summer 2018). The total sample size will significantly increase by 2019 when data collection for ISRD3 ends.

The primary sampling units used in the ISRD project are seventh-, eighth-, and ninth-grade classrooms (paralleling 12- to 15-year-old students), stratified by school type. Although a major challenge was to obtain permission to access schools, most participating countries took great pains to randomly sample schools in the selected cities, followed by a random selection of classes within these schools, resulting in a fair representation of the school-attending population in grades seven to nine.

Data Standardization

In order to ensure the standardization of the translated questionnaires, most participants used the EFS-Survey software provided by Unipark (www.unipark.com/en/). In some countries, Fluid-Survey software (an offline computer program) was used, rather than the EFS-Survey software for online surveys. Data from paper-and-pencil questionnaires were entered by using the EpiData software. Standardized syntax was used to transfer data from EpiData to SPSS for each country that used paper-and-pencil administration, and to create all variables included in the core ISRD3 questionnaire (from definitions, to codes, to checking for out-of-bound questionnaire responses). These procedures resulted in comparable country data files with identical variable names and codes, which are merged into a large international database, currently including 27 countries (n = 62,636) (see Figure 78.1 in next section).

FINDINGS

In general, we have found that the ISRD results are quite compatible with other internationally available crime data. For example, comparisons of ISRD2 offending and victimization rates with those of the other two main sources of internationally available crime statistics (i.e., International Crime Victimization Survey and European Sourcebook data) suggest a moderate level of support for a convergence of different measures (Enzmann et al., 2010). A large number of publications based on the ISRD2 merged data set, now available to the larger scientific community, report results that are generally in line with theoretical expectations derived from social bonding, self-control, social disorganization, and lifestyle theories (see https://web.northeastern.edu/isrd/ for a listing of publications, as well as Enzmann et al., 2018, pp. 3–4).

Since data collection for ISRD3 will not be completed until 2019, we will present only some early findings from the available data. A major concern of ISRD3 has been to explore the effect of social desirability on self-reported levels of offending, and how this factor differs systematically between countries. The so-called response integrity question, as well as the openness question, suggest that there are large national differences in willingness to be open about delinquent behavior (see Enzmann et al., 2018, chapter 3). The effects of social desirability are likely to be strongest on self-reported offending rather than self-reported victimization, therefore we will present estimates of *victimization* across countries (cf. Enzmann et al., 2018). Figure 78.1 presents the incidence rates of being the victim of *core crimes* (assault, robbery, and theft, combined) for 27 countries, grouped in seven country clusters: 1) Nordic countries (Denmark, Finland; n = 3,861); 2) Western Europe (Austria, Belgium, Germany, Switzerland, the UK; n = 21,007); 3) Southern Europe (France, Italy, Portugal; n = 7,174); 4) post-Socialist Eastern European countries (Armenia, the Czech Republic, Estonia, Lithuania, the Slovak Republic, Ukraine; n = 14,795); 5) the Balkans (Bosnia and Herzegovina, Croatia, Macedonia, Kosovo, Serbia; n = 7,691); 6) other non-European countries (Cape Verde, India, Indonesia, Venezuela; n = 6,188); and 7) the USA (n = 1,920). The ordering of the clusters is determined by the combined victimizations in each cluster; within each cluster, the countries have been ranked according to the same victimization rate. Theft is the most typical victimization in all countries; robbery and assault occur less frequently among all samples. Levels of victimization by "core crimes" do vary among countries and country clusters. Overall, non-EU countries, Western Europe, and the USA appear to have higher levels of victimization by "core crimes" (defined as theft, assault, and robbery), whereas the post-Socialist countries appear to have the lowest levels of victimization.

Compared to other crime types, the prevalence of *hate crime* victimization (not shown) is not high. Across the entire sample, 4 percent reported such victimization over the past year. Of the country clusters, Western Europe showed the highest level of hate crime (6 percent), with the post-Socialist cluster (3 percent), Southern Europe, and the Balkans (4 percent) the lowest. In the full sample, 14 percent of the students have experienced *cyberbullying* during the 12-month recall period (not shown). Countries with high prevalence rates include Indonesia (30 percent), the USA (19 percent), and the Netherlands (19 percent). On the other hand, Portugal (6 percent), Armenia and India (7 percent) reported the lowest cyberbullying rates.

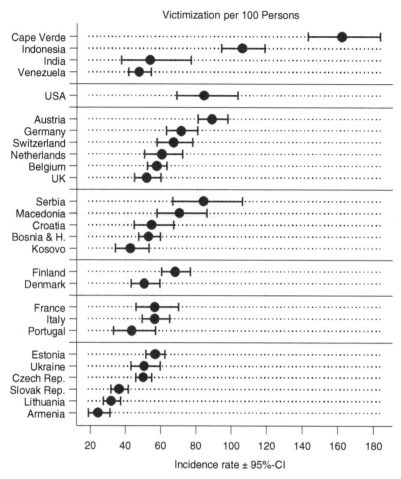

Figure 78.1. "Last year" victimization by theft, assault, and robbery.

Important findings concern the *use of physical force* by parents against their children. About one in five children reported that they have experienced parental physical force (i.e., hitting, slapping, or shoving) in the last year. There is a substantial amount of variation in the use of parental physical force; the Czech Republic (39 percent), Indonesia (31 percent), France and Italy (27 percent), Serbia (26 percent), and the USA (24 percent) rank relatively high, while only 4 percent of Danish youth reported being slapped or hit by parents.

Two other early findings (reported in Enzmann et al., 2018) based on analysis of ISRD3 data are worthy of mentioning. First, ISRD3 has incorporated a test of the impact of cultural variability on self-report responses to questions about offending. The results show that concerns about cultural variability in willingness to respond honestly are empirically supported. For example, there is substantial variation in the percentage of students who indicated that they would (definitely or probably) not admit to socially undesirable behavior such as using marijuana. Second, only a small proportion of all victimizations are reported to the police, which is consistent with other research. However, it is important to mention that there are significant national differences in the likelihood of police notification, which reinforces the caution that we should be wary of using official police records as a comparative measure of crime (Enzmann et al., 2018, p. 64).

CONCLUSIONS

The self-report method is regarded as a reliable and valid method to study delinquency and victimization (Junger-Tas & Marshall, 1999; Krohn et al., 2010). There is no doubt that the ISRD project supports this conclusion, albeit with some qualifications. In the early beginnings, ISRD1 strived towards maximum standardization in design; ISRD2 rephrased this as *flexible* standardization (Junger-Tas et al., 2010, 2012), and experiences with ISRD3 reinforce the importance of recognizing the need for incorporating culture-specific investigations (Rodríguez et al., 2016). An important lesson learned from the ISRD is that estimates of offending should not be directly compared across nations, but rather one should use estimates of victimization instead. The greatest strength of a cross-national survey such as the ISRD is in its contribution to theory-testing (Gottfredson, 2018). As the third sweep of the ISRD draws to a close, the scholarly community may be looking forward to the analysis of a large treasure trove of data on young people's experiences with crime and victimization in a range of countries across the globe.

REFERENCES

Enzmann, D., Kivivuori, J., Marshall, I. H., Steketee, M., Hough, M., & Killias, M. (2018). *A global perspective on young people as offenders and victims: First results from the ISRD3 study.* New York: Springer.

Enzmann, D., Marshall, I. H., Killias, M., Junger-Tas, J., Steketee, M., & Gruszczynska, B. (2010). Self-reported youth delinquency in Europe and beyond: First results of the Second International Self-Report Delinquency (ISRD) study in the context of police and victimization data. *European Journal of Criminology,* 7(2), 159–183.

Gottfredson, M. (2018). Foreword. In Enzmann, D., Kivivuori, J., Marshall, I. H., Steketee, M., Hough, M., & Killias, M. (Eds.), *A global perspective on young people as offenders and victims. First results from the ISRD3 study* (pp. v–viii). New York: Springer.

Junger-Tas, J. & Marshall, I. H. (1999). The self-report methodology in crime research. In M. Tonry (Ed.), *Crime and justice: A review of research* (Vol. 25, pp. 291–367). Chicago: University of Chicago Press.

Junger-Tas, J., Marshall, I. H., Enzmann, D., Killias, M., Steketee, M., & Gruszcynska, B. (Eds.). (2010). *Juvenile delinquency in Europe and beyond: Results of the Second International Self-Report Delinquency study.* Berlin and New York: Springer.

Junger-Tas, J., Marshall, I. H., Enzmann, D., Killias, M., Steketee M., & Gruszczynska, B. (2012). *The many faces of youth crime: Contrasting theoretical perspectives on juvenile delinquency across countries and cultures.* New York: Springer.

Junger-Tas, J. & Ribeaud, D., with the collaboration of Killias, M. W., Terlouw, G. J., Bruining, N., Born, M., He, N., Marshall, C., & Gatti, U. (2003). *Delinquency in an international perspective: The International Self-Reported Delinquency Study.* Amsterdam: Kugler Publications.

Junger-Tas, J., Terlouw, G. J., & Klein, M. W. (1994). *Delinquent behaviour among young people in the Western world: First results of the International Self-Report Delinquency Study.* Amsterdam: Kugler Publications.

Krohn, M. D., Thornberry, T. P., Gibson, C. L., & Baldwin, J. M. (2010). The development and impact of self-report measures of crime and delinquency. *Journal of Quantitative Criminology*, 26, 509–525.

Rodríguez, R. J., Pérez-Santiago, N., & Birkbeck, C. (2015). Surveys as cultural artefacts: Applying the International Self-Report Delinquency Study to Latin American adolescents. *European Journal of Criminology*, 12(4), 420–436.

Data Availability

The data for ISRD2 are *now freely available for download* for researchers at participating institutions on the ICPSR (Inter-university Consortium for Political and Social Research) website, including all pertinent documentation on the questionnaire and sampling procedures.

79 Advancing International and Transnational Research about Crime and Justice with Qualitative Comparative Analysis

Gregory J. Howard, Martin Gottschalk, and Graeme Newman

INTRODUCTION

Whether it is news that drone attacks in Yemen have killed civilians attending a wedding ceremony or that Russian operatives have interfered with national elections, those interested in the practice of comparative criminology can find significant fodder for their investigations in various news sources. For example, the BBC recently reported on the conviction of a South African man who killed his former girlfriend and sought to conceal the crime by burning her remains (BBC, 2018). The case highlighted South Africa's sad distinction as one of the nations with the highest rates of rape and murder of women. The BBC story cited data from 2016 that women are killed in South Africa every four hours and that more than half of these deaths are authored by intimate partners. While the global rate of femicide in 2015 was 2.4 per 100,000, the rate in South Africa was considerably higher, at 9.6 per 100,000. Why are women in South Africa victimized in this way so frequently? Are the causes of gender-based violence in South Africa the same as those in El Salvador, Jamaica, and Guatemala, where the femicide rate is even higher? What are the conditions in those countries with the lowest rates of gender-based violence? Can those conditions be replicated in other nations to prevent violence against women? We contend that criminologists engaged in comparative inquiry must employ rigorous methods to produce defensible answers to questions such as these.

This chapter will unfold in the following manner. First, drawing on the definition provided by Edwin Sutherland and Donald Cressey ([1924] 1960), the project of criminology will be unpacked. Second, attention will be directed toward the concept of comparative method, especially as it has been articulated by Charles Ragin (1987). Third, an application of Ragin's qualitative comparative analysis to the study of violent conflict over renewable resources in the global South will be considered. Finally, the chapter will advance some of the ways that qualitative comparative analysis is poised to advance international and transnational research about crime and justice.

CRIMINOLOGY AND THE COMPARATIVE METHOD

While there is considerable debate about the nature of criminology, one of the more famous declarations of the criminological project was offered by Sutherland and Cressey ([1924] 1960). According to these luminaries:

> Criminology is the body of knowledge regarding crime as a social phenomenon. It includes within its scope the processes of making laws, of breaking laws, and of reacting toward the breaking of laws [...] The objective of criminology is the development of a body of general and verified principles and of other types of knowledge regarding this process of law, crime, and treatment or prevention. (Sutherland & Cressey, 1960, p. 3)

On this view, a criminologist understands crime to be inherently social in that only some acts are deemed offensive by a collectivity through its political process. Of the limited number of acts declared criminal, some folks will persist in carrying them out; however, only a portion of these criminal trespasses will yield a social reaction in the form of an arrest or punishment. The aim of a criminologist, therefore, is to explain how criminal laws are fashioned, how some people violate these laws, and how crime control authorities sanction some of these violations. In short, law creation, criminal behavior, and social control can be called the primary dependent variables of criminology, or the social phenomena that a criminologist wishes to explain. Undertaking such an explanation, a criminologist typically employs theory. A theoretical perspective provides a criminologist with a variety of independent variables, or a set of factors that might account for the dependent variable. The promise of a comparative method is that it can guide a criminologist as she or he tries to unravel the relationship between a dependent variable and some set of independent variables (Howard, Newman, & Pridemore, 2000).

Since comparative work in criminology has been informed by developments in sociology, it might be helpful to make a brief tour of that discipline. Émile Durkheim ([1895] 1982, p. 157), who declared that "comparative sociology is [...] sociology itself," insisted that a comparative analysis should examine co-variation among social facts in various species of society. In other words, he maintained that social studies should search for an association between some dependent variable (e.g., social fact "y," say, crime) and some independent variable (e.g., social fact "x," say, income inequality) in various types of societies. For Durkheim, the comparative method was essentially a variable-based enterprise in that it relied upon statistical analysis. On the other hand, Max Weber (1949) adopted a case-based pursuit that stressed historical detail. Specifying an "ideal type" or an "ideal typical developmental sequence," a social researcher might compare actual events in a particular historical setting to this logically derived imaginative statement to reveal the special causal factors at work in a situated society. While Weber's comparative method sought social explanations for historically unique phenomena, Durkheim's comparative method pursued social explanations for universal phenomena (Kapsis, 1977). Although these two classical theorists' approaches to comparative method differed with respect to technique and theoretical objective, they agreed that the aim of the comparative method was to develop social explanations. Similarly, comparative criminology accounts for the relationship between a dependent variable, like law creation, criminal behavior, or social reaction, and an independent variable by claiming there is a special social characteristic at work (e.g., the society is democratic or religiously tolerant). Thus, "whenever an investigator's explanation makes explicit use of societal or systems level similarities or difference, he/she is engaging in comparative sociology" (Ragin, 1981, p. 107).

Although Durkheim's variable-based and Weber's case-based comparative methods have found wide application in criminology, Ragin (1987) has identified a number of shortcomings with each approach and has developed a hybrid technique that he calls "qualitative comparative analysis." While variable-based methods split cases into parts, making it difficult to understand cases as historically unique wholes and to identify multiple or conjunctional causes for phenomena, case-based methods suffer from an embarrassment of richness as the historical complexity of a case makes it tough to examine more than a handful of cases at a time and to offer generalized explanations for social phenomena. With qualitative comparative analysis, Ragin (1987, p. x) retains the advantages of a case-based strategy in that it can specify how "different conditions combine in different and sometimes contradictory ways to produce the same or similar outcomes" and he provides a means by which researchers can study hundreds of cases simultaneously, making it possible to arrive at general theoretical claims. The key to Ragin's (1987, p. 84) method is the comparison of "wholes as configurations of parts" through the use of Boolean algebra. The basic method uses dichotomous dependent and independent variables, although more sophisticated techniques such as fuzzy sets and multivalue qualitative analysis permit the use of variables with more than two categories. For each case "the typical Boolean-based comparative analysis addresses the presence/absence of conditions under which a certain outcome is obtained (that is, is true)" (Ragin, 1987, p. 86). An analysis proceeds by first constructing a "truth table" to summarize the data and then by applying the logical techniques of Boolean algebra to the data to work "from the bottom up, simplifying complexity in a methodical, stepwise manner" (Ragin, 1987, p. 101).

Ragin's qualitative comparative analysis is not without shortcomings. First, its dependence on dichotomous variables requires that a researcher divide the world into the presence or absence of theoretically meaningful features, although the complexity of the world sometimes makes this all-or-nothing rendering difficult to defend. Techniques have been developed to overcome the shortcomings of dichotomous variables, but the use of fuzzy sets and multivalue variables raises other challenges (Ide, 2015). Second, because Ragin's method stresses the combination of conditions that leads to an outcome of interest, it is not suitable for identifying the unique contribution of a particular variable to that outcome, holding constant the influence of other relevant variables. Finally, although there have been efforts to improve the ability of qualitative comparative analysis to consider the temporal aspects of variables, the method has some difficulty accounting for social change.

Using qualitative comparative analysis, Ide (2015) studied 20 cases in the global South in which intergroup conflict emerged over renewable resources such as land, water, fish, or forests. In seven of these cases, the conflict exploded into open violence in which lives were lost, while in the balance of the cases violence was not forthcoming. Given this variation, Ide (2015, p. 62) sought "to detect the conditions under which conflicts around scarce renewable resources turn violent." Building on the research literature, Ide (2015) posited that structural and triggering conditions are linked to violent conflict escalation. Structural conditions, Ide (2015, p. 62) explained, are "largely static and invariant over time," while triggering conditions "refer to short-term dynamics or 'precipitating events.'" More specifically, Ide

(2015, p. 65) nominated two structural conditions, including "negative othering" (i.e., where the majority of groups involved in a conflict see members of the other groups as "existential threats" or "vastly inferior") and "high power differences" (i.e., where one group enjoys an advantage in "hard and relational power"), as well as two triggering conditions, including "external resource appropriation" (i.e., where "access of local groups to a renewable resource" is compromised by commercialization, privatization, or state intervention) and "recent political change" (i.e., major shifts in both the "political system," such as a move to autocracy from democracy, and the "regime concerning the disputed resource," such as the legalization of communal land sales). In line with the general expectation of qualitative comparative analysis, Ide (2015, pp. 68–69) learned from his investigation that no particular condition on its own was instrumental to the outbreak of violent conflict; instead, "the simultaneous presence of two structural conditions (negative othering and low power differences) and one triggering condition (recent political change) is sufficient for the violent escalation of renewable resource conflicts." The significance of Ide's study resides in its discovery that renewable resource scarcity does not inevitably lead to violent conflict. Further, from a policy perspective, results showing that a combination of conditions prepare the ground for violent intergroup encounters suggest that it might be possible to arrest the outbreak of violence by successfully ameliorating only one of these conditions.

The applicability of the qualitative comparative method to criminology should be apparent. A criminologist would articulate an outcome for which she or he seeks an explanation (e.g., the presence or absence of the death penalty). The criminologist would then nominate the conditions thought to be associated with the outcome by considering hypotheses in the extant literature. Equipped with a set of theoretically informed dependent and independent variables, and a sense of the relationships between them, a criminologist would then examine historically situated cases. Using the procedures of Boolean algebra to simplify the complexity of the world in a theoretically defensible fashion, qualitative comparative analysis would permit a criminologist to advance elegantly the "dialogue of ideas and evidence in social research" (Ragin, 1987, p. xv).

Qualitative comparative analysis promises to advance international and transnational crime and justice research in a variety of ways. First, the technique encourages movement away from existing quantitative databases like those assembled by the United Nations and the World Health Organization with their known threats to reliability and validity (Howard, Newman, & Pridemore, 2000). Second, qualitative comparative analysis promotes a deeper appreciation for the cases under consideration so analyses are less vague and abstract (Ragin, 1987). Third, in its focus on actual outcomes, analyses conducted in the tradition of qualitative comparative analysis make it more likely that research findings will be sensible to policy makers (Bara, 2014). Fourth, with its concern for equifinality, qualitative comparative analysis stresses the possibility that multiple pathways to an outcome of interest exist (Ide, 2015). Fifth, linked to equifinality, qualitative comparative analysis recognizes that specific conditions in the world may not in themselves produce outcomes of interest, but when they are combined with other conditions, causal influence may emerge (Ide, 2015). Finally, by considering the presence and absence of an outcome of interest as independent explanatory problems, qualitative comparative analysis encourages researchers to appreciate that the absence of an outcome is not necessarily produced by the obverse of conditions that yield the presence of the outcome (Ide, 2015). Taken together, the chief advantages of qualitative comparative analysis are its capacity to manage the complexity of the world while developing in the researcher a sophisticated understanding of the particulars related to the cases under analysis.

CONCLUSION

This chapter has briefly discussed comparative criminology. After identifying several reasons for pursuing comparative inquiry, the chapter defined the criminological project and then discussed comparative method. While there are different comparative methods, common to this form of inquiry is the use of societal characteristics to explain relationships between dependent and independent variables. The chapter focused on Ragin's (1987, p. 168) qualitative comparative analysis since its synthesis of variable-based and case-based approaches to social inquiry "allows investigators both to digest many cases and to assess causal complexity." After reviewing a specific application of qualitative comparative analysis, the chapter concluded by suggesting that Ragin's comparative analysis might promote the "dialogue of ideas and evidence" in criminology and secure specific advantages for researchers engaged in international and transnational inquiries.

REFERENCES

Bara, C. (2014). Incentives and opportunities: A complexity-oriented explanation of violent ethic conflict. *Journal of Peace Research*, 51, 696–710.

BBC. (2018, May 2). South Africa's Sandile Mantsoe guilty of Karabo Mokoena murder. Retrieved from www.bbc.com/news/world-africa-43979207.

Durkheim, É. ([1895] 1982). *The rules of sociological method*. (W.D. Halls, Trans.) New York: The Free Press.

Howard, G. J., Newman, G., & Pridemore, W. A. (2000). Theory, method, and data in comparative criminology. In D. Duffee (Ed.), *Criminal justice 2000: Measurement and analysis of crime and justice*. (Vol. 4., pp. 139–211). Washington, DC: National Institute of Justice.

Ide, T. (2015). Why do conflicts over scare renewable resources turn violent? A qualitative comparative analysis. *Global Environmental Change*, 33, 61–70.

Kapsis, R. E. (1977). Weber, Durkheim, and the comparative method. *Journal of the History of the Behavioral Sciences*, 13, 354–368.

Ragin, C. C. (1981). Comparative sociology and the comparative method. *International Journal of Comparative Sociology*, 22, 102–120.

     (1987). *The comparative method: Moving beyond qualitative a quantitative strategies*. Berkeley, CA: University of California Press.

Sutherland, E. H. & Cressey, D. R. ([1924] 1960). *Principles of criminology*. Sixth Edition. Chicago: J. B. Lippincott.

Weber, M. (1949). *The methodology of the social sciences*. (E. A. Shils & H. A. Finch, Trans.) New York: The Free Press.

Cross-National Comparisons Based on Official Statistics of Crime

Marcelo F. Aebi

INTRODUCTION

This chapter presents the main methodological challenges faced by cross-national comparisons based on official statistics of crime, which include police, prosecution, conviction, and correctional statistics. As these statistics measure the reaction to crime and not crime itself, comparisons based on them are usually called comparisons of recorded crime.

Each country has its own specific rules for constructing and producing official crime statistics. As a consequence, cross-national differences in recorded crime rates – commonly presented in the form of rates of offences, suspects, offenders, inmates, or sanctions and measures imposed per 100,000 inhabitants – do not reflect actual differences in the *levels* of crime, but on the construction of the statistics. Hence, the main task of the criminologists working in this kind of comparison is to collect *metadata*, which consist of information about the way in which official crime statistics are elaborated in the countries under study.

BACKGROUND INFORMATION

The main sources for cross-national comparisons of recorded crime are presented in another section of this book. We have illustrated this chapter with examples from the *European Sourcebook of Crime and Criminal Justice Statistics* (Aebi et al., 2014), the *United Nations Surveys on Crime Trends and the Operations of Criminal Justice Systems* (UNCTS) (Harrendorf et al., 2010), and the *Council of Europe Annual Penal Statistics* (SPACE) (Aebi et al., 2018). The *European Sourcebook* was the first collection to include, in 1999, a methodological section with *metadata*. That section, which presents the main rules applied in each country for the construction of its official statistics, was later incorporated to the UNCTS. Since the 2004 annual survey, SPACE also includes a methodological section with metadata that allows understanding how prison statistics are elaborated in different countries.

FACTORS INFLUENCING THE OUTCOME OF OFFICIAL CRIME STATISTICS

Difficulties in cross-national comparisons based on official statistics are due to the influence of four types of factors: legal, statistical, criminal policy, and substantive (Aebi, 2010).

- *Legal factors* refer to the way in which offences are defined in the criminal law of different countries and to the characteristics of their criminal justice systems.
- *Statistical factors* refer to the way in which crime statistics are elaborated. In that context we define the statistical counting rules as the rules applied in each country to count the offences and offenders that will be included in official statistics.
- *Criminal policy factors* relate to the crime and crime prevention policies applied in a country.
- *Substantive factors* refer to the actual levels of crime in each country – which are in fact the ones that the researcher is trying to compare – as well as to the propensity to report offences by the population and the propensity to record offences by the police or other recording authorities.

These factors introduce artificial differences in the levels of recorded crime. As a consequence, before conducting any comparison, researchers must scrutinize the way in which they affect the statistics of the countries under study.

METHODOLOGICAL PROBLEMS RELATED TO THE COMPARISON OF OFFICIAL CRIME STATISTICS

This section presents the main ways in which the previous four factors, acting alone or in combination, introduce distortions in national crime rates. The aim is to provide the researcher with concrete examples of the issues that need to be controlled for when conducting any comparison of crime rates. These examples are taken mainly from Aebi and Linde (2010 and 2012), Farrington et al. (2004), Jehle and Aebi (2018), Robert (2009), and Wade and Jehle (2008).

- **Offence Type**
  Most countries have two main categories of offences: crimes and misdemeanors. Usually – but not always – both are presented separately in police statistics, and, typically, the ones used for cross-national comparisons are the ones that include only crimes. Nevertheless, the criteria applied to distinguish crimes from misdemeanors vary across countries and across time. For example, since 1999, the total number of recorded crimes in Finland is extremely high because it includes all road traffic violations, while in other countries the vast majority of these violations are counted as misdemeanors.
- **Definitions of Offences**
  Manslaughter is a typical example of how legal definitions vary from country to country. This is a common-law offence, but it is not conceptualized homogeneously in the USA, the UK, Australia, and Canada. Consequently, it can fall into different categories when the researcher tries to find its equivalent in civil law countries, where it could correspond to *praeter-intentional* homicide, which only exists in a few countries, to assault leading to death, or to negligent or involuntary homicide.
  Indeed, the translation of the name of some offences is a problem in itself. For example, robbery is considered a violent crime in common law countries and a crime against property (often known as theft with violence against persons) in civil law countries. Similarly, burglary requires the intention to commit any offence in common law

countries, but in civil law nations the most similar concept would be theft with force against property, which by definition requires that the intention is to commit a theft.

- **Subcategories Included in Each Offence**
  The subcategories of the offences included in official statistics can vary according to the legal definitions of the offences or the statistical counting rules applied in each country. For example, the total number of rapes may or may not include violent intramarital intercourse, sexual intercourse with force – or without force – with a minor or a helpless person, homosexual rape, incest, and acts that the country considers as comparable to sexual intercourse. Sweden includes all these subcategories and consequently has the highest European rate of officially recorded rape.

- **Attempts**
  In Scotland or the Netherlands, attempts usually represent more than 80 percent of the total number of intentional homicides registered in police statistics, while in Ireland or Lithuania they usually represent less than 10 percent of them, and in the USA they are not included in the total. Thus, crime rates are affected not only by the inclusion or exclusion of attempts, but also by the rules applied in each country to decide whether a behavior should be counted as an attempt of the most serious offence at stake (e.g., homicide) or as a completed offence of a less serious kind (e.g., aggravated assault).

- **Overarching Offences**
  The rise of cybercrime since the 1990s passed almost unnoticed by criminologists, who were focused on explaining the drop in traditional crime. Cybercrime poses a problem because it is an overarching category that includes *cyber-dependent crimes*, which can only be committed through the Internet (like hacking, viruses, or malware infections), as well as *cyber-enabled crimes*, which correspond to traditional crimes that are committed through the Internet (like cyberbullying, online child pornography, or financial and credit card fraud). The latter can also be committed partially online and partially offline. This leads to a tripartite classification of offences in offline (or traditional), online, and hybrid (which combine an offline and an online component) crimes (Caneppele & Aebi, 2017). The same is true for domestic violence, which also includes a wide set of behaviors, ranging from verbal threats to homicide. A promising solution that is being implemented in some countries is to *flag* in police statistics the crimes that have a cyber component, or that take place between current or former intimate partners, in order to establish at least the proportion of such crimes.

- **Time of Data Recording for Statistical Purposes**
  In some countries, data are recorded in police statistics when the offence is reported to the police (input statistics); in others, data are recorded when the police have completed the investigation (output statistics); in between these extremes, some countries record data at an intermediate stage of the police investigation (intermediate statistics). In that perspective, research has shown that, since the number of offences registered by official measures of crime decreases as the criminal process advances, countries using input statistics tend to present higher crime rates than countries using output statistics.

- **Counting Unit**
  As police statistics usually inform about the number of offences as well as the number of offenders, it would seem logical to presume that they use, respectively, the offence and the offender as their counting units. However, that is not necessarily true. For example,

in the case of homicides, many countries use the victim as the counting unit. Similarly, in court statistics, the counting unit can be the person convicted or the conviction, which may include several persons.

- **Principal Offence Rule**
  If in the course of theft an offender also produces damages to the property and tries to kill a person, official statistics of countries applying a principal offence rule will show only one – the most serious – offence (i.e., attempted homicide), while in countries where there is no such rule, each offence (attempted homicide, damages to the property, and theft) will be counted separately.

- **Serial Offences**
  Offences of the same kind committed by the same person during a certain time can be counted in different ways. For example, if a woman reports to the police that her partner has beaten her 24 times during the last 12 months, Germany will count only one offence, but Sweden will count 24 offences.

- **Multiple Offenders**
  In some countries, the number of offenders engaged in an offence can play a role in the number of offences recorded. Thus, if a gang of five young people attacks one person, most countries will count one offence, but some will count five.

- **Categories of Persons Included in the Total Number of Offenders**
  In their police statistics, some countries include minors and others exclude them; moreover, the lower and upper limits to be considered a minor vary across countries. In correctional statistics, differences arise from the inclusion or exclusion of some categories of persons in the total number of prisoners, namely pre-trial detainees, persons held in facilities that do not depend on the prison administration (e.g., police stations), persons held in units for juvenile offenders, persons held in institutions for drug-addicted offenders, offenders with psychological disorders, asylum seekers or illegal aliens held for administrative reasons, and offenders serving their sentence under electronic monitoring.

- **Opportunity and Legality Principle**
  Some countries apply the opportunity principle, which consists in giving the prosecution authorities discretionary powers that allow them to refrain from prosecution for some offences and under certain conditions, or to apply diversion measures or alternatives to prosecution. Other countries apply the legality principle, which forces the prosecuting authorities to prosecute whenever an offence has been committed and there is a suspect.

- **Reporting Rates**
  Victimization surveys have shown that the rate of offences reported to the police varies according to the offence, but also across countries and across time. Thus, the researcher can improve comparability by weighting the official statistics according to the percentage of offences reported to the police in each country.

- **Recording Rates**
  The few empirical studies available on this topic suggest that the percentage of reported offences that are effectively recorded by the police can vary according to the offence. In particular, property offences are registered far more frequently than personal offences.

- **Changes in Legal, Statistical, or Criminal Policy Factors**
  These changes modify the time series for an offence in such a way that sometimes it is impossible to establish the evolution of the offence during the period studied. For example, the introduction of a zero-tolerance policy should lead, at least in the short term, to an increase in the number of offences recorded by the police, because each minor offence will be included in the statistics. Similarly, the introduction of a new statistical program to register offences usually leads to artificial changes in crime rates. Sometimes, these factors combine themselves, as it happened in Spain, where domestic violence became a criminal policy priority since the late 1990s. This led to an increase in the number of domestic violence-related assaults reported to the police, to a stricter recording of them in police statistics, and to several changes in the law that implied extending the categories of acts and victims included under that heading, as well as transforming all misdemeanors into crimes. As a consequence, the number of such assaults recorded in police statistics was multiplied by four from 2002 to 2010.

SUMMARY AND CONCLUSION

As a rule, differences in recorded crime rates across countries are explained by the way in which official statistics are constructed, which in turn depends on legal, statistical, criminal policy, and substantive factors. This means that differences in recorded crime rates do not reflect actual differences in the levels of crime, but are mainly due to methodological reasons.

Hence, for comparative criminologists, metadata are as important as data. Metadata on the influence of the four factors mentioned above on official statistics is fundamental because it allows applying some corrections to the official crime rates in order to improve comparability. For example, it is sometimes possible to compare countries that use similar statistical counting rules, or to adapt the data of different countries by keeping only some specific subcategories of offences. Thus, it is reasonable to compare completed intentional homicide – excluding attempts – through official statistics, especially if they are counterchecked with data from the WHO Mortality Database. Another interesting technique in order to improve cross-national comparisons consists in using data from victimization surveys to weight the number of offences recorded by the police according to their reporting rates. Finally, official statistics are particularly useful for the study of crime trends provided the researcher collects information that allows controlling for changes across time in the factors presented in this chapter.

REFERENCES

Aebi, M. F. (2010). Methodological issues in the comparison of police recorded crime rates. In S. Shoham, P. Knepper, & M. Kett (Eds.), *International handbook of criminology* (pp. 209–226). London: Routledge.

Aebi, M. F. & Linde, A. (2010). Is there a crime drop in Western Europe? *European Journal on Criminal Policy and Research*, 16(4), 251–277.

(2012). Conviction statistics as an indicator of crime trends in Europe from 1990 to 2006. *European Journal on Criminal Policy and Research*, 18(1), 103–144.

Aebi, M. F., Akdeniz, G., Barclay, G., Campistol, C., Caneppele, S., Harrendorf, B., ... & Kensey, A. (2014). *European sourcebook of crime and criminal justice statistics 2014*. Fifth Edition. HEUNI Publication Series 80. Helsinki: Heuni.

Aebi, M. F., Tiago, M. M., Berger-Kolopp, L., & Burkhardt, C.(2018). *Council of Europe annual penal statistics*. Strasbourg: Council of Europe.

Caneppele, S. & Aebi, M. F. (2017). Crime drop or police recording flop? On the relationship between the decrease of offline crime and the increase of online and hybrid crimes. *Policing: A Journal of Policy and Practice*. Online first.

Farrington D. P., Langan, P. A., & Tonry, M. (Eds.). (2004) *Cross-national studies in crime and justice*. Washington, DC: Bureau of Justice Statistics, US Department of Justice.

Harrendorf, S., Heiskanen, M., & Malby, S. (2010). *International statistics on crime and justice*. HEUNI Publication Series 64. Helsinki and Vienna: HEUNI and UNODC.

Jehle, J.-M. & Aebi, M. F. (Eds.). (2018). Special issue on crime and criminal justice in Europe. *European Journal on Criminal Policy and Research*, 24(1), 3–119.

Robert, P. (Ed.). (2009). *Comparing crime data in Europe: Official crime statistics and survey based data*. Brussels: VUBPRESS Brussels University Press.

Wade, M. & Jehle, J. M. (Eds.). (2008). Special issue on prosecution and diversion within criminal justice systems in Europe. *European Journal on Criminal Policy and Research*, 14(2–3), 161–237.

81   Cross-National Measures of Punitiveness

Alfred Blumstein

Punitiveness is often an issue that enters political debate in a country, with the liberal Left usually calling for less, and the conservative Right usually demanding more. As with most issues that enter polarizing debate, there could well be conflict over how to measure "punitiveness."

Incarceration rate, or prisoners per capita, is typically used as the primary measure of a nation's punitiveness. But measuring punitiveness is inherently more complicated. It is possible, for example, that a country developed a high incarceration rate because it has a high crime rate. That might encourage one to measure punitiveness as the incarceration rate per serious crime. But it may be that solving crimes in that country is particularly difficult because police are less competent, or perhaps because the public is less helpful to the police in solving crimes. Thus, one might augment the measures with incarceration rates per arrest. Even this measure will depend on the discretion allowed police in moving cases forward to prosecution. If such constraints are very stringent, then one might turn to the incarceration probability per conviction as a tighter measure of punitiveness. Going still further, a reasonable measure of punitiveness could be the expected time served per crime or per conviction. This last measure would take account of the duration of the sentence as well as the probability of commitment conditional on a crime, an arrest, or a conviction.

This chapter will provide an array of measures that have been explored cross-nationally in Blumstein et al. (2005), based on cross-national data collected by Tonry and Farrington (2005). Their data covers eight countries (the UK, Scotland, the USA, Australia, Canada, Sweden, the Netherlands, and Switzerland) and six crime types (homicide, rape, robbery, vehicle theft, residential burglary, and assault). One limitation is that some crime-type definitions vary across the different countries. For example, some countries include under robbery all thefts while others include only thefts associated with force or threat of force.

MEASURES BY CRIME TYPE

Figures 81.1a, 81.1b, and 81.1c provide different measures of punitiveness for three different crime types: murder, robbery, and burglary. In each figure we present the expected time served per crime and per conviction. For murder (Figure 81.1a), we see that the clearance rate is fairly high in all the countries, and the transition of expected time served from crime to conviction is not very large. That suggests that clearance rates are fairly high (perhaps somewhat lower in the USA and Australia), and the expected time served for most of the countries

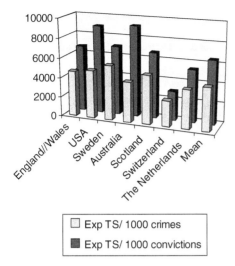

Figure 81.1.a Expected time served per 1,000 murder crimes and convictions (years).

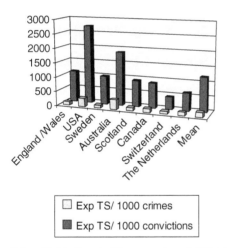

Figure 81.1.b Expected time served per 1,000 robbery crimes and convictions.

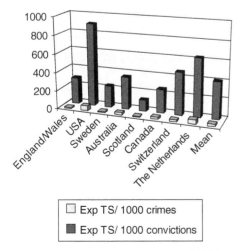

Figure 81.1.c Expected time served per 1,000 burglary crimes.

averages about seven years. Switzerland is the least punitive for murder, averaging about 2.5 years per conviction and almost as much per crime, suggesting a very high clearance and conviction rate.

For robbery (Figure 81.1b), we see that the USA is the most punitive per conviction (about 2.5 years) and also fairly high, along with Australia, for punitiveness per crime. In contrast to murder, where the two measures are fairly close, there is a much greater discrepancy between the punitiveness per conviction and the punitiveness per crime, largely reflecting much greater failures of arrest and conviction for robbery compared to murder. For burglary (Figure 81.1c), where the probability of commitment per conviction is relatively low, the expected time served is appreciably less, covering a range of about 0.1 years per conviction in Scotland and 0.9 years in the USA. Here, the difference between expected time served per crime and per conviction is much greater than for robbery, largely reflecting the fact that clearance rates for burglary are very low and, even for those convicted, incarceration is less than likely. While the various countries seem quite comparable in their punitiveness for murder (except, possibly, Switzerland), as we move to the less serious crimes where there is much greater room for discretion, we see much greater variation across the different countries. Here, the USA continues to stay on top with the highest expected time served per crime and per conviction.

FACTORS ACCOUNTING FOR THE RISE OF INCARCERATION

The growth of incarceration is attributed largely to changes in the political environment associated with crime. It is possible, however, that other factors, such as an increase in crime, could be contributing, and, if that were the case, then the growth of incarceration would not necessarily be indicative of a growth in punitiveness. Blumstein and Beck (1999, 2005) examined this issue in the USA by identifying factors that could be contributing to the rise in incarceration from 1980. They examined the growth in incarceration for six crime types (murder, robbery, assault, sexual assault, burglary, and drug offenses), which account for 75–80 percent of the prison population. The incarceration rate per 100,000 adults in the USA for each of these crime types over the period 1980–2001 indicates that each of these crime types increased over that period, with the growth of drug offenders in prison being the most dramatic.

Blumstein and Beck then examined for each of these crime types whether the growth was attributable to more crime, to more arrests per crime, to more commitments per arrest, or to longer time served in prison, including time served by parole violators. The basic conclusion was that the entire growth came from more commitments per arrest and from longer time served, the two major policy choices. In the early part of the period (1980–1993), these two policy factors contributed roughly equally to the growth in incarceration, but with a stronger emphasis on commitment; in the later period (1994–2001), the contribution of time served was about twice that of commitments per arrest. Initially, the effect was seen as sending more people to prison and later a reflection that they are spending more time in prison. There was no net effect of changes in crimes (some went up and others went down) and there was absolutely no trend in arrests per crime. This lack of an effect of arrests per crime was somewhat surprising, since we anticipated that improvements in policing (e.g., more education, more research on police operations, more skillful management, better forensics) would have shown themselves in an increase in arrests per crime, but that did not seem to occur.

The most striking observation is the dramatic ten-fold growth of incarceration for drug offenses. This reflected a response to increasing pressure from the public for the political system to "do something" about the drug problem, and the only response the political system seemed able to find was to increase incarceration. In contrast to many European countries, which saw the drug problem as a public health issue, the USA posed it as a moral issue, and so the natural response was incarceration.

Another feature of the political environment surrounding punitiveness in the USA is the emergence of what has been called a "prison-industrial complex" (Schlosser, 1998), drawing on the metaphor used by President Eisenhower in his warning of a "military-industrial complex" in his presidential address. When incarceration rates were low and under the control of the criminal justice system, then the politics of those with a stake in incarceration were relatively weak. As incarceration has grown as an economic activity, the influence of those involved in that activity has grown correspondingly. In California, for example, the prison guards' union is known to be the largest contributor to gubernatorial campaigns. In New York, where prison populations have recently declined, a newly elected governor felt he could find resources to meet the state's other needs by closing some prisons. He was met with vigorous criticism by many of the rural legislators of his state who emphasized the importance of prisons to the economic vitality of their regions, and especially those regions which had lost significant manufacturing industry to other countries (Confessore, 2007). The economic interests of a growing number of stakeholders can thus rally with the always-present public concern about crime (in accord with the observation of journalism that "if it bleeds, it leads") and the resulting call for more punishment of offenders.

Rallying support for punishment is much easier if the public thinks of the offenders as an identifiable separate group, and especially if they can point to such groups as comprising a different ethnicity. The USA is composed of a wide range of ethnic subpopulations. One of the largest of such groups are the African-Americans, who are visually distinguishable and are disproportionately incarcerated. Their incarceration rate is about seven times that of whites, although the comparison group of whites includes Hispanics (another significant minority-population group that may even be larger than African-Americans) with a higher incarceration rate than non-Hispanic whites. This heterogeneity could thus be an important factor affecting the majority public's interest in accepting a high incarceration rate.

Alesina and Glaeser (2004) have shown that homogeneous societies provide more welfare services and public goods than do the more heterogeneous societies. As it is put by Alesina and La Ferrara (2005), "altruism does not travel well across ethnic lines." It is easy to see how such concepts could apply to punitiveness. In a more homogeneous society it is easy to be merciful or "altruistic" to others who are similar but may have sinned. To the extent that the sinner is of a different ethnicity, it becomes much easier to bring the differences to mind, to attribute the failings to a group failing, and to treat the offender with greater abstraction and harshness. This phenomenon opens an important potential area for research. One might examine the ethnic heterogeneity of different states and assess their relationship to the state's punitiveness, considering the differential punitiveness to the majority and minority offenders in each state or nation.

CONCERN ABOUT OTHER COUNTRIES PATTERNING THEIR PUNITIVENESS ON THE US MODEL

Given its role as a leader in entertainment and media generally, and in news media particularly, it seems reasonable to be concerned about the degree to which patterns of punitiveness established in the USA are transmitted internationally. As politicians in other democracies see the political success of the "tough on crime" rhetoric, it seems reasonable to anticipate that they could be tempted to follow similar patterns. There is already some indication that these trends are working their way internationally from incarceration data maintained by the World Prison Brief at King's College, London. Using these data, Table 81.1 provides information on incarceration rates (prisoners per 100,000 population) for industrialized democratic countries in 1992 and 2009. Table 81.1 presents the percentage change over those 17 years. The groupings are two countries with low rates initially, two countries with high rates, the Scandinavian countries with relatively homogeneous low rates, and a variety of other countries in Europe. Within each group, the countries are ranked by their percentage change.

The first observation from Table 81.1 is that all of the 18 countries, except Switzerland (with a 4-percent decrease) and Denmark (with no change), had a positive increase over that 17-year interval, and all but one (Finland, with a 3-percent increase) with double digits. Only one had a decline (although some did have declines within the interval but ended up with a net positive growth). The two countries with very low rates in 1992, the Netherlands and Japan, ended up with very high rates of growth; the Netherlands' rate grew by 104 percent and Japan's rate grew by 66 percent, and Japan was exceeded only by Turkey (with a growth rate of 85 percent), Spain (grew by 80 percent), and England/Wales (grew by 74 percent). The two countries with very high rates, the USA and Russia, far exceeded all the others with rates of 723 per 100,000 for the USA and 587 for Russia; however, their growth rates over this interval were relatively modest.

It is clear from this table that incarceration rates increased widely over that interval, very modestly in some places but rather sharply in others. The sharpest increases seem to have occurred in some places that started with the lowest rates, and those low rates could well have provided the ammunition to the political process for demanding increases. While the table certainly does not indicate that political escalation of punitiveness is universal, it does indicate that some European countries, with the likely exception of Scandinavia, do seem to be breaking out of what had previously been a reasonably homeostatic process into a politicized one.

Examination of later data from the 2018 World Prison Brief permits deeper examination of these processes. The later rates are in between the 1992 and 2009 rates for the two low-rate countries, but their earlier rates left plenty of in-between room for that. Among the high-rate countries, the USA came down to an in-between rate of 655 and Russia came just below its earlier rate with 411. In Scandinavia, the rates were in the same range as previously, with Norway slightly above 2009 and the others slightly below 1992. The "Other Europe" countries were predominantly in-between, which means below the 2009 rates, except that France, Portugal, and Switzerland, which had small changes between 1992 and 2009, had small positive changes in 2018. The striking exception to this pattern of small changes was Turkey; its dramatic political changes brought another increase of 78 percent to a rate of 287, the highest

Table 81.1. Trends in incarceration rates in various countries

	1992 Rates	2009 Rates	% Change
Low Rates in 1992			
The Netherlands	49	100	104%
Japan	38	63	66%
Average	*43.5*	*81.5*	*85%*
High Rates in 1992			
The USA	505	723	50%
Russia	487	587	27%
Average	*496*	*655*	*39%*
Scandinavia			
Sweden	63	74	17%
Norway	58	70	21%
Finland	65	67	3%
Denmark	66	66	0%
Average	*63*	*69.25*	*10%*
Other Europe			
Turkey	54	161	198%
Spain	90	162	80%
England/Wales	88	153	74%
Poland	153	224	46%
Scotland	105	148	41%
Germany	71	90	27%
Italy	81	97	20%
France	84	96	14%
Portugal	93	104	12%
Switzerland	79	76	-4%
Average	*89.8*	*131.1*	*51%*

in Europe other than Russia. Further political analysis of the processes in the individual countries will provide for a sharper assessment of the factors contributing to the changes.

SUMMARY AND CONCLUSIONS

While punitiveness is most often measured by incarceration rates, there can be many components other than a desire for punishment contributing to a high incarceration rate. These can include more crime, greater police effectiveness in solving crimes, and more aggressive prosecution. The most direct effects on incarceration rate as indicators of punitiveness would include longer sentences given by judges and more restriction on release and resentencing by parole officials. The problem in a democracy, when the public becomes anxious about crime and presses elected officials to "do something" about the crime problem, the response from the very limited repertoire of available responses almost always shows itself as greater punitiveness by sending more people to prison and for a longer time. This has certainly characterized the USA, which had a stable imprisonment rate of 110 per 100,000 population for at least 50 years while punishment was under the control of the criminal justice system, but which now has a rate that is much more influenced by the political environment and is subsequently almost five times higher, making it the world leader in incarceration rate. Because this stance of being "tough on crime" has worked so well for political officials in the USA, there is considerable concern and some reasonable indications that this model has propagated to other countries. One would hope that fiscal pressures at least would serve to restrain those propagating influences.

Note: this chapter draws heavily on Blumstein, A., "The roots of punitiveness in a democracy," *Journal of Scandinavian Studies in Criminology and Crime Prevention*, 8, 2–16 (2007), which was based on the author's plenary address upon receiving the 2007 Stockholm Prize in Criminology.

REFERENCES

Alesina, A. & Glaeser, E. (2004). *Fighting poverty in the US and Europe: A world of difference.* Oxford: Oxford University Press.

Alesina, A. & La Ferrara, E. (2005). Ethnic diversity and economic performance. *Journal of Economic Literature*, 43(2), 762–800.

Blumstein, A. & Beck, A. J. (1999). Population growth in US prisons, 1980–1996. In M. Tonry & J. Petersilia (Eds.), *Crime and justice* (Vol. 26, pp. 17–61). Chicago: University of Chicago Press.

  (2005). Reentry as a transient state between liberty and recommitment. In J. Travis & C. Visher (Eds.), *Prisoner reentry and crime in America.* (pp. 50–79). Cambridge: Cambridge University Press.

Blumstein, A., Tonry, M., & Van Ness, A. (2005). Criminal justice processing as measures of punitiveness. In M. Tonry & D. P. Farrington (Ed.), *Crime and justice: An annual review of research* (Vol. 33, pp. 347–376). Chicago: University of Chicago Press.

Confessore, N. (2007, February 5). Spitzer seeks ways to find state prisons he can close. *The New York Times.*

Schlosser, E. (1998, December). The prison-industrial complex. *Atlantic Monthly.*

Tonry, M. & Farrington, D. P. (2005). Punishment and crime across space and time. *Crime and Justice*, 33, 1–39.

Phyllis A. Schultze

INTRODUCTION

The World Criminal Justice Library Network (WCJLN) is a group of librarians and information specialists with members from more than 30 countries, representing academic institutions, government and nongovernment organizations, and research institutes, together with individual scholars. The Network was established at a meeting at Rutgers University, Newark, New Jersey, in April 1991 and has grown to be an influential contributor to the communication and the dissemination of information in the field of criminology and criminal justice. This paper provides background to the establishment of the Network, a description of its services, and an outline of the development of its services.

ESTABLISHMENT OF THE WORLD CRIMINAL JUSTICE LIBRARY NETWORK

The specific idea for establishing the network was the brainchild of Ronald V. Clarke, then Dean of the School of Criminal Justice at Rutgers University, Newark, New Jersey, and, prior to that, head of the Criminal Justice Research Department of the British Home Office. He was joined by Professor Graeme Newman, a distinguished professor in the School of Criminal Justice at the State University of New York at Albany. Both had a substantial standing in the criminal justice community and are prolific scholars. They were well aware of the need for the dissemination of a wide range of criminal justice literature for practitioners, academics, think-tank researchers, and other interested parties.

The Don M. Gottfredson Library of Criminal Justice at Rutgers University was chosen as the venue for the first meeting of the network. This library is considered to be a leading academic information provider in the area of criminology and criminal justice in the USA. Librarians from around the world attended this initial meeting, and the network was firmly established. Subsequent meetings were held every two years, with the last physical meeting being held in 2010. However, with the utilization of the Internet, emails, and blogs, the network continues to be a vital resource for all of its members.

So, why was the network started? Realizing that not all libraries have access to the vast range of criminal justice literature, WCJLN was established to address this issue. This was one of the primary mandates emanating from the initial meeting. Although many of the libraries represented include outstanding criminal justice collections, a number of others were from smaller universities that would greatly enhance their resources by drawing upon the collections and expertise of specialized libraries.

So, what is done by the organization? We started out as a small group in 1991 that wanted to share information more broadly. For some, this meant direct communication between members. For others, it represented an opportunity to exchange documents via interlibrary loans, reports, and related information that would serve our clientele with the research that they needed to perform their academic research. For some, it meant sending out an occasional blog or newsletter to inform the wider community of happenings in their particular country, or even of important reports from the wider world. A few started a "gray" literature database, thus creating a virtual catalog of documents not generally available via the traditional cataloging and abstracting/indexing services.

WORLD CRIMINAL JUSTICE LIBRARY ELECTRONIC NETWORK

The Network was enhanced greatly by the development of a WCJLN website hosted at Rutgers University. The website, entitled The World Criminal Justice Library Network, benefits Network members as well as students and academics researching international criminal justice topics. For members there is a directory of WCJLN member libraries; in addition, there are features such as links to online library catalogs, statistical resources, general reference sources, bibliographies, online periodicals, online databases, and information on forthcoming conferences.

The links to the online catalogs of major criminal justice libraries are an important feature of the website. These catalogs include those for the Australian Institute of Criminology, the Institute of Criminology at Cambridge, the US National Institute of Corrections, and the Rutgers Law Library Catalog at Newark (incorporating the Criminal Justice Library holdings), as well as several other noteworthy collections.

As well as listing library holdings, some of the catalogs also provide links to full-text documents or abstracts of materials contained in their collection.

The Australian Institute of Criminology provides links to a number of bibliographies, a listing of online journals and reports, and other databases and online resources. The Library of the National Institute of Corrections (Robert J. Kutak Memorial Library) regularly abstracts unpublished materials; in addition, a link is provided to the full-text for most documents. Library items include research reports, program evaluations, journal articles, monographs, and published books.

Another feature of the WCJLN website are the links it provides to online periodicals. An increasing number of periodicals are providing access to at least an abstract of their articles, and, in some cases, access to the full text of the publication. Some of these are web-based only, with no print edition available.

INTERACTING WITH ONE ANOTHER

Here are a few of the ways that we are interacting with each other and some of the libraries involved.

Australian Institute of Criminology (J.V. Barry Library). This Library was established in 1974 with a focus on research, training, and information work. The Institute publishes a number of documents, most notably the *Trends & Issues in Crime and Criminal Justice*. The library produces a reference database, CINCH, The Australian Criminology Database, which includes materials covering all aspects of Australian criminal justice. The database includes books, journal articles, and reports that are indexed, abstracted, and made available through the library catalog. A new initiative of the library with support from the Australasian Libraries in Emergency and Security (ALIES) is the establishment of an open-access, full-text database of gray literature focusing on policing and law enforcement.

University of Tuebingen, Institute of Criminology. Since 1969, the Institute of Criminology, in close cooperation with the Tuebingen University Library, has been responsible for the German national criminology library (*Bibliotheksschwerpunkt Kriminologie*). Together with a range of services, the library has developed the KrimDok database with references to more than 100,000 documents (German-language and foreign). Access to the database is free of charge through the Institute's website. Professor Hans-Jürgen Kerner is Director of the Institute of Criminology, and full Professor at the Faculty of Law, University of Tuebingen (Germany), with special responsibility for the fields of criminology, juvenile (penal) law, corrections (including prison law), and penal procedure. Professor Kerner helped develop the new *Fachinformationsdienst Kriminologie* (FID-KRIM, Scientific Information and Documentation and Delivery Service Criminology). This is a collaborative endeavor of the University Library and the Institute of Criminology of the University of Tuebingen, Germany. The collaboration is based on a nationwide new system of literature and documentation supply service for scholars of different scientific disciplines and sub-disciplines, as created by the Deutsche Forschungsgemeinschaft DFG (German Research Association, Library and Documentation Division). KRIM-INFO is being broadly conceived, in particular regarding criminology and criminal policy, crime and crime control, youth delinquency and youth justice, crime prevention, victimology, corrections, sentencing, and restorative justice. Open newsletters (any person or institution can subscribe, and always without charge) include *Criminology and Criminal Justice News* (*CCJ-News*), in English, which currently has some 11,000 recipients worldwide.

The newsletter *Kriminologischer Informationsdienst* (*KrimInfo-News*), which is only published in German, has some 3,500 recipients, mainly in Europe.

National Criminal Justice Reference Service (NCJRS)

NCJRS was created in 1972 by the National Institute of Justice, within the US Department of Justice, to provide information for Department of Justice agencies. Since then the NCJRS network has been extended and provides indexes, abstracts, and documents in many areas of criminology and criminal justice. The free *NCJRS Database* indexes journal articles, books, and research reports on criminology and criminal justice back to 1970.

On October 1, 2014, the NCJRS Virtual Library began to focus primarily on the collection of informational materials and resources produced, funded, and/or sponsored by the bureaus and offices of the US Department of Justice, Office of Justice Programs (OJP). All materials housed in the NCJRS Virtual Library prior to October 2014 will remain searchable in the abstracts database and accessible through virtual library services.

Sydney Institute of Criminology, University of Sydney. CrimNet is a weekly electronic criminal justice e-newsletter, sponsored by the Sydney Institute of Criminology at the University of Sydney. It provides regular communication between criminal justice professionals, academics, and students in Australia and overseas.

Rutgers University – Don M. Gottfredson Library of Criminal Justice. Criminal Justice Gray Literature Database. In 2008, the library established a *Criminal Justice Gray Literature Database.* Realizing the importance of providing ready access to the ever-increasing world of "gray" literature, the library took on the task of trying to make these publications freely available to WCJNL members, as well as to the larger criminal justice community. As of 2018, the database includes over 21,000 documents. Each entry includes title, author, and publishing information, as well as a synopsis of the documents and a URL connection to the publication at the time that the entry was made. In addition, a paper copy is added to the Don M. Gottfredson Collection.

In addition, the librarian acts as the managing editor of *Criminal Law and Criminal Justice Books* (clcjbooks.rutgers.edu). This online journal is a joint project of Rutgers School of Law and Rutgers School of Criminal Justice. It features expert and concise reviews of significant books in criminal law, criminal procedure, and criminal justice, written by top scholars in the field. This listserv is open to all.

Institute of Criminology, Cambridge University (Radzinowicz Library). The library was founded in 1960 and named after Sir Leon Radzinowicz, the first director of the Institute (from 1959 to 1972). The library houses the most comprehensive criminology collection in the United Kingdom and is internationally recognized as a world-class criminal justice resource. The library publishes a list of recently cataloged items that is sent to WCJLN members.

WCJLN TODAY

Today, the organization includes over 70 members from all spheres of criminal justice. Although the vast majority of members are librarians, the list includes researchers representing various organizations, criminal justice faculty, and other interested individuals.

In conclusion, Sir Leon Radzinowicz, founding director of the Institute of Criminology at Cambridge University, wrote in his memoirs of the establishment of the Institute's Library:

> At the first meeting on the Advisory Council of the Institute in 1961, Lord Nathan emphat-
> ically stated that "the creation of a library is of the first importance by the Wolfson
> Foundation" [a benefactor offering generous financial support to the Institute]. And Lady
> Wootton reinforced it by "expressing the hope that the library would be made available to
> scholars from all over the world."

Nearly 50 years on, the members of that Advisory Council are likely to have viewed with satisfaction the developments in technology that would now enable the catalog of a library such as the Radzinowicz Library to be searched from different parts of the globe. In addition, they would be encouraged by the cooperative spirit that enables the Institute's librarians to be active contributors to the World Criminal Justice Library Network.

There is no doubting the progress in achieving these ends; the energy and commitment of members, together with unforeseen progress in technological innovation, has meant that the World Criminal Justice Library Network has significantly advanced the dissemination of criminal justice information worldwide.

83 Printed and Electronic Media, Journals, and Professional Associations

Maria Kiriakova

INTRODUCTION

International criminal justice is still a relatively new field of study and, despite the fact that it is closely related to comparative criminal justice, it also includes components from such academic disciplines as politics and economics, sociology and anthropology, criminology and law, gender studies and linguistics, and many others. The multidisciplinary nature of the field makes it practically impossible to provide the researcher with a definite list of resources. This chapter supplies a vast array of library resources and techniques that could assist in international crime and justice research.

LOOKING FOR INFORMATION

Depending on your research topic, you may be able to locate reliable information sources right away; however, some topics will require more time to dig for information. Don't be nervous – there are always academic librarians who will assist you with the library research either in person or by phone, through email or chat.

Where to look for information will depend on the nature of the research question and most of all on the currency of the topic and its interest to the public. The Internet is definitely the first source of information. But don't forget that books still have a value if you are looking for an in-depth treatment of a subject. Subject encyclopedias, for example, will give a general base of knowledge, summarize research already done, and guide you to other possible sources. If you find an article or a book that fits to your topic, read closely through its references or cited works sections. It will suggest other scholarly sources that you might consider using as well. Run a search for these citations in your library system and see if these materials are available to you. Many academic library websites have a citation linker tool, which even allows you to locate citations by a DOI (digital object identifier).

INTERNET SEARCH VERSUS LIBRARY RESOURCES SEARCH

So far, there is no universal search tool that would provide you with all the possible materials available on your topic – books or dissertations, government or agency reports, journal articles, or conference proceedings, just to name a few. Internet browsing in combination with searching specialized library databases will equip you with well-balanced results.

There is nothing wrong with going to the Internet first, especially when choosing search tools that are aimed at academics, such as *Google Scholar* (scholar.google.com), for example. This web crawler is customizable and might bring you to the full texts of academic journals or even ebooks free of charge, provided that you create a profile and set up the links for the library of your affiliation.

More researchers advocate for open digital content and create online repositories of their works available to everybody for free. Open repositories can be organized either by institutions or by subject; precise keyword search is not their strongest point. The biggest players in this new trend are Directory of Open Access Repositories, *OpenDOAR* (www.opendoar.org), its sister organization Directory of Open Access Journals, *DOAJ* (www.doaj.org), and Registry of Open Access Repositories, *ROAR* (roar.eprints.org). Worldwide dissemination of social science research can be found on *Social Science Research Network* (www.ssrn.com/en). Another platform where academics share their research for free is *Academia* (www.academia.edu).

Technical or agency reports, working papers, and conference proceedings that are not commercially published are also known as gray literature. Rutgers University Law School, for example, maintains a *Gray Literature Database* of deeply hidden documents in all aspects of crime and criminal justice, which can be discovered at www.njlaw.rutgers.edu/cj/gray/search.php.

Beware of predatory, or fake, publications available online. Try to see who and where exactly the publisher is, whether the journal is brand-new or has too many articles in one issue; try to cross-reference the author's name and sources of information mentioned in the article.

Libraries provide you with the most trusted resources but you always need to allocate time to find them. Realizing that scholarly research can be onerous, academic libraries quickly adapted by presenting their users with a one-stop search option. Usually, there will be just one search box on the library website that will allow the search inquiry to be performed simultaneously through many library collections (the catalog, multiple specialized databases, digital repositories, media files, etc.). These search mechanisms are known as discovery tools, or federated search, and are not fault-proof. The results of such a search will be a mixed bag of thousands of resources in a variety of formats – print, electronic, microform, audio, visual, etc. – available in your library.

Check how the information is displayed and look for tools to narrow down/filter your search by type, or format, of the document – date range; subjects or topics, etc. In many instances, there will be an option to expand the search to the resources that are not available in your library. If you find a particularly interesting source this way inquire if you can arrange for an interlibrary loan to get it.

Always read the full description of a record in the catalog; see where print copies of the books are located in the library, look for the links for the electronic copies for books or government and agency reports, and check the subject terms in the description of articles that will guide you to more resources on the same topic.

SEARCH TECHNIQUES

One of the most challenging aspects of every research project is the ability to formulate the topic and then describe it in simple terms. Your keyword might be a significant word (such as terrorism or Apartheid), or a combination of words (migrants and crime), or a phrase ("trafficking in small arms"). It is recommended by the majority of the databases to put double quotes (" ") around phrases to keep the search as exact as possible. Use a wildcard (usually *) when the word might have a variant spelling (organi*ed will stand for both organized and organised).

As a rule, online databases will provide the searchers with a thesaurus or a list of controlled subject terms, or descriptors. Using subject terms requires practice and knowledge of the topic. For a novice researcher, it is more beneficial to start with a keyword search. When going through the results, select the most relevant records and open them in full view so subject terms will be displayed as hotlinks. Decide if you would like to see more records that use only these subject headings. The selection of search terms, or keywords, as well as the way they are presented to the online system can either advance or obstruct the search.

SCHOLARLY ARTICLES AND SPECIALIZED LIBRARY DATABASES

Where to look for scholarly articles if they are not freely available on the web? Scholarly articles are a commodity and are available in many instances only in the commercial bibliographic databases – in other words through the library, where you have to be identified as a legitimate user.

The most powerful multi-subject aggregator of peer-reviewed literature such as scientific journals, books, and conference proceedings is *Scopus* (www.scopus.com). It delivers the world's research output in the fields of science, technology, medicine, social sciences, and humanities. Another search tool that allows users to browse through tens of millions of academic journal articles, books, and primary sources in 75 disciplines is *JSTOR* (www.jstor.org).

Below are the names of the well-known subject databases in the area of criminology, law, human rights, and sociology. Many of them will have advanced features that will suggest relevant readings based on your initial search.

Criminal Justice Abstracts is an excellent source of scholarly articles, books, chapters in books, government reports, and dissertations. Some international publications are included with in-depth abstracts in English. The same platform allows access to dozens of other *EBSCO* databases, such as *International Security & Counter Terrorism Reference Center* and *Political Science Complete. Social Sciences Full Text* provides indexing to 625 important journals, 400 of them peer-reviewed, in anthropology, criminology, economics, law, geography, policy studies, psychology, sociology, social work, and urban studies.

Criminal Justice Periodicals Index provides information from practitioners' point of view and includes police and other law enforcement professional, or trade, publications, as well as scholarly journals. *CJPI* is part of the *ProQuest* family of databases that can be searched either separately or simultaneously, depending on your library subscriptions. Another database in the *ProQuest Criminology Collection* is *National Criminal Justice Reference Service*

(*NCJRS*), which covers literature related to research, policy, and practice in criminal and juvenile justice and drug control worldwide, and also has an excellent thesaurus of criminological terms. *NCJRS* can be also accessed free online at www.ncjrs.org.

ProQuest hosts a few politics- and public policy-related databases: *PAIS Index* (public affairs, public and social policies, international relations); *Political Science Database*; *Worldwide Political Science Abstracts. Sociological Abstracts* has an international scope as well. One of the important collections on the *ProQuest* platform is *Dissertations and Theses: Global* (*PQDTGlobal*) that has the world's most comprehensive collection of full-text dissertations and theses.

Project MUSE has full-text versions of scholarly journals and ebooks from many of the world's leading university presses and scholarly societies, with over 120 publishers currently participating.

SAGE Criminology Collection allows users to search for articles in 40 criminal justice journals. This collection can be searched simultaneously with others that are available on the *Sage Knowledge* platform at your library. *Sage Journals* allows users to browse world-class journals by discipline (social sciences and humanities, for example), and then a subject.

Hein Online is the world's largest image-based legal research database. Publications are organized into separate sets based on the US or international focus (for example, European Center for Minority Issues, Foreign and International Law Resources Database, Treaties and Agreements Library, United Nations Law Collection, World Trials Library) and is available in full-text access from cover to cover.

LexisNexis has access to a vast collection of law reviews and news articles in English and some other languages, and US court cases – so does *Westlaw*, but academic libraries might subscribe to abbreviated versions of these databases. UK superior court judgments, Irish case law, and Caribbean, Australian, Canadian, and other international cases can be found in *Justis*.

WorldLII, the *World Legal Information Institute* (www.worldlii.org), is a collection of over 270 databases from 48 jurisdictions in 20 countries that contain case law, legislation, treaties, law reform reports, law journals, and other materials. One of the important collections is the *International Courts & Tribunals Collection* (www.worldlii.org/int/cases), where cases can be searched in 47 different databases.

All library databases will assist your research with many tools: creation of a research profile, links for saving and sharing, creation of citations, or importing them into such systems as *EndNote* or *RefWorks*.

SELECTED INTERNET RESOURCES

Below is a list of some useful websites and homepages of criminal justice research and policy agencies that can guide you to a range of international resources as well as hard-to-find statistical data.

The BJS, Bureau of Justice Statistics (www.bjs.gov) is the major source of criminal justice statistics for the USA.

The CIA World Factbook (www.cia.gov/library/publications/the-world-factbook) is updated weekly and contains data about 267 world entities, with a special section on the countries' involvement in transnational issues.

EUROJUST (www.eurojust.europa.eu) is the European Union's Judicial Cooperation Unit created to fight serious organized crime. Annual reports are available for free. The Press Centre – Useful Links tab on the menu bar will link you to such important resources as: EUR-Lex (eur-lex.europa.eu), a free database of EU law and case law; European Law Enforcement Agency, EUROPOL (www.europol.europa.eu); and POLIS (http://polis .osce.org), the Policing OnLine Information System of the Organization of Security and Co-Operation in Europe (OSCE).

The European Court of Human Rights (www.echr.coe.int) has case law and statistics.

The *European Sourcebook of Crime and Criminal Justice Statistics* (wp.unil.ch/ europeansourcebook) is in its fifth edition and covers the years 2007 to 2011.

The Global Initiative Against Transnational Organized Crime (https://globalinitiative.net) is a not-for-profit organization that attempts to regenerate the debate around countering organized crime, illicit trafficking, and trade. One of its initiatives, UN-TOC Watch, seeks to monitor and analyze how the UN System has been responding to organized crime in the period 2012 to 2017

HEUNI (www.heuni.fi/en) is the European regional institute in the United Nations Criminal Justice and Crime Prevention program network, and allows access to the specialized studies, reports, and statistics in the areas of corruption, human trafficking, victimization, and more.

The UK Home Office (www.gov.uk/government/organisations/home-office) provides crime-related statistics from the United Kingdom prepared by 31 agencies and public bodies.

Human Rights Watch (www.hrw.org) keeps track about the violations of human rights and publishes more than 100 reports and briefings on human rights conditions in some 90 countries.

INCB (www.incb.org), the International Narcotics Control Board, is the independent and quasi-judicial monitoring body for the implementation of the United Nations international drug control conventions.

The International Association of Chiefs of Police (www.theiacp.org) is the world's oldest and largest nonprofit membership organization of police executives, with members in 89 countries. The "Resources & Publications" section of the website has links to the monographs on various policies and best practices.

The International Centre for Criminal Law Reform and Criminal Justice Policy

(icclr.law.ubc.ca) provides advice, information, research, and proposals for policy development and legislation. This Canadian Centre is a component of the UN Crime Prevention and Criminal Justice Programme.

The International Center for the Prevention of Crime (www.crime-prevention-intl.org) promotes research-based policies and practices that work to prevent crime and build community safety.

The International Centre for Prison Studies (www.prisonstudies.org) provides statistics on prison systems and conditions, as well as incarceration rates in more than 200 countries in its free database The World Prison Brief.

The International Court of Justice (www.icj-cij.org) has cases decided by the principal judicial organ of the United Nations.

The International Criminal Court (www.un.org/law/icc) is an independent judicial body established under the Rome Statute with jurisdiction over persons charged with genocide, crimes against humanity, and war crimes.

The International Victimology Institute Tilburg (INTERVICT) (www.tilburguniversity .edu/research/institutes-and-research-groups/intervict) conducts multi-disciplinary, evidence-based research on the victims of crime and abuse of power.

INTERPOL (www.interpol.int) is an international police organization with 192 country members, which facilitates cross-border criminal police cooperation; the website has links to departments of justice throughout the world.

Transparency International (www.transparency.org) is a politically non-partisan organization that raises awareness about corruption on a global level; it also publishes country reports and case studies.

UNICRI (www.unicri.it), the United Nations Interregional Crime and Justice Research Institute, assists intergovernmental, governmental, and nongovernmental organizations in formulating and implementing improved policies in the field of crime prevention and criminal justice.

The United Nations Office on Drugs and Crime, UNODC (www.unodc.org) is the major gateway to information and UN publications on international efforts to fight crime. UNODC regularly updates statistical series on crime, criminal justice, drug trafficking and prices, drug production, and drug use.

SCHOLARLY JOURNALS AND PROFESSIONAL ASSOCIATIONS

Because of the way research is done today – discovering the articles through online searchers rather than browsing specific journals – and the fact that international crime and justice is a multifaceted field, there is no reason to compile a specific list of periodicals. The World Criminal Justice Electronic Library Network (WCJLN) keeps a list of periodicals and databases in the area of international crime and justice that can be found at http://andromeda .rutgers.edu/~wcjlen/WCJ for those who still want to explore core publications.

It is recommended to join a professional association while still a student so that you join a network of peers working in the field of your interest. Usually, there will be a link to the official publications (journals, reports, and conference proceedings) on the society's website. Here are the names of some well-known organizations: Academy of Criminal Justice Sciences, ACJS (www.acjs.org); American Society of Criminology, ASC (www.asc41.com/); American Sociological Association (www.asanet.org); Amnesty International (www.amnestyusa.org); Human Rights Watch (www.hrw.org); International Association for the Study of Organized Crime (www.iasoc.net); International Studies Association (www.isanet.org); World Society of Victimology (www.worldsocietyofvictimology.org).

Beyond the Usual Suspects

Gray Literature in Criminal Justice Research

Phyllis A. Schultze and Estee Marchi

DEFINITION

In doing academic research, one must look beyond journal articles and books as there is a wealth of information produced in other formats. For this, one must look beyond journal indexes and the book catalog and turn to the vast world of "gray" literature that is generally freely available. So what is gray literature? A simple definition is to say that gray literature is that which is published in non-commercial form. This can take the form of conference papers, theses, dissertations, governmental and nongovernmental publications, interest groups, working papers, discussion papers, case studies, project reports, newsletters, technical reports, and research reports. These publications may be produced either in print or digitally – or both. While accessing such documents may be somewhat difficult, they are increasingly important for criminal justice research, policy, and practice, as many of these materials are not indexed or abstracted by commercial indexes.

IMPORTANCE FOR INFORMED POLICY AND PRACTICE

Public policy and practice publications rely on a wide range of resources. There are many issuing agencies, such as think-tanks, university-based institutes, advocacy groups, and other organizations that seek to address policy issues. These resources are often ignored in scholarly literature. It is not unusual to see a research article that does not cite a single gray literature document. Granted, the types of gray literature resources that are available for policy and practice work are many and varied in nature and can be difficult to access, but difficult does not mean impossible.

The current interest in systematic reviews and evidence-based policies for policy and practice requires that policy makers look at evaluations of various interventions or studies in criminal justice. Much of this literature is produced by research agencies, government-supported research, and evaluations of state-run programs. Two such programs that support the efforts to produce evidence-based practices are the Cochrane Collaboration and the Campbell Collaboration. Even a cursory glance at the type of documents examined in their reviews reveals the importance and influence of including gray literature reports.

BENEFITS AND DRAWBACKS

Benefits

A crucial benefit of publishing a report or document online is timeliness. When published online, the document does not have to go through the time-consuming process of finding a place for it to be published, then having it sent out for review, then edited, returned to the author for corrections and additions, and finally being published. And, it is usually free to access. Although it is generally not peer-reviewed, it will go through some internal editing process.

Having a freely accessible document also increases its availability to the user. Not many libraries have access to the ever-increasing number of journals being produced. Making research or policy documents freely available is invaluable to the user. This is especially true for academics in developing countries, which generally have poor access to books and scholarly articles.

Literature addressing current issues such as the opioid epidemic, mass shootings, border security issues, and other hot topics can be made readily available on the Internet, and then disseminated through gray literature databases.

Drawbacks

These documents are generally not peer-reviewed and so can be of varying quality. Academics are often reluctant to have their research published in this format. Tenure processes require that academics publish in peer-reviewed journals, and professors often require students to use peer-reviewed articles exclusively in their research. Although much of gray literature is of high quality, one must determine if a publishing group has their own political or social agenda. With so many organizations producing online material, one must either have knowledge of the disseminating organizations, or must look at the purpose and authority of the organization.

MANAGEMENT

Libraries are often reluctant to introduce the world of "gray" literature to their library holdings, although this is becoming less of a problem as the sheer growth of this type of publication makes it hard to ignore. What is a problem, however, is that it takes time and energy to collect this material, to catalog it, and to make it available to users. Libraries are often short-staffed, increasingly under-budgeted, and so overwhelmed that they can find it thus difficult to take on yet another task. Despite these challenges, research libraries are increasingly aware of the value of the "fugitive" literature out there. Having said this, librarians at academic and research libraries should make their constituents aware of the most promising gray literature databases in their field of interest.

LOCATING GRAY LITERATURE DOCUMENTS

Gray literature can be difficult to search for, identify, and acquire. However, there are a few gray literature databases focusing on criminal justice that should prove very useful. These include the gray literature database at Rutgers University for reports and documents produced after 2008 (https://njlaw.rutgers.edu/cj/gray/index.php) and the NCJRS database for documents published before 2014 (www.ncjrs.gov). Both of these cover the wide range of criminal justice publications. However, there are more specific subject-oriented gray literature databases that can also prove valuable. One place to look for a listing of some of these can be found at www.greynet.org/greysourceindex.html.

Organizations and agencies produce a wide range of documents relevant to criminal justice research. It is also suggested that one consider locating the homepage of such organizations and taking a look at their list of publications. This would include such organizations as the Urban Institute, RAND, the UK Ministry of Justice, the National Institute of Corrections, the World Health Organization, and the United Nations Office on Drugs and Crime, to only mention a few.

Google can be another resource for finding report literature. Besides entering a specific criminal justice subject term, it is useful to add (gray or grey) literature, research, evaluation, or pdf. This will narrow the field.

A PROMINENT GRAY LITERATURE RESOURCE – GREYNET

GreyNet (Grey Literature Network Service) was established in 1992 and relaunched in 2003. GreyNet is dedicated to research, public open access, and education across a wide range of gray literature. Their main activities include hosting an annual international conference, a listserv, and *The Grey Journal*. The conference alternates between Europe and North America, thus maintaining an international focus. This is also a place to find relevant gray literature databases. There are 22 categories listed, ranging from "General" to "Space Technology." This is a leading worldwide organization for the promotion of gray literature and its continuing importance in research and policy.

FUTURE OF GRAY LITERATURE

There is a world of digital revolution taking place. In today's electronic environment, the Internet has greatly changed the world of publishing. There is an endless seam of documents that are freely accessible on the web. These include open journals, open dissertation databases, university-sponsored access to faculty research reports, as well as a host of other materials. Currently, however, these may be difficult to locate, as they are not systematically stored. The following are some of the more promising gray literature websites for criminal justice research.

APO (Analysis & Policy Observatory) is an open-access knowledge hub and information service providing easy access to policy and practice research and resources. APO is updated daily with the latest policy research ensuring that policy makers and analysts can discover and access the best in policy knowledge and evidence. APO includes over 34,000 resources, particularly gray literature reports, articles, and data, over 21,000 authors and nearly 5,000 source organizations with detailed bibliographic information and classification of resources by topic, coverage, and format. It is based in Australia. http://apo.org.au/.

BASE (Bielefeld Academic Search Engine) is one of the world's most voluminous search engines, especially for academic web resources. BASE provides more than 100 million documents from more than 5,000 sources. One can access the full texts of about 60 percent of the indexed documents for free (open access). www.base-search.net/?l=en.

The **Canadian Policing Research Catalogue** consolidates and makes available research material on policing conducted by academics, police services, governments, and other researchers. www.publicsafety.gc.ca/cnt/cntrng-crm/plcng/cnmcs-plcng/rsrch-prtl/index-en.aspx.

The **Criminological Repository**, at the Institute of Criminology, the University of Tuebingen, provides international free access to documents in English, German, and French languages, in the area of crime and rime control. It is new for 2018.

EBSCO Open Dissertations now includes the content from American Doctoral Dissertations (ADD). It is a free database with records for more than 800,000 electronic theses and dissertations from around the world. www.ebsco.com/products/research-databases/american-doctoral-dissertations.

The **Global Policing Database** (GPD) is a web-based, searchable database designed to capture all published and unpublished experimental and quasi-experimental evaluations of policing interventions conducted since 1950. www.gpd.uq.edu.au/search.php.

The **National Criminal Justice Reference Service** (NCJRS) is a federally funded resource established in 1972 offering justice and drug-related information to support research, policy, and program development worldwide. On October 1, 2014, the NCJRS Virtual Library began to focus primarily on the collection of informational materials and resources produced, funded, and/or sponsored by the bureaus and offices of the US Department of Justice, Office of Justice Programs (OJP). All materials housed in the NCJRS Virtual Library prior to October 2014 will remain searchable in the Abstracts Database and accessible through virtual library services. www.ncjrs.gov.

The **OAPEN** library contains freely accessible academic books, mainly in the area of humanities and social sciences. www.oapen.org/home.

OpenGrey System for Information on Grey Literature in Europe provides open access to 700,000 bibliographical references of gray literature (papers) produced in Europe and allows one to export records and locate the documents. The number of social science and humanities entries as of May 2018 is 325,000. www.greynet.org/opengreyrepository.html.

PQDT Open (Proquest) provides the full texts of open-access dissertations and those free of charge. https://pqdtopen.proquest.com/search.html.

The **Rutgers Criminal Justice Gray Literature Database** contains gray literature publications on all aspects of crime and criminal justice that are available online or in the Don M. Gottfredson Library of Criminal Justice. It includes over 21,000 documents, most dating from 2008 to the present. Two places to look for a listing of these can be found at www.greynet.org/greysourceindex and https://njlaw.rutgers.edu/cj/gray/index.php.

Social Care Online (Social Care Institute for Excellence) is the UK's largest database of information and research on all aspects of social care and social work. www.scie-socialcareonline.org.uk/.

The **Social Science Research Network** (SSRN) is a website devoted to the rapid dissemination of scholarly research in the social sciences and humanities. Besides a large number of criminal justice resources, it includes a great number of law review articles and working papers. www.ssrn.com/.

World Map

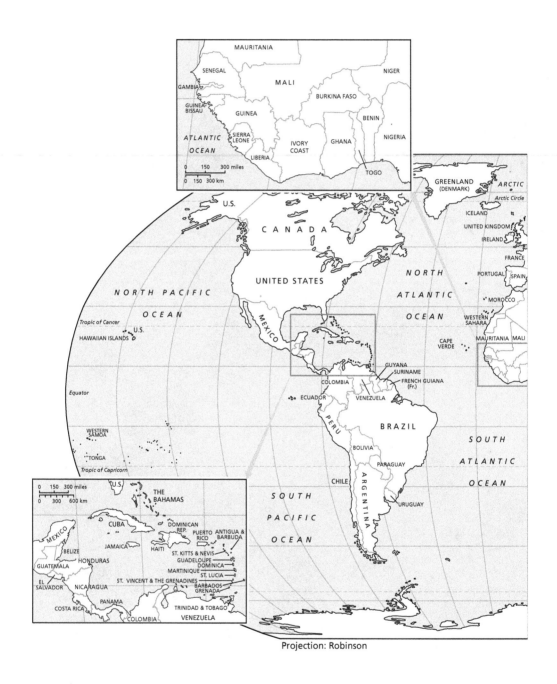

Projection: Robinson

Index

9/11 attack, 148

Abelam of New Guinea, 247
Abu Dhabi Investment Authority, 89
Abu Ghraib incident, 268
abuse of entrusted power for private gain, 138
abuse and neglect, 383, *see also* child maltreatment
Achille Lauro, 120, *see also* maritime piracy
acid attacks
    forms of violence against women, 365, *see also* women
        and international criminal justice
act of aggression, 350
acts of genocide, 327
ad hoc tribunals, 322
    international criminal tribunals, 392, 424
    international war crimes tribunals, 341
administration of punishment
    type, intensity, frequency, and duration, 260
admiralty law, 114
admissibility of evidence, 294
adversarial procedure, 254
Afghanistan, 7, *see also* drug trafficking
African
    continent, 57
    countries, 8, *see also* drug trafficking
    kleptocrat, 89
African Charter on Human and Peoples' Rights, 436
African National Congress (ANC), 345, 440
Afrikaans, 345
aggregate statistics, 14, *see also* human trafficking
aggression
    definition of, 259, 351
Al Bashir, Omar Hassan Ahmad, 325
Al Mahdi case, 322
Al Qaeda, 92, 150, 320, 329, 341
ala kachu, or bride abduction, 247
Albanian, 198
    traffickers, 200
AlphaBay, 70, *see also* cryptocurrencies
Amnesty Committee, 442, *see also* Truth and
        Reconciliation Commission in South Africa
Amnesty International, 451, *see also* nongovernmental
        organizations

amnesty laws, 439, *see also* truth commissions
amphetamine, 7
    amphetamine-type stimulants, 7
Analysis & Policy Observatory, 513, *see also* gray literature
Anderson, Warren, 110
Andes region, 7, *see also* drug trafficking
anomie theory, 477, *see also* international self-report
        delinquency
anonymous corporations, 87
Anti-Boryokudan Law, 207
anti-corruption agencies, 141
anti-shoplifting technology, 313
apartheid, xli, 320, 345, 443, *see also* crimes against
        humanity
    approximation of legislation, 290
apuntada system, 213
Archbishop Desmond Tutu, 441, *see also* Truth and
        Reconciliation Commission in South Africa
Archduke Franz Ferdinand, 155
armed conflict, 390
    international and non-international, 321
    and sexual violence, 365
arms trading
    know-how, 200
ASEANAPOL, 253
assassinations, 193
    by terrorists, 154
Assembly of States Parties (ASP), 353, 410
Association of Chiefs of Police, xxxiii, *see also*
        ASEANOPOL
asylum
    applications, 25
    seekers, 243
asymmetrical warfare, 149
attacks against systems and networks, 61
Auburn system, 265, *see also* prisons
Australian Institute of Criminology, 502, *see also* World
        Criminal Justice Library Network
aut dedere aut judicare, 398, *see also* role of United
        Nations
Autodefensas Gaitanistas de Colombia, 212
Ayyash, Salim Jamil, 431, *see also* Special Tribunal
        for Lebanon

519

CPSIA information can be obtained
at www.ICGtesting.com
Printed in the USA
LVHW052103300622
722456LV00005B/64